Financial planning essentials

SECOND EDITION

Warren McKeown

Marc Olynyk

Lisa Ciancio

Diem La

WILEY

Second edition published 2025 by
John Wiley & Sons Australia, Ltd
310 Edward Street, Brisbane Qld, 4000

Typeset in 10/12pt Times LT Std

Wiley acknowledges the Traditional Custodians of the land on which we operate, live and gather as employees, and
recognise their continuing connection to land, water and community. We pay respect to Elders past, present and emerging.

Creators/contributors
Warren McKeown (Author), Mike Kerry (Author), Marc Olynyk (Author), Lisa Ciancio (Author), Diem La (Author), Diana
Beal (Author, *Personal Finance*), Tom McDonald (Author, *Personal Finance*), Magdy Stephan (Author, *Personal Finance*),
Cynthia Wilson (Author, *Personal Finance*), Jenny Diggle (Author, *Personal Finance*), John Evans (Author, *Personal
Finance*), John Simpson (Author, *Personal Finance*), Tricia Peters (Author, *Personal Finance*), Sinclair Davidson (Author,
Personal Finance), Joan Wells (Author, *Personal Finance*)

Wiley
Mark Levings (Publishing Manager). Jess Carr (Manager, Higher Education Content Management), Laura Brinums
(Publishing Coordinator), Georgina O'Brien (Publishing Coordinator), Ines Yap (Copyright and Image Research), Delia
Sala (Cover Design), John Hamilton (Copyeditor)

Cover image: Worawut / Adobe Stock

Typeset in India by diacriTech

Printed in Singapore
M131201_040724

BRIEF CONTENTS

CONTENTS

Investment choices   109

Fixed interest, shares and property   139

CHAPTER 6

Managed funds, leveraging and buying a house   183

CHAPTER 7

Risk management and insurance   227

CHAPTER 8

Superannuation   267

CHAPTER 9

Retirement planning   313

Development of a statement of advice   415

PREFACE

The financial services industry has evolved significantly over the past 30 years, with changes affecting almost every aspect of the financial planner's professional scope. For many in the profession, the report handed down by the Royal Commission into Misconduct in the Banking, Superannuation and Financial Services Industry on 4 February 2019 was a turning point. One year later, COVID-19 affected the market, causing concern for many investors, and also affected areas like superannuation, where temporary changes were introduced. Now more than ever, Australians need trustworthy, reliable and informed advice from financial planners in order to prepare for their futures.

In authoring this important update, we have sought to inspire the next generation of financial planners to approach their careers with enthusiasm. The financial planning industry is amongst the most dynamic in Australia. Legislation, regulations and financial markets will transform constantly throughout your and your clients' lifetimes, and you will need to continually learn and adapt to thrive in this exciting and challenging environment.

We have prepared this practical and contemporary guide to financial planning to help you guide your future clients throughout their wealth management lifecycles. We have detailed the requisite information and skills, and you will learn to appreciate the options, benefits and risk factors involved in preparing financial advice. Importantly, this text will also equip you with the transferrable language required to provide meaningful and complete guidance for your clients.

Unlike traditional theory-heavy textbooks, *Financial Planning Essentials* is a concise resource with reflective end-of-chapter questions and case examples that illustrate the practical application of financial planning theory.

We wish you well in your studies and hope that this book simulates a lifelong interest in financial planning.

Warren McKeown
Marc Olynyk
Lisa Ciancio
Diem La

May 2024

ABOUT THE AUTHORS

Warren McKeown

Warren McKeown had a career in teaching before joining a Chartered Accounting firm to work in superannuation and financial planning. He moved to the position of Senior Lecturer and Course Director of Financial Planning at RMIT University, where he was responsible for the development of the first financial planning degree program in Australia. During that time, he conducted financial planning courses and workshops for CPA Australia; served as a panel member of the Financial Industry Complaints Service (now AFCA); contributed as a subject expert for the Ethics, Professionalism and Compliance module of the FPAA's (now FAAA) CFP program; and was a founding member of PetersMcKeown Pty. Ltd., an independent financial planning firm. He has degrees in economics and education and a master's degree by research. He has over 30 years' experience in financial planning as a Certified Financial Planner. He has retired from financial planning but is currently a Teaching Fellow in Financial Accounting at the University of Melbourne and is working on a PhD in the fields of agency theory and financial literacy.

Marc Olynyk

Marc Olynyk is a Senior Lecturer in Financial Planning and Program Director of Financial Planning in the Department of Accounting at Deakin University. Marc has significant experience within both academia and industry in the areas of financial planning, superannuation and retirement planning and accounting. He was an Authorised Representative for over 15 years and has more than 20 years of experience as one of Australia's leading academics and educators in the financial planning discipline where he has played a key role in the development, growth and recognition of financial planning within both the university sector and the financial planning profession. He plays a key role in facilitating industry engagement and strengthening the ties between the university sector and industry. Marc has published a number of articles in the areas of financial planning, superannuation and financial literacy.

Marc is a founding committee member and currently Chair of the Financial Planning Education Council (FPEC), is on the TEQSA Register of External Experts in Financial Planning and Financial Services and is regularly called upon to undertake course reviews and accreditations. Marc is a Fellow of the Chartered Accountants of Australia and New Zealand and a member of the Financial Planning Association and Association of Financial Advisers.

Lisa Ciancio

Lisa is the director of Financial Services Learning, a learning and development consultancy that includes facilitation and assessment services for a complete financial services solution for organisations. Lisa was previously a sessional lecturer at Swinburne University for the ethics subject within both the undergraduate and postgraduate Financial Planning qualifications. Prior to joining Swinburne University, Lisa facilitated and assessed a range of financial planning subjects for a number of industry associations and education providers.

Lisa commenced working in financial services in 1997, first as a senior fund administrator and then as a financial adviser until 2002. After this time she moved into technical and management roles for ANZ and NAB until 2011 when she established Financial Services Learning. Since then she has been involved in education committees and advisory groups, providing practical input and audits on educational requirements in specific sectors, such as financial planning, personal trustee services and insurance broking.

Diem La

Diem is a financial planning education specialist with over 25 years' experience in the financial services industry. She began as a practising financial planner in the early 2000s before lecturing in financial planning and economics subjects at Victoria University. The combination of her industry practise and passion for financial planning education led her to managing the Certified Financial Planner (CFP) certification program for almost ten years. Diem was also an Accreditation Assessor on the Financial Planning Education Council (FPEC) and a committee member of the Financial Services Industry Reference Committee in 2019.

Financial planning education remains a passion for Diem and in her current role as an academic program manager, she spearheads the design and delivery of courses tailored to corporate clients' needs while ensuring compliance with regulatory standards. She also plays a pivotal role in advocacy activities, promoting the company's interests with government bodies and professional associations.

Diem holds a Bachelor of Business in Economics and Finance and she is a Certified Financial Planner member of the Financial Advice Association of Australia.

CHAPTER 1

Personal financial planning

LEARNING OBJECTIVES

After studying this chapter, you should be able to:

1.1 describe the concept of personal financial planning

1.2 explain why personal financial planning has gained importance over the past few years

1.3 identify who can be financial planners and what professional standards they must adhere to

1.4 define various types of risk

1.5 describe the general features of the economic environment

1.6 outline the origin of the global financial crisis and describe its impact on Australia

1.7 describe the evolution of the financial planning environment in Australia

1.8 outline the regulatory framework that applies to financial planning in Australia

1.9 identify lessons from history that should be understood by investors and financial planners.

Liz, aged 26, is a primary school teacher and lives by herself in a rental apartment. She has spent the last few years travelling with friends to different countries and exploring new cultures. Now that her friends are beginning to settle down and starting families, Liz feels that she should also think about her future.

Liz receives an inheritance of $20 000 from her late uncle and decides to use this money for a house deposit. Her accountant points out that she would need a larger amount for a house deposit if she wants to buy a property in the inner city suburbs. He suggests that Liz sees a financial planner for advice on how best to invest her $20 000 to achieve this goal. Liz hesitates about seeing a financial planner as she has heard on the news that some 'dodgy' financial planners have given bad advice that has seen many people lose all of their retirement savings. However, she decides to meet with the financial planner that her accountant recommends because she trusts her accountant.

The financial planner, George, discusses Liz's financial goals and asks her to complete a questionnaire that is designed to help George determine what sort of investor Liz is likely to be. George studies Liz's completed questionnaire and determines that she is a long-term investor with a relatively aggressive risk tolerance profile as her main goal is to grow the $20 000 house deposit in 5 or 6 years. George tells Liz that he needs to write a formal proposal for her, called a statement of advice, regarding investments and would get back to her in the next two weeks.

George prepares the statement of advice and recommends that Liz invests the $20 000 in the Australian share market. Some of Liz's friends have made money from their recent investments in the share market so she feels that George's advice is good advice. Liz proceeds with his recommendation. For the first few weeks after investing her money, Liz tracks the performance of the fund and is pleased with the gains. Later in the year, however, she realises that her investment is going down in value and contacts George. George explains that the slight downturn is not unusual towards the end of a year and that her investments are planned for the long term, so short-term ups and downs should not be of concern.

Liz is not entirely reassured by George's reply, however she is relieved to discover that, by the middle of the following year, the value of her share portfolio has risen to $22 500. She has read stories about the global financial crisis (GFC) and is concerned that it would happen again, but is grateful for George's advice that her investments are focused on the long term: that she should not be too concerned about the volatility of the market in the short term, but to keep faith that the market would maintain an upward path over the long term.

Some of the issues to consider in Liz's case include:
- what qualifications her financial planner has obtained in order to give financial advice
- if Liz is assessed as a short-term investor, whether it would make a difference to the advice she is given
- lessons that could be learned from previous share market downturns and the planned term of investment.

These issues are explored throughout this chapter.

Introduction

Financial planning is often said to be a 'new' profession. This chapter provides an overview of what financial planning covers and why personal financial planning is important. Whether you want to become a financial planner/adviser or want to know more about your own finances, this chapter provides a background of basic features that should be considered by all those interested in personal finance. It also includes an outline of the work of financial planners and the professional standards that they must adhere to.

The starting point of anyone's personal financial plan is the preparation of personal financial statements (including a cash budget), followed by the identification of financial goals and the classification of those goals into relative time frames. All investors must have some understanding of risk. Liz's situation described in the opening case study reflects the experience of many people and indicates the inherent risk in investing.

Included in this chapter is an examination of personal financial planning and why it is important. The regulatory framework that encompasses personal financial planning is also outlined. The chapter provides an overview of some of the recent events that have moulded the development of financial planning and which provide valuable lessons about investment markets and financial planning. Later chapters include discussion of personal financial statements and specific types of risk that investors face.

1.1 What is personal financial planning?

LEARNING OBJECTIVE 1.1 Describe the concept of personal financial planning.

The term 'personal financial planning' implies that a person intends to achieve something in a financial sense. Some people do not have a plan or any particular goal. However, when we consider what we would like to set out to do, we often make a 'wish list' of objectives and then apply ourselves to achieving those objectives. Often it makes good sense to consider the list of objectives or goals in three time spans: short, medium and long term. There is no defined length of time for these periods, but the general principle of shorter, medium and longer time frames is a useful approach to setting personal goals.

Short-term goals are those which we intend to achieve over a time frame of about 12 months. You may have a short-term goal of saving enough money to buy a newer car or to travel overseas at the end of your year of study.

Medium-term goals are those we intend to achieve over a period of 2 to 5 years. You may have a medium-term goal of saving enough money for a deposit on a house or to accumulate a share portfolio of, say, $20 000. The level of credit card debt in Australia is cause for some concern, with some people building up a hefty amount of debt and being unable to pay for their purchases soon after placing the debt on their card. So a medium-term goal may also include a plan to retire (pay off) credit card debt by a certain time.

Long-term goals may range from items intended to be achieved in 7 or 8 years up to 40 or more years. Your long-term goals may include the purchase of a two-bedroom home which you can sell in about 10 years to buy a three- or four-bedroom home. You may not have thought much about retirement yet and, with an expectation of 40 years of work ahead of you, the matter of a certain level of retirement income may be of passing interest only. The thought of living another 30 to 40 years after retirement is one which is so far off that the concept of building up funds to last for your lifetime may not have been considered at all. However, the principle of financial planning includes consideration of all time frames. To be realistic, goals should have two components — they should be *specific* or *quantifiable*, and be *referenced to a time frame*.

1.2 Why is personal financial planning important?

LEARNING OBJECTIVE 1.2 Explain why personal financial planning has gained importance over the past few years.

Personal financial planning is about helping people achieve their financial goals. In some respects, it concerns helping people to achieve short-term goals, such as establishing a savings program with the objective of buying a newer car, funding an overseas holiday, generating a deposit for a house or building up a certain amount of wealth by, say, age 40. In other respects, as in Liz's case, it concerns the long-term objectives of the building up of a 'nest egg' or creating sufficient capital to fund retirement. In short, personal financial planning is about setting in place some personal objectives and arranging financial means to satisfy those objectives.

Personal financial planning has its roots in the 'life-cycle' theory of consumption and saving. This economic theory considers the matter of income and expenditure over a lifetime. For a number of years, while in their infancy and youth, people depend on others to expend money on their behalf. Then, during the years of their working lives, sufficient income should be generated to meet current expenditure needs and to provide for the time when little or no income is generated after they have finished working. Figure 1.1 illustrates that the consumption pattern is relatively smooth over a person's life cycle, but that a person's lifetime income profile is quite uneven. It may be argued that a person's expenditure pattern is likely to fall somewhat in retirement as some expenses are likely to be discontinued, such as mortgage repayments and work-related expenses. However, the person's income will also fall in retirement as assets are used to meet consumption needs.

However, the theory of saving sufficient funds to meet retirement expenditure is not always put into practice. Many people do not have specific savings plans and, rather than adopt a disciplined savings habit, are often persuaded through marketing campaigns to spend more than they earn. Compulsory superannuation contributions and more education about the need for savings are still required, in general, to make changes to people's savings behaviour.

In the context of life-cycle theory, personal financial planning is about managing income, expenditure and savings to actively meet a person's short-term and long-term objectives.

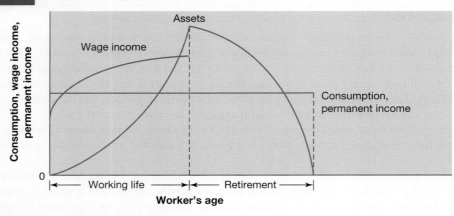

Source: Bateman, Kingston and Piggott 2001.

The Association of Superannuation Funds of Australia (ASFA) regularly prepare a Retirement Standard (RS) which benchmarks the weekly and annual budget needed by Australians to fund either a modest or comfortable standard of living in the retirement years. The ASFA RS was developed to help people know how much they will need to spend each year to fund a lifestyle in their retirement. The standard includes spending needs on such things as communications, energy, food, leisure/recreation, transport, etc. A full explanation of the categories of expenditure is available on the website superannuation.asn. au. Table 1.1 provides an outline of two categories of lifestyle for both a single person and a couple. The table indicates the amount of weekly expenditure needed on various items, on average, for a modest and comfortable lifestyle.

TABLE 1.1 Budgets for various households and living standards (March quarter 2023) for ages 65–85

	Modest lifestyle — single ($)	Modest lifestyle — couple ($)	Comfortable lifestyle — single ($)	Comfortable lifestyle — couple ($)
Housing — ongoing only	111.29	125.13	130.96	136.61
Energy	39.21	52.67	49.68	61.61
Food	106.63	197.69	137.87	239.62
Clothing	20.83	39.60	27.83	51.83
Household goods and services	38.67	45.29	84.35	104.21
Health	55.03	106.35	112.01	209.64
Transport	106.42	113.32	173.91	188.33
Leisure	112.90	177.31	218.92	329.19
Communications	17.92	20.19	22.41	29.17
Total per week	608.91	877.55	957.94	1350.23
Total per year	**31 785**	**45 808**	**50 004**	**70 482**

Note: The figures in each case assume that the retiree(s) own their own home and relate to expenditure by the household. This can be greater than household income after income tax where there is a drawdown on capital over the period of retirement. Single calculations are based on female figures. All calculations are weekly, unless otherwise stated.

Source: Association of Superannuation Funds (ASFA) 2023, pp. 2–3.

When a person has determined the retirement lifestyle they can be comfortable with, the next step is to determine what amount of superannuation capital they need to accumulate to fund that lifestyle. (Note that the modest lifestyle is regarded as marginally better than relying totally on the age pension.) Many Australians are not able to achieve the capital required and rely in varying degrees on the age pension (approximately 80% of retirees rely on the age pension to some extent).

In 2014, the Financial Services Council (FSC) engaged Rice Warner Actuaries to estimate the retirement savings gap (RSG), which is the value of the shortfall the working population will have in building an adequate or reasonable retirement benefit. On an aggregate measure the estimated gap is about $70 100 per person, up from $67 300 in June 2013, indicating the reliance on the age pension for many who are currently close to retirement age. Rice Warner estimated that the average savings in superannuation for males between 55 and 59 is $121 155 and for females between 55 and 59 it is $87 713.

The accepted target benefit at retirement (which includes any entitlement to the age pension) is proposed to be 70% instead of 62.5% of pre-retirement earnings for most of the working population. This is the chosen figure by the FSC because it is within the range nominated by an earlier Senate Select Committee on Superannuation and Financial Services within which people can maintain their standard of living in retirement. The AMP Retirement Adequacy Index also suggests that the figure might be closer to 70%. However, the issue is complex as more spending appears to take place in the initial retirement years and reduces as retirees age. The AMP Retirement Adequacy Index study estimates that the average worker at age 65–69 can now expect to retire on just under $49 000 per annum comprising a combination of superannuation, age pension and other investments.

The focus on superannuation is an important factor behind the increasing importance of personal financial planning over the past few years. The main reasons for the growing importance of personal financial planning include:

- the increasing proportion of people in older age groups, including those who are about to retire
- the increase in longevity
- expected restrictions to reduce access to the age pension
- the introduction of compulsory superannuation
- a greater range of superannuation fund investment choices
- proposed changes to taxation on savings accounts and other government budget announcements.

In summary, the major reason for the increased importance of personal financial planning is the transfer of risk for providing for one's old age from the government (age pensions) and employers (defined benefit superannuation schemes) to individuals.

The increase in numbers in older age groups

A study of demographic trends in Australia shows that we — like many countries throughout the world — are faced with an ageing population. This means that the proportions of the Australian population in the older age groups are increasing relative to the numbers in the younger age groups. Falling birth rates, falling death rates and changing rates of immigration have all contributed to a changing population structure. A significant feature of the structure of our population is the size of the group of people who were born in the period following World War II, from 1945 to about 1960. These people are often referred to as 'baby boomers' (the name reflects a period of significant increase in the birthrate) and are now 63–78 years of age.

Australia's population will change between now and 2050. Note that, when Liz (the young woman from the case study at the start of the chapter) is 75, it is estimated that the numbers in the 75–79 age group will exceed the numbers in the 0–19 age group. Some concern has been expressed about this trend because it is expected that Australia will have a sharp reduction in the number of people of working age compared to the number of retired people. The current ratio is about 5 workers for every person aged 65 years and over, whereas it is predicted that by 2050 this will decline to 2.7 workers for every person aged 65 and over. The expected dependence on fewer workers to supply sufficient taxation revenue to support the age pension and aged healthcare costs has led to a number of policy decisions in recent years, including compulsory superannuation, review of eligibility for the age pension, encouragement for people to defer their retirement, the introduction of the goods and services tax (GST), the government's co-contribution scheme and the changes to tax applied to interest earned on savings.

Figure 1.2 shows the age structure of the Australian population in 2021. Access the ABS website reference to see an interactive age structure where you can move the arrow at the bottom of the diagram to see the estimated changes to Australia's age structure over the years.

FIGURE 1.2   Age structure of the Australian population in 2021

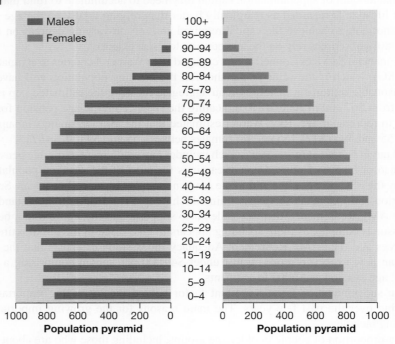

Source: ABS 2023.

The increase in longevity

The 2021 Intergenerational Report, produced by the federal treasury, indicated that Australians' life expectancies remain among the highest in the world. Since 1901, life expectancies have increased from 55.2 to 80.9 years for men and 58.8 to 85.0 years for women. The report projects life expectancies to increase further, reaching 86.8 years for men and 89.3 years for women by 2061 (The Treasury 2021).

One reason for the increase in life expectancy is the vast improvements made in medical science, which have significantly reduced the impact of life-threatening diseases such as typhoid and diphtheria. Other reasons may include changes in dietary habits, with many people being far more aware of the impact of different foods. People are also more conscious of the damaging effects of smoking, as well as the need for regular exercise to reduce the risk of poor health. However, the present diet of many younger people and the reported incidence of childhood obesity may indicate a reversal of the trend to longer lives. To date though, despite the detrimental effects of increased levels of obesity and increases in mortality rates from lung cancer, cardiovascular disease, respiratory and other conditions associated with modern living, there is a gradual rise in the average life expectancy of males and females. The increase in life expectancy has led to increasing numbers of people reaching 100 years of age. However, the increase in longevity has also been accompanied by increased costs of care for elderly people. Health 'is projected to increase from 19.0 per cent of total government spending in 2021–22 to 26.0 per cent in 2060–61' (The Treasury 2021). Hence, it is even more important for individuals to plan for appropriate levels of funding for their retirement years as they will likely have to fund both income and health expenses in their older age.

Restricted access to the age pension

In the past few years, modifications have been made to eligibility for the **age pension**. Gradually, the age of entitlement for the age pension for women has been raised to be the same as that for men.

The federal government offers incentives to people eligible for the age pension to continue working. It omits up to $300 per fortnight of employment income when it assesses eligibility for the age pension under the income test, compared to omitting only about $170 per fortnight of the income earned by a person who is eligible for the age pension and chooses not to work.

In essence, the **work bonus scheme** encourages people over the age pension age to continue working by allowing them to earn a higher amount of income before their age pension payments are reduced. The government has further responded to the long-term cost of demographic change and will progressively increase the qualifying age for men and women to access the age pension. The qualifying age for the age pension is 67 years.

Compulsory superannuation contributions

In 1992, the federal government introduced legislation that made it compulsory for employers to contribute an amount equal to 3% of their employees' salaries or wages to a superannuation fund. Conditions were attached to this rule.

- An employee had to earn more than $450 in a month.
- No contributions were required for employees over 65 years of age.
- An upper limit of income was applied to the requirement to contribute 3% as superannuation.

A graduated scale was introduced at the same time that required a steadily increasing rate of contribution by employers for the next 10 years. Since 2003, employers have been required to contribute an amount over 9% of an employee's remuneration to a superannuation fund.

The purpose of compulsorily requiring employers to contribute to superannuation is to spread the cost of funding retirement incomes to employers while people are actively working. However, estimates conducted by many sources indicated that contributions need to be 3–5% above 9% (i.e. 12–14% p.a.) over a period of 30–40 years of employment in order to produce a retirement income of about 70% of a person's final income from work. In the 2014 federal budget, the treasurer announced that the superannuation guarantee rate will increase progressively from 9% to 12%. It commenced with an increase to 9.25% in 2013–14 and to 9.5% in 2015–16 through to 2021 and thereafter rising to 12% from 2025 and beyond. Thus, it remains likely that a small age pension could still be claimed by people who are not able to accumulate sufficient funds in superannuation even after a lifetime of work. A worrying trend for the government is the need to encourage more people to contribute additional amounts to savings or superannuation as there appears to be an increase in the numbers of people relying on a part age pension. To illustrate, the proportion of the 65–69 age group receiving a full or part rate of age pension increased from 49% in 1991 to 64% in 2008 (ABS 2009). The numbers eligible to receive a part age pension are seen to remain constant at 80% as fewer are able to claim the full age pension (National Commission of Audit March 2014).

Although self-employed people are not required to place any amount into superannuation, a tax deduction is allowed as an encouragement for people who do not have the benefit of employer superannuation contributions to make their own contributions towards their retirement income.

While the current rate of superannuation guarantee contribution may not be sufficient on its own for a person to accumulate the capital required to fund a comfortable retirement, the government encourages people to make additional contributions to their superannuation from their own resources. A salient point in financial planning for retirement is that individuals need to monitor their required income for their retirement years and to make contributions in the years prior to retirement to reach their goals. Many calculators are available on the internet to assist with this — people can nominate their required retirement income and input their contributions and superannuation balance to arrive at a recommended level of contribution to meet their target (see https://moneysmart.gov.au, ASIC's consumer advice website). Although people are unique and have different income needs, the documented guide is that people need between 60% and 70% of their pre-retirement income to meet their income needs in retirement.

Choice of superannuation fund

In 1997, the federal government proposed that individual members of superannuation funds should be given a range of choices for the investment of their superannuation benefits. Industry sources expressed concern about the levels of education being provided to members and the possibility of members making inappropriate investment choices. After lengthy debates, the legislation was passed to operate from 1 July 2005.

Over the period of the debate, many providers of superannuation funds reacted to the proposal by offering members a wider choice of investment within their existing superannuation fund. Many funds did not offer a choice to members or, at best, offered a range of three investment choices: a capital stable fund, a balanced fund and a growth fund. Now it is more common to find up to seven or eight different portfolio mixes and even some investment choices managed by different fund managers being made available to members of the fund. Hence, the main objective of offering a wider investment choice to members of superannuation funds was generally met before the introduction of member choice.

With the introduction of choice of superannuation funds, there was concern among regulators and industry observers that employees would be encouraged to change superannuation funds without proper advice. However, the Financial Planning Association took a strong stance by encouraging its members to ensure that high advice standards were maintained and that indiscriminate changing of funds did not occur. It was expected that many employees might decide not to transfer funds and would remain in the same fund. However, a great deal of marketing encouraged people to think about changing their fund, with new funds being promoted to the public. One expected benefit to consumers was that competition might force the underlying fees to be reduced. This has not occurred to any significant degree. Further, evidence indicates that less than 10% of those eligible to change funds actually did so at the time (Clare 2006; Fry, Heaney & McKeown 2007). To accommodate the needs of employees who do not wish to or do not have the interest in their retirement fund, proposals have been made to provide a low-cost default fund. The review into the governance, efficiency, structure and operation of Australia's superannuation system (commonly known as the Cooper Review), released in June 2010, recommended that a default superannuation fund, called MySuper, be established. The fund is designed to have low fees, and asset allocations that are suitable to the individual employee's age and that reflect the expected term of investment (i.e. a shorter or longer time frame).

Retirement benefits provided by many employers

Those employee groups that had the good fortune to expect retirement benefits from their employment before compulsory superannuation was introduced often were destined to receive their benefit in the form of a defined benefit or promise. In other words, employees would receive a retirement benefit based on a formula comprising the length of service and final average salary. With this type of fund, the employee was not involved in the investment decisions of the superannuation fund, as it was the employer's responsibility to place sufficient contributions into the fund to meet the expected retirement payments. In most funds, the benefit was in the form of a pension which was payable for life.

However, with the combined effect of increased longevity and the increasing numbers looking to retire in the next few years, employers were concerned about their future exposure to funding retirement benefits for an increasing number of years to an increasing number of retirees or their surviving spouses. The answer to this concern was the move to change the form of superannuation fund from a defined benefit or promise fund to a defined contribution or accumulation fund. With this type of fund, the employee receives a superannuation benefit which is the accumulation of the fund after the employer has made the compulsory, and sometimes additional, contributions to the fund. For example, BHP (before it became BHP Billiton) recognised the problem of paying pensions to members or their surviving spouses for longer than expected when the pension fund was established. In the early 1990s and through a series of seminars and information sessions, BHP offered members of the BHP Staff Superannuation Fund who were in receipt of a pension (many of them being the surviving wives of deceased employees) the opportunity to exchange the right to the lifetime pension for a lump sum.

A very important point to note is that along with this change in type of fund went a transfer of the risk of investment from the employer to the employee. With an accumulation fund, it is the member who ultimately bears the risk of the investment choice and the consequent performance of the fund. With the defined benefit fund, it is the employer who has to ensure payments are made to the member and hence carries the risk of both contributions and performance of the fund.

These changes to our socioeconomic circumstances indicate that:
- individuals must take responsibility for their own retirement
- planning must start at an early age
- the complexity of products, rules and decision making mean that people must become far better educated in regard to personal financial decisions.

1.3 Professional standards for financial planners

LEARNING OBJECTIVE 1.3 Identify who can be financial planners and what professional standards they must adhere to.

What is a financial planner?

A financial planner is someone who advises clients on how to manage their money and work towards achieving their specific financial goals. The planner will work with the clients to understand their current financial situation and their financial goals. A tailored strategy will then be developed to help the clients achieve their goals and maintain them. The advice might cover some or all of these areas: insurance, investments, retirement planning, superannuation, estate planning, risk management and tax planning.

Once the client engages the services of a financial planner, the two parties will commence a journey together. Depending on the scope of the engagement, this journey might be a short one or it might be a lifelong one. Along the way, the client will share many personal and sensitive details. Therefore, it's important that the client feels comfortable with the adviser and that trust is established before proceeding.

The financial planning process will vary slightly from one advisor to another, however, it should follow the steps below.

1. Gather client information.
2. Establish financial goals and objectives.
3. Analyse data and identify financial issues.
4. Prepare and develop the statement of advice.
5. Implement the agreed-upon recommendations.
6. Review and revise the statement of advice.

A financial planner needs to collect as much information about the client as possible to have a good understanding of the client's current position before any advice can be given. This information includes personal details such as the client's age, relationship status, children and parents. Information is also collected on the client's employment and income, assets and liabilities, insurance and estate planning matters. Perhaps the most important stage of the financial planning process is establishing the client's goals and objectives, as they will serve as a foundation for developing appropriate strategies. The planner will ask many questions to identify the client's short-, medium- and long-term financial goals.

Sometimes clients set goals that may be unrealistic or difficult to achieve. A financial planner needs to analyse the client's data and identify any financial issues with the stated goals and objectives. This includes conflicting goals such as wanting to achieve high investment returns and avoiding fluctuations in asset valuation. It could also involve a client who wishes to invest their superannuation balance of $100 000 to generate an annual retirement income of $45 000 in five years time for the rest of their life. Once the financial issues are identified and discussed, the financial planner can manage the client's expectations about the goals and objectives.

Using their expertise, the financial planner will design a tailored strategy to help the client achieve their specific goals. The recommendations will be documented in a statement of advice and details the appropriate strategies, products and services. The client should be given ample time and opportunity to ask any questions they might have about the financial plan to help them be comfortable with the strategy.

Once the client is happy with the recommendations, the financial planner will work with the client to implement them. This may involve completing forms to purchase investment products or collaborating with other professionals such as accountants and lawyers to establish appropriate tax structures and estate planning.

Over time, a client's circumstances may change, and their goals and objectives may need to be adjusted accordingly. Also, changes to rules and legislation affecting the client's strategies may also necessitate adjustments to their financial plan. A financial plan should be reviewed on a regular basis to ensure that the client remains on track with achieving their goals.

The six steps of the financial planning process will be explored in more detail later in this text.

Who can be a financial planner?

Personal financial advice can only be provided by a person or an authorised representative of an organisation licensed by the Australian Securities and Investments Commission (ASIC). The names of properly licensed financial planners are listed on ASIC's Financial Adviser Register (FAR).

For a period of time, people who called themselves financial planners ranged from those who were licensed to provide financial advice to those who were not, such as real estate agents who promoted property investments. This caused confusion for many consumers who did not fully understand the role of a financial planner.

During this same time, revelations were made of high-profile financial planner misconduct cases and, together with other factors, they brought the financial planning industry into disrepute. This resulted in legislative reforms designed to recalibrate the education, training and ethical standards for financial planners.

Professional standards for financial planners

In March 2017, reforms were introduced into the *Corporations Act 2001* by the *Corporations Amendment (Professional Standards for Financial Advisers) Act 2017* to raise the education, training and ethical standards for financial advisers.

The terms 'financial adviser' and 'financial planner' have been protected in law since 1 January 2019 and they can only be used by people who are authorised to give financial advice and are listed on the FAR. There are also different professional standards that apply to existing advisers and new entrants.

An existing adviser is a person who was listed as a 'current' adviser on the FAR any time between 1 January 2016 and 1 January 2019. The adviser must not have been prohibited from providing advice as at 1 January 2019. Anyone who does not meet this definition is considered a 'new entrant'.

An existing adviser must:

1. have passed a financial adviser exam by 1 January 2021
2. complete an approved qualification by 1 January 2026
3. meet continuing professional development requirements
4. comply with the Financial Planners and Advisers Code of Ethics.

New entrants wishing to commence a career in financial advice are required to:

1. complete a Financial Adviser Standard (FAS) approved degree
2. undertake a Professional Year
3. pass a financial adviser exam.

New entrants must complete an FAS-approved bachelor degree, a postgraduate diploma or a Master's degree. The degree must be completed before the professional year can commence and new entrants must pass an exam before commencing the second half of the professional year. The Financial Planners and Advisers Code of Ethics applies to financial advisers and therefore, when a new entrant passes the exam and is authorised by their licensee as a Provisional Financial Adviser, they are required to comply with the Code.

On 28 October 2021, the *Financial Sector Reform (Hayne Royal Commission Response – Better Advice) Act 2021* (Better Advice Act) transferred functions relating to the reforms from the Financial Adviser Standards and Ethics Authority (FASEA) to the Minister and to ASIC.

For more information on the financial adviser exam, visit https://asic.gov.au/regulatory-resources/financial-services/financial-advice/educational-requirements/financial-adviser-exam.

For more information on the financial adviser standards, visit https://fas.treasury.gov.au.

1.4 Understanding risk

LEARNING OBJECTIVE 1.4 Define various types of risk.

A very important issue that must be considered in personal financial planning is the understanding of the term 'risk'. To start building an understanding of risk, consider the situation described in illustrative example 1.1.

ILLUSTRATIVE EXAMPLE 1.1

Oliver, aged 24, was given $50 000 from his grandmother's estate and decided to invest the money. 'I wanted to achieve a high return, so I'd have more money to use when I bought a house,' he said.

'When I found a managed share fund that had earned 20% in the last 12 months, and averaged over 15% a year over the past 3 years, I thought "Great — that's perfect!".' What Oliver didn't realise was that higher long-term returns usually go hand in hand with volatility.

In his situation, the share market represented a very risky investment choice. 'Six months later I had found a house and was ready to withdraw my money, but the value of my investment had fallen quite a lot. Of course, I didn't have time to wait for it to recover. I needed the money right away, so I had to accept a $5000 loss.'

In this example, Oliver failed to take into account the risk involved in a short-term investment.

Risk can mean several things. The former Financial Planning Association of Australia (FPA) in conjunction with Macquarie Investment Management Ltd has produced a booklet entitled *The trade-off: Understanding investment risk* (2008) which outlines different types of risk. The following meanings of risk have been adapted from the booklet.

- *Mismatch risk.* This is the mismatching of a person's objectives, investments and time frame. Oliver's situation is a prime example of mismatch risk. The general rule for a time frame and investments to match investment objectives is as follows.

Time frame		Investment
Short term	<1 year	Cash (e.g. cash management trusts)
Medium term	>3 years	Emphasis on fixed interest with some cash and growth assets
Long term	>5 years	Emphasis on growth assets (shares and property) with some access to cash

- *Inflation risk.* This is the risk that the purchasing power of a person's money will be eroded by increases in the cost of living. For example, 50 litres of petrol for a car cost approximately $40 in 2006 but, with the increase in the cost of petrol, a person needed about $70 to buy the same amount of petrol in 2019.
- *Interest-rate risk.* This risk may be considered in two ways.
  - *Reinvestment risk.* When fixed investments mature, an investor needs to consider the interest rates available at the time of reinvestment. If the interest rates have fallen significantly, the investor is faced with a lower income. This occurred in the early 1990s when investors who had invested for a 3- to 5-year period found that the reinvestment interest rate at the time of maturity had fallen from around 12% to about 6%. An investor relying on the interest of $12 000 from a fixed-term investment was then faced with an income of $6000. Similarly, investors who were able to obtain a 4% rate a few years ago are now faced with a fixed-term rate of about 1% p.a.
  - *Market volatility.* Fixed-interest investments usually have a set interest rate for the duration of the term. However, if you sold fixed-interest securities in an emergency and interest rates had risen since you invested, you may find that you would not receive the full value of the investment. For example, a 5-year bond worth $100 000 when interest rates are 5% would be worth approximately $96 000 if interest rates were to rise to 6%. So changes in interest rates can affect not only your reinvestment for income terms but also the capital value of your investment, unless you hold the investment until maturity.
- *Market risk.* All markets have ups and downs. Some are more volatile than others and it is important to be aware of the time frame of the investment in order to be able to ride out the bumps in the performance. Consider the graph in figure 1.3. In the short term, the graph shows the effects of dramatic swings in volatility but the volatility needs to be seen in a longer-term perspective, also shown in the graph. Figure 1.3 shows two sections of a graph of the Dow Jones Industrial Average over the period 2004–13. In panel A, an investor who is concerned in the short term about a portfolio of shares losing value would be very concerned as the index fell from over 12 000 in 2008 to a low of 6500 in 2009, but may have recovered some comfort when the index rose to 10 000 in 2009. Panel B shows that, by holding on to the portfolio, by 2013 the index had reached a new high of nearly 15 000. This illustrates that it is best to hold on to a longer-term strategy rather than to sell in the short term when panic sets in.
- *Market timing risk.* Some people believe that they can time when to get into the market and when to get out of the market. In practice, this is very difficult to achieve and in many cases some market timers end up being worse off. History has shown that, if investors missed the best single month over a 27-year

period to July 2007 on the Australian Securities Exchange, their $10 000 initial investment would have achieved the sum of $272 313, which is 14% below the $316 332 if the funds had remained invested for the whole period. And if the investor missed the best 10 months over that period, the accumulated sum would have been $102 948, which is 67% less than if the funds had remained invested for the duration. The same principle applies for any period of time.

- *Risk of poor diversification.* The main benefit of diversification of investments is to reduce the overall risk of your investment portfolio. Although one market segment has a lower-than-expected return, other market segments may perform better than expected. The key to successful long-term investing with a lower level of risk is to ensure that your investment portfolio is diversified across a range of asset classes.
- *Currency risk.* This risk applies if you hold investments valued in overseas currencies. A rise in the Australian dollar relative to the currency of the country in which you hold some investments will see a fall in the value of your investments. For example, if you had invested A$10 000 in the US share market when the Australian dollar was worth US$0.90 your investment would equal US$9000. When the Australian dollar rose in value to US$1.04, your investment would then be worth A$8654. Of course, if the Australian dollar falls in relation to the US dollar, then your investment would be worth more in Australian dollars. In 2020, the Australian dollar fell to around US$0.67 which meant that your investment would then be worth A$12 916.
- *Liquidity risk.* It is always important to have access to cash for emergency purposes. We can never foresee when we may need the cash, but it is very important to have either cash in the bank available at call or a credit facility that can provide cash at very short notice. Redeeming investments to meet such a need may mean paying an exit fee or selling an investment when market prices are low.
- *Credit risk.* Credit risk applies to investments such as term deposits, debentures, mortgage loans and bonds. It is the risk that the company to which you have lent money will become insolvent and will be unable to meet interest payments or repay your funds. You can guard against this to some degree by seeking information about the company's credit rating, past performance and ownership, which should indicate the quality of the organisation. The international ratings agencies Standard & Poor's (S&P) and Moody's rate various banks and managed investments. The highest rating is AAA. The agencies consider funds rated from AAA to BBB to be 'investment grade'; that is, they have the capacity to pay income and repay funds in a timely manner.
- *Legislative risk.* This refers to the risk of losing your capital or suffering reduced returns due to changes in laws and regulations. Governments may change laws, such as the carbon tax laws, which impact on the firms in which an investor places their money. In adapting to the changed laws, lower profits may be available to be distributed as costs may have increased.
- *Gearing risk.* This is the risk involved in borrowing to invest. Such risks are twofold. First, there is the rate of interest to be paid by the investor which may go up and require an increased amount of repayment to the lender. Second, there is the risk of a severe falling in the value of the assets in which the funds are invested, which may mean the loan or a portion of the loan may need to be repaid immediately.

| FIGURE 1.3 | Don't lose hope in the short term |

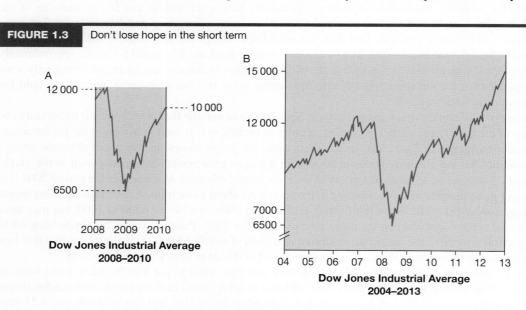

A
Dow Jones Industrial Average
2008–2010

B
Dow Jones Industrial Average
2004–2013

What advice would you give this person?

This is a letter to a financial adviser who responds to readers' queries in a daily newspaper.

Dear Financial Adviser,

I am a 20-year-old university student and have recently inherited $40 000 from the estate of my grandmother. I have decided to keep $10 000 in my bank account to spend on a number of things over the next year or so, but I wish to invest $30 000. My investment time frame is long term, as I do not need the money now. I intend to continue renting a flat with some friends when I complete my degree and start work. I may also go overseas for a year or so with my work, or I may take a year off work to travel in Europe and South America. I am interested in capital growth but am not sure whether I should keep the money in a term deposit in the bank until I decide to use the funds as a deposit for a home unit, or to invest in shares. I am aware of the share market going up and down each day and would be prepared to invest some in this area. Interest rates seem to be fairly low at the moment and the share market seems to be rising despite its daily changes.

What advice do you have as to my best options for investing this money?

Yours sincerely,
A student with a money problem

QUESTIONS

1. Prepare a list of questions that you think should be asked of this student to clarify the meaning of 'my investment time frame is long term'.
2. Describe the investment option, or outline a number of investment options, that you would suggest for this student.

1.5 Features of the economic environment

LEARNING OBJECTIVE 1.5 Describe the general features of the economic environment.

In the early 1990s, Australia had interest rates of 12%, inflation was running at 6%, unemployment was 9% and the annual growth rate was 2%. In mid 2007, Australia's interest rates were around 6%, inflation was down to 3%, unemployment was under 5% and the annual growth rate was around 3%. By 2011, Australia's interest rates, which had declined to below 3% in 2009 had risen again to 4.75%. But in early 2013 interest rates were again 3% p.a. after falling to 2.5% in late 2011. Inflation was 3.3% in 2011 but had fallen to 2.5% in 2013. Unemployment was 4.9% in 2011 but rose to 5.4% in early 2013. The annual growth rate of the Australian economy was 2.7% in 2011 but slightly less at 2.5% in 2013.

The volatility in the economic features that occurred between 2007 and 2013 was due to the impact of the global financial crisis. It should be noted that Australia suffered in a minor way compared to the rest of the developed world. This was a result of federal government stimulus spending and the strength of the demand from China and India for Australian minerals. Current rises in unemployment were considered to be the result of the higher Australian dollar which cheapened goods produced offshore and took away many manufacturing jobs in Australia.

In early 2020, the inflation rate was down to 1.8% with interest rates cut to 0.5% to help stimulate the economy. The economic growth rate was recorded at 2.2% and unemployment at 5.3% (RBA 2020). In contrast, in early 2024, the inflation rate was 3.6%, with the official cash rate 4.35% and unemployment of 4.0%.

We can see that the economic circumstances were quite different 30 years ago. In the context of making financial plans, we need to be very much aware of the economic conditions existing at the time of preparing a plan and the trends which may be occurring in the economy. Over the longer time frame, we are able to see how economies have generally featured in a boom–bust business cycle, as shown in figure 1.4.

FIGURE 1.4 The business cycle

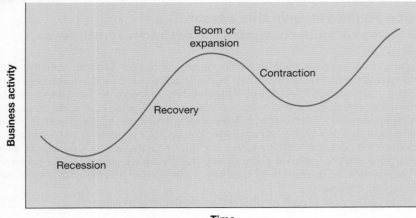

The business cycle may generally be viewed in four stages.
1. *Boom or expansion.* The phase of the business cycle when employment and economic growth are high; an increase in inflation becomes a concern.
2. *Contraction.* The phase when the economic growth rate starts to slow, sales begin to fall, and the level of unemployment starts to rise.
3. *Recession.* The phase when high unemployment is recorded and economic growth slows and may even be negative.
4. *Recovery.* The phase when unemployment begins to fall and economic growth starts to rise.

We cannot consider the Australian economy in isolation. We live in a global economy in which we rely on other countries to supply us with goods and services. Similarly, other countries rely on us for goods and services. We are able to invest in overseas markets and overseas investors can invest in the Australian markets. Decisions that we make can be affected by what goes on in other markets. Large amounts of capital can be transferred from country to country within a few seconds with no regard for the economic consequences for either country.

The federal government uses fiscal or budgetary policies to try to keep the economy from swinging wildly from highs to lows in business cycles through taxation and spending measures to inject into or withdraw money from the general community, depending on the economic conditions at the time. Monetary policy, administered by the Reserve Bank of Australia (RBA), is concerned with control over interest rates and the amount of money in circulation. Monetary policy can be used to stimulate the economy by reducing interest rates or to slow the economy by increasing interest rates when needed. A reduction in interest rates tends to encourage spending and borrowing by consumers and so increases activity throughout the economy. On the other hand, an increase in interest rates tends to restrict borrowing and spending and is designed to slow the growth in the economy.

Fiscal policy is concerned with managing the economy through the use of government-controlled taxation and spending policies. To stimulate the economy, governments may reduce taxation and allow more spending power to remain in the hands of consumers. Governments may also be selective in their spending programs and allocate resources to specific targets such as the elderly or the young unemployed to meet some specific economic or social need. To slow the economy when it appears to be running too strongly, the government may increase taxes and reduce spending programs.

Monetary and fiscal policies are the two main mechanisms by which governments may help to reduce the excesses caused by market cycles. Governments may use a combination of measures to constrain or promote growth in an economy, but the influence of the global economy and what other governments do to control their own economies may also affect what happens in Australia.

Governments and economic commentators monitor gross domestic product (GDP), the consumer price index (CPI), the cash interest rate and unemployment figures along with many other economic indicators to ascertain and understand changes occurring within the economy and to determine whether — and to what extent — government intervention is required.

Knowledge of the economic setting is very important in the framing of any personal financial plan as any decision is made in the context of a dynamic set of conditions; that is, the conditions will change and any financial plan will need to allow for changes. For example, an investor wants to invest in fixed-interest securities for a 5-year period. If interest rates are relatively low and have been for some time, and economic observers note that there are pressures for interest rate rises, it may be advisable to invest for shorter time periods — 3, 6 or 12 months at the most — to take advantage of the rising interest rates that are expected at those maturity dates. In that way, the investor is not committed for the longer term of 5 years at low interest rates when higher rates of interest for the same degree of risk could be obtained at time intervals somewhere during the investor's time frame.

A brief look back at the events of recent years shows the changing economic, financial and social environment that Australians have had to work their way through. Investors must be aware of the need to be flexible and be able to adapt and make changes in response to changing economic circumstances. To develop an appreciation of this need to be aware of changing circumstances, it is worth considering some of our recent investment market history.

Following are some major events that represent lessons from which we can learn:
- 1987 share market crash
- 1990 property trust freeze
- 1991 Pyramid Building Society closure
- 1992 Japanese share market crash
- 1994 bond market crash
- 1997 Asian crisis
- 2000–01 dot.com crash
- 2001 World Trade Center disaster
- 2001–02 corporate collapses
- 2002 falls in world market shares
- 2004 share markets rebound
- 2006 collapse of Westpoint Corporation
- 2006 housing affordability crisis
- 2007–2013 crisis in the US subprime mortgage fund industry and the global financial crisis
- 2010–(ongoing) European debt crisis.

1.6 The global financial crisis and its impact on Australia

LEARNING OBJECTIVE 1.6 Outline the origin of the global financial crisis and describe its impact on Australia.

Anyone studying personal finance issues should have a basic understanding of the financial crisis that impacted on most countries throughout the world in 2007 and beyond. Students should be alert to the origins of the crisis in order to recognise how the genesis of a financial crisis can build up slowly and how it may take some years for the crisis to take full effect. To understand the credit crisis in the United States and its effects on the financial statements of banks, institutions and investors in mortgage-backed securities around the world — in what ultimately became the GFC — it is important to understand the origins of the housing boom in the United States. To help build this understanding, a hypothetical case of Mr and Mrs Smith is used in the following step-by-step explanation.

Mr and Mrs Smith had low-paying jobs, no deposit and wanted to buy a house. The bank would not lend to them so they turned to a mortgage broker who arranged for a loan with no deposit and for a 'honeymoon' (low) rate of interest for 5 years.

Five years later, the interest rate increased by 200%. Mrs Smith also lost her job and the couple struggled with the repayments. They decided to sell their house.

However, the market experienced an increase in the number of properties available for sale and the prices were below what Mr and Mrs Smith paid for the house. The couple returned the house keys to the lender and walked away.

Meanwhile, to mitigate the risks of lending so much money to so many people with no deposit and low income, the finance lenders packaged a number of the loans and sold them to investment banks. These packages were then sold to institutions and other investors.

Investment banks further divided the loans into categories of low risk, medium risk and high risk and were able to obtain favourable ratings from ratings agencies.

Thus, armed with the ratings agencies' approval and bond insurance, and with the backing of mortgage loans on houses, investment banks were able to sell packages of mortgage-backed securities, now called collateralised debt obligations (CDOs), with the promise of high returns (following the 'honeymoon' period) and low risk (based on home mortgages) to willing investors across the world.

However, when people like Mr and Mrs Smith could not afford the repayments on their loans, investors became worried about the interest payments that they were no longer receiving.

When these investors realised that the substance behind the CDOs was non-existent (i.e. no repayments were being made) and the bond insurance was totally inadequate, banks and lending institutions were forced to shut down. The effects of such a withdrawal of credit precipitated a global financial crisis, the scale of which had not been seen before.

While Australia fared better than most other economies, it was not entirely immune to the effects of the GFC. A number of institutions — local councils, superannuation funds and other investment institutions — invested in CDOs offered by the American investment institutions. Hence, such investments lost value. The most severe impact was felt when the Australian banks, which could not obtain funds from overseas banks to lend to businesses in Australia, had to stop lending. This action prompted many people to want to get their funds out of the banks in case the banks closed their doors. It also caused businesses to close because they could not get finance from their bank to carry on normal business practices. As a consequence, the federal government acted swiftly in a number of ways to counteract the effects of the GFC.

- It promised that deposits in banks would be guaranteed by the government.
- It put in place a number of projects to keep businesses going such as building projects in schools, the home insulation scheme, and an increase in first home buyers grants.
- It offered a $900 cash bonus to taxpayers in order to encourage spending in the community.

As a result of these measures, Australia survived the GFC far better than most other developed economies. It recovered far sooner and with far less long-term impact overall.

1.7 The evolution of the financial planning environment

LEARNING OBJECTIVE 1.7 Describe the evolution of the financial planning environment in Australia.

It is useful to reflect on historical developments as it helps us understand aspects of the present. Table 1.2 presents a summary of some of the major changes that have occurred in the financial planning industry since 1980.

TABLE 1.2   Evolution of the financial planning environment

Decade	Selected events in the development of financial planning as a new occupation
1980s	• 1983: Introduction of rollover superannuation funds led to an expansion of superannuation products • 1985: Introduction of capital gains tax led to planning to minimise effect of the tax • 1986: Introduction of fringe benefits tax led to salary packaging • 1987: Creation of imputation credits on company dividends
1990s	• 1992–93: Introduction of compulsory superannuation contributions, gradually rising from 3% to 9% • 1997: Wallis Report recommended many changes to Australia's regulatory system and the operations of the range of financial services offered by institutions such as banks, insurance companies, managed funds, sharebrokers, superannuation funds and friendly societies that operated in the economy
2000s	• 2001: *Financial Services Reform Act 2001* led to many changes in the way financial planning was carried out • 2006–07: 'Simpler Super' proposals introduced by the federal government led to significant changes in superannuation rules • 2007: Changes to the assets and income tests for age pensions • 2008–2010: Three commissions by the federal government: the Ripoll Inquiry into corporate collapses and financial services; the Henry Tax Review to report on new taxation initiatives; and the Cooper Review into the superannuation industry

2010s	• 2011: Future of Financial Advice (FoFA) proposed a range of changes to the way financial planners are remunerated and how financial planners operate their business
	• 2011: MySuper instituted by the federal government to provide a low-cost alternative superannuation fund for investors
	• 2011: RG 175 revision put into operation the changes required by FoFA
	• 2012: FoFA reforms become law and started on voluntary basis
	• 2013: FoFA reforms become mandatory
	• 2013: Update to RG 146 regarding education and training courses
	• 2013: Senate inquiry into the performance of ASIC — whistleblowing, enforceable undertakings, national exam
	• 2013: Australian Government's Financial System Inquiry (The Murray Report) — financial adviser register, financial planner education, general advice, product intervention
	• 2014: Senate Economics Committee starts inquiry into FoFA amendments
	• 2014: Senate Inquiry into Forestry Managed Investment Schemes
	• 2014: Senate Inquiry into Scrutiny of Financial Advice — conflicted remuneration, internal investigations of misconduct, licensee and practice standards
	• 2014: Parliamentary Joint Committee on Corporations and Financial Services — to lift education standards for financial planners, general advice to be renamed product information, financial adviser register
	• 2015: Review of Retail Life Insurance Advice / Trowbridge Report — upfront commissions to be replaced by level commissions combined with an initial advice payment that cannot be paid more than once every 5 years
	• 2015: Tax White Paper — to review CGT and negative gearing, tax system complexity
	• 2016: ASIC RG 221 Facilitating digital financial services disclosures — provided a guide for financial services providers on how to deliver financial product and financial services disclosures to clients via email and on the internet
	• 2016: ASIC RG 255 Providing digital financial product advice to retail clients — outlined some issues in relation to the provision of digital advice (also known as robo-advice or automated advice)
	• 2016: Parliamentary Joint Committee on Corporations and Financial Services Inquiry into Life Insurance Industry — claims handling practices, sales practices, internal dispute resolution, ASIC and oversight of life insurance industry
	• 2016: Parliamentary Joint Committee on Corporations and Financial Services Inquiry into Whistleblower Protections in the Corporate, Public and Not-for-profit Sectors — compensation arrangements, types of wrongdoings, integration of whistleblowing protection regimes and obligations of entities and regulators
	• 2016: Senate Inquiry into Consumer Protection in the Banking, Insurance and Financial Sector — impact of misconduct on victims and consumers, remuneration structures, culture and chain of responsibilities and consumer compensation schemes
	• 2017: *Corporations Amendment (Professional Standards of Financial Advisers) Act 2017* — sets new education and experience standards for financial planners, as well as protecting the terms 'financial planner' and 'financial adviser'
	• 2017: Royal Commission into Misconduct in the Banking, Superannuation and Financial Services Industry — inquiry into the conduct of banks, insurers, financial services providers and superannuation funds (excluding SMSFs). The inquiry also covered the regulator's ability to identify and address misconduct
	• 2018: *Corporations Amendment (Life Insurance Remuneration Arrangements) Act 2017* — changes are made to the amount of upfront and ongoing commissions and volume bonuses paid to advisers for life insurance sales
	• 2018: Productivity Commission inquiry into the competitiveness of the Australian financial system — inquiry into the competitiveness of the Australian financial system with a view to improving consumer outcomes, the productivity and international competitiveness of the financial system and economy
2020s	• 2020: The *Financial Sector Reform (Hayne Royal Commission Response) Act 2020* provides ASIC with some new powers to help them combat corporate crime and bad behaviours by banks
	• 2021: *Financial Sector Reform (Hayne Royal Commission Response — Better Advice) Act 2021* — the Financial Services and Credit Panel is given its own legislative functions and powers to address a range of misconduct by, and circumstances relating to, financial advisers
	• 2022: Quality of Advice Review — a review of the effectiveness of measures to improve the quality of financial advice, with the aim of ensuring Australians have access to high quality, accessible and affordable financial advice

Since the mid 1980s, numerous other changes to tax, social security and superannuation laws and various product developments have resulted in people seeking financial planning advice to better their financial situation. They also led to the continued development of the financial planning industry to the extent that financial planning may now be referred to as a profession. This involved the development of a wider range of skills, education and knowledge for financial planners. ASIC has raised the education standards of financial advisers by requiring them to meet minimum competency standards under regulatory guide RG 146 *Licensing: Training of financial product advisers* and undertake ongoing professional development. The standards were raised further through the introduction of the *Corporations Amendment (Professional Standards of Financial Advisers) Act 2017*.

1.8 The regulatory framework that applies to financial planning

LEARNING OBJECTIVE 1.8 Outline the regulatory framework that applies to financial planning in Australia.

As with any other profession, financial planners are subject to a wide range of regulations and controls. The principal legal regulations and controls that govern the financial planning profession are listed in table 1.3.

TABLE 1.3   **Legal regulations and controls regulating the financial planning industry**

Act	Coverage
Insurance Contracts Act 1984	Insurance contracts
Privacy Act 1988	Covers client confidentiality and dealing with private and sensitive information
Superannuation Industry (Supervision) Act 1993	Legislation concerning superannuation. The Act and its regulations and ancillary legislation are administered by the Australian Prudential Regulation Authority (APRA); other parts administered by ASIC
Superannuation (Resolution of Complaints) Act 1993	Settlement of superannuation complaints. Administered by ASIC
Criminal Code Act 1995	Centrelink fraud covered in this Act. Obtaining a financial advantage by deception
Life Insurance Act 1995	Laws relating to life insurance contracts. Parts are administered by both APRA and ASIC
Income Tax Assessment Act 1997	Laws concerning superannuation, income, deductions and capital gains
Social Security (Administration) Act 1999	Rules around Centrelink benefits
Australian Securities and Investments Commission Act 2001	Laws concerning ASIC's authority and jurisdiction
Corporations Act 2001	Contains prescriptive obligations for the financial services industry. Chapter 7: Financial Services and Markets. Administered by Australian Securities and Investments Commission (ASIC)
Financial Services Reform Act 2001 (FSRA)	ASIC (incorporated into the *Corporations Act 2001*)
Anti-Money Laundering and Counter-Terrorism Financing Act 2006	Deals with identifying clients and the source of funds
Tax Agents Services Act 2009	Financial planners obliged to register as a tax (financial) adviser and the obligation to adhere to the Tax Practitioners Board's Code of Professional Conduct
Competition and Consumer Act 2010	An Act to govern the anti-competitive nature of business practices. Administered by ASIC

Future of Financial Advice 2011	Changes to the laws relating to the provision of financial advice. Administered by ASIC (incorporated into the *Corporations Act 2001*)
Corporations Amendment (Professional Standards for Financial Advisers) Act 2017	Education and experience standards for financial planners, as well as protecting the terms 'financial planner' and 'financial adviser'
Corporations Amendment (Life Insurance Remuneration Arrangements) Act 2017	Removes the exemption from the conflicted remuneration ban on benefits paid in relation to certain life risk insurance products
Financial Sector Reform (Hayne Royal Commission Response) Act 2020	To implement a large number of the Hayne Royal Commission recommendations, including providing ASIC with some new powers to help them combat corporate crime and bad behaviours by banks
Financial Sector Reform (Hayne Royal Commission Response — Better Advice) Act 2021	Introduces a new disciplinary system for financial advisers, including a new disciplinary body, the Financial Services and Credit Panel

Regulatory structure and influences

The recommendations from the 1997 Wallis Inquiry into the financial services industry led to some significant changes in the legislation and regulatory authority covering financial services activity in Australia. The thrust of the changes was to bring a range of financial services which were previously covered by different legislation under the one Act of Parliament. Thus, the *Financial Services Reform Act 2001* was incorporated into the *Corporations Act 2001*.

In addition to the requirement to comply with the Corporations Act, there are a number of other laws that financial advisers need to comply with. These include other Acts of Parliament as well as the common law of negligence and contract.

The key points of each law are listed below.

Corporations Act 2001

A key objective of the Corporations Act is to promote confident and informed decision making by consumers of financial products and services. It also promotes fairness, honesty and professionalism by those who provide financial services, and creates a fair, orderly and transparent market for financial products. The Corporations Act also aims to reduce systematic risk and provide fair and effective services by clearing and settlement facilities.

The main areas of the Corporations Act affecting the financial planning industry include:
- part 7.6, division 5 — licensing regime in the financial products and financial services advice industry
- s. 761 — retail and wholesale clients
- ss. 763–765 — what is a financial product and what is not
- s. 912A — licensee's obligations
- s. 941 — financial services guide
- s. 961 — best interests obligation
- s. 961A — appointment of authorised representatives of licensees.

Common law

Common law deals with civil liability. The general application of common law provides remedies for such matters as contracts and negligent misrepresentation.

The common law provides that in a contractual obligation with a client, for example fee-for-service basis, if the financial planner's services are not performed satisfactorily, the client is entitled to contractual remedies for cost recovery and loss suffered.

Advisers who operate on a fee-for-service basis are under a contractual obligation to the client. If they perform those services in an unsatisfactory or negligent manner, or do not perform those services, the client can seek redress under common law. The adviser has a duty of care that must be exercised under common law. Otherwise, the person relying on that information may be entitled to damages for negligent misrepresentation.

Superannuation Industry (Supervision) Act 1993 (SIS Act)

Superannuation entities must comply with the SIS Act in order to attract concessional tax treatment. Failure by these entities to comply may result in a loss of tax concessions as well as risking civil and/or criminal legal action by an aggrieved person.

Three other pieces of legislation provide for the regulation of superannuation entities.

- *Superannuation Supervisory Levy (Amendment) Act 1995.* This Act imposes a levy on superannuation entities for the purpose of recouping the APRA and ASIC cost of supervision of the superannuation industry.
- *Superannuation (Financial Assistance Funding) Levy Act 1993.* This Act imposes a levy on superannuation entities, which is used to provide financial assistance to funds which have sustained losses due to theft or fraudulent activities.
- *Superannuation (Resolution of Complaints) Act 1993.* This Act established a complaint resolution scheme and the Superannuation Complaints Tribunal.

The SIS Act aims at providing the framework for the prudent management of superannuation funds. It provides the necessary checks, rules and standards that aim to minimise risks to ensure compliance. It sets out rules and clarifies the duties of the trustee, for example external audit requirement, complaints handling, and information disclosure and member participation in the management of superannuation funds.

APRA administers the SIS Act and its regulations and ancillary legislation which regulate the superannuation industry. A main objective of APRA is to properly safeguard the benefits of members and policyholders.

Life Insurance Act 1995

APRA administers the Life Insurance Act which has specific reference to the operations of insurance companies offering life insurance. ASIC also administers the way in which advisers of life insurance conduct their business with clients.

Insurance Act 1973

This Act, administered by APRA, regulates the general way in which insurance companies conduct and operate their business.

Australian Securities and Investments Commission Act 2001

This Act establishes the regulations pertaining to the organisation of ASIC.

The role of ASIC

ASIC aims to maintain public confidence by improving sales and disclosure practices in the financial advisory industry. It is committed to raising standards of financial services and products offered to Australian investors through policy, surveillance, industry campaigns and targeted enforcement. ASIC administers the following legislation.

- *Corporations Act 2001* (including the Corporations Regulations)
- *Australian Securities and Investments Commission Act 2001* (ASIC Act)
- *Insurance Contracts Act 1984*
- *Superannuation (Resolution of Complaints) Act 1993*

It is the role of ASIC to ensure practitioners comply with legal requirements governing the financial planning industry. ASIC does not draft legislation — this is Treasury's role. ASIC's role is to implement the legislation. ASIC is the watchdog for consumer protection laws in financial products and services. Its powers relate to the client:

- receiving financial advice
- putting money into investments, superannuation, life insurance or general insurance, or depositing money with a bank, building society or credit union.

Its powers do not relate to the client in situations that include:

- borrowing money, which is governed by state or territory departments of fair trading or the Australian Competition and Consumer Commission
- having concerns about the actual level of fees; that is, where the client has been clearly told about them and has been charged only what the contract provides for
- buying health insurance
- the merging of banks or closure of their branches.

In meeting the challenge of implementing the reforms of the Corporations Act, ASIC has developed policy and guidance in consultation with industry members and industry bodies to help the advisory services industry apply the legislature provisions to their individual circumstances. Some of the most important regulatory guides related to financial planning are:

- RG 104 *Licensing: Meeting general obligations*
- RG 105 *Licensing: Organisational competence*
- RG 146 *Licensing: Training of financial product advisers*
- RG 165 *Licensing: Internal and external dispute resolution*
- RG 166 *Licensing: Financial requirements*
- RG 167 *Licensing: Discretionary powers*
- RG 168 *Disclosure: Product Disclosure Statements (and other disclosure obligations)*
- RG 169 *Disclosure: Discretionary powers*
- RG 175 *Licensing: Financial product advisers — conduct and disclosure*
- RG 179 *Managed discretionary account services*
- RG 181 *Licensing: Managing conflicts of interest*
- RG 182 *Dollar disclosure*
- RG 183 *Approval of financial services sector codes of conduct*
- RG 184 *Superannuation: Delivery of product disclosure for investment strategies*
- RG 200 *Advice to super fund members*
- RG 221 *Facilitating digital financial services disclosures*
- RG 244 *Giving information, general advice and scaled advice*
- RG 246 *Conflicted remuneration*
- RG 276 *Superannuation forecast: Calculators and retirement estimates*.

Dispute Resolution Scheme

Where a consumer is dissatisfied with the services received from their financial planner or other financial services providers, the following avenues are available for a complaint to be lodged.

1. Seek resolution from the financial planner or financial service provider — a professional financial planner should aim to resolve the dispute with the client promptly and fairly.
2. Approach the person responsible for handling complaints within the organisation — if the client is unhappy with the outcome of dealing with the financial planner, the matter should be brought to the attention of the person who is responsible for handling complaints on behalf of the financial planner's organisation.
3. Contact an external dispute resolution body — this independent body will have the power to investigate and resolve the dispute.
4. Take legal action through the courts — this is the last available avenue for a dissatisfied client to seek redress if the outcome from the external dispute resolution body is unacceptable to the client.

Australian Financial Complaints Authority

The Australian Financial Complaints Authority (AFCA) is a free and independent dispute resolution body that considers complaints about:

- credit, finance and loans
- insurance
- banking deposits and payments
- investments and financial advice
- superannuation.

AFCA's role is to assist consumers and small business to reach agreements with financial firms about how to resolve their complaints. The service is free and impartial, and AFCA do not advocate for either party. Where a complaint cannot be resolved between the parties, AFCA can step in and decide an appropriate outcome that will be binding on the financial firm involved in the complaint. AFCA can also award compensation for losses suffered as a result of a financial firm's error or inappropriate conduct.

Refer to AFCA's website afca.org.au for more details on their role and services.

The government is announcing the biggest financial advice shake-up in years. Here's what it could mean for you

The federal government wants to increase the number of financial advisers in Australia so more households can afford quality financial advice and don't have to rely on advice from 'finfluencers' and unregulated sources online.

The government says 10 000 financial advisers have left the industry since 2019 in the wake of Hayne royal commission, and it has left a vacuum of quality information for people.

It says there are only 16 000 financial advisers left in the country, and the median cost of financial advice has increased by 41% between 2018 and 2021 as a result, leaving quality advice too expensive for too many households.

To deal with the problem, it says it wants to significantly increase the number of financial advisers in Australia and make it easier for superannuation funds to provide advice to their millions of members who are approaching retirement.

It also hopes to encourage financial advisers with at least 10 years' experience — and a clean regulatory record — to stay in the industry by allowing them to keep practising if they don't have a tertiary qualification.

It's part of the government's response to the Quality of Advice Review, the final report of which was released in February.

The government says it has accepted 14 of the review's 22 recommendations 'in full or in-principle', and it will develop legislation over the coming year to deal with them.

It will also introduce legislation to parliament this week aimed at keeping experienced financial advisers in the industry.

The plan to rebuild the financial advice industry

Stephen Jones, Assistant Treasurer and Minister for Financial Services, outlined the government's plans on Tuesday.

He said the government would tackle the problem in three phases.

In the first phase, it will try to streamline the process of giving financial advice through the channels that already exist.

That will involve replacing unwieldy statements-of-advice with something more fit-for-purpose, scrapping the legalistic 'safe harbour' checklist that advisers have to follow to comply with the best interests duty, and improving transparency about the commissions advisers are being paid for certain products.

It will coincide with the government's attempt to encourage experienced financial advisers to stay in the industry.

'This week, I will be introducing legislation to parliament to follow through on the government's election commitment to create a pathway for experienced advisers with a clean record to continue practising without the need to undertake further education,' he said in a speech to the Association of Superannuation Funds of Australia on Tuesday.

The second phase of the plan will involve retirement incomes.

Mr Jones says Australians are now retiring with about 200 000 on average in superannuation, but only 26% of individuals approaching retirement are seeking financial advice.

By 2060, it's projected that one in every three dollars paid out of the super system will be a bequest — that's money being passed to family members.

Mr Jones says the purpose of superannuation is not to leave bequests. An effective retirement system should see Australians drawing down on their super in ways that improve their quality of life in older age.

He says the Retirement Income Covenant, which came into effect in July last year, requires super trustees to develop a retirement income strategy for their members that helps members manage spending of savings through retirement.

But, he says, the current rules constrain super funds from having the exact conversations needed with their members to help them develop those successful retirement income strategies.

'Superannuation funds have told me that they have many retirees who have not switched from the accumulation phase to a tax-free pension account,' Mr Jones said on Tuesday.

'This might be good for the Treasury coffers, but it's not good for members.

I'm also told that there are thousands who miss out on the age pension and other benefits that they are entitled to, simply because they didn't know who to ask. Or because they assumed their super fund was already doing this for them.

'As such, we will adopt the review's recommendation for superannuation funds to expand their provision of advice.

'We will also provide legal certainty for funds on how to collectively charge for advice.

'Super funds are well suited to safely meeting the needs of their members. They are already governed by strong obligations to act in the best financial interests of members and act for the sole purpose of providing retirement benefits to members,' he said.

The third phase of the government's plan will examine the role of other institutions — such as banks and insurers — in providing more information and financial advice.

Mr Jones says as Treasury officials work on implementing the recommendation to allow super funds to provide more financial advice, they will explore with industry what would be required to tailor the model for other institutions.

However, he says, the first two stages of the plan are far more urgent, so the third stage will take a back seat in the government's immediate reforms.

'In terms of priority, I believe it is more urgent that we fix the problems for financial advisers and help the five million Australians, at or approaching retirement, get access to more retirement income advice,' Mr Jones said on Tuesday.

'I'm just not compelled that the same urgency exists in these other spaces.

'There is also a difference between the obligations that cover these institutions and superannuation funds.'

Unregulated advice is filling the information vacuum

Mr Jones said the lack of affordable quality financial advice for Australian households could lead to 'significant consumer harm' as people turned to the unregulated world for information.

'It can lead to even more harm when they try seeking to fill this advice gap with information from the unregulated world,' he said on Tuesday.

'And I don't just mean Uncle Bob at the BBQ. But 'finfluencers'. Unlicensed online advice. And scammers.

'Getting more professional advisers, qualified and into the practice is important. It needs to happen.'

The Council on the Ageing (COTA) said it looked forward to seeing the detail of the government's legislation because reforms to help people approaching retirement to get good retirement income advice are long overdue.

But Patricia Sparrow, COTA's chief executive, said while the changes announced by Mr Jones were positive, she didn't want them to lead to a situation where super fund members would be charged fees for no service.

The Council of Australian Life Insurers (CALI), which was formed last year, also tentatively welcomed the announcement.

It said it supported the government's plan to allow super trustees to provide advice to their members, including on life insurance.

But it said it would like the government to eventually allow life insurers to also provide limited advice to Australians when they asked for it.

'We must address the growing problem of underinsurance that is leaving people unprotected when times get tough,' CALI chief executive Christine Cupitt said.

'For many Australians, getting advice is too expensive or too inaccessible with just 16 000 financial advisers to turn to across the country. Of these advisers, there are just 1000 who are helping people navigate life insurance products, which makes reforms for life insurance advice an urgent priority,' she said.

The finer details of the government plan

The government says it will develop legislation over the coming year to help it implement the recommendations from the final report from the Quality of Advice review.

Here are some of the finer details of its planned changes, following the recommendations.

Phase 1: Removing regulatory red tape

- The 'Safe Harbour' steps will be removed from the Best Interest Duty with consultation to determine implementation details originally designed to protect financial advisers and the implications of adopting the remaining parts of recommendation five (accept in principle part of recommendation five).
- Ongoing fee renewal and consent requirements will be streamlined into a single form, and the requirement to provide a fee disclosure statement will be removed (accept recommendation eight).
- Statements of Advice will be replaced with an advice record that is more fit-for-purpose, with consultation to determine the final design of the replacement (accept in principle recommendation nine).
- Certain exemptions to the ban on conflicted remuneration will be simplified and some removed.
- Standardised consumer consent requirements will be introduced for life, general and consumer credit insurance commissions (accept recommendations 13.7–13.9).

Phase 2: Expand access to retirement income advice

- The restrictions on collective charging will be amended to allow superannuation funds to provide more retirement advice and information to their members (accept in principle recommendation six).

- Superannuation trustees will be provided with legal clarity around current practices for the payment of adviser service fees (accept in principle recommendation seven).

Phase 3: Exploring new channels for advice

The government will explore expanding the provision of advice by other institutions by consulting industry and consumer stakeholders on recommendations to:
- broaden the definition of personal advice (recommendation one)
- remove the general advice warning (recommendation two)
- allow non-relevant providers to provide personal advice (recommendation three)
- introduce a good advice duty (recommendation four)
- amend the Design and Distribution Obligations (recommendations 12.1 and 12.2).
  This consultation will finalise implementation details for:
- the design of the replacement for Statements of Advice
- the implementation details and the implications of adopting the remaining parts of recommendation five
- the Financial Adviser Code of Ethics
- expanding access to affordable retirement advice.

Government consultation will test how these proposals might operate under different advice models, including digital advice models, and across sectors. Consultation will also consider practical policy design and implementation issues, including in relation to consumer protections.

The government will issue its final response on the Delivering Better Financial Outcomes package later in 2023.

Source: Hutchens 2023.

1.9 What investors and financial planners can learn from history

LEARNING OBJECTIVE 1.9 Identify lessons from history that should be understood by investors and financial planners.

The history of the development of the financial planning industry since 1980 contains a vast range of issues that have led to the creation of the 'new profession' of financial planning. The Financial Planning Association Australia (FPAA; see the appendix to this chapter) is taking steps to lift the standards of financial planners so that members of the public will receive a more professional service. Legislative change, economic circumstances, a lack of general financial literacy and a deeper understanding of the risk of investment have all played a part in this development. Recent history contains many lessons for financial planners and investors, including the need for an awareness of:
- market cycles — shares, property and interest rates all experience cycles of high and low returns
- the risks accompanying high returns — recall the adage 'high return equals high risk'
- the benefits of diversification — the benefits of spreading investments over asset classes to reduce risk and obtain more reliable returns
- the underlying portfolio of investment products — a fixed interest return may not be what it seems; an investor needs to know how money is being invested as a product may have a different set of risks than is immediately obvious, even though it may be 'guaranteed'
- scams — they appear quite frequently and ASIC's website (https://moneysmart.gov.au) provides updates and examples to watch out for
- the need to review investments based on economic and legislative changes — changes in the rules and regulations occur frequently and may affect a person's tax position or eligibility for the age pension. Economic changes may indicate a time to re-allocate an investment mix; for example, rising interest rates may mean it is time to move some funds from shares to fixed interest investments
- the need for financial planners to abide by established rules of conduct and regulations; otherwise, government is likely to impose new rules and regulations to address any misbehaviour or practices exhibited by financial planners that are to the detriment of consumers.

SUMMARY

Personal financial planning is about setting in place some personal objectives and arranging financial means to satisfy those objectives. Preparing a personal budget is a starting point in helping people to assess their financial position. Some people need additional help, through the aid of financial planners, in dealing with the complexity of the range of financial services.

Personal financial planning is carried out in an economic environment and investors should be aware of the impact that changes in economic circumstances can have on their financial plans. Business runs in cycles and monetary and fiscal policies are the two main mechanisms by which governments may help to reduce large fluctuations in the business cycle.

Changes in legislation, such as changes to superannuation and social security rules, and changes in the regulatory framework, such as the statement of advice requirements and professional standards for financial planners, have helped to shape the personal financial planning industry/profession. Economic changes over the last 20 or so years, such as share market crashes, overvaluation of property and overseas interest rate increases, have provided some hard lessons and made both financial planners and investors more aware of market cycles, the risks of high returns, the benefits of diversification, the variety of available investment products and the need to regularly review investments.

KEY TERMS

age pension A pension paid to eligible members of the community based on their age and subject to an income and assets test.

subprime mortgage fund A fund that holds mortgage assets that are of low quality; that is, the mortgages have been given to people who are in danger of not being able to make repayments on their mortgage.

work bonus scheme A scheme that encourages people over age pension age to continue working by allowing them to earn a higher amount of income before their age pension payments are reduced.

PROFESSIONAL APPLICATION QUESTIONS

1.1 A client aged 50 says to you, a junior financial planner, 'I would like to retire with a comfortable level of income. Can you help me to do that?' How would you restate the client's request in more definite terms?

1.2 Prepare a table to summarise the different roles carried out by ASIC, APRA and AFCA.

1.3 The Superannuation Guarantee is one reason why personal financial planning has increased in importance in recent years.

(a) Why do you think that many people show a low level of interest in their superannuation fund?

(b) Will you make your decision about setting an investment portfolio choice in an accumulation fund or will you leave it to a default choice where the fund manager nominates one portfolio selection such as 'conservative' for all members who do not nominate their own selection? Write your opinion about making a choice of investments for your own superannuation fund.

1.4 ASIC aims to maintain public confidence by improving sales and disclosure practices in the financial services industry. Which ASIC legislation enables them to achieve this goal?

1.5 Mary is a first year university student who is interested in becoming a financial planner. Describe the education and experience standards that she would need to satisfy before she could become a financial planner.

1.6 Suppose you have a friend who is interested in seeking advice from a financial planner for the first time. Explain to them what the steps of financial planning are.

1.7 Consider the 1987 share market crash; the 1990 property trust freeze; the 1992 Japan share market crash; the 1997 Asian crisis; and the 2000–01 dot.com crash. What common features can you identify in such events?

1.8 What are your own short-term, medium-term and long-term financial goals? Name two for each of the time frames.

PROFESSIONAL APPLICATION EXERCISES

★ BASIC | ★★ MODERATE | ★★★ CHALLENGING

1.9 The global financial crisis   ★

A friend of yours wants to know how the global financial crisis started. Using a diagram and in your own words, provide an answer to your friend.

1.10 A lesson from history — property trust freeze   ★

Suppose you were considering placing an investment in an unlisted property trust at a time when large amounts of funds were invested in the property sector and valuations of the properties held in the trust had increased by 30% over the past year. Explain whether or not you would consider investing in the trust at that time.

1.11 A lesson from history — price–earnings multiples   ★★

Based on the experience seen in the dot.com crash period, write an opinion giving advice to an investor who wonders if he should sell his investment when the price–earnings multiple reaches 60.

1.12 Wholesale and retail clients   ★★

Jennifer has the following financial details.

- Net assets of $2.2 million
- Gross income in the last two financial years are $260 000 and $240 000 respectively
- $550 000 in investment products

According to s. 761G of the Corporations Act, would Jennifer be classified as a wholesale or retail client? Justify your answer.

1.13 Financial planners — professionals?   ★★★

(a) Prepare a list of things that you regard are indicative of a profession.

(b) Do you believe financial planning is now a profession? Justify your answer.

1.14 Retirement income   ★★★

On a personal level, assess the level of income you think you would need — at a minimum — when you retire. Do you agree with the notion of 62.5% of pre-retirement earnings to be an adequate measure? If a person earned $100 000 prior to retirement what level of capital is required to produce 62.5% of such an income? (Assume a rate of return of 6% p.a.)

CASE STUDY 1

RETIREMENT PLANNING

Married couple George and Tina are both 62 years of age and they have been working since their 20s. They have two financially independent adult children and the following joint assets.

- $600 000 home (no mortgage)
- $5000 home contents
- $10 000 car
- $100 000 savings account
- $300 000 superannuation ($180 000 for George and $120 000 for Tina)

Tina recently received an $80 000 inheritance from her late aunt and this amount is included in the $100 000 savings account. The couple is now considering retiring in the next few years and using their assets to generate an annual income of $30 000 to cover their living expenses.

George and Tina approach you, a financial planner, for advice on how they can best plan for their retirement.

QUESTIONS

1 What other information would you like to obtain from George and Tina before you develop a financial plan for them?

2 Discuss how George and Tina's desired annual retirement income compares with ASFA's benchmarked modest lifestyle budget for a couple aged between 65 and 85.

3 How realistic are George and Tina's retirement objectives based on their current financial assets? Discuss.

4 Explain to George and Tina how the age pension and the work bonus scheme may assist them with their retirement income goal.

5 Identify and discuss three types of risks that George and Tina may face when planning for their retirement.

CASE STUDY 2

DISCLOSURE REQUIREMENTS

The following is based on the article 'Retirees' nightmare: anything goes if you disclose' (Long 2013).

The Prime Trust went into liquidation in 2011 with the loss of $550 million of investors' funds. How did the trust lose so much money when it was supposed to be invested in retirement villages and aged care facilities? The answer lies in the small print in the product disclosure statement (PDS) that allowed the manager of the fund to change the constitution (rules) of the trust. The change allowed the manager to charge a range of fees to the trust to cover things like the listing fee on the ASX — some $33 million! The founder also charged management fees to the trust and then sold the management rights to another party associated with the founder of the trust for a total of around $100 million. The cash flow that went to the founder has been directed to family trusts so that the founder has no control over the assets but is a beneficiary.

ASIC's response to an irate investor included: 'we note that the fees you complained of were outlined in the PDS prior to the Trust's listing on the ASX'. ASIC's response also outlined that there was no evidence to suggest that there had been a breach of the trust's statutory obligations.

Similar things have happened in many mortgage funds and other managed investment schemes where investors have lost money. The main issue is whether the operations and fees are disclosed to investors. The writer states 'the absurdity of "disclosure" as a safeguard is evident in the billions that mainly elderly retirees have lost in such funds over the years' (Long 2013).

QUESTIONS

1 Why is the disclosure seen as an absurdity as a safeguard in this situation?
2 If a financial planner had recommended Prime Trust, what obligations under the Corporations Act are placed on the financial adviser in giving advice to a client?
3 The FAAA Professional Code (see appendix) contain principles of how a financial planner should deal with clients. Select three principles from the FAAA Professional Code and discuss how they may have saved retirees from making the investment in Prime Trust or whether, in fact, the FAAA Professional Code would not have made any difference to the advice given to a retiree.
4 What do you think of the ethics of the founder of the trust by charging such a high fee for listing services on the ASX and changing the constitution of the trust without notifying investors?

CASE STUDY 3

STORM FINANCIAL CLIENTS SLAM $140 000 FINE AFTER 3000 INVESTORS LEFT DESTITUTE

Emmanuel and Julie Cassimatis, the husband and wife founders of collapsed company Storm Financial — which left more than 3000 clients destitute — are facing fines of $70 000 each under a Federal Court ruling. The couple copped the penalty for giving inappropriate financial advice to vulnerable cash-strapped investors and have also been banned from managing corporations for seven years. During Federal Court hearings in 2016, it was determined the pair had breached the civil, not criminal, duties of directors stemming from the Corporations Act.

But the fine is seen as a slap in the face to their former clients, who lost more than $800 million when the company went under. Vietnam war veteran Stephen Reynolds was one of them, with the 70-year-old losing his house in Townsville after being left with a $1.2 million debt. At the time he signed up for a Storm Financial margin lending loan he earned just $800 a fortnight. Is this fine enough? Because my legal bill trying to recover money from that was lent by dodgy banks was almost $80 000, Mr Reynolds said. 'This does not make sense to me, this is a fine of only $70 000 when it appears it could just be pocket money for Mr and Mrs Cassimatis. 'Ten years on, with many families destroyed, marriage break-ups, suicides and lots of lots of stress, I cannot see after 10 years this amount of money is enough — it is a slap in the face. 'Many people have lost their life savings, lives have been destroyed — $70 000 is not much money at all.' If he got to meet Mr Cassimatis face to face, Mr Reynolds said he would ask him if he was remorseful — if he understood what he had done to the lives of thousands of people. He said he'd ask him: 'Do you ever think of these people, what about them?'

Many investors were retirees

Townsville-based Storm Financial crashed in 2009 with losses of over $3 billion. The Australian Securities and Investments Commission (ASIC) pursued the directors in civil proceedings, through the courts, alleging they had breached their fiduciary duties. The Storm Financial investment model encouraged investors to borrow against their assets and buy indexed share funds, but the stock market collapse left them owing millions of dollars. Most of the investors were retired, close to retirement, with few assets and little income. They had little hope of rebuilding in the event of significant loss.

Investors 'Stormified' to invest more over time

ASIC has argued that since 1994, Storm Financial has operated a system considered to be one-size-fits-all investment advice for all clients. The advice recommended clients invest substantial amounts of index fund, using the what was called the 'double-gearing Storm' model. This approach involved taking out both a home loan as well as a margin loan in order to create a 'cash dam' and pay Storm's fees. According to ASIC, once the initial investments took place, 'Stormified' clients would be encouraged to take "step" investments over time.

By late 2008 and early 2009, many of Storm's clients had suffered significant losses.

However, ASIC did not allege the model was inappropriate for all investors, rather, flawed for investors who fell into a particular class — those with little or no income and few assets. Mr Cassimatis has always maintained his innocence, claiming it was the global financial crisis (GFC) that led to his company's collapse, not a flawed lending model. But he told a hearing in 2009 he did accept moral responsibility. 'Whilst I believe it was not our doing, nevertheless it happened on our watch,' he said at the time. He later told the ABC TV's Lateline program: 'Till the moment I draw my last breath we are going to work as hard as we can, I am going to work as hard as I possibly can to find justice for all of these individuals.

Maximum fine for Cassimatis breach is $200 000

In a statement, ASIC said Mr and Ms Cassimatis were penalised for not exercising their duties as directors with the degree of care and due diligence that a reasonable person would. The maximum fine for that breach is $200 000. ASIC began the civil proceedings eight years ago, with the trial finally taking place in 2016. But during that time, ASIC entered into settlement agreements with some of the major banks, who signed off on the original loans.

In September 2012, the Commonwealth Bank of Australia made available up to $136 million as compensation for losses suffered on investments made through Storm Financial. It had already provided $132 million to investors under the resolution scheme. In 2013, Macquarie Bank agreed to pay $82.5 million and in September 2014, the Bank of Queensland signed off on a $17 million compensation deal.

Clients unlikely to recover any more funds

Today was the day for justice, but the thousands of clients who lost everything they owned, are unlikely to recover any further funds. Mr Cassimastis said he too suffered, losing his own home. He had run Storm Financial for over 30 years. The once high-profile couple, known for their lavish lifestyle, used to commute via private jet from Townsville to their Brisbane acreage. Today they are rarely seen in public. Lawyers for ASIC and Mr and Mrs Cassimatis have one week to respond to Justice John Dowsett's draft orders.

Source: Hamilton-Smith 2018.

QUESTIONS

1 What part of the Corporations Act indicates that Storm Financial's approach is not in accord with the legislation?
2 What of the requirements of an AFSL holder do you think the Storm advisers did not meet?
3 Why do you think that the collapse of Storm occurred in late 2008? Describe the economic circumstances of the time and their coincidence with Storm's collapse.
4 Why do you think ASIC recommended to the parliamentary inquiry that all forms of commissions be banned?
5 Research the Storm Financial collapse. What did Storm advise clients to do? What did they invest in? How much did they invest? What avenues of redress have clients available to them?

APPENDIX

FAAA PROFESSIONAL CODE

The principles of the Financial Advice Association Australia (FAAA) Professional Code are organised under three pillars: Being, Knowing and Doing. This Code is current as at June 2024.

Being

1. *Client first.* Placing the client's interests first, in line with the requirements of relevant laws and regulations, is a hallmark of professionalism. This requires that financial planning professionals not place personal, employer or licensee gain or advantage before client interests.
2. *Integrity.* This requires honesty and candour in all professional matters. Integrity requires the financial planning professional to observe both the letter and the spirit of relevant rules, regulations and laws - including the FAAA Code. Integrity requires that conduct is approached in a spirit of utmost good faith and that their actions are aligned with promoting a culture that supports and requires integrity in others.
3. *Objectivity.* This requires that financial planning professionals must not allow bias, preference, undue influence, incentives or other inappropriate factors to influence the advice or service they provide to clients, or their dealings with other professionals.
4. *Fairness.* This requires dealing with clients, colleagues and others in the professional sphere in a way that is just, and treating others in the way you would want to be treated. Financial planning professionals will have a far higher level of knowledge than clients and non-industry participants. Fairness requires they use their greater knowledge to enable clients to make fully informed decisions, and never present advice or information in a way that omits or distorts material considerations.

Knowing

5. *Knowledge and skills.* Financial planning professionals must ensure they have the appropriate level of knowledge and skills required to discharge the functions of their role. For those advising clients, this includes the self-awareness to identify when it is appropriate to decline the provision of advice or to refer the client to another suitably qualified professional.
6. *Continuing Professional Development (CPD).* The financial planning profession operates against a background of a quickly moving market and ongoing regulatory change. In order for financial planning professionals to continue to deliver high quality outcomes to their stakeholders it is incumbent on them to keep up to date with changes and meet their CPD requirements as appropriate to their FAAA membership category.

Doing

7. *Professional behaviour.* Financial planning professionals must conduct themselves with dignity and show respect and courtesy to clients, fellow professionals and others in business-related activities. Professional behaviour requires those in the financial planning profession, individually and in cooperation with peers, to enhance and maintain the profession's public image and its ability to serve the public interest. For those in client-facing roles, this will include providing a high level of client service, meeting commitments in a timely way, providing regular updates and appropriately managing client expectations.
8. *Competence.* This requires financial planning professionals to utilise their knowledge and skills to deliver high quality outcomes for stakeholders. In particular, advice delivered to consumers should be accurate, up to date and relevant. Recommendations must be implemented in a timely and thorough manner.
9. *Diligence.* Financial planning professionals must work in a way that is conscientious and exercises a due level of care. They must apply a best practice approach to their dealings with clients and other stakeholders, meeting the standards set out in relevant FAAA guidance as appropriate. In the financial planning context, this will require gaining an appropriate understanding of a client's circumstances and ensuring recommendations are suitable and aligned with the client's needs.
10. *Confidentiality and data protection.* Due to the volume and sensitivity of client data that financial planners and other related professionals are entrusted with, there is an additional level of responsibility on financial planning participants. This arises due to the potential for inappropriate data use or ineffectual data security to cause consumer harm, as well as damage to the image and reputation of the

profession. Client or consumer data must not be shared in a way that is contrary to law or regulation, or otherwise without the client's informed and explicit consent. Client data must be held in a secure manner and professionals must take all reasonable steps to ensure they comply with the requirements to maintain this.

Source: Financial Advice Association Australia (FAAA) 2023.

REFERENCES

ABS 2009, *Australian social trends*, 4102.0.

ABS 2023, 'Population clock and pyramid', www.abs.gov.au/statistics/people/population/population-clock-pyramid.

ASIC n.d., Moneysmart website, https://moneysmart.gov.au.

Association of Superannuation Funds (ASFA) 2023, ASFA *retirement standard: detailed budget breakdowns: March quarter 2023*, https://www.superannuation.asn.au/resources/retirement-standard/.

Bateman, H, Kingston, G & Piggott, J 2001, *Forced saving: Mandating private retirement incomes*, Cambridge University Press, Cambridge.

Clare, R 2006, *The introduction of choice of superannuation fund — results to date*, February, ASFA Research and Resource Centre, Sydney.

Financial Advice Association Australia (FAAA) 2023, 'The FAAA professional code', https://faaa.au/wp-content/uploads/2023/04/FAAA-Professional-Code.pdf.

Financial Planning Association of Australia Limited 2008, *The trade-off: Understanding investment risk*, http://www.beachsidefinancial.com.au/files/FPA%20trade-off.pdf.

Financial Services Council 2014, *Retirement savings gap at June 2013*, Rice Warner, May, www.ricewarner.com/wp-content/uploads/2015/10/fsc-retirement-savings-gap-at-30-june-2013_060520141.pdf.

Fry, T, Heaney, R & McKeown, W 2007, 'Will investors change their superannuation fund given the choice?', *Accounting and Finance*, vol. 47, no. 2, June, pp. 267–283.

Hamilton-Smith, L 2018, 'Storm Financial clients slam $140k fine after 3,000 investors left destitute', ABC News, 22 March, https://www.abc.net.au/news/2018-03-22/storm-financial-founders-fined-140k-over-800m-company-collapse/9576418

Hutchens, G 2023, 'The government is announcing the biggest financial advice shake-up in years. Here's what it could mean for you', *ABC News*, 13 June, www.abc.net.au/news/2023-06-13/financial-advice-reforms-albanese-superannuation-retirement/102472184.

Long, S 2013, *Retirees' nightmare: anything goes if you disclose, ABC News*, 4 March, www.abc.net.au/news/2013-03-04/long-prime-trust-betrayal-disclose/4551422.

Reserve Bank of Australia (RBA) 2020, 'Key economic indicators snapshot', 4 March, www.rba.gov.au/snapshots/economy-indicators-snapshot.

The Treasury 2021, *The 2021 intergenerational report,* Australian Government, 28 June, https://treasury.gov.au/publication/2021-intergenerational-report.

ACKNOWLEDGEMENTS

Extracts: © ABC

Extract: © Financial Advice Association Australia

Figure 1.1: © Cambridge University Press

Figure 1.2: © Australian Bureau of Statistics

Table 1.1: © The Association of Superannuation Funds of Australia Limited

CHAPTER 2

Financial planning skills

LEARNING OBJECTIVES

After studying this chapter, you should be able to:

2.1 prepare personal financial statements

2.2 recognise the role played by financial counsellors in the financial environment

2.3 analyse financial statements using ratio analysis

2.4 demonstrate financial mathematics skills necessary for financial planners

2.5 explain the concept of time value of money and the benefits of compound interest

2.6 compare the difference between nominal and effective interest rates

2.7 explain the concept of net present value

2.8 apply the time value of money concept to different investment choices

2.9 explain the effect of taxation and inflation on the rate of return.

Nina is aged 23. She has finished her apprenticeship and has now started her own landscape gardening business. Her uncle, an accountant, has suggested that she makes sure that she pays herself a small wage from the business and to keep the business income and expenses quite separate from her own bank account. She has had her own savings account for a long time, but when she left school she made regular contributions as personal savings throughout the 4 years of her apprenticeship. Nina has accumulated approximately $6000 from both savings and interest after withdrawing $3000 to buy items of equipment to set up her business. Nina also arranged to borrow another $3000 to buy other items before the prices increased. Her uncle has drawn her attention to the rate of interest that she needs to pay on the loan and the rate of interest that she earns on her savings.

She is somewhat surprised to learn that she earns only 2% on her savings but has to pay 10% on her loan. However, she decided not to use all of her own money to start the business because she was a little uncertain that she would make a success of it. Nina's uncle also suggested using a credit card for the business expenses as a way of keeping business records, but to make sure that she paid the balance by the due date to avoid interest payments at 19%. While she was thinking about her finances, she wondered how she could improve the rate of interest on her own savings. Her uncle suggested that she move most of her savings to an account where the interest is compounded every month rather than every six months as happens with her current bank account. He also said that the cost of living increases and the impact on tax on her savings meant that Nina probably wasn't really saving anything at all.

His comments raised a number of issues that Nina needs to consider. These include the:
- effects of interest rates on saved and borrowed funds
- impact of increasing prices
- use of a credit card
- effect of taxation on her rate of return.

Illustrative examples used throughout this chapter will relate back to Nina's situation.

Introduction

Financial planning requires specialised knowledge across diverse areas including investments, risk management, taxation, estate planning, social security and retirement planning. This chapter looks at some of the technical skills that financial planners require in order to provide appropriate advice, particularly in the area of investments.

In this chapter we consider the essential data that an adviser needs to collect and how to use that data when advising clients. We also consider not only how compounding affects investments and examine ways in which comparisons of investment returns can be made, but also the impact of interest rates on credit cards.

It is important that investments are considered in terms of:
- their returns with regard to the frequency of interest payments
- the time value of money in present value terms
- the effects of inflation and the effects of taxation.

2.1 Preparing personal financial statements

LEARNING OBJECTIVE 2.1 Prepare personal financial statements.

Previously you learned about personal financial goals and their relevant time frames. As you move through various stages of life, and as various events — such as a new job, marriage, the birth of a child, or the death of a parent — change your life, your personal goals may change. Such changes emphasise the importance of ongoing attention to the personal financial planning process and the need to periodically reassess financial goals.

Once we determine what our financial goals are, we need to gather the necessary information and prepare working documents to determine whether such goals are achievable. These working documents involve the preparation of personal cash flow budgets and financial statements.

Personal financial statements consist of a set of information about a person's financial circumstances. Financial statements may be prepared in two parts:
1. a personal cash flow budget or statement, which aims to indicate all the sources of income and expenses to determine the amount of income available for savings or investment or whether, in fact, insufficient income is derived to satisfy the level of expenses

2. a personal **balance sheet**, which aims to indicate the assets or items of value owned by the person and all the liabilities or amounts owed to other people to derive a net worth value of that person.

Personal cash flow budget

The personal cash flow budget sets out the anticipated income from all sources and the items of spending or expenditure which will use up most or, in some cases, all of that income.

Income consists of money received from salary, wages, interest, profits, bonuses, fees charged, dividends, distributions, social security pensions or allowances, or any other earnings. Expenditure consists of payments for food, clothing, gas and electricity, rent, interest on borrowed money, rates, entertainment, holidays, education, pay television, mobile phone and any other items of expense.

Assuming that income exceeds expenditure, the difference is regarded as savings. This may include regular transfers of money to a savings plan with a financial institution, the occasional purchase of shares, or the accumulation of savings in a bank account.

In some cases, there may be a period of negative savings where income does not meet the required level of expenditure. On these occasions, people will draw on past savings, use borrowed money or run up a credit card debt to meet the required level of expenditure. Examples of such circumstances include a period when one partner is out of work or when additional expenses need to be met when income flow is limited. Such a situation should be temporary; otherwise a drastic review of expenditure patterns is needed.

Your personal cash flow budget will be unique to your own circumstances as it depends on your stage in life, your occupation, your attitude to money management and your good fortune with regard to having wealthy parents or being a beneficiary of a deceased estate. Young singles living at home with no dependants are more likely to be able to save fairly high proportions of their income for some time and be able to accumulate some assets. Couples with a young family are more likely to spend more than they earn for a period of time and will have a different cash flow situation.

Suppose we are given the following information on income and expenditure prepared by Qinbo and Feilian Wong in 2019. Qinbo is employed as a telecommunications technician. Feilian works part-time at a migrant centre. Qinbo is aged 43 and Feilian is 42. They have two children aged 15 and 13 years.

The annual cash flow for the Wong family shows a positive result at the end of the year. Note that this illustration focuses on cash flow and does not take into account the end-of-year taxation issues which may result from the income and deductions allowed under the taxation rules for the investments; nor does it take into account any employer superannuation contributions that go directly to a superannuation fund.

Income (2019)	
Qinbo (after PAYG tax)	$ 85 000
Feilian (after PAYG tax)	35 000
Interest and managed fund distribution	3 000
Total income	123 000
Expenses	
Food, car, clothing, utilities and insurances	55 000
School fees, uniforms, other activities, etc.	15 000
Loans and credit card repayments	22 000
Personal contribution to superannuation	6 000
Entertainment, holidays and miscellaneous expenses	18 000
Total expenses	116 000
Surplus/(deficit)	$ 7 000

The Wongs operate their finances with some savings in the bank but have access to additional cash through a home equity draw-down facility. This facility allows Qinbo and Feilian to draw additional cash through an agreement with their bank based on the level of assets they own. Qinbo and Feilian have not bothered to work closely with a personal cash flow statement before, as their joint income was in excess of their needs and they were able to accumulate some cash reserves and other assets before they had children. However, in the past couple of years, they have noticed that they tend to have fewer savings available to spend and are more aware of the impact of school fees and the expenses of a growing family.

Projected cash flow budget/statement

To help clients look ahead to their future cash flow position, we can also prepare a projected cash flow budget/statement which takes into account any significant changes we expect to occur over that time. When we look to the future cash flow position, we may refer to such a work sheet as a budget. A budget is a financial statement showing *expected* income and expenditure, and many people use a budget to help them keep a check on the 'cash in' and 'cash out' situation.

The following shows an abbreviated 5-year cash budget based on forecasts made by the Wongs using a 3% increase in income and expenses as an assumption.

	Year 1	Year 2	Year 3	Year 4	Year 5
Income ($)	123 000	126 690	130 490	134 405	138 438
Expenses ($)	116 000	119 480	123 064	126 756	130 559
Net cash flow ($)	7 000	7 210	7 426	7 649	7 879

In the context of considering the cash budget for the Wong family, we also need to consider their financial goals. In the short term, their objective is to take control of their finances and to show a decrease in the amount they owe the bank. This projection assumes that they do not change their current lifestyle and expenditure pattern. Their medium-term goal is to have sufficient savings to build up their investment portfolio. Their long-term goal is to accumulate sufficient assets to retire at age 65 with an annual income of about $75 000 in today's dollars.

Personal balance sheet

To complete the clients' financial picture, we also need to consider their total financial wellbeing, not just their ongoing finances. To do this, we need to know the health of their personal balance sheet. The preparation of a personal balance sheet requires the listing of all their assets and liabilities to indicate the equity they have, or their net worth (i.e. assets minus liabilities).

Assets are things of value we own. Assets include bank deposits, property, shares, managed funds, motor vehicles, antiques and any other item of value. The assets listed by the Wongs include their house and contents, cash, a managed investment fund, two cars and their superannuation funds.

The Wong's net worth is the difference between their assets and their liabilities. The personal balance sheet is shown below.

The Wongs have been able to accumulate net assets as Qinbo and Feilian have been working since their early twenties and they delayed having children until their late twenties.

Assets		
House and contents		$650 000
Cash in a savings account		12 000
Motor vehicles (2)		32 000
Managed investment fund		23 000
Superannuation funds (combined)		240 000
Total assets		957 000
Liabilities		
Credit card debt	12 000	
Home mortgage	250 000	
Car loans	22 000	
Total		284 000
Net worth		**$673 000**

Liabilities are those amounts of money we owe to other people or institutions. In the example above, the liabilities include the credit card debt, the mortgage on their home and car loans. We need to ensure that we separate the assets from the liabilities so we can determine the difference, which is the person's or household's net worth.

Many people do not have the benefit of net assets like Qinbo and Feilian in the example above; they may have a much lower net worth position with fewer assets and a higher amount of debt. But, again, many may have a much higher net worth position. Personal financial planning is related to our own unique set of financial circumstances — some are more fortunate than others, but the general principle of using these basic data collection tools helps us put each person's financial planning needs into perspective for that person.

The use of a personal cash flow statement and a personal balance sheet is much the same as the use of similar financial documents in business. They are used to monitor the income and expenditure patterns of a business in terms of the goals that are set, and to consider the performance of the enterprise in meeting its short-, medium- and long-term objectives.

The next section considers the use of the information contained in the cash flow statement and the balance sheet, and applying such information using business management tools as a means of monitoring and assessing an individual's financial position.

2.2 The role of the financial counsellor

LEARNING OBJECTIVE 2.2 Recognise the role played by financial counsellors in the financial environment.

In the process of helping people manage and plan their finances, we discover that there are many people who require additional assistance. Before people consult a financial planner, some may need the assistance of a **financial counsellor**. Financial counsellors undertake casework with individuals and provide community education and community development activities. They provide a free, confidential and independent service for people experiencing financial hardship and are usually accessed via local government offices. Financial hardship can arise from any number of factors such as family breakdown, depression, homelessness, physical and mental ill health, and financial stress.

The work of a financial counsellor involves an overall assessment of the individual's or family's financial situation, identification of options to address financial problems, and an exploration of the implications of the available options. The assistance that a financial counsellor can offer may include advice and advocacy on the implications of unpaid bills, debts and fines; assistance to negotiate payments with creditors; assistance with budgeting; and providing other relevant information.

Consumers live in an increasingly complex and expensive financial world and some financial practices impact adversely on low-income and marginalised consumers.

Financial counsellors assist clients across all ages with increasingly complex financial practices. The role of the financial counsellor is quite separate from that of the financial planner/adviser. Rather than advise on investing or dealing with superannuation matters, financial counsellors provide a valuable service to meet the needs of vulnerable people in the community.

Financial planners may refer some clients to a financial counsellor to assist in areas where a client may have little experience. Some of these areas include finding a home, particularly when housing is becoming more unaffordable for many; the use of credit card debt to furnish homes and to acquire the latest television sets; the difficulties of understanding mobile phone company contracts and their charging practices; and the promotion of **reverse mortgages** among the elderly population.

In October 2016, Financial Counselling Australia (FCA), the peak body representing financial counsellors, published a report containing 65 case studies of the positive benefits of financial counselling for people experiencing financial trouble. Although this report was published some time ago, the case studies provide good examples of the value this service provides. Three of the case studies are provided below.

CASE STUDIES

Case study 1 — Caitlin

Caitlin's husband had a high-paying job but left the family. Caitlin is now a single mother with a young daughter and, when she presented for financial counselling, was struggling to make ends meet on a Centrelink parenting payment. Two credit cards in Caitlin's name were with debt collectors and payment was being demanded on the gas bill from a previous house. Caitlin had also been convinced by a salesperson into signing up for an educational pack of $3000 for her daughter. A financial counsellor helped Caitlin to claim all government concessions, claim child support through Centrelink, change the lease on the house to Caitlin's name and change bank accounts so that Caitlin could access a fee-free account. Together Caitlin and the financial counsellor created a budget tailored to Caitlin's circumstances. They explored options for priorities of rent, food, energy, medicine and clothing before tackling debts. The financial counsellor arranged small pro-rata payments for gas and credit card debts and assisted Caitlin to return the Educational Pack, stating it was not suitable for the purpose it was intended and had the contract set aside. As a result, Caitlin grew in confidence and felt empowered to take control over her economic life. Her communication with her daughter improved and her daughter's schooling improved immensely. All debts have now been paid and Caitlin has not relied on child support. Caitlin undertook study and, on graduating with qualifications in aged care, now has full-time employment and cancelled her Centrelink parenting payments. Money that was being paid for debts now goes into a holiday account and Caitlin and her daughter have already been on a holiday. Caitlin has become an authority on home budgeting for her family and friends, and she has upgraded her car using money that she has saved. Caitlin and her daughter are extremely happy. The financial counsellor has been advised by Caitlin that he is no longer needed, however Caitlin requested yearly review appointments. Originally sceptical, Caitlin has since sent two other friends along for financial counselling.

Case study 2 — Pam and Michael

Pam and Michael are a couple in their 70s who had owned a very successful business. They then found out that their accountant defrauded them of millions of dollars over a fifteen year period. This sent Pam and Michael's business into liquidation and resulted in them losing their home. Their solicitor advised them not to pursue the matter through the legal system because it would cost thousands of dollars, which they did not have, and they could not guarantee they would be able to get any money back. The couple were distressed as their many years of hard work had disappeared. Pam and Michael still had extensive debt in their personal names, originally used for business purposes. But there was no money left from the business to pay these out as they had ensured their employees and business creditors were paid out first. Pam and Michael exhausted all avenues to keep themselves financially afloat until they had no money left and needed to apply for the aged pension. They saw a financial counsellor not knowing what else to do.

Initially the best solution seemed to file for bankruptcy as they could not manage any of their debts as most of their money was going on rent, which didn't leave much for basic expenses. They described how they used to live without ever thinking about money and now they didn't have enough money for food. As a very proud couple, Pam and Michael found the prospect of bankruptcy quite demoralising but they had to seriously consider this option to avoid other legal repercussions. After further discussion of their options, it was decided to seek waivers on all debts. So far, the financial counsellor has managed to obtain waivers for $85 000 of their $101 500 debts and is still in negotiation with creditors to waive the remaining debt. Pam and Michael did not believe that this relief was even possible. They are very thankful to the financial counsellor for restoring their dignity and peace of mind knowing they can live the rest of their lives without debts hanging over their heads.

Case study 3 — Peter

Peter was referred to a financial counsellor by his university student-support service after he notified the university of his intention of withdrawing from his studies. Peter's financial situation was desperate and he had been relying on other students for food and borrowing money from his grandmother, an aged pensioner. A major issue for Peter was his expensive mobile phone contract which accounted for the majority of Peter's income. The outstanding debt on Peter's account was in excess of $3000 and increasing, despite Peter's attempt at repayment. A financial counsellor helped Peter to prove that the contract was unfair which eventually resulted in its cancellation and waiver of the arrears. Peter has continued his tertiary studies and will graduate next year with an engineering degree. Peter is overjoyed with the result which turned his life around.

Source: Financial Counselling Australia 2016.

Refer to the FCA website (www.financialcounsellingaustralia.org.au) for more details about financial counselling. Search the media releases on the website to gain a deeper understanding of the work of the FCA.

2.3 Using financial ratios as a planning tool

LEARNING OBJECTIVE 2.3 Analyse financial statements using ratio analysis.

The two financial documents for the Wong family (as described earlier) can be used further to analyse the family's financial position. We will outline briefly four ratios which, in their various ways, provide useful information for evaluating a person's individual set of financial circumstances.

These ratios are:

- equity, or net worth ratio
- liquidity ratio
- savings ratio
- debt service ratio.

You will be able to apply these ratios to exercises in the Professional Application Exercises at the end of this chapter.

Net worth ratio

The first of these ratios is the *equity* or *net worth ratio*. The equity/net worth ratio is the ratio of net worth to total assets, expressed as a percentage. It is found by dividing the net worth by the total assets and multiplying by 100. The formula is as follows.

$$\text{Equity or net worth ratio} = \frac{\text{Net worth}}{\text{Total assets}} \times 100$$

Using the information in the Wong family's circumstances as listed in the personal balance sheet, we find the following.

$$\begin{aligned}\text{Equity or net worth ratio} &= \frac{\text{Net worth}}{\text{Total assets}} \times 100\\ &= \frac{\$673\,000}{\$957\,000} \times 100\\ &= 70.3\%\end{aligned}$$

This means that the Wong family owns 70.3% of the assets that they have acquired, and other people or institutions own 29.7%.

For a young person or couple, it is expected that their equity ratio would be relatively low as they are likely to have a high level of debt. An older couple nearing retirement would be more likely to have a high equity ratio, as they would be trying to eliminate debt completely or to reduce debt to a minimum by the time they retired.

Liquidity ratio

The *liquidity ratio* compares the amount of liquid assets to current debt, expressed as a percentage. Liquid assets are those assets which are in cash form or assetsthat can be easily converted to cash. The Wong's managed investment fund is relatively easy to convert to cash, however the Wong's intend to hold this investment for the long term, and so it does not have to be included in the liquid assets. Current debt represents that amount of debt which is to be repaid within the next 12 months. Thus:

$$\text{Liquidity ratio} = \frac{\text{Liquid assets}}{\text{Current debt}} \times 100$$

Assume that current debt comprises the annual repayments on the credit card, home mortgage and car loan. In this case we have liquid assets of $12 000 (the cash in savings account as listed in the personal balance sheet) and total current debt repayments of $22 000 (as listed in the personal cash flow budget). Thus:

$$\begin{aligned}\text{Liquidity ratio} &= \frac{\text{Liquid assets}}{\text{Current debt}} \times 100\\ &= \frac{\$12\,000}{\$22\,000} \times 100\\ &= 54.5\%\end{aligned}$$

This ratio shows the percentage of liquid assets available to cover current debt. It may be expressed in terms of months by multiplying the ratio by 12 (for months in the year). In the Wong family's case, they have 6.5 months (0.545×12) of liquid assets available to meet their current liabilities. This provides some clarity in knowing how long they can cover their debt repayments from their liquid assets should their income stop.

Savings ratio

The third ratio — the *savings ratio* — shows the level of savings expressed as a percentage of total income. In this case, we need to be careful about defining savings. It is not just the amount left over after deducting expenditure from income, since that would ignore any investments made within the expenditure items. We need to add back the items which may be regarded as investments, such as share purchases, extra superannuation contributions and additional bank deposits. The savings ratio (after tax) is calculated as follows.

$$\text{Savings ratio} = \frac{\text{Savings}}{\text{Net income}} \times 100$$

In this case, we have an estimated $7000 increase in their bank account (savings) as they have a surplus of income over expenses for the year, plus the additional annual superannuation contributions of $6000 (as listed in the personal cash flow budget). The savings ratio for the Wong family after tax is calculated as follows.

$$\begin{aligned}
\text{Savings ratio} &= \frac{\text{Savings}}{\text{Net income}} \times 100 \\
&= \frac{\$13\,000}{\$123\,000} \times 100 \\
&= 10.6\%
\end{aligned}$$

It is likely that a young couple with small children may have a low or negative savings ratio. Similarly, an older couple may also show a low savings ratio. A couple whose children have left home and who are looking forward to 10 years or so of work before retirement may have a high savings ratio. A young couple who have just married and are both intending to work for a few years before starting a family may also have a high savings ratio. There is no hard and fast rule about what the savings ratio should be; the savings ratio should be considered in the context of the set of circumstances under review. The Wong's case may be similar to many people with teenagers at secondary school.

Debt service ratio

The *debt service ratio* shows the debt commitments expressed as a percentage of the after-tax income (as listed in the personal cashflow budget). This ratio can be used to indicate the effect of a particular course of action, such as the impact of a decision either to increase the level of debt significantly by undertaking a new major purchase, or to reduce drastically the level of income by one partner ceasing work or working part-time instead of full-time, or if a rise in interest rates occurs. The ratio is as follows.

$$\text{Debt service ratio} = \frac{\text{Annual debt commitments}}{\text{Annual net income}} \times 100$$

In the Wong family's case:

$$\begin{aligned}
\text{Debt service ratio} &= \frac{\text{Annual debt commitments}}{\text{Annual net income}} \times 100 \\
&= \frac{\$22\,000}{\$123\,000} \times 100 \\
&= 17.9\%
\end{aligned}$$

If the Wong family's income falls because Feilian's job is cut back to 3 days a week and she earns only $15 000 after tax, the debt service ratio will show an increase from 17.9% to 21.4%. This is calculated by reducing total after-tax income for the family from $123 000 to $103 000. By indicating the effect of such a change on their ability to service their debt, Feilian may seek other employment to restore their level of income.

Note that some of these ratios use only the balance sheet and others use a combination of both the balance sheet and the cash flow statement. The use of the ratios on their own may not provide much useful information, but the trend over 2 or 3 years or more can be very useful together with information on the stage of life of the person who is the subject of the review.

Personal finances through a business lens

Let us consider another view of debt ratios. If a family's balance sheet was similar to a firm's balance sheet we would clearly see what was regarded as short-term debt (current liabilities) and long-term debt (non-current liabilities). In this way, we can see the proportion of short-term debt relative to the total assets and also the proportion of long-term debt relative to the amount of family assets. In the Wong family's case, short-term debt may be regarded as their credit card debt and the car loans (total $34 000 as listed on the personal balance sheet). This presumes that they want to pay them fairly quickly.

As a proportion of their assets, this means that their short-term debt is only 3.6% of their total assets (i.e. $34 000 / $957 000 = 3.6%). In a strict accounting sense, short-term debt is that which is required to be paid within the next 12-month period. As it is expected that the Wongs will take about two years or more to pay the credit card debt and the car loans, then the short-term ratio would be less than the amount illustrated above.

Their long-term debt, represented by their mortgage of $250,000 as listed on their personal balance sheet, is 26% of their assets (i.e. $250 000 / $957 000 = 26%).

Most people are aware of the power of using spreadsheets to make computations easier and to save time. However, the investment of time and thought to set up the spreadsheet properly will save even more time and provide for ease of auditing the cell formulae. To learn more about setting up a spreadsheet properly, see the appendix at the end of this chapter. It provides some very useful examples of how to set up a spreadsheet to assist your financial planning.

PROFESSIONAL ADVICE

Newlyweds' net worth

Mehmet and Elif, both aged 34, are newlyweds. Their after-tax salaries are $85 000 and $69 000, respectively. They have been renting a flat since they started work but have decided to buy a house. Their decision has been made easier because Mehmet's parents said that, when they retire at age 65 in one year, they would withdraw $40 000 from their combined superannuation funds and give the money to Mehmet and Elif to help them to buy a house. When Mehmet and Elif approached the bank for a loan they had to provide details of their income, expenses, assets and liabilities to the lending officer. The items provided for their personal balance sheet were as follows.

Assets	
Bank account	$65 000
Furniture/personal effects	18 000
Managed investment fund	30 000
Cars	26 000
Superannuation — Mehmet	86 000
Superannuation — Elif	61 000
Liabilities	
Credit cards	5 500
Car loans	5 000

They also advise the lending officer that their monthly commitments are:
- rent $2280
- car loans $390.

They would prefer not to cash in their managed investment fund at present as the value has fallen by 8% over the last 2 months. They have instructed the fund manager to reinvest the distributions rather than receive them in cash. Their intention is to leave the investment to accumulate to meet the education expenses of the children they hope to have in the future.

They anticipate paying off their credit card debt in full next month and they would also have paid off the car loans in the next 12 months. They also advise the lending officer that their current rate of household expenses (not including the rent and repayments) is about $2400 per month.

▶

2.4 Financial mathematical skills applied in financial planning

LEARNING OBJECTIVE 2.4 Demonstrate financial mathematics skills necessary for financial planners.

When will I be able to retire? Will my investments provide me with sufficient income for my retirement? How much will I need to invest so that I can afford to send my children to private schools? If I have $300 000 in my superannuation in 8 years, what is that equivalent to in today's money terms? Is it preferable to pay off my mortgage or invest any surplus funds? Financial planners are constantly faced with questions such as these. In order to provide answers to such questions, financial planners need to have a strong working knowledge of fundamental mathematical concepts that relate to investment and retirement planning as well as the taxation consequences of any investment decision.

The skills required include a basic understanding of the nature of compounding and the time value of money. A simple example to demonstrate the need to understand the concept of 'time value of money' is the use of a projected superannuation balance or retirement income produced on some superannuation fund statements provided to members. When a projected figure of say, $1 million, is provided on such a statement it needs to be understood in the context of whether the impact of inflation has been taken into account in delivering such a figure. If the $1 million is a projected figure we need to know whether it represents $1 million at today's dollar value (the real value) or a dollar figure of some future time. The difference can be quite misleading. An understanding of these concepts will enable financial planners to determine both present and future values of capital amounts and to assess alternative income streams so that different investment options can be compared.

In practice, financial planners can often access computer packages which, with a click of the mouse, can determine present and future capital values, and compare alternative income streams. However, computer packages cannot equip financial planners with the skills to explain to clients the basis on which their advice is determined. Financial planning is a relationship profession built on trust and responsibility. It is imperative that financial planners provide clients not only with solutions but also with the assurance that the advice given is based on a thorough understanding of the factors that give rise to these solutions.

2.5 Compound interest and the time value of money

LEARNING OBJECTIVE 2.5 Explain the concept of time value of money and the benefits of compound interest.

Most financial decisions involve benefits and costs that are spread out over time. The concept of the time value of money establishes a relationship between cash flows received and/or paid at different points in time. If you are offered the alternative of receiving $1000 at the end of four years or receiving $1000 today, a rational response would be to choose to receive the money today. There are possibly three reasons you might prefer the money today.

1. The person promising you the money in 4 years may not fulfil the promise — there is an element of risk in that there is some uncertainty that you will receive the money.

2. If you have the money now, you can invest the $1000 and earn a return — if you wait for 4 years, there is an opportunity cost (that is, the return you could have achieved in another investment).

3. If you have the money now, you can use it for present consumption.

Because there is risk, an opportunity cost and the postponement of present consumption, people prefer cash now rather than later. This is called the 'time preference for money' and it highlights the idea that a dollar today is worth more than a dollar to be received in some future period of time. In order for us to be indifferent to the receipt of the $1000 now or in four years, we would need to be compensated for undertaking the risk, forgoing the opportunity to invest the money now and delaying our ability to use the funds for consumption. The compensation we require is equal to our opportunity cost; that is, the best rate of return we could earn from investing the $1000 for 4 years. If we could earn 8% p.a. from investing these funds for 4 years, our opportunity cost would be 8% p.a. This compensation or opportunity cost is often described as the interest rate required, the rate of return required, the **discount rate** or the time preference rate.

We have discussed why a dollar in hand today is worth more than a dollar to be received at some future date. If we know what our opportunity cost (or rate of return requirement) is, we can determine what amount of money we would require in 4 years in order for us to be indifferent about receiving the $1000 now or receiving the $1000 plus compensation at a later time. This can be termed the **future value** (often abbreviated as *FV*) of our investment. Using a financial calculator and this example, we can input the following values to determine the future value of the investment.

$$PV = \text{amount of the present sum of money (\$1000)}$$
$$i = \text{interest rate per period (8\%)}$$
$$N = \text{number of periods (4)}$$

If we select the future value key (*FV*) on the financial calculator, we will know that if our opportunity cost is 8% we will require $1360.49 in 4 years to be indifferent about receiving the money today or waiting for the 4 years.

This sum of money comprises the initial sum of money, $1000, plus interest earned over the 4-year period (see the table below).

Initial sum	$1 000.00
Interest in year 1 = 8% × $1000	80.00
Interest in year 2 = 8% × ($1000 + $80)	86.40
Interest in year 3 = 8% × ($1000 + $80 + $86.40)	93.31
Interest in year 4 = 8% × ($1000 + $80 + $86.40 + $93.31)	100.78
	$1 360.49

From this example, we can see that in years 2, 3 and 4 we are earning a return not only on the original capital sum, but also on any accumulated interest. That is, in year 2 we earn interest on year 1's interest. In year 3, we earn interest on the interest from years 1 and 2. In year 4, we earn interest on the interest earned in years 1, 2 and 3.

This is the nature of compounding. This is what Nina learned when she discovered that she was earning 'interest on her interest'. The longer the time that funds are invested and the higher the interest rate, the more significant is the effect of compounding on the value of those funds at some future period of time.

Table 2.1 shows future values at different interest rates. We can see that an investment of $100 invested for 2 years at 5% p.a. grows to $110.25, whereas that same investment will grow to $127.63 if it is invested at 5% p.a. for 5 years. If the time frame is 4 years, we can see that, the higher the interest rate, the greater will be the value of our investment.

TABLE 2.1 **Future values at different interest rates**

	Future value of $100 at various interest rates			
No. years	5%	10%	15%	20%
1	$105.00	$110.00	$115.00	$120.00
2	$110.25	$121.00	$132.25	$144.00
3	$115.76	$133.10	$152.09	$172.80
4	$121.55	$146.41	$174.90	$207.36
5	$127.63	$161.05	$201.14	$248.83

We can also use a formula to determine the future value of an amount invested today. This formula is as follows.

$$FV = PV(1 + i)^n$$

where PV = amount of the present sum of money ($1000)
$\quad\quad i$ = interest rate per period (8%)
$\quad\quad n$ = number of periods (4)

$$FV = \$1000(1 + 0.08)^4$$
$$= \$1360.49$$

Because of the nature of compounding, we can see why we say that money has a time value. That is, a dollar in one time period has a different value from a dollar received or paid in a different time period. This same notion of the time value of money can enable us to determine what an amount to be received at a future date is worth in today's money terms. Comparing the future value of two cash flow streams, or comparing the **present value** — that is, the value in today's money terms of those same cash flow streams — will always result in the same conclusion as to which is best.

For example, Grace asks your advice about two options. Option A and Option B will generate the following cash flows.

	End year 1	End year 2	End year 3	End year 4	End year 5
Option A	nil	nil	$27 000	$8 000	nil
Option B	nil	nil	nil	nil	$40 000

In order to compare these investment options, it is necessary to consider the cash flows at a common time period. If we compare these two investment options at the end of year 5 — that is, the future value of both Option A and Option B — we can evaluate which investment option is preferable.

Using a financial calculator and this example, assume the opportunity cost is 8%. We can input the following values to determine the future value of the investment.

Option A
(We need to do this calculation in two parts.)
Part 1 — To calculate the future value of the $27 000 after 2 years
$\quad PV$ = amount of the initial sum of money ($27 000)
$\quad\quad i$ = opportunity cost or interest rate per period (8%)
$\quad\quad n$ = number of periods (2)
If we select the future value key (FV) on the financial calculator, we will know that, if our opportunity cost is 8%, $27 000 to be received in 3 years is equivalent to receiving $31 492.80 in 5 years.

Part 2 — To calculate the future value of the $8000 in 1 year
$\quad PV$ = amount of the initial sum of money ($8000)
$\quad\quad i$ = opportunity cost or interest rate per period (8%)
$\quad\quad n$ = number of periods (1)
If we select the future value key (FV) on the financial calculator, we will know that, if our opportunity cost is 8%, $8000 to be received in 4 years is equivalent to receiving $8640 in 5 years.

The future value of both cash flows, $27 000 to be received in 3 years and $8000 to be received in 4 years is equivalent to receiving $40 132.80 in 5 years (adding Parts 1 and 2 together: $31 492.80 + $8640 = $40 132.80).

Option B
The future value of $40 000 to be received in 5 years is $40 000.

Our advice to Grace would be to explain that, because of the time value of money, she is better off accepting Option A because it provides her with more money in future dollar terms.

If we had compared Option A with Option B on the basis of the value in today's dollar terms, we would arrive at exactly the same conclusion. We can determine the present value of the investment by inputting the values shown below.

Option A
(Again, we need to work this out in two parts because of the different amounts of money to be received in different years.)

Part 1 — To calculate the present value of the $27 000 to be received in 3 years

FV = amount of the initial sum of money ($27 000)

i = interest rate per period (8%)

n = number of periods (3)

If we select the present value key (PV) on the financial calculator, we will know that, if our opportunity cost is 8%, $27 000 to be received in 3 years is equivalent to receiving $21 433.47 in today's money terms.

Part 2 — To calculate the present value of the $8000 to be received in 4 years

FV = amount of the future sum of money ($8000)

i = interest rate per period (8%)

n = number of periods (4)

If we select the present value key (PV) on the financial calculator, we will know that, if our opportunity cost is 8%, $8000 to be received in 4 years is equivalent to receiving $5880.24 in today's money terms.

The present value of both cash flows, $27 000 to be received in 3 years and $8000 to be received in 4 years, is equivalent to receiving $27 313.71 in today's money terms (adding Part 1, $21 433.47, and Part 2, $5880.24, = $27 313.71).

Option B

FV = amount of the future sum of money ($40 000)

i = interest rate per period (8%)

n = number of periods (5)

If we select the present value key (PV) on the financial calculator, we will know that, if our opportunity cost is 8%, $40 000 to be received in 5 years is equivalent to receiving $27 223.33 in today's money terms.

Again our advice to Grace would be to explain that, because of the time value of money, she is better off accepting Option A. In this analysis, it is because it is providing her with more money in today's dollar terms.

The formula to determine the present value of future sums of money can be used to assess Grace's question. This formula is the inverse of the formula used to determine a future value from a present sum.

$$PV = FV(1 + i)^{-n}$$

Or it may be expressed as follows.

$$PV = FV/(1 + i)^n$$

where FV = amount of the future sum of money

i = interest rate per period

n = number of periods

Applying this formula to the example for Grace, we can determine the present value of each cash flow stream.

Option A

$$PV = \$27\,000(1 + 0.08)^{-3} + \$8000(1 + 0.08)^{-4}$$
$$= \$27\,313.71$$

Option B

$$PV = \$40\,000(1 + 0.08)^{-5}$$
$$= \$27\,223.33$$

Obviously, our advice to Grace would be the same, as the lump sums are identical to those which we derived by using a financial calculator.

So far, we have considered only the future value and the present value of single sums of money. A related issue is the determination of the future value and present value of an identical stream of receipts/payments occurring in every period for a specified time. A series of cash flows that are identical in amount and occur at the end of consecutive time periods is called an ordinary annuity.

Consider the following annuity with an interest rate required of 7%.

End year 1	End year 2	End year 3	End year 4	End year 5
$500	$500	$500	$500	$500

If we wish to find the accumulated value (future value) of this annuity at the end of 5 years, we can input the following values in our financial calculator to determine the future value of the investment.

   PMT = amount of the annuity ($500)

      i = interest rate per period (7%)

      n = number of periods (5)

If we select the future value key (*FV*) on the financial calculator, we will know that if our opportunity cost is 7% we will require $2875.37 in 5 years to be indifferent about receiving $500 each year for 5 years and receiving $2875.37 in 5 years.

Alternatively, we can use the formula for the future value of an annuity to determine the accumulated value at the end of the 5 years. This formula is as follows.

$$FV = \frac{PMT\,[(1+i)^n - 1]}{i}$$

$$= \frac{\$500\,[(1+0.07)^5 - 1]}{0.07}$$

$$= \$2875.37$$

Using the same example, we can determine the present value of this income stream. To calculate the present value, we would input the following values into a financial calculator or use the formula for the present value of an annuity.

   PMT = amount of the annuity ($500)

      i = interest rate per period (7%)

      n = number of periods (5)

If we select the present value key (*PV*) on the financial calculator, we will know that if our opportunity cost is 7% we would be indifferent about receiving $2050.10 today and receiving $500 each year for 5 years. Using the formula:

$$PV = \frac{PMT\,[1 - (1+i)^{-n}]}{i}$$

Hence:

$$PV = \frac{\$500\,[1 - (1+0.07)^{-5}]}{0.07}$$

$$= \$2050.10$$

Understanding the concepts of compounding and the time value of money enables us to consider the types of questions that might commonly be asked of a financial planner. Consider the following situation to illustrate how these concepts are applied.

ILLUSTRATIVE EXAMPLE 2.1

Lawrence has just turned 40 and is seeking your advice about his retirement plans. Lawrence would like to retire at 65, and wants to have $1.25 million in an investment account by then in order to maintain his current lifestyle. He has determined that he can afford to invest $9000 each year (for the next 15 years) towards his retirement. At age 55, he will need to withdraw $25 000 as he intends to invest in a healthy food retail outlet venture. If Lawrence's retirement account earns 12% compounded annually, how much will Lawrence need to deposit into the account each year for the last 10 years (between ages 55 and 65) to meet his goal of having $1.25 million? To tackle Lawrence's concerns, we could take the following steps.

Step 1

Determine how much Lawrence's account will be worth at age 55. We know:

   PMT = amount of the annuity ($9000)

      i = interest rate per period (12%)

      n = number of periods (15)

If we input these data and then select the future value key (*FV*) on the financial calculator, we will know that the value of Lawrence's account in 15 years when he turns 55 will be $335 517.

Once we deduct the cost of the investment in the healthy food retail outlet ($25 000), the balance of the account will be $310 517.

Figure 2.1 provides an illustration of the impact of compounding interest and the time value of money in a different context. In this situation, the mortgagee has already paid off their home and, at around age 70, decides to undertake a new mortgage called a **reverse mortgage** under which the lender will provide ongoing payments or a lump sum. In most cases, no repayments on the mortgage are made and the interest accumulates and therefore compounds over the period of the loan. Figure 2.1 illustrates the effect of compound interest for someone who takes out a reverse mortgage. Note the illustration which represents the percentage amount of the house that the owner has over a period of time and the increasing effect of the unpaid interest on the loan as the interest builds upon the previous unpaid interest. Go to moneysmart.gov.au and input different variables in the reverse mortgage calculator to see the impact of compound interest for people who commence a reverse mortgage.

FIGURE 2.1	The effect of compound interest on a reverse mortgage over time

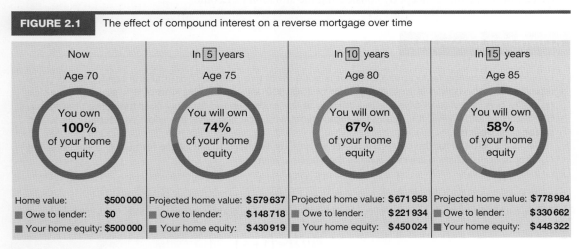

Now	In 5 years	In 10 years	In 15 years
Age 70	Age 75	Age 80	Age 85
You own **100%** of your home equity	You will own **74%** of your home equity	You will own **67%** of your home equity	You will own **58%** of your home equity
Home value: $500 000	Projected home value: $579 637	Projected home value: $671 958	Projected home value: $778 984
Owe to lender: $0	Owe to lender: $148 718	Owe to lender: $221 934	Owe to lender: $330 662
Your home equity: $500 000	Your home equity: $430 919	Your home equity: $450 024	Your home equity: $448 322

Source: ASIC 2023a.

The example in figure 2.1 is based on a 70-year-old person living alone whose house is valued at $500 000 with an anticipated increase in value of 3% p.a. The reverse mortgage rate is 8% p.a. The person requires a lump sum of $100 000 in 1 month and the fee is $12 per month.

In another example, Nina's grandmother, Anne, is 80 years of age and living alone in a home worth $650 000 with an anticipated increase in value of 3% p.a. Instead of a lump sum, Anne requires an extra $300 per month to help with some medical and rehabilitation expenses as she is getting frailer in her old age. Assuming the rate is 8% p.a. and monthly fee is $12, the reverse mortgage calculator demonstrates that in 5 years her total debt would be $22 925. Anne's home would be worth $753 528 but her equity $730 603, or 97% of the house's value. In 10 years Anne's equity in the home will fall to 93% (assuming a growth rate in the home of 3% p.a.). Anne is quite pleased that her family will gain a large share of the house when she dies, so thinks that her life will be much easier if she goes ahead with the reverse mortgage monthly payments.

2.6 Nominal and effective interest rates

LEARNING OBJECTIVE 2.6 Compare the difference between nominal and effective interest rates.

So far, we have assumed that compound interest rates are determined on an annual basis. These are the nominal or stated rates of interest that a bank might quote as the interest rate applicable to your mortgage. If, however, the interest is calculated more than once a year, the value of any investment or loan is affected by the frequency of those interest rate determinations. When nominal interest rates are compounded more than once a year, the convention is to determine the periodic interest rate, i, as follows.

$$i = \frac{j}{m}$$

where j = the nominal rate of interest
$\quad m$ = the number of compounding periods per year

For example, the nominal interest rate for a year is $j = 0.09$ (or 9% p.a.) and we are told that interest is compounded each quarter. If $m = 4$ quarters each year in a 4-year period, you now have:

$$m \times n = 4 \times 4 \text{ or } 16 \text{ periods of 1 quarter each}$$

with a quarterly interest rate of:

$$i = \frac{j}{m}$$
$$= \frac{0.09}{4}$$
$$= 0.0225 \text{ per period of 1 quarter}$$

We can illustrate this concept by considering the situation of Leonie.

ILLUSTRATIVE EXAMPLE 2.2

Leonie is considering taking out a loan but is not sure of two main options that she has for meeting the repayments. One option is to take the loan of $100 000 with an interest rate of 9% p.a. compounded quarterly over a period of 5 years; the other is at 9% compounded monthly over the same time frame. She wants to know what the size of the repayments would be and what the effective interest rate would be for each option.

Using the formula for the present value of an annuity, we need to adjust the formula to reflect that the number of compounding periods is more than once a year.

$$PV = \frac{PMT[1 - (1 + i)^{-n}]}{i}$$

The same formula adjusted to reflect the fact that interest is compounded quarterly is as follows.

$$PV = \frac{PMT\left[1 - \left(1 + \frac{j}{m}\right)^{-m \times n}\right]}{\frac{j}{m}}$$

$$\$100 000 = \frac{PMT[1 - (1 + 0.0225)^{-20}]}{0.0225}$$

$$PMT = \$6264.21 \text{ per quarter}$$

When interest is compounded more frequently than once a year, Leonie is actually paying more than the nominal interest rate quoted. In order to have a clearer picture of how much interest she will pay, we use the measure called the effective rate of interest. This is the interest rate that would be charged if the interest had been compounded once a year.

The formula to determine the effective interest rate is given by the following.

$$i = \left(1 + \frac{j}{m}\right)^m - 1$$

In our numerical example we have:

$$i = \left(1 + \frac{0.09}{4}\right)^4 - 1$$

$$= 9.31\%$$

The nominal interest rate of 9% p.a. quoted to Leonie is actually an effective rate of 9.31% p.a. when we take into account that the interest is compounded quarterly.

We need to compare the two options for Leonie by using the same formula and calculating the repayments based on 60 payments (5 years of 12 monthly payments). In this case the repayments are $2075.84 per month.

$$PV = \frac{PMT\left[1 - \left(1 + \frac{j}{m}\right)^{-m \times n}\right]}{\frac{j}{m}}$$

$$\$100\,000 = \frac{PMT[1 - (1 + 0.0075)^{-60}]}{0.0075}$$

$$PMT = \$2075.84 \text{ per month}$$

The effective interest rate for the monthly repayments is as follows.

$$i = \left(1 + \frac{j}{m}\right)^m - 1$$

$$= \left(1 + \frac{0.09}{12}\right)^{12} - 1$$

$$= 9.38\%$$

In this case, Leonie would have to choose either to pay an effective interest rate of 9.31% if she is able to make repayments of $6264.21 per quarter for 5 years, or to pay $2075.84 per month each month for 5 years at an effective interest rate of 9.38%. Note that the effect of the higher number of compounding periods per annum results in a lower total sum to be repaid ($124\,550.40 = $2075.84 × 60 monthly repayments and $125\,284.20 = $6264.21 × 20 quarterly repayments) despite having a higher effective interest rate (9.38% compared to 9.31%).

The following scenario illustrates the importance of understanding the difference between nominal interest rates and effective interest rates.

Consider the interest rates charged by two banks, where:
- Bank X charges 8.25% p.a., compounded daily
- Bank Y charges 8.5% p.a., compounded annually.

To determine which bank is charging the lower interest rate, we need to compare interest rates on an annual basis, that is, compare the effective interest rates being charged.

The effective interest rate being charged by Bank X is calculated as follows.

$$i = \left(1 + \frac{0.0825}{365}\right)^{365} - 1 = 8.6\%$$

The interest rate of 8.5% p.a. charged by Bank Y is compounded annually so this will be identical to its effective interest rate, that is, 8.5% p.a.

We can see, therefore, that 8.5% compounded annually is lower interest than 8.25% compounded daily (with an effective interest rate of 8.6% p.a.).

If we extend this issue further, we can illustrate the importance of understanding the difference between nominal and effective interest rates by considering the following interest rates quoted by three banks.
- Bank A: 15%, compounded daily

- Bank B: 15.5%, compounded quarterly
- Bank C: 16%, compounded annually

The effective interest rates for these three banks are as follows.

$$\text{Bank A} = \left(1 + \frac{0.15}{365}\right)^{365} - 1 = 16.18\%$$

$$\text{Bank B} = \left(1 + \frac{0.155}{4}\right)^{4} - 1 = 16.42\%$$

$$\text{Bank C} = \left(1 + \frac{0.16}{1}\right)^{1} - 1 = 16\%$$

Which bank is offering the best rate? For a saver, Bank B offers the best (highest) interest rate. For a borrower, Bank C offers the best (lowest) interest rate. Nina (from the case study at the start of the chapter) would be delighted to know that, as a saver, a higher interest rate may be earned over the year when the interest is paid on a more frequent basis as well as the interest gaining the benefit of being compounded.

What we can see from this situation is that the highest nominal interest rate is not necessarily the best interest rate for an investor, and compounding during the year can lead to a significant difference between the nominal interest rate and the effective interest rate. Any comparison of interest rates should be made on the basis of effective interest rates.

To consider the notion of effective interest rates in a specific context that impacts on most people, let us look at the interest rates charged on the use of credit cards.

Credit cards

Credit card lending has grown strongly over the past three decades. Credit cards are offered by many organisations, not just banks, and nearly everyone has one if not two cards. Basically, they work this way — lines of credit are approved and can be drawn on by the borrower in the form of cash advances, or they may be used to purchase goods and services directly.

Credit card charges vary. Some charges are based on an annual fee combined with an interest charge on the outstanding balance after a certain interest moratorium period. For example, interest might not be charged to the account if the outstanding balance is settled within 30 days of the issue of the credit card statement. Additional fees are usually levied for cash advances.

Tables 2.2 and 2.3 give some examples of credit cards with some of the common features available today.

TABLE 2.2   **Examples of credit cards with features relating to transfers**

Company name	Purchase rate	Interest free months	Annual fee	Credit limit	Balance transfer fee
Virgin Money VISA	11.99%	15, then 21.69%	$99	$30 000	1% of balance transfer
NAB VISA	19.74%	12, then 21.74%	$90	No limit	3% of balance transfer
ANZ Low Rate	12.49%	28, then 21.24%	$0 for 12 months, then $58	No limit	2% of balance transfer

Source: Tindall 2023.

TABLE 2.3   Examples of credit cards with features relating to annual and late payment fees

Company name	Interest rate	Annual fee	Max free days	Late payment fee
ING Orange One Low Rate VISA	11.99%	$0	45	$20
Virgin Money VISA	11.99%	$99	55	$30
Westpac Mastercard	13.74%	$59	55	$25
Coles Mastercard	12.99%	$58	55	$30
Great Southern Bank Mastercard	11.99%	$49	55	$12.50

Source: Tindall 2023.

Credit card facilities are provided by banks, building societies and credit unions. Australians are starting to realise what a credit card actually costs them. An interesting observation is that $2.45 billion was wiped of credit card debt nationally in the 12 months from November 2018 to November 2019. Two significant factors can be attributed to this considerable reduction in credit card debt; improving credit to attain home loans and new credit (Gordon 2020).

The RBA published data in January 2020 that the current level of personal credit card debt at $27.20 billion was actually the lowest it had been since December 2006. Comparing this type of credit with business and housing, it is noted that, since 2015, personal credit has had negative growth (RBA 2020).

Credit cards are a good example of open-ended lending. Such credit can be used repeatedly until a prearranged limit is reached. Credit cards are generally issued by financial intermediaries. Similar instruments, technically charge cards, are issued by American Express, Diners' Club and bodies such as major retailers for use in their stores only, and by specific-purpose providers such as MotorCharge for vehicle fuel accounts and vehicle servicing. With all credit cards, the borrower decides the amount and timing of credit to use up to the prearranged limit.

Consumers are attracted to credit cards for automatic billing because of the convenience, the inducements such as frequent flyer points and customer loyalty rewards programs, and because they have more control over their spending.

Interest rates on credit cards are generally quoted as effective interest rates. Effective interest rates allow for the impact of compounding. Following on from the previous section on effective interest rates: if we owe $100 on a credit card which charges interest at the rate of 1.6% per month, at the end of the first month we will owe $1.60 in interest and our balance will be $101.60. At the end of the second month, we will owe interest on our original $100 and interest on our interest, which is the essence of compounding. This process would continue month by month until the end of the year. At the end of the year, we will owe $120.98 on the credit card, which means the effective rate of interest is 20.98% p.a. Recall the formula for the effective rate of interest.

$$\text{Effective rate of interest} = (1 + 0.016)^{12} - 1$$

$$= 20.98\%$$

A credit card might typically charge an effective annual rate of 20.98% on purchases (and a higher rate on cash advances), which means the monthly interest rate is 1.6%. Therefore, any outstanding balance on a credit card will grow by 1.6% per month. All credit card providers insist on a minimum monthly payment which is a percentage of the outstanding balance — the minimum will vary between card providers but 2% would be a typical figure.

The amount owing on a loan, which increases by 1.6% per month and decreases (if only minimum payments are made) by 2% per month, is unlikely to fall very rapidly, if at all. Indeed, if the credit limit has not been reached then even one or two credit purchases during the next month will most likely mean that the individual owes more this month than last month. The cycle can be a vicious one, with one commentator suggesting that people who mismanage credit cards will spend a year of their life working just to pay off the interest on their cards.

Junia is 22 and owes $3000 on her credit card. The current interest rate is 1.6% per month. If Junia makes no additional purchases on her credit card and pays $60 per month off her debt, Junia will be 30 when she makes her last payment and she will have paid more than $3000 in interest. If Junia's credit card provider charges an annual fee of $59 to her account each December, after 8 years of payments of $60 per month, Junia, at age 30, will still owe more than $1000 and she will have paid more than $3600 in interest.

As we can see, minimum payments barely cover the ongoing interest commitment. Making minimum payments leaves the individual exposed to very high interest rates. Individuals need a plan which discharges credit card debt as quickly as possible. This might include:

- making payments greater than the minimum
- consolidating credit card debt with other debt which attracts a lower rate of interest
- switching to a credit card which offers a lower rate of interest, including taking advantage of cards that offer a low honeymoon rate — although clients must be clear on the interest rate consequences once the honeymoon period is over.

Using the Credit Card Calculator available on the Moneysmart website, we can inform Junia of the effects of a nominal interest rate. If Junia owes $3000 with an annual interest rate of 18.5% and minimal repayments of 2% or $20 per month then she will pay a total of $10 227 over 26 years and 9 months. The calculator is available at: https://moneysmart.gov.au/credit-cards/credit-card-calculator. The effective interest rate using the above formula is 20.152%. However, if she is able to increase her repayments to $148 per month, she will pay only $3557 over 2 years and save a total of $6670.

The following article is one of a number of informative articles provided by ASIC on the Moneysmart website.

Pay off your credit cards

Pay on time

Check your credit card statement for the due date and make sure you pay on or before that date. By doing this, you'll avoid paying extra interest or late fees and also help keep your credit score healthy.

An easy way to pay is by direct debit or automatic transfer from your bank account each month. Set it for the day after your pay goes in, so you have enough money to cover it.

You can also set up a reminder to pay in your calendar

Pay as much as you can each month

If you can make higher repayments each month, you will pay off the debt faster and save money. If you only pay the minimum, you'll pay a lot of interest and it will take years to pay off your debt in full.

If you're finding it hard to pay the minimum amount, contact your bank or credit provider straight away or talk to a free financial counsellor. Taking action early stops a small money problem from getting bigger.

Cut back on your credit cards

If you have multiple credit cards, plan to reduce the number you have. Try setting yourself a goal to pay off one card at a time. Start with either of these.

Smallest debt

Paying off the card with the smallest debt first helps motivate you to keep going. Once you've paid that off, move onto the next smallest debt.

Highest interest rate

If one of your cards has a much higher interest rate, consider paying off that one first. Then pay off your other cards one by one.

Whichever option you choose:

- keep making the minimum payments on all your cards
- use only one of your cards, and try to keep it just for emergencies
- cancel each credit card once you've paid it off.

Reduce your credit limit

To avoid the temptation to overspend on your card, ask your credit provider to reduce your credit limit. You can do this online, by phone or by visiting a branch. In most cases, it takes between one and two business days.

If you need to increase your limit to buy something special, aim to pay it off quickly. Then reduce your limit again to a manageable amount.

2.7 Net present value

LEARNING OBJECTIVE 2.7 Explain the concept of net present value.

Net present value (otherwise referred to as NPV) is a means to determine whether an investment is worth undertaking. This concerns the comparison of what is proposed to be outlaid or invested in today's dollars with what the investment is predicted to return in today's dollars.

NPV is the sum of the present value of cash inflows less cash outflows. The expected future cash inflows are adjusted for the time value of money by discounting those cash flows by a discount rate — this gives a present value. The discount rate is usually determined by the rate of return on the investment required by the investor. It sometimes is referred to as the cost of capital. By undertaking this process, we can make a direct comparison between alternative investments or investment projects.

NPV is calculated as follows.

NPV = PV (Future cash flows) – Investment today

NPV may also be expressed in a formula as follows.

$$NPV = -CF_0 + \frac{CF_1}{(1+r)^1} + \frac{CF_2}{(1+r)^2} + \cdots + \frac{CF_n}{(1+r)^n}$$

$$= \sum \frac{CF_i}{(1+r)^i} - CF_0$$

where

NPV = net present value of the project

CF_0 = the initial outlay of the investment

CF_i = the future cash flows over the period i

r = the discount rate or cost of capital

i = number of periods

n = the number of the last year of the project

Note that if the NPV of an investment is:

< 0 then the investment is generally financially unacceptable

$= 0$ then the investment may be regarded as marginal

> 0 then the investment is generally regarded as financially acceptable.

The process of discounting is based on the reverse of compounding. If you expect to receive $100 in 1 year with a discount rate of 10% p.a. the present day value of the $100 in 1 year is $91. So, if an investment costs $300 today and is expected to return $100 at the end of each of the next 4 years with an interest rate of 10% p.a. then we can calculate the NPV as follows.

$$NPV = -300 + \frac{100}{(1+0.1)^1} + \frac{100}{(1+0.1)^2} + \frac{100}{(1+0.1)^3} + \frac{100}{(1+0.1)^4}$$

Note the initial investment is shown as a minus figure to indicate that it is an outflow. We can see the result in the following table.

Year	0	1	2	3	4
Cash flow	−300	100	100	100	100
Discount factor	1	0.9091	0.8264	0.7513	0.6831
Discounted cash flow	−300	90.91	82.64	75.13	68.31

The discount factors may be found in tables in most finance textbooks. Alternatively, the discount factor can be calculated using the formula:

$$\frac{1}{(1+r)^n}$$

Thus the discount factor for 1 year is:

$$\frac{1}{(1+0.1)^1} = 0.909\,090\,9$$

and the NPV in the above example is:

$$NPV = -300 + 90.91 + 82.64 + 75.13 + 68.31$$
$$= \$16.99$$

Thus, as the NPV is a positive amount, the investment proposal may be regarded as financially acceptable.

The NPV technique is widely used to compare and evaluate investment options for investors.

2.8 Further applications of the time value of money concept

LEARNING OBJECTIVE 2.8 Apply the time value of money concept to different investment choices.

The time value of money concept has a number of applications further to the above situations, and a financial adviser needs to be well versed in understanding the concept and how it may be applied. We will consider two of these applications in this section, namely, the internal rate of return and the valuation of fixed-interest securities.

The internal rate of return

Often, investors and financial advisers use the **internal rate of return** (IRR) on an investment as the investment yield or return on an investment. The IRR is the discount rate at which the NPV is zero. That is, the IRR is the rate of return at which the present values of cash inflows and outflows are equal. The discount rate at which the NPV is zero is given by the following formulae.

$$NPV = -CF_0 + \sum \frac{CF_i}{(1+r)^i} = 0$$

or

$$CF_0 = \sum \frac{CF_i}{(1+r)^i}$$

where CF_0 = the initial outlay of the investment
CF_i = the future cash flows over the period i
r = the discount rate
i = number of periods
n = the number of the last year of the project

The IRR is usually calculated by using a financial calculator or a spreadsheet. However, it is possible to calculate IRR by using a linear interpolation method by following these steps.

$$IRR = r_A + \frac{(r_A - r_B) \times NPV_A}{(NPV_B - NPV_A)}$$

Step 1. Apply an estimated discount rate, say $r_A = 10\%$.

Step 2. Calculate NPV_A using this discount rate. In the example in the previous section, $NPV_A = \$16.99$.

Step 3. Estimate a second discount rate r_B that could produce a negative NPV, say $r_B = 15\%$.

Step 4. Calculate NPV_B for the discount rate r_B (as shown in the table below).

Year	0	1	2	3	4
Cash flow	−300	100	100	100	100
Discount factor	1	0.8696	0.7561	0.6575	0.5718
Discounted cash flows	−300	86.96	75.61	65.75	57.18

Therefore:

$$NPV_B = -300 + 86.96 + 75.61 + 65.75 + 57.18 = -14.5$$

If the result does not produce a negative result, you need to try again with another discount rate.

Step 5. Calculate the IRR using the formula provided above.

$$IRR = 10 + \frac{(10 - 15) \times 16.99}{(-14.5 - 16.99)}$$
$$= 10 + \frac{(-5 \times 16.99)}{-31.49}$$
$$= 10 + 2.7$$
$$= 12.7\%$$

The variation of NPV is represented in figure 2.2 which shows that the NPV is positive at all discount rates less than the IRR (12.7%) and negative for discount rates above the IRR. The concept of IRR differs from the discount rate because the IRR is the return that will be made from the investment and the discount rate is the rate that is applied to compare different investments.

FIGURE 2.2	The variation in NPV at different discount rates

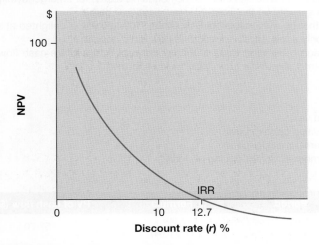

An investment is attractive when the investment's IRR has a positive NPV and its return is higher than the discount rate.

So, if the IRR of an investment is:

  $< r$ then the investment is generally financially unacceptable

  $= r$ then the investment is marginal

  $> r$ then the investment is generally financially acceptable.

A note of caution: Where there is only one sign change in cash inflows and outflows there will be only one IRR value. When there are multiple sign changes in cash inflows and cash outflows this can result in multiple IRR values at which NPV = 0 or no IRR value at all. In these cases, a financial adviser should use NPV analysis rather than IRR.

Fixed-interest securities

Investors in fixed-interest securities lend money to the security issuer, so the investors are, in effect, investing in debt because the issuer will relend the funds for some purpose to another party. In return for their investment, the issuer will pay the investors a fixed rate of interest for a set period of time. The regular interest rate is termed the 'coupon rate'.

All goes well for an investor as long as the issuer pays the interest on time and repays the full amount at the maturity date. However, if the investor needed to sell the security prior to the maturity date then the value of the security may not be the same as agreed. The value that the investor receives will depend on the interest rates prevailing in the economy at the time the investor needs to sell the fixed-interest security.

How the value of the security is determined relates to the time value of money concept because the method used to calculate the market value of the security is known as the discount method. This method refers to the rate of return required by the investor and is the rate at which future cash flows are discounted back to the present value.

ILLUSTRATIVE EXAMPLE 2.4

A security agreement is made on the basis of 12% interest (6% each half year) for a period of 2 years. Thus, during the course of the 2 years, the investor, Howard, will receive interest payments of 6% each 6 months and, at the end of the 2 years, he will also receive the amount of the original investment. Suppose Howard invests $1000 under the above terms.

The contract will stipulate the following payments.

Period	6 months	1 year	18 months	2 years
Future returns	$60	$60	$60	$60 + $1000

However, only a few days after the security is invested, the interest rates in the economy change and for a similar 2-year investment period the interest rate falls to 8% p.a. or 4% every 6 months. Howard's own situation changes too and he decides that he needs his $1000 for emergency expenses on his home. He decides to sell his security on the fixed-interest securities market.

Howard discovers that he will receive not $1000 but $1072.60. He is delighted at such a quick gain on his investment after only a few days and wonders how did it happen?

The answer is based on the time value of money concept of the future cash flows under the original agreement. The present value of the future returns is as follows.

$$PV = \frac{FV}{(1 + i)^n}$$

where PV = present value
FV = future value or cash flows
i = the interest rate per period
n = the number of compounding periods
In Howard's case:

Period	Formula	PV of cash flow ($)
1	$\dfrac{60}{(1 + 0.04)}$	57.70
2	$\dfrac{60}{(1 + 0.04)^2}$	55.50
3	$\dfrac{60}{(1 + 0.04)^3}$	53.30
4	$\dfrac{1060}{(1 + 0.04)^4}$	906.10
Total		1072.60

Note that the future cash flows of $60 and the return of the principal amount of $1000 are set future cash flows. The difference is that the prevailing interest rate has changed and provides a lower discount rate. Hence, Howard is able to sell his security, nominally valued at $1000, for a market price of $1072.60. If Howard was able to hold on to his investment for the 2 years, he would receive interest at a higher rate than the 4% the market offered after he had made his investment.

The critical point in this example is that the prevailing interest rates can affect the market price of the security and can result in a capital gain or a loss if the interest rates increase.

Suppose an investor is faced with the choice of two fixed-interest investments. Option A offers a fixed interest rate at 5% p.a. for 1 year and Option B offers a fixed interest rate of 6% p.a. for 2 years. Also, assume that the investor wants to invest for a period of 2 years. Is it better for our investor to choose Option B and receive a guaranteed 6% p.a. for 2 years, or to invest in Option A to get 5% p.a. for 1 year and take a chance on the interest rate for the second year — which may be higher or lower than 5% p.a? Which option is the investor more likely to choose? How can a financial adviser offer advice to an investor facing such a choice?

One way of resolving this dilemma is to solve for the rate at which the second year of investment for Option A is expected to represent the same outcome as for Option B. This is known as the **forward rate**.

For this example, let f_2 be the future interest rate for Year 2 that an investor choosing Option A would need to obtain in order to receive the same outcome as an investor who chose Option B.

$$f_2 = \frac{(1 + r_2)^2}{(1 + r_1)} - 1$$

$$= \frac{(1 + 0.06)^2}{(1 + 0.05)} - 1$$

$$= 0.07 \text{ or } 7.0\% \text{ (rounded)}$$

where f_2 = the future rate of interest in the second year for Option A

r_1 = the interest rate for the 1-year investment for Option A

r_2 = the interest rate for the 2-year investment for Option B

To explain this further, we will consider an investment of $1. For Option B, the compound interest for the 2 years is $(1.06)^2 = \$1.12$ (rounded).

For Option A, the return after one year is $1.05. If, at the end of Year 1, the investor of Option A obtains an interest rate of 7.0% and reinvests, the return would be $1.05 \times 1.07 = \$1.12$ (rounded). If the interest rate for Year 2 went down to 4% then the Option A investor would realise $1.05 \times 1.04 = \$1.09$ at the end of Year 2. If the interest rate in Year 2 went up to 8.0%, then the Option A investor would receive $1.05 \times 1.08 = \$1.13$.

So, in the case described above, there is no difference in the investment choices as long as the interest rate that is available for the second year at the maturity of the 1-year fixed term is at least 7.0%.

However, investment choice depends on the investor's view of the future interest rate. If interest rates move down after one year, Option B would be the better choice. If interest rates move up in the second year, Option A would be the better choice, as long as the rate increases to above 7.0%. So, it depends on the expectation of what the future interest rate is likely to be and, in many respects, the view about the trend of inflation. If, for a 1-year term, the interest rate is 5% and, for a 2-year term, it is 6% it may be likely that, at the outset, the view is that the future rate will be 7.5% after 1 year. By choosing the 2-year security an investor might miss out on possible higher interest rates.

The use of the forward rate approach may act as a guide in helping to resolve such a dilemma but economic conditions are changeable and future interest rates are difficult to predict with accuracy.

2.9 Effect of tax and inflation on the rate of return

LEARNING OBJECTIVE 2.9 Explain the effect of taxation and inflation on the rate of return.

When advising clients, an adviser needs to inform their client of the effects of both inflation and taxation on the net return on investments. In other words, an adviser needs to indicate the real rate of return after the *nominal* return is reduced by taxation and the effect of inflation. The nominal rate of return is the return stated by an investment; for example, 7% p.a. fixed interest. The real rate of return is the actual return to the investor after deducting the taxation to be paid by the investor and the rate of inflation. The repayments for fixed-interest investments, in particular, are prone to be overestimated when the effects of inflation and taxation are ignored. Table 2.4 indicates in simple form the effects of inflation and taxation on the real rate of return on a fixed-interest investment. Note that this table does not take into account the timing of the interest or tax payments which both may affect the real rate of return and indicate an even lower rate of return than that illustrated.

TABLE 2.4	Effect of inflation and taxation on the real rate of return on a fixed-interest investment			
Tax rate %	18.0	32.0	39.0	47.0
Interest %	8.0	8.0	8.0	8.0
Tax on interest %	(1.44)	(2.56)	(3.12)	(3.76)
After-tax return %	6.56	5.44	4.88	4.24
Inflation %	(5.0)	(5.0)	(5.0)	(5.0)
Real rate of return %	1.56	0.44	−0.12	−0.76

Note: This example assumes: interest rate = 8% p.a., inflation rate = 5% p.a., tax rates include 2.0% Medicare levy and are based on the rates applying in 2023–2024.

Assuming Nina was happy with a fixed interest rate of return, she may be less happy when she considers that she may lose some of the value of her interest if she pays personal income tax and when the cost of living increases, which reduces what she can buy with her money.

SUMMARY

Financial planners need to assist their clients in achieving their financial goals. They do this by helping clients to determine how much money is required and in what time frame. They then need to apply a number of skills such as the preparation of personal financial statements and applying ratio analysis to advise their clients on how they may reach their objectives and to assist clients to understand the impact of certain events on their family budget. Financial planners also need to explain to clients how money has different values in different time periods. A dollar in hand now is worth more than a dollar received in a year. This notion is referred to as the time value of money. The longer the time that money is invested, the greater will be the future value of that investment. The increase in value comes about because any interest received on the original investment will itself earn interest in subsequent time periods. This is the nature of compounding.

Other knowledge and skills that the financial planner needs to have in order to explain concepts of finance to clients include the need to understand the difference between nominal and effective interest rates and the use of the present value method to evaluate different investment choices. In particular, financial advisers need to alert clients about the effective interest rates charged on credit cards when the full amount is not paid by the due date. Finally, the financial adviser needs to understand and to relate to clients the effects of inflation and taxation on the returns that they will actually gain and how this may differ to the stated returns.

KEY TERMS

balance sheet A statement of assets and liabilities; the net result is the owner's value.

discount rate The rate of return required by an investor from an investment.

financial counsellor A person who is not a financial planner, but who assists people who have difficulties with managing their money.

forward rate The interest rate that is required to be achieved in a later year when choosing between a short-term and longer term fixed-interest investment.

future value An amount of money at some future time.

internal rate of return The rate of return at which the cash inflow and cash outflow of an investment is zero.

net present value The present value of a stream of income payments after deducting the cost of the stream of income payments.

present value An amount of money at today's value.

reverse mortgage An arrangement to mortgage a home in order to receive payments from the fund provider in return for a percentage ownership in the home or an accumulated debt to be paid when the home is sold.

PROFESSIONAL APPLICATION QUESTIONS

2.1 Suppose your friend lost their job, was unable to pay the electricity account when it was due and the electricity supply was disconnected. How could a financial counsellor assist your friend?

2.2 Review the Professional Advice feature in this chapter. Consider the impact on Mehmet and Elif's financial circumstances if both were to continue working but Elif's after-tax income was increased by 30% for a period of 2 years while she takes on a more responsible position. How will this affect their savings ratio and their net wealth? (Assume that Elif decided to delay having children until after the 2-year period of higher payment.)

2.3 Explain in your own words why $100 today will buy more goods and services than $100 in 3 years.

2.4 An advertisement offers a fixed term deposit for 4 years with an interest rate of 3.50% p.a. compounded annually or a fixed deposit for 4 years with an interest rate of 3.35% p.a. compounded quarterly. Which one would you choose? Explain why.

2.5 This question has two parts.
   (a) A credit card is a virtual requirement in today's society. Do you agree or disagree with this statement? Explain.
   (b) Find out the nominal interest rate on your own credit card and calculate the effective rate of interest.

2.6 Your uncle invested $50 000 in a 5-year fixed term security 2 years ago when the interest rate was 5.5% p.a. payable half yearly. He now needs to get his money back as an emergency situation has arisen. He asks a broker to sell the security on the securities exchange market and is delighted to receive the sum of $53 000. Explain why your uncle has received more than he originally invested.

2.7 Edmond has a dilemma. He has a choice of investing $10 000 for 5 years at an interest rate of 5.25% p.a. with interest payable quarterly or investing for 6 years at an interest rate of 5.5% p.a. with interest payable quarterly. Edmond does not need the $10 000 for a 6-year period. What will determine whether Edmond chooses one or the other investment period?

2.8 Jerry and Carol are aged 81 and 78 respectively and they own their own home. They do not have much spare capital to undertake repairs and renovations on their home but intend to sell their home in the next 3 years and move into a residential unit where they will have easy access to care as they age. They believe that their home will gain a better price if they spend about $60 000 on updating their bathroom and kitchen and re-painting. Consider the proposal of borrowing the funds as a reverse mortgage with no repayments made until they sell their house. What factors do they need to consider in making their decision?

2.9 Brad and Nerida are considering two alternative investments. Option 1 requires an outlay of $10 000 and after 2 years is expected to bring a cash flow of $1500 p.a. for the next 3 years. Then the investment would be terminated and they would get their $10 000 back. Option 2 requires an outlay of $15 000 and is expected to bring a cash flow of $1200 for each of the next 5 years. They would then expect to sell the investment for $17 500. Explain how net present value calculations would help them to decide on the best investment choice.

2.10 Thuy, one of your clients, invested $80 000 into a fixed term security at a rate of 6% p.a. Thuy earns income that puts her in the 37% marginal tax bracket. She wonders why you have mentioned that she needs to understand the effects of inflation and taxation on her 'real' rate of return. Calculate the real rate of return to Thuy if inflation is 2.5% and write a brief explanation to Thuy to demonstrate the real rate of return on her investment.

PROFESSIONAL APPLICATION EXERCISES

★ BASIC | ★★ MODERATE | ★★★ CHALLENGING

2.11 Ratio calculations ★

Tim and Laura provide the following financial information.

Assets	Home $400 000
	Bank account $4000
	Car $15 000
Liabilities	Home loan $300 000
Income p.a. (after tax)	Laura $58 000; Tim $80 000
Home loan repayments	$25 000 p.a.

(a) Calculate their net worth ratio.
(b) Calculate their debt service ratio.
(c) Calculate Tim and Laura's debt service ratio if a rise in interest rates causes their home loan repayments to increase to $30 000 without any change in their income.

2.12 Credit card switch ★

Yasmin has received an offer in the mail to transfer her $7500 credit card balance to a new provider. The offer is 'low rate and no fees'. The rate offered is 3.49% p.a. compounded monthly for 6 months with no application fees or transaction fees. However, in the terms and conditions it says:
- after the 6-month introductory period, the interest rate will revert to 21.5% p.a., which is a variable rate
- the transferred balance will be repaid first
- government charges and a late payment fee may apply
- minimum monthly repayments are required to be 3% of the outstanding loan amount or $30, whichever is the greater.
(a) What advice can you give Yasmin?
(b) Why might Yasmin consider switching to the new provider?

2.13 Investment returns ★★★

Effie has been given a chance to invest in her sister's frozen fruit juice company which needs some 'seed' capital so that production can commence. Her sister, Libby, estimates that an investment of $50 000 to buy 50 000 shares is needed. Libby estimates that each share will be worth $5.00 in 5 years.

(a) Nominally, what is the rate of return that Effie can expect to earn?

(b) What is the present value of the expected sum in 5 years if Effie sells her shares?

(c) In present value terms, what is the rate of return that Effie can expect to earn?

2.14 Savings needed ★★★

Zak wants to accumulate the sum of $70 000 in 4 years when he anticipates using the sum as a deposit on a home unit. He plans to have an annual holiday which he can fund from other savings. Zak has an initial starting amount of $8000 in an investment fund. If he expects an average annual rate of return of 7.5% on his investment, how much will he need to save each year to reach his objective?

2.15 Credit card interest ★★★

Pedro always thought that his credit card company charged a monthly interest rate. He has just checked his credit card statement and was surprised to learn that the company charges a daily interest rate of 0.000 52%. Pedro believes that, when you allow for 365 periods of compounding, the interest rate would be astronomical. What is the effective annual rate?

2.16 Evaluating a potential project ★★★

GreenBean Ltd's ambitious finance manager provides the following information with regards to a possible new project and wants you to evaluate whether the company should proceed with the project.

Purchase price of equipment	$4 million
Expected life of equipment	6 years
Tax depreciation of equipment	$0.5 million p.a.
Scrap value of equipment after 6 years	$280 000
Company tax rate	30% p.a.
Required rate of return	11% p.a.
Expected sales	$3.2 million p.a.
Operating costs (excl. interest and depreciation)	$1.1 million p.a.
Finance for the equipment	8-year bank loan with interest @ 7.5% p.a.

2.17 A savings plan ★★★

Raoul and Zara have a newborn baby, Isla. Generous grandparents have made a gift of $20 000 for Isla. Raoul and Zara have decided to invest this in trust for Isla so that on her 21st birthday she will have a deposit to potentially buy a one-bedroom home unit.

Raoul and Zara are considering making additional annual payments to the trust account, in order to increase the deposit amount to 40% of the expected price of the unit. Assume that the current price of a one-bedroom home unit is $320 000 and that property prices grow at 4% p.a. Assume that the trust account earnings are 7.5% p.a.

(a) What is the projected amount that will be available to Isla, when she turns 21, from the gift that is being held in trust?

(b) How much must Raoul and Zara contribute each year to achieve the desired deposit amount of 40% of the unit's expected purchase price?

(c) Discuss what factors may affect the achievement of Raoul and Zara's objective.

2.18 Choosing an investment term ★★★

Your aunt seeks your advice about investing $40 000 for a period of 3 years with interest paid half yearly at a rate of 5.2% p.a., or for 2 years with interest paid half yearly at a rate of 5.6% p.a. Calculate the rate of interest your aunt would need to get in the third year to be content with either investment choice.

2.19 Changing interest rates ★★★

Tyler borrowed $280 000 (mortgage) from the bank to be repaid over 20 years, at a variable nominal annual rate of interest of 4.5%, compounded monthly. Tyler considered fixing the rate because he was concerned about rising interest rates. However, the fixed rate of interest was set at 6.2% so the initial repayments were cheaper under the variable lending rate. The bank now needs to raise interest rates on all its variable loans and advised Tyler that his interest rate is to be increased to 6.7% p.a. compounded monthly. There are still 17 years to go before the loan is fully repaid.

Tyler asks you to calculate how much extra he will need to pay each month after the interest rate rise.

2.20 Paying off a mortgage early ★★★

Caitlin and Troy have settled on buying a new home for $900 000. They have sold their current home for $600 000 and, after paying the balance on their first home mortgage, have a deposit of $150 000 they can use against the mortgage on their second home. The details of their new home loan are as follows.

Repayments	Monthly
Interest	3.50% p.a. (nominal)
Term of the loan	20 years

(a) What are Caitlin and Troy's minimum monthly payments?

(b) If they wish to pay their loan off within 12 years, what would be the new amount of the monthly payments in order to achieve their goal? (Assume there are no other changes in the loan conditions.)

2.21 Fixed-interest securities in a changing interest market ★★★

Akio invested $40 000 in a fixed-interest security for a period of 3 years on the basis of 6.0% p.a. with interest payments made every 6 months. After 1 year, calculate the market value of the remaining 3-year security if the prevailing interest rates in the economy for 3-year securities with interest paid every 6 months change to:

(a) 4% p.a.

(b) 9% p.a.

CASE STUDY 1

ASSESSING A FINANCIAL SITUATION

Albie and Debra are a young married couple who have one child, Noah, aged 3 years. They have plans to send Noah to a private secondary school when he is 12 years of age and have decided to undertake an investment plan so they can pay for the fees from their investments rather than pay the fees from their salaries at that time. They have not yet put into place any savings plans.

Albie and Debra are undecided about whether they should invest funds over the next 5 years and then let the investments grow for the remaining 4 years, or whether they should wait until Noah is in primary school, when they may be able to afford more money to invest as their salaries should be higher. They are conscious that Debra may not be able to work full-time again until Noah goes to primary school so that is part of the reason why they may not save initially. Hence, they plan to invest $200 per week from now for such a purpose. They know which school they would like to send their children to and have been advised that the fees are $7000 p.a. per student. The bursar at the school also advised them that the fees may be expected to rise by 3% per year. Albie and Debra expect to achieve a long-term rate of 6.5% p.a. on their choice of fund, one that is designed for education funding, because of its tax-free status.

QUESTIONS

1 Calculate the end benefit if Albie and Debra start investing $200 per week for the next 5 years and then leave the investment intact for the following 4 years.

2 Calculate the alternative approach, which requires them to invest nothing for the next 5 years but then $300 per week for the 4 years prior to Noah commencing secondary school.

3 Explain the difference in terms of the impact of compounding.

4 What other issues do you think they need to consider in their analysis?

CASE STUDY 2

SHORT-TERM GOALS

Jenna is 20 years old and has been working as a retail assistant for 2 years. She earns $38 740 per year ($745 per week) in salary after tax.

She shares a flat with two friends. Her weekly payments on average are: rent $170; public transport fares $50; food $140; utility bills $60; mobile/internet phone $30; clothing $50; and entertainment $100. She also makes sure that she is saving some of her income and, for the past 2 years, has arranged for an automatic debit of $450 per month from her bank account into a managed fund. The amount accumulated in the fund comprises the original $3000 she was given for her 18th birthday to start the fund and contributions and earnings of $12 000, making a total sum of about $15 000. The managed fund is a balanced fund.

Any money left over after expenses and automatic debit investment is kept in her bank account, which totals $1000.

Jenna's main goal is to buy a car in the next 6 months. She will use some of the money in her managed fund if she has to, but hopes to buy a car valued at about $17 000 plus insurance of $850 p.a.

QUESTIONS

1 Clearly state Jenna's short-term goal.

2 How would a financial counsellor help Jenna to determine whether she may be on target to meet her goal?

3 Suppose the retail store proposes to reduce Jenna's hours and her annual after tax pay will decrease to $31 000 p.a. How will this affect her living costs and savings target?

4 What advice might a financial counsellor give to Jenna in such circumstances? Is there any other advice you may offer to help her achieve her goal?

5 What are the three main investment risks that Jenna faces given her short-term goal?

CASE STUDY 3

PERSONAL FINANCIAL STATEMENTS AND RATIO ANALYSIS

Refer to the discussion of Qinbo and Feilian Wong in the chapter. Assume the Wongs are given $50 000 from an inheritance.

QUESTIONS

1 Suggest three options (with reasons) that they may consider for the funds.

2 Select one option and prepare a personal cashflow budget and personal balance sheet for the Wongs.

3 Undertake ratio analysis for the Wong's changed situation.

CASE STUDY 4

REVERSE MORTGAGES

Barbara is a widow aged 72 who lives alone. Barbara requires $50 000 to renovate her kitchen and bathroom and to undertake some additional repairs to the guttering on her home. She does not want to leave her home for at least the next 10 years.

Barbara's home is valued at $400 000. The only other funds she has available are a $20 000 term deposit with her bank and 400 shares in Telstra valued at about $2000. She has no other funds to draw on to enable her to undertake the upgrade of her house as she relies on the full amount of the age pension for her normal living expenses. Hence, Barbara has been advised to consider a reverse mortgage. She understands that if she obtains $50 000 as a reverse mortgage against her home that the interest rate would be 8.3% p.a.

Barbara seeks advice from a reverse mortgage provider and is given a package of documents to consider. The documents require Barbara to seek legal advice from a solicitor and also advice from a financial adviser before she can proceed with her application. Both the financial adviser and the solicitor are each required to sign a document in the package.

QUESTIONS

1 Calculate the debt that Barbara would accumulate over the planned 10-year period.

2 Calculate the estimated growth in the value of Barbara's home if the property market is estimated to increase in value at the rate of 6% p.a.

3 Write a memo to Barbara to outline the consequence of entering into a reverse mortgage in terms of the debt to be paid to the reverse mortgage provider and how much she would have left when she may sell her home in order to buy a smaller home in 10 years or so.

4 Why do you think it is a requirement for a person seeking a reverse mortgage to consult with both a solicitor and a financial adviser and require them to sign about the advice they have given before making an application?

APPENDIX

FINANCIAL MODELLING

Financial advisers need to be proficient in the use of spreadsheets as a means of both 'crunching numbers' and communicating with clients.

Most financial analysis can be quickly modelled by a financial adviser using a spreadsheet. Off-the-shelf products have their place; however, there will be many instances when the needs of a client will not fit the software and should not be made to fit the software. Further, financial advisers need to validate results produced by software using sound estimation skills and by having a thorough appreciation of any assumptions and calculations used by the software. Financial advisers also need to ensure that their clients understand and are comfortable with any financial analysis, whether it be the product of an off-the-shelf software package or the result of an adviser's own spreadsheet skills.

Figure 2.3 is an example of a well-constructed spreadsheet. This spreadsheet can be contrasted with figure 2.4, which is a poorly designed spreadsheet. Take some time to compare the two spreadsheets. In the 'good design' spreadsheet, the formulae used in row 30 are outlined in the box at the bottom of the spreadsheet. In the 'poor design' spreadsheet, the formulae used in row 7 are outlined in the box at the bottom of the spreadsheet.

FIGURE 2.3	Well-designed spreadsheet

A1	B	C	D	E	F	G	H	I	J	K
2							Filename:		Good Design	
3							Author:		Mike	
4							Date created:		10-Feb	
5							Time created:		10.20 am	
6										
7										
8	Data Section									
9										
10										
11	Opening salary						90,000			
12	Opening salary index						1.0			
13	Opening balance of fund						75,000			
14	Age at commencement						45			
15	Year at commencement						2002			
16	Rate of earnings growth						4.2%			
17	Superannuation contribution tax						15.0%			
18	Superannuation earnings tax						15.0%			
19	Rate of employer superannuation guarantee contributions (SGC)						10.0%			
20	Rate of salary sacrifice						10.0%			
21										
22	Working Section									
23										
24										
25	Age	Year	Salary	Opening	Earnings	Earnings	SGC	Salary	Contributions	Closing
26				Balance		Tax		Sacrifice	Tax	Balance
27				of fund						of fund
28										
29	44	2001	90,000							75,000
30	45	2002	90,000	75,000	3,150	(473)	9,000	9,000	(2,700)	92,978
31	46	2003	90,000	92,978	3,905	(586)	9,000	9,000	(2,700)	111,597
32	47	2004	90,000	111,597	4,687	(703)	9,000	9,000	(2,700)	130,881
33	48	2005	90,000	130,881	5,497	(825)	9,000	9,000	(2,700)	150,853
34	49	2006	90,000	150,853	6,336	(950)	9,000	9,000	(2,700)	171,539
35	50	2007	90,000	171,539	7,205	(1,081)	9,000	9,000	(2,700)	192,963
36	51	2008	90,000	192,963	8,104	(1,216)	9,000	9,000	(2,700)	215,151
37	52	2009	90,000	215,151	9,036	(1,355)	9,000	9,000	(2,700)	238,132
38	53	2010	90,000	238,132	10,002	(1,500)	9,000	9,000	(2,700)	261,934
39	54	2011	90,000	261,934	11,001	(1,650)	9,000	9,000	(2,700)	286,585
40	55	2012	90,000	286,585	12,037	(1,805)	9,000	9,000	(2,700)	312,116
41										
42										
43	Explanatory notes:									
44	The earnings tax rate and the contributions tax rate are separate data items to allow for possible superannuation surcharge.									
45	It is assumed that SGC and salary sacrifice occur at year end and therefore do not attract earnings.									
46	Closing balance = opening balance + earnings − earnings tax + SGC + salary sacrifice − contributions tax.									

| 30 | =B29+1 | =C29+1 | =D29*I12 | =K29 | =E30*I16 | =F30*−I18 | =D30*I19 | =D30*I20 | =(H30+I30)*−I17 | =SUM(E30:J30) |

FIGURE 2.4 Poorly designed spreadsheet

A1	B	C	D	E	F	G	H	I	J
2	Poor Design								
3									
4									
5									
6	45	2002	90000	75000	9000	9000	3150	3172.5	92977.5
7	46	2003	90000	92977.5	9000	9000	3905.055	3285.75825	111596.7968
8	47	2004	90000	111596.7968	9000	9000	4687.065464	3403.05982	130880.8024
9	48	2005	90000	130880.8024	9000	9000	5496.993701	3524.549055	150853.247
10	49	2006	90000	150853.247	9000	9000	6335.836376	3650.375456	171538.708
11	50	2007	90000	171538.708	9000	9000	7204.625734	3780.69386	192962.6398
12	51	2008	90000	192962.6398	9000	9000	8104.430873	3915.664631	215151.4061
13	52	2009	90000	215151.4061	9000	9000	9036.359055	4055.453858	238132.3113
14	53	2010	90000	238132.3113	9000	9000	10001.55707	4200.233561	261933.6348
15	54	2011	90000	261933.6348	9000	9000	11001.21266	4350.181899	286584.6655
16	55	2012	90000	286584.6655	9000	9000	12036.55595	4505.483393	312115.7381

7	46	2003	90000 = J6		9000	9000	= E7*0.042	=(H7*0.15)+((F7+G7)*0.15)	=E7+F7+G7+H7–I7

From a client's point of view, it should be readily apparent which spreadsheet is more effective in communicating the assumptions and calculations required to produce the final result. With more direct and easy-to-follow formulae, the client is in a position to understand and, if necessary, question any of the assumptions and calculations. The approaches taken by the two spreadsheets are compared in table 2.5.

It is beyond the scope of this appendix to review all the aspects of good financial modelling — advisers may spend many hours working on their spreadsheets and be satisfied with what they perceive to be a very elegant solution. However, other users of the spreadsheet, including clients, will not devote the same amount of time trying to understand the spreadsheet. Therefore, a spreadsheet should always be 'road tested' on naive users.

Perhaps the most powerful ally and most dangerous enemy in creating spreadsheets is the copy command. With a properly structured data section and working section, the copy command should enable the working section of the spreadsheet to be created quickly. The copy command is at its most powerful with a clear understanding of the difference between absolute and relative cell references. Placing a '$' symbol in front of a column letter or a row number fixes that column letter or row number; placing a '$' symbol in front of *both* the column letter and row number fixes *both* the column letter and the row number. For example, I16 is an absolute cell reference that can be copied anywhere on the spreadsheet and the reference will remain to cell I16. There is usually a shorthand way of fixing a cell reference. For example, on most laptops, a cell reference highlighted in the formulae bar can be converted to an absolute cell reference by pressing the function key F4. In the 'good design' spreadsheet, the rate of earnings growth of 4.2% is located in the data section in cell I16. At the bottom of that spreadsheet are the formulae displayed for row 30 — the formulae for earnings in row 30 are simply copied by virtue of the absolute cell reference I16 to rows 31 through 40. Indeed, once all the formulae have been correctly entered into row 30, the entire row can be highlighted and copied down to row 40 — this is a sign of robust spreadsheet design that is built on an intelligent combination of relative and absolute cell references working in conjunction with a data and working section.

Table 2.5 compares the well-designed spreadsheet and the poorly designed spreadsheet.

TABLE 2.5 Spreadsheet comparison

Characteristic	Good design	Poor design
Separation between data and workings	The spreadsheet has a data section and a working section. All literal values are defined in the data section and no literal values are included in the working section. If a literal value changes then only one cell will need to be changed (e.g. if the rate of earnings growth changes then the only cell that will need to be changed is cell I16).	There is no clear separation between the data and the workings — if the rate of earnings growth changes this value is embedded in cells H6 to H16. There are many other literal values embedded in the spreadsheet making it very difficult to perform 'what if' type analysis.

(continued)

TABLE 2.5 *(continued)*

Characteristic	Good design	Poor design
Spreadsheet looks ahead	The spreadsheet looks ahead and identifies potential future variables (e.g. the current assumption is that the salary will not increase in real terms but it could). By including an opening salary index and multiplying the salary by that index we can provide for this possibility.	The spreadsheet does not look ahead (e.g. if the current salary increases in real terms then the whole structure of the spreadsheet will need to be reworked).
Reference data	The spreadsheet has a filename, author name, date and time created.	No reference data is provided. Assuming that you print out the spreadsheet several times before you get it right, how can you be sure you (or the client) are looking at the latest version?
Column structure	Columns are clearly labelled and are logically organised from left to right. Including the SGC and salary sacrifice columns to the right of the earnings column reinforces the notion that these contributions do not attract earnings in the current year. This is also reinforced by explanatory notes on the spreadsheet.	The columns have no headings. If/when the user has decoded column H as representing earnings, it is not clear whether this is inclusive or exclusive of SGC and salary sacrifice.
Number of columns	Wherever possible a spreadsheet in a financial plan should be contained within an A4 page — if absolutely necessary it can be printed in landscape format. Use as many columns as can reasonably be displayed. Combining too many calculations within one column makes the spreadsheet less transparent. Many financial plans are prepared for people approaching retirement. (The font should not be too small.)	If you look at column I, too many calculations are performed here — the spreadsheet lacks transparency.
Number formatting	The formatting needs to be consistent. If the spreadsheet is calculating values in the thousands of dollars then displaying cents is unnecessary. Percentages should be displayed as percentages and the number of decimal places should be consistent. For large numbers, using a comma to separate the thousands improves readability. If items are to be deducted, show them as negative numbers rather than hiding the subtraction in the formulae.	

REFERENCES

ASIC 2023a, 'Reverse mortgage calculator', Moneysmart, https://moneysmart.gov.au/retirement-income/reverse-mortgage-calculator.

ASIC 2023b, 'Pay off your credit card', Moneysmart, https://moneysmart.gov.au/credit-cards/pay-off-your-credit-card.

Financial Counselling Australia 2016, *Financial counselling — it makes a difference,* October, www.financialcounsellingaustralia.org.au/docs/financial-counselling-it-makes-a-difference.

Gordon, L 2020, 'Aussies wipe $2.45 billion off credit card debts in past year', RateCity, 13 January, www.ratecity.com.au/credit-cards/news/aussies-wipe-usd2-45-billion-off-credit-card-debts-past-year.

RBA 2023, *Chart pack: Credit and money,* 4 March, https://www.rba.gov.au/chart-pack.

Tindall, S 2023, 'Credit card comparison', RateCity, 6 January, www.ratecity.com.au/credit-cards.

ACKNOWLEDGEMENTS

Extract: © Financial Counselling Australia.

Extract: 'Pay off your credit card', Moneysmart, https://moneysmart.gov.au/credit-cards/pay-off-your-credit-card. ASIC MoneySmart website. © Australian Securities & Investments Commission. Reproduced with permission.

Figure 2.1: 'Reverse mortgage calculator', Moneysmart, https://moneysmart.gov.au/retirement-income/reverse-mortgagecalculator.ASIC MoneySmart website. © Australian Securities & Investments Commission. Reproduced with permission.

CHAPTER 3

Taxation planning

LEARNING OBJECTIVES

After studying this chapter, you should be able to:

3.1 identify the source of Australian taxation law

3.2 outline the different components of taxable income

3.3 calculate net tax payable for an individual, including levies and tax offsets

3.4 outline the taxation implications associated with the returns generated from different forms of investment, including capital gains tax

3.5 identify a range of common tax-effective strategies

3.6 explain the taxation implications of income splitting

3.7 explain the taxation implications of income versus capital growth

3.8 identify the various taxable entities, and compare the tax advantages and disadvantages of these different entities

3.9 explain the concept of negative gearing

3.10 explain remuneration planning and understand the taxation implications of salary packaging and fringe benefits tax (FBT)

3.11 explain the goods and services tax (GST).

Frank runs a panel beating business as a sole trader and employs two workers. His pre-tax income after expenses for the current year is $140 000. Frank's spouse Angela works part-time selling sporting goods with a major sports chain. Angela's salary is $42 000 p.a. The couple have 3 children aged 17, 22 and 24.

The couple is seeking some advice on how they are able to minimise their tax and build upon their long-term wealth. They realise that they have not given much attention to their investments over the years but are now committed to building wealth for their retirement.

The couple advises that they are looking to buy a rental apartment close to the city for around $650 000 plus $35 000 of costs associated with the purchase. They would contribute $160 000 from their own funds (a term deposit and selling off part of their share portfolio) and borrow the rest from the bank at a 3.5% interest rate.

The couple provides the following financial information.

Investment	Amount	Cost price	Ownership
Bank account	$ 40 000	$ 40 000	Frank
Term deposit	$ 80 000	$ 80 000	Frank
Share portfolio	$ 225 000	$160 000 (acquired 10 November 2000)	Frank
Superannuation	$ 180 000		Frank
Superannuation	$ 220 000		Angela

The couple's debt amounts to $360 000 and consists of:
- home mortgage — $320 000
- car loan — $30 000
- credit cards — $10 000.

Some of the issues in this case to consider from a tax point of view include the following.
- How much income tax is the couple paying?
- Are the couple's investments held in the name of the most appropriate person to minimise the imposition of tax?
- What are the tax implications of disposing part of their share portfolio?
- Should Frank look at establishing a more tax-effective strategy for running his business, such as a family company or family trust?
- In whose name should the rental property and debt be acquired in? Would it make any difference if the rental property was expected to make a profit or loss each year?
- From a tax perspective, in what order should debt be paid? Is it preferable to pay off the home loan or the rental property loan first?
- Could Angela restructure her remuneration package to minimise tax on her salary?

Illustrative examples used throughout this chapter relate to Frank and Angela's situation.

Introduction

An important factor to consider with any investment or financial decision is the implications of taxation. The amount of tax payable can vary considerably depending on the type and timing of the income and deductions as well as who is liable for the tax. An investment which shows the best return before tax may not necessarily generate the best return after tax has been taken into account. Different strategies and investments can significantly impact upon the amount of tax payable.

Although tax is an important component, it should never be the sole determining factor. A taxpayer needs to weigh up all of the expected benefits compared with the total costs from an after-tax perspective. The investment or strategy must also be consistent with the risk profile of the client (refer to the chapter on personal financial planning).

There is a well-known saying that there are two certainties in life — death and taxes. Death is certain but taxes are not necessarily so, as any tax planner will agree. What is certain, however, is that whatever the tax law is now, it will change — a risk that must be recognised by all investors. Because of the frequency and dimension of these changes, comprehensive tax guides are likely to be useful for only a short time. This chapter concentrates on general taxation principles as they affect personal financial planning rather than the fine details.

As with financial planning, tax planning is very specific to the needs of an investor. For example, a particular tax structure may be of benefit to one investor but detrimental to another. It depends on the tax position of the investor in the years involved.

Taxation planning is the legitimate organisation of an investor's affairs in accordance with taxation laws to minimise tax. *Tax evasion* involves criminal falsification or non-disclosure as a means of reducing tax. *Tax avoidance* fits between the two and although it looks to minimise tax through legal means, the strategies employed are artificial and contrived and have no reason other than obtaining a tax benefit. Tax avoiders run the very real risk of having their schemes struck aside and heavy penalties imposed. Tax evaders run the risk of very heavy fines and long prison terms. In the context of personal financial planning, this chapter is about taxation *planning*, the organisation of an investor's affairs to minimise tax.

3.1 The Australian taxation system

LEARNING OBJECTIVE 3.1 Identify the source of Australian taxation law.

The primary function of most taxes is to redirect economic resources from the private sector to the government to enable it to conduct its various spending programs. Taxation represents the major form of government revenue raising in most countries around the world. Taxation has a number of different functions including:

- to finance the activities of government that modern society expects and that may not be adequately provided by the free market — for example, defence, health, education and roads
- to achieve the government's economic objectives — for example, an increase in taxes can be used to reduce private-sector spending and therefore restrict inflation
- to achieve desirable social objectives — taxation can be used to encourage or discourage spending on particular types of products and services such as imports, tobacco, alcohol and heavily polluting goods
- to redistribute income and wealth — for example, to provide social welfare to families.

A short history of taxation in Australia

Although various forms of taxes have been around for many hundreds of years, the first **income tax** was introduced in England in 1799 to help finance the war against France. At that time, a taxpayer made their own assessments of assessable income and allowable deductions and paid 10% of this to the government. Various models of tax were imposed over the years in England to finance various wars and were withdrawn when hostilities ceased.

The first income tax in Australia was imposed in South Australia in 1884. By the early 1900s, income tax had been introduced by every Australian state. The first Commonwealth income Tax Act was imposed in 1915 largely as a means of financing the war effort during World War I. The 1915 measures continued in force until the 1922 Act was introduced, which was superseded by the 1936 Act which remained in force for many years. Until 1923, both the states and the Commonwealth levied their own income taxes and taxpayers were required to prepare and lodge two sets of income tax returns. The two sets of income tax lasted until 1942 when, due to financial pressures arising from World War II, the Commonwealth Government took over the levying of income tax exclusively.

The Tax Law Improvement Project (TLIP) commenced in 1983 with the objective of redrafting and simplifying the *Income Tax Assessment Act 1936* (ITAA36) which had become cumbersome and complex. The first instalment of the program resulted in the enactment of the *Income Tax Assessment Act 1997* (ITAA97). However, the full number of instalments of this Act were never enacted which means that large parts of the tax law are still contained within the ITAA36 and taxpayers are required to work with two Acts.

In the latter part of the 1980s, a major reform of the income tax law began with a view to broadening the income tax base of the government and attempting to minimise tax avoidance. The statement known as the Reform of the Australian Income Tax System outlined a number of major policy developments including:

- introducing a capital gains tax
- introducing a fringe benefits tax
- introducing a dividend imputation system to eliminate the double taxation that existed on the taxing of dividends received by shareholders
- the non-deductibility of entertainment expenses.

All of these measures have become part of the Australian income tax system over the years and will be discussed in further detail in this chapter.

Taxation bases

In Australia, taxes are imposed at the Commonwealth, state, territory and local government levels. Over the years, taxation has been levied on a range of different activities, transactions and property. Some examples are a tax on income, profits, goods and services, the importation of goods, the production of goods and services, capital profits and even death. Most countries rely upon a range of taxes to raise government revenue and no developed country relies upon a single taxation base.

Income tax (direct tax)

Direct tax is a tax paid directly by the person or organisation on whom it is levied and is payable on most forms of income and profits. Examples include wages and salaries, most forms of income derived from investments and business income. Since the initial Commonwealth income tax was levied in Australia in 1915, there have been continual calls for Australia to broaden its tax base away from just income tax.

Goods and services tax (indirect tax)

The **goods and services tax (GST)** was introduced into Australia from 1 July 2000. It is a broad-based value-added tax on goods and services and is charged at a flat rate of 10% on suppliers and importers. An indirect tax is defined as a tax levied on expenditures, that is, the tax is paid when the good or service is purchased. Examples include sales tax, goods and services tax, excise tax and value-added tax. Indirect tax is collected and paid by a supplier, but it is ultimately borne by the consumer through the charging of higher prices. Other examples include customs duty, which is a tax imposed on an importer for goods imported into Australia, and excise duty, which is a tax on the manufacture of certain goods such as alcohol, tobacco and petrol.

In this chapter, we will be focusing on the determination and calculation of income tax.

Sources of taxation law

The three basic sources of taxation law in Australia are:

- the *Income Tax Assessment Act 1997* (ITAA97) — since the Tax Law Improvement Project, which involved rewriting the old *Income Tax Assessment Act 1936* (ITAA36) into simple English, the readability and usability of the legislation has improved. Many of the improvements are included in legislation as amendments to the 1936 or 1997 Acts. References to taxation law are made sometimes to ITAA97 and sometimes to the old legislation, ITAA36, in addition to the relevant amendment
- case law, where interpretation of legislation by the courts sets precedent
- the Australian Taxation Office (ATO), which gives advice on the application of the law with rulings and determinations.

The ATO legal database website at law.ato.gov.au (see figure 3.1) provides easy access to all sources of taxation law.

FIGURE 3.1   The ATO legal database

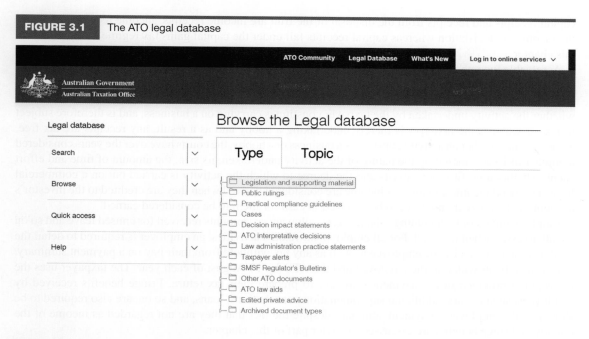

Source: ATO 2024a.

3.2 The components of taxable income

LEARNING OBJECTIVE 3.2 Outline the different components of taxable income.

Income tax in Australia is determined on a financial year basis, which is the period from 1 July to 30 June, and is levied on a range of different entities including individuals, companies, trusts and superannuation funds. The calculation of income tax requires certain tax rates to be applied to the taxable income of the particular entity. Net tax payable is determined as follows.

$$\text{Gross tax payable} = \text{Taxable income} \times \text{Tax rate}$$

$$\text{Net tax payable} = \text{Gross tax payable} - \text{Tax offsets and rebates} + \text{Levies}$$

Taxable income is worked out as follows.

$$\text{Taxable income} = \text{Assessable income} - \text{Allowable deductions}$$

All taxpayers are required to lodge a tax return each year with the ATO. Each individual in Australia is assessed individually and is required to submit an income tax return for income earned and deductions incurred in their own name. Family members are assessed individually and not as a family unit.

Since 1986, Australia has operated under a **self-assessment regime** where the ATO generally accepts information provided by taxpayers in their tax returns and issues tax assessments on this basis. Information supplied by taxpayers in their returns is subject to audits and other verification processes.

Assessable income

Assessable income includes ordinary income and statutory income. Ordinary income is covered under s. 6.5 of ITAA97 and described as 'income according to ordinary concepts'. It includes such income as salary and wages, rent, dividends, sales revenue, interest and annuities. Ordinary income earned from all sources during the financial year is assessed, whether derived in Australia or from overseas.

Ordinary income is not actually defined in the tax legislation but has been interpreted according to its common-law meaning, which basically relates to the realisation of a financial gain. In attempting to explain the characteristics of income, the courts have attempted to distinguish the concepts of income receipts and capital receipts. The best illustration of the difference is the analogy of the tree and the fruit of the tree. To a fruit grower, the tree is capital and the fruit is income. Receipts from the disposal of the trees are capital receipts and receipts from the disposal of the fruit are income receipts. Income receipts fall under the income tax legislation whereas capital receipts fall under the capital gains tax regime covered later in this chapter.

Assessable income is brought to account in the period when it is considered derived. Generally, income is derived by a business when it is earned. Most large businesses work on an accruals basis but many small businesses report on a cash basis. An important issue when considering the taxing of business receipts is whether the activity undertaken by the taxpayer constitutes carrying on a business, and is therefore subject to tax, or whether the taxpayer is merely undertaking a hobby and as a result, any receipts are tax free. To determine whether an activity constitutes a business or a hobby, the courts have over the years considered a number of issues, including the nature of the activity undertaken, its size, the amount of time and effort spent, whether a profit motive exists and the degree to which the activity is carried out on a commercial basis. Dividend income and interest income are considered derived when they are credited to the investor's account, that is, they do not have to be received in cash for them to be considered earned.

Employment income, including salary, wages, allowances, amounts received for unused leave and so on are all assessed when received. For all employment-related activities, an employer is required to detail the total income received by the employee as well as any tax withheld from their pay on a payment summary, which must be provided to the employee and the ATO by 14 August of each year. The taxpayer uses the information provided in the payment summary to prepare their tax return. Fringe benefits received by employees, such as cars, additional superannuation contributions, loans, and so on, are also required to be shown on the employee's payment summary despite the fact that they are not regarded as income of the employee. Fringe benefits are discussed in a later part of this chapter.

While a number of regular government pensions, allowances and benefit payments are assessable income, such as the age pension payment and the JobSeeker payment, most support-type payments are exempt income. Some of the exempt government payments include:

- youth allowance
- family tax benefits
- disability support pension
- ABSTUDY
- carer allowance.

The year in which income is derived is important as it may impact upon when tax is payable as well as how much tax is payable. To minimise tax, it is generally advantageous to defer income to a later period. Consider the following example.

ILLUSTRATIVE EXAMPLE 3.1

Angela, who is employed as a retail assistant, is considering retiring on 30 June (see the opening case study). Upon her retirement, she expects to receive the following payments.

Salary	$ 6 000
Unused annual leave	$ 6 000
Employer termination payment	$12 000

From the point of view of minimising taxation, does it make any difference whether Angela retires on 30 June or 1 July?

It is likely that Angela will be better off if she retires in July of the next financial year. The reason is that Angela's taxable income in the year of retirement will be lower than in the current year when she is fully employed and receiving a salary of $42 000. With a lower taxable income, the rate of tax will be lower, which means her tax payable will be lower. Income tax is charged on a progressive basis in Australia with the result that the more income a person earns, the greater the percentage of tax applied. As a general rule, it is normally advantageous to defer income to a later financial year. Not only does this defer income and the payment of tax, it may also reduce the overall amount of tax payable, as discussed earlier.

In the tax planning process, only income receipts are assessable. Capital appreciation of an investment is not generally regarded as income of the taxpayer. However, when the investment is realised or sold, the gain from the capital appreciation is subject to another form of tax called the capital gains tax (CGT). The CGT legislation is very complex and taxes the gains or profit made from the disposal of most assets and investments. Capital gains tax will be discussed further in a later section of this chapter.

Allowable deductions

Allowable deductions include two types of expenses or outgoings: general deductions and specific deductions. Section 8.1 of ITAA97 covers general deductions and provides that an expense may be classified as an allowable deduction on the basis that it is necessarily incurred in gaining or earning that assessable income. There must be a sufficient connection between the expense incurred and the earning of the assessable income. Examples of the type of expenses that would be considered an allowable general deduction include:

- travelling and car expenses incurred in the course of an employee's work
- subscriptions for professional journals related to the employee's employment
- income protection insurance
- business deductions and interest paid in connection with an activity that generates assessable income.

Deductions are not allowed for outgoings of a private, capital or domestic nature, or for expenses incurred in earning exempt income. For example, travelling costs to and from work are not tax deductible because they are considered to be of a private nature. Expenses incurred in connection with investments are normally allowable deductions as long as they are incurred in the course of earning assessable income from those investments. Thus, interest payable to the bank on funds borrowed to buy an investment property would be deductible as long as the property generated assessable income. On the other hand, interest on borrowings used to finance the purchase of a vacant block of land generating no assessable income is unlikely to be tax deductible. Interest on borrowings used to finance the family home is not deductible as the home is of a private or domestic nature and does not generate assessable income.

The taxation legislation also provides for a number of specific deductions that would not normally be allowed under the general provisions but which have been specifically legislated to be an allowable deduction. Examples include tax preparation expenses with a tax agent, donations and gifts to approved charities, repairs and bad debts. All of these expenses are allowable deductions for a taxpayer, even though they are not directly attributable to earning assessable income.

Deductibility of expenditure is important, and structuring a client's affairs to maximise deductions and therefore minimise taxable income and tax payable is of prime importance.

Substantiation of allowable deductions

Generally, a taxpayer is required to have written evidence for any expense they claim as a deduction, which normally takes the form of an invoice or receipt. Travel diaries are required to be used to verify travel claims. Employees are generally required to be able to substantiate any work-related claims they make in their tax returns, except where the work-related expenses are less than $300 in total. Invoices and receipts are required to be kept for a period of five years from lodgement of the tax return.

PROFESSIONAL ADVICE

Travelling expenses

Phil Stewart joined Let's Fly Away Travel at the start of the financial year as a travel agent. During the current year, he travelled overseas on four occasions and interstate twice as detailed below. The travel arrangements were either supplier-structured or self-structured. In broad terms, supplier-structured involves travel where the itinerary is structured by the supplier of the travel product. With self-structured travel, the traveller structures the itinerary. In the case of supplier-structured arrangements, the travel costs are borne by the supplier. The only cost to Phil is a participation fee and his own personal expenses. In the case of self-structured arrangements, he pays for all his travel costs, including fares and accommodation while on annual leave. In addition to four weeks annual leave, he is eligible for five days paid educational leave. Phil uses his educational leave for his supplier-structured travel.

Details of his travel during the year are as follows.

Date	Destination	Period	Leave type	Itinerary structure
August	Bali	1 week	Educational (& weekend)	Supplier-structured
October	USA and Thailand	1.5 weeks	Annual leave	Self-structured

Date	Destination	Period	Leave type	Itinerary structure
December	Tasmania	1 week	Educational (& weekend)	Supplier-structured
February	Gold Coast	1 week	Educational (& weekend)	Supplier-structured
December	Thailand and Vietnam	2 weeks	Educational (& annual leave)	Supplier-structured
June	Around the world	2 weeks	Annual leave	Self-structured

Phil is claiming a portion of the travel expenses as a tax-deductible claim for an amount of $8000. Phil's rationale for the claim is that on each of the trips he undertook holiday activities, he was employed to sell holiday-related travel products and his employer's business model emphasised 'excellence of service to its customers' based on the personal experiences of the consultant. Phil argues that to survive in the travel industry, you have to be passionate about travel, which he says he is, and you have to travel at every available opportunity, which he does.

QUESTIONS

1. Do you believe Phil is entitled to claim a tax deduction for the costs of the trips that he undertook during the year as a travel agent?

2. Would it make any difference to his claim if Phil took his family with him on the overseas trips?

3. What documentation would Phil need to keep in order to substantiate his claim?

Individual tax rates

Individual taxpayers pay tax at progressive rates where the rate of tax increases with the level of income. These are known as **marginal tax rates**. Marginal tax rates (MTR) for resident individuals as of 1 July 2024 are shown in table 3.1.

TABLE 3.1   Marginal tax rates

Taxable income	Marginal tax rate	Tax payable ($)
$0–$18 200	0%	$Nil
$18 201–$45 000	16%	16% on the excess over $18 200
$45 001–$135 000	30%	$4288 plus 30% on the excess over $45 000
$135 001–$190 000	37%	$31 288 plus 37% on the excess over $135 000
Above $190 000	45%	$51 638 plus 45% on the excess over $190 000

Source: ATO 2024b.

As illustrated in table 3.1, no tax is payable if an individual's taxable income is less than $18 200, known as the tax-free threshold. A 16% marginal tax rate applies to income between $18 200 and $45 000; 30% on any income above $45 000 up to $135 000, and so on. With progressive taxation, the tax effect of additional income or additional deductible expenses depends on the level of taxable income earned.

All individuals pay tax on total taxable income that they have earned during the financial year. Most individuals pay tax on a **pay as you go (PAYG)** basis where tax is pre-paid in instalments to the ATO throughout the year towards payment of their expected final tax liability. Most employers are required to deduct income tax from the pay of their employees on a weekly, fortnightly or monthly basis. At the end of the year, individuals — with the help of a paper-based Tax Pack, online lodgement with myTax, a tax agent or an accountant — submit a tax return. Based on the total taxable income for the financial year, net tax payable is determined by the ATO and tax already paid under the PAYG system is deducted from this net amount. The taxpayer will either need to pay the balance of tax owing to the ATO or will receive a refund of tax.

ILLUSTRATIVE EXAMPLE 3.2

Janet earns assessable income of $84 000 consisting of a salary of $82 000 and bank interest of $2000. Her allowable deductions consist of work-related expenses of $500 plus $100 of donations. Accordingly, her taxable income totals $83 400.

Gross tax payable is determined as follows, using marginal tax rates effective from 1 July 2024.

Janet's taxable income falls in the band of between $45 000 and $135 000. Therefore, her marginal tax rate is assessed at 30%.

Tax on $45 000 (detailed in table 3.1)	$ 4 288.00
Tax on excess income above $45 000	
$38 400 × 30% marginal tax rate	11 520.00
Total gross tax payable	**$15 808.00**

Residency

The imposition of taxation in Australia differs depending on whether an individual is regarded as an Australian resident or non-resident for taxation purposes. A person is regarded as a tax resident if they either permanently reside in Australia, as evidenced by setting up a home, studying or working within Australia, or they satisfy one of three tests. Generally, a period of 6 months of work, study or setting up a home is used to determine tax residency. Other factors that the ATO will consider include: intention and purpose, family, business or employment ties, maintenance and location of assets and social and living arrangements. The consequences of being classified as a tax resident include the following.

- Tax residents apply the marginal tax rates detailed in table 3.1 above whereas non-tax residents do not get the tax-free threshold, nor are they entitled to receive a number of tax rebates and offsets as discussed below.
- Tax residents are taxed on income from all sources, derived both within and outside of Australia, whereas non-residents are taxed only on income derived in Australia.

When an Australian citizen decides to work overseas for a period of time they may lose their Australian residency for tax purposes. Let us consider two examples. Emma takes up a 1-year contract to teach English in Korea. After her contract expires, she intends to travel for the following 3 months before returning to Australia. She will board with a family while she lives in Korea. Emma has a home in Australia that she will rent out while she is away. In the second example, Gail takes up a 3-year contract with an overseas firm with an option to extend for a further period. Gail and her partner decide to rent out their home in Australia while they are away. While overseas, Gail and her partner purchase a property and Gail will receive an accommodation allowance.

From the two examples, Emma is likely to be treated as a resident but Gail is likely to be treated as a non-resident. The significant differences are the length of time that Gail plans to be away from Australia and the establishment of a new home outside of Australia. Being classed as a 'resident' or 'non-resident' for tax purposes needs to be determined on a case-by-case basis via specific tax advice.

Tax rates payable by other entities

Companies

Large companies are levied income tax at a flat rate of 30% on their taxable income for the financial year. There is no tax-free threshold.

Companies classified as base rate entities are subject to a reduced tax rate of 25%. A base rate entity is defined as a company that has:

- an aggregated turnover of less than the $50 million for the income year
- 80% or less of their assessable income is base rate entity passive income.

Base rate entity passive income includes: corporate distributions and franking credits on these distributions, royalties and rent, interest income, capital gains as well a number of other items.

Individuals operating a business as an unincorporated small business with an annual turnover of less than $5 million are also entitled to the small business tax offset which effectively provides an offset of 16% of the tax payable on the business income received subject to a maximum cap of $1000 per year.

Superannuation funds

Complying superannuation funds pay income tax at a flat rate of 15% on their taxable income. Non-complying superannuation funds pay tax at a flat rate of 47%. Again, there is no tax-free threshold for superannuation funds.

Partnerships

A partnership is not a separate legal entity. Accordingly, partnerships are not assessed for tax even though they are required to lodge a tax return. Profits are allocated between the partners who are assessed on their share of the profits at their individual marginal tax rates.

Trusts

All profits earned within a trust structure are generally required to be distributed between the various members having an entitlement to that income, called **beneficiaries**. The income received by a beneficiary is added to any other income earned and taxed at the beneficiary's marginal tax rate. If there is trust income to which no beneficiary is entitled, then the trustee must pay tax on that income at the highest marginal tax rate, currently 45% plus Medicare. This provision is in place to ensure that the trust income is distributed to beneficiaries rather than accumulated within the trust.

3.3 Calculation of net tax payable for an individual resident taxpayer

LEARNING OBJECTIVE 3.3 Calculate net tax payable for an individual, including levies and tax offsets.

Once gross tax payable has been determined, an individual taxpayer may be entitled to a number of tax offsets or rebates, which are used to reduce tax payable. However, a taxpayer may also be subject to a number of levies and charges, which have the effect of increasing the amount of tax payable. As outlined previously, the calculation of net tax payable is determined as follows.

$$\text{Net tax payable} = \text{Gross tax payable} - \text{Tax offsets and rebates} + \text{Levies and charges}$$

Tax offsets

Individual taxpayers may be entitled to claim a reduction in their tax payable through the use of a number of **tax offsets or rebates**. Tax offsets are used by the government to provide social and welfare assistance and support to individuals and families in need, encourage certain kinds of activities and investment, and provide a credit for payments of tax.

Unlike an allowable deduction, which is subtracted from assessable income in order to determine taxable income, a tax offset represents a reduction in the amount of tax that is required to be paid by a taxpayer. Examples of tax offsets include the imputation credit or franking credit offset, low income tax offset, senior Australians tax offset and pension tax offset.

A complete list of possible tax offsets can be found on the ATO website (ato.gov.au). Generally, a tax offset can only be used to eliminate gross tax payable. In most situations, tax offsets cannot exceed a taxpayer's gross tax payable and the excess is not refundable, they cannot be applied against the Medicare levy and cannot be carried forward to future years. One of the main exceptions to this is in respect of the imputation credit, which will be discussed later in this chapter.

Support for low income earners

To assist Australian residents that are low income earners, the government provides support through a tax offset that has the effect of reducing net tax payable. The tax offset is known as the low income tax offset.

The low income tax offset (LITO) is currently set at $700, payable for taxable incomes up to $37 500. Where the taxable income of a taxpayer exceeds $37 500, there are two shade-out thresholds. For a taxable income between $37 501 and $45 000, the $700 offset is reduced by 5 cents for each dollar in excess of $37 500. For a taxable income between $45,001 and $66 667, a taxpayer will be entitled to a maximum offset of $325 minus 1.5 cents for each dollar in excess of $45 000. The offset cuts out completely at a taxable income of $66 667.

The effect of the low income tax offset is that a taxpayer can effectively earn a taxable income of around $21 887 and have a zero tax liability.

The LITO thresholds for the financial years 2018–19 through to 2023–24 are given in table 3.2. At the time of writing LITO thresholds were not available for the 2024–25 financial year.

TABLE 3.2 **LITO thresholds for the financial years 2018–19 through to 2023–24**

Taxable income	Maximum size of tax offset
$0–$37 500	$700
$37 501–$45 000	$700 minus 5 cents for every $1 in excess of $37 000
$45 001–$66 667	$325 minus 1.5 cents for every $1 in excess of $45 000

Source: ATO 2024c.

Example

Katherine's taxable income is $56 000. Katherine's entitlement to the LITO will be calculated as:

$$\$56\,000 - \$45\,000 = \$11\,000$$
$$\$11\,000 \times 0.015 = \$165$$
$$\$325 - \$165 = \$160$$

Levies and charges

The Australian Government imposes a number of levies and charges on individual taxpayers. The most important of these are the Medicare levy, the Medicare levy surcharge and the higher education loan program (HELP) charge.

Medicare levy

Most resident individual taxpayers are required to pay the **Medicare levy** as part of their tax liability. For a number of years, the Medicare levy was set at a rate of 1.5% of taxable income. The Medicare levy is used to fund Australia's national health system. From 1 July 2014, the Medicare levy increased to 2% of taxable income to help fund the National Disability Support Scheme. The Medicare levy is based on the taxable income of the individual. Low-income earners may be entitled to some relief from having to pay the Medicare levy.

Medicare levy surcharge

The Medicare levy surcharge is an additional levy imposed on individual taxpayers that are high-income earners without adequate private health insurance. The surcharge is applied on a sliding scale based on the taxable income of the individual. The income thresholds and rates from 1 July 2024 are provided in table 3.3.

TABLE 3.3 **Medicare levy surcharge rates**

Taxable income		Levy payable
Single income	Family income	
$97 000 or less	$194 000 or less	0%
$97 001–$113 000	$194 001–$226 000	1%
$113 001–$151 000	$226 001–$302 000	1.25%
$151 001 or more	$302 001 or more*	1.5%

*Increase the family income threshold by $1500 for each additional dependent child after the first child.
Source: ATO 2024d.

HECS and HELP charge

In order to assist students pay their higher education fees, the government provides support by making available Commonwealth Government loans. The system, called HECS-HELP (higher education loan program), assists students by allowing them to defer payment of their higher education fees and to repay them at a later time through the taxation system when their taxable income reaches a certain minimum income threshold. Students are only able to access a HECS-HELP loan if they are enrolled in a Commonwealth supported place (CSP). FEE-HELP is a loan scheme for full fee-paying undergraduate and postgraduate students and can be used to pay for course fees. Borrowing limits are placed on the HELP support provided. For 2024, the HELP loan limit is $121 844. Medicine, dentistry and veterinary science have higher loan limits. A student's renewable HELP balance is their available borrowing capacity up to the loan limit.

HELP repayment rates are based on a taxpayers repayment income which is determined as: taxable income plus any total net investment loss (which includes net rental losses), total reportable fringe benefits amounts, reportable super contributions and exempt foreign employment income (Australian Government n.d.).

The repayment rates are based on progressive tax rates, so that the higher the repayment income, the higher the repayment rate. The repayment rate commences at a rate of 1% of reportable income in excess of $51 550 and increases to a repayment rate of 10% for a reportable income in excess of $151 200 (ATO 2024c).

Taxpayers can check their outstanding HELP loan balance and any repayments made through their myGov account.

ILLUSTRATIVE EXAMPLE 3.3

Frank and Angela's daughter, Michelle, is employed as a journalist and earns a wage of $91 000 p.a. She has a HELP loan outstanding of $35 000.

During the current year, she also received $2500 in bank interest and $3000 from a TattsLotto win. Michelle's expenditure for the year is as follows.

Travelling to and from work	$1 200
Travelling costs incurred for work purposes	1 000
Membership to the Media, Entertainment and Arts Alliance	800
Donation to hospital	200
Membership of local tennis club	200
Tax agent's costs (preparation of tax return)	600

Michelle is single and does not have any private health insurance.
What is the net tax payable by Michelle for the 2024–25 financial year, including her HELP repayment?

Assessable income		
Salary	$	91 000
Bank interest		2 500
Total assessable income		93 500
Less: Allowable deductions		
Travelling costs incurred for work purposes		1 000
Membership to the Media, Entertainment and Arts Alliance		800
Donation to hospital		200
Tax agent's costs (preparation of tax return)		600
Total allowable deductions		2 600
Taxable income	**$**	**90 900**
Gross tax payable		$18 058.00
($4 288 + 30% of the excess over $45 000)		
Add: Medicare levy (2.0%)		1 818.00
Add: Medicare levy surcharge (0%)		0.00
Add: HELP repayment (5.5% x $90 900)		4 999.50
Net tax payable		**$24 875.50**

Notes:
- The TattsLotto win is considered to be a windfall gain and normally non–assessable.
- Travelling to and from work is considered to be expenditure of a private nature and not tax deductible.

- Donations or gifts of $2 or more have been specifically legislated to be an allowable deduction.
- Expenditure incurred by a taxpayer in managing their tax affairs has been specifically legislated to be an allowable deduction.
- Although Michelle does not have private health insurance, because her income is below the Medicare levy surcharge income threshold, she is not liable to pay a Medicare levy surcharge.

Taxation of minors

Special tax regulations are in place to prevent taxpayers avoiding tax by directing income to children. Minors are defined as unmarried persons under 18 years of age not in full-time employment. The special tax rules relate to the 'unearned income' of minors. This includes the income from most forms of investments, such as interest, rental income and dividends and income distributed from a family trust. However, income which is considered 'earned' by the minor is excluded from the special rules, and includes employment and business income.

The tax rates payable by minors on unearned income are detailed in table 3.4

TABLE 3.4   **Tax rates payable by minors on unearned income**

Taxable income	Tax rates
$0–$416	$Nil
$417–$1307	$Nil plus 66% of the excess over $416
Over $1308	45% of the total amount of income that is not excepted income

Source: ATO 2024e.

Where a minor is in receipt of unearned income, the first $416 of taxable income is exempt from tax. A rate of 66% applies to income between $417 and $1307, and the top adult marginal tax rate of 45% applies to that part of the income above $1307. The aim of the shading between $416 and $1307 is to achieve a maximum overall rate of 45% — the same as the top marginal rate paid by adult taxpayers. It is therefore evident that it is not particularly tax effective to invest funds or direct funds into the name of minors where income generated on unearned income exceeds $416.

Note that income which is considered earned by the minor, such as employment income, is taxed at normal adult marginal tax rates.

Minors do not have access to the low income tax offset to reduce tax payable on income other than employment income.

ILLUSTRATIVE EXAMPLE 3.4

Frank has a term deposit with the XYZ bank for $40 000 which pays an interest rate of 1.5% p.a. Should Frank invest the term deposit in the name of Grace, his youngest daughter who is aged 17 and working?

Grace can earn only $416 of unearned income before becoming liable to penalty rates of taxation on the interest. Therefore, it would only be worth investing up to $27 733 of the term deposit in the name of Grace ($27 733 × 1.5% = $416).

3.4 Impact of tax on investment income

LEARNING OBJECTIVE 3.4 Outline the taxation implications associated with the returns generated from different forms of investment, including capital gains tax.

Income received from most forms of investment, such as shares, property and bank accounts, is assessable for tax, although some differences in tax treatment do exist. The following sections explain the significance of these differences and helps to explain the importance of understanding the tax impact on income received from different forms of investments. When buying an investment or constructing an investment portfolio, an investor should be analysing and comparing after-tax returns. Income derived from investments is included in a taxpayer's assessable income. Where a taxpayer disposes of an investment that was acquired after 19 September 1985, capital gains tax may also be payable on the gain or loss made. CGT is an important consideration in determining the net return from an investment. The provisions of the capital gains tax legislation will be considered in further detail later in this chapter.

Interest

Interest received by a taxpayer is normally treated as assessable income and subject to tax at the taxpayer's marginal tax rates. Interest is normally assessed when it is actually received by the taxpayer.

Tax is a significant determinant of the net return derived from interest-bearing securities. If an investor earns 1.5% on the money market, the after-tax return of an investor on a marginal tax rate of 45% is .83%. This ignores the effects of inflation. Once inflation is taken into account, the investor is likely to be making a negative real return.

In situations where there is a joint bank account, such as with a husband and wife, interest is normally brought to account based on the couple's beneficial (right to receive) share of the account. If the individual shares are not specified, interest received is normally assessed on a 50/50 basis.

Issues may arise in respect of interest earned on a child's bank account. There may be circumstances where the parent is assessed on the income even though the account is in the name of the child. This may arise where the parent provides the money and is seen to control the use of the funds. For example, a parent sets themselves up as trustee for their child's bank account and makes all investment decisions. Where the ATO is satisfied that the funds effectively belong to the parent and the parent is the one that has a beneficial entitlement to the funds in the bank account, the parent will be assessed on the income, even though the bank account may be in the name of the child. Consideration should also be given to the penalty rates of tax that apply to the unearned income of minors as discussed previously.

Dividend income

Dividends are distributions of company profits to shareholders. Dividend income is fully assessed in the hands of the shareholder, regardless of the source of the company profits. The income is included within the assessable income of the investor when the dividend is paid, credited or distributed to them.

Before the introduction of **dividend imputation** in July 1987, dividends were subject to double taxation — once by the company when the profits were earned, and again by the shareholders when the after-tax dividends were distributed to them. Since the introduction of dividend imputation, an investment in shares has been far more attractive in Australia.

The basis of the dividend imputation system is to ensure that company profits are in effect only subject to tax once in the hands of the shareholder at the shareholder's marginal rate of tax. If the company has already paid tax on the profits from which the dividend has been derived, the shareholder will be entitled to a tax offset for the tax already paid by the company. This is done in order to prevent the double taxation of the dividend.

Before describing the operation of the dividend imputation system, it is worth understanding some of the terms used.
- Where a company has paid full tax on the profits from which a dividend is derived, the dividend is known as a franked dividend.
- In situations where the company has not paid tax on its profits for the year, perhaps due to carried forward tax losses, any dividend paid is known as an unfranked dividend.
- Companies can have a situation where they have paid some tax on their profits, but not the full rate. Any dividends paid from profits in this situation are known as partially franked dividends.

The operation of the dividend imputation system is as follows. A shareholder in receipt of a franked dividend in a financial year will need to include both the dividend received plus a franking or imputation credit, representing the amount of tax previously paid by the company, within their assessable income. The total amount is then assessed at the taxpayer's marginal tax rate. However, to avoid double taxation, the shareholder is then entitled to a tax offset for the amount of the franking credit included within their assessable income. To assist the taxpayer with preparing their tax liability, the company paying the dividend will advise the shareholder of the amount of the attached franking credit. The franking credit is determined as follows.

$$\text{Franking credit} = \text{Dividend received} \times \frac{\text{Company tax rate}}{1.0 - \text{Company tax rate}}$$

$$= \text{Dividend received} \times \frac{0.30}{0.70}$$

For a franked dividend received from a base rate entity (small company), the franking credit is determined as follows.

$$\text{Franking credit} = \text{Dividend received} \times \frac{0.25}{0.75}$$

Where the taxpayer is in receipt of an unfranked dividend, the cash received is fully assessable and the franking credits do not apply. Illustrative example 3.5 demonstrates the operation of the dividend imputation system.

ILLUSTRATIVE EXAMPLE 3.5

Assume that Angela decides to acquire $100 000 worth of shares in Tassie Devil Ltd which pays a dividend of 20 cents per share fully franked. The cash dividend is $2000 and the imputation credit is $857.14 ($2000 × 30/70). Angela also receives a salary of $42 000 for the year.

As Angela is on a 16% marginal tax rate, then the tax implication is as follows.

Salary		$ 42 000
Franked dividend received	$2 000	
Add: Imputation credit	857	2 857
Taxable income		**$ 44 857**
Gross tax payable		$4 265.12
Less: Low income tax offset		(332.15)
Less: Imputation credit		(857.14)
Add: Medicare levy		897.14
Net tax payable		**$3 972.97**

To understand the benefit of dividend imputation, assume that the $2000 dividend is instead received as an unfranked dividend as follows.

Salary	$ 42 000
Unfranked dividend received	2 000
Taxable income	**$ 44 000**
Gross tax payable	$4 128.00
Less: Low income tax offset	(375.00)
Add: Medicare levy	880.00
Net tax payable	**$4 633.00**

With the franked dividend, the taxpayer is better off by an amount of $660.03. This illustrates the importance of franking credits on the after-tax return to investors.

As can be seen in table 3.5, the benefits of the franking credits attached to dividend income vary depending on the tax position of the investor.

Table 3.5 compares the impact of dividend imputation on investors with different tax rates.

TABLE 3.5 Comparison of the impact of dividend imputation on investors

	Low-income investor	Mid-income investor	High-income investor
Dividend received	$ 700	$ 700	$ 700
Franking credit (dividend × 30/70)	$ 300	$ 300	$ 300
Taxable income	$1000	$1000	$1000
Marginal tax rate	16% tax rate on $1000	30% tax rate on $1000	45% tax rate on $1000

(continued)

TABLE 3.5 *(continued)*

	Low-income investor	Mid-income investor	High-income investor
Gross tax payable	$160	$300	$450
Less imputation credit	$300	$300	$300
Net tax payable (refund)	($140)	$ 0	$150
	Because the company has already paid tax at a rate of 30%, the low-income shareholder will be entitled to a refund for the difference between the tax already paid by the company and their marginal tax rate.	Because the company has already paid tax at a rate of 30%, which is the same as the shareholder's marginal tax rate, the shareholder will not need to pay anything further, nor will they be entitled to any refund.	Because the company has already paid tax at a rate of 30%, the high-income earner will need to pay only an additional 15% tax to bring the tax payable to their marginal tax rate.

Dividend imputation means that the receipt of fully franked dividends by shareholders, particularly those on a low marginal tax rate, is particularly tax effective when compared to the receipt of income from most other forms of investment. However, not all dividends are fully franked and a financial planner must take into account variations in the level of franking when recommending and analysing Australian shares.

Dividend reinvestment

Some companies offer a scheme whereby, instead of the investor receiving a cash dividend, the investor is offered the opportunity to acquire additional shares in the company at the value of the cash dividend. The price at which the additional shares are offered to the shareholder varies, but a common discount is around 2% on the average of the market price over the last 5 days. No brokerage or stamp duty is payable by the shareholder, so this is a relatively attractive way of building up a portfolio. It is also attractive for the company as a means of preserving cash within the business.

Regardless of whether the shareholder receives dividends in the form of cash or in the form of additional shares in the company, the dividend is still taxable and is required to be included in the taxable income of the taxpayer.

Rental income

Where a property is held for investment purposes, while any rental income is assessable to tax, any expenditure incurred in earning that income may be an allowable deduction. The main deductions for an owner of rental property are the interest payable on any borrowings used to finance the acquisition of the property, deductions for the decline in the value of certain furniture and fixtures, repairs, commissions paid to managing agents, bank fees, financial institution duties, insurance, rates and land taxes. A number of the more common complex deductions will be discussed in the following section. A taxpayer may be eligible to claim a tax deduction for any net rental loss incurred, that is where expenditure exceeds income.

Interest deductibility

Interest incurred on a loan used to finance any investment may be an allowable deduction as long as it is incurred in earning assessable income. The key issue to be considered is that there must be a clear connection between the borrowing of the funds and the earning of assessable income and the loan must not be of a private, capital or domestic nature. This goes back to s. 8.1 of the ITAA97, covered earlier in this chapter. Interest incurred on a loan used to buy a home which is used as the person's principal residence is not deductible because the expenditure is domestic in nature, nor is interest payable on a loan used to buy vacant land, because it has not generated any assessable income (unless the taxpayer is a land developer). On the other hand, interest payable on a loan taken out to buy an investment property that is generating assessable income will be tax deductible.

An important factor in accumulating wealth is to ensure that loans taken out for private purposes that do not provide any tax benefits, such as for a home or a car, are paid off as quickly as possible when compared to loans that do provide tax benefits.

Where the interest charge together with any other costs incurred exceed any income generated from an investment, this is known as negative gearing and gives rise to a tax loss. On the other hand, where income received exceeds the total costs incurred from an investment, including interest, this is known as positive gearing. Refer to the chapter on managed funds and leveraged investments for a comprehensive coverage of gearing.

Capital works deductions

Where construction on a residential building used for investment purposes commenced after 15 September 1987, a taxpayer is entitled to a capital works deduction at the rate of 2.5% p.a. This was previously a deduction of 4% where construction commenced between 17 July 1985 and 15 September 1987. Other rates will apply depending upon the nature of the construction.

When purchasing a building to use for earning rental income, it is crucial to determine the date of construction, as this entitlement to a deduction passes to the purchaser upon sale. For example, an investor purchased a block of flats on 1 July 2017 for $1 million. The taxpayer will be entitled to an annual tax deduction of $25 000 ($1 000 000 × 2.5%).

Deductions for the decline in value of assets

The cost of acquiring an investment or asset (e.g. a kitchen stove for a rental property) is regarded as capital expenditure and therefore not generally tax deductible in the year of purchase. However, the decline in value of the asset over its effective life is an allowable tax deduction because of the loss of benefits to the taxpayer over time. The deduction comes under the provisions of the Uniform Capital Allowance System, and from 1 July 2001 this system applies to most depreciating assets.

As part of the 2023–24 Budget, the Australian Government announced that small businesses with aggregated turnover of less than $10 million will be able to instantly write off the value of new equipment worth up to $20 000 that is first used or installed ready for use between 1 July 2023 and 30 June 2024. In the 2024 budget it was announced that the instant asset write off will be extended to 30 June 2025. This measure is still before Parliament and is not yet law.

Income from managed investment schemes

Managed investment schemes, commonly known as **managed funds**, are unit trust structures that allow investors (unit holders) to pool their money to invest in an investment that is managed by a professional fund manager. The funds within the structure can be invested into a range of different types of investments, such as shares, cash, fixed interest and property.

Managed funds are a very popular investment vehicle in Australia and can either be listed and traded on the Australian Securities Exchange (ASX), where they are known as a listed investment company (LIC), or they may be unlisted and not able to be traded on the ASX. Unlisted managed funds account for the majority of managed funds that exist in the marketplace. The structure of managed investment schemes is discussed further in the chapter on managed funds and leveraged investments.

Managed funds are a particularly popular investment vehicle for investors who do not have the time or expertise to manage their funds themselves. Funds within the managed investment structure are managed by a professional fund manager and investors have a right to a share of any income and profits generated. Being unit trusts, the managed fund itself is not assessable to tax. All income earned within the fund, such as rental income, interest, fully franked dividends and capital gains made on the sale of investments are distributed to investors of the fund and taxed at the investors' individual marginal tax rates. As well as being taxed on the income and capital gains generated within the trust, the individual unit holder will be taxed on any realised capital gains or losses made on the disposal of the units they hold in the managed fund. The unit price of investing in the fund will reflect the value of the investments held within the managed fund and will increase and decrease over time.

To illustrate the taxation consequences of investing in an unlisted managed fund, consider illustrative example 3.6.

ILLUSTRATIVE EXAMPLE 3.6

On 1 July, Frank takes $10 000 from his savings account to invest into an Australian shares managed fund. However, by the end of the financial year he notes that his investment in the fund has fallen to $9500. He receives a tax statement from the fund which states that during the financial year he received a distribution ▶

from the fund consisting of $400 of income and $600 of capital gains. Frank wonders how he could be liable to a taxable capital gain when the value of the fund had fallen by year end.

The distribution of $400 of income reflects the fact that during the year, the fund generated income from investments held. In addition, the capital gain of $600 would have arisen from the manager selling some investments during the year. Tax will therefore be payable on any realised capital gains made within the fund. The fall in the value of the Australian shares managed fund at year end reflects the fact that investments held within the managed fund have fallen at that time. If the investor does not sell the units in the managed fund, the loss is unrealised and no gain or loss is brought to account at that stage. This shows that an investor may have to report income and a capital gain in a year even when the value of their investments has actually fallen.

Capital gains tax

Prior to the introduction of the **capital gains tax (CGT)** regime on 20 September 1985, profits made upon the disposal of any capital asset, such as shares, property, bonds etc. were not subject to tax because they were not considered to be assessable under the ordinary income provisions of the Income Tax Assessment Act. The introduction of specific statutory provisions of the CGT regime in 1985 were designed to broaden the income base of the government, limit investment speculation and bring capital gains to account as assessable income of the taxpayer.

It should be noted that the CGT provisions do not apply to gains or losses made as part of the business activities of a taxpayer such as a property developer or share trader. Such gains and losses are considered as assessable income under the ordinary income provisions of the ITAA and are fully assessable.

CGT is a tax on realised capital gains. For CGT to apply there must be disposal of an asset that was acquired by the taxpayer after 19 September 1985. The CGT is calculated as the difference between the net disposal value and the net cost of the asset. The assessable capital gain forms part of the taxable income of the taxpayer for the year and is taxed at the taxpayer's marginal tax rate. Where the taxpayer incurs a net capital loss for the year, the amount cannot be claimed as a tax deduction; it can only be offset against a capital gain made in the same year, or if no capital gain is made, it can be carried forward indefinitely to be set off against any future capital gains incurred.

Certain items are exempt from the CGT legislation including:
- the taxpayer's main residence
- passenger motor cars
- gains from lottery wins
- gambling winnings
- insurance proceeds where the compensation is for personal injury
- proceeds from superannuation funds
- assets acquired prior to the introduction of CGT on 20 September 1985.

The CGT legislation is very complex and far reaching and over 50 different kinds of events may trigger a capital gain or loss, including disposal of an asset, a loss, cancellation or destruction of an asset and the end of an option to acquire shares. A disposal includes any change of ownership. Thus, the transfer of shares from one spouse to another or from an individual to their private company or family trust would be considered to be a capital event. Once a capital event is triggered, the capital gain or loss is determined as the difference between the net proceeds from sale and the asset's net cost base. The net proceeds represent the amount of funds received upon sale of the asset less any incidental costs incurred upon the sale of the asset. Examples of incidental costs may include legal costs, brokerage charges and advertising fees. The net cost base of the asset represents the total funds paid to acquire the asset plus any incidental fees incurred in the process of acquiring the asset, such as stamp duty, valuation and legal costs. Other capital expenditure incurred during the period of ownership to increase or improve the value of the asset is also added to the cost base of the asset. Examples of capital expenditure relating to an investment property may include renovations, extensions, major repairs and painting. Expenditure undertaken on the property which is considered a repair rather than a capital expenditure would be treated as an allowable deduction.

Calculating the capital gain or loss

Once a capital gain or loss has occurred, the taxpayer needs to determine that amount to be included in their assessable income. This is known as the assessable capital gain. Where the asset has been held for less than 12 months, the full capital gain is brought to account as part of the taxpayer's assessable income.

Where the asset has been held for more than 12 months, the taxpayer may be entitled to a concession in the method of calculating the capital gain. The two possible methods of calculating the assessable capital gain are the indexation method and the discount method.

1. The indexation method allows for an increase in the cost base by applying an indexation factor based on the increase in the consumer price index (CPI) from the date of acquisition up to 20 September 1999. Under this method, the cost base is indexed by the percentage increase in the CPI for the period commencing from the quarter of the year in which the asset was acquired until the quarter ended September 1999, when the availability to index the cost base ceased. CPI increases after the September 1999 quarter are disregarded so that indexation effectively became frozen at that date. CPI rates are available from the Australian Taxation Office at www.ato.gov.au/Rates/Consumer-price-index.

2. Under the CGT discount method, the capital gain is reduced by a discount factor to determine the net assessable capital gain. The discount factors used to determine the net capital gain are:
   – individual or trust — 50% discount
   – complying superannuation fund — 33.33% discount
   – other entities including companies — 0% discount.

Thus, for an individual, once the 50% discount is applied to the capital gain made, only half of the capital gain is included in the assessable income of the taxpayer.

The selection of the two methods depends upon when the asset was first acquired.

- For assets acquired after 20 September 1985 and before 21 September 1999, the taxpayer has the choice as to which of the two methods they select — the indexation method or the CGT discount method.
- For assets acquired after 21 September 1999, the CGT discount method must be used.

The *normal assessable income rules* are used when the investment has been acquired and disposed of within a 12-month period. A taxpayer is only able to use the indexation method or the CGT discount method where the asset has been owned for at least 12 months.

A capital loss from the sale of an investment is made if the reduced cost base is greater than the proceeds from the sale of the asset. The reduced cost includes the costs of acquisition but excludes any amounts to the extent to which the expenditure is tax deductible. When a capital loss is incurred, no allowance is made for the effects of inflation under the indexation method, nor is the individual entitled to a 50% discount under the CGT discount method.

ILLUSTRATIVE EXAMPLE 3.7

Frank has decided to sell the share portfolio that he acquired on 1 November 1994 for $160 000. Frank sells the shares in July of the current financial year for $225 000. The costs of disposal are $5000. The cost base is $160 000 while the net capital proceeds amount to $220 000 ($225 000 – $5000). The capital gain is therefore $60 000.

As the shares were acquired prior to 20 September 1999, Frank can select from either the indexation method or the CGT discount approach to determine the net assessable capital gain that will form part of his assessable income. Under the indexation method, the value of the property is indexed by CPI from the date of purchase (CPI at that time was 62.8 for the December 1994 quarter) up to the September 1999 quarter when the indexation method was frozen (CPI was 68.7 at that time).

Net capital proceeds	$220 000
Less: Indexed cost base ($160 000 × 68.7/62.8)	175 032
Net assessable capital gain	**$ 44 968**

Under the CGT discount approach, the net capital gain is determined as the difference between the net cost base and the net capital proceeds less the discount factor.

Net capital proceeds	$220 000
Less: Net cost base	160 000
Capital gain	60 000
Less: 50% discount	30 000
Net assessable capital gain	**$ 30 000**

As the CGT discount method provides the lower net capital gain, an amount of $30 000 will be included in the assessable income of Frank and taxed at his marginal tax rate.

Tax planning and capital gains tax

Tax planning is an important consideration with the acquisition and disposal of investments in order to be able to minimise the imposition of any assessable capital gain. Issues to consider in the planning include:

- in whose name or which entity name the asset will be acquired
- the nature of the investment
- the length of time the investment is likely to be held
- the timing of disposal
- the method used to calculate the capital gain or loss.

The structure/entity used to hold the asset is important. The capital gains discount for an individual taxpayer and a trust is 50%. The discount for a superannuation fund is 33.33%. There is no discount for a company. Therefore, it is generally not advisable to hold appreciating assets within a corporate structure.

Where a taxpayer disposes of a capital asset as part of normal trading or business activities, such as with share traders or property developers, capital gains will be fully assessable as ordinary income with no allowance provided for indexation or a discount factor. Just what constitutes a business activity needs to be determined on a case-by-case basis and no one factor determines what constitutes a business. The taxation authorities usually look at a number of factors including the frequency of transactions, profit motive and the commercialisation of the activity. Persons who regularly buy and sell shares or properties may be considered as traders. However, being classified as a share trader or property developer is not necessarily bad news. For an investor, capital losses can be offset only against capital gains, but if a trader makes a loss, it is deductible from the trader's assessable income.

In order to take advantage of the tax concessions available in calculating the assessable capital gain, an investor would be advised to hold an asset for longer than 12 months. Taxation is relevant not only in the decision to invest, but also in the decision to sell that investment as well as the timing of the disposal. If an asset has been held for longer than 12 months, the taxpayer may be entitled to utilise either the indexation method or the discount method, depending on when the asset was acquired. As indexation became frozen in September 1999 (when the index was 68.7), the passage of time will mean the discount method will normally yield the lower assessable capital gain. However, tax planners must consider the application of both methods and choose the one that provides for the lower capital gain. Different methods can be used for each asset sold.

The timing of the disposal of an asset is an important issue in terms of minimising the imposition of taxation. It is normally beneficial to dispose of an asset in the year in which the taxpayer's taxable income is reduced, thereby reducing the marginal tax rate applicable. This might occur during the taxpayer's retirement, for example.

If, during the year, capital gains have been made on the disposal of an asset, the investor may consider different strategies for reducing the impact of the capital gain on their taxable income. For example, the investor may be able to realise capital losses to offset other capital gains made during the year. The taxpayer may also look to see whether they are able to qualify for a tax deduction that can be used to reduce their taxable income. For example, a taxpayer may be entitled to a tax deduction for a personal concessional contribution made to their superannuation fund. See the chapter on superannuation for further details.

PERSONAL FINANCE BULLETIN

Tax headache: CGT and lodgers

Question: I'm about to sell my property and am looking for help on my capital gains tax situation. The problem is that I have had people paying board to bring in some extra cash and I need to work out how much of my capital gain on the house is now subject to CGT.

I had one tenant for 30 weeks and one tenant for 47 weeks, with an overlap of about 2 weeks in the middle (I have two spare rooms, but only really wanted one boarder at a time). I'll have had the property for 6 years when I sell. Is there a formula for working out how much of my capital gain will be taxable? And what rate of tax will I pay?

Answer: Ordinarily, your main residence is exempt from capital gains tax (CGT). To gain this benefit, your home must be used primarily for private or domestic purposes, which means you cannot derive assessable income. If part of your main residence is used to derive assessable income (for instance you lease two rooms) you will be liable to CGT for the period that your home is leased and deriving rental income.

The portion that's liable to CGT is normally determined on an area basis and time basis. For example, if your home consists of ten rooms and you use two rooms to derive assessable income over a 30-week period, under these circumstances, 20% of your main residence is liable to CGT during the 30 weeks the property was leased. Complications can arise where these variables (as in your case) are not consistent.

For more information you can read the Tax Office publication 'Is the dwelling your main residence?', and more particularly the section that sets out the formula for 'Calculating a partial exemption'. You can download a copy from the Tax Office website (ato.gov.au).

Incidentally, as you had owned the property for more than 12 months (in your case 6 years), only 50% of the portion of the capital gain you make on sale is assessable and liable to tax at your marginal rates of tax (which can vary between 0% and 45%) plus the Medicare levy. As this is a rather complex calculation (especially in your case) it's best that you seek advice from a registered tax agent.

Source: Prince 2011.

3.5 Taxation planning

LEARNING OBJECTIVE 3.5 Identify a range of common tax-effective strategies.

One of the more important parts of the financial planning process in helping an individual to meet their financial goals is personal taxation planning. The aim of taxation planning is to develop strategies that will legitimately minimise the imposition of taxation on an individual. That is, it is the process of organising the affairs of a person or family with a view to minimising the amount of overall income and other taxes that are payable.

The financial planning process requires financial planners to undertake a detailed consideration of a client's circumstances and financial position and to develop appropriate recommendations to deliver on the client's objectives. It is important to note that since 2016, financial advisers have been required to be registered with the Tax Practitioners Board (TPB) in order to provide tax (financial) advice services to a client for a fee or other reward.

The financial planner has a **best interest duty** under the Corporations Act to act in the best interests of the client, which includes taking into account the taxation position of the client and the tax ramifications arising from any recommendations put in place. This will mean that the advice must be based on sound principles and the client must be made fully aware of the consequences before acting upon the advice. However, taxation law in Australia is very technical and complex, and financial planners need to ensure that they do not provide taxation advice outside the scope of their experience, training and qualifications. Prior to acting upon advice that has a tax consequence, financial planners need to advise the client to seek the advice of their accountant or tax adviser to confirm the taxation implications of the advice given.

While taxation planning forms an important aspect of the investment strategies developed for an individual, taxation should not be the overriding factor determining investment decisions. However, many people do invest in particular assets because of the tax advantages that the asset offers. Towards the end of the financial year, in particular, various investment schemes and financial products are often promoted as an effective means of reducing the amount of tax a person will have to pay. Examples that have been promoted in the past include investments in pine plantations, almonds, films, aquaculture and structured investments that have a capital protection element to them. It is important in assessing any investment to properly understand how the product works, its risk and return characteristics, and its role in achieving the person's overall financial objectives. While taxation may be an important issue to consider, the investment must stand on its own merits and have the potential to provide real after-tax returns, whether in the form of income and/or capital growth.

The following taxation planning strategies are considered in the remainder of this chapter: income splitting, income versus capital growth, tax structures, negative gearing, and salary packaging and remuneration planning.

3.6 Income splitting

LEARNING OBJECTIVE 3.6 Explain the taxation implications of income splitting.

One of the most common methods of taxation planning is **income splitting** or transferring income from an individual paying tax at a high marginal tax rate to an individual or other entity that is on a lower rate of tax. A number of strategies are available that can assist in achieving the transfer of income. The decision to divert income to another individual, such as a family member, or into a particular tax structure will depend upon a number of factors including the cost, the benefits to be gained, other tax implications involved and the financial understanding of the individuals involved.

Salary or wage income cannot be split. Also, under the personal services income (PSI) regime, income that is earned predominantly from the personal activities of a person cannot be diverted or assigned to another person, entity or structure. In contrast, income derived from the carrying on of a business can be diverted. The range of different structures available to a person to operate a business activity will be discussed later in this chapter.

Normally, the easiest means of diverting income is by transferring investments and other assets to family members earning a lower taxable income. If the other taxpayer has no other income, this strategy will be particularly attractive because of the tax-free threshold of $18 200 that applies to individuals, as well as the opportunity for them to take advantage of tax offsets, such as the low income tax offset.

However, the transfer of investments or other assets to another family member or entity may give rise to a number of issues and tax consequences.

1. Care needs to be taken with the transfer of income to children because of the special penalty rates of tax that apply to the unearned income of minors under the provisions of ITAA36 Div. 6AA (discussed earlier in this chapter). This does not apply to children and other family members over the age of 18.
2. The person to whom the income has been diverted is entitled to demand actual payment of the income and the asset (as it is in their name), which may not be intended or desirable. For example, assets transferred to children.
3. The transfer of an asset to another entity or person, including a family member, is considered a disposal, and accordingly the impact of the CGT provisions must be considered. That is, the amount of any CGT payable on the transfer of the asset would need to be considered in determining the feasibility of the strategy.

3.7 Income versus capital growth

LEARNING OBJECTIVE 3.7 Explain the taxation implications of income versus capital growth.

In many situations, the benefit attached to holding an investment or an asset may be provided in the form of either income or capital growth. The preference for income over capital growth will depend upon a range of factors such as the cash flow needs of a person; their time horizon — that is, whether they are investing for the short term or long term; and the tax consequences associated with each option. From a tax point of view, income earned from an investment or other asset is fully assessable to tax. On the other hand, capital gains generated are taxable under the CGT provisions which might provide for the gain to be assessed in a concessional manner. For example, for an investment that has been held for more than 12 months, an individual is entitled to a 50% discount on the gain under the CGT discount method.

The distinction between the receipt of income and the receipt of capital is therefore important from a tax perspective.

3.8 Tax structures

LEARNING OBJECTIVE 3.8 Identify the various taxable entities, and compare the tax advantages and disadvantages of these different entities.

As discussed earlier, one of the important strategies available to an individual in minimising the imposition of taxation is to attempt to split or divert their investment, business and other income to another individual or tax structure. It is normally beneficial for the individual within a family on the lowest marginal tax rate to receive investment and business income. However, rather than an individual earning the income in their own name, it may be preferable to hold investments or to run a business under an alternative tax structure which might not only minimise the imposition of tax, but also provide other benefits to the investor. The main tax structures available to hold investments or operate a business include sole ownership, partnership, family company, family trust and a superannuation fund.

Each tax structure has its own advantages and disadvantages which need to be carefully considered before its establishment. Two of the most important issues to be considered in deciding which entity should be used to receive income are cost and complexity. Establishing and administering alternative tax structures can be costly and complex. Before setting up an alternative tax structure, an investor needs to ensure there are real gains to be made. The different tax structures — and their advantages and disadvantages — are considered next.

Sole ownership

This is the simplest and cheapest entity for holding investments or running a business. The individual has complete control over the decision making, there are no set-up costs and individuals have an entitlement to an $18 200 tax-free threshold, a range of tax offsets and rebates and a 50% discount on the capital gains made on the sale of assets. Income splitting can occur through investments being held in the name of the individual on the lowest marginal tax rate.

However, sole ownership has a number of disadvantages and limitations. All of the income belongs to the individual and tax is paid at their marginal tax rate. In addition, there is limited asset protection for a sole-owner business and the business has a finite life (based on the owner's capacity to continue the business). When the owner dies, the business and any investments held by the business must be sold or transferred to another party.

Attempts to divert or transfer income to other individuals within a family may be difficult. If an investment is already held in the name of one individual, the transfer of assets to any other individual or entity may incur capital gains tax. In addition, while there may be opportunities to divert investment income to another member of a family, tax regulations do not permit the diversion of income derived from personal services income, such as a salary.

Partnerships

A partnership for tax purposes exists when two or more persons form an association for the purposes of either running a business as partners or for the purposes of receiving income jointly; for example, a couple with a joint bank account. Taxable income in these circumstances can be split between taxpayers — usually members of a family — to minimise tax.

Advantages of forming a partnership include the fact that it can be established quickly, cheaply and simply, and income can be split between the partners. For example, assume that the total investment earnings of the Rajasekaram family are $80 000 for the current year. This is their only source of income. Rather than either one of the couple owning the investments in their own name and having a taxable income of $80 000, the ability to split income between the husband and wife (i.e. $40 000 each) will result in a saving in net tax through each person being on a lower marginal tax rate and each having a tax-free threshold of $18 200 plus offset entitlements.

Disadvantages of a partnership include the fact that it has limited asset protection, control of a business is shared and there is limited flexibility in being able to split income between the different partners. That is, each partner receives a share of the income of the partnership based on their share of their interest or ownership in the partnership.

With respect to investment income where ownership is in joint names, such as with joint bank accounts or a jointly owned investment property, unless the ownership share is specified, the income is normally divided equally between the parties who own the investment. The same principles would apply to income earned from carrying on a business. In conducting a business, normally a partnership agreement would be established to clarify roles, responsibilities and profit splits.

While a partnership is not a separate legal entity and therefore does not pay income tax, a partnership is still required to submit a partnership tax return in order to show to the Australian Taxation Office how the taxable income or loss of the partnership has been distributed among the partners in accordance with the partnership agreement. Income tax is then levied on the partners individually.

Tax payable by entity
— nil
Tax payable by individual partners
— individual marginal tax rates

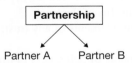

Companies

Companies are a separate legal entity where the directors of the company manage and administer the assets of the company on behalf of the company's owners, who are called shareholders. Companies are taxed in their own right. That is, a company is required to submit a tax return and pay income tax in their own right at a flat rate of 30%, or 25% for small business (base rate) entities. There is no tax-free threshold or graduated level of tax as there is for individuals.

Profits of the company are available to be distributed to the shareholders of the company in the form of dividends. Capital gains on the disposal of assets held by a company are normally fully assessable. The indexing of the cost base or access to the CGT discount are not available for companies which means it is usually advisable for investors *not* to hold investments in a corporate structure.

The advantages of operating through a corporate structure include:

- limited liability of shareholders
- the ability to split income between family members through paying wages and salaries
- the company continues to exist regardless of the death of a shareholder or any changes in shareholders
- imputation credits can be passed onto shareholders through the payment of franked dividends
- profits of the company can be retained within the entity and do not need to be paid out as dividends in a particular financial year. The timing of the payment of dividends can be deferred to a period where the shareholders may be on a lower marginal tax rate, such as upon retirement.

The drawbacks of operating through a company structure include:

- a company is relatively costly to set up and to administer on an ongoing basis
- companies are subject to the rules and regulations of the *Corporations Act 2001* and *Australian Securities and Investments Commission Act 2001* which imposes time and dollar costs on directors and shareholders
- companies have no tax-free threshold, no entitlement to the tax offsets available to individuals and no entitlement to tax concessions on capital gains.

Tax payable by entity
— flat rate of 30%
(25% for small business (base rate) entities)
Tax payable by individual shareholders
— individual marginal tax rates incorporating dividend imputation system

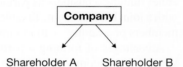

ILLUSTRATIVE EXAMPLE 3.8

Based on the opening case study, assume that Frank or Angela had acquired their share portfolio in the name of their family company rather than in their individual names.

For tax purposes, the company will make a capital gain of $60 000 which is likely to be taxed at a tax rate of 25% — a tax of $15 000. There is no capital discount available to a company. If Frank or Angela had invested in the share portfolio in their individual names, the capital gain would have been reduced by 50%. The tax saving for the individual would depend on their individual marginal rate of tax.

Trusts

A **trust** is governed by a trust deed which sets out the various rights and obligations on the operation of the trust. A trust is a structure that can own and hold assets and investments, or run a business. It is controlled and managed by persons or company (called the trustee) for the benefit of other persons (called beneficiaries). The trustee has legal control over the assets of the trust which means they can buy and sell assets but will never own or enjoy the benefits of ownership, such as the income generated from their use. While the beneficiaries do not legally own the assets within the trust, they are the ones that are entitled to the assets and profits of the trust.

There are four elements of any trust:

1. a trustee
2. property capable of being held in trust
3. one or more beneficiaries
4. a personal obligation attaching to the trust property.

There are two main types of trusts. A unit trust is divided into a fixed number of units, much like shares within a corporate structure, and profits are distributed according to the number of units held. Unit trusts are commonly used in non-family situations where it is important for the ownership of units and distribution of profits to be formalised to prevent disputes. In contrast, a discretionary trust is a far more flexible vehicle and particularly suited to family situations. With a discretionary trust, income is distributed according to the discretion of the trustee. This can be undertaken with a view to minimising the imposition of tax across the family members.

From a tax point of view, trusts are not separately taxed. While a tax return is required to be prepared, this is to show how the income of the trust has been distributed among the various beneficiaries. Trust income is generally taxed in the hands of the beneficiaries at their marginal tax rates. All income, gains and losses are required to be distributed to the beneficiaries, including any tax offsets or rebates associated with the income. This is because of the 'flow through' effect of all transactions to the investor in the trust.

Tax payable by entity
— nil
Tax payable by individual beneficiaries
— individual marginal tax rates

Superannuation funds

A superannuation fund is a scheme for the payment of benefits upon retirement or death. Savings are held in trust until the person satisfies a condition of release, such as retiring or death. It is an invaluable tool for the financial planner and client and is driven considerably by taxation concessions. Complying superannuation funds are levied with a concessional income tax rate of a flat 15% on the fund's taxable income. Employer compulsory superannuation contributions paid for their employees are generally deductible for the employer. Personal superannuation contributions may also be eligible for a tax deduction.

Tax payable by entity
— flat rate of 15%
Tax payable by individual fund members
— no individual tax implications

Table 3.6 shows the advantages and disadvantages of different tax entities.

TABLE 3.6   **Advantages and disadvantages of different tax entities**

Entity	Advantages	Disadvantages
Sole ownership	• Investment income can be split • Main residence exempt from CGT • 50% discount on capital gains • A tax-free threshold of taxable income and a graduated tax scale depending on the size of taxable income • Domestic losses can be carried forward to be offset against assessable income	• Not possible to split salary or wage income • Minors subject to penalty tax • Marginal rates climb to 45% • Medicare levy at certain income levels plus possible Medicare levy surcharge • Unlimited liability
Partnership	• Capacity to split income • Capacity to direct property and therefore income to the partner with the lowest level of income • Losses can be distributed to partners and used to offset against income they have earned from other sources • Relatively simple to administer	• Minors subject to penalty tax • Marginal rates climb to 45% • Medicare levy at certain income levels plus possible Medicare levy surcharge • No flexibility in sharing income as fixed according to partnership agreement • Unlimited liability
Companies	• Flat rate tax of 30% (25% for base rate entities) • Normally, losses can be carried forward • Limited liability of shareholders • The ability to split income between family members	• No tax-free threshold • Losses are kept within the company • No concession on the calculation of capital gains tax

(continued)

TABLE 3.6 *(continued)*

Entity	Advantages	Disadvantages
	• The company continues to exist despite the death or changes in shareholders • Imputation credits can be passed onto shareholders through the payment of franked dividends • Earnings of the company can be retained within the entity thereby deferring the payment of tax on distributions of dividends to a later period	• Costs of administration including preparation of accounts • Subject to a significant amount of government regulation
Trusts	• Capacity to direct income to the beneficiaries with the lowest tax rates • 50% discount on capital gains • The trust continues to exist despite the death of or changes in beneficiaries	• Losses are trapped inside the trust and can be offset only against future trust income • Costs of administration
Superannuation funds	• 15% tax rate on earnings • CGT discount of one-third	• Borrowing not allowed • Costs of administration including the preparation and audit of accounts • Funds cannot be accessed until the member has satisfied a condition of release such as retirement

Note: When a superannuation fund is in pension mode, no tax is payable on income or capital gains.

3.9 Negative gearing

LEARNING OBJECTIVE 3.9 Explain the concept of negative gearing.

Negative gearing arises where the total deductions associated with an investment, including the interest charge, exceed assessable income generated from the investment. That is, a tax loss is generated from the investment which may be able to be claimed as a tax deduction. Negative gearing is a useful tax-effective strategy especially for those on the highest marginal tax rate as the loss can be used to reduce income from other sources, such as wages, and reduce the overall incidence of tax. However, there is little point acquiring an investment that simply generates a loss each year. To be effective, the investment must show an eventual and overall profit. An investor may be willing to generate a tax loss each year as long as there is the potential to generate a capital gain upon disposal of the asset of sufficient amount to compensate for the risk attached to the borrowing, and to cover the tax loss generated over the years from the negatively geared investment.

As with any investment, although taxation is a significant factor to consider, the primary consideration is the ability of the investment to produce a real after-tax return for the investor. Negative gearing is covered in more detail in the chapter on leveraged investments. The benefit of the tax loss depends upon the marginal tax rate of the borrower. This is an important issue to consider when determining which family member should own the investment and take out the borrowing. Thus, in a situation where an investment is negatively geared and generates a tax loss, a family member on a high marginal tax rate will receive a much higher tax benefit from the loss than a family member on a low marginal tax rate.

A situation of **positive gearing**, where the assessable income in a year exceeds all allowable deductions, may still be attractive for an investor despite generating taxable income. Positive gearing is likely to be attractive for those investors requiring an ongoing income and/or where taxation is not a prime consideration. In this case, the debt and borrowing should be held in the name of the family member on the lowest marginal tax rate in order to minimise the payment of tax.

3.10 Salary packaging and remuneration planning

LEARNING OBJECTIVE 3.10 Explain remuneration planning and understand the taxation implications of salary packaging and fringe benefits tax (FBT).

Salary sacrificing, also known as salary packaging, is a common benefit made available by employers and is aimed at providing an employee with their salary in a more tax-effective manner. Salary sacrificing involves substituting part of an employee's future cash salary or wages for non-cash benefits provided by the employer, such as the provision of a car, additional super contributions or a laptop. While not all employers provide a salary-packaging option for their employees, enterprise bargaining is leading to more flexible remuneration packages being negotiated.

The principle behind salary sacrificing is that instead of an employee receiving all of their remuneration from employment in the form of a fully taxed cash salary or wage, they take part of their remuneration in the form of concessionally taxed or tax exempt non-cash benefits. Non-cash benefits received by an employee are not subject to income tax. For salary sacrificing to be effective for the employee, the combined after-tax benefit from the salary and non-cash benefits must be greater than the after-tax benefit from receiving just the cash salary. From an employer's point of view, the aim is to ensure that the total cost of an employee's remuneration package is no greater by providing salary sacrificing as an option.

Depending upon the employer, a number of non-cash benefits may be made available to an employee. The most common benefits provided include:

- superannuation contributions in addition to the mandatory superannuation guarantee (SG) contributions
- the use of a fully maintained car
- paying car-parking costs
- providing reduced-interest or interest-free loans
- paying school fees for the employee's children
- providing a laptop, mobile phone or other electronic device.

A number of these benefits are covered in the next section.

The question of whether a person should salary sacrifice a non-cash benefit, or whether an optimum combination of salary and non-cash benefits exists, will depend on the individual's circumstances. Each person has differing financial circumstances, goals and needs, and a financial plan should determine the optimum package for each person.

ILLUSTRATIVE EXAMPLE 3.9

Angela earns a salary of $42 000 p.a. and her employer has given her the option of salary sacrificing into a $10 000 non-cash benefit. Angela is unsure whether she should salary sacrifice or not.

Some of the issues that Angela will need to consider include the following.

- Tax savings — by salary sacrificing, Angela's gross tax payable and Medicare levy will be based on a cash salary of $32 000 instead of $42 000, resulting in a saving in income tax.
- Need for the benefit — to what extent does Angela really need or want the non-cash benefit?
- Reduction in disposable income — can Angela afford the reduction in her cash salary?
- Fringe benefits tax payable — will the non-cash benefit be subject to fringe benefits tax (see below)?

Fringe benefits tax

Although the provision of non-cash benefits does not form part of the assessable income of an employee and is not subject to income tax, non-cash benefits may be subject to another form of tax called the **fringe benefits tax (FBT)**. The rate of the FBT is currently 47%, based on the highest individual marginal tax rate plus the Medicare levy of 2%. While the tax is payable by the employer, the cost will be passed onto the employee as part of the employee's total remuneration package.

Fringe benefits tax (FBT) was introduced in 1986 to cover the loss of income tax to the government that resulted from employees being paid non-cash benefits instead of fully taxed cash salaries. The FBT legislation was introduced to ensure that the imposition of tax on the individual would be the same regardless of whether the employee receives a cash salary and pays income tax at their marginal tax rate or takes a non-cash benefit and pays the FBT.

Salary sacrificing and the payment of FBT arises as a result of there being an employer–employee relationship. Accordingly, sole traders cannot salary sacrifice. Employers are able to claim a tax deduction for both the cost of the benefit provided to an employee as well as the cost of any FBT paid. The FBT year is based on the period 1 April to 31 March.

FBT is determined under the following process.

- Step 1. Determine the taxable value of the benefit
- Step 2. Apply a gross-up rate = Fringe benefits taxable amount
- Step 3. Apply FBT rate of 47% = FBT payable

The taxable value of a fringe benefit is based on a set of valuation rules — different categories of benefits have specific rules for calculating the taxable value. The purpose of the grossing-up process is to convert the fringe benefits received by an employee to their pre-tax equivalent value so that there is little difference in the taxation treatment between an employee receiving a cash salary, and paying income tax at the highest marginal tax rate of 47%, or the employee receiving a fringe benefit and the employer paying FBT at 47%.

There are two gross-up formulae for calculating the fringe benefits taxable amount. The two gross-up rates are required because of the impact of GST on the cost of non-cash benefits provided to employees. Where an employer does not incur GST on the cost of a benefit, or is not entitled to claim GST credits back from the government, a gross-up rate of 1.8868 is applied. This is known as a type 2 benefit. In situations where GST is payable on a benefit and the employer is able to claim a GST credit from the government, a gross-up rate of 2.0802 is used. This is known as a type 1 benefit. The higher gross-up rate allows for the employer to recover GST credits from the government as a result of providing a fringe benefit to an employee. The amount of FBT payable is calculated on the GST tax-inclusive value of the fringe benefit.

It is most important when a salary package is arranged, that it is undertaken in accordance with Taxation Ruling 2001/10. The ruling reaffirms the ATO's stance that where an employee agrees to forgo future salary and salary sacrifice into a non-cash benefit, an agreement to salary sacrifice must be in force from the outset and not put into place after the employee has become entitled to income or benefit.

ILLUSTRATIVE EXAMPLE 3.10

Frank and Angela's second child, David, is provided with a type 1 fringe benefit of $2800 for holiday airfares. The fringe benefits taxable amount is calculated as follows.

$$\$2800 \times 2.0802 = \$5825$$

In addition, David is provided with a type 2 fringe benefit of $4000 for school fees (GST exempt) for his child. The fringe benefits taxable amount is calculated as follows.

$$\$4000 \times 1.8868 = \$7547$$

David's aggregate grossed-up value of fringe benefits is $5825 + $7547 = $13 372.
The fringe benefits tax payable is $13 372 × 47%= $6285. This amount will be payable by David's employer to the ATO but the employer will deduct this payment from David's remuneration package.

A fringe benefit is defined broadly and is designed to capture most forms of non-cash benefits provided to an employee. Benefits are divided into four main categories for FBT purposes:

- fully taxed fringe benefits
- concessionally taxed fringe benefits
- exempt fringe benefits
- excluded benefits.

Fully taxed fringe benefits

These are benefits provided by an employer where the actual cost or value of the benefit is fully assessable for FBT purposes. Examples of fully taxed fringe benefits include many types of private expenses incurred by the employee such as payment of mortgage loans, school fees, holidays and private telephone expenses.

There is generally no financial benefit to be gained by an employee salary sacrificing into fully taxed benefits. That is, either the employee will pay income tax at their marginal tax rate if they do not salary sacrifice or if they do salary sacrifice and have to pay FBT, a tax rate of 47% will be payable. From this it can be seen that an employee on a marginal tax rate of less than 47% is actually going to be worse off salary sacrificing into fully taxed fringe benefits which are taxed at the highest marginal tax rate.

Taxable value of benefit	$10 000
FBT on grossed-up amount	$10 000 × 1.8868 × 47%
FBT	$8868
Charge against package	$10 000 + $8868 = $18 868

Thus, to receive a $10 000 benefit, the charge against the pre-tax income of the employee is $18 868.

If the employee had paid for the $10 000 benefit from their after-tax income, the amount of pre-tax income they would have required can be determined by the following equation.

$$\$10\,000 \times \frac{1}{1 - \text{MTR}}$$

For an employee on an MTR of 32% (including the 2% Medicare levy), the amount of pre-tax income required would be $10 000 × (1 / 0.68) = $14 706. Thus, the employee would be worse-off salary sacrificing a fully taxed fringe benefit by $4162.

Concessionally taxed fringe benefits

Concessionally taxed fringe benefits are benefits provided by an employer where the taxable value of the benefit is assessed at a lower amount than the actual monetary value. Concessionally taxed fringe benefits provide the most tax advantage to employees on the highest marginal tax rate. However, depending on the circumstances, they may also provide tax benefits for some employees on lower marginal tax rates.

As the provision of a car benefit is one of the most common types of concessionally taxed non-cash benefit provided to employees, this benefit will be covered in some detail.

Motor vehicles

A car fringe benefit arises when a car that is owned or leased by an employer is made available to an employee for private use. Private use arises in situations where the car is used for private purposes or is available for private use. Available for private use would include where the car is garaged at the employee's home overnight.

The value of the benefit is calculated either by the statutory formula method or the operating cost method as follows.

Statutory formula method

Under the statutory formula method, the taxable value of the benefit is determined by applying a statutory rate to the base value of the car. The statutory rate is a fixed rate of 20% regardless of the number of kilometres travelled. Under the statutory formula method, there is no requirement on the employer to establish the percentage of private use of the car by the employee. An allowance is made within the formula for situations where the employee may contribute towards the cost of the benefit.

The taxable value of the benefit is determined under the following formula.

$$\frac{\text{Value}}{\text{of car}} \times \frac{\text{Statutory}}{\text{rate}} \times \frac{\text{Days in the FBT year car used or available for private purposes}}{\text{Days in FBT year}} - \text{Employee contribution}$$

The taxable value of a car benefit is reduced by any employee contribution paid to the employer towards the cost of the benefit. Employee contributions can be an effective strategy for reducing the taxable value of concessionally taxed benefits and therefore the FBT payable by employees on a marginal tax rate less than the FBT rate.

Operating cost method

The operating cost method works out the total cost of operating the car for the year; for example, payment for petrol, servicing and insurance and leasing costs. From there, the employer, with the employee's help, establishes the percentage of private use (such as a weekend drive to the country) as compared to the percentage of business use (travelling from work premises to clients) of the car by the employee.

This is done on the basis of kilometres travelled during a year and is established by the employee keeping a log book of business trips for 12 weeks in the first year in which the employee had use of the car.

Once the percentage of private use is established, it is applied to the costs incurred on the car to establish the taxable value of the benefit (for instance, an operating cost of $8000 with 40% private use would mean a taxable value of $3200).

The higher the proportion of private use of the car, the higher will be the taxable value of the benefit. The formula used for determining the taxable value is as follows.

$$\left[\begin{array}{c} \text{Total operating costs} \\ \text{of car} \end{array} \times \left(100\% - \begin{array}{c} \text{Proportion of business use} \\ \text{for year} \end{array} \right) \right] - \text{Employee contribution}$$

If the car is owned by the employer, rather than being leased, the costs are also required to include a depreciation charge at a rate of 25%. The costs are also required to include an imputed interest charge based on the statutory interest rate. The statutory benchmark interest rate is published annually in an ATO taxation determination. For the FBT year ending 31 March 2024, the benchmark interest rate is 7.77%.

Both the operating cost method and the statutory formula method should be calculated to determine the most cost-effective alternative. Unless there is a large percentage of business use, the statutory formula method will usually result in a lower taxable value and therefore a smaller FBT liability. The operating cost method may provide a lower taxable value when the car does not travel many private kilometres in a year. However, even when the operating cost method does provide a lower taxable value, it still may not be the preferred option because of the need to maintain detailed records to substantiate the costs incurred and the nature of the kilometres travelled.

ILLUSTRATIVE EXAMPLE 3.11

Angela's employer provides her with a car benefit under a leasing arrangement. The car has a value of $32 000 and the leasing arrangement commenced from 1 April 2023. The car was available to Angela for private use for the full year. Angela agrees to pay the employer $3000 in respect of fuel costs incurred. Total kilometres travelled for the FBT year were 30 000. The log book showed the car was used 40% for business purposes and 60% for private purposes. The following car costs were incurred for the year.

Lease payments	$ 8 200
Insurance	980
Registration	750
Repairs	1 000
Fuel	4 800
Total cost of car benefit inclusive of GST	**$15 730**

Under the operating cost method, the taxable value of the benefit is as follows.

$$(\$15\,730 \times 60\%) - \$3000 = \$6438$$

Using the statutory formula method, the taxable value is as follows.

$$(\$32\,000 \times 20\%) - \$3000 = \$3400$$

Calculating the FBT liability on the car benefit

Because the lowest value is used to calculate the FBT liability, the statutory formula method applies in this case. The FBT payable is calculated as follows.

$$\$3400 \times 2.0802 \times 47\% = \$3324$$

The total annual cost charged by the employer to Angela's salary package would be calculated as follows.

$$\$15\,730 \text{ (car running costs)} + \$3324 \text{ (FBT payable)} = \$19\,054$$

Note that an employer may decide to reimburse the employee for the amount of GST included within the costs of the car.

Exempt fringe benefits

A number of fringe benefits provided to employees are exempt from FBT and, accordingly, are particularly attractive to salary sacrifice into. Some eligible work-related benefits include notebooks, laptops and other portable computers; protective clothing (required for employment); briefcases, mobiles and calculators.

The FBT exemption will apply only if the benefits are primarily used within the employee's employment and the exemption is restricted to one item per year. Other common exempt fringe benefits include newspapers and periodicals used for business purposes, minor benefits of up to $300 which are infrequently provided and/or are difficult to record and value (e.g. Christmas gifts or Christmas parties), the cost of a taxi for a single journey to or from work, and certain other work-related items.

Excluded benefits

These are benefits that are specifically excluded under FBT legislation. One of the most common excluded benefits is superannuation which makes it particularly attractive as part of a salary sacrifice arrangement.

Superannuation

Superannuation contributions are an attractive form of salary sacrifice because an employee is provided with tax concessions to assist in accumulating wealth for their retirement. In the case of superannuation, the employee substitutes part of their cash salary through making additional contributions to their superannuation account. These contributions are in addition to the mandatory superannuation guarantee (SG) contributions that employers are required to make for their employees. SG contributions are discussed in more detail in the chapters on superannuation, retirement planning and self-managed superannuation funds.

FBT is not payable on superannuation contributions made to an employee's super fund as part of a salary sacrifice arrangement. However, it is important to note that all superannuation contributions made by an employer to a super fund are subject to a 15% contribution tax payable by the superannuation fund from the employee's account balance. Thus, for each $100 of superannuation contributions made through the SG scheme or through salary sacrificing, $15 is paid as tax to the Australian Taxation Office and only $85 will be left in the member's account. If an employee's adjusted taxable income for a year plus super contributions equals or exceeds $250 000, an additional 15% tax will be levied on the employer super contribution.

For the majority of employees that are on a marginal tax rate greater than 15%, significant tax savings can be made through salary sacrificing into superannuation. While salary sacrificing into superannuation is an effective means of reducing income tax payable, generally the strategy that results in a reduction in taxable income cannot be used to increase a person's entitlement to government benefits or to reduce their government obligations (discussed next).

Reportable fringe benefits

Where the total taxable value of fringe benefits provided to an employee is greater than $2000 in a FBT year, an employer is required to report the grossed-up taxable value of all fringe benefits provided to an employee on their payment summary which is then provided to the Australian Taxation Office. These are known as 'reportable fringe benefits'. The ATO is concerned to ensure that an employee does not use salary sacrificing as a means to reduce their taxable income in order to gain access to certain government benefits or avoid their obligations for a number of government taxes and levies. Some of these government benefits and obligations include the government co-contribution, spouse contribution tax offset (for the receiving spouse), Medicare levy surcharge, child support obligations and entitlement to certain income-tested government benefits.

In determining reportable fringe benefits, the employer is required to use the type 2 gross-up rate of 1.8868, regardless of whether the employer is entitled to claim GST input tax credits.

In addition to reporting the taxable value of fringe benefits, employers also need to include **reportable employer superannuation contributions (RESCs)** on the employee's payment summary. Reportable employer super contributions include salary sacrificed superannuation contributions and contributions an employer makes on behalf of an employee, other than the mandatory SG contributions. This is again designed to ensure that a taxpayer is not able to reduce their taxable income in order to gain access to government benefits or reduce obligations through salary sacrificing into superannuation.

3.11 Goods and services tax

LEARNING OBJECTIVE 3.11 Explain the goods and services tax (GST).

The goods and services tax (GST) was introduced in Australia in July 2000 as part of a major tax reform involving the abolition of wholesale sales tax and the reduction of income tax rates for individuals and companies. The government considered the existing tax system was inadequate to meet the needs of a community which, with its ageing profile, will place a larger and larger burden on the public purse. The GST is based on the value-added tax model adopted in several countries around the world. It is a 10% broad-based tax applied on the consumption of most goods, services and property, including those that are imported, but does not apply to goods or services which are exported or consumed outside Australia.

The investment which bears the greatest impact of GST is property and its impact is broken into four sections as follows.

Rents
- Residential rents are not subject to GST.
- Commercial rents may be subject to GST. However, the GST treatment is dependent upon the GST situation of the landlord.

Expenses
- GST is paid by both residential and commercial landlords on agents' commissions, insurance, investment advice, renovations and repairs. Investors in residential property cannot claim a credit for GST paid on the above expenses, but investors in commercial property can claim against the GST imposed on rent from commercial property.
- GST is not added to water and sewerage charges, council rates and interest costs.

Acquisition of investment
- All new property, residential or commercial, attracts GST on the sale.
- The purchase of non-new property is not subject to GST if it is residential, but is subject to GST if it is commercial. Investors in commercial property can offset the GST paid on purchase against the GST charges on rental income.

Realisation of investment
- GST is not imposed on the sale of residential property by investors but it is imposed on the sale of commercial property. However, if the turnover, that is, annual rentals of commercial property, is less than $75 000 p.a, then investors do not have to register for GST. If they are not registered they do not have to charge GST on their rentals. However, if investors in commercial property are not registered, they cannot claim a credit for GST paid on inputs.

GST, therefore, must be taken into account in any decision on property investment. It is difficult to identify specifically the impact of GST, but investors considering investing in either residential or commercial property must now feel biased towards residential, which does not attract the GST. When considering investing in new or non-new property, residential investors must be biased towards non-new property, as there is no opportunity to offset the GST imposed on new property.

GST does not affect other forms of investment to the same extent, but it is payable on the brokerage charged on the purchase and sale of shares and on such inputs as computers and stationery.

SUMMARY

Like most developed countries, Australia relies upon a range of taxes to raise government revenue. The Australian taxation system has four basic forms of taxation — income tax, capital gains tax, fringe benefits tax, and the goods and services tax.

The taxable income of a taxpayer is determined by subtracting allowable deductions from assessable income. Assessable income is made up of both ordinary income and statutory income and includes income earned from all sources during the financial year, whether derived in Australia or from overseas. Expenditures incurred by the taxpayer will be an allowable deduction only to the extent to which they are incurred in earning assessable income during the financial year.

Individuals are assessed for tax purposes based on marginal rates of tax which means the greater the taxable income of a taxpayer, the greater the rate of tax that applies. Both companies and superannuation funds are assessed on a flat rate of tax regardless of the amount of taxable income earned.

The returns generated from all forms of investment are subject to tax. However, in attempting to maximise after-tax returns, it is important that an investor understands the different tax planning strategies associated with each form of investment. The gains and losses derived from the sale of all forms of investments are subject to the capital gains tax provisions. Due to the concessions attached to the calculation of CGT for individuals, it is important to distinguish between receipts of a revenue nature and those of a capital nature.

Taxation has the potential to reduce substantially the actual return generated from an investment. However, with careful planning, taxpayers have some flexibility and opportunities to structure their affairs so as to minimise the imposition of tax and maximise their after-tax returns.

One of the major decisions facing a taxpayer in establishing a business or acquiring investments is the form of entity that should be utilised. The major tax entities available include sole traders, partnerships, trusts, superannuation funds and companies, and each has its advantages and disadvantages.

Salary sacrificing involves substituting cash salary for non-cash benefits that are subject to a lower imposition of tax. While non-cash benefits are free from income tax, many are subject to the fringe benefits tax. Remuneration planning can be a very effective tool for creating long-term wealth and minimising the imposition of taxation.

The GST is a 10% broad-based tax applied on the consumption of most goods, services and property. The investment which bears the greatest impact of GST is property and it impacts rents, expenses, and the acquisition and realisation of investments. GST, therefore, must be taken into account in any decision on property investment. GST does not affect other forms of investment to the same extent, but it is payable on the brokerage charged on the purchase and sale of shares and on a number of inputs.

KEY TERMS

allowable deductions Expenses incurred by the taxpayer which are deducted from assessable income to derive taxable income.

assessable income Income that is assessable to tax or recognised and measured under taxation law.

beneficiary A person nominated to receive a payout from an insurance policy, a superannuation fund or the assets of an estate.

best interest duty The obligation placed upon the financial planner to act in the best interests of the client.

capital gains tax (CGT) A tax applied when a profit is made on the disposal of a capital asset.

dividend imputation A tax system in which shareholders are entitled to a tax credit for the amount of tax already paid by the company on the profits from which dividends are paid.

fringe benefits tax (FBT) A tax applied to the taxable amount of non-cash benefits provided to an employee.

goods and services tax (GST) An indirect tax imposed on the purchase of goods and services at a flat rate of 10%.

income splitting Shifting income from a person on a high marginal tax rate to a person or entity on a lower tax bracket.

income tax A tax levied on individuals and companies in proportion to the level of income earned.

managed investment schemes (managed funds) Investment schemes where funds are deposited with a fund manager to manage on behalf of investors.

marginal tax rates The percentage of tax paid on each additional dollar of income earned.

Medicare levy A levy on the taxable income of an individual taxpayer to help fund Australia's health system.

negative gearing A situation where the total deductions associated with an investment, including the interest charge, exceed assessable income generated from the investment; in this case, the loss can be claimed as a tax deduction.

pay as you go (PAYG) A system where a taxpayer's expected tax liability is paid progressively during the year by way of instalments.

positive gearing A situation where the assessable income generated from the investment exceeds total deductions incurred, including the interest charges; in this case, tax is payable on the profit.

reportable employer superannuation contributions (RESCs) Additional superannuation contributions made by an employer for an employee which are in addition to the employer superannuation guarantee contributions. The most common example is amounts salary sacrificed into superannuation.

salary sacrificing A strategy that involves an employee substituting part of their cash salary for a non-cash benefit; the most commonly salary sacrificed benefit is superannuation.

self-assessment regime A system whereby the ATO initially accepts taxation information provided by a taxpayer for the purposes of assessing the taxpayer's tax liability.

tax offsets or rebates Reductions in tax payable provided by the government to support or assist individuals or activities.

trust A legal structure where assets are nominally owned and held by a trustee on behalf of beneficiaries.

trustee The person or entity that has the responsibility for holding and managing the assets of the trust on behalf of the beneficiaries.

PROFESSIONAL APPLICATION QUESTIONS

3.1 What are the general conditions that need to be satisfied for an expense to be considered an allowable deduction for tax purposes?

3.2 John and Eve are looking to make a gift of $15 000 to help pay for the future education of each of their three grandchildren. Should the payment be invested in the names of the grandchildren or their parents? Discuss.

3.3 William, aged 17 and a 2nd year building apprentice, receives income from a salary of $32 000 as well as receiving dividends of $3000 from a share portfolio that was bought from an inheritance received. How will William's total income be taxed?

3.4 Tanya and Jon have a joint account worth $20 000 with the Westpac Bank. Jon holds a term deposit worth $60 000 also with the Westpac Bank as well as a portfolio of Australian listed shares worth $100 000 (cost base of $30 000). Jon works full-time and pays tax at the highest marginal rate; Tanya is at home with twin boys aged 14. What is the best way of organising their financial affairs in order to minimise tax? Jon is considering transferring all their investments into Tanya's name. Identify the benefits of doing so and any possible costs.

3.5 What is the difference between the Medicare levy and Medicare levy surcharge? How are the levies determined and are the two levies payable by all types of entities?

3.6 Michael acquired a share portfolio three years ago consisting of 1000 shares in the CBA Bank worth $65 000. During the year he receives fully franked dividends of $3500 and, at the end of the year, the share portfolio has increased in value to $100 000. What amounts will be included in Michael's taxable income for the year?

3.7 Vivian is negotiating her salary package with her new employer, Spindex Ltd. She wants to salary package $10 000 into superannuation, $5000 for private expenses and $2000 for a laptop. Outline the FBT impact on each of the items including advantages and disadvantages.

3.8 Jarred and Sharyn are a married couple and looking to acquire an investment property. Discuss the factors that need to be considered in respect of the following questions raised.
(a) In whose name should the investment property and borrowing be purchased in?
(b) Are all of the income and expenses relating to the property assessable/deductible?
(c) How will any potential capital gains tax on the future disposal of the property be determined?
(d) If the property shows a net rental loss each year, what is the benefit of purchasing the investment property?

3.9 Brigitte buys and sells shares on a regular basis. During the year, she makes a capital gain of $7000 on the sale of one parcel of shares and a loss of $10 000 on the sale of another parcel of shares. What are the tax implications of the capital gain and loss incurred by Brigitte?

3.10 Charmi has acquired a holiday home for an amount of $680 000 and borrowed $480 000 at an interest rate of 3.5% p.a. Her annual loan repayments to the bank amounts to around $36 400 including interest of $16 800. Charmi rents the holiday home out to friends over the Christmas and Easter periods and earns rental income of $9000. Is the rental income from the holiday house assessable? Are the loan repayments of $36 400 payable to the bank tax deductible? Discuss.

3.11 On 15 June 1992, Trang bought $10 000 of Singtech Ltd's shares. On 20 February in the current year, they had tripled in value and Trang realises that she could dispose of these shares to take advantage of this price movement. Given that her marginal tax rate is 30% and the CPI index number for June 1992 is 59.7, calculate CGT under both the CGT discount and indexation methods to advise her which method is most appropriate.

3.12 Patrick is considering purchasing an investment property for $750 000. The property was built in 2010. Patrick hopes to rent out the property for $500 per week. He expects that annual insurance, rates and costs to maintain the property will be approximately $6000 p.a. and interest costs on his loan will be $24 000 for the year. Patrick earns a salary of $50 000 p.a. while his wife earns $205 000 p.a. as an accountant. Outline the income and CGT implications of this investment, including in whose name the investment should be acquired.

3.13 Terry is a landscaper and operates his business as a sole trader. He is aged 48 and married to Mary aged 46 who is a stay-at-home mum. They have 3 children aged 22, 19 and 16. Terry's net income from the business is $200 000 and he also earns $12 000 a year teaching landscaping at the local TAFE college and $10 000 net income from an investment property. Terry is looking at ways of how he might be able to minimise his taxable income for the year. He wants to know the following.
(a) Should his landscaping business be set up under a better tax structure?
(b) Can he divert his salary income from the TAFE college to Mary?
(c) Can he transfer the investment property to Mary so that she earns the income in her name?

PROFESSIONAL APPLICATION EXERCISES

★ BASIC | ★★ MODERATE | ★★★ CHALLENGING

3.14 Dividend imputation ★

Ying Xie has shares in an Australian mining company, JKL Ltd. She has received a final dividend statement for the year. Ying Xie needs you to explain some things about the statement to her. The details are as follows.

Description	Dividend per share (A$)	Number of shares	Franked dividend	Unfranked dividend	Gross payment
Final	24 cents	5 750	$1 104.00	$276.00	$1 380.00
Interim	20 cents	5 750	$ 920.00	$230.00	$1 150.00

Franking credits: Final ($473.14); Interim ($394.29)
(a) Explain the difference between 'franked dividends' and 'unfranked dividends'.
(b) What percentage of the shares is regarded as 'franked'?
(c) Explain how the 'franking credit' would be treated in the calculation of Ying Xie's tax payable for the year.
(d) Suppose Ying Xie earns a salary of $65 000, has no other income apart from the shares and does not have private health insurance. Calculate her tax payable in this situation.

3.15 Tax calculations ★

Nicholas, aged 27, works as a communications technician and earns $75 000 p.a. plus is provided with a fully-paid van to use in his work. Nicholas completed his university degree 4 years ago and has a HECS debt outstanding of $35 000.

Nicholas earns $3000 worth of interest and received $2000 of fully franked dividends during the year. His expenses during the year amount to the following.

Living costs	$26 000
Donations to charity	400
Registration, insurance and petrol spent on his private car which is used on weekends	2 200
Subscriptions to football club	500
Purchase and replacement of work tools	800

Calculate the net tax payable by Nicholas including his HELP repayment.

3.16 Tax calculations ★

George has just commenced employment as a teacher and his first year's income is $75 000. He also receives bank interest of $500. His expenses consist of $500 of subscriptions to the Australian Teacher Education Association, $700 of car expenses in travelling to and from work, and donations of $100. His HELP debt amounts to $30 000. Calculate his net tax payable.

3.17 Capital gains tax ★

Gayle has just sold a property and received $650 000. Her costs of selling the property amounted to $5000. Explain the tax implications of the sale based on the following scenarios.
(a) Gayle lived in the property as her principal residence for the total period of ownership.
(b) Gayle acquired the property for rental purposes in October 2015.
(c) Gayle is in the business of buying properties, renovating them and selling them for a profit.

3.18 Tax calculations ★★

Toby and Emma are a young couple with no children. They are both employed — Toby as a computer programmer and Emma as an accountant. Toby earns a salary of $90 000 and incurs the following expenses.
• Computer society subscription $600 p.a.
• Technical journals $700 p.a.
• Hobby magazines $500 p.a.
• Donations $200 p.a.

In addition, Toby receives investment income of $4000 from investments in a managed fund. The fund distribution includes $1500 of fully franked dividends.

Emma earns a salary of $63 000 and receives $2000 of fully franked dividends and $1000 from unfranked dividends. She also made a profit on the sale of her car recently of $1000. Emma's expenses comprise the following.
• Technical journals $800 p.a.
• Parking expenses (when visiting clients) $900 p.a.
• Accountants' society subscriptions $800 p.a.
• Local craft society subscription $200 p.a.

Calculate the tax payable for both Toby and Emma for the current financial year.

3.19 Tax structures ★★

Howard and Jeanette are planning to purchase an investment property in a bayside suburb of a capital city. The purchase price is $1.2 million. Jeanette was the beneficiary of the sale of her deceased mother's house and has the money available for investment. As Howard and Jeanette are in their mid-fifties and expect to retire in the next 8 years or so, they are wondering how they should purchase the property. They could either buy it in Jeanette's name, in the name of a discretionary family trust or in the name of a family company. Jeanette is on a MTR of 45% whereas Howard is on a MTR of 30%. The couple has 2 children aged 13 and 15. During the period of ownership, the property is expected to earn a net return of 4% p.a.
(a) What are some of the issues you would consider in determining in which name or entity the property should be purchased in?
(b) Would there be any tax benefits to be gained in distributing income earned from the property to the couple's 2 children? Discuss.
(c) What difference would the tax structure have on the way that the capital gain on sale would be calculated and taxed?

3.20 Tax structures ★★

Carol runs a successful restaurant as a sole trader and normally generates a net income of around $240 000 p.a. Her husband Keith is employed as an engineer and earns a taxable income of $120 000 p.a. The couple have 2 children, both aged under 16.

(a) Carol is looking to acquire a car and wants to know whether she is able to salary sacrifice the car through her business.

(b) What are the benefits and drawbacks of running the restaurant through a family company?

(c) If a company structure was set up to operate the business, Carol wants to know how profits would be distributed and whether all the profits of the company would need to be distributed each year.

(d) If the business was set up within a trust structure instead of as a company, would you recommend the establishment of a family unit trust or a discretionary trust? Explain.

(e) Would it make any difference which structure was set up in terms of the distribution of income to their children?

3.21 Tax strategies ★★

Mark and Carolyn are aged in their mid-forties and are seeking some advice on how they can improve their financial position. Carolyn earns a salary of $160 000 p.a. while Mark earns a taxable profit from his business as a self-employed project management consultant of $50 000 p.a. Mark works part-time and looks after the children. The couple's disposable income after tax is $22 000 p.a. The couple have 3 children — Jack, aged 9, Kim, aged 13, and Felicity, aged 15.

The couple's investments are shown as follows.

Item	Market value	Ownership
Bank account	$ 60 000	Carolyn
Platinum international managed fund (acquired in March 2014 for $70 000)	$100 000	Carolyn
Shares		
• acquired 10 months ago for $50 000	$ 70 000	Carolyn
• acquired in March 1998 for $50 000 (CPI factor at that time was 67.0)	$ 80 000	Carolyn

The couple is looking to sell the entire share portfolio over the next few months to pay off their home loan. Carolyn has a carried-forward capital loss of $20 000 from 2 years ago when she sold an investment property. The couple is concerned by the large amount of tax they are currently paying and seek some advice on how they might be able to minimise tax and maximise wealth prior to retirement.

(a) Outline some of the general tax-effective strategies that the couple might consider putting in place in order to minimise their overall tax liability each year.

(b) If the shares are sold, calculate the net assessable capital gain that would be included in Carolyn's assessable income for the year.

(c) In order to minimise taxation, Carolyn has been advised to sell the managed fund portfolio and transfer the funds to Mark to invest. What would be the advantages and drawbacks of this strategy? Discuss.

3.22 Salary sacrifice and fringe benefits tax ★★★

Wendy has decided to salary sacrifice into a car benefit through her employer. The cost of the car is $35 000 and Wendy expects to travel 30 000 kilometres each year, 30% of which are expected to be for business purposes. The costs incurred by the employer in providing the car are as follows.

Leasing costs	$11 000
Repairs	1 000
Petrol	4 500
Registration	800
Insurance	700
Total costs	**$18 000**

All of the costs include GST except for registration. The car is available for private use throughout the FBT year. Wendy contributes $2000 p.a. towards the cost of the benefits provided to the employer. Wendy is also considering salary sacrificing $12 000 into her superannuation fund this year.

(a) Is salary sacrificing an effective strategy for all non-cash benefits and for all employees? Are there circumstances where you would not recommend a salary sacrifice arrangement for a particular employee?

(b) Calculate the FBT payable by Wendy's employer on the total non-cash benefits provided for the current FBT year.

(c) What are the tax benefits of Wendy making a superannuation contribution as part of a salary sacrifice arrangement as compared to making a contribution from her after-tax income?

(d) Could Wendy's husband Dave also salary sacrifice into his superannuation account? Dave is a self-employed builder and is looking to build his superannuation balance in a tax-effective manner.

3.23 Negative gearing ★★★

Carl and Karen are seeking some advice on accumulating wealth for their retirement. The couple has an aggressive risk profile and is prepared to take on further debt. Carl has a salary of $140 000 p.a. and Karen works part-time and earns a salary of $42 000 p.a. They have a home worth $920 000 and a home mortgage of $240 000 charging an interest rate of 3.5% p.a. They also have an outstanding credit card balance of $20 000 which has an interest rate of 17% p.a. and a car loan amounting to $12 000 in Carl's name which has an interest rate of 7% p.a. Carl earns $1500 from bank interest and has work-related expenses of $1200. Karen's work-related expenses total $400. The couple has private health insurance.

The couple is looking to take out a bank loan for $110 000 to acquire a share portfolio. The bank loan would have an interest rate of 6.5% p.a. and it is expected that the shares will generate a 4% p.a. fully franked dividend and capital growth of around 5% p.a. The bank has advised that the annual loan repayments would be $15 300 p.a. with the first year's interest payment being $7150.

(a) In whose name would you recommend that the share portfolio be acquired in? Explain.

(b) Would the interest charged on the bank loan used to acquire the share portfolio be tax deductible? Explain. Are there any circumstances in which interest charged on a loan used to acquire an investment would not be tax deductible to an individual?

Carl decides to take out the bank loan and acquire the share portfolio in his own name. In the following year, assume that the shares generate the expected returns and that there is no change in the salary, other income and work-related expenses of the couple.

(c) If the couple had surplus income after paying off all expenses and were looking to pay off their debt as quickly as possible, what would be the order that you would recommend for the repayment of their debt? Discuss.

(d) Based on the above information, calculate the tax payable for both Carl and Karen for the year using current tax rates.

CASE STUDY 1

TAXATION PLANNING

Nick and Selena are a married couple in their forties. They have 3 children — Tom aged 17, Kate aged 15 and Linda aged 14. Nick works as an office manager and earns $80 000. Selena is a partner in a law firm and earns a salary of $170 000 p.a.

Nick and Selena seek some advice from you in respect of reducing tax payable, especially by Selena, and also on generating wealth. They have not taken an interest in their financial planning to date but want to change this now. The couple provides the following details.

Balance sheet

Assets	
Home and contents	$1 400 000
Cars	55 000
Holiday house (rental income of $6000)	580 000
Bank account (interest rate of 1% p.a.)	70 000
Share portfolio (fully franked dividends of 4% p.a.)	120 000
Superannuation (after-tax return of 6%)	400 000
Total assets	**$2 625 000**
Liabilities	
Mortgage on home (interest rate of 3.5% p.a.)	$ 350 000
Bank loan on share portfolio (interest rate of 6.5% p.a.)	50 000
Credit card (interest rate of 15% p.a.)	10 000
Total liabilities	**$ 410 000**

- All of the assets are owned in the name of Selena except for the bank account and holiday home which are jointly owned.
- The share portfolio was acquired for $100 000 in 2014. Selena took out an interest only loan (no payments are made against the principal owing). Selena has a carried forward capital loss of $7000 relating to some shares she sold 3 years ago.

EXPENSES

In addition to their interest and loan repayments, the couple incurred the following expenses during the year.

Expenditure	Nick	Selena
Work-related expenses	$ 1 000	$ 2 200
Travelling to and from home	1 200	1 500
Child care expenses	0	6 000
Donations	500	0
Living costs	18 000	18 000
Tax agents' fees	700	900

The couple does not have any private health insurance.

QUESTIONS

1 Determine the net tax payable for the current year for both Nick and Selena.
2 The couple is concerned with the amount of overall tax they are paying. Discuss some of the tax-effective strategies that the couple could use.
3 The couple has suggested salary sacrificing into their superannuation account. What is the benefit and drawback of salary sacrificing into superannuation and who would most likely receive the greatest tax benefit?
4 The couple is wondering whether they are able to claim any expenses incurred on the holiday house. Is this possible and how would any entitlement to a tax deduction be determined?
5 The couple has been disappointed with the growth in value of the share portfolio over the past few years and is now looking to sell the entire portfolio and invest the proceeds into an Australian fixed interest bond fund. Based on the current market price and after taking account of estimated selling expenses of $2000, calculate the likely assessable capital gain.

CASE STUDY 2

SALARY PACKAGING

James Zocchi is 28 years old and single. After completing his degree in marketing, like many young Australians, he travelled overseas on a working holiday. After 18 months travelling through Europe and working for some of the time in London, he arrived back in Australia and was offered employment with a large food products distribution company for whom he had worked while overseas. To his surprise, and based on the references he obtained while working for the head office in London, he was offered a gross salary of $100 000 plus superannuation. The personnel manager met with him to work out details of how he would like to be paid as he was given the opportunity to request his employer to package his salary in ways that would benefit him.

James was told that his employer would contribute $12 000 of SG contributions to his superannuation fund regardless of whether James wanted to package any himself. Even though James is fairly young and knows that he is not able to access his superannuation until he is at least 60 years of age — some 32 years away — he knows that he needs to put money aside for his retirement and that by putting a bit more away at an earlier age the benefits of compound interest will work in his favour in the long run. So James decided that he would like to salary package $5000 to his superannuation fund each year in addition to the employer's contribution. When James left to go overseas he gave his laptop computer to a young nephew as it was about 5 years old. After speaking with the personnel manager he decided to take up the offer of salary packaging a new personal laptop computer costing $5000. He could have paid for it himself over a few months but decided to take advantage of the opportunity to acquire it without paying income tax on the amount needed to buy it and without any fringe benefits tax.

As a young marketing professional and with career advancement in sight he decided that there would be benefits for him if he became a member of the Young Marketers Association, which required a membership fee of $850 p.a. He decided that it would be very convenient to have his employer pay the fee on his behalf as a salary package item as he might forget to pay the membership fees when they fell due. So, even though he could get a full personal tax deduction for the membership fee, he decided that for convenience reasons he would package the amount from his salary.

When James arrived home from his overseas travels, he found his old car waiting for him in the garage at his parents' house. His car was 15 years old, dripped oil, did not run smoothly and needed about $3000 spent on it to maintain its roadworthiness. He decided that with his newly acquired employment and with such a generous starting salary he should drive a more modern car. As he had just arrived back in Australia after spending the savings that he had accumulated, he did not have sufficient funds to buy a car immediately and did not want to borrow his mother's new car as she needed it almost every day. However, the personnel manager advised him that he could take up the option of salary packaging a car through his employment. The personnel manager gave him a list of vehicles from a car dealer and a list of various costs so that James could consider the type of car and range of costs that would suit him and his salary package. James considered the list and costs and provided the following details in respect of the car: cost of car $35 000; lease costs $12 000 p.a.; and petrol and service costs estimated to be $4000 p.a. He estimated that he will travel about 24 000 kilometres in the 12-month period and he will have the car for private use for the whole year. He selected a particular type and model of vehicle and gave the information to the personnel manager, along with his preferred colours for the car and interior. Within a few weeks, James was contacted to collect the vehicle and to complete all the required paperwork.

QUESTIONS

1 Why would the employer want to offer James the opportunity to enter into a salary packaging arrangement?
2 Under what circumstances would you recommend that salary sacrificing is not an appropriate strategy for a client?
3 Rather than salary sacrificing, what other options could James consider in order to obtain a new car?
4 Calculate the FBT liability for the current FBT year and the total cost charged by the employer against the salary of James if all of the above non-cash benefits are salary sacrificed.
5 What is the effect on the FBT if James decides to contribute $3200 of his after-tax income to his employer towards the cost of the vehicle package? Is it worth doing?

CASE STUDY 3

NEGATIVE GEARING

Fiona, aged 32 and single, is employed as a teacher earning $75 000 p.a. She is currently renting. Fiona has quite an aggressive risk profile and is looking to buy into an investment property. The plan is that after six years, Fiona would move into the property herself and make it her home. Fiona approaches you for some advice on how best to structure the purchase.

Fiona is looking to purchase a property for around $760 000 and take out a bank loan for $480 000. Fiona is able to get the loan for a period of 20 years at an interest rate of 3.2% p.a. She has saved a total of \$300 000 including an amount of \$180 000 which is currently sitting in a share portfolio. She inherited the majority of the shares 8 years ago from her grandfather who purchased them in 2008. The shares have a cost base of \$100 000. Fiona provides the following information relating to the estimated income and expenses of the property in the first year.

Estimated rental income	\$24 000
Estimated expenses:	
Rates	2 500
Insurance	800
Interest and loan repayments (interest component is \$15 360)	32 900
Depreciation on fixtures and fittings	3 000
Installation of carport	8 000

Fiona also incurs work-related expenses of \$1500 and tax agents' fees of \$600. She still has an outstanding HELP loan of \$15 000.

QUESTIONS

1 Should the property be purchased in the name of a family company or trust or be acquired in the personal name of Fiona? Discuss.
2 Discuss the likely tax treatment of the installation of the carport in respect of the property purchase.
3 Calculate the capital gain or loss on disposal of the shares.
4 Based on the investment property purchase and the sale of shares, calculate the net tax payable by Fiona for the year.
5 What would be the tax implications if Fiona was to move into the property after six years and use it as his principal residence? She has heard that there is no CGT payable if the house disposed of is used as a principle residence?

REFERENCES

ATO 2024a, 'Browse the legal database', Australian Government, www.ato.gov.au/law/#Law/browse.
ATO 2024b, 'Individual income tax rates and threshold changes', Australian Government, 6 March, www.ato.gov.au/about-ato/new-legislation/in-detail/individuals/individual-income-tax-rates-and-threshold-changes.
ATO 2024c, 'Low income tax offset (LITO)', 2 June, www.ato.gov.au/individuals-and-families/income-deductions-offsets-and-records/tax-offsets/low-and-middle-income-earner-tax-offsets#Lowincometaxoffset.
ATO 2024d, 'Medicare levy surcharge income, thresholds and rates', 15 March, www.ato.gov.au/individuals-and-families/medicare-and-private-health-insurance/medicare-levy-surcharge/medicare-levy-surcharge-income-thresholds-and-rates.
ATO 2024e, 'Study and training loan repayment thresholds and rates', Australian Government, 16 June, www.ato.gov.au/Rates/HELP,-TSL-and-SFSS-repayment-thresholds-and-rates/#HELPandTSLrepaymentthresholdsandrates201.
Australian Government n.d., 'HECS-HELP', www.studyassist.gov.au/help-loans/hecs-help.
Prince 2011, 'Tax heading: CGT and lodgers', *Your Investment Property*, 14 December, www.yourinvestmentpropertymag.com.au/tax-strategy/tax-headache-cgt-and-lodgers.

ACKNOWLEDGEMENTS

Extract: © 'Tax headache: CGT and lodgers', *Your Investment Property*, retrieved from www.yourinvestmentpropertymag.com.au/article/tax-headache-cgt-and-lodgers-120888.aspx.
Figure 3.1: © Australian Taxation Office.
Table 3.1: © Australian Taxation Office.
Table 3.2: © Australian Taxation Office.
Table 3.3: © Australian Taxation Office.
Table 3.4: © Australian Taxation Office.

CHAPTER 4

Investment choices

LEARNING OBJECTIVES

After studying this chapter, you should be able to:

4.1 consider the general attributes of investors

4.2 explain the broad investment classes

4.3 understand the risk and return relationship

4.4 understand the benefits of diversification

4.5 appreciate the performance history of the various asset classes

4.6 understand general investment strategies

4.7 gain an awareness of behavioural finance

4.8 develop an awareness of investment scams

4.9 identify information sources for investment choices.

Ava is 19 and a retail shop assistant in a large city department store. She is quite pleased as her manager has recommended her to become a trainee manager specialising in women's clothing. After going to the football one weekend with some friends they go to a bar to have a few drinks before heading to a night club after dinner. Atticus, who works in real estate, started to talk about the capital gains that could be made by buying a property in the right location and 'doing it up'. He indicated that he was considering borrowing a large sum of money to do just that. Caitlin, who works in a bank, agreed it could be a good investment, but was cautious about the changes in the rate of interest that Atticus would have to pay while he was doing up the house with no income coming in. Caitlin said a safer approach to investing would be building up a bank account first so Atticus had a bigger deposit and would have to borrow less. Steve, who is studying to be an accountant, thought that the property investment idea was good but it didn't allow for any flexibility if Atticus needed to get some cash quickly out of his investment. Steve said he preferred to be a bit more flexible and, if he was to borrow money for an investment, he would borrow and buy a parcel of shares so he could buy and sell shares depending on the need for cash or the ups and downs of the share market.

Ava thought about what she had heard from her friends over the next few days and felt that she was fairly ignorant about investing. She asked her uncle, Daniel, who worked in superannuation about investing. Her uncle advised her to start learning about the different forms of investing herself so she would have some knowledge about what people were talking about when investment choices came up in conversation. So Ava decided to buy some books and search on the internet to give herself some background knowledge for future discussions with her friends.

Issues to be considered from this case concerning investment choices include:
- the features of some of the major investment choices
- the return and risks to be expected from such investments.

These and other issues will be considered in this chapter.

Introduction

This chapter deals with investment choices. Just as there are different types of investors there is also a broad range of investments that consumers can choose. Broadly, investors may choose from two forms of investment: direct and indirect. Direct investment occurs when investors make their own decisions about where their funds are ultimately placed, be it in fixed-interest deposit accounts, shares, property or some other form of asset. Indirect investment is when investors place their funds with funds managers who use vehicles such as unit trusts and master funds to consolidate the funds of many investors and then invest the pooled funds according to their own stated investment strategies.

To consider any investment choice, an investor should have an appreciation of the risk and return relationship to understand that the higher the return the higher the level of risk. This chapter also considers the means by which risk may be reduced. Such risks and returns for each investment category also need to be understood in terms of recent performance history and time frames. Such an understanding is fundamental to adopting an investment strategy, as is having an awareness of how some investors behave rationally and how others base investment decisions on lack of information and biases. The chapter also outlines the danger of investment scams. The chapter concludes with an outline of the sources of information for investment choices.

4.1 General attributes of investors

LEARNING OBJECTIVE 4.1 Consider the general attributes of investors.

In 1949, Benjamin Graham, writing in the classic text on value investing *The intelligent investor*, distinguished between two main types of investor: the defensive investor and the enterprising investor. The defensive investor is focused on conserving capital — their main emphasis is on avoiding any serious mistakes or losses, and also on freedom from effort, annoyance and the need for making frequent decisions. The second type, the enterprising or aggressive investor, is characterised not by speculation, but by their willingness to devote time and care to the selection of sound and attractive investments even though they may not be fully trained experts in the field. In summing up his 'intelligent investor', Graham remarks that the enterprising investor will never embark on an investment choice which he does not fully comprehend and which he cannot justify by reference to the results of his personal study or experience.

In many respects, the classification that Graham observed is not dissimilar to the general range of classifications of investors used by financial planners today. Table 4.1 provides an insight into the general classification of investors that may be applied by financial planners. The table indicates some features that may be ascribed to different investment types such as stability of income, tolerance to risk and an approximate investment time frame. Investment classification is also usually matched to a typical asset allocation held by various investors. In the table, the 'growth' investments represent a combination of property investments and share investments which may be invested in domestic or international markets.

TABLE 4.1   A general investor classification

Investor classification	Features	Approximate asset mix
Very conservative	• Household income is unstable and insecure. • No tolerance for loss of capital. • Investing time frame is 2 years or less.	• Cash 60% • Fixed interest 30% • Growth investments 10%
Conservative	• Household income is somewhat unstable and insecure. • Able to tolerate no more than 5% decline in capital value. • Investing time frame is between 2 and 4 years.	• Cash 20% • Fixed interest 40% • Growth investments 40%
Balanced	• Household income is fairly stable and secure. • Able to tolerate a 10% decline in capital value. • Investing time frame is between 4 and 6 years.	• Cash 10% • Fixed interest 30% • Growth investments 60%
Aggressive	• Household income is substantially stable and secure. • Able to tolerate a 15% decline in capital value. • Investing time frame is between 6 and 8 years.	• Cash 5% • Fixed interest 15% • Growth investments 80%
Very aggressive	• Household income is very stable and secure. • Able to tolerate regular fluctuations of 20% or more in capital value. • Investing time frame is between 8 and 10 years.	• Cash 5% • Fixed interest 10% • Growth investments 85%

4.2 Broad investment classes

LEARNING OBJECTIVE 4.2 Explain the broad investment classes.

When faced with deciding what to invest in an investor needs to have a sound understanding of the range of investment choices. This section provides an outline of the main investment choices:

• cash
• fixed interest
• property
• shares/equities.

Cash

A person uses cash to access funds for day-to-day living expenses and emergency situations. However, cash also plays an important role in an investment portfolio as it can be used to manage cash flows into other asset classes and as a safe haven if an investor feels that it is wise to withdraw from one asset class and hold it in cash to avoid a decline in value of that portion of a portfolio.

Cash investments aim to provide income, liquidity and stable returns. Cash investments can include savings accounts, money-market securities and cash-management trusts. Cash has the lowest risk of all asset classes and generally offers a relatively low rate of return. Cash investments are usually referred to as a 'risk-free' investment as there is a very low chance of default by the banking sector. For analysis of investments purposes, the interest rate of the federal government's 90-day Treasury notes is generally regarded as the risk-free rate of return in Australia. Cash investments are less volatile than other types of asset classes because of their short-term nature. Since the time of the global financial crisis, cash deposits up to $250 000 are guaranteed by the federal government. Despite its relative safety, one aspect of cash investments is that there is the risk that capital will not keep pace with inflation and lose value in real terms. Income from cash investments is paid as interest and the amount paid varies as interest rates move up and down with expectations of inflationary trends.

Fixed interest

Fixed-interest investments are investments that are agreed for a certain period of time at a known interest rate. Interest is usually paid on a regular basis, but with some fixed-interest investments the interest payment is factored into the final payment and offered as a discount security or with accumulated interest paid on maturity. Some fixed-interest securities offer a reinvestment of interest to gain the benefit of compounding. Fixed-interest investments can be issued by banks, the Commonwealth Government, state governments, semi-government authorities, overseas banks and authorities, and other corporations. Commonwealth government bonds, called exchange-traded Treasury bonds, are traded on the ASX. This offers a way for investors to buy and sell these securities in the form of CHESS depository interests (CDIs).

Fixed-interest investments usually have longer investment terms than cash investments. For example, Australian bond maturities range from 1 to 15 years while US bonds can extend up to 30 years. Investment in both international and Australian fixed-interest securities increases diversification and lowers overall investment risk. The main types of fixed-interest securities are:
- term deposits — issued by banks
- government and semi-government bonds — issued by governments to fund or help pay for major public projects
- corporate bonds, debentures or notes — issued by large public companies to fund business expansion. Such securities usually offer a higher interest but have less back-up security (assets) behind them. Sometimes, corporations issue hybrid securities which have characteristics of both equity and fixed-interest securities. Convertible bonds/notes, for example, commence as bonds but can be converted into equity at a future date. These types of securities have higher risk than government or corporate bonds as they are less secured.

Fixed-interest securities can be traded on the secondary market before their maturity if an investor needs to convert their investment to cash. Fixed interest is a low- to medium-risk investment suitable for investors with a time frame of three years or more. As well as providing a regular stream of income, fixed interest can provide a stabilising effect on a portfolio during periods of share market volatility. Later, you will learn about the potential capital growth or loss that can occur if a bond needs to be sold prior to maturity.

A big issue for fixed-interest investors is credit risk, which is the risk of an issuer defaulting on repayment of capital. Fixed-interest investments offered by banks have a low level of risk, as such investments are backed by the strength of the banking sector. Some fixed-interest investments may be backed by a guarantee which is supported by the institution. However, the guarantee is only as strong as the institution itself and history has shown that some institutions have not been able to pay the interest and even have lost capital because the institution itself has become bankrupt. Investors should refer to credit ratings which provide a good indication of the risk level associated with the issuer. However, credit ratings are not a guarantee even though a high rating indicates a lower likelihood of the issuer defaulting on repaying capital.

Property

Direct residential property has been the traditional form of investment for many Australians and may be considered separate from an investment portfolio, as many people consider their home to provide shelter and lifestyle benefits rather than viewing it strictly in terms of an investment choice.

Leaving aside the family home until a later chapter, **property** investments can consist of rental properties (residential, commercial, industrial or rural); listed property trusts known as real estate investment trusts (REITs); and unlisted property trusts. Property trusts are pooled investments which hold a basket of properties in one or more of the property sectors and offer units to be purchased by investors.

Property is a long-term investment with higher risk than fixed-interest investments but slightly lower risk, historically, than shares. Direct property offers steady rental income, tax breaks via negative gearing, depreciation and capital appreciation. At the same time, direct property has a number of drawbacks: it takes time to buy and sell; building a diversified property portfolio is an expensive exercise; property exposure is usually limited to one sector; locating and keeping good tenants can be difficult; and there is always the cost of ongoing care and maintenance. There is also the risk of capital loss and lower rentals during times of oversupply.

REITs and unlisted property trusts (both forms of managed investment) provide many of the benefits of direct property investment without some of the constraints. Returns from property trusts can include income in the form of rent received from the underlying properties and capital growth (or loss) from changes in the value of the unit price. Property trusts also offer tax advantages to investors in the form of tax deferred income distributions. Some property trusts hold properties overseas which can provide a further level of diversification to an investment portfolio. Income is derived from rental payments and then distributed as income to unit holders. The income return can be compared to fixed-interest returns but may also vary from time to time depending on the quality of the tenants and the terms of the leases which are managed by the property trust.

Property trusts have similar risks to shares. The value of their units can rise and fall and is subject to changes in investor confidence and other factors affecting the property market. Property investments are usually funded by borrowings and interest is thus paid by the trust to the lender. If the level of borrowing is substantial and the demand for the property falls, the value of the units in the property trust can fall. During the global financial crisis, many property trusts suffered severe falls in value when they could not refinance debt and had to sell off development and other properties at low prices and even at prices lower than the purchase price.

Shares/equities

Shares are a unit holding (i.e. a share of the ownership of a company). Companies may be public or private, but generally when we consider investment portfolios we think of shares in public companies which are listed on the Australian Securities Exchange (ASX) or overseas stock exchanges, such as Wall Street (USA), and DAX (Germany).

Shares listed on the ASX are classified into industry sectors based on the Global Industry Classification Standard (GICS). The Australian share market sectors are energy, materials, industrials, consumer discretionary, consumer staples, healthcare, information technology, telecommunication services, utilities, property trusts and financials. Common measures used in evaluation of the performance of a share portfolio are the various indices created by the ASX, such as the S&P/ASX 200 Energy Index which comprises companies whose businesses are dominated by either of the following activities: the construction or provision of oil rigs, drilling equipment and other energy-related service and equipment, including seismic data collection; or companies engaged in the exploration, production, marketing, refining and/or transportation of oil and gas products, coal and other consumable fuels.

Shares are generally considered a high-risk and high-return investment and are suitable for longer-term investors. Historically, Australian shares have provided long-term growth well above inflation. But in the short term, share market returns have been quite volatile at times. Thus, share market investors can expect a negative return once in every 5 years, which is why shares are suited to longer-term investors (7 years plus). The length of time of the investment greatly reduces, but does not eliminate, the volatility in returns from shares. Share markets move in cycles, reflecting the underlying strength of the economy, political factors, industry trends and market sentiment. On any given day, interest rate and inflation expectations, company profits, dividends, economic growth figures and the rise or fall of the Australian dollar can impact share prices.

Shares provide a good source of income but are also the focus for capital growth. Most companies distribute a proportion of their profits in the form of dividends. Companies that pay high dividends tend to be blue-chip companies such as those in the banking, insurance and retail sectors. Some companies, such as those in the mining sector or newer industries such as biotechnology, may retain dividends to fund future research, expansion or exploration. Dividends can change from year to year depending on the company's profitability. Australian shares can provide tax-effective returns by means of the dividend imputation system under which, given companies have already paid tax at the company tax rate, investors can use franking credits to offset the amount of tax they pay on dividends. The higher the franking level the greater the benefit. Thus, the dividends are imputed to carry the tax credit to the shareholder.

Australian investors can also access international share markets. Investing internationally can increase diversification and provide access to industries and companies not available in Australia. Australia represents less than 3% of the total world share market. By diversifying some portion of an investment portfolio in overseas markets, an investor may benefit from returns generated in countries experiencing different phases of the business cycle than Australia at a particular point in time.

All of the different investment classes can be accessed by investors either directly or indirectly via managed funds.

4.3 The risk and return relationship

LEARNING OBJECTIVE 4.3 Understand the risk and return relationship.

We have all heard the expression 'the higher the return the greater the risk'. This section provides an overview of the relationship between risk and return. John Bogle (founder of the Vanguard Group of Investment Companies), wrote in 1994 that 'the message is to maximize your capital by earning the highest returns you can over the longest period possible . . . However, risk is every bit as central as reward in the establishment of your investment portfolio, so you must carefully consider what risks you are prepared to assume.' The key determinants of the price of an asset are the risk associated with the asset and the returns that the asset is expected to generate. Consequently, all financial decisions must be evaluated in terms of expected risk and expected return. In order to adequately present investment options to clients, financial planners must be very clear about what is meant by investment risk and investment return, and how measures of both risk and return are determined.

Inflation-adjusted rates of return

When we consider the rate of return on an investment, we need to consider the real rate of return not just the nominal rate. The real rate of return allows for the effects of inflation. Inflation causes investors to lose purchasing power when they sell their assets in the future and wish to buy goods and services with the proceeds. Inflation also causes the rate of return on an investment to fall in value. The real rate of return (R real) is calculated as follows.

$$R\,\text{real} = \frac{1 + R\,\text{nom}}{1 + h} - 1$$

where: R nom is the nominal rate of return and h is the inflation rate.

So, if the nominal rate of return is 6.27% after tax and inflation is 5% the real rate of return is as follows.

$$R\,\text{real} = \frac{1.0627}{1.05} - 1 = 0.0121 \text{ or } 1.21\%.$$

Definitions of risk

Some of the more common definitions of risk are the chance of loss of capital, the chance of loss of purchasing power or the variability of the returns associated with the given asset. Return is the total gain or loss experienced by the owner of a financial asset or investment over a given period of time.

The chance of loss of capital

The chance of loss of capital varies for different asset classes. In the past 60 years, a cash investment has always resulted in a positive return to investors, albeit small in some years. Some 20 years ago, cash investments earned over 6% p.a. whereas, at the time of writing, interest on cash was under 2% p.a. There has been no loss of capital. Recall from the previous sections that investments in cash do not always generate a return which maintains its purchasing power. This occurs when the returns are not greater than inflation — the second definition of risk. Consequently, an investment in cash may result in a negative real return.

Investments in shares and some fixed-interest investments such as debentures and unsecured notes can, and have, resulted in a loss of capital value over some time periods. Shares are therefore considered to be riskier than investments in cash. Share investments, although generating negative returns over some time periods, have a decreasing likelihood of negative returns as the time period increases.

During the past 60 years, any period of 10 years generated positive returns. That is, as the length of time for the investment increased, the chance of loss for share investments decreased. However, the risk of some shares and fixed interest investments losing capital altogether remains as a risk of investing.

The chance of loss of purchasing power

Research in 2004 by Russell Investments provides an interesting comparison of the nominal and real returns of three asset classes commonly found in investor portfolios.

> A dollar invested in cash between 1937 and 2002 earned a 6.0% average annual return. Yet, according to the Australian Consumer Price Index, inflation during that same period averaged 5.5%. Cash's real return? Only 0.5%. A dollar invested in Australian bonds over the same period earned a 6.3% average annual return. Less inflation, the real return is 0.8%. Better than cash, but not by much. A dollar invested in Australian shares over this [65 year] period generated an 11.2% average annual return. The real return: 5.7%. That's 7 times better than bonds and almost 12 times better than cash.

A similar story may be found across any long-term period of markets. Most discussions on investment performance focus on nominal returns. Yet, an investor's personal 'bottom line' is how their investments perform after inflation has been allowed for and also after allowing for taxation.

The variability of returns

In order to understand what we mean by variability of returns, consider the position of Gold Ltd and Silver Ltd shown below.

Gold Ltd and its competitor Silver Ltd generated the following returns over the past 5 years.

	Year 1	Year 2	Year 3	Year 4	Year 5
Gold Ltd	12%	17%	8%	11%	22%
Silver Ltd	12%	15%	13%	14%	16%

To determine the expected return for both these companies, we calculate the mean return as follows.

$$\text{Gold Ltd} \quad \frac{(12\% + 17\% + 8\% + 11\% + 22\%)}{5} = 14\%$$

$$\text{Silver Ltd} \quad \frac{(12\% + 15\% + 13\% + 14\% + 16\%)}{5} = 14\%$$

Both Gold Ltd and Silver Ltd have the same mean return or expected return $E(R)$.

In order to choose between the two companies, an investor must evaluate the returns in light of the associated risk. One measure of risk is the variability of returns. Clearly, Gold Ltd has returns which vary to a greater extent around the mean return or expected return than do the returns of Silver Ltd. In financial planning, we can measure this risk by calculating the **standard deviation** of the returns, which measures the variability of returns around the expected return. For Gold Ltd, we can calculate the standard deviation (s) in two stages: (1) calculate the variance, and (2) take the square root of the variance.

$$
\begin{aligned}
s^2 &= \sum_{i=1}^{n} \frac{[X_i - E(R)]^2}{(n-1)} \\
&= \frac{(12-14)^2 + (17-14)^2 + (8-14)^2 + (11-14)^2 + (22-14)^2}{(5-1)} \\
&= \frac{122}{4} \\
&= 30.5
\end{aligned}
$$

where
s^2 = variance
X = value of each return
n = sample size
i = position of each return in the sample

The standard deviation is equal to the square root of the variance so for Gold Ltd the standard deviation is 5.52%, and by following the same process for Silver Ltd, the standard deviation is 1.58%.

What does the standard deviation tell us? No analyst, sharebroker, mathematician or financial planner can tell with any certainty what the returns for a company will be in some future period. At best, they can use their knowledge of past returns to estimate the probability of future returns. The standard deviation is based on probabilities. It is a statistical fact for normal distributions that if we know the standard deviation, we know that roughly two-thirds (66.7%) of the actual returns will lie in the range of expected return plus one standard deviation and expected return minus one standard deviation.

For Gold Ltd and Silver Ltd, this would tell us that two-thirds of the actual returns lie in the following range.

Gold Ltd	8.48% – 19.52%
Silver Ltd	12.42% – 15.58%

That is, in Gold's case: 14% − 5.52 = 8.48% at the low end and 14% + 5.52 = 19.52% at the high end.

If we want more certainty about the likely range of returns that could eventuate, we can again use the standard deviation. To be 95% confident that the actual returns will lie in a given range, we simply determine the values of the expected return plus 2 standard deviations and the expected return minus 2 standard deviations, assuming the returns are normally distributed.

For Gold Ltd and Silver Ltd, this would tell us that 95% of the time we can expect the actual returns to lie in the following range.

Gold Ltd	2.96% – 25.04%
Silver Ltd	10.84% – 17.16%

Using the standard deviation as a measure of risk, we can see that although Gold Ltd and Silver Ltd have identical expected average returns, Gold Ltd is far more risky as there is greater variability of the returns. The standard deviation shows the possible range of returns that may be expected given the history of returns of that asset. Investors in Gold Ltd are likely to receive higher returns in some periods than investors in Silver Ltd, but they are also likely to receive lower returns in some periods than investors in Silver Ltd.

This example highlights only the risk of individual shares. We can also see that the returns we can expect for different asset classes have different degrees of variability or volatility.

In 2008 MLC produced a study of asset performance over 109 years. Figures 4.1 and 4.2 provide a view of the volatility of equity, bonds and cash over that period. Figure 4.1 shows the range of volatility in each of the 3 asset classes over a 1-year period. For instance, Australian shares indicate a wide range of plus 67% to a loss of 40% in 1 year, whereas Australian cash has only recorded a range of between plus 1% and 17% in a 1-year period. However, as shown in figure 4.2, the 10-year average annual returns show that Australian shares have a range of between plus 2% and 24%, indicating that the 1-year volatility of Australian shares is evened out over a longer time frame and records the higher returns over the longer time frame compared to Australian bonds and Australian cash.

With an understanding of the variability of returns (volatility), most investors recognise the importance of diversifying their investments to minimise investment risk. In the next section, we examine how diversification actually results in a reduction in risk.

FIGURE 4.1   Range of 1-year returns over the previous 109 years, ending 31 December 2008. The median return is shown by the dashed line.

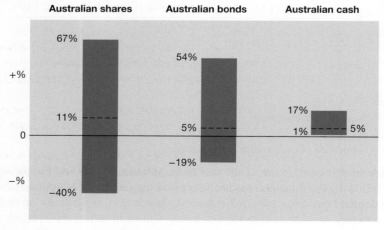

Source: MLC 2008.

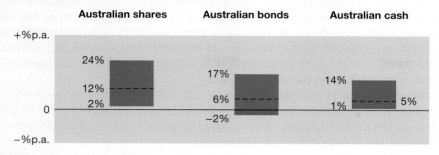

Source: MLC 2008.

Access the 2021 Vanguard Index Chart for 30 years performance from 1991 to illustrate the range of returns shown in both figures 4.1 and 4.2: https://intl.assets.vgdynamic.info/intl/australia/documents/resources/index_chart2021.pdf.

4.4 The benefits of diversification

LEARNING OBJECTIVE 4.4 Understand the benefits of diversification.

How can diversification reduce risk?

As outlined earlier, the risk of a share (the variability of the returns) can be measured by the standard deviation. When a portfolio of shares is held rather than shares in one company only, we have to consider the risk and returns of the portfolio as a whole.

The expected return on a portfolio is simply the weighted average return of the individual shares in the portfolio, where the weights are the fraction of the total portfolio invested in each share.

ILLUSTRATIVE EXAMPLE 4.1

Consider a portfolio that comprises two shares: Share A and Share B.

	Share A	Share B
Expected return	10%	14%
Standard deviation	3%	5%
% of total portfolio	55%	45%

The expected return $E(R)$ for a portfolio comprising 55% Share A and 45% Share B would be as follows.

$$E(R) = 0.55\,(10\%) + 0.45\,(14\%)$$
$$= 11.8\%$$

As you can see, the expected return (mean return) for the portfolio lies between the highest return for all assets in the portfolio and the lowest return for all assets in the portfolio. The minimum possible value of $E(R)$ of 10% occurs when the portfolio contains only Share A. The maximum possible value of $E(R)$ of 14% occurs when the portfolio contains only Share B.

Unlike returns, the riskiness of a portfolio is not simply a weighted average of the standard deviations of the individual shares in the portfolio. Also, the weights used are not simply the fraction of the total portfolio invested in each share. To determine the risk of a portfolio of shares, we need to understand the concept of the correlation between shares. To explain the concept of correlation, consider the following.

When the economy is growing, firms in the building and construction industry tend to do well. Firms which manufacture whitegoods also tend to do well. When the economy is declining, firms in both these industries tend to perform badly. We can say that the returns of these companies tend to move together in the same general direction. When one performs well, the other performs well. When one performs badly, the other performs badly. We can say that the returns from such companies are *positively correlated*.

In a strong economy, the Australian dollar may increase in value. This will have the effect of making our exports more expensive. Firms which rely on exports may not perform as well as they might do in a declining economy. Comparing the performance of companies in the building and construction industry with companies reliant on exports, we may find that when one company performs well, the other performs badly. We could say that the returns of these companies tend to move in the opposite direction. That is, the returns from these companies are *negatively correlated*.

The statistical measure which determines the extent to which two companies are positively or negatively correlated is called the *correlation coefficient*. This measure can take any value between +1 and −1, where +1 indicates that the companies move in exactly the same direction together. A portfolio consisting of two such shares would be just as risky as the individual shares.

A correlation coefficient of −1 would indicate that the two companies move counter-cyclically to each other. When the returns on one share rise, the returns on the other share fall, and vice versa.

With an understanding of the correlation between shares, we can return to the problem of determining the risk of a portfolio of shares. In combining two shares into a portfolio, where the individual shares are quite risky as measured by their standard deviations, it is possible that the risk of the portfolio as a whole will actually be less than the risk of the least risky share in the portfolio. In some situations, it is possible that the portfolio risk can be reduced to close to zero. This will occur when the returns of the shares are perfectly negatively correlated; that is, they have a correlation coefficient of −1.0.

In reality, most shares are positively correlated, but not perfectly so. On average, the correlation coefficient for the returns on two randomly selected shares would lie in the range +0.5 to +0.7. Under such conditions, combining shares into portfolios reduces risk but does not eliminate it completely.

If we return to our previous example, we can see the impact on the portfolio risk (standard deviation of the portfolio) for *different correlation coefficients* between Share A and Share B. (*Note:* The calculations to determine standard deviations of the portfolio are not provided as they are complex and lengthy. Students interested in calculating the standard deviation of a portfolio can find the workings for calculating covariance, correlations and standard deviations in any business finance text.)

	Share A	Share B	Correlation coefficient			
Standard deviation	3%	5%	−1.0%	0.2%	0.6%	1.0%
Portfolio risk (standard deviation of the portfolio)			0.6%	3.0%	3.5%	3.9%

An investor who wants to achieve the mean return of 11.8% by holding a mix of both Share A and Share B will be able to do so, and provided the correlation coefficient between the assets is less than +1.0, the risk of the portfolio will be reduced.

This discussion and illustrative example 4.2 highlight why the concept of diversification for investments is so important. An investment which has a portfolio comprising assets with less than perfectly positive correlation coefficients between the assets will generate weighted average returns but with reduced risk. So, if the correlation coefficient between Shares A and B is 0.2 it means that the standard deviation of the portfolio of the two shares is 3.0%. This is the same risk as having all shares in A, but much less risky than having all shares in B.

ILLUSTRATIVE EXAMPLE 4.2

Consider a different portfolio that comprises two shares: Share C and Share D.

	Share C	Share D
Expected return	10.5%	9.5%
Standard deviation	4.0%	4.0%
% of total portfolio	50.0%	50.0%

In this second example, the expected return for the portfolio comprising both shares is again the weighted average of the returns for each share.

$$E(R) = 0.50\,(10.5\%) + 0.50\,(9.5\%)$$
$$= 10\%$$

The risk of the portfolio will not usually be the weighted average of the risk of each share (4%) but rather it will be less than 4%. Considering several correlation coefficients, notice that except when there is a perfect positive correlation between these two shares, the risk of the portfolio is less than the risk of either individual share.

	Share C	Share D	Correlation coefficient			
Standard deviation	4%	4%	−0.1%	0.2%	0.6%	1.0%
Portfolio risk (standard deviation of the portfolio)			0%	3.1%	3.6%	4%

Again, note that for a correlation coefficient of 0.2 the risk of the portfolio of Shares C and D is 3.1%, which is much below the 4% standard deviation for both Shares C and D; that is, the combination of two riskier shares results in a lower level of risk.

Diversification across asset classes

It is also important to diversify across asset classes — that is, to hold funds in cash, fixed interest, property and shares, because these asset classes are less than perfectly positively correlated. As such, the risk is reduced.

Reilly and Norton (2006) demonstrated the benefits of diversification of asset classes. They placed a $10 000 investment in each of the two investment strategies over a 25-year period. Strategy 1 contained one asset only; Strategy 2 invested $2000 equally in five assets. In Strategy 1, the asset earned an average of 7% p.a. At the end of the period, the total was $54 275 (rounded). Of the five assets in Strategy 2, one asset was a total failure with the $2000 lost completely. The second investment earned no return at all, but the $2000 remained. The third investment earned an average of 5% p.a. over the 25 years. The fourth investment earned an average of 10% p.a. and the fifth investment earned an average of 12% p.a. The total return of the Strategy 2 portfolio is $64 442 (rounded). So, even though some assets performed poorly, the gain of the portfolio containing a number of assets (across asset classes) achieved a return of more than $10 000 over the single asset strategy.

Table 4.2 describes some of the risk, return and correlation attributes associated with the various asset classes. We can see that the asset classes are not perfectly positively correlated and as such we know that the overall risk of the portfolio will be reduced.

The big question, then, revolves around what proportions we place in each asset class. This is an important question because research evidence suggests that this decision is the major determinant of the performance of a portfolio. A study — that has long stood the test of time — by Brinson, Singer and Beebower (1991) examined US pension fund plans and found that the decision as to how much should be allocated between the asset classes explained 91.5% of the variation in a plan's performance. Later studies have confirmed the Brinson, Singer and Beebower finding with similar results.

TABLE 4.2   Risk, return and correlation attributes

	Cash	Fixed interest	Property (direct)	Shares	International investments
Risk (short-term volatility)	Very low	Low	Medium	High	Medium to high but excellent for diversification as natural hedge
Correlation with other asset classes	Low	Low	Low with cash, fixed interest; moderate with shares	Low with cash, fixed interest; moderate with property	Depends on asset class

(continued)

TABLE 4.2 *(continued)*

	Cash	Fixed interest	Property (direct)	Shares	International investments
Returns in the long run	Low	Low to medium	Medium to high	High	Depends on asset class
Ability to beat inflation	Very poor	Poor	Good	Very good	Depends on asset class

Application of the diversification decision

At this stage we need to consider briefly the theory about the best combination of investments for an investor. Figure 4.3 shows a curved line which reflects the trade-off between returns and risk to produce a combination of assets to minimise volatility in a portfolio. If investors limit themselves to low-risk securities, they will be limiting themselves to investments that tend to have low rates of return. So, for better returns, they should include some higher growth, higher risk securities in their portfolio, but combine them in a way so that some of their fluctuations cancel each other out. (In statistical terms, an investor should consider a combined standard deviation that is low, relative to the standard deviations of the individual securities.) The result should provide a high average rate of return, with less of the volatility.

FIGURE 4.3 The efficient frontier

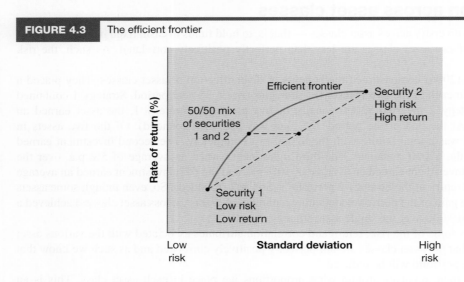

The science of efficient portfolios was based on the research of Harry Markowitz, who received the Nobel Prize for Economic Sciences in 1990. His theory was to assume investors have return and risk data for a collection of securities and they graph the return rates and standard deviations for all the possible combinations of these securities. Markowitz showed that the result will be a region bounded by an upward-sloping, concave curve, which he called the **efficient frontier**. Higgins and Abey (2000) noted that there is no one 'best' portfolio. 'There are, in fact, any number of efficient portfolios, at different points in the trade-off curve'. Thus, in figure 4.4, point A represents the combination of securities that provides the best possible return at the lowest risk. Point B shows the best possible return for the highest risk. Any point along the curve shows the combination of securities that gives the optimal return for the amount of risk that investors would tolerate.

So, for any given value of standard deviation, investors would like to choose a portfolio that gives them the greatest possible rate of return, so they always want a portfolio that lies along the efficient frontier, rather than inside the curve. Inside the curve represents either a lower rate or lower return or both for the particular combination of the two securities. The first important aspect of the efficient frontier is that it identifies where the most efficient portfolios are. The second important aspect of the efficient frontier is that it is a curve. This is the key to how diversification lets investors improve their risk–return ratio. To illustrate, imagine a 50/50 allocation between two securities. Assuming that the performance of these two securities is quite different as their business cycles have not coincided, the standard deviation of the 50/50 allocation will be *less* than the average of the standard deviations of the two securities separately.

Figure 4.4 indicates that this stretches the possible allocations of the two securities from a straight-line relationship *to the left* of the straight line joining the two securities and this forms a curve in the relationship between the two.

FIGURE 4.4 The efficient frontier for a combination of two securities

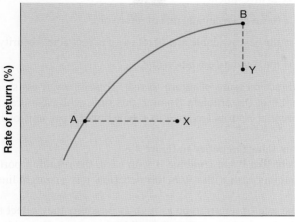

In statistical terms, this effect is due to lack of covariance. This means that the smaller the covariance between the two securities, the smaller the standard deviation of a portfolio that combines them. This indicates a lower level of variation and risk. The ultimate would be to find two securities with *negative* covariance (one security with a very good return and the other with a very poor return).

To explain this further, consider again figure 4.4. The graph shows a conceptual trade-off between risk and return. Points X and Y represent individual securities. The curved line represents the most efficient combination of the investments. Portfolio A is a low risk, low return portfolio for an investor who seeks that level of risk and indicates the best combination to achieve the highest return for that level of risk. Portfolio B is a combination of securities that provides the highest level of return for a higher level of risk that an investor may accept. The individual investments that form the portfolios are less attractive than the portfolios with a combination of each security. Security X produces the same level of return as portfolio A, but with a higher level of risk. Investment Y produces the same level of risk as portfolio B but with a lower level of return. So, the objective of setting an investment strategy requires a trade-off between risk and return to get the best combination that suits the investor.

FIGURE 4.5 Risk and return with the efficient frontier

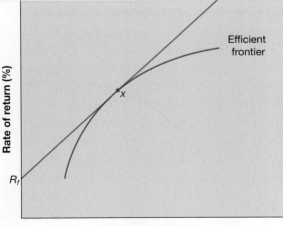

The curve of the efficient frontier shows where the most risk–return efficient portfolios are located but another measure from the field of finance, the Sharpe ratio, identifies the best possible proportions of these securities to use in a portfolio.

The Sharpe ratio is defined as follows.

$$S(x) = \frac{(r_x - R_f)}{StdDev(r_x)}$$

where

x = an investment

r_x = the average annual rate of return of x

R_f = the best available rate of return of a 'risk-free' security (e.g. the cash rate)

$StdDev\left(r_x\right)$ = the standard deviation of r_x

The Sharpe ratio is a direct measure of return to risk. To see how it assists an investor in creating a portfolio, consider figure 4.6 of the efficient frontier, this time with cash drawn in. This ratio indicates the historic average differential returns (relative to a benchmark) per unit of historic variability of the differential return.

There are three important things to notice in figure 4.6.

1. If you take an investment like x and combine it with cash, the resulting portfolio will lie somewhere along the straight line joining cash with x. (On this occasion, it is a straight line and not a curve because cash is riskless.)
2. Since investors want the rate of return to be as high as possible, they select the investment (indicated by x) that gives them the line with the greatest possible slope (as indicated in figure 4.6). The slope of this line is equal to the Sharpe ratio of x. So, in summary, this gives an investor the method for finding the best possible portfolio from this collection of securities. That is, first, find the investment with the highest possible Sharpe ratio. Second, take whatever linear combination of this investment and cash will give an investor the desired value for standard deviation. The result will be the portfolio with the greatest possible rate of return.
3. Markowitz's modern portfolio theory assumes there are only two asset types: risky and risk-free. The key concern for investors is the determination of what proportion of wealth to invest in 'risky' assets and what proportion to invest in 'risk-free' assets. Because of the risk characteristics of cash, fixed interest, property and shares, we can categorise these asset classes as relatively risky or risk-free assets. We can broadly call cash and fixed-interest 'risk-free' assets, although in reality some fixed-interest investments are not risk-free at all. Some fixed-interest securities are subject to credit risk and when interest rates change, substantial gains and losses can be made from investments in traded fixed-interest securities. Cash is not always risk-free either. In this sense, there is always the risk that a cash investment will not outperform inflation. Notwithstanding these limitations, we still consider both cash and fixed-interest securities as 'risk-free' investments within the context of modern portfolio theory. We can broadly call property and shares risky or growth assets. The risky assets have the potential to generate growth in the underlying value of the portfolio.

FIGURE 4.6 Relationship between the efficient frontier and the Sharpe ratio

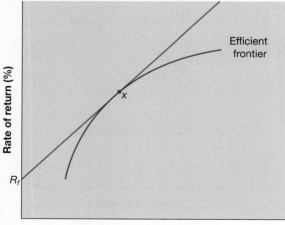

Financial planners need to help their clients make a decision as to what proportion of wealth should be invested in growth assets and what proportion in cash and fixed interest. The asset allocation decision will depend largely on the specific risk attributes of the client. Financial planners should try to help clients become more familiar with the client's own risk characteristics, as the risk characteristics will determine the proportion of the total portfolio that should be invested in cash and fixed interest, and the proportion that should be invested in growth assets. In order to advise on asset allocation, planners need some measure of the client's risk tolerance. Risk profiling by means of questionnaires is discussed in detail in the chapter on the development of a statement of advice. In the following example, assume that we can quantify the client's risk tolerance and establish a standard deviation of portfolio returns that is acceptable to the client. With this information, we can use our understanding of expected return and standard deviation to make the asset allocation decision.

ILLUSTRATIVE EXAMPLE 4.3

Consider two investors, Danielle and Louise, each of whom has $100 000 to invest. Both investors wish to hold a well-diversified portfolio that comprises some cash and fixed interest and some growth assets. They have both selected a growth fund that has an annual expected return of 16% and a standard deviation of 12%. For illustration purposes, assume the return on 90-day Treasury notes is a proxy for the risk-free rate of interest and is 6%. Their concern is in determining the proportion of their investment that they will place in the growth fund and the proportion they will place in cash and fixed interest (risk-free assets). Danielle is relatively risk tolerant and you have been able to determine that she would be comfortable with her total portfolio having a standard deviation of 9%. Louise is relatively risk averse; she is comfortable with a standard deviation in her portfolio of only 5%.

From modern portfolio theory, we can state the risk–return relationship as follows.

$$E\left(R_p\right) = R_f + \left[\frac{E\left(R_{pi}\right) - R_f}{\sigma_{pi}}\right]\sigma_p$$

Where $E\left(R_p\right)$ = expected return on the entire portfolio

$E\left(R_{pi}\right)$ = expected return on the risky fund

σ_p = standard deviation of the entire portfolio

σ_{pi} = standard deviation of the risky fund

R_f = risk-free interest rate

Substituting the values for the risk-free rate, the expected return on the growth fund and the standard deviation of the growth fund, we can express the relationship between the expected return for the entire portfolio and the standard deviation for the entire portfolio.

$$E\left(R_p\right) = R_f + \left[\frac{16\% - 6\%}{12\%}\right]\sigma_p$$
$$= 6\% + 83.3\%\sigma_p$$

Using this formula, we can now substitute Danielle's and Louise's risk tolerances to obtain the proportions of wealth to be included in risky assets (growth assets) and risk-free assets (cash and fixed interest).

Danielle — risk tolerance is 9% standard deviation

$$E\left(R_p\right) = 6\% + 83.3\%\,\sigma_p$$
$$= 6\% + 83.3\%\,(9\%)$$
$$= 13.50\%$$

For a two-asset portfolio (risky assets, risk-free assets), the proportions are:

$$E(R_p) = (X)[E(R_{pi})] + (1 - X)R_f$$

where X = proportion of wealth in risky assets. The equation can be rewritten as follows.

$$E(R_p) = [E(R_{pi}) - R_f]X + R_f$$

If we substitute the expected return for a 9% risk into this model, we obtain the following.

$$13.50\% = [16\% - 6\%]X + 6\%$$

We can rearrange this expression to obtain the solution for X.

$$X = 75\%$$

Thus, 75% will be invested in risky or growth assets. The remaining 25% will be invested in risk-free assets (cash and fixed interest). This combination is the best mix to try to achieve Danielle's target level of 9%.

Louise — risk tolerance is 5% standard deviation
Recall that Louise has a preference for a standard deviation of 5%.

$$E(R_p) = 6\% + 83.3\%\sigma_p$$
$$= 6\% + 83.3\%\,(5\%)$$
$$= 10.17\%$$

Again, for a two-asset portfolio (risky assets, risk-free assets), the proportions are:

$$E(R_p) = (X)[E(R_{pi})] + (1 - X)R_f$$

where X = proportion of wealth in risky assets. The equation can be rewritten as follows.

$$E(R_p) = [E(R_{pi}) - R_f]\,X + R_f$$

Using the values we determined and Louise's expected return:

$$10.17\% = [16\% - 6\%]X + 6\%$$
$$X = 41.7\%$$

Thus 41.7% will be invested in risky or growth assets. The remaining 58.3% will be invested in risk-free assets (cash and fixed interest). This combination should achieve Louise's target risk level of 5%, if future returns mimic past performance.

From this analysis we can summarise the asset allocation decision for Danielle and Louise as follows.

	Cash and fixed interest	Property and shares	Standard deviation of portfolio
Danielle	$25 000	$75 000	9%
Louise	$58 300	$41 700	5%

However, some investors take a different view of investing. They invest in a small number of assets and monitor that small portfolio closely for performance; that is, they say 'put your eggs in a basket and watch that basket!'

4.5 Recent performance of asset classes

LEARNING OBJECTIVE 4.5 Appreciate the performance history of the various asset classes.

In this section, we consider the recent performance of the various classes of assets. The ASX (periodically), many research houses, sharebroking firms, industry associations and fund managers examine the returns from the various asset classes. One set of results is given in table 4.3. Keep in mind that these data reflect diversified portfolios in each asset class. An undiversified portfolio may not perform in a similar manner.

TABLE 4.3   Percentage returns at June 2018 over time

	10 year %	20 year %
Australian shares	4.0	8.8
International shares (hedged)	7.2	7.4
International shares (unhedged)	6.1	5.4
Australian fixed-interest	6.2	5.9
Listed property (A-REITS)	1.8	7.2

| Cash | 3.6 | 4.6 |
| Consumer price index (CPI) | 2.3 | 2.5 |

Source: Adapted from Russell Investments and ASX 2018, pp. 8–9.

These results are more or less what would be expected from finance theory. Over the longer time frames, returns for the risky asset classes are expected to outperform the less risky asset classes because they take more risk. Over the 10- and 20-year time frames, most asset classes experience returns above the CPI to indicate a real rate of return after inflation. The only asset class to fall below inflation are the 10-year performance of A-REITs. But over the 20-year time frame, that asset class has very positive returns on average per annum. The 20-year time frame takes into account a number of business cycles so that where we see the 10-year negative returns in A-REITs we can detect the significant effect of the global financial crisis over the 10-year period. This indicates the different business cycles that the world experiences in terms of short-term performance, but it also indicates the benefit of long-term investment. Note that each year such figures will change on a rolling-time basis. Gradually the severe effects of the 2007–13 period will be diminished and long-term returns will even better reflect the benefit of riskier assets despite the short-term volatility that can depress returns over the shorter time frame.

The 2021 Vanguard Index Chart provides updated returns for most of the items in table 4.3: https://intl.assets.vgdynamic.info/intl/australia/documents/resources/index_chart2021.pdf.

4.6 General investment strategies

LEARNING OBJECTIVE 4.6 Understand general investment strategies.

Investment strategies take a number of forms. Individual investors may use one approach or another; some investors combine the features of several. The initial principle which investors are wise to adopt is *diversification*. Diversification merely reflects the old adage 'don't put all your eggs in one basket' if you don't want to run unnecessary risks. Modern portfolio theory is based on the same premise.

From earlier in this chapter, portfolio theory suggests that risk among a collection of investments, called a portfolio, can be reduced through the judicious selection of appropriate assets. Risk is reduced if the determinants of risk and return among the assets are related to different phenomena. Even more preferable for the risk-averse investor is the case where risk is related to the same underlying determinants but is related in the opposite direction. For example, if the Indonesian economy boomed when the French economy was depressed and vice versa, then an investor could reduce risk by investing in assets in both economies, rather than in one or the other. This reflects the principles of negative correlation.

If diversification is generally considered to be a good thing, then the question arises as to how an investment portfolio should be *allocated* to get the benefits of diversification. As outlined in the discussion of modern portfolio theory previously, investors have to make allocative decisions. Suppose Jane wins $100 000 and decides to invest it. What would she do?

- She might look around and decide not to invest in casinos, coal mining or pine plantations.
- She might decide she is interested in communications, medical technology and banks.

She has, in effect, made some allocative decisions.

The top–down allocation approach is based on the idea that the whole investment scene should be analysed to determine attractive and unattractive areas, for example, sectors likely to enjoy future high growth and potentially depressed sectors, respectively. Once forecasts are made, decisions may then be made about how funds should be split between investment classes and sectors to match each investor's risk preference. For example, an ideal investment spread for an individual may be selected as:

- 40% Australian equities
- 20% international equities
- 30% property
- 10% fixed-interest securities.

Once the allocation decisions are made, the *selection* of appropriate investments, be they Australian listed shares, international shares, properties or fixed-interest securities, involves choosing a few from many thousands of available investments. How does an investor choose appropriate investments? And also, what long-term strategies may be adopted?

Matching investors to products

In portfolio theory, we assume most investors are risk averse, but that investors differ in their degrees of risk averseness. Apart from innate forces which dictate a person's tolerance to risk, it would be reasonable to expect that risk tolerance would be governed by a person's age, income, wealth, gender, years to retirement, past financial experiences and perhaps some other factors. For example, young people are often happy to take on more risk than older people. There are good reasons for this. Youth generally appear to be less risk averse, they have often had less chance of experiencing financial losses when investments have 'gone wrong', and they usually have more years to increase wealth before retirement and thus have more time to recover should things go awry.

Fixed-interest products appeal to more risk-averse people. There are two aspects of this which are worth considering. First, there is the guarantee of the interest payment at a given level, so long as the borrower remains solvent. Selection within this category needs to be carefully scrutinised as many 'guaranteed' products are available. The 'guarantee' offered by some entities may end up being quite worthless. The entity may guarantee the interest and return of capital but, if the entity fails, the 'guarantee' of return of income and capital is only as good as the assets of the entity offering the guarantee. However, overall there is usually little uncertainty about the income from these products. Second, many of these products are capital stable. That is, the value of the capital remains fixed and there is little chance of the loss of capital.

Investment in traded securities such as bonds remains an exception to this rule. A rise in the general level of interest rates will normally promote decreases in the capital values of traded fixed-interest securities. Conversely, holders of these securities will enjoy an appreciation in capital values when the general level of interest rates falls.

Notwithstanding the fact that more risk-averse investors are drawn to fixed-interest products, it is normal for many investors to hold some proportion of fixed-interest securities in their portfolios. The proportions will vary according to the investment strategy. For example, a so-called capital stable portfolio might have 50% fixed interest whereas a growth portfolio may have less than 20%. Host Plus (a superannuation fund for employees in the hospitality, tourism, recreation and sports industries), for example, includes a range of between 30% and 50% fixed-interest and like securities in its conservative portfolio mixes. Other funds managers may include different proportions in their portfolios, according to their assessments of their clients' risk preferences and the investment choices of the managers of the different portfolios in the fund.

Few investors with reasonable wealth do not own their own homes. Property thus often occupies a major position in possibly a majority of portfolios, as we saw earlier. Apart from the family home, property investment appeals to people because of its tangibility and its familiarity. In addition, people are aware that property values generally keep pace with inflation. Thus, unless investors are forced to sell during a downturn in the property cycle, they are likely to retain the purchasing power of their funds and can indeed make large capital gains. In terms of the risk–return trade-off, property appeals to people who can tolerate moderate risk, who are looking for medium rates of return and who have a medium- to long-term investment horizon.

Investors who favour the share market are generally less risk averse than those who favour property, and certainly much less risk averse than those who favour fixed-interest products. However, the range of shares is so large that a wide range of risk averseness can be accommodated by the appropriate selection of shares. An investor wanting relatively lower risk, for example, might select a share in the consumables or retail sector, a class of listed investments which typically shows only small price variations. In contrast, the prices of biotechnology shares and mining stocks have varied tremendously in recent times.

Gibson (2000) studied the effects of **multiple-asset class investing** over a period of 26 years between 1972 and 1998. He used different portfolios of asset classes using cash, bonds, property (REITs) and shares. His research concluded that by using a combination of all four asset classes over a period of time, an investor would achieve a higher long-term average return with a lower level of risk. Gibson discovered that the combination of the four asset classes resulted in a compound average return of 13.77% compared with 13.61%, 13.30% and 12.46%, respectively, for portfolios of three, two and one asset classes. In addition, he found the risk of the portfolios was significantly decreased by holding the four asset classes. The standard deviation for the four-asset class portfolio was 10.55% whereas the standard deviations for the three-, two- and one-asset class portfolios were 11.92%, 14.45% and 20.04%, respectively. The lower risk of the four-asset class portfolio was confirmed by Sharpe ratios. The Sharpe ratios were: 0.66, 0.60, 0.50 and 0.37, respectively, for the four-, three-, two- and one-asset class portfolios. The Sharpe ratio calculation indicates a volatility-adjusted performance for each portfolio with the higher figure representing a higher risk-adjusted return.

Overall, an investor is faced with a vast range of investment choices and combinations. The determination of a strategy is the first step, followed by the combination of asset classes, and then by the selection of components of each asset class.

4.7 Behavioural finance

LEARNING OBJECTIVE 4.7 Gain an awareness of behavioural finance.

The traditional view of studying markets is that there is an assumption that the market is efficient. That means all publicly available information that exists about that company or product is known to all participants in the market and the price determined is an interaction between buyers and sellers. Efficient-market theory, modern portfolio theory and asset-pricing relationships (such as the capital asset pricing model or CAPM) between risk and return are all built on the assumption that investors are rational.

However, over the past 30 years, a number of academics have researched the concept of a relatively inefficient market. They have questioned the rationality of investor behaviour and developed a discipline of studies in behavioural finance. Olsen (1998) wrote that behavioural finance 'seeks to understand and predict systematic financial market implications of psychological decision processes ... behavioural finance is focused on the implication of psychological and economic principles for the improvement of financial decision making.' They have pointed to the bubbles that have occurred in economic history and argued that the occasional huge rise in prices could not have been the result of efficient or rational behaviour. One such bubble is the US dot.com bubble of 2000. In early 2000, analysts were predicting that stock returns would be in the order of 15–25% p.a. over the next few years in response to the rapid and widespread use of the internet. Some companies, keen to get into the market, sold themselves to investors as the next 'hot stocks' as they provided the means to ride on the back of the internet revolution. When many of those companies were trading at 100 times earnings or more (price/earnings ratio), a crash was soon on the horizon. For example, Amazon.com traded at a high US$75.25 in 2000 but fell to US$5.51 in 2001–02 (a percentage decline of almost 93%). Many companies who started late in the 1990s to cash in on the new craze did not survive the crash and went out of business.

What history shows is that there are many periods when markets reached dizzying heights and then crashed to regain a more normal pattern for a few years. Students might care to research Dutch Tulip mania in 1636–37 and the South Seas bubble of 1720. These examples indicate that there are times when investors are less than rational.

PERSONAL FINANCE BULLETIN

Behavioural finance: when what you see is all there is

Imagine a coin is flipped 20 times and heads comes up every time. You're given a large sum of money to bet on the next flip. What would you call?

Many of us would call tails on the basis that it seems 'due'. After all, if a coin is flipped 21 times, then the probability of 21 heads is 1 in 2 097 152. Intuitively, we know that such streaks have low and declining probability. Critically, however, this has no bearing on the next flip of the coin. The coin, much like the roulette wheel that has had a run of red numbers, has no memory. The probability of flipping a head after 20 heads in a row is the same as always: 1/2.

The flawed thinking that draws many of us to tails is known as the gambler's fallacy. The mistake is to expect to see what happens over a much larger (or infinite) sample of flips to be represented at a much smaller sample size. For instance, the coin-toss sequence H-T-H-T-T-H would be considered more likely by many people than H-H-H-T-T-T, simply because it seems more random, or more representative of a random process.

The gambler's fallacy is just one example of a broader cognitive trap known as representativeness. It describes our willingness to judge events by how they appear rather than by how likely they actually are according to the rules of probability. We use stereotypes, individualising or unrepresentative information at the expense of more accurate, yet complex calculations that we think are the sole realm of the statistician. The latter require careful thinking by the rational, calculating part of our brains and the evidence from behavioural surveys is that we much prefer jumping to conclusions than carrying out the math.

The different way our minds treat readily available information and information that is unknown or hard to get is described by behavioural psychologist Daniel Kahneman in the acronym WYSIATI or 'What you ▶

In 1979, the efficient market theory was challenged by two psychologists, Daniel Kahneman and Amos Tversky, who argued that people, at times, display some irrational behaviours. Since then, behavioural finance studies have identified and quantified a number of factors found to create irrational investor behaviour. We will consider some of such factors in the following sections.

Loss aversion

Kahneman and Tversky (1979) described individual behaviour in the face of risky situations where investors faced the prospect of gains and losses. Hence, they termed their theory 'prospect theory'. They argued that individuals place different values on gains and losses, and discovered that losses are considered far more undesirable than the desire for equivalent gains and this was termed **loss aversion**. They conducted experiments based on a gamble of winning $100 or losing $100. They found that losses were 2.5 times more undesirable as equivalent gains were desirable. Even when there was a choice of two losses — a sure loss of $75 or a 75% chance to lose $100 and a 25% chance to lose nothing — they found that people chose to take the gamble.

The studies of behaviour in taking a risk with losses were extended when the trading records of some 10 000 clients were studied and a 'disposition effect' was observed. That is, there was a clear disposition among investors to sell their winning stocks and to hold on to their losing stocks. Selling a stock that had risen enabled an investor to realise a profit. If they sold their losing stocks, they would realise a loss which hurt more than could be offset by the equivalent gain. In fact, investors with losing stocks tended to hold on to them in the hope (the gamble) that the stocks would recover. Hence, it was observed that investors have an aversion to losses which is counter to the efficient market and the rational investor theories. Efficient investor behaviour may be seen in an example where it would be advantageous for an investor to plan to sell losing stocks to offset the capital gains tax levied on winning stocks that they have sold and then later, if they believed that the losing stocks would eventually recover, they could repurchase the losing stocks before that recovery. Yet there seems to be a reluctance to implement this strategy as it would mean realising a loss.

Prospect theory may also be seen in practice in the large number of people who decided not to take any action to change their superannuation investments when 'choice of fund' legislation was passed. No action in such a choice was seen to be an avoidance of a potential loss situation.

Herding

Some behavioural finance research indicates that groups tend to make better decisions than individuals, known as **herding**. This is based on the belief that if information is shared and all points of view are considered then, on balance, the wisdom of the group prevails in the decision-making process. This may provide a well-informed market and result in a relatively efficient market. Yet, group behaviour may lead to incorrect decision making and turn into 'group think'. This was illustrated by a study where a person stood on a street corner and looked up at the sky. A few people stopped to look up too but when five people stood and looked up the number of observers grew four times. When the researcher placed 15 people on the corner, almost every passer-by looked up. The 2000 dot.com bubble was an example of when people made incorrect decisions and acted as a herd, forcing prices up to unrealistic levels. Many did not want to miss out on the action and bought stocks on the basis that they were rising and would keep on rising.

Robert Shiller, author of *Irrational Exuberance* (2000), noted that the process feeds on itself in a 'positive feedback loop'. Fund managers are not immune from this behaviour: as the market rises, more investors may pour more funds into managed funds which may be seen to encourage the managers to invest further into a rising market when their other instincts may suggest that they should not. It is suggested that they may also succumb to the herd mentality despite their investment management responsibilities.

Overconfidence

Research indicates that people deviate from rational thinking in making judgements where there is an element of uncertainty. This can be seen in the overconfidence sometimes portrayed by people about their own personal beliefs and abilities or an overoptimistic view of the future.

Experiments where a class of students was asked about their level of competence in relation to the average driver in the group invariably resulted in about 80–90% of students estimating that they were above the average. Other experiments indicate that 25% of the class believed they were in the top 1% of the population in terms of getting along with others and in judging athletic ability, and at least 60% of the students believed they were in the top quartile. Such results have also been observed to explain investor behaviour. The results indicate that many individual investors are mistakenly convinced that they can beat the market. As a result, they tend to speculate more than they should and end up trading too much. In fact, research by Barber and Odean (2001) studying the trading records of a large discount broker discovered that, the more individual investors traded, the worse they did. The researchers also found that male traders did worse than female traders.

The fact that many investors exhibit levels of overconfidence may be based on hindsight bias; that is, it is argued that investors tend to have a selective memory of their own successes which translates into any future success being perceived as the result of their own attributes. Investors then rationalise that poor results were the product of external events over which they had no control. Observers of market performance note that there tends to be an overvaluation of 'growth' stocks because many investors think that those stocks will perform better and hence put their money into such stocks and drive the prices higher. When the forecasts of some stocks are not realised and the projected earnings are subdued, investors may decide to seek better value elsewhere and sell such stocks. Thus, the prices of such growth stocks are likely to record a fall in value and then, as often happens when projections are not realised, may underperform the more solid stocks (with less expectations of rapid growth) otherwise known as 'value' stocks.

Biased judgements

Biased judgements refers to when investors' decisions are sometimes clouded by a bias which runs against sound probabilistic thinking. An illustration of this is shown in the famous Tversky and Kahneman (1982) experiment where a description was given of a young lady. The young lady was aged 31, single, outspoken and very bright. She majored in philosophy and, as a student, she was deeply concerned with issues of discrimination and social justice. She also participated in anti-nuclear demonstrations. Participants in the experiment were then asked to rate different statements about her. One statement was that she 'was a bank teller' and another was that she 'was a bank teller and active in the feminist movement'. More than 85% of participants judged that she 'was both a bank teller and active in the feminist movement' rather than simply a 'bank teller'. In terms of probability theory, the probability that somebody belongs to both category A and category B is more than or equal to the probability that she belongs to category A alone. Because the description of the young lady made her seem like a feminist, the choice that she was both a bank teller and a feminist was perceived as being more representative of her than just being a bank teller.

This 'representativeness' leads to a number of other biases in investors' judgement such as investors who chase 'hot funds' (those that have performed well in the past year or so) or who extrapolate from recent evidence. The bias towards investing in housing in the United States (prior to the global financial crisis) was seen in comments made by advisers that 'house prices never go down!'

PROFESSIONAL ADVICE

Max was having coffee with two of his old school friends, James and Simon, and the conversation turned to the share market. Both James and Simon said that they had bought into Slick Oil Company when the price per share was 25 cents and now the shares were worth $30 each.

'Wow,' said Max. 'That's for me. I'll buy some!'

James said that the shares were still on the rise even though the company had not paid a dividend yet, and that the company was sure to declare a distribution soon. Simon said the price–earnings ratio was ▶

---

about 120 to 1 but that was not really anything to worry about as it was a growth stock and did not need to worry about earnings in the short term.

....

QUESTIONS

1. What sort of investor behaviour do you think Max is exhibiting?

2. What sort of investor behaviour do you think James and Simon are exhibiting?

3. What advice would you offer to the three friends?

Two behavioural economists, Hersh Shefrin and Meir Statman (2000), suggested that most investors seek to balance security with the small chance of winning the lottery. They proposed a behavioural portfolio based on mental accounts formed into a layered pyramid with each layer treated as a separate mental account. The base layers represent assets designed to be highly secure and protected from loss. The higher layers represent risky assets which are invested in the hope of high returns. This explains why some investors may buy shares in blue-chip companies and also some small-cap shares. They want the security of the solid and consistent performing large company and the riskiness of the new small company. The layers of riskiness of the mental accounts may also be seen in the context of diversification.

4.8 Investment scams

LEARNING OBJECTIVE 4.8 Develop an awareness of investment scams.

This chapter is concerned with investment choices. So, it would be remiss if we did not consider the lessons from the past about investment schemes that have been promoted to investors and have, instead of being valid investment opportunities, in fact been **investment scams**. The following examples are sourced from MoneySmart, the Australian Securities and Investments Commission's (ASIC) financial tips and safety checks website (https://moneysmart.gov.au). The website lists scams relating to investors; superannuation; banking and credit; other scams; how to avoid and report scams and how to recover losses.

Some factors are common to all investment scams, such as:
- they do not have a product disclosure document
- they promise high returns
- most require the prospective investee to provide a password or bank account details
- the investments are often based overseas or must be kept a 'secret', presumably so other people don't find out about the offer and invest as well.

The simplest, yet most effective (devastating) scams perpetrated on unsuspecting investors for many years have been 'Ponzi' schemes. Such schemes require only a few victims in their early stages to be successful. The promoter promises a very high return on the investment and says it is secure. Part of the money deposited by early investors is then used to pay the first dividend cheques or interest payments. The victims are more than happy to receive high dividends. The scammer continues paying dividends for a couple of months until the investors are more comfortable with their investments, and decide to invest more. Investors typically then begin to urge their friends and relatives to invest as well, usually at the behest of the promoter of the scheme. Soon there is a steady flow of funds into the scheme and the number of investors grows. (The classic and largest Ponzi scheme which came unstuck during the global financial crisis concerned the fund management activities of Bernard Madoff. Search the internet for details.) See the ASIC Podcast Episode 47 *The Power of a Ponzi Scheme*.

Provided the scammer is disciplined about how much money is left in the account to pay 'interest' or 'dividends', the scam can continue for years. Theoretically, if the scheme continues to draw in new investors, it could go on indefinitely. In practice such schemes generally fall over because the promoter starts to spend the money too quickly or the pool of investors starts to decline. A classic Ponzi scheme was operated by Mr. M who offered people investment returns of between 3% and 6% per month. Mr. M's illegal scheme received $216.9 million from investors who ultimately lost $76 million. Many of the investors were from the local community who became aware of the scheme through family and friends. This is typical of how many people become involved in a Ponzi scheme. Mr. M served a 5-year jail term.

Another scheme in recent times concerns 'Nigerian letter scams' where letters or emails are sent from a person claiming to represent a government agency in Nigeria. The letter asks the person to give their bank account details so that their bank account can be used for offloading many millions of dollars offshore — for which the person will be paid a generous commission. ASIC's advice is to ignore these letters and not to give the scammers any banking details. All that happens is that the scammer withdraws the balance out of the person's account. ASIC reports that at least six people who provided their account details travelled to Nigeria to investigate the scheme and were murdered.

Bushfire relief scams

In early 2020, there were a wide range of appeals raising funds for people and animals affected by the bushfires. Unfortunately, some of these were scams.

Scammers pretended to be legitimate charities and even impersonated people impacted by the bushfires. They used cold-calling, direct messaging and social media to raise funds (ACCC 2020).

Details can be found at www.scamwatch.gov.au/news/bushfires-and-scams.

Other scams

The Australian Competition and Consumer Commission (ACCC) publish a little black book that provides examples of scams. Examples of such scams are as follows.

Scams targeting computers and mobile devices

How the scam works

Remote access scammers call you on the phone claiming that your computer is infected by viruses. If you follow their instructions, it will allow them to access and control your computer where they can steal information or install malware. They may also try to convince you to purchase 'anti-virus' software, which usually turns out to be overpriced or freely available on the internet.

Malware is a term for any malicious software that can be installed on your computer or other devices including viruses, spyware, ransomware, trojan horses and keystroke loggers.

Keystroke loggers and spyware allow scammers to record exactly what you type on your keyboard to find out passwords and bank details or access personal information and send this anywhere they want. Once installed, scammers can control your email and social media accounts and grab whatever information is on your device, including passwords. They can also use your accounts to send more scams to your friends and family.

Investment and superannuation scams

Investment scams come in many forms including cryptocurrency purchase, binary options trading, business ventures, superannuation schemes, managed funds and the sale or purchase of shares or property. Scammers dress up 'opportunities' with professional looking brochures and websites to mask their fraudulent operations. They often begin with a phone call or email out of the blue from a scammer offering a 'not-to-be-missed', 'high return' or 'guaranteed' opportunity. The scammer usually operates from overseas, and will not have an Australian Financial Services licence.

Superannuation scams offer to give you early access to your super fund, often through a self-managed super fund or for a fee. The scammer may ask you to agree to a story to allow the early release of your money and then, acting as your financial adviser, they will deceive your superannuation company into paying out your super benefits directly to them. Once they have your money, the scammer may take large 'fees' or leave you with nothing at all.

Source: ACCC 2016, pp. 6, 8, 16.

Despite warnings about the scam nature of the investment, many people hang on to the belief that there is gold at the end of the rainbow and are prepared to take the risk. Even when alerted to the fact the money may have been transferred from their account, some people insist on the fact that the promised rewards will arrive. All consumers need to be aware of basic risk and return principles and be prepared to treat such offers with scepticism.

4.9 Information sources for investment choices

LEARNING OBJECTIVE 4.9 Identify information sources for investment choices.

When an investor undertakes their own research into appropriate investments, they will be confronted with a wide range of information. The information can be considered in different categories:
* the economy — current and forecast economic conditions, both domestic and international
* the industry — background, competitors and outlook for a particular industry sector

- the institution/company — specific information about the background and prospects for an institution or company
- prices/quotations — current prices and the recent trend in prices/quotations of the specific investment alternatives.
  Investors may gain information from a number of sources which include:
- ASIC's website
- the business sections of the daily newspapers and finance journals
- monthly magazines focusing on investments and strategies
- government publications such as the Reserve Bank Bulletin
- securities exchange releases
- annual reports issued by companies and institutions
- analysts' reports usually available by subscription or through stockbrokers
- published industry data
- ASX prices
- the internet using a search engine to find investment information websites, some of which may be free but otherwise by subscription.

SUMMARY

There are many forms of investment, offering various promises of return and carrying varying degrees of risk. Investors carry their own individual attitudes to the risk and return features of investing. Whether investing directly or indirectly, an investor needs to understand the basic features of the asset class. To consider investment choices, an investor should have an appreciation of the risk and return relationship to understand that the higher the return the higher the level of risk. Risk may be reduced by diversification of assets. Efficient market theory describes the trade-off required between risk and return for the most efficient investment portfolio to achieve the highest return for a given level of acceptable risk by an investor. The risks and returns for each investment category also need to be understood in terms of recent performance history and time frames. Such an understanding is fundamental to adopting a suitable investment strategy. However, an investor's strategy may be influenced by certain types of investor behaviour. Behavioural finance research has found various reasons that many investors may not behave rationally in their investment choices at all times. A number of common investment scams take advantage of this fact.

KEY TERMS

biased judgements Investors' decisions are sometimes affected by a bias against or towards something.

efficient frontier The curved line that represents the optimal mix of return and risk for a portfolio of investments given a required level of risk.

herding When an individual follows group behaviour in the belief that the group has made the right decision.

investment scam An investment opportunity that is promoted to investors which has no substance other than to benefit the promoter of the investment.

loss aversion Investors place more value on losing than gaining.

multiple-asset class investing A mixture of asset classes in an investment portfolio.

property An investment into the asset class that covers real estate in its many forms.

shares An investment holding in a company.

standard deviation A measure of the riskiness of an investment.

PROFESSIONAL APPLICATION QUESTIONS

4.1 What are the main differences between a 'conservative' and an 'aggressive' investor?

4.2 What are the general features of a fixed-interest investment?

4.3 What is the significance of a standard deviation and how would you explain its meaning to a client? Write your response as if you were drafting a letter to a client.

4.4 Why does a diversified portfolio rely on assets that are negatively correlated?

4.5 What was the main feature of Gibson's findings about multi-asset class investing?

4.6 What is meant by the explanation that investors treat gains and losses differently as described by the 'loss aversion' view of investor behaviour?

4.7 Consider the following investments and rank them based on Shefrin and Statman's proposition about how people think about investing: buying a $20 000 car, buying a $300 000 property, buying a $50 lottery ticket, investing $20 000 in a fixed interest security, investing $20 000 in new technology stocks. Rank the investments in order of most secure to riskiest. Explain your ranking.

4.8 What are the four main factors identified as common to all investment scams?

4.9 From your reading of this chapter, write a short briefing memo to Ava (from the opening case study) about the key investment messages that she should consider when investing over the next few years.

PROFESSIONAL APPLICATION EXERCISES

★ BASIC | ★★ MODERATE | ★★★ CHALLENGING

4.10 Designing a suitable portfolio ★

Access the Vanguard 'Asset class tool' which shows the annual returns for selected asset classes ranked in order of performance in each year: https://insights.vanguard.com.au/static/asset-class/app.html

Construct a suitable investment portfolio for an investor who is considered to be a 'balanced' investor using the Australian asset classes listed and applying a percentage to each category to be included in the portfolio, Then calculate the average return from 2009 to the current year.

4.11 The ASX website ★

(a) Prepare a table of the sectors under the GICS and search the ASX website to nominate two companies that fit into each sector.

(b) Identify the P/E ratios and year highest and lowest prices for each company.

(c) Select one of the sectors and research the two companies you have nominated to explore their similarities and differences.

4.12 Investment advice ★★

Examine the following returns of the portfolios of two investors, Emerald and Diamond.

	Year 1	Year 2	Year 3	Year 4	Year 5
Emerald	10%	18%	7%	9%	23%
Diamond	11%	16%	6%	9%	19%

(a) Calculate the expected returns for both Emerald and Diamond.

(b) Calculate the standard deviations for both Emerald and Diamond.

(c) Discuss which is the riskiest portfolio to invest in.

4.13 Nominal and real rates of return ★★

Benedict told his friend Henry that he expected to receive an investment return of 9.5%. Henry suggested to his friend that 9.5% might not actually be the real return on the investment. Henry told Benedict that he had forgotten to consider the effect of inflation.

(a) Calculate the real rate of return for Benedict if inflation was 3.4%.

(b) Suppose the rate of return of another investment that Benedict was considering was 4.5%. What then would be the real rate of return?

4.14 Return expected from a portfolio ★★★

Assume a portfolio has two investment choices as per below.

	Apples	Oranges
Expected return	7%	13%
Standard deviation	3%	8%
Percentage of portfolio	70%	30%

Calculate the expected return for the portfolio.

4.15 Portfolio efficiency ★★★

The figure indicates two different portfolio choices, A and B. Explain why portfolio A is less efficient than portfolio B.

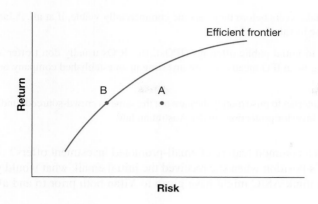

4.16 Choosing a portfolio ★★★

The figure below indicates two different portfolio choices, C and D. Explain why portfolio D is the preferred option to portfolio C.

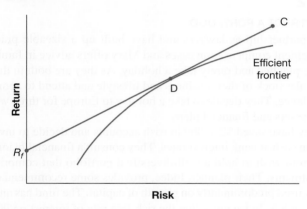

4.17 The behaviour of an irrational investor ★★★

'Herding' and 'loss aversion' have been identified as two forms of behaviour that indicate that investors do not always act rationally in making investment decisions. Write a brief memo to explain each one.

CASE STUDY 1

AN INVESTMENT OPPORTUNITY NOT TO BE MISSED

Yifan was attracted to an email inviting her to invest in an initial coin offering (ICO). She received information about the ICO and the project that it is funding with an outline of the likely profits to be earned by the project. The deal was that, by investing in an ICO, she would receive digital tokens related to the project that was on offer. Yifan considered that the likely returns were worth the risk of investing as the tokens may rise in value.

Moneysmart (n.d.) provides the following information.

How initial coin offerings (ICOs) work

An ICO is a way a project can raise money over the internet. You invest in an ICO by sending money or cryptocurrency to a blockchain project. In return you receive digital tokens related to that project.

ICOs are speculative, high-risk investments. Many ICOs are for projects that:

• are experimental
• are at a very early stage of development
• may not have even started yet.

Some projects may take years before they become commercially viable, if at all. A large number of ICOs fail or do not increase in value.

ICOs sound similar to initial public offerings (IPOs). But ICOs usually don't offer any legal rights and protections. Investing in an IPO means you are investing in an established company or asset, rather than a project.

While ICOs use the internet to raise money they are not the same as crowd-sourced funding. Crowd-sourced funding offers basic investor protections under Australian law.

QUESTIONS

1 What do you think is a common feature of email-promoted investment offers?
2 If you were in Yifan's position when she received the initial email, what would you have done?
3 What advice do you think ASIC might have given to Yifan both prior to and after Yifan had invested her money?
4 Write a note of advice that you could give someone who is faced with a similar tempting offer.

CASE STUDY 2

MARY AND ANDY CONSTRUCT A PORTFOLIO

Mary and Andy are in partnership as lawyers and have built up a sizeable practice over a number of years. Andy works in accident compensation cases and Mary offers advice in family law. They both work exceptionally hard in the practice and rarely take a holiday. As they are both in their mid-forties, a friend has suggested that they take stock of their business and lifestyle and attend to some of the things in life to restore some sense of balance. They decide to take a holiday to Europe for three weeks and to take a week to review their personal assets and financial plans.

They discover that they have saved $250 000 in cash accounts and decide to invest the funds to achieve a better rate of return than cash at bank interest rates. They consult a financial planner who discovers at the joint meeting that they both wish to hold a well-diversified portfolio that comprises cash, fixed-interest, property and share investments. Their planner, Indee, provides some recommendations for them and they agree on a fund that is focused predominantly on growth of capital. The fund has an expected return of 12% and a standard deviation of 8%. Indee notes that the risk-free rate of interest on 90-day Treasury bonds is currently 3% and both Andy and Mary agree that they are prepared to take some risks in achieving capital growth over the next 5 years. They know that they will both continue to work in the practice for at least 10 more years. However, they still want to maintain some measure of stability in their investment and do not want to subject their $250 000 completely to the wide swings of property and share investments. They discuss this matter with Indee. Their concern is in determining the proportion of their investment that they will place in the growth fund and the proportion they will place in risk-free assets, namely cash and fixed interest.

Mary is relatively risk tolerant compared with Andy, and Indee has been able to determine that Mary would be comfortable with her total portfolio having a standard deviation of 7%. Andy is relatively risk averse in contrast to Mary and is more comfortable with a standard deviation in the portfolio of only 6%.

QUESTIONS

1 Using the formula for the risk–return relationship calculate the expected return for the portfolio and the standard deviation for the portfolio.
2 Using the results from (1), substitute Mary's risk tolerances to obtain the portions of funds to be included in risky assets (property and shares) and risk-free assets (cash and fixed interest).
3 Using the results from (1), substitute Andy's risk tolerances to obtain the portions of funds to be included in risky assets (property and shares) and risk-free assets (cash and fixed interest).
4 From the results calculated in your analysis, prepare a table as indicated below to summarise the asset allocation decision for Andy and Mary.

	Cash and fixed interest $	Property and shares $	Standard deviation of portfolio
Mary			
Andy			

REFERENCES

ACCC 2016, *The little black book of scams: a pocket-sized guide so you can spot, avoid, and protect yourself against scams*, Commonwealth of Australia, https://www.accc.gov.au/about-us/publications/the-little-black-book-of-scams

ACCC 2020, 'Bushfires and scams', Scamwatch, 6 January, www.scamwatch.gov.au/news/bushfires-and-scams.

ASIC 2019, Podcast Episode 47 *The Power of a Ponzi Scheme*, https://asic.podbean.com/e/episode-47-the-power-of-a-ponzi-scheme/

Barber, BM & Odean, T 2001, 'Boys will be boys: gender, overconfidence, and common stock investment', *Quarterly Journal of Economics*, February, pp. 261–92.

Bogle, J 1994, *Bogle on mutual funds*, Irwin, Chicago.

Brinson, GP, Singer, BD & Beebower, GL 1991, 'Determinants of portfolio performance II: an update', *Financial Analysis Journal*, May–June.

Fidelity International 2018, 'Behavioural finance: when what you see is all there is', 13 June, https://www.fidelity.com.au/insights/investment-articles/behavioural-finance-when-what-you-see-is-all-there-is/

Gibson, R 2000, *Asset allocation — balancing financial risk*, Irwin, New York.

Graham, B 1949, *The intelligent investor*, HarperCollins, New York.

Higgins, E & Abey, A 2000, *Fortune strategy*, 2nd edn, Allen & Unwin, Sydney.

Kahneman, D & Tversky, A 1979, 'Prospect theory: an analysis of decision under risk', *Econometrica*, vol. 47, no. 2, pp. 263–92.

MLC 2008, 'How much returns vary through time', www.mlc.com.au.

Olsen, RA 1998, 'Behavioural finance and its implications for stock-price volatility', *Financial Analysts Journal*, vol. 54, no. 2, March–April, pp. 10–18.

Reilly, FK & Norton, EA 2006, *Investments*, 7th edn, Thomson South-Western, Mason.

Russell Investments & ASX 2018, 2018 Russell Investments/ASX long term investing report: the journey matters as much as the destination: June 2018, www.asx.com.au/documents/research/russell-asx-long-term-investing-report-2018.pdf.

Shefrin, H & Statman, M 2000, 'Behavioral portfolio theory', *Journal of Financial and Quantitative Analysis*, vol. 35, no. 2, pp. 127–51.

Shiller, R 2000, *Irrational exuberance*, Princeton University Press.

Tversky, A & Kahneman, D 1982, 'Judgments of and by representativeness', in D Kahneman, P Slovic & A Tversky (eds), *Judgment under uncertainty: heuristics and biases*, Cambridge University Press, pp. 84–98.

Vanguard Investments 2023, 'Realistic sharemarket expectations', https://www.vanguard.com.au/adviser/learn/insights/markets-and-economy/setting-realistic-expectations-vanguard-asset-class-forecasts-2024

ACKNOWLEDGEMENTS

Figures 4.1 and 4.2: © MLC

Extract: © Russell Investments

CHAPTER 5

Fixed interest, shares and property

LEARNING OBJECTIVES

After studying this chapter, you should be able to:

5.1 distinguish between cash and fixed-interest securities

5.2 understand the nature of, and participants in, the fixed-interest investment market

5.3 understand the different forms of fixed-interest investments

5.4 appreciate the difference between discount and coupon securities and the effect of a change in interest rates

5.5 understand the nature of, and participants in, the share market

5.6 consider the influences on share prices

5.7 understand the capital asset pricing model (CAPM)

5.8 apply some basic valuation models to value shares

5.9 appreciate the existence of other forms of direct investment

5.10 outline the qualities and characteristics of property for investment

5.11 describe the different forms of property investment

5.12 describe the features and benefits of property funds

5.13 explain the taxation effects of investing in property

5.14 apply valuation methods to an investment in property.

Lila, now aged 28, graduated as a medical doctor and after three years working in a city-based hospital she decided to gain more medical and surgical experience by spending a year in the Antarctic as a medical officer on a government-sponsored scientific expedition. As a very busy person while working at the city hospital, Lila had not attended to all her personal financial affairs and her savings had accumulated to about $30 000 which she had sitting in a savings account held at her bank. In the week before she left, she transferred her savings to a 12-month term deposit at the same bank.

While Lila was in the Antarctic she gained the benefit of being in a low income-tax zone and much of her salary was saved because meals, accommodation and other items were supplied. So, at the end of her year away, she arrived home knowing that her savings had grown by another $100 000.

Lila now wants to offer her medical skills in a new field and has decided to work for the next 12 months in Africa with Médecins Sans Frontières. However, before she starts work she has decided to better order her finances and consults a financial planner about her savings and what alternatives she has. She is not interested in acquiring a property yet but wants her savings to grow more than the inflation level that eats into the value of her savings.

She consults Rebecca, a financial planner. Rebecca discusses matters of riskiness of investments with Lila and suggests that Lila is a reasonably conservative investor but willing to invest in shares that are in the top 50 companies. Lila's first thought is to maintain her term deposits with her bank but Rebecca suggests that instead of remaining as a customer of the bank she could become an owner of the bank by buying some bank shares.

Lila's situation raises some issues to consider about direct investments. These include:
- whether to hold fixed-interest securities directly
- whether to hold shares of the riskier securities directly
- the risks and opportunities of investing directly in the fixed-interest market
- the risks and opportunities of investing directly in the share market.

This chapter will explore these issues.

Introduction

This chapter deals mainly with direct investment into three main asset classes — fixed-interest securities, equities or shares, and property — and considers the investment issues of other forms of direct investment. Direct investment occurs when investors make their own decisions about where funds are ultimately placed, be it in fixed-interest deposit accounts, shares, property or some other form of asset. The opposite case occurs when investors place their funds with funds managers who use vehicles such as unit trusts and master funds to consolidate the funds of many investors and then invest the pooled funds according to their own stated investment strategies. A managed fixed-interest fund is a pooled investment in which the manager invests in a range of fixed-interest securities. Likewise, a share fund is where a manager invests in a range of shares and manages that portfolio by buying and selling shares to make a profit. A property fund is one in which a number of properties is held for both income producing purposes and **capital gain**.

Most people have an account at a financial institution where some savings or working funds are kept. Also, many people own shares directly such as in Telstra or the Commonwealth Bank as a result of subscribing for shares when government-owned institutions became public companies. Many people also own shares directly in a wide variety of companies, in industries including mining, retailing, banking and pharmaceuticals as part of their portfolio mix of investments. Many people have a direct investment in property being their own home. Yet others may own more than one property as their preferred choice of direct investment. Some people prefer to hold some investments in the form of coins, collectable items or works of art. These too are direct forms of investment and may have some different features even though investors hold such investments to achieve long-term capital appreciation. For example, collectables differ in an investment sense, in that they often suffer from a market that has too few buyers (otherwise known as a 'thin' market), are relatively scarce and they may suffer from theft or deterioration.

Each section of the chapter attempts to give an appreciation of the nature and structure of the relevant markets, the participants in the markets and the products on offer.

5.1 Cash and fixed-interest securities

LEARNING OBJECTIVE 5.1 Distinguish between cash and fixed-interest securities.

Deregulation of the Australian financial system accelerated in the early 1980s in response to global financial forces. Deregulation was the removal of many legal controls and regulations which had stifled innovation and hindered the adjustment mechanisms and operations of the various financial markets. For example, the price of the Australian dollar (the exchange rate) had been fixed in terms of other currencies until December 1983 and the government managed its price by making periodic adjustments. After the floating of the dollar, the operations of the various foreign exchange markets set the price of the Australian dollar according to market forces. Volatility increased. For example, the value of the Australian dollar in terms of the US dollar fell from the US80–90 cents range in the early 1980s to less than US50 cents in the early 2000s, and continued to experience rises and falls over the next few years. It rose to a high point of US110.55 cents in July 2011, retreating to US106 cents in 2012 then further to US96 cents in June 2013 and US67 cents in June 2024.

Deregulation does not mean that the economy is entirely left to the market with no regulation of the financial system at all. There is still plenty of regulation or at least prudential oversight. Bodies such as the Reserve Bank of Australia (RBA), the Australian Securities and Investments Commission (ASIC) and the Australian Prudential Regulation Authority (APRA) are concerned with the stability of the economy, the achievement of macroeconomic goals and the maintenance of public confidence in the financial system and its institutions. This is to help investors and others participate in the financial system in a well-informed and confident fashion.

Partly as a consequence of deregulation, the 1980s saw rapid growth in all forms of debt in Australia, with both individual and corporate borrowers participating in the rush. The dollar value of debt increased markedly. However, more importantly from the point of view of the investor, the range of fixed-interest products available to those people who wanted to place funds in these types of investments increased rapidly.

Before reviewing the types of products available to investors looking for fixed-interest rates underlying the income they earn on their funds, we need to explain the concept of cash and to develop an understanding of the participants in the fixed-interest markets and how all the pieces in the markets fit together.

Cash as a term in finance has many meanings. Cash can be the money in our pockets or purses, or the money held under our mattresses. This sort of cash earns no return. No one pays us a rent for the use of the money. Cash held in a short-term account, on the other hand, can be just as available and we can arrange our affairs so that people pay us for the use of those funds. Large investors typically are paid interest on funds lent overnight. Thus, the overnight rate of interest is the 'cash' rate. Accordingly, we will think of cash as a short-term loan rather than as coins or notes in our pockets.

Fixed interest is a term used to describe an investment, whether it be for a short or longer time frame, where a set rate of interest is agreed on for the fixed period of time of the investment. So, typically a bank may offer a term deposit at, for example, 5.3% p.a. for a 2-year time frame. The contract means that the investor lends money to the bank for 2 years for an interest return of 5.3% p.a. with the return of both interest paid either after each year or at the end of 2 years, plus the return of the initial capital sum invested. Fixed interest investments may use some variation of the above and also be offered by different institutions seeking to borrow money from the public.

5.2 The nature of, and participants in, the fixed-interest market

LEARNING OBJECTIVE 5.2 Understand the nature of, and participants in, the fixed-interest investment market.

The nature of fixed-interest markets and products

The essential features of most fixed-interest securities are that:
1. the interest rate, which is the price of the loan of funds to the borrower, is set at the start of the loan period
2. the face value (the principal) is fixed.
    Interest is payable at the start, during or at the end of the loan period.

The interest rate on fixed-interest securities varies according to the maturity of the debt and the perceived riskiness of the borrower. All interest rates stem from the base of the *cash rate*. Margins are then added to compensate lenders for increased risk and time until maturity. However, we also need to consider the difference between the cash rate and the real cash rate after allowing for inflation. We are aware that the rate of inflation is more commonly measured by the Consumer Price Index (CPI) which means that $100 in the future will not buy as much as $100 today. So, we need to distinguish between the nominal rate of interest and the real rate of interest.

The general formula for converting a nominal cash amount at a future period t to a real cash amount is as follows.

$$\text{Real cash amount} = \frac{\text{Nominal cash amount}}{(1 + \text{Inflation rate})^t}$$

As an example, if the interest rate is 10% and the inflation rate is 5%, you are only better off by 4.67% at the end of the year, as shown below.

$$1.0476 = \frac{1.10}{1.05}$$

This means that, if you invested $1000 in a 10-year fixed-term investment at 10% p.a., you receive interest of $100 in each of the ten years. Then, when the term deposit matures, your final payment would be $1100 ($1000 + $100). With an inflation rate of, for example, 5% p.a., the real value of that final payment in 10 years would be $675.30 (i.e. the nominal amount of $1000 plus $100 discounted by 5% for 10 years ($1100 / 1.05^{10})).

The cash rate is the interest rate which the RBA directly manages through its management of money supply. The RBA buys or sells securities to inject or withdraw funds from the Australian economy so that appropriate amounts of cash are available on a daily basis in the economy. The board of the RBA determines when the cash rate should change. For example, during 2006–07, the board announced two cash rate increases of 0.25% from 5.75% in order to damp down activity in the economy and to try to avert increasing inflation. On each occasion, the cash rate quickly settled on or near the new target as the managed supply of funds was closely matched with expected demand. In the period 2007–09, the RBA dropped the cash rate to encourage people to borrow and to stimulate the economy, but in 2009–10 the RBA sought to gradually increase rates again to contain inflation. However, in 2011 the RBA again reduced the cash rate from 5% to 3% to attempt to stimulate the economy and in 2015 the cash rate was again reduced to 2% to further stimulate the economy. In March 2020, the RBA reduced the cash rate from 0.5% to 0.25% in an attempt to boost the flagging economy. In November 2020 there was a further decrease to 0.10%. However, in the subsequent 3 years the cash rate was increased 13 times, sitting at 4.35% as of June 2024. To see the latest graphs on interest rates refer to the RBA quarterly Chart Pack publication, 'The Australian Economy and Financial Markets'. Figure 5.1 shows the cash rate over the period 1993 to 2019.

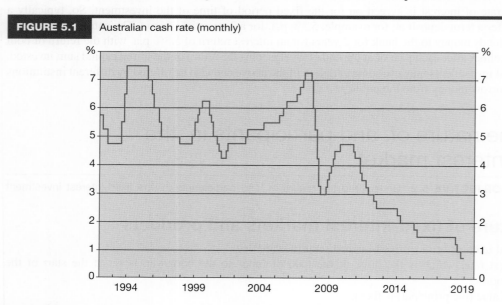

FIGURE 5.1 Australian cash rate (monthly)

Source: RBA 2020, p. 18.

Participants in the fixed-interest markets

The participants in the fixed-interest markets are principally the authorised deposit-taking institutions (ADIs) (including the banks and the non-bank financial institutions (NBFIs)), other finance sector firms such as insurance companies and fund managers, private individuals, trading companies ('ordinary businesses') and governments. Some of these participants come to the markets as lenders, some as borrowers and some as both. Many of the financial institutions act as intermediaries; that is, they facilitate the operation of the markets by, for example, collecting and pooling funds for investment in large projects or by matching lenders with borrowers.

It is worthwhile to note that, increasingly, the old divisions between market participants are becoming blurred. Twenty or more years ago, a bank housed itself in buildings of typical architecture that we knew meant a 'bank', and it offered opening times that were somewhat restricted. Now, 'banks' or at least banking services can be found in supermarkets, department stores, fruit shops, petrol outlets, holes in brick walls and many other places, and service is available 24 hours a day, 7 days a week. Additionally, banking services are available via phone or the internet.

5.3 Different forms of fixed-interest investments

LEARNING OBJECTIVE 5.3 Understand the different forms of fixed-interest investments.

The terms of fixed-interest investments can vary from 'at call' (immediate access) to very long maturities of perhaps up to 20 years. There is a good deal of interdependence between all the instruments available in the markets, and this interdependence tends to keep interest rates aligned reasonably tightly, even though there may be significant differences in perceived riskiness and maturities. Some fixed-interest providers may offer higher rates of return to investors because the providers may use the funds for riskier projects such as lending to property developers. In these cases the rate of interest may be 3–4% higher than offered by the banking sector, indicating the relative riskiness of such projects — on occasions the rates of interest have failed to be met and a failure to repay the capital has occurred. An example of a failure of the non-bank lending sector is Banksia Securities which collapsed in 2012. Investors received only 82 cents of every dollar they had invested (the last part payment was made in 2014). Investors lent money to the firm on a fixed interest basis but the money was used to fund property investments where the developers failed to make repayments. Figure 5.2 indicates the relative closeness between the cash rate and the 90-day bank bill rate which are generally regarded as 'risk-free' rates of return.

FIGURE 5.2 Comparison between the cash rate and the 90-day bank bill rate

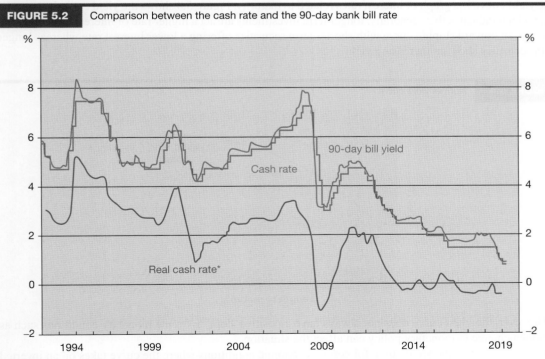

* Calculated using average of year-ended weighted median inflation and year-ended trimmed mean inflation.

Source: RBA 2020, p. 18.

Figure 5.3 indicates the variation between a longer-dated bond (10 years) and the cash rate to illustrate the difference between the interest rates. To help clarify the nature of trading being undertaken, the fixed-interest markets are normally divided into two major classes — the *money market* where securities of up to one year's duration are traded and the *capital market* where longer-dated securities are traded.

FIGURE 5.3 Spread between the Australian 10-year bond yield and the cash rate

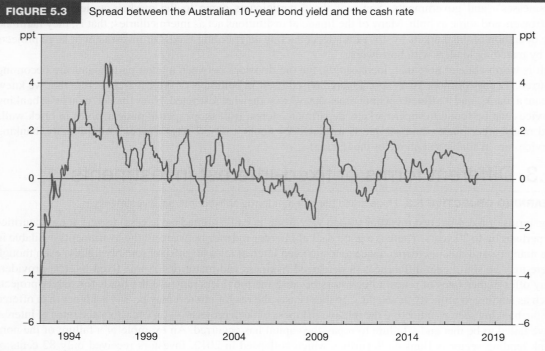

Source: RBA 2020, p. 20.

Longer maturity securities usually, but not always, offer a higher interest rate, because there can be higher risk attached to longer periods. Instruments with perceived higher risk, such as personal unsecured loans, attract higher interest rates than a bank-accepted (guaranteed) commercial bill or a government loan. The **yield curve** is a graph of interest rates related to maturity. Figure 5.4 shows the yield curve in a normal state which indicates that, generally, longer term investments attract a higher rate of interest. You will note that it is an upward sloping curve with shorter term securities offering a lower interest rate whereas longer term securities show an increasing yield.

FIGURE 5.4 Normal yield curve

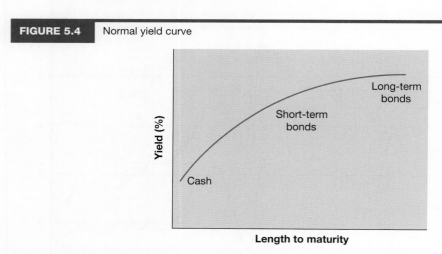

However, the yield curve does not always have a positive slope. Extreme monetary conditions such as a sudden change in monetary policy can affect the situation.

Figure 5.5 shows the yield curve for certain economic conditions where the curve takes on an inverted or downward sloping shape. This indicates that short-term interest rates are higher than long-term rates. This may occur when the RBA raises interest rates in the short term to curtail an inflationary trend.

A higher interest rate for the short term will encourage people to deposit money in a bank and discourage people from borrowing, thereby reducing the pressure on prices. At other times the yield curve may be flat when short-term and long-term rates are virtually the same, and a humped yield curve may occur when medium-term rates are higher. Anticipating the features of the business cycle can reward the astute investor who watches interest-rate movements.

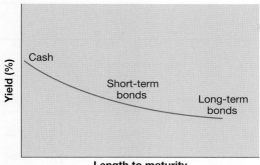

FIGURE 5.5 Inverse yield curve

Even though it could be argued that accounts at ADIs are not strictly direct investments, they act like direct investments. That is, these accounts give investors immediate access to their funds, but very little return in the way of interest payments. Many of these products pay interest at between 0.0% and 1.0%.

Term deposits are available at ADIs for varying terms from one month to several years. The interest rates offered usually increase with maturity, although expectations that interest rates may fall will dampen the marginal increases in rates as terms increase. Because of the high credit ratings that Australian ADIs enjoy, there is little risk associated with these products.

Investors wanting higher risk and returns may invest in commercial bills, corporate debentures and unsecured notes offered by finance companies and others. Commercial bills usually have 90- or 180-day durations. Banks often bring investors and borrowers together and the bank guarantees repayment to the investor in return for a fee paid by the borrower. These are bank-accepted bills (BABs) which allow individual investors to take on higher risk and enjoy higher returns.

A debenture is a form of corporate bond which is a long-term security that pays regular interest at a fixed rate on the face value. The face value is repaid in full at maturity. Debentures are usually secured by a charge over a group of assets owned by the issuer. Unsecured notes are similar securities except with more risk and higher interest rates. However, some firms offering debentures and unsecured notes have failed in the past and have been unable to meet their promise to pay interest and repay capital amounts to investors. Recall the old maxim 'the higher the return, the higher the risk'! (Search the internet for news about Australian Capital Reserve, Fincorp and South Eastern Secured Investments Ltd.)

The fixed-interest rate attached to the bond is usually payable 6-monthly or annually, and is often called the coupon. This is a quaint term which stems from the old practice of having coupons (tickets or receipts) printed on the physical bond. When a periodic interest payment was made, the coupon was cut from the bond which the lender held and was given to the borrower as proof that the payment had been made. The coupon was thus a receipt for the payment.

Investors with reasonably large sums of money may invest directly in bonds offered by governments, semi-government authorities and corporations. In Australia, bonds offered by the government (Commonwealth Government securities or CGS) enjoy very good security ratings, and the state governments and semi-government authorities have slightly lower, but still good, risk ratings. The Commonwealth Government in recent years has made it a budget strategy to repay outstanding debt, so that it has no net debt. As a result, access to Commonwealth bonds on issue has been limited; essentially only a few financial institutions hold CGS. Investors wanting to hold bonds have been forced to the corporate bond market.

Corporate bonds have increased in popularity over the last decade as figures 5.6 and 5.7 show. Only a few years ago the Commonwealth Government introduced retail bonds to small-scale investors with a nominal value of $1000. Two types are available — Treasury Fixed Coupon Bonds and Treasury Capital Indexed Bonds — and investors may purchase bonds in lots of $1000 up to $250 000. They may be purchased on the Australian Securities Exchange (ASX). These bonds are now known as exchange-traded AGBs (Australian

Government Bonds) and can be purchased as either exchange-traded Treasury bonds or exchange-traded Treasury indexed bonds.

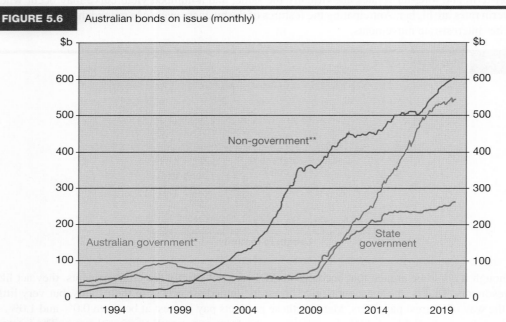

FIGURE 5.6 Australian bonds on issue (monthly)

* Excludes bonds purchased by the Australian Government.
** Excludes ADIs' self-securitisations, includes government guaranteed bonds.
Source: RBA 2020, p. 24.

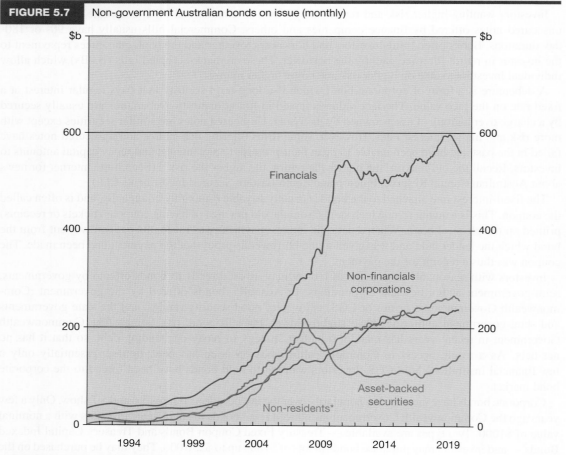

FIGURE 5.7 Non-government Australian bonds on issue (monthly)

* Australian dollar-denominated bonds only
Source: RBA 2020, p. 24.

The yield from corporate bonds is higher than that from CGS, as can be seen in figure 5.8. Corporate bonds are rated for risk, with the lowest risks rated AAA and the highest BBB. The highest risk corporations must offer investors greater compensation, as figure 5.9 shows. Many banks and large financial institutions offer securities which have hybrid income qualities between fixed interest and the variable returns of equities. These are called floating rate notes (FRNs). These securities have a floating interest rate normally set 0.75% to 3% above the bank bill rate (to compensate for the higher risks involved) with interest paid quarterly and no fixed maturity date. They are listed on the ASX.

| FIGURE 5.8 | Australian corporate bond yields (monthly) |

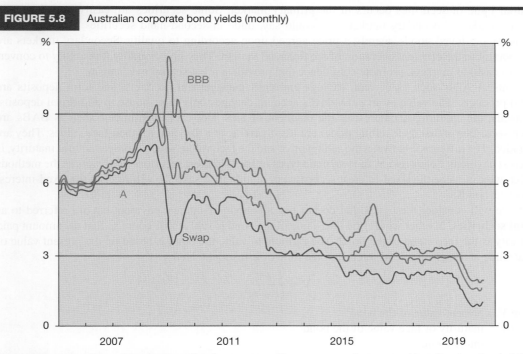

Note: Yields on bonds issued by the Australian Government and swap rates are 3-year maturities. Corporate bond yields are a weighted average of senior bonds with remaining maturities of 1 to 5 years, including financial and non-financial corporations.
Source: RBA 2020, p. 20.

| FIGURE 5.9 | Australian corporate bond spreads (spread over government yields; monthly) |

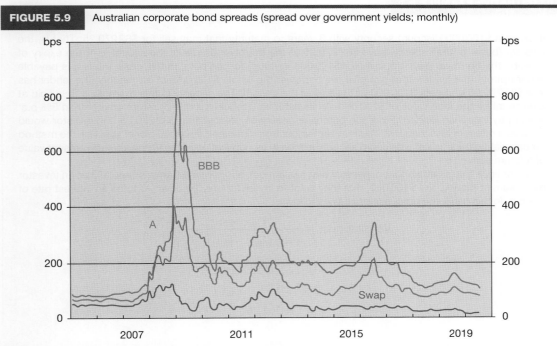

Note: Swap spreads are for 3-year maturity. Corporate bond spreads are a weighted average of bonds with remaining maturities of 1 to 5 years; they include financial and non-financial corporates.
Source: RBA 2020, p. 20.

5.4 Discount and coupon securities and a change in interest rates

LEARNING OBJECTIVE 5.4 Appreciate the difference between discount and coupon securities and the effect of a change in interest rates.

Discount and coupon securities

The initial issue of securities occurs in the primary market. Some securities are easily traded later in secondary markets. Secondary markets, we could say, trade in second-hand securities, but there is no discount for pre-loved goods, merely a price agreed upon according to quality. Secondary markets are very important to the efficient operation of the financial system. They give liquidity (the ability to convert easily into cash) to markets, promote confidence and provide a price-setting mechanism.

Accounts at ADIs such as current, savings and cash management accounts, and term deposits are untraded products. The value of an individual's account changes only in response to additional deposits, withdrawals, the crediting of interest or the payment of fees. However, instruments such as BABs are discount securities in that their selling prices are less than (i.e. at a discount to) their face values. They are often traded. The difference between the selling price and the face value, which is redeemable at maturity, is the interest payment. Let us review the two main types of fixed-interest securities and examine the methods by which we can value the fixed-interest security. For simplicity's sake we will refer to the fixed-interest securities as bonds.

First, we will consider the bonds that do not pay a coupon or interest payment but are referred to as **discount securities**. In other words, the face value of the bond is sold at a discount so that the amount paid on maturity is the face value of the bond. The formula to value the bond is based on the present value of the face value at the given rate of interest at the time of investment. Hence:

$$V = \frac{FV}{(1 + r)^n}$$

where V = present value of the bond

FV = maturity or face value of the bond

r = interest rate

n = number of periods

ILLUSTRATIVE EXAMPLE 5.1

Imagine a $100 000 discount security with 3 years to maturity that may sell for $82 270.25. That is, the investor (buyer of the security) pays $82 270.25 to the borrower (issuer of the security). At the expiry of 3 years, the borrower pays the investor $100 000 in return for the note. In this case, interest is payable either upfront (the lender does not give the borrower the whole $100 000) or at maturity (the lender has lent $82 270.25 and gets $100 000 at the end of the period). The security in this example is thus sold at a discount on the face value of $100 000. An investor who requires a rate of return greater than 5% p.a. would pay less than $82 270.25. If the purchase price was greater than $82 270.25, the investor would achieve a return of less than 5%. You may remember from chapter 2 (financial planning skills), the method for calculating the price of a discount security is merely an application of the formula for the present value of a future sum.

To continue this example for an investor that has a much shorter time frame, suppose that an investor has a sum of money, say $100 000, that they want to invest for only 90 days. Assume an interest rate of 7% p.a. In this case, the purchase price is as follows.

$$\text{Purchase price} = \frac{\text{Face value}}{1 + \left(\text{Interest rate} \times \frac{90}{365}\right)}$$

$$= \frac{\$100\,000}{1 + \left(0.07 \times \frac{90}{365}\right)}$$

$$= \$98\,303.26$$

And, if the investor did not know what the interest rate was when the financial institution offered a price for the $100 000 in 90 days then the investor's return on the investment is given by the following.

$$\text{Return on investment} = \frac{\text{Face value} - \text{Purchase price}}{\text{Purchase price}} \times \frac{365}{90} \times \frac{100}{1}$$

$$= \frac{\$100\,000 - \$98\,303.26}{\$98\,303.26} \times \frac{36\,500}{90}$$

$$= 7\%$$

Second, we need to consider the form of fixed-interest security that pays a coupon or interest payment at predetermined times. These are known as **coupon securities**. Such fixed-interest securities are more common and are often traded. They are initially issued in the primary market by the borrower, but may be sold later by the lender in the secondary market. Each time such a security is sold, the traders involved make a judgement about interest rates in general and the riskiness of the particular instrument. Regardless of the coupon rate, the price settled on at each trade governs the effective interest rate of the instrument. This is because the dollar value of the interest payments is fixed. Thus, the yield or effective interest rate depends on the price of invested funds. The price of a bond is calculated using the formulae for the present value of both a future sum and of an annuity.

ILLUSTRATIVE EXAMPLE 5.2

As an example, a $100 000 bond is due in 2 years with a 5% coupon. It pays $2500 every 6 months for the remainder of its 2-year life. In addition, the bond issuer promises to repay the $100 000 principal at maturity in 2 years time.

The valuation of the bond is the present value (PV) of the interest payments (an annuity) and the PV of the principal due in 2 years. If the rate of return required by an investor is 6% then the PV of the annuity payments is $9291.63 and the PV of the future lump sum is $88 849.40. If we add the two together we get the sum of $98 141.22, which represents the present value of the bond at 6% and that is how much the investor requiring 6% will pay to acquire the bond paying coupons at 5% for 2 years. The investor will offer to pay less if an investor requires a higher rate of return, say 7%.

This calculation is based on a combination of the PV of a stream of interest payments and the PV of the face value of the bond. The formula to produce the above figures is:

$$PV = \frac{PMT}{i} \times \left[1 - \frac{1}{(1+i)^n} \right]$$

Plus:

$$PV = \frac{FV}{(1+i)^n}$$

Substituting the data into the equations, gives:

$$PV = \frac{2500}{0.03} \times \left[1 - \frac{1}{(1+0.03)^4} \right]$$

$$= \$83\,333 \times 0.1115$$

$$= \$9291.63$$

Plus:

$$PV = \frac{\$100\,000}{(1+0.03)^4}$$

$$= \$88\,849.40$$

Total:

$$= \$98\,141.03$$

Accessing fixed-interest markets

Investors wanting access to these markets can approach many types of firms operating in the finance industry. ADIs offer current, savings, cash management and term accounts. Some institutions now offer a slightly higher-interest and fee-free internet account which attracts many investors.

Finance companies offer debentures and unsecured notes direct to the public. Semi-government and government notes and bonds may be bought or sold through professional brokers and Commonwealth bonds may be purchased directly via the ASX. Investors may thus gain access to these securities by purchasing in the secondary market or by buying when the securities are first issued.

The effect of a change in interest rates

We may make an assumption that most investors are risk averse, but that investors differ in their degrees of risk averseness. Apart from innate forces which dictate a person's tolerance to risk, it would be reasonable to expect risk tolerance to be governed by a person's age, income, wealth, years to retirement, past financial experiences and perhaps some other factors. For example, young people are often happy to take on more risk than older people. Youth are generally less risk averse, they have often had less chance of experiencing financial losses when investments have 'gone wrong', and they have usually more years to increase wealth before retirement and thus have more time to recover should things go awry. A retired person in their mid-sixties on the other hand may decide that fixed-interest investments will provide more security for their retirement than the risk of investing in shares that may not recover for some years after a share market crash.

Fixed-interest products appeal to more risk-averse people. There are two aspects of this which are worth consideration. First, there is the guarantee of the interest payment at a given level, so long as the borrower remains solvent. (*Note:* ASIC researched the profile of debenture holders to understand how better to protect small investors. They found that a typical investor was aged in their mid-sixties and was attracted by the perceived security of the rate of interest and capital protection of the investments.) Generally, there is little uncertainty about the income from these products. Secondly, many of these products are capital stable. That is, the value of the capital remains fixed, and there may be little chance of the loss of capital. However, investment in traded securities such as bonds remains an exception to this rule. A rise in the general level of interest rates will normally promote decreases in the capital values of traded fixed-interest securities. Conversely, holders of these securities will enjoy an appreciation in capital values when the general level of interest rates falls.

As an example, let us consider this situation. Suppose Lucy buys a discount bond for $10 000 that will pay $15 000 in 5 years. The expected return is equivalent to an interest rate of 10%. However, imagine that Lucy must sell the bond on the market in 2 years because she has an emergency need for the money, and the prevailing interest rates in 2 years have gone up to 15%. Lucy will not be able to sell the bond for $12 000 which would represent the original 10% yield over the 2 years. A purchaser, Mike, would offer Lucy only the present value of the bond based on the maturity value and the present value of the remaining interest payment stream based on the 15% interest rate. If Mike paid $12 000, he would get a return of only about 8% which is about half of the prevailing interest rate. The only way Lucy could sell the bond is to lower the price so that the yield is equal to the prevailing interest rate. If she offered the bond at $10 400, this means that Mike would earn $4600 over the remaining 3 years to maturity which represents a yield of 15%. So Lucy would make a return of only $400 or 2% instead of the 10% that she wanted when she bought the bond 2 years before.

This situation is an example of the fact that a very poor return may be made on a bond investment if a person has to sell prior to the maturity date. Then again, if the prevailing interest rates fall below the coupon rate, a seller can also make a gain on the sale. To follow Lucy's example further, if the prevailing interest rates had fallen to 5% when Lucy needed the money and had to sell the bond and Mike was able to buy the bond from Lucy for $10 400, the bond would continue to pay coupons at 10%. If Mike then held the bond to maturity to obtain the $15 000, this represents the return on his acquisition of the bond at the equivalent of 15%, despite the fall in the prevailing interest rate. Of course, if Lucy realised the impact on the bond value of the fall in interest rates, Mike would have to pay more than $10 400 to acquire the bond from Lucy (as it would be in high demand) which would lower the return on his investment to equal the prevailing interest rate.

Notwithstanding the fact that more risk-averse investors are drawn to fixed-interest products, it is normal for many investors to hold some proportion of fixed-interest securities in their portfolios. The proportions will vary according to their own investment strategy. In addition to the funds which investors keep in their investment portfolios, many people also have separate accounts where they keep working funds and precautionary balances. Working funds for day-to-day living expenses may be kept in a current account with credit and debit card access, and precautionary balances are kept in an easily accessed account such as a cash management trust (CMT). Precautionary balances are sums of money that people keep for emergencies. Although these working funds and precautionary balances may not be thought of as part of investment nest eggs, they do, in fact, increase the proportion of net wealth invested in fixed-interest products.

5.5 The nature of, and participants in, the share market

LEARNING OBJECTIVE 5.5 Understand the nature of, and participants in, the share market.

Shares are also known as 'equities' in Australia and 'common stock' in the United States. Investment in equities or shares in Australia has become markedly more common in the last two decades. The increase in popularity is due to the almost unbroken steady climb in average share prices since the crash in October 1987 and the spate of privatisations of government businesses until the global financial crisis of 2007–13. The steep decline in prices following the September 11, 2001 terrorist attacks in the United States was quickly reversed by returning confidence and rising demand but was then washed away by the fall in global markets when the impact of the credit crisis across the world caused many investors to sell shares and withdraw to the safety of cash. The ASX 200 recorded its highest point of 7132.7 in January 2020, overtaking the previous high point of 6829 in November 2007. By March 2020, the ASX 200 had fallen back to around 5000 as a result of the economic impact of the Coronavirus pandemic, but in subsequent years it recovered to record a new high point of 7919.60 in April 2024.

Initial public offers (IPOs) of shares, including those issued in privatisations of government businesses, are often, but not always, a way of enjoying good capital gains. One reason for this is that, before a business is subjected to the scrutiny of the whole of the investing public, it is difficult to put a realistic price on the whole of it and consequently on its shares. IPOs are thus often underpriced in order to ensure that the 'float' of the business is a success.

Another factor which has been important in government floats is that members of the government, who ultimately decide on the initial price of these shares, are unwilling to bear the electoral backlash that would ensue if shares were priced so highly that they traded on the market initially at a discount to the offer price. Even though initial investors need not sell and crystallise such losses, there would still be public protest.

Take the case of Telstra, for example. The issue price for the second tranche at $7.80 per share was over optimistic following the successful first sale of shares at $3.30 per share. For some years, prices in the secondary market for Telstra shares had been consistently about $3 lower than the offer price. Investors were not pleased. The third tranche was offered in two parts at a total price of $3.60. In December 2010, Telstra shares were trading at around $2.80 per share — far below the price paid by those who bought in the second tranche and below the price paid by those in the first and third tranches. But, by June 2013, Telstra's share price had risen to $4.70, a gain of 68% since December 2010. By October 2016, Telstra's share price had risen further to $5.05, representing a rise of 80% since December 2010 and was trading at $3.43 in February 2020 based on the expected fall of 40% in net profit amid costs associated with the National Broadband Network (NBN) (Duke 2019).

The nature of the share market

Shares may be sold privately or by brokers who specialise in non-listed shares. However, the bulk of trading occurs on stock exchanges. In Australia, the ASX currently has a virtual monopoly on the trading of listed shares, but there are a couple of minor markets, such as the National Stock Exchange of Australia (formerly the Stock Exchange of Newcastle), which have only a fraction of the capitalisation and turnover of the ASX.

The ASX requires companies to satisfy its regulations before they can be listed and traded. For example, companies are required to meet the continuous disclosure rules so that the market can be fully informed of any significant events that might affect the decision making of investors about holding shares in that particular company. The market is clearly divided between the industrial sector companies in areas such as building, household goods, food processing, banks, transport, media and insurance (which collectively account for about 80% of the market), and the resources sector. Most trading is executed by members of the exchange on behalf of themselves or their clients.

The market price of traded shares is determined by the interaction of demand and supply, and the market is highly susceptible to movements of capital to and from Australia. There is normally a reaction in the value of Australian shares when there is a strong movement in prices on the United States' Wall Street. Additionally, the value of the Australian dollar and international demand for Australian products (commodities in particular) are major determinants of the strength of the market. Figure 5.10 shows how the Australian market (ASX 200) has moved in relation to the US and world markets (S&P 500 and MSCI World, respectively). Figure 5.10 shows the changes between 1994 and 2020.

FIGURE 5.10 Australian, US and world share price indices, monthly (end December 1994 = 100)

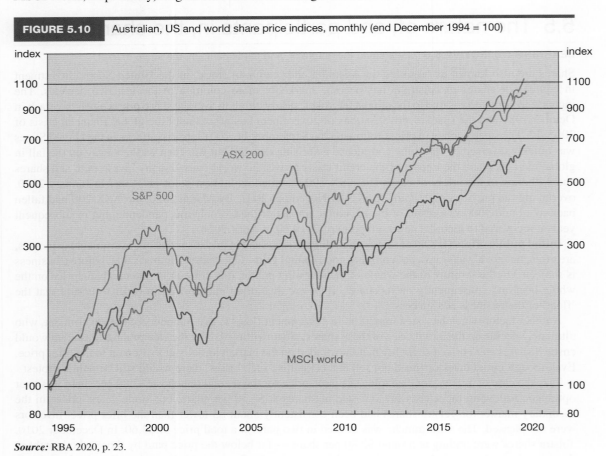

Source: RBA 2020, p. 23.

Publicly listed companies can issue new shares and the number of shares issued can be changed at an Annual General Meeting of shareholders. Once issued in the primary market, the issued shares may then be traded in the secondary market. The forms in which capital may be raised are determined by the *Corporations Act 2001*.

Capital may be issued in any of the following forms. Ordinary shares are the most common class of shares. Holders of ordinary shares share the ownership of the corporation with other holders of ordinary shares. Holders share the profits by receiving cash dividends or more shares in lieu of cash, or (theoretically) an increase in the value of each share where profits are not distributed. Holders also share losses through reductions in share prices or underlying value. Shareholders of limited liability companies risk only the amount of their investment; they cannot be made to repay debt owed by an insolvent corporation.

Contributing shares are not completely paid up when they are initially issued. A company may not require full payment immediately if it does not need the funds, and this makes the issue more attractive to potential investors. When the full amount owing has been called (requested) and paid, these shares become fully paid ordinary shares. As a variation of this theme, many of the large privatisations such as Telstra and Suncorp-Metway used a two-stage process to issue shares in an attractive manner to small shareholders. These have involved a fixed first payment which attracts either a dividend or interest, followed by a further payment, either fixed or set by the market, to complete the sale of each share.

Preference shares may be ordinary, cumulative, participating or redeemable. Preference shareholders have preference over ordinary shareholders with respect to claims on profits, dividends and the firm's assets should the company be wound up or liquidated. Holders of these shares usually have limited voting rights and shares have a fixed rate of return or dividend.

Characteristics of the various types of preference shares differ. Ordinary preference shareholders have a claim only on profits for a particular year. Cumulative shareholders retain priority over profits until all outstanding dividends have been paid. Participating holders have priority for dividends and have access to additional dividends after ordinary shareholders have been paid. Redeemable holders can have their shares bought back or redeemed at their face value at the discretion of the company at a certain date.

Deferred dividend shares are shares issued on the understanding that dividends will not be payable until a future specified date when a particular project becomes profitable. These shares usually trade at less than ordinary shares to reflect the dividend difference or the time shareholders must wait before they can expect to receive a dividend. In addition, corporations may issue options with varying conditions which grant rights to the holders to purchase new shares in the future.

Participants in the share market

The participants in the share market are listed corporations, investors and brokers who facilitate trading. Corporations are mainly interested in the primary role of the share market as a means of raising capital. They also use the secondary market to purchase shares in other companies, either for reasons of strategic alliance, takeover or for investment purposes. The latter is particularly true of institutional investors, such as managed funds, who play a critical role in the secondary market.

Investors, as we know, are individuals and firms that buy and sell financial assets mainly for the income they receive from holding the asset. The Australian investor survey in 2023 found that typical investors were about 58% male and 42% female.. The survey found that 51% of Australians held investments in 2023, with the average investor aged 47. Thie average age is trending downwards — 58% of investors are now aged under 49. The COVID-19 pandemic saw a surge of new investors, with a 13% growth in investors since 2020. (ASX 2023).

Purchasers of shares are not always involved for the purposes of participating in ownership of companies and earning income. They may have a number of different motivations. Hedgers are individuals and firms who hold two or more financial assets in the expectation that offsetting price movements, due to non-random events, will help eliminate risk. Thus, a jewellery manufacturing business which buys tonnes of gold each year might buy shares in a gold mine so that, as its gold input costs rise, it earns extra income through the additional profit made by the mine. Speculators are individuals and firms, with profit as their major motive, who hold financial assets for resale at a higher price. There are often many of these buyers operating in share markets every day. Finally, there are arbitrageurs who are individuals and firms who simultaneously buy and sell similar financial assets in different markets to profit from unequal prices.

Investors, hedgers, speculators and arbitrageurs all perform useful functions within financial markets. They provide a depth of buying and selling which tends to make markets more efficient. Appropriate prices are set more easily. Consider the operation of an auction. Suppose the 'correct' price for the good is $1000. If there is only one buyer, the highest price bid may be $600 and the seller may decline to sell or, if desperate, sell knowing that the 'proper' price is much higher. If there are two or more keen potential buyers, the bids will rise towards $1000, may stop around that price or may indeed exceed it. However, if the good is not unique, the price will not rise much above $1000, because the bidders know they will be able to get a supply elsewhere. Hence, the more depth there is in a market on both the buying and selling sides, the more accurate is the price-setting mechanism.

5.6 The influences on share prices

LEARNING OBJECTIVE 5.6 Consider the influences on share prices.

Analysis of share prices

Market forces determine the prices of shares when traded in the secondary market. From 2000 to 2007, Australian share prices rose quite steeply as earnings increased and funds poured into the share market by superannuation funds managers. Figure 5.11 shows the rise in share prices of industrial, financial and resource companies. However, you can also see the fall in prices from late 2007 as the global financial crisis caused many investors both in Australia and overseas to withdraw from the market and to hold greater amounts in cash and fixed-interest investments. A recovery has been made between 2007 and 2020, however, the COVID-19 pandemic in 2020 caused share markets around the world to fall by over 20%. However, by August 2023 share markets had recovered from the COVID-19 pandemic, with an increase of some 22%.

FIGURE 5.11 Australian share prices (end December 1994 = 100)

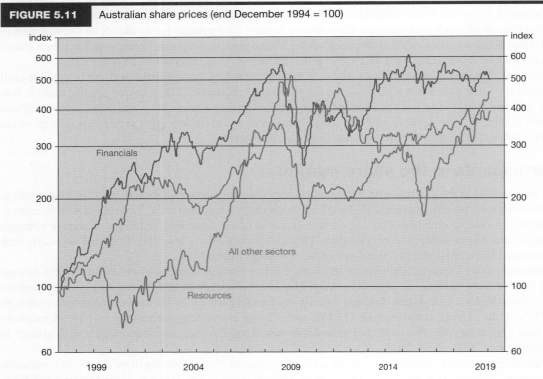

Source: RBA 2020, p. 23.

Many factors are likely to affect the price of shares. Essentially, if there is more buying pressure than selling pressure, prices will rise. If the converse applies, prices will fall. It is difficult to list every factor which may influence an investor's decision to buy or sell shares, but rational decision making usually dictates that the factors that may be of some consequence are:

- interest rate levels
- inflation
- taxation
- theoretical price levels
- earnings and dividends
- quality of management
- company reports and announcements
- profit reports
- changes in commodity prices
- industry events
- government policy and announcements
- takeover activity
- economic expectations
- domestic and international economic fluctuations.

Methods of analysis

There are two broad approaches to the analysis of share prices. Fundamental analysis uses objective measures to analyse a company's current financial situation. It also attempts to forecast the effects of future events on those measures. Technical analysis, on the other hand, is more concerned with how recent market perception of the worth of an investment has been translated into market prices.

Although it is important that individual investors are aware of macro factors likely to affect the return on an investment in a particular share, fundamental analysts think it critical that objective examination at the individual corporation level be conducted to ascertain expected profitability and the degree of risk associated with the investment. Analysis can involve many measures, and should at least consider liquidity, capital structure, profitability, market valuation and risk analysis.

Liquidity

The liquidity of a company can be defined as its capacity to continue to meet its short-term financial obligations and hence to continue trading. The liquidity of a company is often measured by the current ratio; that is, the ratio of current assets to current liabilities. A ratio of 2:1 is generally regarded as desirable but it does depend on the industry sector.

A wide range of current ratios is usually noticeable among industry groups. One of the main reasons is the inherent differences between industries. Some industries require a large investment in accounts receivable or inventory (e.g. textiles) and will therefore have much higher current ratios than companies with almost no inventory (e.g. transport).

Capital structure

The capital structure of a company describes the proportion of its funding derived from three broad sources:
1. borrowings (funds provided by financial creditors through bank loans, mortgages, debentures, unsecured notes etc.)
2. trade and other miscellaneous creditors
3. shareholders' funds.

Capital structure can be measured by the debt–equity ratio or, alternatively, by the proprietorship ratio which is the proportion of shareholders' funds to total assets.

Industry differences are again an important influence on capital structure. At one extreme are finance companies. Their business is to borrow funds in order to lend and they inevitably display a much higher dependence on outside financing than industrial companies. At the other extreme are companies in capital goods industries. Their fortunes are strongly influenced by the trade cycle and they must therefore adopt a conservative long-term financing structure.

Profitability

The most common measure of profitability for shareholders is the ratio of after-tax earnings to shareholders' funds. This is usually referred to as the return on shareholders' funds or rate of return on invested capital (RRIC) and is obviously an important ratio for investors. Again, there are wide differences in profitability between industries. Caution should be used in interpreting the figures because of differences in definitions and accounting procedures. Investors should be interested in the returns they receive from their shareholding — both in terms of dividend received and capital gain in the value of their shares — remembering too that different shares will carry more risk and may provide a higher return.

The profitability of a company can be measured in many ways. A useful measure of the return on a company's assets is provided by the EBIT ratio — earnings before interest and tax (EBIT) to total funds (shareholders' funds plus borrowings). This ratio allows comparisons between companies with different capital structures, as earnings are being considered before the impact of funding decisions. The ratio should also be compared with prevailing interest rates and, as a minimum (except in agriculture where returns are low), the company's return on funds should exceed the cost of borrowing. Short-term funding is often excluded in calculating the ratio to eliminate the distortions from seasonal funding fluctuations.

Investors are interested in dividends paid by corporations. Thus, dividend yield is an important measure. Dividend yield is dividend per share divided by the current price of the share. The value of dividend yields varies widely at any time over the range of listed corporations, from zero to perhaps 8%. This measure allows the returns from individual shares to be compared with those both of other shares and of other types of investments. Figure 5.12 shows average Australian and USA dividend yields from 1940 to 2019. Note that Australian shares have generally provided higher average dividend yields. This does not necessarily mean that Australian companies have been more profitable. Dividend policy of companies is affected by taxation law and other issues. For example, US companies put less emphasis on dividends and more emphasis on capital gain as methods to reward their shareholders.

Market valuation

The market valuation (or capitalisation) of a company is the number of ordinary shares on issue multiplied by the market price per share. The market valuation represents the consensus of investor opinion as to the present value of the future dividends expected from the company. In practice, it varies according to the outlook for earnings, and thus dividends, and with takeover prospects.

A measure commonly used as an indicator of share market value is the price-earnings (P/E) ratio. The P/E ratio is the share market price of a company's shares divided by earnings per share. The ratio reflects investors' valuation of future prospects, rather than present performance. Where there is promise of strong earnings gains, the P/E ratio will tend to be high. When earnings growth is not expected to be strong, or where earnings in the industry are cyclical, the P/E ratio may be slow to respond to variation in earnings if investors hesitate to sell the shares. Figure 5.13 shows times such as 1968–70 and 1998–2002 when investors allowed their exuberance to run ahead of earnings as they bid share prices up to far greater relative heights to be followed by share price falls.

| FIGURE 5.12 | Average Australian and USA dividend yields 1940–2019 |

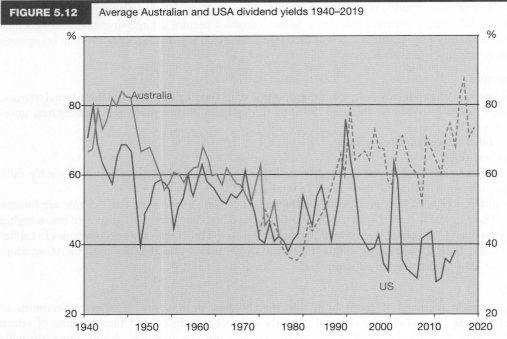

Source: Mathews 2019, p. 8.

| FIGURE 5.13 | Trailing P/E ratios |

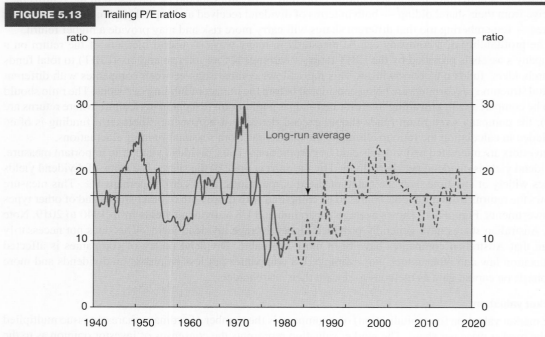

Source: Mathews 2019, p. 25.

Although the measure is widely used in the market, it is not without ambiguity. For example, the P/E ratio for the same share can vary widely from one analyst to another, depending on whether past or future earnings are used. Where future earnings are used, the figure may be more 'relevant' but the estimate of future earnings may vary widely from analyst to analyst.

Technical analysis or charting is concerned with graphing the price history of an asset over a relevant period of time and analysing the pattern of price movements. As graphs are more accurate and useful when there is a large amount of relevant data, the method is widely used with shares, for which there are appropriate and readily available price data.

Chartists look for recurring patterns in price movements and have developed a jargon to describe these patterns. Terms include *trends, support levels, resistance levels, symmetrical triangles, descending triangles, pennants, flags, shoulders* and *breakouts*. Supposedly, all known market information is incorporated in these price movements and buy or sell points can be isolated.

Figure 5.14 illustrates one tool of the chartist — trendlines. A line is drawn between at least three points. In an upward movement the low points are connected to form an upward line. The trendline gains more importance when the number of price extremes that can be connected by a single line indicates an increase. In this analysis, it is assumed that the market will continue in the direction of the trend until the trend is broken. In the case of an uptrend, buying opportunities are presented when the price is above the trend line. If the trendline has just been tested — which means that the price has moved down to the trendline, touched it and then rallied and moved higher — it may be taken as a signal to buy. Conversely, a break of that same upward-sloping trendline might be interpreted as a signal to sell. Hence, further research needs to be undertaken in a trading situation.

FIGURE 5.14	Trendlines

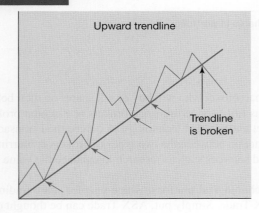

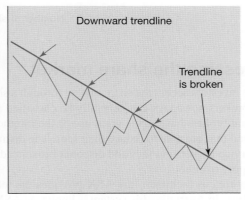

A chartist saying is 'up by the stairs and down via the elevator'. This means that a falling market can often be extremely vicious. This is typical of a bear market, but a low point can often denote the end of a trend. Trendline theory argues that an investor should wait until the trendline is actually broken before it can be said that the up or down trend has finished. A trendline is broken when, in the case of the downtrend, the price moves above the trend. Some analysts use a 2-day rule to verify a break in the trend and require a close of the relevant price to be above the trendline, which will often save the trader from 'whiplash'. Whiplash means getting taken out of the market when a trend is 'broken' only to find the trend immediately resumes and had not really been broken.

Many people follow the chartist theories whereas others stick more closely to fundamental valuation methods. Some analysts focus on using fundamental analysis as a filter and then look towards technical analysis to determine buy and sell points.

Risk analysis

In recent years, portfolio managers have given increasing attention to the role of risk factors in constructing portfolios. This has been brought about by the development of portfolio theory which has supplied a rigorous framework of analysis where formerly intuition prevailed. In portfolio theory, investment risk is broken down into two components:

1. 'market' or 'systematic' risk
2. unsystematic risk.

The first, market or systematic risk, is the variation because of general market movement due, for example, to the impact of such general forces as interest-rate movements, a severe downturn in the global economy, a war, the collapse of a country's currency, or an event such as the tsunami that hit Japan in early 2011. The second component, unsystematic risk, comprises those factors which are peculiar to an individual company such as statements made by the chief executive officer, the decisions made by management or union activities designed to win a pay rise or better conditions. These latter elements are 'random' in their impact and their individual effects may be removed through diversification. The 'market risk', on the other hand, cannot be diversified away. Investment managers thus select shares to remove as much risk as possible. Figure 5.15 shows the conceptual relationship between risk and the number of investments held in a portfolio.

FIGURE 5.15 | Systematic and unsystematic risk

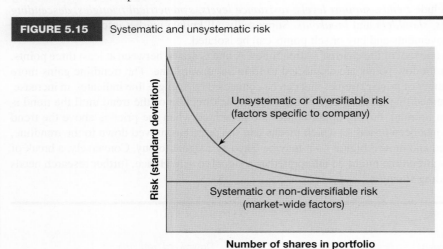

Number of shares in portfolio

Accessing the share market

Private investors access the share market through a sharebroker who will buy or sell shares on their behalf. Sharebrokers nowadays can generally be classified as full-service/full-price brokers or discount brokers. Discount brokers have made great use of the internet and modern technology to reduce their transaction costs and thus are able to reduce their fees. The distinction between the two types of brokers is blurring as full-service brokers cut fees and discount brokers add services such as research to enhance the value they can supply to clients.

In its role as facilitator, the ASX provides the technological platform which enables share trading to take place. In Australia, this system is known as ASX Trade. Simply put, ASX Trade can be thought of as a public auction, whereby market participants can place their orders to buy and sell shares by specifying a desired quantity and price. If you imagine a marketplace with thousands of such people continuously entering their 'bids' (if they are looking to buy) and 'offers' (if they are looking to sell), you will have a rough idea of the size and scale of the ASX Trade system.

Orders placed within the ASX Trade system are prioritised based on price-time priority. This is best illustrated with an example. If we have two investors looking to buy or sell a particular share, and each enters the desired quantity and price they are willing to pay or offer, the order with the 'best' price will have priority. The 'best' price is defined as the higher price if the person is looking to buy, or the lower price if they are looking to sell. The next logical question then is, 'What if two investors are looking to buy or sell shares at the same price?' In this case, priority is based on a 'first come first serve' basis, whereby the order received in the market first will have priority.

The cost of trading shares depends on whether an investor uses a broker to trade shares or trades personally using an online trading facility. The cost of personal trading online ranges from $10 to $20 for a transaction. A full service broker fee may cost a minimum of $70 per trade up to $10 000 value and then about 0.2–0.3% on large trades of, say, $1 million. There is a wide range of fees and options that exist in the market depending on the level of advice required by the investor. Many brokers now insist that clients hold funds in accounts accessible by the broker to settle buy transactions and that they, the brokers, have proof that shares are owned before a sale transaction is affected. Transactions must be settled by the third day after the day of the transaction or a substantial fine is levied.

Because the old method of a printed share certificate has been abandoned, investors have their shareholdings substantiated by statements issued by registrars such as CHESS (Clearing House Electronic Subregister System), an electronic transfer and settlement system. Entries in this system are sponsored by the brokers with whom clients are registered. Alternatively, companies outsource or maintain their own electronic registers. Coupled with electronic transfer of cash, uncertificated holdings speed transactions and cut transaction costs. Thus, the ASX trades solely by way of linked computers and market activity can be viewed only on computer screens, and not like on television where you may see brokers working at the New York Stock Exchange.

The effects of technological change and globalisation are nowhere more apparent than in the equity markets. Until the end of the 1990s, investors who wanted to expand and diversify their portfolios to include international equities were virtually forced to use the services of funds managers because it was difficult to obtain timely investment information and to trade on markets other than the ASX. However, during 1999, internet brokers started to provide investors with direct access to trade on US markets.

Risk and return

Recall from the case study at the start of this chapter that Lila required some financial advice and consulted with Rebecca, the financial planner. They held a wide-ranging conversation about potential investments and the risks Lila was prepared to take. As a part of that conversation, Rebecca suggested to Lila that she buy some shares in her bank to become an owner rather than just a customer. As part of her explanation, Rebecca advised that the term deposit that the bank was offering for a 12-month period was 4.5%, but that shares in the bank were paying a dividend of 3.2%. At first Lila could not see that there was an advantage in investing where the return was lower and with more risk. But then Rebecca showed Lila a chart which showed the risk in interest rate returns over time and also that the dividend paid by the bank tended to rise by 3% p.a.

QUESTIONS

1. Suggest an argument why Lila might prefer to invest in the bank's term deposits.
2. Suggest an argument why Lila might prefer to invest in the bank's shares.
3. What would your advice be if Lila's investment time frame was at least 3 years?
4. What would your advice be if Lila's investment time frame was at least 7 years?

5.7 The capital asset pricing model (CAPM)

LEARNING OBJECTIVE 5.7 Understand the capital asset pricing model (CAPM).

So far, we have noted that there is a relationship between systematic risk and return. What we have not shown is the exact relationship. The capital asset pricing model (CAPM, pronounced 'cap-em') attempts to establish the relationship between systematic risk and return. The CAPM proposes a variable for *relative* systematic risk. This variable, beta (β), measures the risk of a share relative to the total market risk (remember, 'market risk' is 'systematic risk'). The variability of share returns relative to market returns is a measure of the share's systematic risk. The CAPM gives the following relationship between return and risk.

$$R_i = R_f + \beta_i(R_m - R_f)$$

where R_i = the expected or required return on share i
R_f = a risk-free rate
β_i = the beta of share i
$R_m - R_f$ = the risk premium (the margin for equity-market risk or, the difference between the market rate and the risk-free rate).

This model says that the expected return on a share is equal to the risk-free rate (the rate offered by a government security) plus the amount of risk (beta) multiplied by the price of risk (the risk premium). If investors wish to buy a particular share, the expected return must, at least, be equal to the return they would earn if they invested in a risk-free asset (such as a government bond or bank deposit). In addition, we know that owning shares is risky, so investors need to be compensated for that risk. They will not be compensated for total risk, just the systematic risk. Beta measures the systematic risk of the share and the risk premium measures the price of risk. In the CAPM, the beta of the market as a whole is always 1. Therefore, a share with a beta of less than 1 is less risky than the market as a whole, and a share with a beta of more than 1 is more risky than the market as a whole. Many mining and exploration companies have betas higher than 1 whereas companies providing more stability such as retailing or banking services have betas less than 1.

A Ltd and B Ltd have betas of 0.8 and 1.2 respectively. The risk-free rate is 4% and the risk premium is 6%. What is the expected return on each share?

$$A\,Ltd\ R_i = R_f + \beta_i(R_m - R_f)$$
$$= 4\% + 0.8(6\%)$$
$$= 8.8\%$$
$$B\,Ltd\ R_i = R_f + \beta_i(R_m - R_f)$$
$$= 4\% + 1.2(6\%)$$
$$= 11.2\%$$

It is important to note that the only difference between these two shares is their beta. The risk-free rate and risk premium for the two are the same; indeed, they are the same for all shares on any particular market (but not for shares listed on different markets). The difference in expected returns is determined only by their betas.

When all shares are correctly priced as per the CAPM, we expect to see the relationship shown in figure 5.16.

FIGURE 5.16 Graphical representation of the CAPM

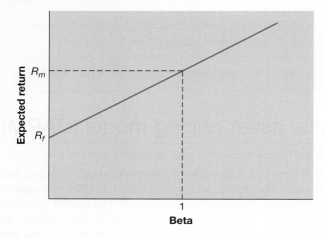

In figure 5.16, we see an upward-sloping relationship between systematic risk and return. This upward-sloping line is called the *securities market line* (SML). Figure 5.16 also shows that the beta of the market return is 1. After all, the relative risk of the market as a whole relative to itself must be 1. The SML can be used to identify undervalued and overvalued shares. In the case of A Ltd and B Ltd, imagine we believed that A Ltd would actually provide a return of 15% and B Ltd would actually provide a return of 10%. Their expected returns given by the CAPM are 8.8% and 11.2% respectively. This situation is shown in figure 5.17.

As shown in figure 5.17, A Ltd is offering a higher return than we would expect given the CAPM. Similarly, B Ltd is offering a lower return than we would expect given the CAPM. Investors who discovered this would buy A Ltd because, for low risk, they can get high returns. As they continued to buy A Ltd, its price would rise and, for a given future price and future dividends, the return would fall until it was offering the expected CAPM return (8.8%). Similarly, investors would sell B Ltd. As they continued to sell, the price of B Ltd would fall. For a given future price and future dividends, the return of B Ltd would rise until it reached the expected CAPM return.

Looking at figure 5.17, we see that A Ltd plots above the SML, while B Ltd plots below the SML. All shares that plot *above* the line are *undervalued*, and those that plot *below* the line are *overvalued*.

FIGURE 5.17 Undervalued and overvalued shares and the SML

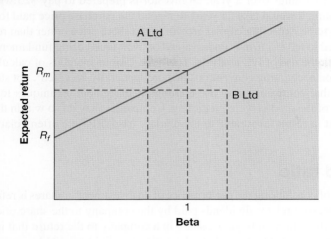

The two basic functions of the CAPM are to estimate expected returns (using the basic formula) and to identify undervalued and overvalued shares. Those practitioners who use the CAPM, however, use it for estimating expected returns — few use it to identify undervalued and overvalued shares. In order to make practical use of the CAPM, three pieces of information are needed — the risk-free rate, the market risk premium (note that these two pieces of information are the same for all shares on any one market), and the share beta.

The risk-free rate is usually taken to be the returns on a short-term government bond, although some practitioners make use of long-term government bonds. The market risk premium is the difference between the market return and the risk-free rate. Each of these variables can be forecast, or historical data can be used. As long as usage is consistent, there is no reason either of these approaches is better than the other. Estimating the share beta, however, is more complex and most practitioners make use of a statistical procedure called regression analysis.

5.8 Basic valuation models to value shares

LEARNING OBJECTIVE 5.8 Apply some basic valuation models to value shares.

In the following sections, three basic valuation models are introduced — the P/E ratio, the dividend yield ratio and the residual income model. There are other valuation models that you may learn in finance classes such as: the dividend discount model (which uses CAPM), the free cash flow method and other variations of the P/E ratio.

Price-earnings ratio

One of the simplest valuation techniques used is the price-earnings ratio (P/E). The P/E ratio is simple to calculate and easy to understand.

$$P/E = \frac{\text{Price per share}}{\text{Earnings per share}}$$

Consider the P/E ratio in the situation of FGH Ltd and Stefano the analyst. If the price per share of FGH Ltd was $10 and the expected earnings per share $1, then we would say that FGH Ltd was trading at 10 times earnings.

There are at least two ways this ratio can be used. The most common way is to calculate the P/E of a particular firm, and then assume that this P/E will be stable over time and use it as a forecast of whether prices are overvalued or undervalued on the market.

Stefano is valuing FGH Ltd which historically has had a P/E of 10. He has estimated that earnings per share (EPS) will be $1.20 next year. He therefore expects that the share price should be $12 per share. This is a simple form of valuation, which is quite popular and widespread. A potential problem with this type of valuation is that there is no indication that P/Es are stable over time. Indeed, the evidence seems to suggest that they are not stable over time.

The P/E ratio is an indicator of whether a share is overvalued or undervalued. For example, a P/E of 25 indicates that, for $1 of earnings over a year, an investor is prepared to pay $25 which could also mean that, to earn $1 per annum, it would take 25 years to recoup the purchase price paid for the share. Thus, the investor is more likely to be expecting capital growth in the share price rather than relying on dividends.

P/E ratios can be used to tell if a firm is undervalued or overvalued using fundamentals. In general, there are some problems with the use of P/E analysis. There are various methods of calculating EPS, and these methods are all based on accounting conventions that are 'generally accepted', not standardised. Investors should also be aware that companies may use earnings management techniques to provide an earnings result that the analysts of the market were predicting. Companies may do so within the generally accepted accounting rules to 'tilt' a result favourable to the market. Also, EPS are often volatile over time and can often be negative.

Dividend yield ratio

Another common way of considering the performance of an investment in shares is referring to a company's dividend yield. This measure relates dividends paid by the company to the share price of the company. It is a way of comparing the return on buying a share in a company to the return that is paid by, say, a term deposit or any other investment. The formula to determine the dividend yield is as follows.

$$\text{Dividend yield} = \frac{\text{Price dividends received over the year}}{\text{Share price}}$$

So, suppose a company pays a dividend of $2 per share over the year and its share price is $40. The return on the share would be 5% (i.e. $2 / $40 = 5%). This represents the return that an investor may expect when buying a share at $40. If the share price was $45 then the dividend yield would be 4.44%.

Figure 5.18 represents the history of dividend yields from 1920 to 2020 and indicates a general lessening of dividend yields over time as the relative price of shares has increased.

FIGURE 5.18 Dividend yields

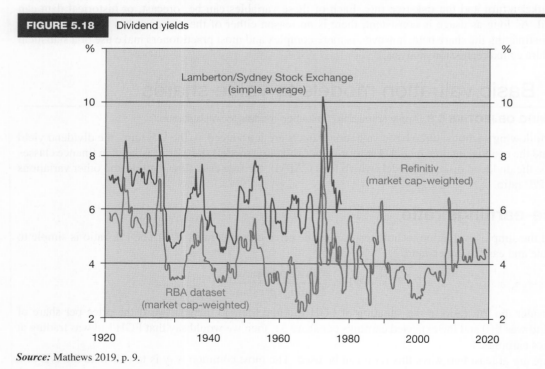

Source: Mathews 2019, p. 9.

The residual income model

A relatively simple way of valuing a company is to apply the residual income valuation model. It is an approach to valuation of the equity in a company that takes into consideration an expected rate of return on the net assets of the company. 'Residual' is the excess of any value that is measured relative to the book value of shareholders' equity after allowing for a cost of capital. This approach is like the EVA approach and the abnormal earnings model which can also be researched further as a method of valuation.

The basis behind the residual income model is that the portion of a share's price which is usually above (or sometimes below) the book value of a company is attributable to the company's extra hidden value or expertise of the management team. Thus, the model is a tool for calculating what a more realistic value of a share is.

To calculate the value of a company, the net assets or equity of the company at the beginning of the year are multiplied by the expected or desired rate of return of the company and then compared against the net income earned by the company over the year. The difference is the residual income.

The basic formula to calculate the residual income is as follows.

$$\text{RI (end)} = \text{Net income (end)} - (\text{Net assets (begin)} \times \text{Required rate of return})$$

And the simplified model to value the company is as follows.

$$V\,Beg = BV\,Beg + \frac{\sum RI_t}{(1+r)^t}$$

To restate: the residual income model measures the net income that an investment earns above the threshold established by the minimum rate of return assigned to the investment. Also, when share investors settle on a price they will pay for each share, they consider future expectations of the success or otherwise of a company.

Let's consider how it works in the following example.

ILLUSTRATIVE EXAMPLE 5.4

Adi Company has net equity or book value at the beginning of the year (BV beg) of $400 per share and its owners require a 10% return of capital (i.e. a return of $40 per share). Suppose the firm had earnings of $50 per share (EPS) then the residual income (RI) would be $10 per share. But if Adi Company paid a $5 dividend per share (DPS) to shareholders, the residual income would be reduced to $5 per share and the equity of the firm at the end of the year (BV end) would be $405 per share.

In the next year, suppose the RI is $6 per share and, the year after, it is $8 per share. The next step is to discount the future RI to a present value so we can assess the price at which share investors are willing to pay for a share in Adi Company.

Table 5.1 provides this information in tabular form.

TABLE 5.1   Adi company — book value

	BV Beg 1	End year 1	End year 2	End year 3
BV Beg	$ 400	$ 405	$ 418.50	$ 448.65
EPS		$ 50	$ 60	$ 80
DPS		$ 5	$ 6	$ 8
Required return BV Beg × 10%		$ 40	$ 40.50	$ 41.85
RI		$ 5	$ 13.5	$ 30.15
Discount factor at 10%*		0.9091	0.8264	0.7514
Present value of future earnings		$4.5455	$11.1564	$22.6517
Total of future earnings	$ 38.35			
Value of firm (Beg BV + PV of future earnings)	$438.35			

* Discount factors can be found in most finance text books

Table 5.2 gives this information in short form.

TABLE 5.2   Adi company — residual income per share

Value of firm at Beginning =	Book value at beginning +	Residual income per share end Year 1 +	Residual income per share end Year 2 +	Residual income per share end Year 3
	$ 400	$ 5	$ 13.50	$ 30.15
Discount factor		1.10	1.10	1.10
PV of residual income p.a.		$4.5455	$11.1654	$22.6517
Total PV of residual income p.a.	$ 38.35			
Value per share	$438.35			

Value of the firm at Beg   =   BV Beg + $400 + $5 + $13.50 + $30.15
Value Beg   = $400 + $4.5455 + $11.1564 + $22.6517
  = $438.35 per share

As forecasted residual earnings are positive, the shares of this firm are valued at $438.35 which is a premium over the current book value $400 per share. If the share price on the market was above $400 per share, the residual income model indicates that the share is worth more than the market price. If, however, the model showed the value to be below $400 per share, it means the shares are trading at a discount.

As with all valuation models, the residual income model relies very much on the forecast of future earnings.

Other methods may also be used to value shares. Two methods, the free cash flow and the dividend discount methods use fundamental accounting reports and a discounting approach to make estimations of the value of shares. All the methods suffer from an infinite time horizon used to discount future earnings. Hence, when a time horizon is imposed, any model is affected by assumptions about estimates and forecasts about future earnings. Generally, the valuation methods arrive at a similar outcome with reasonable consistency in the valuation of companies.

'Growth' versus 'value' investment

As we have seen, measures such as the P/E ratio and return or dividend yield have been deemed to be important guides to investment. However, opinions differ about the 'best' way to use these tools.

One school of thought is that *growth* investments with high P/E ratios and related low yields have potential for future high growth and therefore should be purchased now to enjoy future gains. In these cases, the market, through the extent of buying, has bid the price up so that the price has grown at a faster rate than earnings. This seems to indicate expectations of significant future growth. John Maynard Keynes, the famous economist, is said to have followed this investment principle to his financial advantage, even though he believed buying for value to be more rational. Success with this strategy depends on being able to sell the investment before other investors realise the price has outstripped the investment's ability to make a reasonable return on committed funds. For example, some US technology shares were priced so high in late 1999 that they needed to increase profits and dividends by 25% each year for the next 100 years in order to make average returns.

Consider a share like CSL (Commonwealth Serum Laboratories). In March 2002, its price was $42, its P/E was about 80 and its dividend yield was 0.62%. When CSL was privatised by the Commonwealth Government, the share became a favourite of the market and the price was pushed up by the weight of buying pressure. The price outran the growth in earnings at that time. Nevertheless, buyers still thought there was scope for the company to increase its profits in the reasonable future. However, the world price for blood products fell and CSL's earning potential was no longer so rosy. The share price fell to less than $20, but later recovered to about $30. In July 2005, the price was about $35, the P/E was 23 and the dividend yield was 1.2%. Two years later in July 2007, after much good news about vaccine sales and research results, the price was about $89, the P/E was 31 and the yield 1%. The share had been as high as $98 in the preceding 12 months. In October 2007, the shareholders approved a 3-for-1 share split which effectively tripled the number of shares and reduced the price per share by one-third. The share split was intended to benefit shareholders by increasing the liquidity and affordability to retail investors. By 2010, CSL's share price was around $33.75, its P/E was 18.2 and the dividend yield was 2.37%. By June 2013, the price was $59.60, its P/E was 27.5 and its dividend yield was 1.61. In June 2016 the share price was $108.09, its P/E was 26.23 and its dividend yield was 1.58. In June 2024 CSL shares were $282.78, P/E was 36.75 and dividend yield was 1.16%.

Some of the reasons for the growth in share price of CSL are: people are prepared to pay more for quality health products; there is a limited number of suppliers of such products (hence, few competitors); more products have been developed increasing the market share; and an ageing population requires more healthcare products. Hence, with the rise in price and fall in dividend yield, the company may be seen as relatively expensive but investors are focused on the growth prospects of the firm.

The other investment strategy is to buy with *value* in mind always. Is the asset apparently underpriced in relation to value norms? If it is a business, how many years of current profits are necessary to pay back the purchase price? If it is a share, is the P/E ratio lower than the current market average and is the dividend yield higher than the current market average? If this is so, and the asset does seem to be priced so that its purchase would give good value, is there some known future detriment or liability that is depressing the current price? If not, this asset may well be a good investment.

Many recent studies have suggested that portfolios consisting of shares which were purchased with low P/E and high dividend yields eventually perform well. Moreover, the selection of shares within those attribute constraints does not require any great skill — selection may be *random*.

If investing on the basis of value is such a sure winner, the question must be asked as to why 'value' shares languish on the market for extended periods of time before they start to enjoy price increases. The answer must surely be that there is a deal of fashion and herd mentality in all asset markets, and especially on the share market. Keynes observed that professional investors and speculators seemed to be far more concerned with forecasting short-term speculative gains which result from market enthusiasms. They are less concerned with real value and probable yields in the long term.

5.9 Alternative direct investments

LEARNING OBJECTIVE 5.9 Appreciate the existence of other forms of direct investment.

'Alternative investments' is the name currently being generally applied to investments in assets such as infrastructure (e.g. toll roads, railways, airports and water supplies), property development trusts, residential property trusts, private equity and hedge funds. Where the vehicles owning these assets are listed, such as listed property trusts, they may be considered by the potential investor as much the same as listed equities. Another alternative investment, private equity, will now be considered.

While private equity has received a great deal of media attention in the last few years because of the raising of high levels of debt, the takeover of well-known companies and brands, and the increase in risk for all stakeholders, this sort of private equity investment is outside the world of the personal investor. In contrast, private equity, in the sense of owning your own business (e.g. owning a service station, newsagency or bottle shop, or running your own accountancy firm, dental practice or legal firm) has always been in the realm of the private investor. In many cases, the owner(s) may organise their business as a company with the shareholding held by one, two or more people. The value of the shares will then represent the value of the entity. When a small business owner wishes to sell their business, it is likely that the shares in the company will be sold to another small business operator and the business will continue on.

Other markets

Precious metals such as gold, silver and platinum are used as investment assets. It is possible to accumulate these metals in the form of collectables such as coins and crafted wares including jugs and plates, but people also collect ingots which have value but not much beauty. Precious metals are seen as a hedge against inflation, but their prices are also subject to supply and demand pressures and do not rise in a consistent fashion.

In addition to the conventional asset classes, there are other types of assets where people invest funds. Many of these markets started as hobbies which grew and 'got out of hand'. Some of these markets trade wines, art, antiques, stamps, bank notes, coins and various other collectables. Things become assets with market value when several people are willing to buy them. For example, the share certificates (scrip) of nineteenth century railway schemes, gold mines and like ventures were often highly ornate. Collectors became interested in collecting these intrinsically worthless pieces of paper and a new asset class was born. The hobby is called scripophily (love of scrip). Another example is the bond certificates issued by the Confederate States of America to finance the fighting of the American Civil War in 1861–65. These are worth nothing even though the South still owes money to the holders, but they are actively traded among scripophiles. The problem with markets of such items is that they may be quite 'thin', where the price may be made by relatively few buyers.

Another class of investment involves various agricultural schemes. These schemes have a long history in Australia and have involved emus, ostriches, goats, stud cattle, stud sheep, racing horses, llamas, trees for timber, trees for pulp, paulownia, aloe vera, nuts, jojoba; and the flowers, foliage and fruits of Australian native vegetation species. The schemes are often promoted as a means of having access to the simpler and more 'pure' country lifestyle with the added attraction of reducing tax. Many of these schemes have resulted in losses rather than increases in wealth. Government rulings have taken away significant tax advantages and, combined with the effect of the global financial crisis, where very little new money was invested in the schemes and loan money was not available to support the schemes, many schemes went into administration and liquidation.

Ethical investment

Reflecting a shift in societal values, ethical or social investment has emerged as an identifiable force in the last decade or so. The term 'ethical investment' tends to be used in the United Kingdom and Australia, whereas alternative names such as environmental, 'green' and socially responsible investment (SRI) are used mainly in the United States.

Ethical investments have characteristics which allow investors to integrate their personal values and social concerns with their investment objectives. Thus, businesses actively supported by such investments ('investees') operate in industries or carry out activities the investors approve of and want to support.

Ethical investors interested in putting their funds to work in companies they approve of are rather limited in the scope of activities and number of investees. Additionally, the lack of ready information about all the activities of corporations is a constraint to investment. Investors may invest directly in the primary or secondary market when they find a company they approve of. They may use the growing number of investment brokers who offer a service in screening the corporate world for likely ethical investments, or they may invest in trust funds especially set up to attract the ethical investor.

Surveys have found that environmental concerns are high in priority for Australian ethical investors. The issues with highest priority are active rather than reactive in nature, being environmental protection, sustainable land use, forest logging/woodchipping, reafforestation, and efficiency of energy and resource use. Of lesser importance, but still of concern, are the screening out of armaments, repressive regimes, unfair work practices, uranium and nuclear industries, and racism and discrimination. One issue to consider when choosing to invest in ethical investments is that an investor might increase the risk of investment because of a reduction in diversification; that is, the investor is choosing a portfolio based on a restricted number of shares in the total market.

5.10 Qualities and characteristics of property

LEARNING OBJECTIVE 5.10 Outline the qualities and characteristics of property for investment.

The term 'property investment' covers a wide asset class with many ways in which a person may invest as part of a broad-based investment portfolio. An obvious property investment is in one's own home, which will be discussed more in the next chapter. Another form of property investment is to purchase an investment property and use negative gearing as the financing method. This is discussed further in the chapter on taxation planning. Of course there are other ways of investing in propertyin the form of an investment company or an investment trust. There is a wide range of property investments to consider.

Although investment in property principally consists of an investment in buildings to produce an income stream and capital growth in the longer term, it has a great deal to do with the scarcity of land. In capital cities, we often see the purchase of a property followed by the demolition of the building and the construction of a new building. In many such cases, the purchase has been based solely on the position of the land and hence its value, and not on the building. So, it is the scarcity value of land that is the substantial reason for the escalation in prices of many properties.

Property, as an asset class for investment, has a number of particular characteristics. The main characteristics of property include the following.

- It is generally regarded as a solid, tangible form of investment — some investors argue that they are investing in 'bricks and mortar' rather than a piece of paper representing a share certificate.
- Land is a scarce commodity and subject to changes in value according to demand.
- An investment in property is generally illiquid — part of it cannot be sold easily.
- Diversification is limited if a large proportion of a portfolio is invested in one location.
- Returns are less volatile than dividends paid from shares and capital values are relatively stable compared to shares.
- Returns may comprise both capital and income.
- Entry costs and exit costs can be relatively high.
- Management and maintenance costs can be expensive.
- A higher level of gearing is possible as lenders prefer to lend against property investments.
- Taxation advantages, such as depreciation allowances, provide investment incentives.
- Some property investments can offer diversification across a range of property classes as well as diversification of asset portfolios.
- Property market values are not subjected to daily valuations, unlike the share market.
- Property markets exhibit pronounced cycles which may not coincide with other sectors of the share market such as media, retailing, beverages or consumer services.
- Property markets may be affected by different cycles of values. For example, holiday houses tend to take a longer time to recover from a slump in the economy or rise in interest rates than residential property.

5.11 Different forms of property investment

LEARNING OBJECTIVE 5.11 Describe the different forms of property investment.

When deciding to invest in property, a person has a wide range of choices. They can invest in a direct form or an indirect form and can select from a range of options within these forms. The decision to invest directly or indirectly is based, principally, on the amount of funds available for investment and also on the requirement for diversification.

Direct property investment

A person may own property directly in freehold form when they have bought a property at auction or by private sale and they, or a related entity such as a trust, are the registered proprietor; that is, the person or entity whose name appears on the title.

Direct property investment can be broken down into a variety of classes. These include residential (the most numerous and familiar type of direct property holding), retail, commercial, agricultural and industrial properties. Then it is also possible to identify types of each class of property. For example, commercial property can be divided into suburban strip commercial, regional shopping centres, CBD office buildings, hotels, motels, entertainment centres and so on.

Indirect property investment

Indirect property investments are other forms of property investments where the property is owned via a third party. Indirect property investment is most frequently seen in the following forms.

- Listed real estate investment trusts (REITs) — formerly known as listed property trusts (LPTs), these are property trusts that are traded on the ASX.
- Unlisted property trusts (UPTs) — property funds that are not listed on the securities exchange.
- Property securities funds — unlisted trusts that hold investments in listed property trusts and other unlisted property trusts.
- Mortgage funds — trusts that hold mortgages over properties.
- Mixed funds — funds that hold some properties, as well as a range of other asset classes such as convertible notes.
- Private property syndicates — small groups of investors who form to purchase property.

These entities tend to invest in property other than residential property, although in recent times some small property syndicates have formed to buy and hold residential properties. Indirect property investment provides the means by which people can invest small amounts of capital but gain the benefits of diversification of investment in the property market.

As property investment can cover a very wide field, this section of the chapter will focus on property investment that financial planners are more likely to consider as part of a financial plan for most clients. Residential property is a favoured form of property investment for many people and is usually undertaken directly. The more favoured indirect form of investing in property is conducted via funds that focus mostly on commercial property. These two types of property investment are considered more closely next.

Residential property

Residential property has, generally, had a significant rise in capital value since the early 2000s. Traditionally, in the long term, residential property has provided rates of return lower than Australian and international shares. However, downturns in share markets and a boom in housing prices have seen some areas of residential property attain high rates of capital growth. The rapid rise in some housing areas may be considered to be a study of land economics. In brief, this consists of a limited supply of undeveloped land for housing development (based on government zoning plans); the cost of local government charges; costs of surveying; infrastructure costs, such as street lighting, drainage and road construction (some of which may be subsidised by government); and availability of finance at low interest rates to undertake the total development.

Some argue that a rise in capital city house prices is because state governments limit supply of land around capital cities by means of zoning (which means that tracts of land are not available for housing development). Others argue it is a function of our high levels of immigration with many people settling permanently in Australia. Others suggest it is a consequence of policies such as the continuation of negative gearing and a lowering of the capital gains tax which encourage investment in property as part of an investment strategy. The truth may be that the cause of the rise in capital city house prices is a mixture of all three.

Of course, not all sectors of the residential property market have seen substantial rises in values. Many houses in regional centres and towns have not experienced the same rate of this growth. The point to note is that different sectors of all property markets have cycles of demand and supply peculiar to the sector and not all types of property perform equally at the same time.

Commercial property

Commercial property investment is largely the domain of institutional investment groups or high net-wealth individuals. This is largely due to the capital required to undertake a commercial property acquisition and the knowledge and experience that is necessary to determine a sound investment.

Commercial property includes a wide range of real estate such as CBD, suburban strips and regional centres in the form of offices, retail, industrial factory, warehouse, farming, infrastructure, or leisure and tourism properties. Each has different risk and return characteristics, and income and capital growth features. Commercial property can cost millions of dollars, which means that most investors are unlikely to invest directly with such large sums of money required to purchase these buildings.

There are several factors to consider in buying a commercial property, such as the local geographic area, the trend in consumer demand and labour supply, lease covenants, zoning restrictions, redevelopment potential and specific information relating to the property itself (such as the amount of rent, terms of leases, vacancy levels and expected yields). In addition, the purchaser needs to have a comparative basis for the value of the property or some other means to ensure the property is purchased at a fair value.

It is interesting to note that the yield (the return of income expressed as a percentage of the value of the property) and the income security available from commercial property is usually superior to residential property. For example, the highest yields generally are available from industrial property, say at 9% to 10%. A well-located retail or office property may yield 7% to 8% while residential property would usually command about 5% to 6%.

Income security is also greater with longer-term leases, which in general have built-in rent increases and provisions to recover outgoings. In some cases, leases are secured with bank guarantees to cover up to 6 months rent in case of a lessee default.

An investment risk is that the tenant may cease trading or that, for some reason, the tenant will not renew the lease at the expiry of the current lease. This means a big part of the investment decision process is finding out about the current tenant as well as how easy it may be to obtain another tenant for the property if, for any reason, the property becomes vacant. Hence, the property manager considers the matter of 'future maintainable rent'; that is, not the current rent but the rent that could realistically be achieved if the property was placed on the market should the current tenant leave.

Property funds provide for easy access in terms of low-cost entry and wide diversification benefits. The next chapter will look at managed funds; however, in this section we will consider property funds as a form of investment in property.

5.12 Features and benefits of property funds

LEARNING OBJECTIVE 5.12 Describe the features and benefits of property funds.

Property funds are pooled investments where the property assets are divided into units for investors. They are set up as trusts with investors as 'unit holders' and beneficial owners of the properties in the trust, with the legal owner of the properties as the trustee of the trust. The sections which follow describe the features and different forms of property fund.

Real estate investment trusts

The units in a listed real estate investment trust (REIT — formerly known as a listed property trust or LPT) are listed on the ASX like shares in companies. In Australia, such a trust is referred to as an **A-REIT**. The owners of the trust (unit holders) can trade their units on the ASX in the same way as they would any share or other listed security. Investors owning units in the trust receive benefits from distributions, tax advantages and capital gains in the price of traded units. The managers of the trust (otherwise known as the responsible entity or RE) buy, sell and manage property assets with a view to maximising returns for unit holders.

To measure the performance of A-REITs, investors can compare the performance of a particular A-REIT against the property trust average and against other assets. The most appropriate measure is the S&P/ASX 200 Property Trust Index, which is a weighted average of unit prices in A-REITs listed on the ASX.

Unlisted property trusts

'The essential guide to investing in Unlisted Property Trusts' (Green 2019) outlines a number of features of an unlisted property trust (UPT). UPT is not listed on the securities exchange. They are usually 'open-ended' trusts; this means they can expand by issuing new units which can then be used to purchase new properties or to retire debt. Some UPTs require a notification period for withdrawal of an investment amount; it may take between 10 and 30 days, and in some cases months, to redeem an investment. In that sense, a UPT is a relatively illiquid investment. Whereas A-REIT unit prices may constantly change as units are publicly traded on the securities exchange and may act more like shares, the prices of UPTs reflect a more stable form of investment value and may be likened to a fixed-interest investment.

UPTs are usually smaller than A-REITs, hold a less substantial property portfolio and, generally, carry higher amounts of debt to fund the purchase of properties.

Lessons from the late 1980s, early 1990s and the GFC are instructive. In the earlier period, UPTs suffered severe setbacks when record high interest rates and falling demand for property saw most UPTs facing serious liquidity problems. When investors tried to redeem their investments and get their money back, the managers could not sell the properties without realising a loss and, in fact, some could not even find a buyer. Managers froze redemptions for up to two years and some unlisted property trusts closed altogether, leaving some investors with a significant capital loss. Again, in the global financial crisis, some UPTs curtailed redemptions from the fund which restricted a possible closure of the funds altogether. Some funds only allowed redemptions to be made by investors over a period of 2–3 years to avoid dramatic losses for the investors who remained in the fund.

As a result of past liquidity problems, most UPTs now have strategies in place to deal with a repeat of a rush of redemption requests. In many cases, these funds have evolved into hybrid funds where significant amounts are invested in A-REITs as well as direct property. The A-REIT investments are principally held in property but since the units are traded on the ASX they are far more liquid, which in turn makes the UPT a relatively more liquid investment than previously was the case.

Property syndicates

The high entry price for commercial property means it is often purchased by pooling the resources of more than one investor. Property syndicates are designed to have a shorter life than UPTs (typically 5 to 7 years) and invest in office, retail and industrial properties. Examples of the types of commercial property a syndicate might invest in include entertainment venues, caravan parks, healthcare projects and retirement villages. Consider an example of a small investor syndicate. To illustrate the workings of a syndicate assume four people join together to buy a factory costing $2 million. Each contributes $100 000 of their own money (possibly borrowed from their bank against the security of their home), then they each borrow $400 000 from a separate bank secured against the factory and the owners' personal guarantees.

An advantage of this arrangement is that each of the four owners has been able to access an investment that may have been beyond them individually. However, they need to agree to hold the investment for a stated period of time as they would be relying on each other to buy the other out if some issue arose and they needed to sell their share within the agreed time frame.

Usually property syndicates are formed for a set period of time with an objective of selling the property at the end of that period, after realising an expected capital growth and high levels of rental income during the period. A feature of the small property syndicate is that, provided certain conditions are met, a small number of investors may combine to buy one or more properties without having to satisfy the rules of the Corporations Act regarding licensing of responsible entities and the issuing of product disclosure statements and other regulatory requirements.

Property securities funds

Property securities funds hold a portfolio of units in A-REITs, other types of property funds and cash. They offer liquidity to investors as they do not hold property directly but provide for an investment in property to fit an investor's portfolio. Some specialise by sector, such as retail properties, but most are diversified.

Some of these funds do not try to outperform an index but are passive investments as they track an index of A-REIT performance. They suit most investors as they provide for diversification without having to choose or monitor an individual A-REIT and without an additional level of fees.

Mortgage funds

Mortgage funds enable investors to invest in a fund which holds a number of mortgages over property. Investments in mortgage funds are relatively illiquid with many requiring a 12-month investment period before redemption of the original investment. They are unlisted funds which hold mortgages over property against borrowers of the funds raised by the mortgage fund.

Returns are provided to investors in the form of a fixed interest payment based on the repayments of interest and loans by the mortgagors (borrowers). No capital growth is expected from an investment in a mortgage fund. The unit holder shares in the risk of default by a mortgagor and the effectiveness of the manager of the fund to lend responsibly to borrowers. Mortgage funds usually hold first mortgages up to 65% of the loan-to-valuation ratio (LVR) to limit the exposure to any default.

Mezzanine funds

A mezzanine fund lends money to developers who need to borrow more than they can borrow from the banking sector. Banks lend to a certain level of the value of a property development but the developers may require additional borrowings to fund the project. Such funds may be raised from investors with the promise of higher rates of interest as the manager of the fund lends the money to developers at a higher rate. However, the prospect of higher returns comes with an additional level of risk that the developer may not succeed with the plans of the project on time, if at all.

Hybrid funds

A hybrid fund is one which invests in a mixture of units in A-REITs, UPTs, syndicates and other forms of property funds, convertible notes, as well as cash. These funds offer diversification of property investment across listed and unlisted property funds and also between debt and equity forms of investment. A hybrid fund may also gear the fund by borrowing funds to achieve a higher rate of return.

A hybrid fund offers investors the chance of comparable returns of property fund investment but, above all, the benefits of liquidity and diversification.

Unit pricing of property funds

To invest in a property fund, an investor purchases units in the fund. Most funds require an initial investment of \$5 000, which buys a certain number of units. The price of each unit depends on the type of property fund but generally represents a portion of the market value of the properties in the fund.

A-REIT unit prices are determined by the same market forces that determine the price of any security. The unit price is equal to the market value of the underlying properties less any debt, divided by the number of units on issue, as shown in table 5.3.

TABLE 5.3   A-REIT unit prices

Market value of property held by the fund	\$40 000 000
Less: Mortgage debt owed to lenders	\$15 000 000
Equals net asset value	\$25 000 000
Divided by number of issued units	12 500 000
Equals price per unit	\$ 2.00

Because properties are not revalued on a daily basis, units of A-REITs may trade at a premium or discount to the net asset value of the fund depending on the market's assessment of the property trust's prospects. In practice, the net asset value used is the net tangible asset (NTA) backing of the fund. The NTA is derived from the net asset value by deducting intangible assets such as goodwill, brand names and copyright.

Factors relevant to the market's assessment of unit prices may include:
- the A-REIT's income yield — that is, net income expressed as a percentage of the property's current market value, relative to some benchmark such as current interest rates
- expected rental growth and capital growth, which largely depends on the quality of the underlying properties and the strength of the A-REIT's management team
- general economic conditions in Australia and the rest of the world.

Units of UPTs are bought and sold via the manager; that is, a management company appointed by the unit holders to manage the property trust's affairs including the transfer, issue and redemption of its units and the maintenance of all unit-holder records.

An unlisted property trust's unit price will be set by the manager in a similar way as the determination of an A-REIT unit price. However, the fund manager deducts a manager's fee for handling the redemption or transfer of units.

The value of units in mortgage funds usually does not change as they reflect the characteristics of a fixed-interest investment whereby the original capital invested at the start is returned at the expiry of a predetermined period of time.

Summary of benefits of investing in a property fund

Property funds provide the opportunity to invest in a number of properties, allowing investors to diversify their portfolio by location, size and sector (e.g. office, industrial, shops and hotels) and also to avoid cyclical fluctuations in unit prices by owning properties in several of these categories. The cost of such diversification may be gained for a relatively small initial outlay.

An investment in a property fund is a 'unitised' investment, allowing the buyer to purchase a parcel of units representing a pro rata entitlement to the distribution of income — derived generally from rent from the fund's properties. If an investor chooses to reinvest the distribution of income they will be allocated more units in the fund.

In addition, property funds do not require management by the unit holder because the ongoing maintenance and management of the trust is undertaken by the responsible entity. The manager of the fund does not own properties. The properties are owned by the unit holders and are held in trust on their behalf by the manager/responsible entity. The manager of a property fund is, in effect, a contracted employee of unit holders and can typically be removed by a majority vote of unit holders. Management fees vary from about 0.5% to 1.5% p.a. of the gross value of the assets of the trust. In addition, the manager may be entitled to property management fees and performance incentives. Such fees are an extra layer of costs that are levied. The manager, for example, may obtain a fee for arranging new leases, monitoring tenants to ensure the building is well maintained according to their contract and dealing with other such property management matters. The only decisions required by the investor are the buy or sell decision and those related to voting at general meetings.

Another apartment?

Bruno is a 36-year-old middle manager with a no-nonsense attitude in a large firm. He says he has been too busy attending to his career to be much concerned with his finances, but over the Christmas holidays has decided to take stock and make some wealth accumulation plans. He is single and has no plans for marriage in the near future. He wants to take an annual holiday to Europe and he can comfortably afford to with his salary level. He expects promotion within his firm in the next 2 years, where he anticipates an increase in his salary of about 25%. He currently is paid a gross salary of $170 000.

Bruno lived with his parents until he was 25 years of age, when he purchased a one-bedroom apartment for $240 000. He has now paid off the outstanding loan and has even more income surplus to his needs as he can now save the mortgage repayments that he was paying to the bank. He has about $30 000 in a cash account and, in a special savings account (established since he repaid his loan some months ago), he has $20 000 available for investment.

He has now come to you for advice. Bruno estimates that his apartment is now valued at about $640 000 and that he can allocate about $1000 per fortnight to his next venture into wealth accumulation. For his superannuation fund, he has nominated the Australian shares option so he considers that he has enough exposure to shares. He decides that he wants to invest more in the property market as he has seen how the value of his apartment has increased in the past few years. He is wondering if he should invest in another apartment in the same building where he lives as an apartment has just come onto the market for $600 000.

QUESTIONS

1. Calculate the interest that Bruno would have to pay based on an interest-only loan of 4.5% p.a. when he has to borrow the full amount. Identify other costs that he would be required to pay, both upfront and ongoing.

2. Suppose Bruno was able to let the property for $600 per week and allocate the extra savings of $1000 per fortnight to the financing of the project. Ascertain whether it is affordable without consideration of any taxation advantages. Prepare a table to illustrate the advantages and disadvantages of the proposal in question 2 (draw on the information in question 1) compared to an alternative proposal to invest the savings into a property trust (or property trusts) assuming that Bruno borrows 100% of the $600 000 on an interest-only basis to invest in the alternative proposal.

5.13 Taxation of property investments

LEARNING OBJECTIVE 5.13 Explain the taxation effects of investing in property.

Property investments are subject to the same income and capital gains tax rules as other investments. Property investors benefit from the discount available on capital gains before tax and they also benefit through the depreciation allowance rules to reduce assessable income. Thus, there are two specific taxation advantages of investing in property.

Property funds are in the legal form of trusts. Trusts provide a 'flow through' of the income and capital gain derived by the trust and provide tax benefits in the form of tax-free and tax-deferred income. They are very tax effective for investors. Consider the tax consequences of someone who has an investment property. The income to be declared in the income statement is the gross rental or lease income from the tenant. The deductions that can offset the income include:

- loan interest — most property investors borrow money to acquire an investment property and, under taxation rules, are allowed to deduct the interest as a cost of earning the income
- borrowing costs of loan — the set-up costs of borrowing funds are allowed to be deducted over a 5-year period
- depreciation — depending on when the property was built, a capital depreciation allowance of 2.5% p.a. of the cost of the building is allowable if the building commenced after August 1979, except for the period between August 1984 and September 1987 when it was 4%

- depreciation of furniture, fittings and appliances according to the various depreciation rates, which range from 5% to 20% p.a. depending on the item, as determined by the ATO
- rates and insurance
- agent fees
- repairs (but not capital expenses, which must be depreciated)
- other costs that may be incurred in earning the rental income.

In many situations, investors purchase an investment property as a negative gearing strategy where the expenses will exceed the income. The ATO allows for the loss to be claimed because it is assumed that, in the long run when the property is sold, tax will be levied on the capital gain. Refer to the chapter on taxation planning to review the capital gains tax rules and taxation on real estate. With this strategy, however, there is the matter of the **cost base** of the property. When the property is sold, the cost base or original cost is reduced by the accumulated depreciation for the building that has been claimed as an expense over the years of ownership. The reduction in the cost base tends to increase the capital gain and hence the amount of tax to be paid on sale of the property. Of course, while it is assumed the property will be held for the purposes of achieving a capital gain, there are occasions when the sale of a property may result in a capital loss.

Tax advantages of a property fund

Trusts are not taxpaying entities, so cannot benefit from tax deductions that arise in the normal course of business. Therefore, the passing on of these tax benefits to the unit holder gives rise to a 'tax advantaged' component to dividend distributions received by the investor. The tax-free component relates to certain deductions available to the trust and the tax-deferred element derives from building depreciation allowances. In this case, tax is paid including the tax-deferred component only when the unit holder disposes of their units. The value of this tax-advantaged component compared with the distribution actually paid can be quite high for investors in high tax brackets.

Illustrative example 5.5 shows both the tax for a year's income and the tax on the gain on sale of the property after holding the property for 5 years. It illustrates the effect of the reduced cost base when units in an unlisted property trust are sold. When income is distributed from a property trust, the income is assessable income to an individual. However, some of the income is classified as tax-exempt and some is tax-deferred. To repeat, the tax-deferred income is, in effect, the depreciation allowances for the building that need to be deducted from the original cost base when the units are sold.

ILLUSTRATIVE EXAMPLE 5.5

Sally wanted to invest in a property so she could increase her long-term wealth. She purchased a newly constructed unit which cost $500 000 and $26 800 for stamp duty and associated legal fees. Sally had $126 800 of her own money and borrowed $400 000 on the basis of interest-only at a rate of 4.5% p.a. She asked her accountant about how the income from the unit would be taxed and the after-tax cash flow effect. The accountant produced a schedule to show the income received and the deductions allowed for Sally's newly constructed rental property (table 5.4).

TABLE 5.4   Income and deductions schedule

Cash flow	$
Gross rent $2300 per month	27 600
Less: Property expenses paid in cash (e.g. rates, repairs)	(12 000)
Less: Interest payments on loan	(18 000)
Net cash flow before tax	(2400)
Tax effect	
Net cash flow before tax	(2400)
Less: Depreciation of building $500 000 @ 2.5%	(12 500)

(continued)

▶

TABLE 5.4   (continued)

Less: Depreciation of furniture, fittings etc. (assume)	(5000)
Less: Allocation of one-fifth of borrowing costs (assume $2000)	(400)
Taxable income	(20 300)
Tax loss (i.e. tax savings) assuming 47% tax rate	9541
After-tax cash flow ($9541 – $2400)	7141

You will note that, in this situation, if Sally has negatively geared the investment, she is able to use the tax loss as a tax deduction against other income, resulting in tax savings to offset the negative cash flow (refer to the chapter on taxation planning).

Sally decides to sell the property after 5 years and the sale price is $700 000. Her accountant now produces a schedule to show the taxation liability and the after-tax proceeds on the sale of the property (table 5.5).

TABLE 5.5   Taxation liability and after-tax proceeds

Net sale proceeds before tax	$
Sale proceeds	700 000
Less: Selling costs (assume)	(25 000)
Net sale proceeds	675 000
Less: Repayment of loan	(400 000)
Net proceeds before tax	275 000
Tax liability	
Net sale proceeds	675 000
Less: Purchase price (including stamp duty)	(526 800)
Less: Accumulated building depreciation (5 years)	(62 500)
Reduced cost base	(464 300)
Capital gain (net sale proceeds less reduced cost base)	210 700
Taxable gain (capital gain less 50% discount)	105 350
Tax on capital gain (assuming 47% tax rate)	(49 514.50)
After-tax proceeds on sale of property	225 485.50

Note that if the investor's marginal tax rate is lower than the highest rate then the tax savings are less.

Tax-advantaged distributions

Unlisted property trusts pay distributions most often on a quarterly basis, while some pay monthly distributions. Often a significant proportion of the distributions paid to investors is tax deferred. The tax-deferred distribution is often a selling point made to investors, as most investors are keen to defer — if not avoid — paying income tax. However, the tax deferral is often not understood clearly, as the real basis for deferral lies in the impact of the depreciation and consequent reduction in the purchase price of the asset itself when it comes to calculating the tax to pay in the future.

Tax-deferred distributions are not required to be declared as taxable income by the investor in the year they are received, but they will reduce the closing tax value (previously known as the cost base) of the investor's units in the trust. This reduction in the closing tax value is likely to result in a higher taxable capital gain on disposal of the investment, depending on the investor's marginal tax rate.

If the units are held by a superannuation fund and it is in pension phase (i.e. all assets of the fund are being used to support the pension payments), the income and capital gains of the fund are not assessable for income tax, making such investments very tax effective. Thus, for a superannuation fund investor, there is the likelihood of tax-deferred distributions while the fund is in the accumulation phase and nil tax on the distributions and capital gains when it is in the pension phase.

The impact of tax deferral

The distribution of income in a tax-deferred form may be seen as a relatively efficient form of investment. In fact, a trust may undertake property investments to gain the advantages of tax-deferred income and can offer up to 100% tax-deferred income for the first few years based on the substantial depreciation charges available from building refurbishment. To illustrate, suppose a trust invests in a commercial property and an investor on the highest marginal tax rate invests $100 000 into the trust. The fund can provide both tax deferral and tax halving. Table 5.6 shows the projected returns over a 5-year period.

TABLE 5.6 Projected returns over a 5-year period

	Year 1	Year 2	Year 3	Year 4	Year 5	Totals
Forecast returns	8.00%	8.00%	8.00%	8.00%	8.00%	
Forecast tax deferred	80%	80%	80%	80%	75%	
Amount distributed	$8000	$8000	$8100	$8200	$8320	$40 620
Tax-deferred distribution	$6400	$6400	$6480	$6560	$6240	$32 080
Assessable income	$1600	$1600	$1620	$1640	$2080	$ 8540
Tax payable (45% + 2% Medicare)	$ 752	$ 752	$ 761	$ 771	$ 978	$ 4014
Net after-tax distribution	$7248	$7248	$7339	$7437	$7353	$36 606
After-tax yield	7.25%	7.25%	7.34%	7.43%	7.35%	
Equivalent pre-tax yield	13.7%*	13.7%	13.8%	14.0%	13.8%	

* Calculated as 7.26% / (1 − 0.47) (The after-tax yield is divided by 1 minus a tax marginal rate of say, 45% plus 2.0% Medicare levy, to determine the equivalent before-tax return for an investor on such a high marginal tax rate.)

In the first year of income, the amount forecast to be distributed is 8%. The tax deferral means that the income is 80% sheltered from tax in that year. The investor can then use that income for other purposes such as investing or reducing debt. Suppose then that the investor sells their units in the property trust and that the value of the investments at the end of year 5 is $120 000. In that case, the capital gains tax calculation is shown in table 5.7.

TABLE 5.7 Capital gains tax calculation

	$
Step 1. Establish the cost base	
Purchase price	100 000
Less: Total tax-deferred amount	(32 080)
= Reduced cost base	67 920
Step 2. Establish the taxable capital gain	
Sales proceeds	120 000
Less: Reduced cost base	(67 920)
= Taxable capital gain	52 080

(continued)

TABLE 5.7   *(continued)*

	$
Step 3. Apply discount to taxable gain	
Taxable capital gain	52 080
Less: 50% discount	26 040
= Assessable amount	26 040
Step 4. Calculate tax	
Assessable amount	26 040
× Tax rate	47%
= Tax on capital gain	12 238.80

The total tax paid by the investor in this case is $12 238.80 plus $3955 = $16 193.80. Compare this with other investments, such as simply placing the funds in fixed interest for 5 years at an interest rate of 8.0%; the amount of tax on the income over 5 years at a high marginal tax rate totals $18 600. The tax rate for a highest marginal rate tax payer in 2024–25 is 45% + 2% Medicare. Not only has the investor gained income each year with minimal tax payable, but the tax on the capital gain after the 5-year period is also very tax-advantaged and the investor has benefited by capital growth in the amount of the original investment.

However, if the trust bought and sold properties within the 5-year period, the investor may have to pay capital gains tax, as the capital gains are distributed to the investor as they occur. If an investor in a property fund did not sell any of their units in the fund but the fund actually sold a property held in its portfolio, then the investor may have a capital gains item to declare in their own tax return even though they did not make the decision to sell the property. Such is the hidden issue faced by investors in a managed fund.

5.14 Property valuation methods

LEARNING OBJECTIVE 5.14   Apply valuation methods to an investment in property.

Valuing property is different to valuing shares and bonds. Each property is unique and the actual terms and conditions of a sale may vary substantially. Information conveyed to the market such as projected yields and capital growth forecasts may be less than perfect, properties may not be readily saleable and buyers may need to purchase a property relatively quickly without being able to establish a comparative price. Given all these factors, the 'actual' value of a property may not really reflect the market price. So, to offset such features, how do property investors place a value on a real estate investment? There are two main ways — estimating a market value and performing an investment analysis.

Estimating a market value

Three methods that may be used to estimate a market value are as follows.
1. *The cost approach.* The basis of this approach is to determine the cost of building the property at the current costs of land, labour, design and materials. However, for older buildings, this approach provides a less-than-perfect valuation method. It is difficult to place a value on the uniqueness of some older buildings, including considerations as their heritage value. Also, a valuation of older buildings needs to allow for depreciation of the structure.
2. *The direct comparison approach.* Although every property may have unique qualities, some properties may be quite similar in design, location, age and condition. Comparable sale prices can provide a representation of a market value for a particular property.
3. *The capitalisation approach.* An estimated market value is made by comparing recent sales figures to provide a rate of return currently required by investors based on the income stream paid to investors (i.e. the rent charged to tenants) less normal operating expenses. The market value can then be estimated.
   As an example of the capitalisation approach, suppose there were three recent sales of rental property recorded in a similar location, shown in table 5.8.

TABLE 5.8   Example of the capitalisation approach

Similar property	Net income	Sale price	Rate of return (capitalisation rate)
123 Smith Street	$30 000	$360 000	0.0833
139 Smith Street	$33 000	$400 000	0.0825
151 Smith Street	$32 500	$380 000	0.0855

Using this information, the capitalisation rate on average is 0.0837. So, if the net income for the property is projected to be $31 400, then the market value would be calculated as shown.

$$\text{Market value} = \$31\,400 / 0.0837 = \$375\,150$$

Similarly, this method can be used to determine the net income that can be demanded from a tenant. Suppose a person paid $500 000 for a rental property and required a return of 8.5% p.a. from the investment. By rearranging the formula we can determine the net income to be as follows.

$$\text{Net income} = \$500\,000 \times 0.085 = \$42\,500$$

(Note that an estimate of expenses would need to be made and added to the net income to arrive at a gross rent figure to be required from a tenant.)

Net present value investment analysis

As well as considering the estimates of market values of property, investors may also use methods of investment analysis which principally revolve around a net present value (NPV) approach. From the chapter on financial planning skills, you may recall the time value of money concept — how a dollar today is worth more than a dollar in the future. So, to calculate a net present value we need to know the future cash flow arising from a rental contract and then discount the future dollar amounts based on a discount rate representing the rate of return available on similar forms of investment.

ILLUSTRATIVE EXAMPLE 5.6

Stella wants to invest in a property (Property A) for a 3-year time frame. She intends to outlay $400 000 now and then to sell the property at the end of 3 years for $600 000. Stella expects to receive rising net income each year, starting with $20 000 in year 1. She is also considering an alternative property (Property B) for the same amount which has a lower expected sale price ($560 000) at the end of year 3 but a higher income stream over the 3 years. By considering these two investment choices we can see how the investment analysis method can be applied. If Stella did not want to invest in either of the two properties, she would invest the $400 000 in a managed fund which is expected to pay a rate of return of 8% p.a. The expected net income flows are shown in table 5.9.

TABLE 5.9   Net income flows

	Year 1	Year 2	Year 3
Property A	$20 000	$21 000	$22 000
Property B	$28 000	$30 000	$32 000

Recall the formula to arrive at the present value of a lump sum from the chapter that looks at financial planning skills. The following provides an example of application of the formula.

$$\text{NPV of Property A} = (\$400\,000) + \$20\,000 / 1.08 + 21\,000 / 1.08^2 + 22\,000 / 1.08^3$$

Note that the denominator is taken to the power based on the number of years because the net income needs to be discounted to a present value. So, in year 2 the net income needs to be discounted from the end of year 2 back to the start of year 1 to enable Stella to compare the two investment choices.

▶

The initial outlay is in brackets as it represents an outlay of funds and the $600 000 sale price after year 3 is a positive figure as it represents a return of funds at the end of year 3.

Thus

$$\text{NPV of Property A} = (\$400\,000) + \$18\,518 + \$17\,996 + \$17\,468 + \$476\,400$$
$$= \$130\,382$$
$$\text{NPV of Property B} = (\$400\,000) + \$25\,928 + \$25\,712 + \$25\,408 + \$444\,640$$
$$= \$121\,688$$

This analysis using the net present value method tells Stella that it would be better to invest in Property A as it is expected to return a positive and higher current cash value than Property B. Also, because it shows a positive return, the investment should be proceeded with. If the NPV was negative, which may occur if the sale price after 3 years was estimated to be a much lower figure, the investment proposal may be abandoned and Stella should then invest in the managed fund.

This analysis assumes a known projection of income, a future sale price and a stable rate of return for an alternative investment. However, it does provide a means of evaluating an investment proposal despite its assumptions. By substituting other figures for expected sales prices, income projections and a rate of return, this method can provide a means of considering the value of prospective investments under different scenarios.

SUMMARY

Direct investment occurs when investors make their own decisions where funds are placed. Direct investments may be made in three main areas — fixed interest, shares and property — as well as in niche markets.

The fixed-interest markets are dominated by the financial institutions and governments. The financial institutions principally act as intermediaries which facilitate the operations of the markets by pooling funds for large projects and matching lenders with borrowers. Fixed-interest securities come with different terms, different rates of interest and features. Interest rates on fixed-interest securities are fixed for the contracted maturity and may be of two types — a discounted security or a coupon security. Fixed-interest investment generally appeals to more risk-averse investors.

Share investment has gained increasing interest by investors over the past two decades. This interest stems from the privatisation of public assets, a rising share market for most of the recent past, the internet boom, increased numbers of flotations of corporations and more general interest in investment. Shares in listed Australian companies are traded on the ASX and investors are able to buy and sell their shares online or by using the service of sharebrokers. Investors decide on the shares they will trade after undertaking analyses of current prices and current and future earnings. Investors attracted to shares are generally less risk averse than other investors.

Investment in property is an essential ingredient of a diversified investment portfolio to achieve both income and capital growth objectives. Property investment covers a wide range and includes residential, commercial, agricultural and industrial and the many variations of property contained within those broad classes. The development of property trusts and the growth in the numbers of property funds offered on the market has enabled many investors with limited means to invest indirectly in a diversified range of properties both in Australia and overseas. The advantage of being able to make relatively small investments coupled with the liquidity aspects of investing in property funds has led to the significant diversity in the property trust industry. Investors in property obtain taxation benefits to minimise the taxation effects of their investment.

Other forms of direct investment include coins, stamps and works of art. The markets for such investments may be rewarding but also may suffer from lack of depth and liquidity.

KEY TERMS

A-REIT A property trust listed on the ASX.

capital gain Includes the initial cost of the asset plus any other costs that are added to the initial cost.

cost base The various costs of an asset that are included in the calculation of a taxable value.

coupon securities Fixed-interest securities that pay interest at set periods of time during the life of the contract.

discount securities Fixed-interest securities that are priced to include interest which is not paid in separate payments.

initial public offer (IPO) The first offer of shares to the public, sometimes referred to as a 'float' of shares.

yield curve A line representing the interest rates for different time frames of investment.

PROFESSIONAL APPLICATION QUESTIONS

5.1 Why is a nominal cash return not equal to the real return on a cash investment?

5.2 What does the upward sloping yield curve represent?

5.3 Why does an investor gain a greater level of security with a Treasury Fixed Coupon Bond than a corporate bond?

5.4 What is the likely effect of the general prices of shares of an announcement by the RBA of a decrease in the cash rate?

5.5 Explain the difference between systematic and unsystematic risk.

5.6 Suppose a person was considering an investment in a term deposit or a share investment and was told that the interest rate of the term deposit and the dividend yield of the share investment was the same. How would you explain the differences in the two investment choices?

5.7 Provide a reason why an investor might buy shares that are selling on a very high P/E ratio.

5.8 If you were planning to invest in property as a general asset class, list three positive characteristics and two negative characteristics that property investments are likely to possess.

5.9 Compare the features of investing in an A-REIT and a UPT.

5.10 Describe the risk and return of investing in a mezzanine fund.

PROFESSIONAL APPLICATION EXERCISES

★ BASIC | ★★ MODERATE | ★★★ CHALLENGING

5.11 Real gain from a term deposit

Assume that you invest $75 000 in a 1-year term deposit at 4.5%. How much is repaid to you at maturity? If inflation is 1.75%, what is your real gain in today's prices?

5.12 Calculating the price of a 90-day bond ★

A 90-day $100 000 BAB (Commercial Bill) security yields 6.6%. Calculate its price.

5.13 Calculating the price of a 180-day bond ★

A 180-day $100 000 BAB (Commercial Bill) security is sold for $98 120. Calculate its yield.

5.14 Choosing a share to invest in ★

Fiona is considering investing in either Share Apple or Share Pear. She has the following information.

Economy	Share Apple	Share Pear	Probability
Slowing	7%	8%	0.25
Steady	19%	17%	0.6
Expanding	27%	28%	0.15

What is the expected return on each share?

5.15 Does the price of a bond change? ★★

A 6%, 10-year bond pays a coupon once a year and yields 5% per annum. If the yield remains unchanged, what will be its price in 1 year?

5.16 Calculating a P/E ratio ★

(a) Calculate the missing figures in the table below.

Share price per share $	Earnings per share $	Price/Earnings ratio %
15	2.00	
	0.5	45
65		15
120		20

(b) Research the P/E ratio to form a view about what ratio of share price to earnings indicate whether the market is underpriced or overpriced on a long-term average.

5.17 A company reported net profit of $16.3 million. It has 2.8 million ordinary shareholders. ★★

(a) Calculate the company's EPS.

(b) Assuming the share is priced at $52.90 per share, calculate the company's dividend yield if the company paid $2.65 dividend per share to shareholders.

5.18 Calculating the residual income and return on equity ★★

The following table shows the earnings and dividend forecasts made at the end of 2020 for a firm with $40.00 book value per share in 2020. The firm requires 12% return on equity.

Forecast	2021	2022	2023
EPS	6.00	7.20	8.20
DPS	1.25	1.50	2.00

(a) Follow the method set out in the chapter to determine whether the residual income is positive or negative and calculate the forecast return on equity for each year.

(b) If the share price at the end of 2020 was $45, discuss whether the company's share price is under- or overvalued.

5.19 Calculating rental returns ★

Nerida recently purchased a rental property for $525 000. She expects that she should be able to charge a rent based on a gross return of 6% p.a.

(a) What is the amount of gross rent that she would charge?

(b) If Nerida is told that ongoing costs of owning the property (without considering the interest costs on a loan) amount to $5259 p.a., calculate her net income return after costs.

(c) Assuming Nerida has not borrowed any funds to acquire the property and her marginal tax rate is 30% (ignore Medicare levy), calculate her after-tax return on the rental income.

(d) If instead, Nerida borrowed $300 000 on interest-only terms to acquire the property and has to pay interest of 4.5% p.a., what is the taxation implication for Nerida?

5.20 Calculating the value of a property ★

Foula has inherited a rental property from her father. The property is in a regional town that Foula visits only occasionally so she is not familiar with the prices of property in the area. She visits a local real estate agent who advises that if she wants to rent the property, then she could expect to receive a rental income of $400 per week. Foula also wonders what the value of the property is expected to be if she decides to sell it. The agent advises that according to recent sales of similar properties, an average capitalisation rate of 7.0% could be applied.

(a) Calculate the expected market value of the property.

(b) How might the agent have arrived at an average capitalisation rate of 7.0%?

(c) List the factors that Foula is likely to take into account in making her decision to rent the property or to sell it.

(d) If you were in Foula's position, what might you decide to do? Explain.

CASE STUDY 1

CONSIDERING A TERM DEPOSIT

Kate Turner has sold her house and, after repaying the amount outstanding on her home loan, has $200 000 available to invest. Kate does not want to buy another house for at least three years as she has decided to work overseas for that time. However, she does not want to take undue risks with her funds and does not want to put the money in the share market. Kate goes to her bank and asks for the interest rates on term deposits for the 3-year period. She is given a rate chart that shows the following.

Term	Interest rate (per annum)
30 days	1.7%
6 months	1.65%
12 months	1.65%
24 months	1.40%
36 months	1.40%

Kate wonders what she should do with her $200 000. Should she put it all into a 3-year term deposit and forget about it until she returns or should she consider putting it into shorter-term fixed interest and then communicate with the bank as the term expires?

QUESTIONS

1 How would you describe the interest rate yield curve? Explain why.

2 Calculate the amount of interest that Kate would receive if she invests it all in the 3-year term.

3 Calculate the present value of the interest and return of the principal in 3 years if the inflation rate is 2% p.a.

4 Suppose Kate decides to take the highest return and invests all her money for 30 days. What risk does she take when the term matures and she then needs to reinvest the funds?

5 Suggest a possible solution to assist Kate with her investment plans.

CASE STUDY 2

COMPARING PROPERTY INVESTMENTS

Todd and Wesley are two friends who met at university and, during their summer vacation, decided to develop a property together. Their plan is to buy a property that they can renovate and paint, then obtain a tenant and sell the property in 3 years when, with improved value, the property could be sold for a substantial gain.

They are currently considering two property choices. The anticipated net income for each property for each year is shown in the following table.

	Year 1	Year 2	Year 3
Property A	$28 000	$30 000	$32 000
Property B	$30 000	$32 000	$34 000

Todd and Wesley will borrow most of the funds required to purchase whichever property that they decide to develop but, regardless of interest payments, they want to know which property is the best value for them to invest in.

Property A requires an outlay of $580 000 to acquire the property and initial costs of $60 000 to upgrade the property before it could be rented. It is expected that they can sell the property at the end of the 3-year period for $680 000.

Property B requires an outlay of $550 000 and initial costs of $40 000. They expect to sell the property in 3 years for $640 000.

The rate of return that they could obtain from an alternative investment choice is 5% p.a.

QUESTIONS

1 Calculate the net present value of acquiring, developing and selling property A.
2 Calculate the net present value of acquiring, developing and selling property B.
3 Which property would you advise them to purchase? Explain why.
4 What questions would you consider if they decided not to undertake the property purchase but to invest in an alternative investment choice?

REFERENCES

ASX 2023, 'Australian investor study 2023', www.asx.com.au/investors/investment-tools-and-resources/australian-investor-study.

Duke, J 2019, 'Telstra profit down 40 per cent, warns of big impact from NBN in 2020', *The Sydney Morning Herald,* 19 August, www.smh.com.au/business/companies/telstra-profit-down-40-per-cent-warns-of-big-impact-from-nbn-in-2020-20190815-p52h8k.html.

Green, J 2019, 'The essential guide to investing in unlisted property trusts', Cromwell Property Group, 9 December, www.cromwell.com.au/wp-content/uploads/sites/2/2023/04/Essential-Guide.pdf.

Mathews, T 2019, 'A history of Australian equities', Research Discussion Paper 2019-04, Domestic Markets Department, Reserve Bank of Australia, June, www.rba.gov.au/publications/rdp/2019/pdf/rdp2019-04.pdf.

RBA 2024, 'The Australian economy and financial markets', *Chart pack, March*, www.rba.gov.au/chart-pack/pdf/chart-pack.pdf?v=2024-04-12-11-00-10.

Scutt, D 2020, 'ASX posts largest weekly fall since GFC', *The Sydney Morning Herald*, 20 March, www.smh.com.au/business/markets/asx-posts-largest-weekly-fall-since-gfc-20200320-p54cd0.html.

ACKNOWLEDGEMENTS

Figures 5.1–5.3; 5.6–5.13; 5.18: © Reserve Bank of Australia

Managed funds, leveraging and buying a house

Jake and Sarah acquired three different Australian equity managed funds a number of years ago on the advice of a financial planner. However, they have never understood the types of funds they have invested in or why they needed to invest in three different funds. The couple is looking to dispose of two managed funds (B and C) and invest all into Fund A on the basis of it producing the best 1-year return. The fees and returns for all three funds, together with a summary of their investment style, are provided below.

Fund	Total return		Management fee (ICR)
A	1 year 3 years 5 years	46.71% −4.38% 3.6%	0.85% p.a.
B	1 year 3 years 5 years	18.2% −4.10% 7.79%	0.5% p.a.
C	1 year 3 years 5 years	14.4% −3.35% 7.1%	1.22% p.a.

Fund A

Investment style

Passive ⬜⬜⬛⬜ Active

Value ⬜⬛⬜⬜ Growth

Small cap ⬛⬜⬜⬜ Large cap

Fund B

Investment style

Passive ⬛⬜⬜⬜ Active

Value ⬜⬛⬜⬜ Growth

Small cap ⬜⬛⬜⬜ Large cap

Fund C

Investment style

Passive ⬜⬜⬜⬛ Active

Value ⬜⬛⬜⬜ Growth

Small cap ⬜⬛⬜⬜ Large cap

Some issues to consider from this case include the following.
- What are the benefits of investing into a managed fund?
- What do the different investment styles refer to within the three managed funds?
- Is there any value in the couple retaining all three managed funds or should all monies be consolidated into the one managed fund account?
- What issues would need to be considered if the couple decided to sell one or more of the funds?
  Illustrative examples used throughout this chapter will relate back to the information contained within this case study.

Introduction

This chapter will cover three separate but related topics. First, it will provide an overview of the managed funds industry. Managed funds allow investors to pool their money together and invest into a variety of asset classes. Funds are managed by a team of professional fund managers and may offer investments in a portfolio mix of fixed interest, shares and property or as a single asset class. Investors can select from a wide range of asset classes and management styles, to make either periodic payments or lump-sum contributions, and to determine the desired level of risk they are prepared to accept within their investment portfolios.

Second, this chapter considers the impact of using borrowed money to invest into shares and property. Borrowing money is also known as gearing or leveraging. Some people use leverage as an investment strategy and borrow a larger sum of money to buy a property or buy a larger portfolio of shares. The terms, negative gearing and margin lending are two aspects of this strategy which will be explored in this chapter. In Australia, most people's first experience of gearing is via the purchase of their first home; few people can accumulate enough capital to buy their first house and, as a result, use gearing to assist with the purchase.

Third, this chapter considers the matter of buying a home or renting. To buy a home is to invest in property but it first requires a deposit and a steady income stream to pay back the amount borrowed plus interest. Many are not able to afford to buy a home and need to rent a property owned by someone else and, then, some may choose to rent and invest their savings in other investments. This chapter will consider the issues relating to financing the purchase of a home.

6.1 Characteristics of managed funds

LEARNING OBJECTIVE 6.1 Provide an overview of the managed funds industry.

According to the Australian Securities and Investments Commission (ASIC) (2020), a managed investment scheme (MIS), commonly known as a managed fund, exists where:

- people are brought together to contribute money to get an interest in the scheme ('interests' in a scheme are a type of 'financial product' and are regulated by the *Corporations Act 2001*)
- money is pooled together with other investors (that often number in the many hundreds or thousands) or used in a common enterprise
- a 'responsible entity' operates the scheme. Investors do not have day-to-day control over the operation of the scheme.

A managed fund operates under a trust structure where investors pool their money with many other investors in order to buy into a portfolio of assets that are managed by a professional manager. The funds are managed on behalf of the investors according to the stated investment goals of the fund. For example, the objective of an equity fund may be to invest in a concentrated portfolio of Australian shares that aims to offer long-term returns in excess of the cash rate plus 4% p.a. over a rolling 5-year period.

Investors buy units in a fund, similar to buying shares in a company, and as the value of the investments within the fund rises or falls, the price of the units move accordingly. Investors have **beneficial interest** in the pool of investments based on the proportion of the total investments they hold. Income and capital gains generated within the fund are distributed to investors in proportion to the number of units held. Unit holders may also incur capital gains and losses when they sell their units.

For example, Fund M collects $10 million from investors to invest into Australian shares. The fund manager will issue 10 million units each at $1. If an investor invests $10 000, they will receive 10 000 units in the fund. Let's say after 5 years the value of the fund is now $20 million due to an increase in the value of the investments held. Thus the investor's investment has doubled from $1 per unit to $2 per unit, an effective doubling of the original worth of their investment. In addition to the capital growth during the period, Fund M is also likely to have earned and distributed income to its investors based on the proportion of units held.

Characteristics of managed funds

A managed fund is an unlisted investment vehicle (i.e. not listed on the ASX) where a financial organisation invites investors to invest monies with them with the objective of purchasing and managing a portfolio of investments in order to generate returns for the investors. The fund is managed by a professional fund manager who charges a management fee for undertaking their work. The fund generates earnings from its investments and distributes the earnings to the unit holders in the form of income, capital growth or a combination of both. A managed fund is characterised by the type of assets the fund invests in, the management structure, the tax concessions and tax structure available, and the regulatory structure required for the operation of the fund. A managed fund is purpose-built, where the rules and regulations for the operation of the fund, including the assets to be invested in, are established within a **trust deed** before potential investors are invited to invest. Interests in a managed investment scheme are a type of financial product and are regulated under the Corporations Act.

Managed funds, over time, may collect a substantial amount of funds from investors. Some of the large funds manage portfolios worth over $1 billion. At 31 December 2023, the managed funds industry had $4751 billion funds under management, an increase of $176 billion (3.9%) on the September quarter 2023 figure of $4574 billion. The significant amount of funds raised allows a fund manager to invest in a large and varied range of investments, some of which would be difficult for the individual to invest in directly. Examples include international shares, office property, ethical investments, commodities and infrastructure assets such as airports, tollways and wind farms. Managed funds offer investors the potential to invest across all of the main asset classes including:

- cash management trusts
- Australian and international equity (share) trusts
- Australian and international property (REITs) trusts
- Australian and international fixed interest
- alternative investments such as commodities and infrastructure.

These funds will be discussed further later in this chapter but it's worth noting that the same risk and return relationship exists for investing into the various asset classes, no matter whether investing directly or indirectly through managed funds (figure 6.1).

FIGURE 6.1 Risk/return relationship

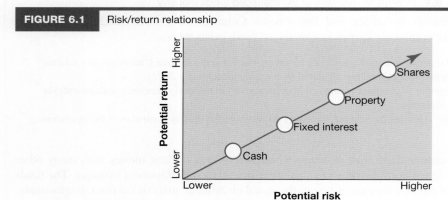

Managed funds are popular because they allow investors to gain access to a wide range of different asset classes (cash, fixed interest, property and shares), exposure to different industry segments (e.g. commercial property or Asian shares) and effective diversification across a range of different investment types (e.g. a balanced fund which invests across all of the main asset classes).

In the absence of this type of investment vehicle, many of these assets or portfolio mixes would be unavailable or difficult for the individual investor to acquire.

However, many investors prefer to invest directly into the actual asset such as shares, retail property or term deposits. There are a number of benefits of investing directly, including the ability to control the actual investment (what to buy, when to buy and when to sell); management and administration costs may be less in many instances; and the investor has the ability to better control the taxation aspects of their investments (the decision of when to sell and incur capital gains tax will impact upon the taxation position of the investor). Figure 6.2 contrasts direct and indirect investments.

FIGURE 6.2 Direct versus indirect investing

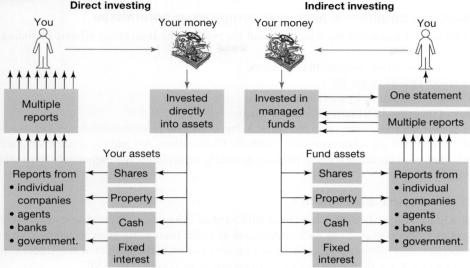

6.2 The regulation and structure of managed funds in Australia

LEARNING OBJECTIVE 6.2 Describe the regulation and structure of managed funds in Australia.

This section provides a brief overview of the structure of managed investment schemes (MISs) and how they operate, and the Australian regulatory environment for MISs.

The regulation of managed funds

The managed fund industry is administered by ASIC. ASIC monitors the industry and ensures compliance with the relevant legislation. ASIC regularly issues policy statements and policy proposal papers to industry participants, outlining changes and alerting the industry to areas of concern.

Chapter 5C of the Corporations Act regulates the operation of an MIS. If it is intended that an MIS is to be available to retail investors, s. 601ED of the Act requires that an MIS with more than 20 members be registered with ASIC. A registered MIS must be operated by a responsible entity. The responsible entity of the fund is required to be a public company and hold an Australian Financial Services Licence (AFSL) under s. 601FA. Accordingly, MISs are subject to a number of general obligations that apply to all AFSL holders under s. 912A of the Act. Investment products available to retail clients are subject to the disclosure requirements set out in Chapter 7 of the Act, including the need to provide a **product disclosure statement (PDS)**.

Under the Managed Investments Act a fund must:
- be operated by a responsible entity (RE)
- have a **constitution**
- have a compliance plan
- issue a PDS
- conduct independent audits.

The single responsible entity

A managed fund is required to appoint a single RE which has the dual role of being both trustee and manager of the scheme.

The RE must:
1. be a public company holding an Australian Financial Services Licence (AFSL)
2. have minimum net tangible assets of 0.5% of the value of its overall assets, with a minimum requirement of $50 000 and a maximum requirement of $5 million (see Regulatory Guide RG 166 *Licensing: Financial requirements*).

Breaches of duties by an RE are civil wrongs which may attract penalties of up to $1 million for the RE and up to $200 000 each for its officers.

Constitution, compliance plan and compliance committee

Each MIS must have a constitution which sets out the rules of the investment scheme including matters such as:
- how much it costs to buy interests in the scheme
- the investment powers of the RE
- how to resolve complaints by investors
- the rights of investors to withdraw from the scheme.

An MIS is also required to prepare a compliance plan as part of its responsibilities, which would set out how the RE will ensure the scheme complies with the Corporations Act and the scheme's constitution. It covers such matters as ensuring scheme property is clearly identifiable, held separately from other assets and is regularly valued.

Product disclosure statements

Holders of AFSLs who wish to offer units in an MIS to retail investors must provide investors with a PDS. The purpose of a PDS is to disclose such information as might reasonably be expected to have a material influence on a potential investor's decision about whether to invest in the product or not. Under s. 1013D(1) of the Corporations Act, a PDS must meet certain criteria to be accepted by ASIC.

Some of the requirements include:
- details of the significant benefits of the product
- details of the risk of the product
- the cost of the product
- disclosure of all fees and charges (plus a worked example if the amounts are unknown because costs are calculated on the amount invested)
- whether the product will generate a return to the investor
- significant characteristics and features of the product
- information about dispute resolution systems investors can use if they are unhappy with the product or the performance of the product.

Unit holders

Unit holders are the investors in the fund or scheme and are the beneficiaries of the fund. They do not own the assets of the fund; they are simply investing in the ability of the fund's assets to generate a return. The structure of managed funds with more than 20 unit holders is explained in figure 6.3.

FIGURE 6.3 Structure of managed funds with more than 20 unit holders

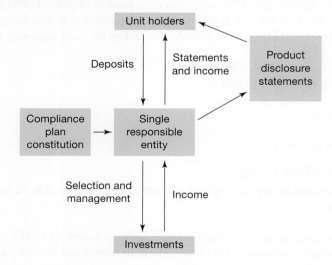

Current managed fund structure — managed investment schemes

6.3 Investing into managed funds — advantages, downsides and risks

LEARNING OBJECTIVE 6.3 Outline the advantages, downsides and risks associated with investing into managed funds.

Advantages of investing in managed funds

The benefits of investing through a managed fund can be summarised as:

- able to access investments with only a small amount of funds
- provides access to a wide range of asset classes and investments
- provides investment opportunities that would normally be out of reach of the average investor
- funds are managed by a professional fund manager
- consolidation of reporting
- ability to achieve effective diversification across asset classes, fund managers with different styles, investment sectors and countries.

While many investors prefer to have control over their investments, the task of selecting appropriate investments and managing them effectively is often a very resource- and time-intensive exercise. Also, many individual investors do not have the experience or expertise to manage investments themselves. For these investors, managed funds may be a viable alternative to direct investing as these funds are managed by professional investment managers who are paid for their skills, experience, processes and resources. Further, managing the administration, reporting and taxation aspects of direct investments can be difficult and time consuming. Managed funds consolidate the reporting on transactions, balances, withdrawals, income, capital gains and taxation for investors of the fund, thereby making the record keeping associated with investing a lot easier.

Using managed funds as a diversification strategy

Investing in managed funds provides investors with a greater choice of assets for a given amount of capital than can be achieved through direct investing thereby making it easier to build an effectively diversified portfolio of investments.

The choice available in the managed fund industry today is continually increasing as fund managers look for investment opportunities that are likely to appeal to investors.

Benefits of diversification

Diversification is the spreading of investment capital across different asset classes so the positive performance of some investments neutralises the negative performance of others. Diversifying a portfolio into different investments allows the investor to take advantage of the full cycle of growth in an economy and helps reduce the effect of a negative return from holding any one particular sector or asset class.

The large pool of funds controlled by a managed fund also allows the investor to access investments that they may not otherwise be affordable or that may not be available to individual investors. Thus, by investing in an Australian share fund, an investor may have an interest in the top 300 Australian shares. Similarly, with a property fund, an individual investor may have access to commercial property, such as shopping centres that would normally be unaffordable or unattainable.

A managed fund allows access to a widely diversified portfolio with only a small amount of capital. Most retail funds (those funds open to investors with relatively small amounts of money) have a minimum initial contribution of $2000–$5000. Most managed funds also provide a regular savings or investment plan. Thus, an investor does not need to wait to save a significant amount of money before they can invest.

As explained in the following sections, diversification can take place at different levels.

Diversification across asset classes

While all investors would like to invest in the best performing asset class, evidence shows that it is virtually impossible to predict which asset class is likely to outperform in any particular year. Investors should construct their investment portfolios based on their particular goals and objectives and the level of risk they are prepared to accept. Evidence from portfolio theory suggests that investing across a range of asset classes enables an investor to reduce risk for a given level of return. Constructing a fully diversified investment portfolio across all asset classes by means of direct investing is extremely difficult unless the investor has large amounts of money to invest.

Some fund managers specialise in individual asset classes and an investor is able to invest into a number of different managed funds to achieve diversification; for example, large cap Australian shares, international bonds, Australian property and infrastructure. Other fund managers invest across a number of different asset classes within the one fund; for example, a balanced fund or a growth fund. The benefit of this is that diversification can be achieved by investing into just one fund and the manager will continually re-weight the portfolio to ensure that the different asset classes remain properly diversified. This is a simple and effective way for investors to be able to achieve effective diversification.

Diversification across managers with different management styles

There are hundreds of different managed funds in the marketplace. Investors have the ability to select from different funds and fund managers based on the particular management style that suits their goals, needs and objectives.

Some of the styles available include:

- holding and managing a large number of securities within the fund or concentrating on just a few securities
- adopting an **active investment** approach to investing or a **passive investment** approach to investing
- selecting investments based on a value or growth approach or a combination of both
- utilising a tactical asset allocation approach, where the manager times the entry and exit of investments to take advantage of changes in the economic and market outlook, or a strategic asset allocation approach where the manager sets long-term target allocations across the various asset classes.

Diversification across investment sectors

Using a managed fund to diversify across asset sectors means that the investor can achieve exposure to different sectors within asset classes. Examples may include healthcare, consumer staples, financial services, global resources or construction.

Diversification across countries

Research into international investing has shown that investors can enhance the returns of their portfolio by diversifying investment capital across countries. This can be achieved if the countries chosen have different economic cycles. The benefits of this strategy are evidenced by the significant ownership of Australian assets by international investors.

Downsides of investing in managed funds

The downside of investing into a managed fund can be summarised as follows.

- Fund managers charge fees for managing and administering the investment portfolio.
- There is a lack of control over investment and timing decisions.
- There is a lack of transparency in a number of aspects including determining fees, returns and investment approach.
- The variety of managed funds in the marketplace makes it difficult to select and analyse an appropriate fund.

Many funds charge an entry and/or exit fee, charge an annual management fee, known as the **indirect cost ratio** or ICR (previously known as management expense ratio or MER) which typically falls in the range from 0.5% p.a. to 2% p.a., and the fund may also pay the investor's financial adviser a fee out of the fund balance as payment towards the cost of providing advice. The sale of investments by the fund manager may lead to assessable capital gains and the payment of tax by the investor.

Another problem that investors face when investing into managed funds is that there is now such a variety of investing combinations that it is often difficult for individual investors to choose the most appropriate fund manager for their circumstances. There are a number of ways of analysing and assessing fund managers, and these are discussed later in this chapter.

Risks of investing in managed funds

By investing into a portfolio of different securities, managed funds can reduce the risk of being exposed to a single security, country or asset class. However, there are still risks associated with investing into any investment or investment structure that investors need to be aware of. The risks will be determined by the nature of the asset class and the selection of the investments made by the fund manager. Some of the risks that investors need to be aware of include:

- *market risk* — all markets and asset classes are subject to the risk of price and return volatility
- *security risk* — the individual securities or investments selected within a managed fund's portfolio will be subject to specific risks that will affect the performance of the fund

- *currency risk* — international investments are subject to movements in the exchange rate which can adversely impact upon the value of the investment portfolio
- *liquidity risk* — there is a risk in investing in unlisted managed funds in that the investor may not be able to redeem their units because of lack of liquidity held by the fund. This applies particularly to property and mortgage funds. Listed investments generally have low liquidity risk because of the ability to transact through the Australian Securities Exchange (ASX)
- *gearing risk* — some managed funds have the ability to borrow funds which can magnify potential gains made by a fund. However, gearing also has the potential to magnify potential losses
- *taxation risk* — there is a risk that the government may change laws as they relate to the taxing of managed funds that may negatively impact upon the after-tax returns received by investors
- *beta risk* — investments in an index fund, such as exchange traded funds which are discussed later in the chapter, will only match the performance of the specific index that it tracks. There is no chance of the fund manager's selection skill generating returns above the market's performance.

6.4 Typical fee structures of MISs

LEARNING OBJECTIVE 6.4 Explain the typical fee structure of a managed fund.

ASIC has released a number of Regulatory Guides (RGs) and other guidance notes to assist REs in issuing adequate and comparable fee information to investors. RG 168 gives guidance on the framework and detail necessary to be disclosed in PDSs. RG 182 Dollar disclosure explains the minimum disclosure standards for fees and commissions. With few exceptions, all funds managers and advisers must disclose as a dollar amount all the fees that may affect the returns to investors. The intent behind RG 182 is to allow clients to compare fees more easily.

Types of fees

Various fees have enjoyed different names over the years. In its enhanced fee disclosure documentation, ASIC has suggested standard names to aid comparison.
- *Establishment fee.* An establishment fee is charged for processing the investor's application and establishing the investor's account. This is often nil, but may be a percentage of the initial deposit or a flat entry fee as a dollar amount.
- *Contribution fee.* Contribution fees are for the initial and every subsequent investment to cover the cost of processing. This fee may vary from nil up to about 4%. It may be deducted from each contribution or a fee may be charged directly by the adviser.
- *Withdrawal fee.* These are fees charged by the fund for each withdrawal. Each fee may be nil up to a flat dollar amount of, for example, $50.
- *Termination fee.* This is the fee charged for closing the account. It is often nil, but a withdrawal fee may be charged.
- *Ongoing fees or management costs.* These are fees charged for the ongoing maintenance of the investor's account and cover such things as investor updates, account management, taxation summaries, and overheads for the management of the fund. They are normally charged as a percentage of asset values and vary depending on the complexity of the investment strategies.
- *Switching fee.* This is a fee charged when investors change their asset mix or their fund within the same managed group.
- *Adviser service fee.* Some funds managers pay financial planners ongoing fees for every year a client's funds remain in their MIS but dependent upon the annual service fee agreed to by the investor.

The payment of any fee reduces the overall returns to the investor and therefore is an important consideration when selecting a particular managed fund. Due to increasing competition and transparency within the industry, few fund managers now charge an establishment or contribution fee.

Indirect cost ratio

Among the individual fees listed in the previous section, you will have noted ongoing fees or management costs. These are the costs that funds managers incur to finance the operation of the fund and this must be disclosed to investors. They include costs of purchasing investments, external funds management, performance fees and investment-related legal, accounting, auditing and other operational and compliance costs. They are deducted from investment returns before the returns for any period are declared.

The indirect cost ratio (ICR) is the ratio of management costs not deducted directly from investors' account balances expressed as a proportion of the average net assets of the fund. ICRs generally range from about 0.3% to 2% p.a. Some MISs call these costs 'management costs'. The ICR enables investors to compare the fees charged by a particular fund against others in the marketplace on a consistent basis.

ILLUSTRATIVE EXAMPLE 6.1

Referring to the case study presented at the commencement of this chapter, the three different funds (Funds A, B, and C) each have different indirect cost ratios (ICRs). Is it better to always select the fund with the lowest ICR and avoid the expensive funds?

While a consideration of the ICR is important, it is also important to note that it is only one of a number of issues that must be considered. The investments undertaken by some funds are, by their nature, more expensive to operate than others. Managing a fund that invests internationally, especially in emerging markets, is much more expensive than investments undertaken in Australia. Other factors to consider include the returns the fund generates, its management style and investment objectives.

6.5 The differences in managed funds

LEARNING OBJECTIVE 6.5 Discuss the differences in managed funds.

There are a vast number of managed funds in the marketplace that have been established to suit the needs, objectives and risk profiles of most types of investors. Managed funds can be categorised based on a number of criteria such as:

- the unique investment objective and philosophy of the fund
- whether the funds are listed or unlisted
- the type of investments held by the fund
- the investment structure of the fund.

These differences will determine the particular investment decision-making processes adopted by the managed fund and impact upon the type of investments selected, overall performance, risk characteristics and costs. It is important that investors properly understand and appreciate these issues before they invest.

Investment objectives

Each managed fund has a specific investment objective. It is important that the fund's particular investment objective and philosophy is detailed so that investors can determine whether the fund is appropriate for them. Investor attitude to risk can vary and, as a result, it is important for fund managers to set out their specific investment strategy in advance, allowing investors to select funds that are consistent with their risk profile and invest into assets classes and investment segments that suit their needs. Fund objectives cover a wide range of issues including the time horizon; whether the emphasis is on income, growth or a combination or both; the level of volatility attached to the fund; and the type of investments targeted by the fund.

Differences in the investment objectives of managed funds can be illustrated by the following two types of funds.

1. *Australian share fund.* Objective: to provide long-term growth with moderate tax-effective income. The assets are actively managed with a focus on flexible sector management and adequate diversification to minimise risk. The investment philosophy is to target both mid and small cap stocks which possess potential for superior growth.
2. *Australian bond fund.* Objective: to provide investors with fixed-interest returns from investment grade Australian bond investments with an aim to outperform **benchmark** returns over any rolling 3-year period.

Listed and unlisted managed funds

Investors have the choice of investing into managed funds that are either listed on the Australian Securities Exchange (ASX) or are unlisted. Before investing into either of these structures, investors need to have a very clear idea of what they are investing in the type of scheme being offered, the nature of the investments available and whether the fund meets the particular needs and objectives of the investor.

Unlisted managed funds

Unlisted managed funds are the most common type of managed investment scheme available in Australia. With **unlisted managed funds,** investors deal directly with the fund manager when they want to buy units or redeem (sell) their units. These funds are open-ended structures, meaning that the fund can continually issue new units as funds are received from investors and buy back existing units from available cash holdings when an investor wishes to sell their units. Unlisted managed funds operate as trust structures and issue units to investors. An investor will purchase and sell units in the fund directly from the fund itself rather than from existing members or unit holders. As a result, unlisted funds need to be concerned with liquidity and their ability to fund investor redemptions from available cash or from selling investments

Unlisted managed funds do not pay tax in their own right but are required to distribute all income as distributions to unit holders, including a share of any capital gains made and franking credits received within the fund. These funds receive income from their investments, which may be in the form of dividends, interest and rental income, and this income is then paid across to investors after costs.

The underlying value of the units in the fund is based on the prevailing market value of the fund's investment portfolio. This is represented by the fund's net asset value (NAV). NAV is the value of the fund's assets less the value of its liabilities. Each time units are sold or redeemed, investments within the fund are sold at current market selling prices.

The NAV is determined as follows.

$$NAV = \frac{Fund\ assets - Fund\ liabilities}{Number\ of\ units\ issued}$$

ILLUSTRATIVE EXAMPLE 6.2

A fund manager provides investors with the following information.

	($ million)
Assets	
Cash	30
Bonds	60
Equities	120
Property	30
International equities	60
Liabilities	
Debentures (loans)	35
Number of current units issued	16 101 324

The unit price of the fund is therefore as follows.

$$Unit\ price = \frac{\$300\ million - \$35\ million}{16\ 101\ 324}$$

$$= \$16.46$$

Most unlisted funds have a separate buying (offer) price and selling (bid) price. This is known as the fund's **spread** or **bid-offer spread**. The buying price is higher than the selling price to allow for transaction costs incurred by the fund in buying and selling investments, which is passed onto incoming unit holders.

Listed managed funds

The objective of **listed managed funds** is similar to that of unlisted funds with these schemes also providing investors with the opportunity to invest in a diversified portfolio of investments managed by a professional fund manager. The main difference with a listed fund is that investors can buy and sell units or shares through the ASX in the same way they can with other shares and other listed securities. Listed funds also offer investment opportunities across a wide range of asset classes and management styles to suit the particular investment requirements of most investors.

The four main types of listed managed fund structures operating through the ASX are:
1. listed investment companies (LICs)
2. listed investment trusts (LITs)
3. real estate investment trusts (REITs)
4. exchange traded funds (ETFs).

A **listed investment company (LIC)** raises funds by issuing shares in the same way as any other listed company. Funds are used to establish an investment portfolio and investors can trade in the LIC via the ASX. The fund operates with a fixed number of shares on offer and a fixed amount of funds under management. It does not regularly issue new units or cancel existing units. This type of fund is known as a closed-end structure. Just like any other listed company the fund may, over time, decide to raise more funds by issuing more shares or reduce the size of the fund by cancelling shares. Managers of listed funds are not as concerned with their liquidity holdings as unlisted fund structures, as investors wanting to sell their units in a listed fund trade through the ASX rather than having funds repaid from the cash holdings of the fund. LICs pay returns to investors in the form of dividends, which may be franked or unfranked.

A **listed investment trust (LIT)** operates in a similar manner to an LIC, except that the fund issues units rather than shares. LITs can be both open-ended structures, where investors buy and sell units through the fund itself, or closed-end structures that allow investors to trade through the ASX.

Real estate investment trusts (REITs) provide investors with the opportunity to invest into a managed portfolio of diversified Australian real estate. The manager selects and manages the investment properties. Returns to investors are distributions of rental income plus increases in the underlying value of the properties contained within the fund. REITs provide investors with the opportunity to gain exposure to property that would normally be inaccessible due to such factors as cost, size and geographic region. The types of property available within REITs include industrial, office, retail, hotels and leisure, and aged care. REITs do not normally offer residential property.

Exchange traded funds (ETFs) ETFs are listed on the ASX and traded in the same way as any other share. While the majority of listed and unlisted managed funds adopt an active management style, that is the fund manager selects and trades in individual shares that they believe will outperform the market, the objective of an ETF is to track and duplicate as closely as possible the performance of a selected share market index. This is known as a passive or index management style. The different management styles are discussed in greater detail later in this chapter. Thus, ETFs provide investors with the opportunity to invest into a broad and diversified portfolio of investments matching a particular market index with a single transaction.

While the value of a listed managed fund portfolio is generally based on the value of its NAV, its actual value on the ASX is determined on a day-to-day basis by normal market influences, and demand and supply factors. Depending on such factors as current market conditions, expectations and sentiment, the value of listed managed funds may trade at a discount, premium or at par to its net tangible asset (NTA) backing.

(For more details see https://moneysmart.gov.au/managed-funds-and-etfs and, for ETFs and ETPs, www.asx.com.au/products/etf-and-other-etp.htm.)

Types of investments undertaken by funds

Single sector funds

These funds concentrate on a particular asset class as listed below.

1. Cash management funds invest in:
   - overnight or 24-hour cash deposits
   - short-term government securities
   - a mix of short- and medium-term government securities
   - an international mix of short-term government securities
   - a mix of short-term government, banking and corporate debt, which may be either within Australia or internationally.
2. Fixed-interest funds invest in:
   - short- to medium-term government bonds
   - government bonds across all maturities
   - international government bonds
   - mortgage loans
   - a mix of government, banking and corporate bonds.

   In addition, fixed-interest funds may hedge their international portfolios (i.e. reduce the exposure to changes in interest rates) using swaps, options or futures, if allowed for in their constitution and compliance plan.
3. Property funds invest across different sectors of the property market including commercial, industrial, retail and residential. Most property funds hold a diversified portfolio of assets spread by location and

activity undertaken within the property category. Large property funds are sometimes involved in the development of new properties such as housing estates or retail shopping centres.

4. Share or equity funds can be divided into the many different categories of shares, including:
   - *index funds* — the manager exactly matches a share market index (such as the All Ordinaries)
   - *sub-sector funds* — the manager chooses equities from a particular type of company such as from the industrial, telecommunications, property development or banking sector
   - *developing or emerging markets funds* — the manager chooses equities from countries where the share markets or capital markets are still developing
   - *high-growth funds* — the manager chooses equities that are likely to experience high growth in the short to medium term; they are just as likely to achieve no growth in the same period, so these funds are high-risk funds and the returns should compensate the investor for that risk
   - *small cap funds* — the manager chooses companies that have a small market capitalisation compared with the larger companies on the stock exchange, hoping to see the companies grow to larger firms of the future
   - *ethical funds* — the manager applies ethical, social or responsible screening to the selection of investments within the fund which may involve actively seeking out commercial activities that bring social or environmental benefits, and avoiding investments in activities which are socially or environmentally harmful.
5. International funds can be divided into:
   - *regions* — such as Asia–Pacific, Asian Tigers, European, G7, Americas, Emerging Markets
   - *countries* — such as local neighbours of Australia, major trading partners of Australia, or simply the United States, the United Kingdom or Europe
   - *sectors* — within the country the manager may choose specific types of investments such as property in the central business district, industrial equities, mining and resources equities, or government bonds.

Diversified (multi-sector) funds

While the majority of funds are single-sector funds, a number of diversified or multi-sector funds exist that invest across a wide range of different asset classes. The fund manager determines a broad asset allocation and determines the proportion of funds to be invested into each asset class. The advantages of this type of fund are that the investor can achieve effective densification across all or a number of asset classes within the one managed fund and the manager periodically reweights the investments within the fund to ensure the specified asset allocation is maintained. This reduces the need for the investor to rebalance their investments themselves.

Various types of diversified funds exist, covering a range of investor risk profiles.

- *Conservative funds* are designed for investors with a low risk profile who require investments with relatively low volatility and a low chance of negative returns. The funds aim to provide investors with income and some short- to medium-term capital growth through exposure to a diversified investment portfolio that holds a significant amount of their funds in cash and fixed interest. Typically, around 40–60% of the fund is invested into such defensive investments.

- *Balanced funds* aim to provide investors with a mix of medium-term capital growth and income. The aim is to generate a return higher than conservative funds while restricting the level of risk or volatility by holding a portfolio of both growth-type assets, such as shares and property, and defensive-type assets, such as cash and fixed interest. Generally, around 50–70% of the fund's assets are invested into shares and property.

- *Growth funds* aim to achieve long-term capital growth and some income through investment into a diversified investment portfolio with an emphasis on share investments. The fund may also invest in a range of other, more high-risk investments such as small companies, private equity funds and emerging markets in order to chase higher returns. Because of the nature of their investments, the risk exposure of growth funds is relatively high and suitable, therefore, for more aggressive investors willing to take on risk in order to potentially achieve higher returns. Typically, around 70–90% of the fund's investments are allocated to growth-type investments.

Search the internet to find examples of the asset allocations for each of the various types of diversified funds as described above.

Different management and investment styles

Understanding the investment style of funds can help investors match their own risk profile to that of the fund. A manager's style or investment philosophy is a reflection of their fundamental approach to investing. The PDS and constitution of a fund will provide details of the particular management style adopted by the fund. The main investment styles are categorised under the headings of active and passive management styles and these are described below. Figure 6.4 illustrates the relationship between the various active management styles.

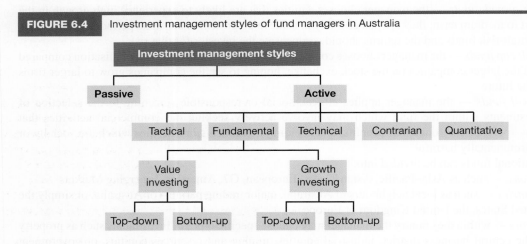

FIGURE 6.4 Investment management styles of fund managers in Australia

Active fund management styles

An active management style refers to a strategy that involves the fund manager selecting specific investments to be held within a portfolio with the objective of outperforming the market or the particular benchmark index. A traditional active-managed fund attempts to meet this goal through a combination of stock picking, market timing and asset allocation decisions. The active fund manager's style is generally categorised as either value or growth oriented, although a number of other styles exist in the marketplace. The active fund manager uses a particular method to determine the appropriate asset mix for the fund. Some examples of these methods include the following.

- *Tactical analysis.* Fund managers use two main methods when they purport to be tactical managers or tactical asset allocators (TAAs) and look to actively move investments around in order to maximise returns. The first is to over-weight or under-weight an individual investment (increase or decrease the percentage of the portfolio's holding) in order to take advantage of likely future changes in the investment's value. The second is to try to 'time' the market to determine the best time to buy or sell an asset.
- *Fundamental analysis.* Fund managers evaluate the available accounting and reported data with a view to determining those companies or other specific investments that may be undervalued for the given circumstances (and therefore the fund manager would buy these assets), or overvalued given the information available in the market (and therefore the fund manager would sell these assets). These data are known as 'fundamental data'.
- *Technical analysis.* The oldest form of analysis is to predict future price movements from past price movements. Technical analysis is the study of price and value data to determine patterns in past price movements. Decisions to buy or sell an asset are based on past history.
- *Contrarian analysis.* This is where a fund manager buys when prices are falling and sells when prices are rising. Managers are not trying to pick the top or the bottom of the market — overall, they are hoping their average buy prices will be lower than their average sell prices.
- *Quantitative analysis.* 'Quants' use statistics and models to measure risk and expected returns from an investment/asset, with a view to constructing a portfolio of the highest expected return for the lowest possible risk.

Value funds managers

A basic method of assessing the value of an investment is to determine if the asset is undervalued (and therefore a buy) or overvalued (and therefore a sell). This analysis focuses on the ability of the asset to generate income, both now and in the near future. **Value funds managers** believe that markets are affected by many factors, such as emotion, momentum, rumours and market sentiment which results in shares trading above and below their fair value at differing times. Value managers target neglected and out-of-favour companies that they believe are undervalued and underpriced by the market. Value managers attempt to exploit market conditions by buying companies that are underpriced and selling them once they become overpriced.

Growth funds managers

The focus for **growth funds managers** is capital growth or gain. Income streams are not as important to these managers as the capital appreciation of the investment. This style of fund manager also uses the top-down or bottom-up approach to asset selection and analysis. With a top-down approach, the fund manager studies macroeconomic variables and trends relating to an individual country as well as the global economy such as GDP, trade balances, currency movements, inflation and interest rates in order to determine where to invest and in what types of investments and companies. A bottom-up approach concentrates on the fundamental analysis of the company and examines factors such as the company's sales growth, profitability, market share, cash flow and debt position. Growth managers concentrate on shares that have the potential to provide superior future growth. Typically, growth managers search out companies in high-growth or developing sectors and industries and also concentrate on the quality of the management of these companies to continue to provide continued excess growth.

There is often a debate as to which style provides the best returns for investors. Over differing periods in the market cycle, value managers will outperform growth managers and vice versa. While some investors may prefer to invest in a particular investment style, others may decide to blend value and growth investments by either selecting a combination of value and growth fund managers within their portfolio or otherwise selecting a fund that already combines the two types of investment styles. Some analysts argue that categorising investment styles is simply a way for fund managers to differentiate themselves from each other when in fact value and growth are simply two sides of the same coin, meaning that all managers will consider both value and growth considerations in their investment selections.

ILLUSTRATIVE EXAMPLE 6.3

Referring to the case study detailed at the commencement of this chapter, one of the factors which Jake and Sarah will need to consider in determining which funds to keep and which to dispose of is whether they prefer value managers, growth managers or some other variation. Which of the investment styles provides better long-term returns and is it better to stick with one investment style or invest so as to capture both styles?

One of the factors affecting the performance of a particular investment style is the state of the economy and financial markets. In times of market growth and expansion in the economy, growth managers may tend to outperform because they invest in corporations and market segments that have the potential for significant future growth. Examples may include technology, healthcare and the resources sector. In times of economic and market contraction, there is usually a trend toward the more secure blue-chip companies that value managers typically invest in. As it is extremely difficult to forecast future economic and market conditions, it may be advisable to select funds that utilise different investment styles. This utilises the principles of diversification. Within the case study, reference to the investment styles of the three funds reveals that whereas Fund C is more value oriented, Funds A and B are very similar and therefore, holding both funds may not significantly improve the diversification benefit.

Passive fund management or indexed funds

Passive funds managers do not attempt to outperform an index or benchmark; they simply try to replicate the performance of the index. The main object of an index fund is to produce returns in line with the index of that particular asset class, minus their fees. Securities are held within the portfolio in proportion to the individual securities making up the index. For example, if we assume that the Commonwealth Bank makes up 10% of the ASX All-Ordinaries Accumulation Index, an index manager would hold approximately 10% of the bank within their share portfolio. From time to time, companies making up the index change, and move in and out of the index. If the value of the overall index changes, index managers will need to purchase or sell shares in individual companies to ensure the proportional holdings of those companies remain the same.

The argument for adopting a passive investment style is that the average performance of all investors is the same as the market (the benchmark index) and therefore the aggregate return of all investors in the market will equal the market return. That is, it is impossible for everyone to beat the market — half the investors will beat the market while half will receive returns lower than the market return. Thus, while active managers attempt to beat the market and incur trading fees in attempting to do so, only about half will generate returns (before fees) in excess of the market. Once fees are taken into account, active funds as a group may underperform the index.

'Indexing' involves building a portfolio of investments that replicates a widely publicised index. The index should be easily recognised in the market and information about its construction should be readily available to all market participants. The index should reflect all securities available in a market sector; for example, all federal government bonds, all equities, all property. Exchange traded funds (ETFs), discussed previously, are a form of index fund. Examples of well-known indexes are the ASX All-Ordinaries Accumulation Index, the suite of S&P/ASX indices and the Dow Jones industrial index. Most of these indexes are reported in the daily financial media.

ILLUSTRATIVE EXAMPLE 6.4

Again referring to the case study of Jake and Sarah detailed at the start of the chapter, the investment profile of managed Fund B indicates that it has a passive investment style whereas Fund C has an active management style. Fund A adopts a management style that is predominantly active. Which management style is preferable? Is one management style better than the other? Is it necessary to have funds covering all management styles?

This issue of which management style outperforms the other has been the subject of academic debate for many years. To date, there is no conclusive evidence one way or the other. A number of financial planners have adopted an investment process known as a core-satellite approach which looks to invest the major share of the investment portfolio (the core) in cheaper index funds, especially in asset classes where it is difficult to outperform the market such as cash and fixed interest and shares in large companies. The planner may then invest a proportion of the portfolio in a number of funds that use an active management style (the satellite funds) in an attempt to find returns in excess of the market. Examples may include investments in the shares of small companies and in emerging markets such as China and India.

Retail and wholesale managed funds

Unlisted managed funds are typically offered to investors at a retail and/or a wholesale level. There is very little difference in the actual investments undertaken between **wholesale managed funds** and **retail managed funds** as they often have the same names and invest in exactly the same investments. The main difference is that wholesale managed funds charge lower management fees and tend to have a much higher minimum entry amount.

Investment structures and platforms

Investment platforms allow investors to access a range of different investment options under the one administrative structure. Not only do many of these platforms offer a range of different managed funds covering different asset classes and fund managers, they also commonly allow investors to invest directly into shares, term deposits and even property syndicates. Investment platforms provide investors with the ability to select from a wide range of investments that suit their particular needs, objectives and risk profile. In return, they charge the investor an additional fee to be able to access the diverse range of investments.

The two main types of investment platforms are master funds and wrap accounts, described in the following two sections.

Master funds

A **master fund** is an administration service that pools money together from investors and provides access to a range of different fund managers and other investment options. Within this structure, investors are able to access wholesale managed funds. The master fund provider may have a product list containing many different managed funds to select from. The funds selected by the investor from this approved product list are consolidated under the one account and held on behalf of the investor by the trustee of the master fund who is the legal owner. The investor receives one consolidated report covering all investments held within their account.

Wrap accounts

Wrap accounts are similar to master funds in that they also provide an administrative structure to hold a diverse range of investments under the one account. However, wrap accounts are different in their structure. Investments held within a wrap account are held in the name of the investor. As a result, investments within a wrap account can be transferred between different wrap providers and even to the direct ownership of the investor without triggering any capital gains tax. A modern wrap account can provide investors with access to not only a diverse range of different managed funds, but also to a number of direct investments such as direct shares and term deposits. Again, the wrap provider will charge the investor an additional fee.

Benefits and drawbacks

The benefits of investing through a master fund or wrap account are that:

- the investor only deals with the one organisation for all of their investment transactions
- there are cost savings because the managed funds can be accessed at wholesale ICRs
- the investor can access funds that may not be available at a retail level
- the investor receives one consolidated report detailing all of their investments held within the master or wrap account and summarising overall asset allocation, performance and tax reporting.

While some investors prefer to manage their investments themselves, many others are happy to pay for the administrative services provided by investment platforms. The main drawback of these types of products is that they come at a cost. Apart from the ICR charged by each individual fund manager, the platform provider itself will also charge an administration fee to cover their costs. This fee will vary depending upon the funds under management but will typically range between 0.5% and 1% p.a.

PROFESSIONAL ADVICE

Setting up an investment strategy

Barry works with the local council as a leisure services manager. He is aged 42, married with two young children and earns an annual salary of $75 000. Barry's wife is not currently employed. Barry would like to start investing into quality investments outside of his superannuation account to fund his children's education, to pay for a home extension that will be required in the next few years as the children get older, and to put some money aside to support his retirement.

Barry believes he has a moderate risk profile. He has little investment experience and is busy with his job and family. He does not have much of an interest in managing his finances. He is prepared to take on some risk in order to chase higher returns but does not want to borrow or invest in high-risk products. He owns a few shares in the Commonwealth Bank and has $10 000 in a cash account.

Barry will shortly inherit a small investment portfolio from his grandmother consisting of $30 000 cash and $40 000 in three managed funds as follows.

Australian Share Index Fund $20 000	(ICR 2.0%)
Australian Bond Fund $10 000	(ICR 1.2%)
Australian Infrastructure Fund $10 000	(ICR 2.4%)

Barry is looking to sell all three managed funds, and invest the money into a direct share portfolio. He doesn't know anything about managed funds but believes he has the ability to outperform fund managers and generate higher returns.

···

QUESTIONS

1. Determine the type of investments that an Australian infrastructure fund would invest into.

2. Would it be worth Barry holding his investments within a master fund or wrap account structure? What are the advantages and disadvantages of this approach?

3. Would you recommend that Barry sell the three funds in order to trade in direct shares?

6.6 Measuring returns and analysing the performance of managed funds

LEARNING OBJECTIVE 6.6 Outline some of the methods used for measuring returns and analysing performance of managed funds.

A number of methods are used to assess the performance of a managed fund. Some methods are aimed at assessing the absolute return of the fund, whereas other methods analyse the overall performance of the fund relative to a benchmark or in terms of the risk taken by the fund managers to generate that return.

Measuring returns from a change in unit price

For the investor, information about the performance of the fund is contained in the daily unit price. The absolute returns from investing in a managed fund are calculated as follows.

$$r = \frac{(\text{Sale price or Current market value}) - \text{Purchase price}}{\text{Purchase price}} \times 100$$

ILLUSTRATIVE EXAMPLE 6.5

Joe purchased 2000 units in the Infrastructure Trust on 30 June 2019 at a unit price of $1.85. The market value one year later is $2.36. The absolute return is as follows.

$$r = \frac{\text{Current market value} - \text{Purchase price}}{\text{Purchase price}} \times 100$$

$$= \frac{\$2.36 - \$1.85}{\$1.85} \times 100$$

$$= 27.57\%$$

Of course, this is not the real return — Joe would need to sell his units at $2.36, then subtract taxes and fees to determine his real return.

A more sophisticated formula for measuring the fund's return is:

$$R_p = \frac{(MV_1 - MV_0) + D - C}{MV_0} \times 100$$

where R_p = return on the fund

MV_1 = market value of the investor's units at the end of the evaluation period

MV_0 = market value of the investor's units at the beginning of the evaluation period

D = any distribution (redemptions or income distributions) from the portfolio to the investor during the evaluation period

C = contributions to the fund during the period by the investor

Once a fund's return has been calculated, it is compared with the return on the benchmark portfolio or index for the same period. There are a range of sources available to assist investors in keeping up-to-date with the performance of their funds, including the financial press, the finance pages of the general press, the fund's webpage, and the unit holder statements distributed by the fund.

ILLUSTRATIVE EXAMPLE 6.6

Consider this portfolio information.

	$ million
Market value of the portfolio at 1 March 2019	6 960
Market value of the portfolio at 1 March 2020	7 260
Contributions to the fund during the year	320
Distributions paid during the year from the fund	300

In this case, the formula indicated before can be modified to reflect a total fund return and the return on the fund can be calculated as follows.

$$R_p = \frac{(7260 - 6960) + 300 - 320}{6960} \times 100$$

$$= 4.02\% \text{p.a.}$$

As discussed earlier, it would be important to determine if the return of the fund is inclusive or exclusive of fees.

Analysing and assessing managed fund performance

With the hundreds of managed funds in existence, investors require a means of being able to effectively review, assess and compare the risk and return characteristics of the various funds. Investors need to be able to review and monitor ongoing fund performance. To do this, investors should:

- compare the performance against the fund's objectives
- compare the performance against that of other managed funds
- compare the performance against benchmarks
- refer to managed fund research
- undertake an assessment and interpretation of financial ratios.

All managed funds provide regular performance reports that provide the basis for the investor's analysis. There is a natural tendency to concentrate on the short-term performance, whether good or bad, and use that as the basis for analysing fund performance and making investment decisions. However, assessing returns over a longer time frame may provide the investor with a better indication of long-term average performance. Choosing a longer time period that covers different economic cycles and market conditions will provide the investor with a better historical assessment of how the manager has performed and therefore how they may perform in the future.

Comparison of performance against benchmarks

Looking at total returns from a fund does not provide much information about how the returns were generated by the fund manager. Using a benchmark, a point of reference used for comparison purposes, investors can compare the fund manager's performance with the performance of the market overall and determine how much of the declared return comes simply from being invested in the asset class. Excess return above the benchmark is often attributed to the skill of the manager. To be a fair and accurate comparison, the benchmark index must be consistent with the fund's management objectives and the structure of the index must be well known. Common benchmarks used to compare the performance of a particular fund against market index are as follows.

Australian shares	ASX All Ordinaries Accumulation Index
International shares	MSCI World Index
Property	S&P/ASX 300 A-REIT Accumulation Index
Fixed interest	UBS Warburg Composite Bond Index
Cash	UBS Warburg Bank Bill Index

The fund's stated objectives will be based around the benchmark and usually expressed in the form of outperforming the benchmark by a percentage or over a rolling period. For example, a fund's objective may be to outperform benchmark returns over any rolling 3-year period.

ILLUSTRATIVE EXAMPLE 6.7

With the vast array of managed funds covering different asset classes, markets, management styles and investment styles, how does an investor determine which is the best fund to invest in? This is the problem facing Jake and Sarah in the case study at the start of the chapter. One of the techniques that Jake and Sarah can consider is to determine what asset classes their three funds invest in and, by comparing the fund's performance against the appropriate benchmark, determine the extent to which the cost of the fund outweighs the returns relative to the index. Thus, if Fund C's performance prior to fees is 7.1% over the past 5 years whereas the index or benchmark is 7.5%, the fund has underperformed and an investor may feel that the relatively high ICR being charged is not justified.

Reference to managed fund research

A number of research houses exist in Australia with the aim of researching and providing recommendations on the main managed funds in the marketplace. These organisations undertake extensive research on managed funds covering aspects such as performance, financial viability, the quality of the management team, whether the fund is true to its label (i.e. whether it sticks to its management style), and the financial backing and resources of the organisation.

Some of the research house players in Australia include Lonsec, Standard & Poor's, Zenith Investment Partners and Morningstar, and they provide a significant amount of detailed information on many managed funds. Much of the detailed information is, however, only available to financial planners and sophisticated investors through a subscription service.

While this chapter thus far has looked at some basic techniques to analyse managed funds, a range of more sophisticated techniques are available and can be beneficial in revealing further information concerning the risk and return characteristics of the fund. The following discussion will draw on the information provided in table 6.1.

TABLE 6.1   Equity fund performance

Analysis	1 year	3 years	5 years
Performance (p.a.)	12.8%	1.8%	10.2%
Standard deviation (p.a.)	16.5%	16.0%	17.2%
Excess return (p.a.)	4.1%	3.04%	6.52%
Tracking error (p.a.)	5.8%	5.5%	6.7%
Information ratio	0.7	0.6	1.0
Sharpe ratio	0.5	−0.2	0.3

Note: The benchmark used for the calculation of ratios is the S&P/ASX 300 Accumulation Index.

Table 6.1 is an example of the type of information typically provided by the research houses on managed fund performance and risk. The data in table 6.1 relates to a hypothetical Australian share fund.

What does the information tell us about the performance and risk characteristics of the fund? Apart from the performance over time, a number of measures are provided. These measures can be utilised by both financial planners and clients to help improve their investment decision making in respect of a particular fund as well as relative to comparable funds. One of the more common means of analysis included in table 6.1 is described next.

Excess return

The excess return is the return generated by the fund relative to its benchmark. Thus for the 3, 5 and 10-year periods, the particular fund has achieved a return that is over the particular benchmark used by the fund. But, for the 6 month and 1-year returns the fund has not achieved its index benchmark.

6.7 Leveraged investing

LEARNING OBJECTIVE 6.7 Explain the concept of leveraged investing.

An investor uses money to acquire an asset with the objective of increasing wealth through the expected growth in the value of the asset. For example, Kevin buys 1000 shares in a company for $2 per share. He expects that the price of the share will increase to $3 per share in twelve months when his investment would then be worth $3000, an increase of $1000 in his personal wealth. In addition, as well as an increase in the asset's value, he may also receive some income in the form of dividends.

Leveraging an investment means that an investor uses borrowed money to acquire more of an asset. The terms leveraging, gearing, debt financing and borrowings all mean the same thing — using borrowed money. The investor might use some of their own money but borrow the remainder.

In Kevin's case, suppose he uses $2000 of his own money and borrows $4000 from a family member so that he invests $6000 and acquires 3000 shares. When the share price rises to $3 per share, the value of his shares rises to $9000, but he also owes $4000 so his net wealth is now $5000.

As we shall see, leveraging does have risks. In this chapter we will not cover some of the more sophisticated methods of leveraging such as contracts for difference, futures, options and warrants. They will be covered in finance texts.

6.8 Gearing, income taxes and geared investments

LEARNING OBJECTIVE 6.8 Outline how gearing can be used to magnify returns and discuss the income tax effects of gearing.

Gearing describes the use of borrowed money to buy assets. 'Gearing' investments might sound like a peculiar use of a word that is more often used with your bike or car, but the concept is actually exactly the same. Gearing essentially changes the ratio of inputs to outputs. With bikes or cars, a high gear allows you to get higher speed out of the engine. With investments, high gearing allows higher returns (either positive or negative).

In using borrowed funds, investors aim to achieve a return higher than the cost of those borrowed funds. The return can come by means of annual income and by means of a capital gain when the asset is eventually sold. Investors most commonly use gearing to assist with the purchase of share portfolios, managed funds and investment properties.

ILLUSTRATIVE EXAMPLE 6.8

Matthew believes that the price of two-bedroom units in his suburb is likely to increase so he decides to go long by buying a $300 000 unit. He already has a substantial asset base, and his bank is happy to provide an interest-only loan up to the full purchase price at a rate of 8% p.a.

Matthew expects that he can rent the unit for $400 per week. He also expects that the unit will appreciate in value over the next 12 months by 10%. Matthew is not sure how much of his own capital he should contribute to the purchase. If Matthew sells the unit in 12 months, what is the expected return on capital invested for various levels of gearing (ignoring the impact of taxes at this stage)? The details are shown in table 6.2.

TABLE 6.2   Matthew: no taxes, and returns > costs

	No gearing $	Low level of gearing $	Medium level of gearing $	High level of gearing $
Capital	300 000	200 000	100 000	30 000
Borrowing		100 000	200 000	270 000
Total	300 000	300 000	300 000	300 000
Rental income	20 800	20 800	20 800	20 800
Less: Interest		8 000	16 000	21 600
Net income	20 800	12 800	4 800	−800
Capital gain	30 000	30 000	30 000	30 000
Total return	50 800	42 800	34 800	29 200
Capital invested	300 000	200 000	100 000	30 000
Return on capital invested	17%	21%	35%	97%

As long as the rate of return, which includes both income and capital gains, is greater than the cost of borrowed funds then increasing the level of gearing will increase the percentage return on capital invested. In this case, the rental income was 7% ($20 800 / $300 000) and the capital gain was 10% for a total return of 17%. The cost of borrowed funds was 8%.

If Matthew could be guaranteed the returns outlined above, he should borrow as much as possible to fund the purchase of the unit. However, guaranteed investment returns are very hard to find — if the total return falls below 8% then increasing the level of gearing will, in fact, magnify Matthew's losses.

▶

If we assume that Matthew's rental income is only $5000 and that the capital appreciation is only 3% what is the expected return on capital invested for various levels of gearing (ignoring the impact of taxes at this stage)? This is shown in table 6.3.

TABLE 6.3   Matthew: no taxes, and returns < costs

	No gearing $	Low level of gearing $	Medium level of gearing $	High level of gearing $
Capital	300 000	200 000	100 000	30 000
Borrowing		100 000	200 000	270 000
Total	300 000	300 000	300 000	300 000
Rental income	5 000	5 000	5 000	5 000
Less: Interest		8 000	16 000	21 600
Net income	5 000	–3 000	–11 000	–16 600
Capital gain	9 000	9 000	9 000	9 000
Total return	14 000	6 000	–2 000	–7 600
Capital invested	300 000	200 000	100 000	30 000
Return on capital invested	5%	3%	–2%	–25%

In this case, the rental income was 2% ($5000 / $300 000) and the capital gain was 3% for a total return of 5%. The cost of borrowed funds was 8%. Gearing has magnified losses rather than gains.

When an investor invests in an income-producing asset, that income is assessable for tax purposes. The expenses associated with the income-producing asset are tax deductible. Where an asset is highly geared, interest will be a significant deductible expense. Depending on the nature of the asset, there will be other deductible expenses, particularly where the investment is in property. The Australian Taxation Office (ATO) provides details of all the expenses investors may claim against the income of a rental property. These include, among other things, council rates, cleaning, repairs and maintenance. An expense will be deductible when it is an outgoing necessity incurred in earning income. If asked by the ATO, taxpayers must be able to produce the source documentation which proves that the expense has been paid, or risk fines.

Positive gearing

When the annual income from an investment is greater than the deductible expenses it is said to be positively geared. The excess income is taxed at the investor's marginal tax rate. Because annual income exceeds expenses, positive gearing is considered less risky than negative gearing which we will discuss shortly. Positively geared investors are able to meet their interest commitments through their investment income. Where interest-only financing is used, no call is made on any other income of the investor during the investment period. Positively geared investors can undertake a number of positively geared investments at the same time. If we refer back to the example of Matthew in table 6.2 the 'low' and 'medium' scenarios are examples of positive gearing; that is, the net income is positive.

Consider the case of Sally. Sally has noticed that houses in the suburb of Deadville are very cheap compared to neighbouring suburbs. After checking with local real estate agents, she has found out that the capital appreciation of the houses in Deadville in the last 10 years has averaged 1% p.a.. Demand for rental accommodation, however, is high in Deadville with rental yields averaging 10%. If Sally can borrow at 8% and use the purchased house as security, she can produce positively geared returns. Moreover, Sally might be in a position to buy several houses in Deadville.

Negative gearing

When the annual income from an investment is less than the deductible expenses, it is said to be negatively geared. This loss provides a valuable tax shield. The value of this tax shield should be added to the other cash flows associated with holding the asset in determining the net gain from holding the asset.

If we refer back to the example of Matthew in table 6.2, the 'high' scenario is an example of negative gearing; that is, the assessable income of $20 800 and allowable deductions of $21 600 result in negative net income of $800. If we assume Matthew earns a salary of $100 000 p.a. and his marginal tax rate is 30% (2024–25 rates), then this $800 'loss' can be used to reduce his assessable income from $100 000 to

$99 200 and save him $240 in tax ($800 × 0.30). This $240 saving is effectively a positive cash flow which emerges from Matthew holding the income-producing asset — if he did not own the asset, he would be $240 worse off.

Table 6.4 shows the tax Matthew would pay on the 'all equity', 'low' and 'medium' scenarios. Paying tax reduces the total return. Comparing the return on capital invested for each of the scenarios in tables 6.2 to 6.4 shows that the percentage returns have decreased. Table 6.4 also shows that the negatively geared 'high' scenario results in $240 less tax being paid than would otherwise be the case. This effectively improves Matthew's annual return on the investment.

TABLE 6.4 Matthew: impact of income tax

	No gearing $	Low level of gearing $	Medium level of gearing $	High level of gearing $
Capital	300 000	200 000	100 000	30 000
Borrowing		100 000	200 000	270 000
Total	300 000	300 000	300 000	300 000
Rental income	20 800	20 800	20 800	20 800
Less: Interest		8000	16 000	21 600
Net income	20 800	12 800	4 800	−800
Tax paid/shielded (2024–25 tax rates)	−6 240	−3 840	−1 440	240
Net income after tax	13 104	8 064	3 024	−504
Capital gain	30 000	30 000	30 000	30 000
Total return	43 104	38 064	33 024	29 496
Capital invested	300 000	200 000	100 000	30 000
Return on capital invested	14%	19%	33%	98%

The value of the tax shield is a function of the investor's marginal tax rate — the higher the marginal tax rate, the more valuable the shield. This is illustrated in table 6.5.

Why would an investor want to hold an investment, which on an annual basis loses money? The investor must be hoping for a capital gain which will more than offset the accumulated annual losses associated with the investment.

TABLE 6.5 Tax dollars saved where deductible expenses exceed assessable income by $10 000 (2024–25 tax rates)

Marginal tax rate	Tax saved
16.0%	$1 600
30.0%	$3 000
37.0%	$3 700
45.0%	$4 500

Risks of negative gearing

The primary risk associated with gearing, particularly high levels of gearing, is that borrowing repayments need to be serviced. The burden of repayments can be reduced if the lender is prepared to lend on an interest-only basis; however, sooner or later, the principal amount of the loan will have to be repaid. The risk for an investor of not servicing the loan is that the lender has the right to sell the asset at its current market value if the investor breaks the loan terms and conditions. The current market value may be less than the purchase price or the amount of debt outstanding. The investor/borrower is then obliged to repay the balance of the loan outstanding or face bankruptcy.

The risks of gearing are almost the opposite of the benefits of gearing, and include the following.

- The anticipated annual income is lower than expected. For example, a company may pay lower than expected dividends; a rental property may be vacant for a period of time.
- The anticipated annual expenses are higher than expected. For example, variable interest rates might rise; a rental property might need significant repairs.
- If the loan must be rolled over, the lender may change the rules or conditions of the loan which will affect the benefits of the gearing exercise. An example is an increase in the amount of capital the investor/borrower must contribute.

- The investor loses their job or earns less income, resulting in a lower marginal tax rate which, in turn, makes the tax shield benefits of negative gearing less attractive. The investor might also struggle to generate the cash flow to service the outgoings, particularly loan repayments.
- Circumstances force the investor to sell the asset in less-than-favourable conditions.
- Asset-specific factors adversely affect the investment asset. For example, bad tenants significantly damage a rental property; changes in government legislation negatively impact a listed company.
- The asset does not generate the capital gain anticipated. This is the critical success factor, particularly for negatively geared investments — why sustain annual losses unless the ultimate capital gain more than offsets them?

Gearing ratio and loan-to-valuation ratios

The gearing ratio is used to measure the amount of debt in relation to the current market value of the investor's capital contribution. Some lenders set a gearing ratio as part of their debt agreement for borrowers to maintain during the life of the loan. A lower gearing ratio means there is a lower level of risk for the lender. The gearing ratio is calculated as follows.

$$\text{Gearing ratio} = \frac{\text{Borrowed funds}}{\text{Current market value of the investor's capital contribution}}$$

Returning to the example of Matthew, table 6.6 shows the gearing ratio for the various scenarios we have discussed.

TABLE 6.6   Matthew: gearing ratios

	No gearing $	Low level of gearing $	Medium level of gearing $	High level of gearing $
Capital	300 000	200 000	100 000	30 000
Borrowing		100 000	200 000	270 000
Total	300 000	300 000	300 000	300 000
Gearing ratio		0.5	2	9

The gearing ratio, as its name suggests, generally expresses the ratio of debt to capital. As shown in table 6.6 in the 'high' scenario, Matthew had $9 of debt for every $1 of capital.

Many lenders prefer to use the loan-to-valuation ratio (LVR) measure as their means of determining an appropriate limit for the amount of borrowing by the investor. The LVR uses the same inputs as the gearing ratio; however, contrary to what its name suggests, it is generally expressed as a percentage. The LVR is calculated as follows.

$$\text{LVR} = \frac{\text{Debt}}{\text{Current market value of the investor's capital contribution} + \text{Debt}}$$

6.9 Margin lending

LEARNING OBJECTIVE 6.9 Outline how margin lending works.

Margin lending is a geared investment where the lender advances funds to the investor/borrower and the amount borrowed is secured by the investment assets themselves rather than by a mortgage over property. Typically, margin lending is offered to share market investors, although it is not limited to share market investing. As with most loans, there is interest to pay, but usually the loans are not for any fixed maximum term and principal repayments are optional during the life of the contract. Interest on margin loans is normally 1–2% higher than mortgage loan rates. Lenders seek to limit the amount of risk investors are exposed to by using conservative LVRs.

Margin lending increased dramatically in the 2000s. In September 2000, outstanding margin lending debt was $7 billion. By December 2007, pushed on by a buoyant share market, this amount had risen to $38 billion (RBA 2016). However, the GFC resulted in significant falls in world share markets in 2008. First, in an environment of falling share prices, it became less attractive to commence a new margin lending facility. Second, falling share prices resulted in people with existing margin lending facilities receiving margin calls (discussed later in the chapter) which led to the repayment of debt. By September 2009, the level of outstanding margin lending debt had contracted to $18 billion (RBA 2016). The rapid growth of the industry followed by the sudden contraction is not unexpected and reflects the inherent risk in any form of geared investment. While asset prices are increasing and investor confidence is high, the level of margin lending would be expected to increase. When asset prices are falling and/or investor confidence is not so high, the level of outstanding margin lending would be expected to decrease. By March 2016 margin lending had further contracted to $12 billion (RBA 2016).

With a margin loan, a borrower must maintain a given LVR of the assets used as security. For example, if a lender specifies an LVR of 80% the value of the loan cannot exceed 80% of the value of the asset pledged as security. The specified LVR varies slightly between lenders. Generally, lenders set LVRs according to their perception of the underlying risk and inherent price volatility of the individual asset. The less the perceived underlying risk and the lower inherent price volatility, the higher the LVR and the more the lender is willing to lend. Typically, LVRs range from 40% to 80%. The significant reduction in margin lending in 2008 was accompanied by a widespread reduction in LVRs as lenders reassessed the inherent price volatility of all assets in the market, and this lower level of LVRs has persisted as world economic conditions remain uncertain. Any widespread reduction in LVRs must constrain the growth of the margin lending market.

All of the major banks provide margin lending facilities; the Commonwealth Bank, for example, has an extensive list of Australian Securities Exchange (ASX) listed equities that are approved for margin lending purposes.

ILLUSTRATIVE EXAMPLE 6.9

Penny wishes to create a $100 000 share portfolio by using some of her own capital and by commencing a margin loan facility. She intends to use $35 000 of her own money and borrow $65 000 through a margin lending facility.

She wishes to invest in the shares of two publicly listed companies, Newstock Bank and Bright Copper. Her lender advises that Newstock has an LVR of 70% and Bright Copper has an LVR of 60%.

Penny wishes to buy $50 000 of Newstock shares and $50 000 of Bright Copper shares. Her lender will recognise the following security value.

Stock	Current value	LVR	Security value
Newstock	$50 000	70%	$35 000
Bright Copper	50 000	60%	30 000
Total	$100 000		$65 000

One of the benefits of margin lending is that borrowers can also pledge existing assets as security for a margin loan provided they are on the lender's approved list.

If Penny already held $35 000 in shares, $17 500 in Newstock and $17 500 in Bright Copper, the analysis would be exactly the same as the above.

From the point of view of the lender, Penny's LVR is 65%. That means if the loan value of her portfolio rises above 65%, she will then face a margin call. This could happen if the value of her shares falls and the value of her portfolio falls to say $90 000. Then the LVR would be 72% and the bank would require the sale of shares or the deposit of more funds to reduce the LVR to 65%. The movements in individual share prices could affect the amount of security value offered. For example, compare the table below with the previous one. The value of Newstock has decreased whereas the value of Bright Copper has increased. This results in an overall lower LVR.

Stock	Current value	LVR	Security value
Newstock	$25 000	70%	$17 500
Bright Copper	75 000	60%	45 000
Total	$100 000		$62 500

Borrowers must actively monitor their margin loan accounts. By regularly checking changes in the portfolio value, individual security value and loan balance, customers can better manage the chance of receiving a margin call. Naturally, lenders will monitor this as well.

Safety margin

Most lenders will insist that an investor maintains a safety margin of security over and above the value of their loan. The size of the margin will vary from lender to lender. For example, a client might need to maintain a safety margin or buffer of 5%. The safety margin or buffer is there to protect the lender, particularly when asset prices are volatile. If prices fall, the lender will make a margin call to ensure that the safety margin is re-established.

The safety margin is also a source of comfort and reassurance for the individual investor. While the lender might insist on a safety margin of 5%, the individual investor may have a safety margin which far exceeds this in order to further reduce the likelihood of margin calls.

We can calculate the safety margin as follows.

$$\text{Safety margin} = 1 - \frac{\text{Borrowing}}{\text{Security value recognised by lender}}$$

If we return to the example of Penny, and assume that the stock market has been performing well, she now has the following portfolio.

Stock	Current value	LVR	Security value
Newstock	$60 000	70%	$42 000
Bright Copper	75 000	60%	45 000
Total	$135 000		$87 000

Penny's safety margin would be as follows.

$$\text{Safety margin} = 1 - \frac{\$65\,000}{\$87\,000}$$
$$= 25.3\%$$

Margin calls

If the value of the security pledged falls below the value required by the lender, a margin call will be triggered. Margin calls normally have to be satisfied within 24 hours. Margin calls can be satisfied in one of three ways.

1. The borrower contributes cash which effectively reduces the outstanding balance of the loan and re-establishes a safety margin.
2. The borrower uses existing assets which are not currently pledged as security for the loan to increase the level of security offered and increase the safety margin.
3. The borrower sells some of the assets which are currently pledged as security for the loan and uses the cash proceeds from these sales to reduce the outstanding loan and increase the safety margin.

In a rapidly falling stock market, the margin calls can be large and frequent. Highly leveraged individuals may find it hard to satisfy a margin call by the first two means above. This means that they may be forced to sell their assets during a period of falling market prices. Moreover, if a large number of individuals are in a similar position, the selling pressure in the market will drive prices lower and increase the likelihood of further margin calls. If we return to the example of Penny and assume that the stock market has been performing poorly, she now has the following portfolio.

Stock	Current value	LVR	Security
Newstock	$45 000	70%	$31 500
Bright Copper	43 000	60%	25 800
Total	$88 000		$57 300

Her safety margin would be as follows.

$$\text{Safety margin} = 1 - \frac{\$65\,000}{\$57\,300}$$
$$= -13.4\%$$

In this situation, the lender will make a margin call which Penny must satisfy within 24 hours by one of the following means.

- Reducing the outstanding value of the loan by paying $7700 in cash to reduce the balance from $65 000 to $57 300.

- Pledging additional assets as security:

$$\text{Amount needed to be pledged} = \frac{\text{Cash required}}{\text{LVR}} \qquad \textbf{6.1}$$

$$= \frac{\$7700}{0.7} \text{ (assuming LVR is 0.7)}$$

$$= \$11\,000$$

- Selling existing assets and using the proceeds to reduce the value of the loan:

$$\text{Amount needed to be sold} = \frac{\text{Cash required}}{1 - \text{LVR}} \qquad \textbf{6.2}$$

If Penny sold Newstock:

$$\text{Amount needed to be sold} = \frac{\text{Cash required}}{1 - \text{LVR}}$$

$$= \frac{\$7700}{1 - 0.7} \qquad \textbf{6.3}$$

$$= \$25\,667$$

Alternatively, Penny may sell some Bright Copper or some combination of Newstock and Bright Copper.

6.10 Benefits and risks of margin lending

LEARNING OBJECTIVE 6.10 Explain the benefits and risks of margin lending.

There are a number of benefits of margin lending for an investor, including greater access to wealth-creating assets, diversification, liquidity, tax benefits and direct investing opportunities. The main risk of margin lending is associated with meeting margin calls. A number of other risks are also associated with margin lending for the investor.

Benefits of margin lending

Margin lending allows investors to purchase assets that are of a higher value than they could afford using their existing funds. This increases the wealth-creation potential for the investor. Margin lending allows investors to spread their risk across a number of asset types and sectors. The ability to spread the investment capital across different asset types is known as diversification, which is a common risk-reduction strategy undertaken by investors.

Selling shares and repaying a margin loan takes less time than selling property, and can be achieved for a much lower transaction cost. Although most margin lenders charge a fee for early repayment of a loan, most also allow the full repayment of the loan without penalty after a certain period has elapsed. This allows investors ready access to any gains made on their portfolio.

There may be some income tax benefits of margin lending through deductibility of the interest charged on the loan, as well as deferring capital gains tax by not selling shares in a certain financial year. Margin lending allows investors to choose which shares they will invest in (within some limits set by the lending institution) and therefore allows investors to be actively involved in the management of their share portfolio. This may be preferable over managed funds for some investors, and may also reduce management fees.

Risks of margin lending

In addition to the risks associated with meeting margin calls there are a number of other risks associated with margin lending for the investor.

Traditionally, Australian shares have provided between 60% and 80% and managed funds between 20% and 40% of the security for margin loans. For the investor, using shares or managed funds as security for a margin loan provides the assurance that only the investment assets subject to the margin loan are at risk and there is no recourse to other assets owned by the investor. Post global financial crisis (GFC), however, we did see the increased use of margin loans secured by residential property. Partially, this was a response to the GFC-induced share market falls where investors with significant margin lending exposure were unwilling or unable to meet their margin call commitments through the various means we have described in this chapter. It could also be argued that residential property has seen less price volatility than the equity markets and as such, provides a more stable level of security and therefore reduces the likelihood of margin calls. However, it is vital that investors understand that their residential property investments, including possibly the family home, are at risk when they are pledged as security for a margin loan.

There are three sources of risk for interest payments on margin loans — timing, servicing ability and tax.

- Timing issues arise when investors use dividend payments to pay for the interest expense on a margin loan and the dividend payments do not coincide with when the interest payments are due.
- The loan servicing ability of investors for repayments of the loan from existing income is also a risk to be considered, particularly where variable interest rate loans are used.
- Investors often negatively gear a margin lending facility and therefore derive a tax shield from the annual losses incurred. The tax shield is more valuable the higher the marginal tax rate of the investor. While the investor might have the cash resources to service the loan, any sudden and significant reduction in the client's marginal tax rate could seriously diminish the attractiveness of the overall investment.

Finally, the LVR must be maintained at an agreed level. Fluctuating values in the share market are normal and require constant monitoring by investors. Lenders mostly assign the onus of monitoring daily LVRs to their clients, and clients must immediately rectify the situation, under the terms of the contracts, even though the lenders may not have issued margin calls. The effect of this condition is a high level of stress for borrowers if their LVRs are close to the contracted levels; they must monitor the trading results of the share market every day. The way to alleviate the situation is, of course, for borrowers to maintain a comfortable buffer or cushion between their actual or expected LVRs and the contracted levels.

PERSONAL FINANCE BULLETIN

Margin lenders improve lending standards following ASIC review

Following an ASIC review, margin lenders have moved to better address the different levels of risk for investors seeking margin loans, especially in relation to double geared margin loans.

ASIC reviewed the lending practices of six margin lenders, covering 90% of the market, and found that five of the six margin lenders approved 'double geared' margin loans. Double geared margin loans are where a consumer borrows money (using another asset as security, such as their home) to purchase shares, and then obtains a margin loan on these shares to purchase additional shares. Because of the extra risks associated with double gearing, the law requires margin lenders to meet responsible lending obligations.

ASIC found that in certain circumstances, four of the five margin lenders who approved double geared margin loans did not take additional steps when approving such loans, despite the additional risks associated with double geared margin loans.

Following ASIC's review, one margin lender decided to cease offering double geared loans. The remaining four lenders have made several commitments to reduce risks, including ensuring that their policies have, or continue to have, the following requirements for double geared borrowers:

- extra buffers to allow for interest rate rises and/or changes in expenses
- lower maximum allowable loan amounts
- lower loan to value ratios.

ASIC's review also identified two lenders that provided double geared margin loans in circumstances where the borrower would not be able to fully service the margin loan relying only on their available income. Instead, such borrowers would need to sell assets in order to meet their ongoing interest payments. While 'asset-lend' margin loans are not prohibited, ASIC considers that such margin loans are significantly more likely to be unsuitable. Following ASIC's review, both margin lenders agreed to cease approving double geared asset-lend margin loans. 'ASIC is pleased with the industry's response to our proactive review and its commitment to standards that give appropriate consideration to the potentially significant risks that a double geared investment strategy might pose to investors', said ASIC Deputy Chair Peter Kell.

'However, given the clear need for better standards, ASIC will continue to monitor the margin lending sector. Should we find inappropriate lending we will take regulatory action to address consumer risks', he said.

Mr Kell also emphasised the importance for investors to fully understand the risks and costs of margin loans as well as the potential benefits. ASIC's Moneysmart website has guidance to help investors understand how margin loans work and the risks involved.

Source: ASIC 2016.

Derivatives

In addition to margin lending, a number of investment products or instruments in the market derive their value from underlying assets. These are called derivatives. Derivative products allow the investor to be exposed to the price movements of underlying assets without paying the full purchase price of these assets. In this way, they are a form of leveraged investment. Some investors use derivatives purely for speculative purposes; that is, they are not trying to manage the risk associated with some pre-existing position. Other investors use derivatives to hedge risks that they currently face. Whether the investor is speculating or hedging, the mechanics of how these derivatives work does not alter. This chapter will not cover derivatives as they will be covered in a finance textbook. Derivatives that are commonly used include:

- contracts for difference (CFD)
- futures contracts
- options (both Call and Put)
- warrants.

The ASX provides a range of free and publicly-available online short courses that take individual learners from basic concepts through to a more complex and sophisticated analysis of particular products traded on the ASX.

6.11 Mortgages

LEARNING OBJECTIVE 6.11 Explain how mortgages work.

Mortgages are secured geared investments where the mortgage document is the contract between the lender and the borrower. A mortgage contract is a pledge of real estate to secure the payment of a loan. Mortgages can be secured by either residential or non-residential real estate. The mortgage contract gives the lender (**mortgagee**) the right to foreclose on the loan and take ownership of the property in order to ensure that the loan is paid off if the borrower (**mortgagor**) fails to make the contracted payments. Lenders prefer borrowers to have substantial deposits so that the LVR is less than 80–85%.

In Australia, the most common mortgage loans are standard variable-rate loans (SVL) and fixed-rate loans. A standard variable-rate mortgage is one in which the interest rate on the loan is adjusted periodically. Recent trends have shown that the trigger for changing interest rates is the announcement of a change (an increase or a decrease) in the cash rate by the Reserve Bank of Australia (RBA).

Fixed-rate loans have fixed rates of interest for an agreed period. At the end of this period they generally convert to variable-rate loans. Normally borrowers must decide on a time period for their fixed rate contract and usually it will be up to 10 years. After the expiry of that period, an investor may refinance and contract for a fixed rate for a further period. The decision, of course, rests on the likelihood of a rise in interest rates and the premium being charged by the lending institution for the fixed rate over the current variable rate.

With the deregulation of the finance industry, the use of mortgages for investing has become quite sophisticated at the retail level. Some variations on the standard interest-and-principal mortgage repayment schemes include:

- interest-only loans with the entire **principal** payable at the end of the loan
- **equity** release loans, where surplus equity above agreed levels may be withdrawn
- reverse mortgages, where no repayments are made until the contract is settled when the homeowner dies or leaves the property
- second-mortgage loans for investing in other income-generating assets such as shares or other property.

All these styles of lending for investing using mortgages have the same underlying operational characteristics as a standard mortgage including the:

- pledging of real estate to the lender until the debt is repaid
- need to service the debt regularly (e.g. monthly, annually), at the beginning of the loan (e.g. up-front interest payments) or at the end of the loan (e.g. reverse mortgages).

There are a number of benefits of using assets as **security** for borrowings.

- It reduces the risk to the lender that the capital will not be returned. Should the borrower default on the loan, the lender has the right to sell the asset that is securing the loan at its current value, using the proceeds to repay the loan and to cover any costs incurred in selling the asset.
- It allows the borrower to access funds that would not normally be available if the borrower was providing only a promise to repay the loan.

- It allows the borrower to access funds at a cheaper rate than if the borrower was only providing a promise to repay the loan.
- It provides both borrower and lender with a safety net of value. As long as the asset is worth more than the loan, there is a barrier between the value of the debt and the amount that could be raised to repay the debt once the asset is sold.

The disadvantages of using assets as security for borrowing include the:
- risk for the borrower that the particular asset will be seized and sold by the lender
- costs of preparing documentation for the loan; for example, the additional costs in obtaining an independent valuation for the asset
- borrower cannot use the asset that is used as security for the loan for any other purposes without the express written permission of the lender; for example, to secure another loan, to sell the asset, or to demolish and rebuild the property.

6.12 Advantages and disadvantages of home ownership

LEARNING OBJECTIVE 6.12 Identify advantages and disadvantages of home ownership.

In this section we will focus on using a mortgage to acquire a property and then consider the matter of buying a home or renting.

Advantages of home ownership

Purchasing your own home provides a number of advantages.
- *Locational and financial stability* — even the best landlords are seldom willing to enter contracts to let residential property for periods greater than 2–3 years. Hence, tenants have no greater assurance of stability than the agreed terms of contracts. Additionally, an owner-occupier will be aware that costs of ownership will gradually rise, but will not be subject to a rent review where the owner can insist on an unreasonable increase in the rent. Such increases may be grudgingly agreed to by tenants unwilling to undergo the trauma of shifting to a new location.
- *A form of disciplined saving* — many people need the strength of an external force to compel them into regular saving. Having to satisfy a financial institution with regular payments of interest and part of the principal of the loan (or risk expulsion) provides that discipline. In addition, in many relationships, there are differences in savings behaviour of the partners. Again, externally applied discipline can help achieve savings where otherwise it would not be possible.
- *A useful asset base* — houses usually rise in value over the long term and therefore are often a good investment in themselves. Many successful businesspeople have started businesses with little capital but good ideas. Having a fully paid house or at least substantial equity in a house can help to finance business development and expansion. The house equity reassures financial institutions that applicants for loans have financial discipline and, additionally, it can be used as security for a loan. Generally, it is not advisable to use the security in your home for a business loan.
- *Personal freedom regarding living conditions* — an owned home can be altered or added to at the whim of the owner, subject to local government regulations and any covenants entered into at purchase. For example, owners who want to install spa baths or swimming pools may do so, but tenants may not.
- *Taxation concessions and advantages* — there is no capital gains tax (CGT) on the main residence or improvements to it. However, if the homeowner needs to move from their home and rent it for a period of time then a portion of the gain on sale may be taxable. Also, if the homeowner uses their home for business purposes and makes claims for deductions for improvements then, when the house is sold, a portion of the gain may be subject to capital gains tax.

Disadvantages of home ownership

Home ownership has several disadvantages.
- Property investment is best suited to medium- to long-term planning horizons and owner-occupied homes are no different from other property investments. Hence, an owner forced to sell for various reasons at an inopportune time can lose capital, especially if the investment has been held for a relatively short time. Over the longer time frame, and assuming there have been some periods of relatively high inflation, property prices generally will rise, usually to match or exceed inflation.

- Property investment is non-liquid, so owners needing ready cash are disadvantaged relative to, say, owners of shares. On the other hand, cash can be quickly gained by application for a loan on the security of home equity.
- Property investment is commonly the major asset in the total basket of individual wealth with owner-occupied housing comprising about 60% or more of average household assets in Australia.
- There is an opportunity cost in having wealth tied up in a home. Whether there is net cost or net benefit (taking into account forgone alternative investment benefits, avoided rental payments, costs of ownership etc.) depends on individual circumstances. However, usually rents are closely tied to housing costs, so owners who have $500 000 loan commitment in their homes must remember that interest is about $500 per week and rents for comparable housing may also be $500 per week.
- Some people with particular income streams and financial circumstances find it beneficial to rent their main residence but to own other residential property. These strategies rely usually on taxation advantages rather than the pure economics of the situation. For example, negative gearing brings income tax deductions on income-producing property but not on owner-occupied housing. However, negative gearing often requires asset price inflation to be a reasonable proposition and brings additional risk for the investor. On the other hand, there are CGT advantages stemming from owner-occupation of residential property.

6.13 Financial implications of home ownership versus renting

LEARNING OBJECTIVE 6.13 Discuss financial implications of home ownership versus renting.

In this section, we look at the actual decision to rent or buy, assuming the householder has satisfied concerns about the given location, size of dwelling and so on. The decision to rent or to buy can depend on a number of factors.

Firstly, there may be a cultural or environmental determinant. A new householder raised in a family which always lived in its own home perhaps cannot imagine living for very long in rented premises, 'A waste of good money!' Some may prefer to rent and have priorities such as pursing sporting or other social activities rather than mow the lawn every weekend. A person raised in rented premises may not think of buying a home even when it is financially possible.

Secondly, purchase decisions are more likely to be made when a reasonably sized deposit is available to give the new home purchaser some immediate equity in the house. What's a reasonable size? Around 20–30% of the total purchase cost would be useful. A deposit of 10% should be considered an absolute minimum.

Why would it be unwise to enter a house contract, supposing you could arrange finance, with less than 10% deposit? Over time, housing schemes have been implemented by both state and federal governments. Their goals have been the common one of trying to help people get started in paying off a home. Some of these schemes have been more successful than others. The least successful have been the 'no-deposit' schemes, where low-income earners with no saved funds are assisted. There are at least two reasons for this lack of success. People with no saved funds are less likely to have learned the skills which enable them to save. You might argue that they can't save because they do not have enough income. The counterargument to this is that people who are savers manage to save no matter what their income. Thus, people without saving skills are likely to suffer financial emergencies when they are unable to pay the housing instalments and fall behind in their payment schedules.

People falling into arrears in their payment schedules may soon find that they owe more than the amount of the original loan if the shortfall in payments occurs early in the loan period. This is because the interest on the loan continues to accrue and is capitalised, thus increasing the total amount owed. Should the property market be falling at the same time, the question of equity in the home (the proportion of the total value of the house actually owned by the householder) becomes important. It is possible for the new homeowner to owe more than the house is worth.

Equity provides a buffer between the market value and the loan principal. If the market is falling, the householder's equity falls, because the financial institution's stake in the house is a fixed dollar value (the loan principal), which falls only as the loan is repaid. If the market rises, on the other hand, the householder enjoys a windfall gain and equity rises. However, a householder's equity of reasonable size keeps the financial institution happy, because it is assured of being repaid should the house have to be sold.

A further advantage of a larger equity in your home is that financial institutions insist on mortgage insurance if the equity value falls below a certain level, generally less than 20%. The premium for the insurance cover is paid by the householder. It thus increases costs and reduces the amount of savings which can be applied to the reduction of the loan principal and loan period. Mortgage insurance on a $500 000 loan may cost around $4000.

Finally, there are the financial considerations. If the homeowner had to live elsewhere for a period and rent the house out, it is likely that a $600 000 house could be rented for about 5% of its value (i.e. about $30 000 p.a. or almost $600 per week).

Of course, the amount of rent that could be charged depends on the particular location at any given time will depend on the supply of, and demand for, unoccupied housing and for rental housing. Thus, the prospective householder should examine the actual values for particular situations if confronted by this decision. Other factors apart from supply and demand which will have a significant impact are the interest-rate structure and expectations of future interest-rate changes.

ILLUSTRATIVE EXAMPLE 6.10

Charli is 24 years of age and has just graduated with a law degree. She lived at home with her parents while she was at university. Charli is about to commence her first job as an articled clerk before she is admitted to the bar as a lawyer. Charli has followed her parents' example and has built up some savings from her part-time work and invested in some blue-chip shares.

Charli now has a dilemma, should she stay at home with her parents and pay a modest board, or rent a flat with a friend for a couple of years? She knows that if she rents with a friend it will be close to her work and she will become more involved in the inner-city social scene. Her decision is compounded by her need to save for a deposit so she can afford to buy her own home unit in a few years before prices become too expensive. She expects to earn $75 000 in her first year of employment but her salary will increase to $90 000 after she has obtained her practising certificate. If she rents a flat with a friend, she knows she will be paying about $300 per week or $15 000 p.a. to a landlord. If she stays at home, she will pay $100 per week or $5000 p.a. to her parents to help meet the costs of the family household. However, if she stays at home, she will have additional travel costs of about $60 per week or $3000 p.a. as well as the burden of two hours travel time each day. Charli rationalises that the travel time may also be productive time where she can do some extra work-related reading and thinking. So, by staying with her parents, she thinks she will save a deposit more quickly than if she rents with a friend.

6.14 Financing a house purchase

LEARNING OBJECTIVE 6.14 Discuss financing a house purchase.

If a buyer has the necessary funds, the easiest way to finance a house purchase is with the buyer's own cash. The advantages of this approach are the:
- speed of settling the transaction
- freedom to make decisions without being fettered by a financial institution
- absence of the fees associated with loan approvals
- tax advantages in paying cash for an investor's own home and borrowing to invest elsewhere, rather than investing cash elsewhere and borrowing to purchase the home.

Unfortunately, the majority of investors are not in a position to purchase a house for cash — they must obtain a loan. The usual method is by way of a mortgage loan, and with a mortgaged property the lender has rights only over the capital asset, not the income from it or the use of it or, in this case, the right to live in it.

Matching financial capacity to borrowings

How does a potential borrower decide the amount to borrow under a mortgage loan? Does it depend on the amount needed, personal income or current savings? The amount needed depends on the price of the house. How should a buyer decide which houses are too expensive? Are some houses too cheap and unsuitable for a buyer with given financial worth?

Let us look at the last question first. Some houses may be too cheap. They may be in poor condition and need much expenditure to bring them up to standard, they may be in an unsuitable area for the buyer, or they may be of an unsuitable design for the buyer's needs.

Can a house be too expensive? Yes, many houses, although suitable in size and condition, are too expensive for the potential buyer's financial capabilities. How do we know the right price? It all comes back to affordability. Affordability relates the repayments to the borrower's income. As figure 6.5 shows, affordability in recent years has increased in most Australian capital cities except for Melbourne and Sydney. Another factor which must be considered is other indebtedness. If borrowers have no other debts, they can afford higher mortgage repayments and hence can contract for larger loans. There are many ways to judge affordability. Some financial institutions prefer that a borrower's contracted mortgage repayments do not exceed about 30% of before-tax income and that the total of all loan repayments does not exceed 35% of before-tax income. Others suggest the mortgage repayments should not exceed 50% of the surplus funds after normal living expenses and taxes are met. These ratios set the upper limits of available contracted loans.

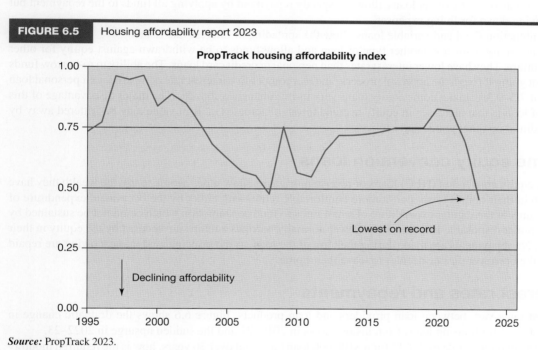

FIGURE 6.5 Housing affordability report 2023

Source: PropTrack 2023.

The use of the term 'normal' in the affordability criterion is interesting. Financial institutions are aware that many people lack financial discipline. Thus, whereas some people are able to make an extraordinary effort to save money and pay off a larger-than-usual loan, others cannot sustain the effort for very long and eventually default. Lenders bow to the inevitable for the community as a whole and suggest loans should be smaller or loan periods should be longer so that regular repayment amounts are smaller. Notwithstanding the norm of community behaviour, some people make an extraordinary financial effort and pay off loans very quickly. This sort of effort, incorporating supreme savings endeavour (i.e. cutting consumption), an appropriate loan structure and perhaps additional work to increase income, is the basis for books with titles like 'How I paid off my mortgage in five years'. People with this discipline can acquire assets very quickly.

The amount of current savings will determine the size of the deposit and thus the amount which can be paid for a property. Financial institutions prefer people to have a sizeable deposit. As many young people find it difficult to raise the deposit required to buy a home — and as prices rise, a higher deposit is required — many parents use some of their superannuation money or mortgage their own home to help their children raise the required deposit. The availability of a good deposit (about 20% or more) will influence the loan decision in a positive manner and will also reduce costs as mortgage insurance to cover the lender against default may not be required. In calculating the amount of savings which can be used as a deposit, buyers should remember that there will be loan establishment fees (up to $1000), conveyancing fees, and other transaction costs such as survey fees and stamp duty to be paid. In addition, an emergency cash balance should be kept to insure against unforeseen circumstances.

Figure 6.5 indicates the housing affordability index for Australia since 1995. The declining trend provides concerns for many young people looking to buy a home.

Loan types

Once all the side issues have been looked after, there are the major issues of interest rates and types of loans available.

- Standard variable loans (SVLs) usually extend for 20–25 years but allow for faster repayment, with the interest rate varying with the market (variations in types of variable loans also may exist from providers).
- Fixed-rate loans have rates and repayments that are fixed for 1–5 years, then become variable with penalties for earlier repayment.
- Capped loans have a cap on rate increases that can be applied for 1 year, then default to SVL conditions.
- Introductory 'honeymoon' loans have approximately 1.0% lower rates for 1–2 years, then revert to SVL conditions.
- All-in-one or 100% offset loans allow for speedy repayment by applying all funds to the repayment but drawing down for living expenses.
  Combination fixed and variable loans allow the spreading of interest-rate risk.

Home equity loans are another type of loan and allow funds to be withdrawn against equity for other expenditure. They have lower interest rates than personal or credit card loans. The ability to re-borrow funds without going through the approval process, and at a competitive interest rate compared with personal loan rates of 7.5–9.5%, make home equity loans very useful financial products. The major disadvantage of this type of loan is that increases in equity accrued through increases in asset value may be frittered away by expenditure on other goods and services.

Home equity conversion loans

Home equity conversion (HEC) loans or reverse mortgages allow older people to use the wealth they have tied up in their homes to support a more comfortable retirement, either by the occasional expenditure of lump sums or the regular expenditure of small sums to fund consumption which could not be sustained by their regular disposable incomes. A borrower normally borrows a lump sum secured by the equity in their house. No repayments are made during the term of the loan, as the principal and interest owing are repaid when the borrower dies or decides to leave their home.

Interest rates and repayments

Interest rates vary between loan providers and loan products. Figure 6.6 shows the dramatic change in interest rates for housing loans from historic lows in 2019–21 and the sudden upsurge in 2022–23.

Given an interest rate of 2.95% for a \$100 000 loan taken out over 30 years, how is the required monthly repayment calculated? This is an annuity calculation. The \$100 000 is the present value of an annuity. The formula, as we saw in the chapter on financial planning skills, is:

$$PV = \frac{C[1 - (1 + i)^{-n}]}{i}$$

where PV = present value

C = regular payment (or PMT if using a financial calculator)

i = interest rate per period

n = number of periods

Thus:

$$C = \frac{PV}{[1 - (1 + i)^{-n}] / i}$$

The first thing to calculate is the interest rate per period, which is the annual rate (2.95%) divided by 12 months for 12 monthly payment periods per year.

$$\frac{0.0295}{12} = 0.002458333$$

FIGURE 6.6 Average housing interest rates

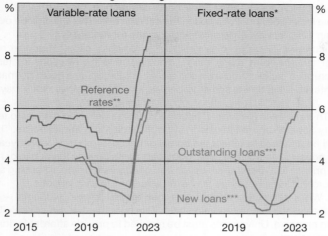

Average housing interest rates

*   Weighted average interest rate across all fixed-rate periods.
** Major banks' standard reference rates for owner-occupier
    variable-rate loans.
*** Series break in July 2019; thereafter, data based on EFS
    collection.

Source: RBA 2024.

There are 360 months in 30 years, so n is 360. Substituting into the equation:

$$(1 + i)^{-n} = (1.002458333)^{-360}$$

$$= \frac{1}{(1.002458333)^{360}}$$

$$= \frac{1}{2.420354}$$

$$= 0.413163$$

$$= \frac{1 - 0.413163}{0.002458333}$$

$$= 238.7138$$

therefore:

$$C = \frac{\$100\ 000}{238.7138}$$

$$= \$418.91$$

PERSONAL FINANCE BULLETIN

Australia's housing crisis is deepening. Here are 10 policies to get us out of it

As Australia's housing crisis deepens, governments at all levels are being called on to help. The federal budget will be handed down today, and housing will be a key talking point.

The current public debate about housing is focused on 'silver bullet' solutions. What is needed instead is a comprehensive package of bold interventions, coordinated between all levels of government and the private sector.

While home ownership has been the Australian tradition, it should not be the only option for secure and affordable housing. Tenants, particularly long-term or life-long tenants, must be supported as much as aspiring homeowners. Rental housing policies, as opposed to policies aimed at construction, have an immediate widespread impact on housing affordability and security of tenure.

▶

Five policies for rental housing

Here are five key measures for the rental market.

1. *Caps on annual rent increases.* These have been common in Western Europe and parts of North America. Allowable increases should be tied to the inflation rate. This will provide owners with adequate income to maintain the property while providing security for renters.
2. *No-fault eviction controls.* Such policies typically accompany caps on annual rent increases. They protect long-term tenants from many risks, including revenge evictions of tenants who make a complaint and disruptive digital platforms such as Airbnb. Exceptions could be made in cases in which owners and tenants are living on the same properties, since such transactions may be personal as well as financial.
3. *Rent assistance.* This can be in the form of housing vouchers delivered directly to tenants. The National Rental Affordability Scheme approach of working with landlords is also effective. The amounts of rental assistance should be adjusted to reflect the actual rental cost trends of recent years.
4. *Social and public housing rentals.* These include apartments built by the public or non-profit sectors to rent at affordable prices. To avoid stigmatisation and ghettoisation, social housing should house people on a range of incomes. Some buildings may even offer rent-to-own options.
5. *Student housing.* While education is Australia's third-largest export, students — both domestic and international — receive little accommodation help. This puts them at risk of exploitation and increases the overall housing pressure. Universities must be required to provide affordable dormitories on campus for the students they enrol.

Five policies for home ownership

Assistance for people who wish to buy a home but have low incomes and lack access to the 'bank of mum and dad' must be guided by the principle that affordable housing is a necessity, just like healthcare and schooling. With that in mind, the government should prioritise the following measures.

1. *Increases in market-rate housing supply.* If enough housing is built to meet buyer demand, and the population remains stable in an area, house prices at the metropolitan level will reduce. That's the law of supply and demand.

   Height bonuses and tax incentives should be provided to developers who build dense housing — especially in inner cities and next to public transport stations. New housing should be in the form of townhouses, condominium towers of varied sizes, and even tiny houses and co-housing compounds where households live as a community with shared spaces.

   The negative phenomenon of NIMBYism should be resisted. It stems from upper-income classes who cast themselves as progressives defending the local character while in fact they seek exclusivity.
2. *Auxiliary units.* Where larger lots cannot be assembled for higher-density housing, the construction of small secondary units next to (or even within) existing houses should be encouraged. To this end, requirements around minimum lot sizes and parking provision should be relaxed. Auxiliary units can serve, among other things, to house older homeowners who wish to downsize — hence their traditional name 'granny flat'.
3. *Inclusionary units.* These are units in new developments that are sold at below-market rates to qualifying lower-income households. Offering a percentage of inclusionary units in large-scale developments should be required nationwide. Inclusionary housing would lead to adjustments in land values rather than making projects unviable.
4. *Transition housing.* This type of housing is for people in crisis situations, such as victims of domestic violence, or who are homeless. It must be free and combined with support services. It largely pays for itself because it offsets the social costs of homelessness and offers major benefits for the beneficiaries.
5. *Financial sticks and carrots.* Governments should offer assistance with both down payments and loans for first-time buyers. At the same time, investment properties and inheritance properties should be taxed at a higher rate to avoid market distortions and property hoarding by small-scale speculators. Tax rules such as negative gearing should be abolished.

The risks of sticking to the status quo

Why haven't the problems with our housing system been fixed yet? Why was the crisis allowed to develop in the first place? Because many profit a great deal from a broken housing system — disregarding the inequalities and gentrification waves that come about as a result.

Australian society should come to share an understanding that a dwelling is a space needed for living. It is not a vehicle to store and showcase wealth and extract excessive rents from the 'houseless'. Nor is its purpose to sustain class divisions from one generation to the next.

Ignoring the housing crisis will result in the Brazilianization of Australia, changing us into a country of high inequality and exclusion in our lifetime. This represents a dark future in which Australia's long-held myth of a classless society will be shattered.

Source: Pojani 2023.

SUMMARY

This chapter covered three separate topics. Firstly, we considered an overview of the managed funds industry where we learned that managed funds allow investors to pool their money together and invest into a portfolio mix of fixed interest, shares and property or as a single asset class where the fund is managed by a professional investment team. Investors can also select from a wide range of asset classes and management styles to suit the desired level of risk they are prepared to accept within their investment portfolios.

Secondly, this chapter considered the impact of using borrowed money to invest into shares and property. Borrowing money is also known as gearing or leveraging. Negative gearing into property or shares is a common investment strategy with an intention of capital gain but also subject to risk. Margin lending was demonstrated as a use of leverage with both return and risk features.

Thirdly, this section of the chapter considered the matter of buying a home or renting and followed on with the use of leveraging to buy a home. Buying a home is an investment in property but it first requires a deposit and a steady income stream to pay back the amount borrowed plus interest. Most home purchases involve a mortgage which requires a lender to hold the title to a property until the debt is satisfied. The decision of what form of loan to borrow was also explored. As many are not able to afford to buy a home and some may choose not to buy a home then the issues associated with renting were examined.

KEY TERMS

active investment An investment approach which is based on an investment manager selecting and trading in securities with the goal of outperforming an index.

benchmark Normally an index or other measure against which the performance of a managed fund or other investment portfolio is measured.

beneficial interest The entitlement to receive benefits generated by assets held in the name of another entity.

capital gain A gain that arises when the price of an asset increases.

derivative A financial product that has no inherent value; its value or price is derived from some other asset.

diversification The spread of different assets held in a portfolio.

equity The client's capital as opposed to borrowed funds.

exchange traded fund (ETF) A fund listed on a stock exchange that has the objective of managing investments on behalf of investors based on tracking a particular index.

fixed-rate loan A loan whereby the interest rate is fixed by a length of time and/or by a fixed interest rate.

gearing The use of borrowed money to assist in the purchase of assets.

gearing ratio The ratio of debt to capital.

growth funds manager An investment management style where investments are selected and traded on the basis of superior future growth.

home equity conversion (HEC) loan (reverse mortgage) A loan or an amount by which a home owner may draw funds based on the equity or ownership value of the home.

indirect cost ratio (ICR) An aggregation of all management costs (MER) and other indirect costs which cannot be attributed to individual member accounts expressed as a percentage of funds under management.

leverage Use a small amount of capital to access a larger amount of an asset.

listed investment company (LIC) An investment company listed on a stock exchange that has the objective of managing investments on behalf of investors.

listed investment trust (LIT) An investment trust listed on a stock exchange that has the objective of managing investments on behalf of investors.

listed managed fund A managed fund that is listed and traded on a stock exchange.

loan-to-valuation ratio (LVR) The amount of debt expressed as a percentage of the total asset value.

margin call Where a lender asks for an additional contribution by a borrower because the current level of the security they are offering has fallen below an agreed threshold.

margin lending Lending for investment where the loan is secured by the investment.

marking to market Constantly reassessing the financial obligations of buyers and sellers as the market price of an asset changes.

master fund An investment fund which enables investors to invest in a number of funds via one fund; sometimes referred to as an investment platform.

mortgage A contract between a lender and a borrower which pledges real estate as security for a loan.

mortgagee The person who receives the mortgage — the lender.

mortgagor The person who offers the mortgage — the borrower.

negative gearing A situation where the total deductions associated with an investment, including the interest charge, exceed assessable income generated from the investment; in this case, the loss can be claimed as a tax deduction.

net tangible assets The total assets of a company, minus any intangible assets and less all liabilities of the company.

passive investment An investment approach which is based on selecting investments within a portfolio based on replicating an index.

positive gearing A situation where the assessable income generated from the investment exceeds total deductions incurred, including the interest charges; in this case, tax is payable on the profit.

principal The amount of a loan which is outstanding.

product disclosure statement (PDS) An offer document designed to provide information about a managed investment scheme to investors, including its risks, costs, return objectives and other information.

public unit trust A trust that issues units to the general public for the purpose of investing monies raised.

real estate investment trust (REIT) An investment trust listed on a stock exchange that has the objective of managing a portfolio of property on behalf of investors.

residential property Property which is designed for and occupied by residents as a home.

responsible entity (RE) A public company that holds an Australian Financial Services Licence authorising it to operate and manage a registered managed investment scheme or managed fund.

retail managed fund A fund that is targeted at individual retail investors with small amounts of money to invest.

safety margin A margin of security which must be maintained above the level required to meet the outstanding value of the loan.

security The promise of assets, including real estate, in the case of loan default.

spread or bid-offer spread The difference between the buying and selling price of units in a managed fund or other security.

standard deviation A measure of the riskiness of an investment.

tax shield Where the annual loss on an investment reduces the amount of tax otherwise payable.

unlisted managed fund A managed fund that is not listed on a stock exchange.

value funds manager An investment management style where investments are selected and traded based on the extent to which they are believed to be underpriced or overpriced.

variable loan A loan that may vary in terms of interest rate charged to the borrower.

wholesale managed fund A fund that is targeted at institutional investors or individual investors that are deemed to be professional or financially sophisticated with large amounts of money to invest.

wrap account An administration service that provides access to a range of different managed funds and other direct investment options and wraps the various investments into one account for an investor. Also known as an investment platform.

PROFESSIONAL APPLICATION QUESTIONS

6.1 What are the advantages and disadvantages of investing in managed funds?

6.2 What factors should an investor consider before deciding to invest in a managed fund?

6.3 What is the difference in management style between an active fund manager and a passive (index) fund manager? Why would an investor want to invest in an actively managed fund if its ICR was higher than that of an index fund?

6.4 Why have wrap accounts and master funds become such popular investment vehicles with clients and especially financial planners?

6.5 How would your selection of a portfolio of managed funds differ between a conservative investor and an aggressive investor?

6.6 What are the advantages of investing in one managed fund that invests across all asset classes compared with investing in a number of different managed funds where each invest in a separate asset class?

6.7 What does the standard deviation of a managed fund indicate about the fund?

6.8 What is the difference between positive and negative gearing?

6.9 What are the risks associated with gearing?

6.10 An investor wishes to buy some shares by using a combination of their own money and borrowed funds. They are unsure whether they should take out a margin loan which is secured against the shares or take out a mortgage against the family home. What are the advantages/disadvantages of each approach?

6.11 Outline three ways that an investor can satisfy a margin call.

6.12 In your own words, write a paragraph about the advantages of home ownership.

6.13 Explain why a mortgage lender might refuse to lend over 90% of the price of a new home.

6.14 A financial institution offers Fatima the choice between a standard variable loan (SVL) of 5.23% or a 2-year fixed rate at 4.89% and then SVL after 2 years. Advise her of the possible issues with each option, and which loan she should accept.

6.15 Managed fund characteristics ★

A managed fund owns the following assets.

Cash/fixed interest	$60 million
Property	$15 million
Shares	$25 million

(a) What type of investor is likely to be attracted to this particular fund, on a scale of 1–5 with 1 being very risk averse?

(b) What long-term real return objective (in excess of inflation) would you expect this fund to have?

6.16 Calculating unit price ★

Calculate the unit price of this fund using the following information.

	$ million
Asset allocation	
Cash and deposits	30
Short-term securities	30
Long-term securities	50
Equities and units in trust	175
Land and buildings	10
Liabilities	110
Number of units issued	11 109 657

6.17 Management styles ★

You receive the following query from a friend.

I have just inherited $140 000 and wish to invest the amount into managed funds. Although I require a little income from the funds, I am mainly interested in long-term growth, so have decided to invest in Australian domestic shares. I have no other shareholding in my investment portfolio. I would classify myself as a moderately aggressive investor.

There are three funds that I am interested in investing in and these are the:

- Second State growth fund — an 'active growth manager'
- Syndal value fund — an 'active value manager'
- Rearguard index fund — a 'passive fund manager'.

Explain to your friend the difference in styles between the three funds. Advise them on whether it is better to invest the $140 000 into one fund or across all three funds and, if so, in what proportions. Explain your advice.

6.18 Analysing managed funds ★

You are looking to invest in a managed fund but note that the ICR is 1.58% which you believe is quite high. You have seen another fund that invests into fixed interests that has an ICR of only 0.9%.

After researching the managed fund you're looking to invest into, you note the following information: net assets ($million) — $623.

The management style of the fund is described as a 'long-term high-conviction portfolio that differs markedly from the index'.

Returns	6 month	1 year	3 year	5 year
Total %	14.35	17.67	9.96	6.53
Income %	0.00	1.94	3.44	2.64
Growth %	14.35	15.72	6.52	3.89
Index %	15.97	11.70	4.42	0.19

Risk	Standard deviation	Risk relative to category
3 year	9.73	Below average
5 year	15.07	Above average

Break-up of investments	% assets
Domestic equity	0.00
Intl equity	97.97
Listed property	0.00
Unlisted property	0.00
Mortgages	0.00
Dom fixed interest	0.00
Intl fixed interest	0.00
Cash	2.03
Other	0.00

(a) What does the information provided tell you about the nature and characteristics of the fund?
(b) What are the reasons behind why this fund might have a higher ICR than a fixed interest fund?
(c) Describe the management style of this fund which describes itself as a 'high conviction' fund.

6.19 Analysing performance ★★

The fund return, benchmark performance and standard deviation are provided for the following three funds.

Fund	Average 3-year return	Benchmark (index) performance	Standard deviation	Tracking error
Fund A	12.0%	10.1%	11.1%	2.6%
Fund B	12.5%	13.6%	12.3%	0.6%
Fund C	12.8%	14.2%	13.5%	6.1%

(a) Explain what the standard deviation tells an investor about the performance of each of the three managed funds.
(b) Does the information contained within the table provide any indication of the likely management investment style adopted by each of the three managed funds? Explain.
(c) Does the information in the table provide us with the basis for selecting the most appropriate fund?

6.20 Selecting managed funds ★★★

Investors have the choice of investing indirectly in securities through either listed managed funds or unlisted managed funds.

(a) Explain the difference between an ETF and an LIC. (Reference can be made to the Australian Securities Exchange — asx.com.au.)
(b) What are some of the reasons that might account for the increasing popularity of ETFs both in Australia and internationally?
(c) Explain how a listed investment company might be listed on the ASX at a market price of $5.20 but have a net asset backing (NAB) of $5.95. What does this tell us about the attractiveness of purchasing units in the fund?
(d) What factors should be analysed in determining the attractiveness of acquiring shares in a listed investment company?

6.21 Impact of gearing on returns: magnified gains ★

Your client, Jason, wants to start a share portfolio using the $50 000 in equity that he has already saved and possibly combine this with some borrowed funds. Assume the following.

- Interest rates at 8%
- Grossed-up dividend income of 6%
- Annual capital gain of 4%
- MTR 37%

What will be Jason's net return in both dollar and percentage terms for the following levels of gearing if he sells the investment asset one year and one day after he buys it?

(a) 100% equity ($50 000 in equity)

(b) 50% equity ($50 000 in equity and $50 000 in debt)

(c) 10% equity ($50 000 in equity and $450 000 in debt)

6.22 Impact of gearing on returns: magnified losses ★

Recalculate your answers to exercise 6.21 using the following assumptions.

- Interest rates at 9%
- Grossed-up dividend income of 5%
- Annual capital gain of 2%
- MTR 37%

6.23 Safety margin ★

Your client, Malala, has the following portfolio which she has financed through a $200 000 margin loan. What is her safety margin?

Company	Market value	LVR	Security
AGK	$80 000	75%	$60 000
BOQ	80 000	70%	56 000
DOW	80 000	65%	52 000
CSL	80 000	75%	60 000
	$320 000		$228 000

6.24 Margin call ★★

Assume that the stock market has suffered considerable falls. Malala's portfolio from exercise 6.23 is now as follows.

Company	Market value	LVR	Security
AGK	$70 000	75%	$52 500
BOQ	65 000	70%	45 500
DOW	85 000	65%	55 250
CSL	50 000	75%	37 500
	$270 000		$190 750

Her lender has made a margin call. Malala does not have any cash to meet the margin call nor does she have any additional assets to pledge as security. For each of the shares in her portfolio, calculate how much she would need to sell to satisfy the margin call.

6.25 Repayments on a home loan ★★★

Georgie and Teresa are contemplating buying a house for which they will need a $200 000 loan. They find a suitable lender who offers them the funds at a nominal annual 6.5% fixed rate and advises a 25-year loan. What is the monthly repayment for a 25-year loan?

6.26 Paying off a loan early ★★★

Deng decides to pay off his $200 000 20-year 6.0% loan faster by paying fortnightly instead of monthly. By how much will the loan term be shortened (to the nearest full year) if he pays about the same amount per month in total, but pays fortnightly instead of once per month?

6.27 Repayment frequency ★★★

Therese contracts for a $250 000 loan at 6.5% p.a. nominal interest rate. What would the periodic repayments be over 25 years if the repayments were made:

(a) fortnightly?

(b) monthly?

CASE STUDY 1

GIVING INVESTMENT ADVICE

Heidi is aged 45 and is married to Scott, aged 48. Both are self-employed, running their own small business, and earn a combined taxable income of around $170 000 p.a. The couple have three children all under the age of 20. Heidi and Scott have a reasonable knowledge of investments and over the years have put together an investment portfolio consisting of direct shares, term deposits and a range of managed funds. The couple's investments are contained within the Alright Wrap account which was set up upon the advice of their previous financial planner; they hold very little in superannuation.

The couple feel that they would like to fully retire in around 10 years. The couple has some interest in the financial market and are prepared to take on some risk in order to achieve a higher rate of return. They realise that there will be some short-term volatility in financial markets and are prepared to invest for the long term. They also realise that their current investment allocation and plan is unlikely to provide them with an appropriate nest egg upon retirement.

The couple is not particularly happy with the performance of their investments and is seeking some assistance. From the website of the Alright Wrap Service, the couple's investments consist of the following.

Direct shares

Commonwealth Bank (cost $45 000 in 1999)	$80 000
ANZ Bank (cost $18 000 in 2001)	$32 000
Bank of Crocker (cost $24 000 in 2009)	$18 000

Term deposits (fixed interest)

6-month term deposit (2.0% p.a.)	$50 000
12-month term deposit (2.1% p.a.)	$85 000

Managed funds

Name of fund (wholesale)	Cost price	Current value	Management style	Tracking error	ICR
Allcash cash fund	$52 000	$52 000	Invests in wholesale money market	0.5%	0.2%
ABC Australian share fund	$32 000	$25 000	Active value manager investing in large caps	2.4%	1.5%
BEB Australian share fund	$27 000	$32 000	Active value manager investing in large caps	2.2%	1.4%
China share fund	$45 000	$62 000	Active value manager investing in large caps	5.2%	2.1%
The Shopping Centre Retail trust	$30 000	$12 000	Active manager investing in shopping centres based in the United States	8.2%	1.4%

All returns from the managed funds are invested directly into the Allcash cash account. The Alright Wrap account charges an annual administration charge of 1.1% p.a. on top of the ICR charged by the managed funds. All managed funds were acquired in 2006, except for the BEB Australian share fund that was purchased 9 months ago.

QUESTIONS

1 Given the couple's financial circumstances and needs, determine what you believe is the appropriate risk profile of the couple and assess whether their current overall asset allocation is consistent with their risk profile.

Prepare a table of their existing investments allocated across the main asset classes. You should use the following table to determine the allocation.

2 Based on your assessment of the couple's risk profile and financial circumstances, determine what you believe is an appropriate asset allocation for the couple (detail in overall dollar and percentage terms).

3 Explain the advantages to the couple of investing through a wrap account.

4 Analyse the investment holdings of the couple and provide recommendations for change or improvement.

5 Calculate the assessable capital gains if the couple were to dispose of all of the managed funds held within the Alright Wrap Service.

Name of investment	Cash	Fixed interest	Australian shares	International shares	Property	Total
Total funds						
– $						
– %						

CASE STUDY 2

TAKING OUT A MARGIN LOAN

Aradhana is 26 and has just received a promotion at work. She now earns $135 001 which is more than the threshold at which the 37% marginal tax rate cuts in. Aradhana is unhappy at losing 37% of her money in tax. She hopes that by investing in a share portfolio she will be able to reduce this tax liability.

Aradhana has spoken to a margin lender who has suggested that she negatively gear her share portfolio by concentrating on stocks that place more emphasis on capital gains rather than income. The lender has recommended a portfolio with a weighted LVR of 70% and Aradhana is happy to contribute $60 000 of her own money and borrow the maximum amount that this equity contribution allows using an interest-only loan.

Aradhana lives with her partner in rented accommodation. They like renting as this gives them the freedom to move around, take holidays and not worry about maintaining a house and meeting mortgage repayments. Aradhana believes that her investment time horizon is about 7 years and would like you to do some financial projections on this basis.

Aradhana provides you with the following information and assumptions.

- Grossed-up dividend income will be 2% p.a.
- Capital gain will be 10% p.a.
- Interest cost will be 8% p.a.
- For the sake of arithmetic simplicity, MTR will stay at 37% even when capital gains are realised.

QUESTIONS

1 If Aradhana does decide to take out the margin loan, what will be the:
  (a) net annual gain or loss?
  (b) accumulated net annual gain or loss over 7 years?
  (c) compounded capital gain over 7 years?
  (d) compounded capital gain net of CGT based on the assumption that she sells the share portfolio after 7 years?
  (e) total net gain (the accumulated net annual loss and the compounded capital gain net of CGT) 7 years after the principal of the loan has been repaid?
  (f) annualised rate of return on equity?

2 Redo the calculations in question 1, above, based on the assumption that Aradhana does not borrow any money and instead invests her $60 000 in equity only.

3 How does the annualised return on equity differ between scenarios 1 and 2 above? Write a brief report to Aradhana which explains why these figures differ.

4 Outline to Aradhana the risks inherent in her margin lending strategy.

5 Assuming that Aradhana is not satisfied with the annualised return on equity via the margin lending strategy, what leveraged derivative instruments are available to her in order to pursue a more aggressive strategy?

REFERENCES

ASIC 2016, '16-010MR Margin lenders improve lending standards following ASIC review', media release, 21 January, https://asic.gov.au/about-asic/media-centre/find-a-media-release/2016-releases/16-010mr-margin-lenders-improve-lending -standards-following-asic-review.

ASIC 2020, 'Funds management', 26 May, https://asic.gov.au/regulatory-resources/funds-management.

ASX 2020, 'ETFs and other ETPs', www.asx.com.au/products/etf-and-other-etp.htm.

Johnson, B 2019, 'How actively and passively managed funds performed: year-end 2018', Morningstar, 12 February, www.morningstar.com/insights/2019/02/12/active-passive-funds.

Moneysmart n.d., 'Managed funds and ETFs', https://moneysmart.gov.au/managed-funds-and-etfs.

Morningstar 2016, www.morningstar.com.

Pojani, D 2023, 'Australia's housing crisis is deepening. Here ar 10 policies to get us out of it', The Conversation, 8 May, https://theconversation.com/australias-housing-crisis-is-deepening-here-are-10-policies-to-get-us-out-of-it-204026.

Prop Track 2023, 'PropTrack housing affordability report – 2023', https://www.proptrack.com.au/insights-hub/proptrack-housing-affordability-report-2023.

RBA 2024, 'Average housing interest rates', *Chart pack*, 3 January, www.rba.gov.au/chart-pack/interest-rates.html.

Westpac Banking Corporation 2016, 'Westpac Balanced Growth Fund — NEF: April 2016', www.westpac.com.au.

ACKNOWLEDGEMENTS

Extract: © The Conversation

Extracts: © ASIC

Figure 6.5: © PropTrack

Figure 6.6: © Reserve Bank of Australia

CHAPTER 7

Risk management and insurance

LEARNING OBJECTIVES

After studying this chapter, you should be able to:

7.1 explain how risk can be classified and describe the risk management process

7.2 explain the key concepts that underpin insurance

7.3 identify and evaluate the personal risks to which individuals are exposed

7.4 identify and evaluate property risks in relation to house and contents

7.5 identify and evaluate property risks in relation to motor vehicles

7.6 identify and evaluate personal and property risks with respect to sickness and accident, consumer credit and travel insurance

7.7 identify and evaluate liability risks

7.8 explain the need for an ongoing review process for insurance and risk.

Phoebe and Joshua Smithfield, both aged 34, are married with a 6-year-old son. They have recently purchased a house in regional Victoria to be closer to Phoebe's family. At $600 000, the purchase price was much higher than what the couple had hoped to pay. However, Phoebe and Joshua feel that the convenience of having Phoebe's parents assist with caring for their young son is worth the higher purchase price. The house cost $600 000 and they have a mortgage of $540 000. They have insured the house for $400 000 and the contents for $10 000.

The property is in a flood-prone area; however, Phoebe and Joshua are not concerned as it has been almost a decade since a flood last occurred there. Also, they are confident that their home insurance policy will cover floods.

Joshua is concerned that they have only $10 000 in contents cover. Phoebe reminds him that the premium savings from taking out a smaller home contents cover than their actual contents value could be used to pay down the mortgage as soon as possible. Also, the value of household goods tends to depreciate, so it could be a waste of money to insure for things that are worth less over time.

Phoebe and Joshua have noticed that, with their son starting school this year, their living expenses are starting to increase. They are now considering increasing their personal insurance and taking up private health insurance as they have heard that these could be paid for using their superannuation funds. Joshua is worried that his past medical history might prevent him from getting additional coverage.

Issues to consider from this case include the following.

- Is flood cover now included in all house insurance policies?
- To the extent that flood cover is included in a policy, is all flood cover the same or do different insurance companies provide different types of cover?
- Is Phoebe right about the depreciation of household goods and is it worth insuring home contents? Assess the adequacy of the couple's contents coverage of $10 000. If fire, flood or some other disaster were to hit would $10 000 be adequate insurance?
- Should Joshua organise his life insurance inside or outside his superannuation fund?
- Should Joshua accurately declare his past medical history in his life insurance application? What are the possible consequences if he doesn't?
- How would Joshua meet their mortgage repayment obligations over the next 5 years if Phoebe were to pass away?
- What factors should Phoebe and Joshua take into account when considering private health insurance for their family?

These issues will be explored in this chapter.

Introduction

Planning is easy in a world without risk. However, risk comes in many forms and unexpected events disrupt our plans. Sometimes the disruption is a minor inconvenience and by working a bit harder or spending a few extra dollars the inconvenience can be overcome. However, there are times when the disruption is more than minor and it has a significant impact on our lives and the lives of people who we care for.

A financial plan sets out the steps by which a person can obtain financial security. This plan must take into account the possibility that risks such as disability and premature death may occur, thereby disrupting the plan. Therefore, part of the development plan will include the analysis of those risks and steps to minimise or eliminate their occurrence or reduce the effect of those risks should they occur.

In this chapter we will identify the types of risk that can occur, and consider a systematic approach that can be used to manage those risks. The process is known as risk management. We will primarily concentrate on personal risks in terms of health, property and liability. (A detailed analysis of business risk is beyond the scope of this chapter, with the exception of the health-related risks of business owners and key employees.)

7.1 Risk and risk management

LEARNING OBJECTIVE 7.1 Explain how risk can be classified and describe the risk management process.

Risk can be classified in a number of ways. Speculative risk and pure risk are two classifications.

Speculative risk arises where there is a chance of a loss or a gain. Gambling is a good example of a speculative risk. Once the bet is placed, there can only be a win or a loss. Setting up a business comes into the same category — the business will succeed or fail. The risks associated with investments fall into this category.

Pure risk arises where there is only a possibility of loss or no loss. Pure risks are normally provided for by insurance. Pure risks can arise from the premature death of the breadwinner, which leaves the dependent family without an income, or loss or damage to an asset such as a house or car. The event will either occur or not occur. Within a financial plan, both types of risk are experienced.

Pure risk can be categorised as follows.

- *Personal* — matters that affect the individual. Death, illness, incapacity or unemployment cause income to cease or be reduced.
- *Property* — loss or damage to property, such as a building burning down or car damage in an accident.
- *Liability* — losses suffered as a result of a legal accountability incurred.

Risk management is a branch of management that has gained considerable prominence over the last 30 years and provides a systematic approach to the management of pure risk. Personal risk management is the adaptation of this process to the individual. The greatest benefit it provides is the systematic approach which helps ensure that all risk are identified and addressed.

The risk management process can be divided into five broad steps as shown in figure 7.1.

FIGURE 7.1   The risk management process

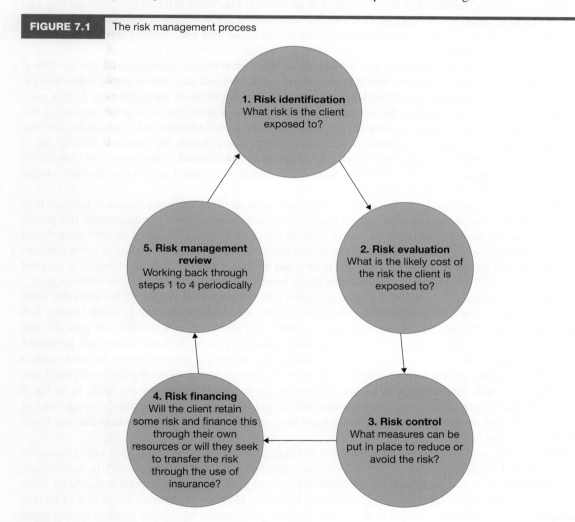

1. **Risk identification**
What risk is the client exposed to?

2. **Risk evaluation**
What is the likely cost of the risk the client is exposed to?

3. **Risk control**
What measures can be put in place to reduce or avoid the risk?

4. **Risk financing**
Will the client retain some risk and finance this through their own resources or will they seek to transfer the risk through the use of insurance?

5. **Risk management review**
Working back through steps 1 to 4 periodically

Shortly we will discuss the risk management process in relation to personal, domestic property and liability risk. However, before we do that we should review a number of important concepts that underpin how insurance can be used in risk management.

7.2 Key concepts in insurance

LEARNING OBJECTIVE 7.2 Explain the key concepts that underpin insurance.

This section reviews a number of key concepts in insurance including how risk is pooled (shared), how the insurance market is structured, the obligation to act in the utmost of good faith and the use of terms, conditions and severity limitations in insurance contracts.

The pooling of risk

Insurance is based on the principle of pooling risk where individuals contribute resources to a fund that is used to pay for the adverse consequences suffered by some members of the pool. Such insurance is normally organised through an insurance company and the contribution to the pool is generally referred to as a **premium**.

Pooling is based on the premise that each entrant into the fund comes with a similar level of risk. If we know the mean risk level of the population, and if our pool is a sufficiently large random sample selected from that population, then actuaries can estimate with reasonable confidence the likelihood of claims being made against the pool and can set premiums accordingly. For example, if we know that 1% of vehicles are likely to be involved in a major accident each year and our insurance pool covers 100 000 vehicles then this gives actuaries enough information to determine the applicable premiums.

We did note above that we assume that each entrant into the pool has a similar level of risk; however, this does not mean that they have an identical level of risk. As we know, inexperienced drivers under the age of 25 have a greater likelihood of being involved in an accident than older drivers, and therefore they can expect to pay a higher than average premium and/or be subject to other limiting conditions such as having a higher *excess* on their policy. Separating the pool into risk categories and charging different premiums is known as *underwriting*.

If a particular insurance company did not charge higher premiums for inexperienced drivers then it is likely that inexperienced drivers would be attracted to that fund and this in turn would mean that the mean risk profile of the fund would be higher than the mean risk profile of the population. In this case, inexperienced drivers are making an *adverse selection against the fund*, that is they are increasing the fund's mean risk profile. More experienced drivers in the fund would effectively be *subsidising* the less experienced drivers. Eventually, premiums would have to increase to match the increased level of risk in the fund, which in turn would eventually drive away the more experienced drivers who could obtain the same level of insurance at a lower cost elsewhere in the market. All general insurers in Australia charge higher premiums for inexperienced drivers.

The insurance market in Australia is very competitive and if an insurer prices a premium too high they are likely to miss out on business. One way of keeping premiums lower is to reduce the average risk profile of entrants to the pool. For example, if people over 50 are more likely to be retired or semi-retired, and therefore likely to spend more time at home, it is also likely that their risk with respect to home contents insurance would also be lower. In this case the insurer has narrowed the size of the pool, however the pool is still large enough for actuaries to estimate the likely losses and therefore set premiums accordingly.

Selectively reducing the size of the pool can reduce the average risk profile of the fund but there is a limit to how small the pool can be reduced to. As we noted above, pooling is about sharing risk and applying probabilities to outcomes in order to determine premiums. The smaller the pool the less confidence actuaries will have in determining the likely commitments of the fund. As a result, premiums would eventually have to rise to reflect that uncertainty. In a theoretical extreme where the pool reduces to one (for example, an opera singer may wish to insure their voice for an upcoming tour) such insurance is available through insurers such as Lloyds of London. However, the premiums are likely to be far in excess of what the probability would suggest that they should be simply because actuaries have no way of averaging this risk over a larger pool where they can have more confidence in the amounts they are likely to have to pay out.

Reducing the size of the pool to reduce the average risk profile of the fund also raises issues of equity. Should we discriminate on the basis of race, gender, age, lifestyle and so on? In some cases, discrimination is a valid ingredient of the insurance offer; for example, life insurance should be more expensive as people get older and the mortality risk increases. However, sometimes the notion of what is acceptable discrimination is harder to determine. Federal government regulations prohibit certain types of discrimination for some insurance products, for example, registered health insurance providers are not allowed to charge an additional premium for people who smoke, drink or are obese. A November 2012 Health Insurance Research report by CoreData (coredata.com.au) indicated that 73% of respondents believed that smokers should pay more for health insurance than non-smokers.

The insurance marketplace

This section briefly considers the players in the marketplace, their role and a broad view of the legislation governing the marketplace. The marketplace comprises insurers, intermediaries, clients and regulators.

Insurers

There are broadly three types of insurers operating in the market.

1. *Life insurers provide a range of risk and investment products.* Risk products include those where a benefit is paid in the event of death or disablement of the person insured. Today, the major part of a life insurer's business relates to investment products which include superannuation. The *Life Insurance Act 1995* relates to the licensing, control and, to some extent, the conduct of insurers.

   Life insurance products are examples of *non-indemnity* type products; that is, the amount paid out by the insurer does not necessarily relate to the actual loss incurred. For example, a life insurance policy may pay out $1 million on the death of the insured — there is really no way of relating this amount to the actual loss incurred, nor does the amount paid out vary according to the circumstances relating to the loss. This can be contrasted to most general insurance products which are *indemnity* type products where the payout by the insurer is directly related to the actual loss incurred. For example, a person might have their household contents valued at $100 000 under a general insurance policy however, they will be able to claim only the value of their actual loss.

   Life insurers were traditionally mutual companies. *Mutual* companies or organisations are businesses owned by their members and run for the benefit of their members. Over the last 20 years, most life insurers have *demutualised* and listed on the stock exchange, so they are now owned by their shareholders and run for the benefit of those shareholders. Some of the life insurance companies that operate in Australia include AIA, Clearview, Metlife, MLC and OnePath.

2. *General insurers provide risk products.* The policies cover all types of risks, including disability risks but excluding life covers. Examples of the types of risks covered are property insurance that covers damage to property by a range of different perils, and liability insurance that provides cover for situations where the insured is legally liable to others as a result of injury/damage or having given wrong advice. The legislative licensing and control measures for general insurers are contained in the *Insurance Act 1973*. Some of the general insurance companies that operate in Australia include IAG, Suncorp, QBE, Allianz and Youi.

3. *Health insurers provide hospital and medical benefits cover.* Medibank Private is the largest private health insurer in Australia. Medibank Private was previously owned by the Federal government and is now a private company listed on the ASX. The other providers include a mixture of for profit (e.g. Australian Unity) and mutual organisations (e.g. BUPA). The legislative licensing and control measures for health insurers are contained in the *Health Insurance Act 2007*.

Intermediaries

Intermediaries are agents and brokers who arrange insurances for a client.

The **agent** is the insurer's representative whose function is to arrange covers for clients with the insurer. The **broker** is the insured's representative whose function is to ascertain the client's needs and, being an expert in the insurance market, arrange the best terms for the client.

These intermediaries are controlled by the *Corporations Act 2001*. The Act provides a framework for a single licensing regime and for disclosure standards. The provisions of the Act were covered in more detail in the chapter on personal financial planning. The Act seeks to protect the public. It does this by requiring full disclosure on the part of those in the financial services industry and by making organisations responsible for the actions of their agents and representatives. When an agent has acted beyond his or her authority, the principal is liable but can seek redress from the agent or representative.

Clients

The consumerism which swept through most areas of commerce in the 1970s and 1980s also came to the insurance market. A number of pieces of legislation were introduced and industry codes of practice were established. The objective of these was to produce an environment where the client could be reasonably sure of the solvency of the insurers and intermediaries and that the conduct of insurers and intermediaries would be fair.

The *Insurance Contracts Act 1984* governs practice in the insurance market and provides protection to the client. The Act states that its purpose is to reform and modernise the law in relation to insurance contracts so that a fair balance is struck between those insured and insurers, and that policy provisions and insurers' practices operate fairly.

The Life Insurance Code of Practice (LICOP), launched in late 2016 by the Financial Services Council (FSC), is a binding set of standards for life insurance companies, focusing on improving customer experiences. The Code covers various aspects of the insurance process, from buying policies and payments to changing policies and handling claims. Insurers committed to transparency, timely claims processing, limited surveillance use and support for vulnerable customers. A revised version of the Code, LICOP 2.0, came into effect on 1 July 2023, with over 50 new consumer protections. The revisions were prompted by concerns raised by regulatory bodies and industry inquiries, such as ASIC and the Royal Commission into Misconduct in the Banking, Superannuation and Financial Services Industry. The updated Code enhances obligations around product design, sales practices, customer communication, claims handling and support for vulnerable customers. While mandatory for FSC member insurers, it's not yet enforceable under ASIC's regime, though future enforceability is anticipated. The key changes include reinforcing product suitability, improving advertising and sales practices, enhancing customer communication clarity, revising claims handling timelines, and focusing on aiding vulnerable customers and those facing financial hardship. Insurers need to align their practices with the revised Code's requirements.

The General Insurance Code of Practice mandates insurers and industry participants who have adopted the Code to provide services to customers in a fair, transparent and truthful manner. It covers various aspects of the customer-insurer relationship, including purchasing insurance, making claims and handling complaints. The Code also requires insurers to assist individuals facing financial hardship, such as those struggling to pay excess amounts or individuals who owe money due to uninsured damages. The Code, owned and published by the Insurance Council of Australia, was effective from 1 July 2021. It applies to a range of general insurance products but not to certain types like workers compensation, marine insurance and life/health insurance. Code subscribers are listed on the Insurance Council of Australia's register and monitoring of compliance is performed by the General Insurance Code Governance Committee, with support from the Code Compliance and Monitoring team at the Australian Financial Complaints Authority.

Regulators

The insurance industry is controlled by two main regulators — the Australian Prudential Regulation Authority (APRA) and the Australian Securities and Investments Commission (ASIC). ASIC deals with consumer-oriented matters and APRA handles prudential regulation. ASIC is responsible for the Corporations Act and liaises with industry bodies in relation to improving the services provided by advisers to consumers.

Insurance policies and the principle of utmost good faith

A fundamental feature of an insurance policy is that it is a contract between the insurer and the insured. The contract relies on the principle of each party entering the agreement with the **utmost good faith**. Section 13 of the *Insurance Contracts Act* states that:

> A contract of insurance is a contract based on the utmost good faith and there is implied in such a contract a provision requiring each party to it to act towards the other party, in respect of any matter arising under or in relation to it, with the utmost good faith.

This means that the highest degree of honesty is imposed on both parties to the insurance contract. Insurers accept the contract for insurance at certain rates of premium under certain terms and conditions based on statements made by the applicant for insurance. Likewise, the applicant enters into an insurance contract in reliance on the promise by the insurer to pay if loss occurs according to the terms and conditions stipulated in the insurance contract.

Thus, there is a duty of disclosure on the applicant to disclose to the insurer all the **material facts** that would influence a reasonable and prudent insurer in accepting a risk or in setting a premium given those particular facts.

The duty of disclosure requires the applicant to disclose all material facts except:

- facts known to the insurer, or those which it may reasonably be presumed are known to the insurer
- facts which diminished the risk insured against
- facts of public notoriety
- facts which the insurer decided to personally ascertain
- facts which may be regarded as superfluous by reason of an express or implied warranty in the policy which covers the circumstances
- facts of which the insurer was deemed to have constructive knowledge (e.g. facts the insurer would have discovered in its ordinary course of business).

The duty of disclosure exists during the negotiations and up to the time when a binding contract of insurance is concluded. It also exists at the time of renewal of the contract. If the applicant does not reveal a material fact to the insurer or deliberately withholds material information from the insurer the contract may be voidable at the option of the insurer. The insurer may also be entitled to reduce the level of liability that the insurer would otherwise be liable for if a claim is made under the contract.

Misrepresentation occurs when an inaccurate or untrue statement is made by the insured or the insured's agent prior to the conclusion of the contract. Two types of misrepresentation are recognised:

1. **innocent misrepresentation** — where the statement is inaccurate but made without fraudulent intent
2. **fraudulent misrepresentation** — where the statement was inaccurate but made knowingly, believing it to be untrue, or where the statement was made recklessly.

Innocent misrepresentation of a material fact renders the contract voidable at the option of the insurer; fraudulent misrepresentation renders the contract void from inception of the contract.

Section 21A of the *Insurance Contracts Act* requires the insurer to inform the applicants for insurance of their duty of disclosure. It also requires the insurer to assist the consumer to discharge their duty by requesting the applicant to answer specific questions relevant to the insurer's decision to accept the risk. In addition it requires the insurer to request the consumer to disclose any exceptional circumstance known to the insured that a reasonable person in the circumstances could be expected to know would be relevant to the insurer's decision.

PERSONAL FINANCE BULLETIN

ASIC takes insurer to court over claims handling 'failure'

The Australian Securities and Investments Commission (ASIC) has filed court proceedings seeking financial penalties against an insurer for allegedly breaching its duty to act with utmost good faith during claims handling.

The legal action against OnePath Life alleges the insurer 'failed' in a number of areas when it decided not to pay out an income protection (IP) policy on the basis that the insured had acted fraudulently.

Its list of failures includes not informing the insured she had the right to appeal through OnePath Life's internal dispute resolution process or by filing a complaint with the Australian Financial Complaints Authority, ASIC says in a statement today.

ASIC has previously taken action against insurers for claims handling failures but the proceedings in the Federal Court seeking financial penalties are its first since new provisions were introduced in March 2019.

The provisions allow the regulator to pursue 'harsher civil penalties and criminal sanctions' under ASIC-administered legislation, including the Insurance Contracts Act, ASIC says in a statement today.

'Insurers play an important role in providing financial security to consumers, particularly in times of crisis,' ASIC Deputy Chair Sarah Court said.

'Consumers need to be confident that their insurer will act in good faith and provide procedural fairness when handling their claims.

'Now more than ever, Australian insurers need to focus on their claims handling procedures and ensure they are meeting their legal obligations.'

According to ASIC, the insured acquired the IP and life insurance policy in 2016 through an ANZ financial adviser. At that time, OnePath Life was owned by the bank until May 2019, when Zurich acquired the business.

The insured submitted an IP claim in November 2018 for a shoulder injury she had sustained in February 2017, which OnePath accepted and began paying the benefits accruing from June that year.

But the insurer then commenced a 'non-disclosure investigation' into an earlier injury, also on the shoulder, that the insured had before she bought the OnePath policy. OnePath did not inform the insured about this investigation.

▶

> The concise statement from ASIC says OnePath Life subsequently sought more information from the insured about the earlier shoulder injury and medical records from her GP and orthopaedic specialist.
>
> OnePath Life obtained a statement of claims from the insured's previous health fund containing references to admissions to hospital between May 2001 and November 2005.
>
> Records that OnePath Life obtained from the hospital showed six admissions during the period 2001 to 2005 'variously referred to as being for suicidal ideations, overdose and self-harm', the concise statement says.
>
> OnePath Life later sought a retrospective underwriting opinion that concluded had the insurer been aware of the hospital admissions, it would have declined the insured's request for IP and life insurance cover at standard rates.
>
> 'Ultimately, OnePath Life decided not to pay out the policy on the basis that the customer has acted fraudulently by failing to disclose the hospitalisation,' ASIC says.
>
> The ASIC concise statement says OnePath failed to make clear to the customer it was concerned that the lack of disclosure was fraudulent and failed to fully investigate her explanation for the non-disclosure, including failing to speak to the ANZ adviser about the completion of the application for the insurance.
>
> 'If an insurer is concerned a customer has engaged in fraudulent non-disclosure, they must make their concerns explicit, give the customer the opportunity to respond and make proper inquiries into any explanation given by the customer before concluding that fraud has occurred,' Ms Court said.
>
> Zurich says it acknowledges the court proceedings and is 'considering the matters raised by ASIC in its concise statement and is committed to working constructively through the court process'.
>
> 'Zurich will not be providing further comment given the matter is now before the court,' the insurer says.
>
> *Source:* Insurance News 2022.

Terms, standard terms and severity limitations

Purchasing insurance requires the client and the insurer to enter into a contract of insurance. All contracts have terms and conditions which set out the rights and responsibilities of the respective parties. All contracts are based on the principle that both parties have willingly entered into an agreement and are aware of the terms and conditions that apply. Unfortunately, often the first time a client reads the terms and conditions associated with their insurance policy is when they want to make a claim. Insurers have made significant improvements in recent years in improving the way they communicate the applicable terms and conditions; however, insurance contracts rely on very detailed terms and conditions which inevitably produce a considerable volume of fine print which most clients find daunting.

As we discussed earlier, the *Insurance Contracts Act 1984* governs practice in the insurance market and provides protection to the consumer. Section 35 of the Act prescribes a range of insurance policies for which standard cover will be assumed to be part of those policies. For example, home contents insurance is a prescribed policy under the Act. The Act also outlines the range of cover for each of the prescribed insurance policies. For example, a home contents insurance policy is assumed to cover loss that is caused by '. . . storm, tempest, flood, the action of the sea, high water, tsunami, erosion or landslide or subsidence'.

The standard terms and conditions that fall under the standard cover are enacted via the *Insurance Contract Regulations 1985*. The consumer can therefore have confidence that the standard terms and conditions which have been drafted and enacted by government, in consultation with the insurance industry and consumer groups, represent a fair basis upon which to enter into an insurance agreement.

The use of standard cover and standard terms and conditions does not, however, obviate the need for the consumer to be thoroughly aware of the extent of the cover and the terms and conditions that apply. As we noted above, standard cover for a home contents insurance policy includes storm, tempest, flood etc. However, until relatively recently there was no standard definition of flood in the regulations which many people in Queensland and New South Wales found out to their peril.

PERSONAL FINANCE BULLETIN

Insurers move to clear up flood definition

When is a storm, not a storm?

The weeks following the severe weather event, which devastated parts of New South Wales and Queensland, is not really a time to be solving riddles.

But that is the position many insurance policy holders find themselves in as they struggle through the fine print of their insurance policies.

For Merryn Edwards from South Murwillumbah, it is a straightforward answer when she is asked what was responsible for the destruction of her family's roofing and plumbing business.

'A storm, Cyclone Debbie and that storm raised the river levels which came over the levee bank, so it's definitely a storm — there's just no question about it, it's definitely storm damage,' Ms Edwards said.

Mick William's one-man steel fabrication business is his life's work, his weekly wage, and his superannuation.

He vowed to take on the insurance company's definition of the Murwillumbah disaster after being told by his insurer that he was not covered.

'On the disaster relief website it has been declared "flood" but you ask anyone in Murwillumbah and they say we got hit by a cyclone,' he said.

'It's been declared as a flood, similarly for Lismore, but you look at the radar images, it spells cyclone and if it wasn't a cyclone, it was a damn good storm.'

At the height of the storm, winds on the coast reached 'storm force', according to Cape Byron Marine Rescue's recordings.

What is a flood? What is a storm?

After an unprecedented spate of natural disasters, the Federal Government introduced a standard definition of flood in 2012, to provide greater certainty for insurers and policyholders.

It applies to household and small business insurance policies.

The definition of flood is:

> The covering of normally dry land by water that has escaped or been released from the normal confines of: any lake, or any river, creek or other natural watercourse, whether or not altered or modified; or any reservoir, canal, or dam.

Campbell Fuller from the Insurance Council of Australia said the difference between storm damage and flood damage was clear.

'The storm might fill the river, but once the river overflows, that's a flood,' Mr Fuller said.

Now the Insurance Council is stepping in to clarify that for policy holders and will hold special forums in late April and early May in flood-damaged regions of Queensland and New South Wales.

Also present will be key insurance companies, Legal Aid, and the Financial Ombudsman Service.

Mr Fuller said policy holders could question the decisions made by insurance assessors.

'Consumers have many avenues to follow, the first is seek internal dispute resolution with the company and that means their claim will be assessed by a different team within the insurance company and sometimes claims are changed at that point,' he said.

If the consumer is still not satisfied after an internal dispute resolution, the next step is to speak to the independent financial ombudsman service.

'It will independently review the claim and it will seek to mediate between the consumer and the insurance company, and if it needs to step in and make a determination that is then binding on the insurance company,' Mr Fuller said.

The consumer could also take legal action against the company.

Who decides if it is a flood or a storm?

The Insurance Council of Australia said it was possible some policy holders on the far-north coast suffered both flood and storm damage.

Mr Fuller said specialist hydrologists could determine what caused inundation.

'They are experts at determining where water came from, when it caused damage to premises, and under some circumstances the damage may have been caused by storm water and by river water or flood waters,' he said.

But that's what the hydrologists do with those reports to the insurer and the insurer will then make that determination.

But even when granted, insurance claims are the short-term solution to the long-term problem of natural disasters.

'Insurance is the canary in the gold mine here, insurers send signals to individuals and to government that communities are flood prone, cyclonic prone or bush fire prone,' Mr Fuller said.

'Insurance companies aren't in charge of trying to prevent those disasters occurring.'

Mr Fuller said there was little doubt that the flood levees at Murwillumbah and Lismore helped curb an even bigger disaster.

Many shop owners in Lismore and Murwillumbah have told the ABC flood insurance is not affordable, and can cost more than $15 000 a year.

Mr Fuller said the problem in Lismore was with a levee that could only contain relatively minor floods.

'If it had been built to withstand a one-in-50 or one-in-100-year flood event then those premiums would have been dramatically lower.

▶

Roma in Queensland only completed a flood levee a couple of years ago and for the most exposed properties in that town premiums fell by 80-90 per cent.'

'If the levee was raised and the flood data showed the risk had been significantly reduced then insurers would respond by lowering the premiums; it's a direct equation,' Mr Fuller said.

The Productivity Commission recommended the Federal Government spend $200 million a year, matched by state and territory governments on mitigation measures to avoid precisely this situation.

Local, State and Federal Governments need to work together to protect those communities.

The conversations we need to have

That question was put to the New South Wales Deputy Premier as he visited Lismore.

John Barilaro said it was time to have a conversation about flood and disaster mitigation.

'It is governments' role both local, state and federal to prepare communities and if it is about building levees, then they are the conversations we have to have,' Mr Barilaro said.

The Mayor of Lismore has already ruled out raising the city's levee calling it a 'Berlin Wall', something Mr Barilaro was aware of.

'The community may not want larger levees or the sort of investment and infrastructure that could protect it, but we have to have those conversations,' he said.

'I know the conversation about levees has been a big issue in Murwillumbah and there are some who don't want to see higher walls, but if that is the cost of protection maybe we need to have that conversation.'

'Conversation' on disaster prevention seems to be the key word, but planning issues are also on the Deputy's mind.

'It is a zoning issue? Why have we got business districts or homes in areas that are now prone and maybe with a chance for greater natural disasters? Is there an issue around zoning? Are we building things in the wrong place?'

Source: Farrow-Smith and Harper 2017.

A consumer reading the above article may believe from its title that they are now protected from flood as it is defined in the regulations. However, it is still at the discretion of the individual insurers as to whether they adopt this definition.

An insurer is able to limit or exclude their liability which would otherwise be provided under standard cover provided they clearly inform the consumer that such cover is limited or excluded. Generally the inclusion in a product disclosure statement (PDS) that the level of standard cover has been modified is seen as sufficient notification notwithstanding the fact that PDS documents are often long, complicated and unread by the consumer.

It is also worth reiterating that not all insurance contracts are prescribed under the Act. For those insurance contracts which are prescribed under the Act, not all contingencies for which the consumer seeks cover might be captured under the standard cover and standard terms and conditions. It is still very much a case of buyer beware.

The terms and conditions included in insurance contracts are one means by which insurers seek to limit their liability. Insurers may also seek to limit their liability through the use of severity limitations such as the use of policy excesses and waiting periods. Severity limitations mean that some of the risk is retained by the individual rather than transferred to the insurer. For example, a policy might have a $1000 **excess**. For a $5000 claim this would mean $1000 is paid (retained) by the individual and $4000 is transferred to the insurer. On a disability policy, a person may elect to exclude the first 4 weeks of any incapacity — the incentive for doing this is a reduced premium under those policies.

7.3 Life, disability, trauma and health risks

LEARNING OBJECTIVE 7.3 Identify and evaluate the personal risks to which individuals are exposed.

This section discusses the identification and evaluation of life, disability, trauma and health risks as well as the control and financing measures for these personal risks.

Identification of personal risks

The following areas need to be considered in the scope of personal risk: premature death, prolonged illness or injury, medical costs and business risks.

Premature death

The effects of a premature death will vary according to a person's responsibilities as far as **dependants** are concerned. A dependant is a person who relies on another, financially, emotionally or in some other capacity. The definition of dependant will vary due to legislation and trust deeds. Generally, dependants are treated more generously than non-dependants with respect to insurance and superannuation payouts.

Consider the following situations.

- *Single person, no dependants.* There is little need for cover. An allowance for final medical and burial expenses is the extent of any need. Where there are any debts to be met, these need to be included also. In most but not all cases, the party to whom the debt is owed will either have security for the debt or have already required a term life cover to be effected for the amount of the debt.
- *Single-parent families.* This category has a considerable need. The income producer has dependants who need to be provided for in the event of premature death. Unlike the situation in two-income families, no alternative income is available should the income producer die prematurely. Although the loss of one income stream in a two-income family will leave a reduced income, at least there is still some income. In the event of the death of a single parent, there needs to be a provision for the children until they reach an age when they can become self-supporting. This provision needs to include an allowance for education and other such expenses to ensure a reasonable standard of living. Many in this category have a low income and their ability to provide for losses (i.e. to pay the insurance premiums) is limited.
- *Two-income families.* The majority of families with dependants fall into this group. In the event of the premature death of either or both breadwinners, the family will suffer a loss of income and with it a fall in living standard. Provision needs to be made so that funds are available to provide ongoing support for the family.
- *One-income families.* The same need that existed for two-income families exists here. The need may be seen to be greater, since if the sole breadwinner dies the sole income stream is lost. At least with two-income families, if only one of the breadwinners dies, one income stream remains.
- *Additional dependants.* Dependants are normally thought of as children, but they can be parents or other relatives. This needs to be considered when assessing future provisions, as these dependants may not always be clearly identifiable, since they may not be dependants at the time the assessment of future income needs is made.

Prolonged illness or injury

For illnesses of short duration, most people are able to call on existing resources and not suffer any significant fall in their standard of living. But when the incapacity is of longer duration, the living standard can be affected. The extent to which people are affected depends on whether they are employees or self-employed.

Employees are normally provided with sick leave by their employer and receive full pay, but how long this is provided for is the significant factor. In the event of a workplace accident, workers compensation benefits are provided. In contrast, those most exposed are the self-employed. Their income can be directly dependent on their efforts, and when their efforts cease, such as with illness, their income may cease also. It may be that the business can still function and provide the same income by employing someone to continue it, but funds will be needed to employ that person.

Medical costs

Medical costs can vary considerably, depending on the injury or illness suffered. Where an injury is work related or arises from a motor accident, then the medical costs arising from those injuries may be met by workers compensation insurance or by compulsory third-party insurance. These schemes set out the level of benefits payable and the extent of medical expenses to be paid and should cover most, if not all, costs. In the case of self-employed people, however, workers compensation insurance may not apply. Outside these areas, the choices are to use the public health system, have some type of health insurance cover, or meet the costs from the individual's own funds.

Each option has its own problems. It is argued that the public health system is overburdened; there can be extensive waiting lists for treatment unless the condition is life threatening. Private health insurance comes at a cost. If people meet their own costs it can be very expensive, and it would be necessary to have funds set aside for this purpose.

Business risks

There are several risks for business, and these need to be recognised and provided for.

- *Partnership.* A partnership agreement may specify that, in the event of the death of a partner, the remaining partners will buy out the deceased partner's share of the business. In most cases, the remaining partners may not have the ready funds available to meet such a cost. If term life policies are taken out on the lives of the partners, the funds are then available to enable the remaining partners to buy out the deceased partner's share.
- *Key employee.* Where a business has a key employee (i.e. one who would be difficult to replace), a term life cover can be used to meet the cost of hiring and training a replacement employee. Multiple replacements may be needed, or a significant amount of training may be necessary.
- *Business loans.* Cover can be effected to meet the outstanding amount of a business loan. Take, for example, a small business where the involvement of the owner, manager or a key employee is vital for the success of the business. The business may be able to obtain a loan at more attractive interest rates or a **creditor** may feel more secure in providing a loan if there is a term life cover in force for the amount of the loan. Should the principal or key employee die, then the loan can be repaid from the policy proceeds. These policies are often referred to as 'key person' policies.

Evaluation of personal risks

In establishing an adequate sum insured, three areas need to be considered.

- A lump sum amount to meet costs at the time of premature death of the income earner.
- A provision to meet the needs of dependants for the period of their dependency after premature death of the income earner.
- A provision to meet the needs of dependants and the income earner in the event of disablement of the income earner.

Lump sum costs

At the time of death a number of expenses may arise and provision needs to be made to meet these costs. The more common items are burial and associated expenses, **estate** administration costs, legal expenses, taxes (e.g. death is a trigger to incur capital gains tax), final medical and associated care expenses, debt clearing and adjustment expenses.

- *Burial and associated expenses.* These expenses will vary but an amount in the vicinity of $10 000 is reasonable. A check with a funeral director at the time of establishing a sum insured will help ensure adequacy. Keep in mind that provision is being made for an event in the future, so allow for inflation. It is common for many people to prepay for a funeral via means of a funeral bond. This type of bond is a form of investment fund that allows for the prepayment to increase in value to ensure that a rise in future costs is covered.
- *Estate administration costs.* The amount to be allowed here will vary according to the size and complexity of the estate. Allow not only for the estate administration costs but also for legal expenses, including any associated taxes or other costs. For example, the situation where one **beneficiary** is left property and another is left cash may result in an unfair distribution, since a future liability for CGT could arise in the case of the property. This can be overcome by providing for the CGT amount in the term life policy sum insured.
- *Final medical and associated care expenses.* The medical and care expenses associated with death can be considerable. Health insurance will reduce the costs but keep in mind that hospital and medical expenses covered under a health insurance policy will not always cover all costs. For example, specialised nursing supervision outside of hospital may be necessary, and the cost of obtaining the service may be greater than the cover provides for.
- *Debt clearing.* The repayment of debts and associated interest places an additional strain on the dependant's income. Having all outstanding debts paid at the time of death reduces the level of income needed to maintain the family's standard of living. These debts might include outstanding balance on mortgages, amounts owed on loans, and outstanding balances on credit cards and charge accounts. Remember that the amount being calculated is to provide for the future. Where there are future plans that involve debt, this should be allowed for also.
- *Adjustment expenses.* Following a death, the family members have to adjust to their new circumstances. This may involve a reduction in their standard of living. The adjustment to this new standard can be helped by a lump sum that supplements their income during, say, a 6-month transition period.

Provision for dependants

To this point, the discussion has related to providing for lump sum amounts that usually need to be met at the time of death. Provision must also be made for the needs of dependants. Two approaches are commonly used to calculate this amount — the multiple approach and the needs approach.

The multiple approach

This approach is quite a simple one and, at times, is used to calculate the entire amount of cover. As the lump sum needs can vary considerably from one person to another, that component is better calculated separately. The multiple approach simply seeks to replace the insured's income by providing an amount that, when invested, will produce for the dependants the amount of income the insured was earning. For example, in the event of the premature death of a person whose income is $50 000 p.a., and assuming a future investment rate of 6%, the necessary sum insured can be arrived at by dividing the salary by the interest rate, or 0.06 in this case. This produces a sum insured of $835 000. This amount, when invested at 6%, will provide an income of approximately $50 000 in perpetuity. A more sophisticated version of this approach involves a table which gives a range of multiples to be used. The table takes into account the age of the dependants and income.

The simplicity of the approach is its downfall. It assumes everyone's situation is the same and does not consider the circumstances of the individual. It ignores the individual's resources and commitments, and relies on investment rates in the future being similar to those applying at the time the sum insured is calculated. Interest rates can vary considerably over time. Dependencies can last for 20 years or more. If the rate used to calculate the future investment return is high there is every possibility that in a future period these same rates will not be available so the return will be less than initially planned, leaving the dependants in a difficult position. This approach also ignores the effects of inflation. Over time the purchasing power of the income generated will diminish.

The preferred approach is to do a detailed analysis of the dependants' needs and establish more precisely the amount of cover needed. When using the multiple approach, there could well be a tendency to look on the amount estimated as being unduly high but, by doing a detailed analysis, a family can see how that amount is compiled and the necessity for each item.

In order to be in a position to recommend a particular program to clients, financial advisers need to have a good understanding of their clients' financial and family circumstances. In the chapter on personal financial planning you read that advisers need to comply with s. 961B of the Corporations Act, which requires that advisers need to act in the best interests of the client so it is just as important to assess a client's needs for risk protection as it is to ascertain a client's tolerance of risk of investment.

The needs approach

The needs approach requires a more detailed analysis, including the compilation of a budget of the costs that would be incurred in the future. The position will, of course, continually change, so it is necessary to recalculate the figures periodically to check that the amount remains adequate.

Keep in mind that what is being calculated is the provision to be made for the dependants. Those provided for under this heading are usually dependent children. Their financial needs will increase as they grow older.

In a two-income family, the income of the surviving partner is deducted from the income needed in each period. Also brought into account is any income received from pensions or benefits to which the surviving partner may be eligible, for example, parenting payment, widow's allowance. These benefits or allowances are subject to assets and income tests and, in most cases, those who have insurance cover to provide for such situations are not eligible. The benefit paid under the policy would exceed the limits set down in the assets test.

In a single-income family, the premature death of the non-earning partner needs to be considered. Provision must be made to cover the cost of employing someone to undertake the non-earning partner's contribution, for example cooking, cleaning and child care.

This section has considered the provision of an income for the dependants. The amount provided will not be needed immediately so most of it can be invested, generating further income. This will be necessary as the buying power of the lump sum amount will be eroded over time with inflation. By generating investment income the effects of inflation will be offset. Under the multiple approach, the interest income is used to generate the dependants' income. As a result, that approach produce a diminishing income over time (in terms of buying power) as the effects of inflation set in.

Karlee Abbott is aged 38 and earns $120 000 per annum. Steve Abbott, her husband, is aged 42. Steve has part-time work and looks after the house and raises their 3 children (Jessica, aged 8, Louise, aged 6, and James, aged 4). The Abbotts own their house which has a value of $900 000 and a mortgage of $620 000. They have 2 cars, one of which is subject to a finance agreement and currently has $8000 to be repaid. Other outstanding debts, including credit cards, amount to $10 000. Karlee has $95 000 in a superannuation account and Steve has $50 000 in superannuation. The Abbotts have estimated that their monthly expenses are $3500 plus $550 per child. This figure has been adjusted to take into account rising costs as the children get older. This amount will be needed until the children are 21.

The expenses that are expected to arise at the time of Karlee's death are:
- funeral and associated expenses $14 000
- legal and associated costs $4000
- emergency funds $15 000.

When the house mortgage was arranged, a term life cover of $250 000 was taken out for Karlee.

Determining the sum insured for term life insurance for Karlee using the multiple approach (assuming a 5% investment rate) is as follows.

Item	Calculation	Amount $
Replacement of income flow	$\dfrac{\$120\,000}{0.05}$	$2 400 000
Less: Term life insurance in force		(250 000)
Less: Superannuation		(95 000)
Sum insured		2 055 000

Determining the sum insured for term life insurance for Karlee using the needs approach is as follows.

Item	Calculation	Amount $
Cost of dependency: Jessica	13 years × 12 months × $550	85 800
Cost of dependency: Louise	15 years × 12 months × $550	99 000
Cost of dependency: James	17 years × 12 months × $550	112 200
Cost of dependency: Steve[a]	23 years × 12 months × $3500	966 000
Funeral and associated expenses		14 000
Legal and associated costs		4 000
Emergency funds		15 000
Repay debts: mortgage		620 000
Repay debts: car finance		8 000
Repay debts: credit cards		10 000
Total amount required		**1 934 000**
Less: Term life insurance in force		(250 000)
Less: Superannuation		(95 000)
Sum insured		1 589 000

[a] This figure is based on Steve's dependency until age 65. Steve might remain dependent for less time and return to work once the children are older. Conversely if Steve does not return to work and the monthly costs do not include some provision for contributions to superannuation the period of dependency could be longer.

From the analysis above it is clear that the needs and multiple approaches can produce very different results. Both methods are highly contingent on the assumptions that underpin them, particularly the rate of investment return and the period of dependency.

Disablement

The discussion to this point has been in relation to the effects on dependants of the death of an income producer. However, if the income earner becomes disabled and unable to work, a similar problem arises but this time with the added need to provide for the income earner.

Disablement can vary from a minor injury or illness that incapacitates for a short period of time to one that is permanent. The costs that need to be met will vary, but can include the following.
- *Medical expenses.* If health insurance is in place, much of the cost may be met but policies do not cover all areas. There may, for example, be a need for specialised nursing that goes beyond the amounts provided by health insurance.
- *Other costs associated with the disability.* These may include the need for house alterations, the provision of prostheses, and the purchase of wheelchairs and other aids.

- *Provision of an income to support the dependants.* This will differ from the calculation for death, as provision will need to be made for the income earner.

The elimination of debts must be included in the calculation of a sum insured as these will place a drain on the income. An amount to provide immediate funds to help during the adjustment period should also be included.

Two covers can meet these costs. A total and permanent disablement (TPD) extension on a term life insurance policy will meet the lump sum amounts, and an income protection policy can provide a regular monthly income.

Control measures for personal risks

Control measures look at what can be done to eliminate the occurrence of risks or to reduce the impact should the risk occur. In relation to personal risks, these measures are mainly lifestyle matters, such as keeping fit, eating sensibly and avoiding risk factors such as smoking and drinking too much.

Financing of personal risks

If, despite the control measures, a loss occurs, then provision needs to be made for the financing of those losses. These losses can be financed by retention or transfer.

Retention

With retention, losses are met from an individual's own resources. This approach is used for smaller losses that the person is able to afford. The most common method is to use an excess on an insurance policy. An excess is the amount of insurance risk which is retained by the individual rather than transferred through insurance.

Transfer

Transfer of risks involves passing financial responsibility for the loss to another party. The main form of transfer is by insurance. In return for a premium, the insurer agrees to meet the cost of certain specified risks. In relation to personal risks, the policies used are term life policies, disability policies and health policies. Term life insurance policies provide a lump sum amount in the event of death, TPD and specified traumas. Income-replacement policies provide a monthly income in the event of disability, even if it is temporary.

PERSONAL FINANCE BULLETIN

Australians skipping genetic screening tests out of fear it will affect life insurance coverage

Genetic researchers fear Australians are skipping genetic screening tests that could detect disease risks early, out of concern that it might affect their life insurance coverage.

Genetic tests are considered a useful tool in the early detection and prevention of serious conditions such as cancer and heart disease.

However a recent report found some Australians were choosing not to have tests or partake in medical research because the results might affect their life insurance premiums or prevent them from accessing certain coverage.

Lead author Dr Jane Tiller told the ABC that decision could be dangerous for some.

'We talk about certain genes, like the BRCA1 gene, which increases the risk of breast and ovarian cancer,' she said.

'Someone knowing they have that gene can take significant risk reducing measures, such as regular screening and preventative surgery.

'But if people don't know about that risk, they can't do anything to prevent it and people deciding they don't want genetic testing, because they're worried about insurance is really a tragedy.'

In some cases, insurance providers can require the results of a person's genetic tests and either deny the level of cover requested or charge higher premiums based on the findings.

▶

Rules in place don't go far enough

A federal parliament committee in 2018 recommended a ban on the use of predictive genetic test results in life insurance underwriting.

The Financial Services Council (FSC), which oversees the insurance industry, introduced a self-regulated moratorium in 2019 to prevent genetic discrimination.

Under the guidelines, genetic tests can't be collected by the insurer for policies up to $500 000.

A group of Australian researchers from several universities monitored the effectiveness of the moratorium and found genetic discrimination in life insurance was still occurring.

Of the health professionals surveyed, 76 per cent felt the moratorium resolved some of their concerns about genetic discrimination, but the majority agreed government intervention was needed, as did the vast majority of patients who were surveyed.

While more than half of genomic researchers were concerned life insurance was a barrier in finding research participants.

Funded through a Medical Research Futures Fund research grant, the Australian Genetics & Life Insurance Moratorium: Monitoring the Effectiveness and Response (A-GLIMMER) report has now been handed to government with two recommendations.

It has called for changes to the Disability Discrimination Act so that insurers cannot use genetic or genomic tests results for any policy and for the Australian Human Rights Commission to be provided with more resources to enforce the new obligations.

Dr Jane Tiller said change is needed.

'Our research shows, overwhelmingly, that Australian stakeholders believe current protections against genetic discrimination are inadequate, and that legislation is required,' she said.

'We are calling on the government to legislate to protect consumers from genetic discrimination and remove the barrier to genetic testing and genomic medicine.'

'Discriminated against for trying to survive'

Judy Honor has a gene mutation that means she has an increased chance of developing cancer.

The Queensland mother of three has fought bowel, liver and breast cancer and encouraged her children to get tested.

She is now taking on the insurance industry, because one of her sons is struggling to get the level of cover he wants.

'He's had no cancer or anything, but because of my genetic thing he's been discriminated against in gaining insurance.'

'We got genetic testing for the survival of our families.

'We feel we are discriminated against trying to do something for our family to survive.'

Her son Dwayne Honor gets regular colonoscopies due to his mother's history but has not undergone genetic testing because he is concerned about life insurance restrictions.

'I don't want to live in a country where we're judged by our genetic makeup, how we're born,' he said.

He said the current moratorium with a $500,000 limit wasn't adequate.

'No one in their right mind would reasonably suggest that if you wanted to get a life insurance protection of $500,000 that that would be sufficiently enough to cover your liabilities . . . it's well below average.'

He said the restrictions on life insurance also impacted people's willingness to partake in medical research.

'I would definitely be involved in research if we could access life insurance and not be genetically discriminated against,' he said.

'I think that in itself would take a lot of pressure off the public health system by allowing us to do good evidence-based preventative health and screening, without the consequence of the financial service industry impacting on your treatment.'

Australia 'more susceptible' to genetic discrimination

The A-GLIMMER report pointed to models in other countries, such as the UK and Canada that better protected consumers and stated Australia was behind.

'Australian consumers are more susceptible to genetic discrimination in life insurance than their counterparts in many other countries,' the report said.

Dr Tiller rebuffed concerns that government intervention would see life insurance costs rise for the general population.

'In every country where this has been done, the insurers raised the argument that people will take out too much life insurance, that risk won't be priced accordingly and that insurance will become unsustainable or unaffordable,' she said.

'We haven't seen that happen in any other country where this has occurred.'

The report has been given to the government. Assistant Treasurer and Minister for Financial Services Stephen Jones said he would consider the report and its findings.

'We don't want people to avoid having genetic tests which could detect life threatening conditions because of a fear it may affect access to insurance,' he said in a statement.

'Early detection can lead to life saving interventions. That's in everyone's interest.'

A spokesperson for the FSC defended the system and said if a consumer was concerned they should contact the Life Code Compliance Committee.

'The genetics moratorium has been reviewed and strengthened, and has been extended indefinitely as part of the Life Insurance Code of Practice from 1 July, 2023,' the statement said.

'The expanded genetics moratorium will be independently enforced and overseen by the Life Code Compliance Committee, which will also have the power to impose financial sanctions on subscribing life insurance companies that do not comply with their obligations under the code, including the moratorium.'

Source: Borys 2023.

Term life policies

A term life policy was the original form of life policy. It paid the nominated death benefit when the person whose life was insured died during the period of insurance. In early times, the period of insurance would have been about a year.

A term life policy as it is offered today usually includes a terminal illness benefit as part of the basic cover. The terminal illness benefit provides that, in the event of the insured person being diagnosed with an illness or disease or sustaining an injury which is likely to lead to death within 12 months, the specified lump-sum benefit is payable. This lump sum is the same as the death benefit in the policy with one proviso — the company usually specifies a maximum amount it will pay in relation to all policies with that company. The amount varies, with most companies specifying $1 million. Any amount paid reduces the death benefit that will eventually become payable. The reasoning behind this premature payment of the death benefit is to make available funds that can help the family during such a trying time with medical and other costs.

Policy features

The basic term life policy has, over time, developed a number of features designed to make it more attractive to clients. Those described in the following sections are found in most policies.

- *Indexed sum insured.* It is usual for policies to have the sum insured indexed so the insured has the option of an increase in the sum insured each year. The advantage of these increases is that they are automatic and do not need a medical examination. Companies generally provide that, in the event of the indexed increase being declined three times in succession by the insured, the automatic index benefit ceases. It can, on request, be reinstated at a future date but is subject to a medical check.

- *Special sum insured increase.* Another benefit often found in policies is a provision that allows for an increase in the sum insured at other times, again without the need for a medical check. The ability to do this arises at the occurrence of certain specified events, such as marriage of the insured, the birth of a child or taking out a mortgage. The policy provision usually specifies minimum and maximum amounts for the increase and the frequency with which these increases can be made. The main value of this benefit lies in the fact that a medical check is not required. If, after effecting the policy, the insured acquires a condition that would be a bar from effecting further cover, this policy provision allows the insured to obtain sum-insured increases.

- *Guaranteed renewal.* This provision means the policy will remain in force continuously, subject to any specified age limit, with the insured only having the right to terminate the policy. This means that the cover cannot be altered or changed if the insured develops any adverse condition; this includes any premium increase related to the condition. Premium rates applied to all those insured are not guaranteed to remain unaltered from year to year as standard premiums can change according to the cost of risks as assessed by underwriters. However, once an adverse condition is experienced, such as the onset of diabetes, the insurance company cannot impose an additional loading to the normal premium.

- *Multiple lives.* Most insurers will allow more than one life to be covered under the one policy. The benefit here is that only one policy fee applies. Where a husband and wife and other family members are all covered under the one policy, a saving in multiple policy fees can be made.

- *Policy duration.* Generally the policy can be taken out for any period of time ranging from 1 day to a term that continues until the insured turns 95 years. Premiums are either stepped premiums or level premiums.

– *Stepped premiums.* These are calculated annually and rise each year in accordance with the increased death risk that results as the insured gets older. Table 7.1 shows typical term life insurance annual policy premiums at different ages for a professional person with a sum insured of $250 000. Premiums are given for both males and females and for smokers and non-smokers.

TABLE 7.1 Stepped premiums — professional person, $250 000 sum insured

Age	Male non-smoker $	Male smoker $	Female non-smoker $	Female smoker $
35	240	440	200	330
40	290	550	230	420
45	400	840	300	570
55	1 120	2 500	820	1 420

– *Level premiums.* Stepped premiums are good if the cover is needed for only a small number of years. The problem with a stepped premium is that, if the insurance is needed for a long period of time, the premiums will rise each year in accordance with the increased risk of death (as seen in table 7.1). By the time the insured reaches 60 years of age, the premium will become quite large and may start to become unaffordable. The level premium offers a solution to this problem. The cost of the premium is averaged over the lifetime of the policy. In the early years, the amounts paid will be greater than the stepped premium for the same year, but in the later years the amount payable will be less. The amount paid in excess of the 'death risk' amount in the early years is invested and the interest along with the surplus is used to supplement the amount paid in the later years, so the full risk premium is still received by the insurer. Table 7.2 compares typical level and stepped premiums for a $500 000 term life policy.

TABLE 7.2 Comparison of stepped and level premiums — $500 000 term life policy

Age	Stepped premium $	Level premium $
30	370	600
40	460	600
50	1 200	600
55	2 200	600

The point that needs to be kept in mind is how long the insured expects to keep the cover in place. If a policy is effected to age 65 using level premiums and, after 6 years, the cover is cancelled, then the insured would have paid an excessive price for the policy. Look at the amounts shown in table 7.3, where the two situations are compared. This would mean an overpayment of $1230 for the period in question. Although taking out a cover to age 65 spreads the premium burden, it may come at a price.

TABLE 7.3 Typical premium differences between stepped and level premiums over 6 years

Age	Stepped premium $	Level premium $
30	370	600
31	380	600
32	390	600
33	400	600
34	410	600
35	420	600
Total	2 370	3 600

- *Convertibility.* There is generally a provision that allows you to convert the policy to any other type of policy with the insurer so long as the sum insured is the same. No medical examination is needed. This can be done at any time to age 95 (although most life companies set the maximum age for such a conversion to 65 or 70), and could be of value in a situation where a person's health deteriorates and a medical examination would mean that cover may not be attainable, or could be effected only at an increased premium. This provision allows people to change the cover to one that better suits their needs at the time. For example, the initial cover may be a term life policy with a stepped premium. People contracting an ailment that precludes them from obtaining further cover may wish to convert to a policy with a level premium so that, at a future time, the premiums do not become prohibitive.
- *Optional benefits.* Companies provide a range of optional benefits as follows.
  - *Total and permanent disablement.* This benefit is described in more detail in the next section on disability policies. Under this benefit, a lump sum is paid if the person insured becomes totally and permanently disabled.
  - *Trauma cover.* This cover is also discussed in more detail in the section on disability policies. Briefly, it provides for the payment of a nominated lump sum in the event of the insured being diagnosed with any number of life-threatening/major illnesses or diseases that would change the person's life.
  - **Future insurability**. This optional benefit gives the insured the opportunity to purchase more cover at future nominated dates without providing further evidence of health status. This is of particular value where an insured has developed a health condition which would preclude further cover being provided. There could be as many as 5 opportunities until the insured person's 45th birthday. The dates on which the option can be exercised are nominated in the policy, but, in the event of certain nominated events such as a house purchase or birth of a child, the date may be brought forward. The benefit usually has a maximum amount of additional cover that is available.

Policy exclusions

In a term life policy, the exclusions are few. For example, most term life insurance policies will exclude suicide for the first 13 months of insurance coverage. Suicide is one exclusion that is common to all policies. Other exclusions vary between insurers.

- *Terminal illness.* Cover is not provided where the terminal illness is a result of an intentional self-inflicted injury or disease.
- *Other exclusions.* These are not found in all policies and, in fact, some insurers will have only the suicide exclusion. Other exclusions may include:
  - death resulting from war, warlike activities, civil commotions and other similar events
  - death resulting from a pre-existing condition that was not disclosed to the insurer before entering into the cover.

In both these situations, cover may still not be granted on policies that do not have such exclusions. An insured going into a war zone could be regarded as non-disclosure of a material fact, due to the increased risk. Similarly, the non-disclosure of a pre-existing condition may fall into the same category.

Policy ownership

A term life policy can be in the name of:
- the life insured
- the life insured but with a beneficiary nominated for the proceeds to be paid to
- a person or company on the life of the person insured.

In the case of the policy being in the name of the life insured, the benefits are paid to the life insured's estate in the event of death. Thus, any distribution of funds needs to wait until probate is granted, which can be some time later. If a creditor has required the insured to effect a policy to cover a debt, the creditor may not ultimately receive payment as the estate debts may exceed the estate funds (including the term life policy proceeds).

Where a beneficiary is nominated, or the owner is a person other than the insured, then the proceeds are paid directly to that person. The advantage of this approach is that the benefit is paid straight away. In the case of creditors or a situation where the insured wants a certain party to receive the funds, the policy should be effected in the name of that party.

Disability policies

Life insurers and, in respect of some policies, general insurers offer a range of disability policies. The cover afforded by these policies revolves around the concept of incapacity as a result of injury or illness.

Some provide cover by way of a lump sum, and others provide cover by way of monthly payments. The four covers examined in this section are:

- total and permanent disablement insurance
- trauma insurance
- income protection insurance
- business overheads insurance.

Total and permanent disablement (TPD) insurance

This cover is usually taken as an extension of a trauma or term life insurance policy. The benefit provides that, in the event of the person insured becoming totally and permanently disabled, the policy will pay the nominated amount. On payment of a TPD benefit, the remaining amount of cover is reduced by the amount of the benefit. The definition of total and permanent disablement is the critical aspect of the cover and the policy definition needs to be considered carefully. Not all policies are the same and some are quite restrictive. The more restrictive definitions usually carry a lower premium but this may be little consolation if, in the event of a claim, it is too restrictive to meet the loss.

An example of a commonly used definition of total and permanent disablement is where an applicant satisfies either of the following two criteria. If either part is satisfied, the benefit is payable.

- The total and permanent loss of any of the following:
  - the use of both hands
  - the use of both feet
  - the use of one hand and one foot
  - the sight of both eyes
  - the use of one hand and the sight of one eye
  - the use of one foot and the sight of one eye.
- Injury or disease which, in the opinion of the insurer, has wholly prevented the insured person from performing the principal duties of their usual occupation for a continuous period of at least 6 months and which, despite the insured person receiving treatment or rehabilitation, will continue to prevent them from ever again performing those duties or the principal duties of any other full-time occupation that they were engaged in during the 5 years prior to the cessation of work. For the purpose of this definition, it does not matter if the occupation is paid or unpaid.

The circumstances in which the benefit is paid occur infrequently. In the first part of the definition, two limbs or faculties are involved. Bear in mind that the phrase used is 'loss of use of'. If, for example, a foot is badly damaged so that it is not usable on its own, the courts have decided that this does not constitute loss of use if the foot is usable with a prosthesis. However, the wording of the latter part of the definition is quite important. It relates to the insured's usual occupation or one they have undertaken over the past 5 years.

The broadest definition is one referred to as the 'own occupation' definition. This is usually available only in professional white-collar occupations. It stipulates that the insured is unable to work in their occupation for at least 6 consecutive months and is so incapacitated that in the opinion of the insurer's professional adviser the insured is unlikely to be able to resume his or her own profession or occupation ever again. Under this definition for example, a surgeon who lost a hand would meet the definition requirements and therefore would be entitled to a payout under the policy and would still be able to lecture in surgery at a university.

The following is an example of a restrictive definition.

> Total disablement arising from illness, accident or injury, which we believe causes the insured person to be unable to engage in any occupation, employment or business for remuneration or profit.

The use of the words 'any occupation' leaves very few situations where the conditions of the definition could be met. Referring back to the earlier example, the surgeon would not be able to make a claim.

Trauma insurance

The purpose of trauma cover is to provide a lump sum in the event of the diagnosis of any of the listed traumas. The cover can be purchased as an extension of a term life policy or as a stand-alone policy. The trauma cover is generally offered in two forms — basic trauma cover includes a few traumas only; broader trauma cover provides a more extensive list.

Basic trauma cover generally includes the following traumas:

- cancer — malignant tumours
- heart attack

- coronary artery surgery
- stroke
- terminal illness.

Some insurers will also cover paraplegia, quadriplegia and occupationally acquired HIV under their basic trauma cover. The list for broader trauma cover also varies between insurers. Of all claims reported, more than 90% are for traumas that are covered under the basic cover. Problems arise because insurers differ in their definitions of trauma. The problems are further compounded by the complex medical terminology which is used to define the trauma but will not mean a great deal to the average person.

Some benefits require qualifying periods, that is, the policy will not apply if the condition becomes apparent within 90 days of the commencement of the policy. In the list above, cancer (malignant tumours), coronary artery surgery, heart attack and stroke may fall into this category. The insurer imposes the waiting period to eliminate any traumas that are present but have not yet become apparent at the time the cover is effected.

The benefits under the cover are usually indexed to the **consumer price index (CPI)** subject to a ceiling, which is usually set at around 5%. Cover is generally available from age 15 to 65, on renewal to age 70. Premium payment can be stepped or level. Trauma policies generally exclude suicide within 13 months of the policy commencement, intentional self-injury or intentional infection, and trauma from war or civil commotion. Most companies seem to provide a maximum amount of cover of $1 million.

Combined term life, trauma and TPD policies

Life insurance, trauma insurance and TPD insurance can each be taken out as stand-alone (un-bundled) policies. TPD insurance is frequently included as an additional benefit within a life insurance policy. This additional benefit is sometimes referred to as rider benefit. Combining two or more insurances into the one policy is generally referred to as bundling.

Trauma insurance can also be included as a rider benefit within a life insurance policy. In a bundled insurance policy the sum insured under the rider benefit cannot exceed the death benefit specified in the life policy. Any payment under the rider will reduce the amount payable under the policy overall. For example, a life insurance policy with a sum insured of $1 million includes a trauma rider — if the insured subsequently makes a trauma claim of $200 000, the life insurance sum insured will now be limited to $800 000. Most insurers will provide the insured with the opportunity to buy back some additional coverage after a claim.

ILLUSTRATIVE EXAMPLE 7.2

Lucy is single and has no dependants. She has no need for life insurance and therefore a bundled policy which includes life, TPD and trauma is probably not the best choice for her. She should consider TPD and trauma as stand-alone policies and/or she should consider an insurance policy which bundles TPD and trauma cover together.

Income protection insurance

Income protection insurance, also known as salary continuance insurance or disability income insurance, provides cover in the event of the insured being unable to work as a result of accident or sickness. The benefit of income protection depends on your annual salary, waiting period before receiving the benefit and the duration of the benefit payment.

Benefit. The policy provides a monthly income benefit if the person insured becomes totally disabled by injury or sickness. This benefit can be an amount that is agreed on at the time the policy is effected and is generally set at a maximum of 75% of pre-tax monthly income derived from personal exertion. Alternatively, the benefit amount can be equivalent to an indemnity value. This is where the maximum monthly benefit is agreed on at the commencement of the policy and the actual monthly benefit is assessed at the time a claim is made. The indemnity value is based on the insured's average earnings over the last 12 months. In both cases, investment income is not taken into account as this will continue regardless of incapacity. As with other personal risk products, there are variations. Some insurers may offer a fortnightly benefit. The benefit payable under the policy is reduced by any sick-leave payment, workers compensation or motor accident compensation, or payments from other insurance for sickness or accident.

Benefit period. This is the length of time the insurer will pay the benefit for. The more common periods are 2 or 5 years or to age 65 years. This latter benefit is the one that should be most seriously considered.

The main purpose of an insurance cover is to provide for a catastrophe. An event that disables for a long period of time completely changes a person's lifestyle and, in most cases, severely so. Where incapacity lasts for 5 years, in most cases it will be permanent.

In the case of a benefit to age 65, this is usually only available to low-hazard occupations such as white-collar professionals.

Waiting period. All policies have a waiting period where no cover is provided. The length of the waiting period is decided by the insured and can range from 14 days to 2 years. In deciding on a waiting period, people need to take into account the reason they are effecting the cover. Most accidents and illnesses are of short duration. Employees have sick leave, and self-employed people will, generally, be able to manage for a short time — they may have set aside an emergency fund for this purpose. The major problem arises when the illness is prolonged, because loss of income cannot be sustained for the long term. Each case needs to be judged on its merits, and people need to work out how long they could manage without an income before deciding on the length of the waiting period. The longer the waiting period the lower the premium.

ILLUSTRATIVE EXAMPLE 7.3

Jason, a non-smoker, is a 30-year-old accountant with an annual gross salary of $86 000 plus 9.5% superannuation. He applies for income protection insurance with an agreed monthly benefit payment of $5375. The monthly premium will vary, depending on his waiting period and benefit payment period, as shown in table 7.4 below.

TABLE 7.4   Jason's monthly income protection insurance premium

Waiting period	Benefit payment period	Premium
14 days	6 months	$ 71.78
	12 months	$ 86.70
	24 months	$104.28
28 days	6 months	$ 49.01
	12 months	$ 60.02
	24 months	$ 74.54

Guaranteed renewal. The insurer guarantees renewal of the policy each year until a specified age. The premium rate is changed only if the premiums for the whole underwriting class are increased.

Total disablement. The benefit under the policy is paid in the event of the insured person becoming totally disabled during the policy period. An example of a commonly used definition in policies is that you are totally disabled if, due to injury or sickness, you:

- cannot do at least one of the income-producing duties of your occupation
- are not working and are under medical care.

For those in manual occupations, the definition used is that you are totally disabled if, due to injury or sickness:

- during the first 2 years, you cannot do at least one of the income-producing duties of your occupation
- after the first 2 years, because of the same injury or sickness, you are unable to perform any occupation for which you are reasonably suited by education, training or experience
- you are not working and are under medical care.

An even more restrictive wording rarely seen today states:

> You are totally disabled if, due to injury or sickness, you are unable to perform any occupation.

Care needs to be exercised in the choice of policy taken. The wording that indicates you will be considered disabled only if you are unable to perform any occupation allows the insurance company greater scope in avoiding payment. Such policies will be offered at quite a cheap premium, but this is of little value if it does not provide the cover needed when a serious incapacity occurs.

Partial disablement. With rehabilitation, an insured person may be able to return to partial duties some time before a full recovery is made. Most policies recognise this position and provide a partial benefit in this event. Where the period of total disablement has existed for at least 14 days, after which the insured person is able to return to work in a reduced capacity, a proportionate benefit will be paid from the end of the waiting period. The benefit is calculated by a formula similar to the following.

$$\text{Benefit payable} = \frac{\text{Pre-disablement income} - \text{Post-disablement income}}{\text{Pre-disablement income}} \times \text{Monthly income benefit}$$

ILLUSTRATIVE EXAMPLE 7.4

Samantha is a television journalist. She fell and broke her arm badly. For 8 weeks she was unable to work, but after that she was able to undertake some light duties. Her pre-accident income was $12 000 per month. Following the accident, her income dropped to $4000. The monthly benefit under the policy is $9000. Applying the formula results in a benefit payable of $6000.

$$\text{Benefit payable} = \frac{\$12\,000 - \$4000}{\$12\,000} \times \$9000$$
$$= \$6000$$

Additional benefits. Insurers may add several extras to their coverage, including rehabilitation expenses, CPI indexation of benefits, and payments to cover superannuation contributions.

Changes to income protection insurance
APRA has implemented the following changes to the income protection insurance market:
- from 1 April 2020, agreed value income protection policies ceased to be offered (indemnity value policies can continue to be offered)
- from 1 July 2021:
  - benefit payments to be based on earnings within 12 months of claim
  - benefit payments not to exceed 90% of earnings at the time of claim for the first 6 months
  - benefit payments not to exceed 75% of earnings after the first 6 months
  - guaranteed renewal policies ceased to be offered — benefit payment period to be a maximum of 5 years
  - life insurance companies to have effective controls in place to manage risks associated with long benefit periods (such as to age 65 for policies taken out prior to 30 March 2020).

Business overheads (expenses) insurance

This cover is a variation of the income protection policy. Cover under both policies revolves around the fact that the insured person must be incapacitated by accident or illness. Where the income protection policy provides cover for loss of income, the business overheads policy provides cover for eligible business overheads that accrue while the insured person is incapacitated, less any income received during that period. The amount payable, however, cannot exceed the monthly benefit figure nominated by the insured when the policy was taken out.

The policy defines eligible business overheads as recurring costs incurred in the normal day-to-day running of the business, such as electricity, rent and lease costs. Eligible expenses do not include costs such as capital expenditures and depreciation on land and buildings.

There are several important points to remember about the cover. Unlike the income protection policy, the amount paid is not the benefit stated in the policy. The benefit stated represents the maximum amount payable. The amount paid is the total of the eligible expenses that accrue in that month. Cover can be obtained for 100% of the eligible expenses. Unlike the income protection policy, the benefits under this policy are paid only while the insured person is unable to work — no partial benefit is available.

Business overheads insurance seeks to protect the revenue of the business. Since the policy is for a revenue purpose, the premium will be tax deductible for the business; however, this also means that any payout from the policy will be taxable.

Health insurance policies

Health insurance in Australia is provided in two areas. The public system (Medicare) is available to all Australian residents. In addition to Medicare, there is private health insurance. This is available only to those who purchase insurance from a licensed health insurer.

Medicare

Medicare provides free treatment as a public patient in a public hospital and subsidised treatment by health professionals such as doctors, specialists and optometrists for certain services.

Medicare provides a range of medical and hospital benefits.

- *Medical benefits.* This includes fees for doctors, specialists, obstetricians, optometrists and other specified specialists, and the cost of X-rays and pathology tests.
- *Hospital benefits.* Cover is provided for Medicare patients (public patients) in a public hospital. This means that the patient is attended by doctors and specialists nominated by the hospital. Most of the cost is met by Medicare. This includes any physiotherapy, occupational therapy and pharmaceuticals provided by the hospital while the person is an in-patient at the hospital.

The benefit paid by Medicare is 85% of the schedule fee. The remaining 15% is met by the patient. Note that many doctors charge an amount greater than the schedule fee. In those cases, patients must bear the cost of the excess themselves.

Medicare is paid for by way of a levy on income and it is collected with a person's income tax. For more detailed coverage of Medicare, visit its website at medicare.gov.au.

Private health insurance

Private health insurance provides greater flexibility in where and by whom a person is treated. It also provides cover for services not covered by Medicare. With private health insurance, patients are able to choose the hospital to be treated in and the specialist who will provide the treatment. In addition, they have access to private wards and, if available, individual rooms.

Health insurers must be licensed and provide cover within the framework of the health insurance legislation. Health insurers must accept cover from all applicants and the premium rates they apply, which must be approved by government, cannot be loaded for poor health. Waiting periods are imposed by funds for pre-existing or other conditions on first taking out health insurance but this is for a maximum of 12 months.

Private health insurance covers a wide range of areas including hospital costs in a public or private hospital as a private patient. 'Extras' can be added which provide cover for dental treatment, chiropractic, ambulance, home nursing, podiatry and a range of therapies including physiotherapy, occupational therapy and speech therapy. In addition, private health insurance can cover the cost of prostheses, glasses and contact lenses.

As well as providing the extras cover, funds offer a range of different hospital covers that suit the needs of people and may allow them to obtain a lower premium. The hospital benefit provided can vary from one that meets the full cost to one where the patient pays a portion of the cost. In addition, covers are available that may exclude some conditions such as obstetrics, heart surgery or hip replacement.

Policies that have an excess are also available (i.e. the patient pays the initial amount of any claim). This is applied only in relation to hospital covers, where an excess of up to $500 for singles ($1000 for couples) a year can be taken.

Private health insurance is not cheap. Spiralling medical costs brought the cover to a near crisis point in the late 1990s. As costs rose, more people dropped out. Those who stayed included the people who were in poor health. This meant that the claims costs were shared by fewer people and premiums rose further. At the same time, the people who withdrew were now using Medicare and the increased numbers were causing a strain on the public health system. Once the participation rate for private health insurance dropped to 30%, the government stepped in with measures aimed at stalling this drop.

Three measures were introduced: the health insurance rebate, the Medicare levy surcharge and the premium loading.

The federal government health rebate provides individuals and their families with a rebate of their health insurance premiums. The size of the rebate depends on age and income as shown in table 7.5.

TABLE 7.5	Federal government health rebate effective for the period 1 July 2024 to 30 June 2025			
	Below threshold	**Tier 1**	**Tier 2**	**Tier 3**
Singles	$97 000 or less	$97 001–113 000	$113 001–151 000	$151 001 or more
Families	$194 000 or less	$194 001–226 000	$226 001–302 000	$302 001 or more
Rebate				
Aged under 65	24.6%	16.4%	8.2%	0%

Aged 65–69	28.7%	20.5%	12.3%	0%
Aged 70 or over	32.8%	24.6%	16.4%	0%

Source: Adapted from ATO 2024a.

Income includes taxable income, reportable fringe benefits and reportable employer superannuation contributions. The income thresholds above apply for the 2024–2 financial year.

The Medicare levy surcharge is in addition to the 2% Medicare levy. The surcharge is applied to people without private health insurance who earn a high income, as described in table 7.6.

TABLE 7.6   **Medicare levy surcharge for the 2024–25 financial year**

	Below threshold	Tier 1	Tier 2	Tier 3
Singles	$97 000 or less	$97 001–$113 000	$113 001–$151 000	$151 001 or more
Families	$194 000 or less	$194 001–$226 000	$226 001–$302 000	$302 001 or more
Medicare levy surcharge				
Rate	0.0%	1.0%	1.25%	1.5%

Source: Adapted from ATO 2024b.

A premium loading of 2% applies for each year a person delays joining a health insurance fund after they turn 30 years of age. With the wide range of covers now available and the high premiums involved, choosing a cover can be a daunting task. This has led to the advent of health insurance advisers who research the market and provide guidance on the cover that best suits a person's needs and at the most competitive price. These advisers are often able to secure significant savings. A number of websites have questionnaires to assist in the process of selecting a suitable health insurance fund/policy. However, it is important to note that most websites will only list a selected number of health funds/policies and that these websites are generally funded by the health funds themselves.

PROFESSIONAL ADVICE

Choosing health insurance

As a financial adviser, you want to see your clients achieve their financial goals. As such, it can be tempting to encourage clients to insure for every possible contingency. Such a level of insurance will be expensive and limit the funds available to the client for investment and potentially day-to-day expenditure.

While you may have a personal view about whether health insurance is suitable for your own circumstances, it is important not to impose this view on your clients. In what circumstances is health insurance of value to a client?

Successive federal governments have introduced measures aimed at reducing pressure on the public hospital system primarily by encouraging individuals to take out private health insurance and to use the private health system.

Decisions with respect to health insurance go beyond purely financial considerations. Some clients will place a very high value on the choice that private health insurance generally provides. Some clients will be perfectly fit and make very little use of medical facilities over their lifetime, making health insurance less necessary. The problem, as with all insurance, is how can you tell, with foresight rather than hindsight, whether a client will need health insurance? This is easier to do for clients who have a history of medical problems or anticipate making more use of medical facilities in the future, in which case health insurance will have a higher value.

....

QUESTIONS

Your client, Kathy, is a healthy 29-year-old single female earning $100 000 a year. She has no private health insurance. What are the financial and non-financial arguments for Kathy taking out private health insurance? What would you recommend for this client?

Arranging personal risk management insurance through a superannuation fund

Some personal risk insurance policies, such as term life insurance, can be arranged via the individual's superannuation fund and paid out of pre-tax dollars rather than after-tax dollars.

Vanessa is 37 years old and wishes to take out a $1 million term life insurance policy. The annual premium on this policy is $1800. Vanessa's marginal tax rate (MTR) is 32.5%. She has the opportunity to hold the policy outside of superannuation and pay the premiums using her after-tax dollars. Alternatively, she could have the policy within her superannuation fund, sacrifice part of her salary to her superannuation fund and ask the fund to pay the premium using her pre-tax income. Table 7.7 compares the pre-tax income required to pay life insurance premium when holding the policy within superannuation and outside of superannuation.

TABLE 7.7   **Holding life insurance inside or outside of superannuation**

Policy outside of superannuation	Policy within superannuation
Pre-tax income required to pay premium	Pre-tax income required to pay premium
= premium / (1 − MTR)	= $1800
= $1800 / (1 − 0.325)	
= $2667	

Vanessa would be $867 ($2667 − $1800) better off in pre-tax income by taking out the term life insurance within her superannuation. This would be equivalent to $585 ($867 × (1 − MTR)) of after-tax income, a savings amount that she could use to purchase additional term life insurance or she might just enjoy more cash in her pocket.

Term life insurance through superannuation

When a person first joins a superannuation fund, the balance will be quite small, but over time this will grow. Having the term insurance arranged through a superannuation fund ensures that in the event of death or serious disability there will always be an adequate amount in the fund to provide for dependants and beneficiaries. A minimum level of term life insurance is an automatic requirement of some funds.

Bob is 35 years old and has $100 000 in superannuation. Bob also has a $900 000 term life insurance policy which he has arranged through his superannuation fund. If Bob passed away, $1 million would be available in his superannuation fund to provide for dependants and beneficiaries. When Bob is 45 years old, he might have $400 000 in superannuation in which case he might reduce his term life insurance coverage to $600 000 — if he passed away, $1 million would still be available in the fund. The idea is that insurance coverage is higher when superannuation balances are lower (and insurance premiums are lower) and insurance coverage is lower when superannuation balances are higher (and insurance premiums are higher). Refer to figure 7.2.

FIGURE 7.2   Term life insurance through superannuation

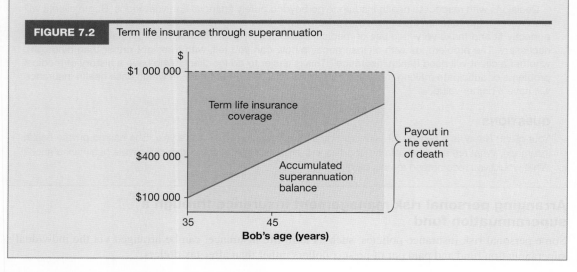

Pre-tax **salary sacrifice** contributions made to superannuation are normally taxed at 15%; however, when the contribution is for the purpose of paying a term life insurance premium the contribution itself is not added to the taxable income of the superannuation fund. It thereby avoids tax which means the full contribution can go to paying the term life insurance premium.

When the term life insurance premium is paid by the fund, any payout on that policy as a result of the death of the individual is to the superannuation fund and not to the estate of the deceased. The death of the member is, however, a **condition of release** which allows the trustees of the superannuation fund to pay out the member's account balance which also includes the proceeds of the insurance payout. The trustees will either be bound to pay out the balance to a nominated individual because the deceased had made a binding death benefit nomination, or the trustees will use their discretion to pay out the account to an individual or to the deceased's estate.

If the trustee pays out the account to a dependant of the member, the money will be received by the dependant tax free. If the trustee pays out the account to a non-dependant, tax will be payable. The amount of tax payable depends on the composition of the account. The account may comprise a tax-free component, a taxed component and an untaxed component. The taxation treatment of these components is discussed in the chapter on retirement planning.

Given the taxation implications, if an individual seeks to save money by arranging their term life insurance through their superannuation fund, if possible, it would be better to leave this money to a dependant and redirect other estate assets to non-dependants. If an individual does arrange their term life insurance through their superannuation fund and this money is then left to a non-dependant, they should understand that some of their tax savings will be lost when the funds are paid out. If an individual arranges their term life insurance outside a superannuation environment using after-tax dollars to pay the premium, any payout on the policy is not taxed in the hands of the beneficiary regardless of whether the beneficiary is a dependant or not. However, when the beneficiary invests that money and begins to generate investment earnings, those earnings will be taxable.

Total and permanent disability insurance through superannuation

As discussed previously, TPD insurance tends to be an add-on to a term life insurance policy. Premiums for a combined term life and TPD policy can be salary sacrificed resulting in tax savings. Any payout on a TPD policy is to the superannuation fund not the individual.

Since 1 July 2014 superannuation fund trustees can only offer insurance to their members which is consistent with satisfying a condition of release. Prior to 2014 it was possible to purchase an own-occupation TPD policy through superannuation. This, however, could result in an unsatisfactory situation where an individual receives a payout into their superannuation fund as a result of a disability which they could not access because they had not satisfied a condition of release from superannuation. This could be a significant problem if the person was considerably younger than their **preservation age**. Preservation age is discussed in the chapter on superannuation.

If term life and TPD policy premiums are paid from after-tax dollars, they are not tax deductible for the individual, nor is any payout taxable. If term life and TPD premiums are paid via a superannuation fund, any TPD benefits paid to recipients over the age of 60 will be received tax free. If TPD benefits are paid to a recipient under 60 years of age some tax will be payable. The amount of tax payable depends on the composition of the superannuation account and whether the payout is a lump sum or an income stream.

Income protection through superannuation

An individual may decide to pay their income protection insurance premiums via pre-tax salary sacrifice contributions to their superannuation fund. Provided the income protection policy covers a period of temporary disability which lasts more than 2 years, the contributions will be a deductible expense to the fund. As a consequence, the full contribution (premium) would pass through the superannuation fund to the insurer.

As noted above, since 1 July 2014 superannuation fund trustees can only offer insurance to their members that is consistent with satisfying a condition of release. All income protection policies must ensure that the conditions for any payout on the policy are consistent with the SIS temporary incapacity conditions of release.

Income protection premiums are tax deductible when paid by an individual out of after-tax dollars, so the tax savings previously discussed in relation to term life and TPD insurance are not applicable here.

Any payout on an income protection policy is assessable income for the individual regardless of whether the premium was paid by the superannuation fund or the individual. An individual may still decide to organise their income protection policy through their superannuation fund because the fund has some buying power with insurers, which means that the fund can achieve lower premiums than the individual could.

Term life, TPD and income protection policies are all designed to protect against a loss of future income. As such, for some people it makes sense to consolidate these policies and hold them all within a superannuation environment.

Group underwriting

Insurance policies can be either individually underwritten or underwritten as a group. A group policy occurs when individuals who have a specific relationship with each other are collectively underwritten. For example, an employer may take out a group policy for employees, or a superannuation fund trustee might take out a group policy which covers members of the fund. Where a group policy is taken out by an employer, the employer is generally the owner of the policy. Similarly, where a group policy is taken out by a superannuation fund trustee, the trustee is generally the owner of the policy. Group policies are available for term life, TPD and income protection. Many large superannuation funds provide a base level of group term life and TPD cover.

In **underwriting** a group policy, the insurer calculates the group's characteristics and sets premiums accordingly. Group insurance does not take into account the risk associated with particular individuals and, as such, it is a useful means by which individuals with particular health risks can achieve cover at a reasonable price. However, this means that group insurance involves some cross-subsidy from healthy to less healthy individuals. The insurer attempts to manage this risk by insisting on the following.

- *A minimum rate of acceptance.* If only 10% of new members accept the group insurance, it is likely these would be 'unhealthy' people (attempting to take advantage of the reasonable price despite their individual health risks). This is often referred to as **adverse selection against the fund**. To avoid this adverse selection the underwriter might insist, for example, that at least 75% of new members accept the insurance.
- *Acceptance within a set time.* New members have a limited period of time to accept the insurance. If no time limit was specified, individuals may wait until they are unhealthy before joining the fund.
- *The amount of insurance is fixed.* If the amount of insurance was not fixed, unhealthy members could significantly increase their level of insurance and thereby make an adverse selection against the fund. Some superannuation funds allow individuals to buy additional units of insurance, but the number of additional units is usually limited. If an individual wishes to increase their insurance beyond this level, it would need to be done on an individually underwritten basis.

If a policy for an employer-sponsored group pays a benefit, the benefit is paid to the employer who in turn will pass this benefit on to the employee. The employee will receive the benefit in the form of an employment termination payment. If a policy for a superannuation fund trustee-sponsored group pays a benefit, the benefit is paid to the superannuation fund. The release of the benefit to members and the taxation treatment of the benefit are as previously discussed under the section on arranging insurance through a superannuation fund.

If an individual leaves a superannuation fund, they may not be able to transfer their insurance. This means they would need to take out new cover which might be assessed at their current age and health condition. This is an important consideration for anyone considering exercising their right of choice to move to a new superannuation fund. The promise of lower management fees in a new fund could be more than offset by a higher cost of insurance.

7.4 House and contents risk management

LEARNING OBJECTIVE 7.4 Identify and evaluate property risks in relation to house and contents.

This section discusses the identification and evaluation of house and contents risks, the control measures for house and contents risks and the financing of house and contents risks.

Identification of house and contents risks

A range of perils can cause damage to these assets, such as fire, storm, water damage, burglary, impact by vehicles and earthquake. Items of a more fragile nature are subject to breakage.

Evaluation of house and contents risks

In most cases, the value of an item can be easily ascertained. With a house, the value relates only to the building, and does not include the land, since the land will not normally suffer damage. The question to be asked is what amount will be needed to meet any loss. In the event of a total loss, the building will need to be replaced, so a sum sufficient to rebuild the property will be needed. This may well be greater than the market value of the building. As a building gets older its value will diminish, but maintenance and extensions can change this. The value of the land is what principally keeps property prices increasing. With house contents, the same will apply. A 5-year-old washing machine will have a lower value than a new one. In the event of a loss, there needs to be sufficient funds to purchase a new one.

Control measures for house and contents risks

Measures can be taken to minimise the damage that can occur, such as the use of smoke detectors which gain attention and facilitate summons of help to put out a fire. Burglar alarms, deadlocks and other fixed protection on the house reduce the risk of burglary. An important point to bear in mind is that, by making a house more difficult for a burglar to gain entry, the more likely it is that the burglar will move on to another property that is easier to gain access to.

Financing measures for house and contents risks

Control measures will not stop all losses occurring so there is the need to provide financing should a loss occur. This is generally achieved by insurance. Some amount of retention can be undertaken by using an excess. Care needs to be taken in arriving at a sum insured so that in the event of a major loss the sum insured is sufficient to replace the property that has been damaged or destroyed.

Two types of policies are available in the marketplace. The more common one is a replacement value policy (often referred to as a new for old policy). In the event of a loss, this cover provides new items to replace those lost or destroyed, even though the items lost may be several years old. The same also applies to the house — the policy will provide a new house in the event of a loss. The other type of policy is an indemnity value policy. This cover, which was the original type of cover, pays only the value of the property at the time of the loss — depreciation is taken into account.

In arriving at a sum insured under the replacement value cover, the property covered by the policy needs to be included at its replacement value price. In the case of contents insurance, this will include all the contents of the client's house. It is necessary to do a detailed calculation to arrive at an adequate sum insured. The result invariably surprises. Keep in mind that, when calculating replacement value, you are using current prices even though the original purchase price may have been somewhat lower and the item is now several years old. Contents that were purchased some years ago for $50 000 may well have a replacement value today of $100 000. There is no shortcut to the calculation — it is necessary to go through the house room by room and calculate the total value. Some insurers have guides that list items commonly found in different rooms to help you calculate the total amount.

A builder will be able to give an indication of the replacement cost of a building. Working on a standard figure per square may not be accurate as it does not take into account the quality of the fittings and the finish to the house. When considering policies, you must be aware that some policies incorporate a **co-insurance clause** (or average clause). The purpose of this clause is to penalise policy-holders if they fail to insure for the full value of the property. The use by insurers of this clause is diminishing — many are electing not to include it in their policies. Where it is used, the effect of this clause is to reduce the amount of the loss in proportion to the amount of **underinsurance**. The calculation recognises the difficulty in arriving at an accurate sum insured, so the calculation is made on only 80% of the full value.

The application of the clause is shown in the case where a house, the full value of which is $300 000, is insured for only $160 000, but the partial damage amounts to $150 000. The calculation is as follows.

$$\frac{\$160\,000}{80\% \times \$300\,000} \times \$150\,000 = \$100\,000$$

The insurance company would cover only $100 000 of the $150 000 loss, leaving the owners of the house with an amount of $50 000 to cover from their own resources.

Keep in mind that many insurers do not use this clause so check the policy before taking it out.

The importance of insurance and using an adequate sum insured must be stressed. Following major bushfires and widespread storm damage, the fact invariably emerges that many people have no insurance or are underinsured by as much as 50%. Particularly with bushfires, the outcome may be a total loss, so the owners are looking at a considerable shortfall in the policy payout. In the 2009 Victorian Black Saturday bushfires, tragically 173 people lost their lives and 2029 homes were destroyed. It has been estimated that 25% of the homes were uninsured. Of those homes that were insured, 80% were underinsured.

Domestic policies are usually offered in a package which includes house, contents and liability insurance.

House and contents insurance

There are broadly three types of policies used in the area of house and contents insurance. A brief description of each follows.

- A policy that covers all risks of loss or damage. Its cover is very broad and the premium is more expensive.
- A policy with **listed perils** to be covered. The following are included in most covers:
  - fire
  - explosion
  - lightning or thunderbolt
  - earthquake
  - theft
  - vandalism
  - water or other liquid
  - falling trees, branches or aerials
  - damage by animals
  - riot
  - storm, rain or flash flood
  - glass breakage.
- A policy that provides a cover for all risks of loss or damage in relation to valuables only. This cover is taken in conjunction with the listed perils policy where a broader cover is required for property at and away from the premises.

  The main policy exclusions include:
- damage when property has been left unoccupied for more than 60 days
- where the loss or damage is deliberately caused with intent to defraud
- damage caused by structural defects and faulty workmanship in the construction of the building or lack of maintenance to the building
- damage to property caused by tree lopping or the actions of trees, plants or their roots
- accidental damage to TV screens, ceramic stove tops, glass in picture frames, radios and clocks.

House cover

The cover on the house is usually for replacement value, and is often referred to as new for old cover. There are some variations of this in the marketplace. The original type of cover was an indemnity value policy which provided cover for market value. In other words, depreciation was taken into account. The market value would, in most cases, be lower than the cost to rebuild the house. Since the point of replacement value cover is to provide the insured person with sufficient funds to rebuild the house, the market value or indemnity value policy would not achieve this.

Contents cover

Cover is normally provided on a replacement value basis (new for old). In addition to cover against the listed perils, the policy may also provide for temporary accommodation, where the insured premises are uninhabitable due to an insured peril. As well, cover is often provided for credit card fraud, food spoilage and burning out of electric motors.

Liability insurance

Public liability covers liability arising out of the ownership or occupation of the property and is usually for a fairly large amount, for example $10 million. Bear in mind that awards for bodily injury can run into several million dollars. One not unusual case concerned a tenant left paraplegic after he fell from an upper floor balcony of a block of flats where the external lighting was not working. The damages were assessed at $4 million and legal costs were around $600 000. Suddenly $10 million doesn't seem such a large amount after all.

7.5 Motor vehicle risk management

LEARNING OBJECTIVE 7.5 Identify and evaluate property risks in relation to motor vehicles.

This section discusses the identification, and evaluation of, and control measures and financing for motor vehicle risks.

Identification and evaluation of motor vehicle risks

There are two types of motor vehicle risks — damage to the vehicle itself and loss or damage to third parties or their property. The former is limited to the amount of the repairs and will probably not exceed the value of the vehicle. The latter can run into millions of dollars; serious bodily injury to a third party could result in very large losses if legal liability is established.

Control measures and financing for motor vehicle risks

Control measures involve fitting the vehicle with a car alarm and undertaking advanced driving courses to improve vehicle handling skills. Financing measures are mainly through the use of insurance policies. Retention would be considered in relation to small losses only; this can be achieved by taking an excess on the motor policy.

Types of motor vehicle insurance policies

There are four main types of motor vehicle insurance policies. Compulsory third party (CTP) insurance, as its name implies is compulsory by law. Comprehensive motor insurance (CMI), fire, theft and third-party property damage insurance (FTTPPD) and third-party property only (TPPO) insurance are not compulsory.

It is necessary to apply to an insurer for cover, with the insurer deciding acceptance in each case and advising the terms and conditions. Each of these policies is briefly described in the following sections.

Compulsory third party (CTP) insurance

This policy is compulsory by law and is effected, usually, at the same time as the vehicle's registration. The policy provides for the legal liability of the driver arising out of the use of the vehicle. The nature of the legal liability varies from state to state. In some states, the scheme is a 'no fault' one. This means that it is not necessary to prove fault on the part of the driver. It is necessary to show only that the injury arose out of the use of the vehicle. In other states, the scheme is fault-based or partially fault-based.

Regardless of the type of scheme, the compensation paid is by way of a weekly benefit. The injured party's medical and hospital expenses are met as well. Where compensation is sought for permanent impairment, the schemes will provide compensation only for serious permanent injury, which is defined by each state Act, and the amount payable is limited.

Comprehensive motor insurance (CMI)

This is the broadest of the policies and has two main sections.

1. *Damage to the vehicle itself.* This section provides cover for damage to the vehicle, whether for repairs or if the vehicle is a total loss. Under a motor policy, a total loss applies when the cost of repairs exceeds the value of the vehicle. As the vehicle gets older and its value reduces, a situation could arise where the vehicle is quite repairable but the cost of the repairs exceeds the value of the vehicle. The insurer's liability, however, is limited to the vehicle's value therefore the sum insured on a motor policy is usually expressed as market value. The insurer uses the value of the vehicle in the market at the time of the loss. It is possible, however, to have an **agreed value cover**. This is used in a situation where the insured feels that the condition of the vehicle is such that its value is greater than that of similar vehicles in the market. In such a case, the insured and insurer agree on the value of the vehicle.

   Common exclusions in this section of the policy include:
   - contents of the vehicle other than standard tools and accessories
   - claims for loss of use or any consequential losses
   - wear and tear and mechanical or electrical breakdown.

2. *Third-party liability.* This section provides cover for the insured or the driver (driving with the insured's consent) for their legal liability in relation to property damage as a result of an accident arising out of the use of the vehicle. In addition this section pays, legal costs incurred in defending the action. The amount of cover provided is large — $50 million is not unusual.

The following provisions are the main ones that apply to both sections of the policy.

- The driver must be licensed.
- The blood-alcohol level of the driver must not exceed the limit permitted by law.
- The driver must have the insured's consent to drive the vehicle. (If not, it would be theft, which is still covered, but the insurer could bring an action against the driver for the cost of the claim.)
- The vehicle must not carry more passengers than is permitted by law (the number is specified in the vehicle registration).
- The policy is subject to an excess. This is the initial amount of any loss that must be borne by the insured. There is a basic excess to which an age and/or new driver excess amount may be added.

Fire, theft and third-party property damage insurance (FTTPPD)

This cover contains the two sections of the comprehensive policy but the own damage section cover is limited to fire and theft of the owner's vehicle. This policy is used for an older vehicle where the value is lower. The premium is cheaper than the comprehensive cover.

Third-party property cover only (TPPO)

This policy provides cover for third-party property damage only. It also is used for older vehicles.

Uninsured motorists extension cover can also be included in either the FTTPPD or TPPO covers. It provides cover when the insured's vehicle is damaged as the result of an accident where the driver of the other vehicle is uninsured. If the insured is not at fault, and provided the name and address of the other driver are supplied to the insurer, the damage to the insured's vehicle is covered up to a specified amount. This is usually around $3000.

7.6 Other insurances

LEARNING OBJECTIVE 7.6 Identify and evaluate personal and property risks with respect to sickness and accident, consumer credit and travel insurance.

A range of other non-business general insurances are available including sickness and accident insurance, consumer credit insurance and travel insurance. Each of these insurances is discussed briefly below.

Sickness and accident insurance

This cover is a restricted form of an income protection policy provided by life insurers. The policy provides cover for both capital and weekly benefits. Capital benefits provide cover for death or total disablement as a result of an accident. The weekly benefits are provided in the event of temporary disablement as a result of accident or illness. In the case of illness, the incapacity must be of more than 7 days duration.

The main difference between this policy and an income protection policy is that the sickness and accident policy defines an accident as being of violent, accidental, external and visible means. The income protection policy does not define 'accident' and is therefore much wider in the events it provides cover for. The sickness and accident policy usually has a maximum benefit period of 2 years for sickness. Another important difference relates to the cancellation provision. A sickness and accident policy contains a cancellation clause and must be renewed each year. The insurer can refuse renewal. Income protection policies cannot be cancelled by the insurer.

The main exclusions are injuries from war, nuclear weapons or radiation, deliberate self-injury, conditions sustained while under the influence of alcohol or drugs, professional sporting activities, and flying other than as a passenger in a licensed plane.

Consumer credit insurance

This is a sickness and accident cover designed for a specific purpose. It provides protection for those who have entered into any type of consumer finance contract where they are required to make regular payments. The policy includes an unemployment benefit also.

The policy provides for the payment of the periodic instalment if the insured person is incapacitated by way of accident, sickness or unemployment. In the event of death, the policy will pay out the contract.

The main exclusions are:

- a deliberately self-inflicted injury
- drug or alcohol addiction
- the insured becoming voluntarily unemployed or unemployment resulting from a contract expiring.

Travel insurance

Travel insurance policies are a collection of different covers in the one policy, including the following.

- *Luggage and personal effects*. This provides cover for loss or damage to the traveller's luggage and personal effects. The policy usually excludes damage to the baggage (not contents), including chipping, denting, and mechanical or electrical breakdown. The policy also generally excludes the loss of currency, travellers cheques and similar forms of payment. Lost or stolen items must be reported to the police within 24 hours before a claim can be made.
- *Medical expenses*. This cover includes medical expenses incurred on a trip, including hospital, medical, surgical and associated treatment provided by a qualified practitioner, as well as travel and accommodation expenses incurred as a result of illness or injury. Cover is also provided for the non-refundable section of the accommodation and travel costs in the event of the cancellation of the trip owing to the death or disablement. This includes the death or disablement of the insured or an accompanying traveller, the death in Australia of a specified person or the collapse of the tour operator.
- *Personal liability*. Included is a personal liability policy that provides cover for any negligent act involving bodily injury or property damage. The policy excludes damage to property in the insured's custody or control, the use of a motor vehicle, contractual liability and liability arising from AIDS.

7.7 Liability risk management

LEARNING OBJECTIVE 7.7 Identify and evaluate liability risks.

There are three broad areas from which a legal liability can arise.

- *Common law*. The most common area in which liability can be incurred here is due to negligence, for example, where a financial adviser was negligent in giving advice.
- *Statute law*. This refers to liability arising under an Act of Parliament. For example, liability in relation to an injury resulting from a faulty product may exist under the *Competition and Consumer Act 2010*.
- *Contract*. People can make themselves liable beyond the areas covered by common law or statute law by agreeing under a contract to be liable for any loss or damage.

This section discusses the identification and evaluation of, and the control measures and financing for liability risks.

Identification and evaluation of liability risks

Liability at the personal level is increasing. People sustaining injury or suffering damage to property are more prepared to pursue a legal action. This is in part encouraged by the legal fraternity and firms that provide representation on a 'no win no fee' basis. A significant rise in the number of negligence actions has resulted in the liability crisis of recent years and large premium increases for liability insurance. The importance of having adequate liability insurance is now evident.

Control measures and financing for liability risks

With liability risks, an effective control measure is simply taking steps to minimise the chance of loss in relation to potential loss situations that have been identified. For example, in a financial planner's office, the use of a checklist helps ensure that nothing has been overlooked in gathering information in order to provide advice to a client. An area overlooked can result in incorrect advice and possible legal action. Because of the amounts that can be involved, insurance is the best means of handling liability risks. Liability losses do not occur often, but when they do the amounts involved are rarely small. To this end, retention is not usually appropriate.

Regulations of the Corporations Act were amended in 2007 with respect to professional indemnity (PI) insurance. Holders of an Australian Financial Services Licence (AFSL) must have adequate professional indemnity insurance. ASIC Regulatory Guide RG 126 *Compensation and insurance arrangements for AFS licensees* provides guidance on the minimum requirements for PI insurance cover as follows.

> Where a financial services licensee has revenue from retail clients of less than $2 million they should have PI cover of at least $2 million which includes the ability to meet an individual claim of up to $2 million. Where a financial services licensee has revenue from retail clients of more than $2 million they should have PI cover at least equal to their expected revenue from financial services which includes the ability to meet an individual claim of up to $2 million.

PI insurance is a form of business insurance to assist a business in meeting any claims which are made against it. The primary purpose of PI insurance is not to act as a form of consumer compensation scheme. In some cases a consumer may make a valid claim against a business; however, the claim is not covered by the terms of the PI insurance in which case the business will need to fund the compensation from their own resources. In some cases the amount paid out by the PI insurer may be less than the amount the business has to pay in settlement with the consumer, in which case the business will need to fund the difference. This problem is further compounded when the business has insufficient capital to fund the payment and in extreme cases where the business itself has collapsed. The collapse of high profile financial advisory firms such as Storm Financial, Opes Prime and Westpoint highlighted the need for advisers to have adequate PI insurance and also raised the issue over whether there should be a national compensation arrangement for consumers of financial services.

In 2010, the federal government commissioned a review of compensation arrangements for consumers of financial services and in 2011, as part of the Future of Financial Advice (FOFA) reform process, published that review. The review recognised the difficulty of trying to transform what is essentially a PI insurance service to business into an insurance compensation scheme for consumers. The review suggested a number of means by which consumers could be better protected within the current PI framework, including strengthening the capital adequacy of financial advisers so that they have the financial capacity to meet claims as they fall due. With subsequent federal elections, changes in government and the devastating effects of Storm, Opes Prime and Westpoint receding from memory, the impetus to create an insurance compensation scheme for consumers of financial services has waned. There is, however, still considerable uncertainty associated with the provision of financial advice pursuant to the FOFA and other reforms and for insurers uncertainty is generally reflected in higher premiums.

It is important to remember that PI insurance does not, in any circumstances, cover the adverse consequences for an investor of a significant downturn in investment markets.

7.8 Implementation and review

LEARNING OBJECTIVE 7.8 Explain the need for an ongoing review process for insurance and risk.

With risks identified, control and financing measures are developed and implemented to enable the systematic management of the identified risks.

The next step, a very important one, is the ongoing review of the program. The changes people experience bring with them a need to change the financial plan. A financial planner needs to systematically revise a client's financial plan to take into account the effects of any changes in circumstances. A periodic review should be undertaken, and it is important to review the pure risk aspects of the plan at the same time. A common premium instalment date on the insurance cover is an ideal time to undertake the review.

SUMMARY

It is worth reflecting on the case study of Joshua and Phoebe that we introduced at the start of this chapter. Risk management is a systematic approach to the identification and management of risks faced. Joshua and Phoebe need to identify and quantify the risks they face including personal and property risks. Having identified the risks they need to plan how to control and manage those risks. Even so, some risk remains and it needs to be financed or transferred. Where a risk is relatively small it might be financed from the savings of Joshua and Phoebe; however, many risks will be too expensive to finance through personal savings and will need to be transferred via insurance. The death of Joshua or Phoebe would seriously compromise the capacity of the remaining partner to meet their mortgage commitments. However, insurance comes at a cost and a decision must be made over whether the cost is affordable and if it represents a fair trade for the risk being exchanged.

Joshua and Phoebe face a wide range of insurable risks. In this chapter we have reviewed the need for personal risk, property, motor vehicle and liability insurance policies as well as the main characteristics of these policies. To the extent that Joshua and Phoebe manage their risk exposure through insurance they will need to deal with insurers by acting with the utmost good faith. To do otherwise might result in the insurer not paying the claim and therefore leaving Joshua and Phoebe still exposed to risk.

Joshua and Phoebe should also consider arranging some or all of their personal insurance requirements through their respective superannuation funds in order to pay their premiums in the most tax-effective manner.

Having developed a risk management plan, the plan must be implemented and regularly reviewed. At the time that Joshua and Phoebe pay their annual insurance premiums they should review the adequacy of their insurance coverage in light of any changes in their circumstances.

We have discussed in this chapter some of the ways that risk can be controlled and financed without the use of insurance. Nonetheless insurance remains the principal means of providing for the potential of serious losses.

KEY TERMS

adverse selection against the fund Where individuals are able to make choices which alter the risk profile of a fund and which can potentially limit the fund's ability to meet its commitments and/or unfairly shift obligations between members.

agent Insurer's representative who directly organises insurance for clients.

agreed value cover Generally applies to motor vehicle insurance where the insured believes their vehicle is worth more than market value and therefore they reach an agreement with the insurer to insure the vehicle at a higher value with a commensurately higher premium.

beneficiary A person nominated to receive a payout from an insurance policy, a superannuation fund or the assets of an estate.

broker Insured's representative who determines the client's insurance needs.

co-insurance clause A clause in an insurance contract which reduces the claimable loss in proportion to the amount of underinsurance.

condition of release Criteria that, if satisfied, enables an individual to withdraw their money from superannuation.

consumer price index (CPI) An index used to measure inflation; that is, the general increase in prices.

creditor A person to whom money is owed.

dependant A person who relies on another, financially, emotionally or in some other capacity.

estate The deceased's assets which have not been directly passed to beneficiaries.

excess The amount of insurance risk which is retained by the individual rather than transferred through insurance.

fraudulent misrepresentation An inaccurate statement made knowingly believing it to be untrue, or an inaccurate statement made recklessly.

future insurability A clause in an insurance contract which provides the insured with the opportunity to purchase more cover at future nominated dates without providing further evidence of health status.

innocent misrepresentation An inaccurate statement made without fraudulent intent.

intermediaries Agents and brokers who arrange insurances for a client.

listed perils An insurance contract which lists the events (perils) covered. Therefore, events not listed are not covered.

material fact A fact that would influence a reasonable and prudent insurer in accepting a risk or in setting a premium given those particular facts.

premium The cost of taking out insurance.

preservation age The minimum age at which funds can be withdrawn from superannuation.

pure risk Where there is chance of loss or no loss; for example, your house might burn down this year or it might not.

risk management A branch of management that provides a systematic approach to the management of pure risk.

salary sacrifice Where an employee asks their employer to take some of their income and redirect this to pay for a benefit on behalf of the employee; the most commonly salary sacrificed benefit is superannuation.

speculative risk Where there is a chance of a loss or gain, for example, in gambling or investing.

underinsurance Where the payout from an insurance policy as a result of an event is not able to restore the individual to the financial position they were in prior to the event.

underwriting The process by which the insurer assesses the risk associated with an individual or a group of individuals and provides insurance coverage at a price commensurate with the risk.

utmost good faith Under the *Insurance Contract Act 1984* both parties to an insurance contract must display the highest degree of honesty.

PROFESSIONAL APPLICATION QUESTIONS

7.1 Explain if premature death is a pure risk or a speculative risk.

7.2 The Potters, Jack and Emily, ages 41 and 43 respectively, have 2 children aged 10 and 14. Jack is a high school teacher and Emily runs a bookkeeping service from home. Emily's business has been growing quite steadily and currently produces an annual income of $42 000. The Potters own their house, which is valued at $950 000. Their mortgage is $650 000. They have 2 cars, a current model Prado and a 7-year-old Honda. Identify and discuss the various risks to which the Potters are exposed.

7.3 What traumas are usually included in a basic trauma cover? What issues should clients be aware of when considering taking out trauma insurance?

7.4 What is risk pooling? How can insurers reduce the size of the pool in order to reduce the average level of risk within the pool? Is there any limit to how small the pool can be?

7.5 Who are the main regulators in the insurance industry and what are their individual responsibilities?

7.6 Justine has $80 000 of life insurance provided through her superannuation fund. She is thinking of applying for additional coverage but is worried about filling in an application form and/or having to attend a medical examination. Several months ago, Justine was diagnosed with diabetes and she has since been very careful with her diet. She is quite confident that her health has improved as a result although she has not been back to a doctor to confirm this. Given her improved health, Justine is considering not mentioning the diabetes in any application, but she is unsure of the consequences of failing to declare her medical history correctly. Advise Justine.

7.7 Describe how the three types of insurers differ in the market.

7.8 Your client, Quyen, is 25 years old, single and a non-smoker. She has just received a quote from an insurance company for $1 million in term life insurance. The annual premium would be $1345. In your opinion, is it worth it?

7.9 Which policy is likely to attract the higher premium: a TPD 'own' occupation insurance or a TPD 'any' occupation insurance?

7.10 Leonie and Mark are both aged 32 years, both earn the same level of income ($75 000) and both work in the same occupation. Leonie is upset to learn that her quote for income protection insurance is more expensive than Mark's. The quotes the couple received were as follows. For a benefit of $50 000 p.a. (for each of Leonie and Mark), Leonie's quote was $634.80 for a 30-day delay before the insurance would be paid and $429.60 for a 60-day delay. Mark's was $368.40 for a 30-day delay and $203.40 for a 60-day delay. Provide reasons why Leonie's quote for income protection insurance is more expensive than Mark's.

7.11 Jemima has an annual income of $69 000. She has savings in a bank account of $1200 and has accumulated 18 days of unused sick leave. What amount would you recommend Jemima take as a monthly benefit under an income protection policy and what deferment period might he select before insurance cover would be provided? Give reasons for your answer.

7.12 Rick has recently saved enough money to purchase a 2010 hatchback for $4500 and he would like to minimise the cost of car insurance. Rick is considering between compulsory third party insurance and third-party property cover only. Advise Rick how these two types of insurance differ. Which car insurance cover you would recommend for him and why?

PROFESSIONAL APPLICATION EXERCISES

★ BASIC | ★★ MODERATE | ★★★ CHALLENGING

7.13 Term life insurance — multiple approach ★

Harry earns $92 000 per annum and has $67 000 in superannuation. He does not currently have any life insurance. Using the multiple approach, calculate Harry's sum insured based on an investment rate of 4%.

7.14 Co-insurance ★

The market value of the Nguyen's home and contents is $850 000. However, Mr Nguyen insured the home and contents for only $600 000. If fire caused $300 000 damage, what amount is the insurance company liable to pay if the policy included a co-insurance clause and the company required a market value of 80%?

7.15 Income protection insurance — agreed value versus indemnity policy ★

Danni is earning $8000 per month and takes out a fixed benefit (agreed value) income protection policy for 60% of her monthly income. Six months after commencing the policy her income falls to $6000 per month. After several months of earning $6000 per month she falls ill and is unable to work.

(a) What will be the monthly benefit under the policy?

(b) If Danni had an indemnity policy rather than a fixed benefit policy what would be the monthly benefit under the policy?

7.16 Term life insurance premiums ★★

KGB Insurance offer term life insurance under the following terms.

• guaranteed renewal
• cover to age 75
• sum insured remains constant.

The indicative monthly premiums for $1 million coverage are as follows.

Age	21 to 34	35 to 39	40 to 44	45 to 49	50 to 54
Non-smoker	$101	$112	$148	$223	$387
Smoker	$161	$225	$285	$485	$808

(a) Why do the premiums increase as the age of the insured increases?

(b) In percentage terms, approximately how much more expensive is term life insurance for a smoker than a non-smoker?

(c) If the renewal of the policy was at the discretion of the insurer, would you expect the premiums to be higher or lower? Why?

(d) If the sum insured was indexed to CPI, would you expect the premiums to be higher or lower? Why?

(e) If the term of the insurance was to age 65 rather than age 75, would you expect the premiums to be higher or lower? Why?

(f) Ashleigh and her husband are both 45, non-smokers and considering term life insurance. Ashleigh believes she is being discriminated against by being asked to pay the same premium as her husband. Why does she hold this view? Do you agree?

7.17 Paying term life insurance through superannuation ★★

(a) If a term life insurance premium is $2500 and the client decides to pay their premium out of after-tax dollars, how much pre-tax income will an individual need if their marginal tax rate is:

(i) 0%?

(ii) 19.0%?

(iii) 32.5%?

(iv) 37.0%?

(v) 45.0%?

(b) If a term life insurance premium is $2500, how much pre-tax income will an individual need if they decide to salary sacrifice their premium into superannuation?

(c) Besides the cost differential between (a) and (b), what are the advantages/disadvantages of paying term life insurance premiums through a superannuation fund versus paying for them out of after-tax dollars?

7.18 Stepped versus level premium ★★

GAI Insurance are offering the following insurance premiums to a 30-year-old male non-smoker with a sum insured of $1 000 000.

Age	Stepped $	Level $
30	740	1200
31	750	1200
32	761	1200
33	773	1200
34	787	1200
35	803	1200
36	821	1200
37	842	1200
38	866	1200
39	894	1200
40	926	1200
50	2150	1200
55	4400	1200

(a) Why do stepped insurance premiums differ from level insurance premiums?

(b) Gavin is 37 years old and is unsure if he has a long-term need for life insurance. Should he take out a stepped or level premium policy?

(c) If Gavin was 52 years old, how would your advice change, if at all?

7.19 Health insurance ★★★

Longwei is 33 years old and single. He is looking to take out some health insurance coverage. Longwei earns $112 000 per year and has not had health insurance coverage in the past. He has entered his personal details and preferences into the iselect.com.au website and has been given a quote of $178 per month before any loadings or rebates are applied.

(a) Given that Longwei is over 30 years of age how will premium loading be applied?

(b) How much health rebate will Longwei be entitled to?

(c) What will be the net annual cost of the insurance after allowing for (a) and (b) above?

(d) If Longwei decides not to take out health insurance how much Medicare levy surcharge will he have to pay?

7.20 The multiple approach to determining the sum insured ★★★

Sylvia is married and has four teenage children. She has a detailed retirement plan in place. She is 43 years old and she hopes to retire 17 years from now when she is 60 by which time his superannuation should be sufficient to afford a comfortable life in retirement for herself and her partner. Sylvia is, however, concerned that she has insufficient life insurance and she would like to ensure that she has sufficient to cover any loss of earnings caused by her death during that 17-year period. She currently earns $150 000 per annum.

(a) Using a simple multiple approach, how much life insurance coverage will Sylvia need to cover her loss of earnings for the 17-year period?

(b) If Sylvia were to pass away in the first year and the amount calculated in (a) above was invested at 2% for 17 years, what would be the present value of this insurance payout?

(c) If Sylvia were to pass away in the first year and the amount calculated in (a) above was invested at 2% for 17 years and the inflation rate was 3%, what would be the present value of this insurance payout?

(d) If the rate at which funds are invested is greater (less) than the inflation rate, what implications does this have for the sum insured?

(e) Assuming that Sylvia does not pass away in the first year of insurance, what implications does this have for the sum insured (see figure 7.2)?

CASE STUDY

ESTABLISHING PERSONAL INSURANCE NEEDS

Eddie and Kaye Turner, aged 39 and 37 respectively, have 4 children aged 4, 6, 8 and 10. They own their home, which has a current market value of $500 000, and have a mortgage of $150 000. Eddie is a self-employed butcher who employs 3 staff. Eddie and Kaye are in partnership and share profits equally. Eddie's annual income is $80 000. Kaye works part-time helping in the butcher's shop and also part-time as a school's teacher aide; she also receives $15 000 as a salary from the school.

Both Eddie and Kaye contribute to superannuation funds. Eddie has an accumulation fund which currently has a balance of $250 000. Kaye joined her fund more recently and has a balance of $100 500. Eddie has effected a term life cover on his life for $200 000 with Kaye named as the beneficiary. Kaye does not have any term life insurance cover.

Eddie and Kaye have assets which are mainly in the butcher's shop, totalling $150 000. The Turners have a car each. Eddie's is a 2014 model which is leased and has $30 000 outstanding on it at present. Kaye has a 2009 van so that she can transport the children to school and various sporting clubs. Her van is valued at $10 000 and is fully paid for. Personal loans, credit cards and other outstanding debts amount to $20 000.

The family's monthly expenses amount to $8000. The Turners feel that all their children should receive a university education and expect them to be dependent until they turn 21 years of age. They expect to contribute a total of $200 000 to the cost of the children's university education. As each child ceases to be dependent, the monthly expenses will reduce by $1000 a month. Eddie's life expectancy is 82 and Kaye's is 86.

QUESTIONS

1 Calculate the amount of cover required to provide for the family's future needs in the event of:
  (a) Eddie's death
  (b) Kaye's death.

2 You have advised the Turners of the amount of insurance cover they need. They find it hard to believe that such a large amount is needed. They say that by insuring for a lower amount and investing the funds the required amount could be achieved. Explain to them the problem with this approach.

3 Discuss the need for the following covers for both Eddie and Kaye.
  (a) Total and permanent disability
  (b) Trauma
  (c) Income protection

4 When talking about income protection insurance, Eddie and Kaye ask if there is some way they could cover their business overheads against a time when the butcher's shop would have to close for a month or so as a result of some unknown health risk. Explain business overheads insurance and advise the amount of cover that should be taken.

5 When completing the personal health questionnaire Kaye indicates that she has had no history of breast cancer. However, 3 months after completion of the contract, Kaye has tests which confirm some minor breast cancer tumours. Discuss whether Kaye's term life insurance is still valid.

6 Outline insurances other than the personal risk covers discussed so far in this case study that Eddie and Kaye should have as part of their overall risk protection plan.

REFERENCES

ATO 2023a, 'Income thresholds and rates for the private health insurance rebate', Australian Government, 26 August, www.ato.gov.au/Individuals/Medicare-and-private-health-insurance/Private-health-insurance-rebate/Income-thresholds-and-rates-for-the-private-health-insurance-rebate/

ATO 2023b, 'Medicare levy surcharge', Australian Government, 26 August, www.ato.gov.au/Individuals/Medicare-and-private-health-insurance/Medicare-levy-surcharge/Medicare-levy-surcharge-income,-thresholds-and-rates/#Incomethresholdandrates20232324

Biti, L 2019, 'Chapter 7: Life and personal risk insurance' in CCH (ed.), *Australian master financial planning guide 2019/20*, 22nd edn, Wolters Kluwer.

Borys, S 2023, 'Australians skipping genetic screening tests out of fear it will affect life insurance coverage, 30 June, ABC News,www.abc.net.au/news/2023-06-30/australians-skipping-genetic-tests-being-used-by-life-insurers/102540960

Farrow-Smith, E & Harper, D 2017, 'Insurers move to clear up flood definition', 11 April, ABC News, www.abc.net.au/news/2017-04-11/flood-insurance-versus-storm-insurance/8434452.

Insurance News 2022, 'ASIC takes insurer to court over claims handling 'failure', 8 December, www.insurancenews.com.au/daily/asic-takes-insurer-to-court-over-claims-handling-failure

USEFUL WEBSITES

Australian and New Zealand Institute of Insurance and Finance, anziif.com

Australian Financial Complaints Authority, afca.org.au

Australian Prudential Regulation Authority, apra.gov.au

Australian Securities and Investments Commission, asic.gov.au

Financial Advice Association Australia, faaa.au

Insurance Council of Australia, insurancecouncil.com.au

National Insurance Brokers Association, niba.com.au

ACKNOWLEDGEMENTS

Extract: © Creative Commons

Boxes: © ABC

Box: © Insurance News

CHAPTER 8

Superannuation

LEARNING OBJECTIVES

After studying this chapter, you should be able to:

8.1 explain what superannuation is and why Australians need it

8.2 describe the *three pillars* policy of superannuation

8.3 outline the main legislative provisions that regulate superannuation

8.4 differentiate between accumulation accounts and defined benefit schemes and discuss the major providers of superannuation funds

8.5 outline the historical development of the Australian superannuation system

8.6 differentiate between concessional and non-concessional contributions to superannuation

8.7 discuss the main investment constraints that apply to superannuation

8.8 demonstrate how superannuation funds are taxed

8.9 understand how superannuation is divided in the case of a relationship breakdown

8.10 outline the various fees and charges which apply to superannuation

8.11 model how much a person might accumulate in superannuation.

Amanda is 45 years old, recently divorced and wants to buy a home for herself. She has been working as a university lecturer for the past 15 years. When she started work, her superannuation contributions were automatically directed to a defined benefits superannuation plan, whereby Amanda will receive a predetermined retirement benefit amount at age 65. Her superannuation fund recently wrote to her explaining that she needs to decide if she wants to swap from the defined benefit plan to an accumulation plan where she will be given a total balance amount and have to choose investments she would like to hold in superannuation. Once Amanda decides to swap to accumulation, the decision will be irreversible.

Amanda has asked her friends for advice about what she should do.

- Zane suggested Amanda stay in the defined benefit plan because there is zero risk; however, Amanda is not so sure about this.
- Khalidra suggested Amanda swap into the accumulation plan because she should be able to achieve much better investment returns given that the defined benefit plan has a fixed predetermined retirement benefit amount.
- Fred suggested that, regardless of whether she stays in the defined benefit plan or moves to the accumulation plan, Amanda should salary sacrifice as much as possible.
- Rosa strongly disagrees with Fred's suggestion to salary sacrifice. Rosa argues that a dollar in Amanda's pocket is more useful to her than a dollar locked away in superannuation, especially to purchase a house. Rosa goes on to explain that a property is more likely to increase her wealth in the longer term than salary sacrificing into superannuation.

Asking her friends for advice hasn't really helped much. Some of the issues that Amanda needs to consider include the following.

- What is Amanda's attitude to investment risk? Do defined benefit plans cater for a different risk appetite than accumulation plans?
- How have the superannuation rules changed in the past? How are they likely to change in the future? How will these likely changes impact on Amanda?
- How long will her money be locked away inside superannuation and is there any way she can release it if her circumstances change?
- What does salary sacrifice actually mean and why do people recommend it as a way of contributing to superannuation? How much can Amanda salary sacrifice over and above what her employer currently contributes to superannuation?
- How does superannuation fit into Amanda's overall financial plans? How will she prioritise current expenditure over deferred expenditure, that is, expenditure in retirement?
- How much will she need to accumulate in superannuation to fund her retirement and how does this compare with what she is likely to accumulate given her current circumstances?

The issues facing Amanda in deciding how to approach superannuation are examined throughout this chapter.

Introduction

In March 2023, there was more than $3.5 trillion invested in superannuation and therefore, just in financial terms alone, superannuation is of vital importance to Australians. We need to investigate what superannuation is and why it has become such a topic of interest in recent times (APRA 2023).

In this chapter we will focus primarily on superannuation from the individual's perspective (i.e. a superannuation fund member); however, it is impossible to do this without some overall understanding of the superannuation industry itself. Therefore, we need to examine the legislative environment in which superannuation operates.

Keeping up to date in a capricious superannuation environment is difficult; however, anticipating changes is made easier by understanding the factors that have led us to the superannuation environment as it is today. To do this, we need to review the themes that have historically threaded their way through the evolution of the superannuation environment.

Money and assets can enter the superannuation environment by being contributed or transferred into a superannuation fund. If money is contributed to superannuation it needs to be invested to generate earnings for the member. Superannuation is most commonly misunderstood as being its own separate asset class when in fact is just an investment structure, like a trust, that assets can be held within.

Contributions to superannuation and earnings from the investments inside superannuation are subject to tax. We will review the means by which funds are contributed, invested and taxed inside a superannuation environment.

This chapter concentrates on the accumulation phase of superannuation. The next chapter concentrates on the pension phase of superannuation where money is withdrawn from a superannuation environment as an income stream or lump sum amounts.

Figure 8.1 summarises the sequential development of material covered.

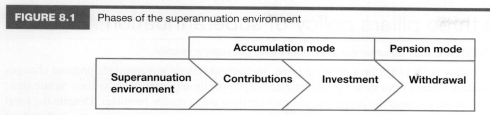

FIGURE 8.1 Phases of the superannuation environment

Figure 8.1 will be expanded at the end of each section of our discussion; for example, at the end of the discussion on the superannuation environment, a figure will briefly summarise that section. By moving between each of the expanded sections of figure 8.1 you will be able to see the bigger picture of superannuation and how the various components are linked.

8.1 What is superannuation?

LEARNING OBJECTIVE 8.1 Explain what superannuation is and why Australians need it.

Superannuation is a vehicle of saving and investing to accumulate and generate wealth to fund retirement, usually in the form of a retirement income stream. Throughout this chapter and the next we will focus primarily on Australia's superannuation system, which is the product of government legislation and is subject to government supervision through a variety of agencies. Retirement funding does not, however, have to be formalised via superannuation — many individuals make saving and investment decisions outside the superannuation environment as a way of building wealth for retirement. For example, an individual might invest in shares, managed funds or rental properties with the view of progressively selling these down or using the earnings to fund retirement in the future.

While the term superannuation is widely used in Australia and is synonymous with retirement planning, the word 'superannuation' is not common overseas. Other countries describe such funds as pension plans, pensions, provident funds and, in the US, citizens talk about their '401k plans' named after the section of the tax act that regulates the plans. Whatever it is called, the intent remains the same — a tax concessional environment designed to encourage people to save for their retirement.

Why the need for superannuation?

Australians are living longer and the baby boomers who were born in the years after World War II are now reaching retirement age. That is, Australia's population is getting older. In 2020, 16% of Australians were over the age of 65 (AIHW 2023).

The tax revenue collected from people in the workforce helps the federal government to meet its social security commitments, particularly its commitment to pay the government assistance payments and the age pension.

In 1974–75, there were 7.3 people in the workforce for each person aged over 65. The federal government's *2021 Intergenerational Report* predicts that, in 2054–55, there will be only 2.7 people in the workforce for each person aged over 65 (The Treasury 2021). The report is published every 5 years with the next edition due to be published July 2026 and will be accessible on the Treasury website www.treasury.gov.au. As a result, the government will not have the tax revenue base to afford its social security commitments unless changes are made. One key change required is to reduce the reliance on the age pension by implementing a number of policies to support that change. For example, the government has implemented concessional tax incentives to encourage individuals to invest more in their superannuation and increased the age pension age requirement from age 65 to 67.

The other key change would be to increase the number of people in the workforce in order to increase the tax revenue base. However, fertility rates continue to fall. However, Australia's total fertility rates have been under the replacement rate — the rate required for a generation to replace itself — since 1976 and continue to fall. The fertility rate in 2022 was 1.63.

Migration is also unlikely to significantly change the average age of the Australian population. Australia's migration policy immediately after World War II encouraged many young unskilled workers with families to migrate to Australia. Australia's migration policy now encourages skilled migrants who, on average, tend to be older. Family reunions as part of the migration policy, where older relatives from overseas join younger family members in Australia, also increase the average age of migrants. Moreover, many of the countries that Australia has traditionally taken migrants from are experiencing the same ageing population problem as Australia and are therefore resistant to losing their skilled worker base.

8.2 The three pillars policy of superannuation

LEARNING OBJECTIVE 8.2 Describe the *three pillars* policy of superannuation.

Superannuation policy will always be a political issue. Incumbent federal governments propose changes to the superannuation system prior to an upcoming election. Opposition parties, who by their nature must oppose the government, discount the proposals and provide their own counter promises. Despite the ideal of having stability in superannuation so that individuals can construct a retirement plan, the hallmark of superannuation in Australia has been the constant changes since it was introduced.

The key aspect of Australia's superannuation system, which does have bipartisan support, is the three pillars (or tiers) policy of superannuation.
- Tier 1 — a taxpayer funded social security pension (a safety net) that is means tested.
- Tier 2 — compulsory employer contributions to superannuation for employees.
- Tier 3 — tax incentives for voluntary contributions to superannuation.

The basic structure of Australia's three pillar system ensures clear direction and any proposal for change must still be based on the three pillars.

8.3 The legislative context for superannuation

LEARNING OBJECTIVE 8.3 Outline the main legislative provisions that regulate superannuation.

The federal government, through use of its section 51 constitutional powers to control taxation, pensions and corporations, has effectively gained legislative control of superannuation in Australia. The cornerstone of this legislative framework is the *Superannuation Industry (Supervision) Act 1993* (SIS Act).

For a superannuation fund to be able to claim the tax concessions associated with being a superannuation fund it must be a complying superannuation fund. To be a **complying superannuation fund**, the fund must:
- reside in Australia
- have made an irrevocable election to be regulated by the SIS Act
- meet the conditions for compliance as outlined in the SIS Act.

A superannuation fund is a form of trust and as such it is administered by **trustees**. Individuals can act as trustees and it is also possible to have a corporate trustee. The **fiduciary responsibilities** of trustees have been developed by the courts through common law principles over many years. Fiduciary means to act in good faith and to put the interests of others (members) ahead of your own. The SIS Act has been seen to largely **codify** fiduciary responsibilities of superannuation fund trustees, although some common law principles still remain. Trustees have a wide range of responsibilities and the role of trustee should not be undertaken lightly. The SIS Act contains a range of penalties for trustees who breach specific provisions of the Act.

As a form of trust, a superannuation fund is governed by its trust deed. The trust deed of a superannuation fund will generally incorporate the terms of the SIS Act and the Superannuation Industry (Supervision) Regulations (SISR). Many trust deeds also include a provision which automatically incorporates any changes to the SIS Act and SISR in order to avoid the expense and inconvenience of the trust deed having to be changed every time the legislation or the regulations change.

A trust deed can be more restrictive than the SIS Act and still be a complying superannuation fund; however, a trust deed cannot override the SIS Act provisions. If it does, the fund will be a non-complying superannuation fund. A complying superannuation fund enjoys a range of tax advantages which will be outlined later in this chapter. A non-complying fund has all its income taxed at the highest marginal tax rate.

The SIS Act is based on a number of underlying principles which include the following.
- The trustees remain responsible for all decisions of the fund. The trustees might decide to delegate some decision making and/or outsource some functions but the trustees are ultimately responsible for all decisions made.
- Wherever possible, members of superannuation funds should participate in decision-making processes via elected membership on trustee boards. The SIS Act is also very prescriptive about the communication required by the fund with members as a means of encouraging their active participation in the fund.

- All investment decisions must be directed towards funding retirement. Superannuation should not be simply a tax haven.
- Superannuation is a regulated and controlled investment environment; however, compliance with the SIS Act does not guarantee the performance or financial viability of the fund.

Reiterating the point above that superannuation is for the purpose of retirement funding, contributions and the earnings on those contributions are preserved inside the superannuation environment until a member satisfies a **condition of release**.

The most common conditions of release for access to superannuation benefits are for a member who:
- reaches age 65, regardless of their work status
- reaches age 60 and changes their employer
- reaches their preservation age (explained below) and permanently retires
- reaches their preservation age and continues to work, but is limited to accessing a retirement income stream rather than the total benefit
- dies (at any age) and their super benefit is paid to their beneficiaries/estate
- has a terminal illness (at any age) where the prognosis is less than 24 months of life
- is permanently incapacitated (at any age) with a diagnosis of being unlikely to ever work again.

The preservation age for individuals born before 1 July 1960 is 55; for individuals born after 30 June 1964, the preservation age is 60; for people born between 1960 and 1964 the preservation age progressively increases from 55 to 60.

There are other conditions of release that are not as common and these include:
- temporary incapacity (at any age), but access is limited to an income stream
- a temporary resident's permanent departure from Australia
- severe financial hardship, and access is limited to a lump sum of $10 000
- compassionate grounds, and access is limited to paying some personal expenses
- the first home super saver scheme (FHSS), and access is limited to $50 000.

In this last list of extended conditions of release there are two particular examples where the government has deviated from the three pillar policy mentioned earlier in this chapter.

In the unprecedented circumstances of early 2020, the government's responses to COVID-19 had a significant impact on the economy, which led the government to announce a temporary measure similar to the severe financial hardship condition of release. This allowed a member to access $10 000 of their superannuation in 2019–20 and $10 000 in 2020–21 financial years. The financial hardship eligibility required that the member was unemployed, or receiving JobSeeker allowance, or had their working hours reduced by 20% or more. Generally, financial hardship provisions are more challenging, requiring the member to receive government assistance payments for 26 consecutive weeks and being unable to pay immediate family living expenses.

Second, the first home super saver (FHSS) scheme was introduced from 1 July 2017 as a measure to assist first home buyers with a contribution to their deposit for purchasing a home in Australia. Individuals can apply to have a maximum of $15 000 of voluntary contributions from any one financial year to be released under the scheme. FHSS is limited to a total of $50 000 for each member across all years. This would allow a couple who plan on purchasing their first home to access $100 000 combined. It should be noted that the government restricts access to voluntary contributions only, and not the compulsory superannuation contributions made by employers on behalf of members. Also, since the withdrawal is not related to retirement, the lump sum FHSS scheme payment may be taxed at the member's marginal tax rate with a tax offset of 30%, and the application must be made to the ATO in the first instance, who will instruct the superannuation fund to release the benefit or not. For more information on the FHSS you can refer the ATO website and search for 'first home super saver scheme'.

Four bodies are primarily charged with the regulation and control of the superannuation industry.

1. The Australian Prudential Regulation Authority (APRA) is the prudential regulator for deposit-taking institutions, insurance and superannuation. APRA is the prudential regulator for all superannuation funds other than self-managed superannuation funds (SMSFs). The term **prudential** generally means the monitoring of risk-taking behaviour. In this context, a very important part of APRA's role is to monitor the risk-taking behaviour of individual superannuation funds.

   All trustees of APRA-supervised superannuation funds must hold a Registrable Superannuation Entities (RSE) licence. The formulation of, and adherence to, a risk-management strategy is an important part of the licensing system.

2. The Australian Securities and Investments Commission (ASIC) regulates market conduct and disclosure. It is part of ASIC's role to ensure consumers are protected and that markets, including the market for superannuation funds, are conducted in a fair, orderly and transparent manner.

Superannuation funds are often called upon to give information to members. Where information stops and advice starts is often a difficult line to draw. A superannuation fund must decide whether to refer members to third parties for advice or to provide the advice themselves. If a superannuation fund provides financial advice, it needs to be licensed to do so. Most large superannuation funds hold their own Australian Financial Services Licence (AFSL), which is issued by ASIC.

3. The Australian Taxation Office (ATO) performs a variety of roles, which include:
   - acting as the regulator of SMSFs
   - collecting tax from superannuation funds and conducting audits to ensure that assessable income is properly disclosed
   - administering the tax concessions available to individuals
   - auditing employers to ensure that they meet their requirements under the *Superannuation Guarantee (Administration) Act 1992* (SGAA) (discussed later in this chapter)
   - collaborating with the state collectors of unclaimed superannuation funds.

4. The Australian Financial Complaints Authority (AFCA), previously the Superannuation Complaints Tribunal, deals with complaints by members against the decisions of trustees. Section 101 of the SIS Act requires that a complying superannuation fund has an established complaints resolution process. An individual member is obliged to use this process first. If unsuccessful, they have access to AFCA. In determining a case, AFCA effectively substitutes itself for the trustee and, in exercising the discretion of the trustee, they may:
   - agree with the original decision of the trustee
   - refer the matter back to the trustee for further consideration based on advice from the tribunal
   - modify the decision of the trustee
   - cancel the decision of the trustee and substitute their own decision.

While we have primarily concentrated on the impact of the SIS Act and the SISR on superannuation, many other legislative provisions impact on superannuation. Superannuation trustees need to be particularly mindful of discrimination, privacy and family law legislation. However, changes to the superannuation environment can be driven by many factors. For instance, the *Same-Sex Relationships (Equal treatment in Commonwealth laws–Superannuation) Act 2008* had a significant impact on superannuation funds. Trustees need to be vigilant to ensure that they are up to date with the legislative environment within which superannuation sits.

8.4 Types of superannuation funds and who provides them

LEARNING OBJECTIVE 8.4 Differentiate between accumulation accounts and defined benefit schemes and discuss the major providers of superannuation funds.

Superannuation is a large industry that can be viewed from a number of different perspectives. We will examine two views here. One view is to look at the types of accounts that are held by individuals; accumulation accounts or defined benefits. A second view is to examine the major providers of superannuation funds, that is, corporate, industry, public sector, retail and small superannuation funds.

Accumulation accounts and defined benefit schemes

The most common type of superannuation account held by an individual is an **accumulation account**. Contributions by an individual's employer and the individual's own personal contributions increase the balance of their accumulation account. In addition to contributions, positive investment returns of the superannuation fund's underlying investment assets also increase the individual's balance.

However, negative investment returns reduce the balance of the individual's accumulation account. In this type of superannuation account the investment risk associated with the superannuation account is borne by the individual and ultimately the retirement benefit amount is simply the balance of the account. In Australia, approximately 80% of all superannuation assets are held in accumulation-style accounts.

Less common, but still a significant part of the superannuation industry, are **defined benefit (DB) schemes**. Under these schemes, contributions are made by an employer into a pooled fund which is designed to cover the predetermined entitlements accruing to members. These schemes can require the employee, as part of their industrial award or agreement, to contribute a percentage of their pre-tax income to the scheme.

The superannuation entitlement for an individual member of a defined benefit scheme is defined by a formula rather than by the balance of their account (as under an accumulation account). The nature of the formula will vary. For example, a defined benefit entitlement might equal 'final average salary' multiplied by a 'factor' multiplied by the number of years worked with that employer. Final average salary is usually calculated as the average salary over the last three years of working, and the factor is often related to the amount of contributions made by the employee.

For example, Mahesh is in a defined benefit fund and has a final average salary of $100 000. He has worked for 20 years and contributed 5% of his pre-tax salary to superannuation which entitles him to a factor of 17%. Mahesh will be entitled to a superannuation payout of $340 000 ($100 000 × 17% × 20).

Detailed **actuarial calculations** are required to determine the factors. If the actuaries get it right, the total value of the defined benefit scheme, which is a product of the contributions made and the investment earnings generated, will match the predetermined entitlements accruing to members. If the actuaries get it wrong, the danger is that the defined benefit scheme is underfunded due to the total value being less than the total sum of the predetermined entitlements. In most cases, the employer has to cover the shortfall by making additional contributions. Therefore, unlike accumulation fund members, defined benefit scheme members bear no investment risk. They will always have certainty about what their superannuation benefit is.

PERSONAL FINANCE BULLETIN

Superannuation: make income the outcome

Having led the world in the 1990s in embracing defined contribution retirement plans, Australia now is rightly reviewing whether the design of its retirement income system is meeting the needs of Australians living in retirement.

David Murray's interim report into Australia's financial systems noted the particular strengths of this three-pillar system, which comprises the age pension, compulsory superannuation guarantee and voluntary private savings. With more than A$1.8 trillion of assets under management, Australia now has the fourth largest private pension pool in the world. The questions, as the Murray report identified, are around the complexity, efficiency and efficacy of the system.

The fact is Australians are not only living longer, they are seeking greater choice and control in managing their retirement arrangements and need cost-effective products that meet their income needs over many decades after stopping full-time work.

The problems with the current system, as I see it, are two-fold: One is around the lack of meaningful information given to consumers and the other is around the stated lump sum goal of most superannuation plans. Unlike the old employer-sponsored defined benefit plans, the defined contribution (DC) plans that dominate in Australia and in the US market transfer the investment and other risks from companies to employees.

My view is that putting relatively complex decisions in the hands of individuals with little or no financial expertise is problematic. While some say the answer is increased financial literacy, it is simply unrealistic to expect people to make decisions about strategies that challenge even seasoned investment professionals. To use an analogy, when we service our cars, the mechanic does not expect us to be able to understand how the fuel injection system works. Most of us just want a vehicle that gets us safely and reliably to our desired destination.

It's the same with our retirement plans. It really makes no sense to ask individuals to make complex choices about risk exposures and asset allocation, for instance.

The second problem is the goal itself. The language around DC investment is about asset value. People are trained to see the key metric as the size of their fund pool, when what really matters to them is whether they will have sufficient income in retirement to live the lives they want to live.

If an individual's pension savings are invested to maximise capital value at time of retirement and her personal goal is to achieve a reasonable level of retirement income, there is a clear mismatch involved.

In the view of the superannuation fund, the relevant risk is portfolio value. But the risk for the individual is uncertainty around retirement income. How do we solve this dilemma? The answer is to adopt a liability-driven investment strategy that is equivalent to how an insurer hedges an annuity contract or how pension funds hedge their liabilities for future retirement payments to members. Nearly a quarter of a century since Australia moved to compulsory super, the financial technology now exists to invest individual super contributions this way. Each fund member would still get a pot of money at retirement and would still have the same choice over their savings they have under current DC arrangements. The difference is the value of the pot would be obtained through a strategy meant to maximise the likelihood of achieving the desired income stream.

Moving to this income-focused strategy would require changes not only to the way super plans actually invest their members' money but also to how they engage and communicate with savers.

▶

Instead of being asked complex (and meaningless) questions about asset allocation, members would be asked three simple questions — their retirement income goal, how much they can contribute from current income and how long they plan to work. Of course, the asset allocation is important, but this only a factor for achieving success. It is not a meaningful input for the choices the consumer actually makes. Once these variables are known, the fund need only regularly communicate to the member the probability of reaching her goal. To increase that probability, the fund member has only three choices — save more, work longer or take more risk. There are no other ways.

The gap between what exists and what Australians need was highlighted by the Murray inquiry interim report, which noted that the current focus on lump sum balances in the superannuation system is evident in the absence of retirement income projections from annual statements to members.

'For many people, income projections, while difficult to calculate, would be far more useful than total accrued balances,' Murray said.

As someone who has spent much of his professional life researching this issue, I can only agree. Ultimately, what Australia needs is an approach to superannuation that uses smarter products rather than trying to make consumers smarter about finance.

Source: Merton 2014.

Major providers of superannuation funds

APRA, which oversees all superannuation funds in Australia other than SMSFs, gathers and publishes data on the superannuation industry. APRA disaggregates the industry into five types of providers. Figure 8.2 highlights the assets held by each provider type.

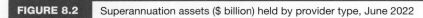

FIGURE 8.2 Superannuation assets ($ billion) held by provider type, June 2022

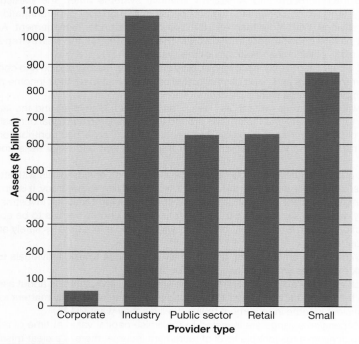

Source: Adapted from APRA 2023, Table 1.

In the past 10 years, **industry funds**, **retail funds** and **small superannuation funds** (includes **self-managed superannuation funds** and **small-APRA funds**) have significantly increased the value of the total assets under management. Over the same period, the value of funds under management in **corporate superannuation funds** has remained relatively constant as some companies have closed down their superannuation schemes and transferred employees to retail funds. This trend in corporate funds has also been fuelled by some companies not wishing to retain the investment risk associated with defined benefit schemes.

Figure 8.2 includes mostly funded superannuation schemes. Funded means that contributions have been made progressively into the superannuation fund over the working lives of the individual members. All corporate, industry, retail and small superannuation funds are funded schemes.

However, not all **public-sector funds** are **fully funded schemes**. It was estimated that, at 30 June 2019, the federal government had an **unfunded** liability to pay public servants superannuation equivalent to $224 billion (Parliament of Australia 2019, p. 41).

In July 2005, the Public Sector Superannuation Accumulation Plan was introduced and provides fully funded accumulation benefits for new civilian employees. However, the unfunded obligation to military personnel and public servants who joined their superannuation fund before July 2005 means that the total unfunded liability is expected to grow further. Successive federal governments have tried to reduce this unfunded liability — the Future Fund was established as a savings plan designed to accumulate wealth over time to offset this unfunded superannuation liability. Part of the privatisation proceeds from the sale of Telstra was paid into the Future Fund. At 31 December 2019, the Future Fund held $168.1 billion in assets (Future Fund 2020).

8.5 History of superannuation in Australia

LEARNING OBJECTIVE 8.5 Outline the historical development of the Australian superannuation system.

The most traditional way of recalling a history is to recount events in chronological order; however, sometimes themes are more instructive than dates. Many themes run through the historical development of superannuation. These themes have led us to where we are today and are useful in providing an insight into where we might go in the future.

Some of the themes to consider in the development of the superannuation system in Australia include:
* the change from white collar to blue collar to no collar
* the need to stay in the workforce longer
* taking lump sums from superannuation
* the tax-concessional environment — do we control the inputs or the outputs?
* is everybody treated equally?

From white collar to blue collar to no collar

The beginnings of formal employer-sponsored superannuation schemes can be traced back to the latter half of the nineteenth century in Australia. The schemes tended to be called provident funds rather than superannuation funds and were mainly confined to white collar employees in banks and public service. To be eligible for a payout from the provident fund, employees had to stay with the same employer until retirement — a concept which today seems quite alien. For the banks, the provident fund was also a means of ensuring good behaviour and character from their employees because conviction for an offence such as theft and/or dismissal would generally result in the employee forfeiting their payout from the fund. Superannuation is often referred to as a 'golden handshake' and sometimes less seriously as a 'golden handcuff' — which could be the case for employees whose entitlements are tied to staying with a job they may not particularly like doing.

By the mid-1980s, approximately 40% of the Australian workforce was covered by superannuation. Coverage was still largely confined to white collar employees. Often, women were excluded from superannuation schemes after they were married — again a concept which seems out of place today.

The federal government has commissioned four inquiries into superannuation — 1928, 1938, 1976 and the Cooper Inquiry of 2010. The 1928, 1938 and 1976 inquiries all supported the concept of a national contributory superannuation scheme; however, all three failed to generate the political impetus for such a scheme.

In 1985, the Australian Council of Trade Unions (ACTU), with the support of the Hawke–Keating government, petitioned the then Arbitration Commission for a 3% wage increase payable in the form of a superannuation contribution. The commission accepted the argument but left unions and individual companies with the responsibility of negotiating the superannuation contribution as a result of improved productivity on a case-by-case basis. The decision extended the reach of superannuation; however, the coverage of the workforce was still patchy and inconsistent. In 1992, the Hawke–Keating government introduced the **superannuation guarantee** (SG) system, which obliged all employers to contribute 3% of each employee's income to superannuation. This rate of contribution was progressively increased to 9% by 2002. In 2010 the Rudd–Swan government announced that the SG contribution rate would progressively increase from 9% to 12%. The timetable for this change was slowed somewhat with the 12% ratet due for introduction in the 2025–26 financial year. Superannuation coverage now extends to well over 90% of the workforce and includes both white- and blue-collar employees.

In 1997, the federal government introduced the eligible spouse rebate/offset for superannuation. We will discuss the operation of the rebate later in this chapter; however, in financial terms it provides a small tax rebate when a person makes a contribution for a low-income or no-income spouse. No income means not in paid employment, and the rebate is often seen as a signal that superannuation coverage needs to extend beyond the workforce and apply to all Australians. In 2004, the Howard–Costello government took this a step further by removing the work test for people under the age of 65, resulting in white collar, blue collar and no collar (not working) people being eligible to contribute to superannuation. The removal of the work test was extended to age 74 on 1 July 2022.

This broadening of the base of people eligible to contribute to superannuation appears to be a consistent trend — in an environment of an ageing population and concern over meeting the funding requirements of the age pension, it seems unlikely that public policy will narrow the base of people entitled to contribute to superannuation in the future.

The need to stay in the workforce longer

The longer people stay in the workforce the more opportunity they have to accumulate more superannuation to fund their retirement. Staying in the workforce also means there is a shorter period actually in retirement that needs to be funded.

As discussed in more detail in the chapter on social security, in 1909 the age pension was introduced for men in Australia. To be eligible for the age pension you needed to be 65 years of age. Given that the life expectancy of males at birth in 1908 was approximately 55 years of age, only a very small percentage of the male population lived long enough to claim the pension. For the next 100 years, the entitlement age remained at 65; however, male life expectancy at birth increased to 80.7 which has resulted in a significant proportion of the male population reaching the entitlement age (Australian Bureau of Statistics 2019). This increasing social security burden has been an important factor driving successive federal governments to create a superannuation environment which encourages us to work longer.

Policy initiatives include:
- a progressive increase in the age pension entitlement age for women from 60 to 65
- an increase in the age pension entitlement age from 65 to 67 for both men and women over the period 2017 to 2023
- the introduction of a **transition to retirement (TTR) income stream**
- the introduction of the **work bonus scheme**
- a progressive increase in the minimum age at which funds can be released from superannuation from 55 to 60
- superannuation changes by the Howard–Costello government in 2007 to encourage people to keep working until at least 60 years of age in order to release money from superannuation tax free
- public policy discussions about aligning the minimum age at which funds can be released from superannuation and the age pension entitlement age.

Policy initiatives in recent years have consistently encouraged us to work longer. It is hard to see this trend changing. Based on the current rules, how old will you be before you can access your superannuation and be entitled to the age pension? Will the rules change before you get there?

Taking lump sums from superannuation

Many countries in the world do not allow individuals to take their money out of superannuation as a lump sum. Some might argue that the ability to withdraw superannuation as a lump sum is an Australian right which cannot be interfered with. Others would argue that allowing individuals to withdraw their money in a lump sum, and possibly spend it quickly and ultimately rely on the age pension, is poor public policy. This has not, however, stopped federal governments from taxing such lump sum withdrawals.

Prior to 1983, it was possible to take money out of superannuation as a lump sum and only 5% of the amount taken was taxable at the individual's marginal tax rate. Even if an individual's marginal rate was as high as 50% the effective tax rate on lump sum withdrawals was 2.5% (50% × 5%) which is hardly a disincentive to withdraw superannuation as a lump sum.

The Hawke–Keating government decided to tax superannuation accrued after 30 June 1983 and subsequently withdrawn as a lump sum at 15% after a particular tax-free threshold had been reached. Some would argue that 15% was not a sufficient tax penalty to discourage people from taking their money out of superannuation but it was more of a penalty than the pre-1983 regime. In 2007, the Howard–Costello government introduced the Simpler Super reforms, which allowed individuals over the age of 60 to withdraw their superannuation as a lump sum completely tax free. It also introduced tax-free pension mode superannuation so that individuals over 60 could draw an income stream from superannuation tax free. Investment earnings on the underlying assets would also be tax free once the superannuation was in pension mode.

Over the longer term, will we see a backflip on taxing lump sums to discourage people from withdrawing them? With likely significant budgetary pressures in the future, will governments be able to afford the tax revenue forgone by not taxing lump sums for those over the age of 60?

The tax-concessional environment — do we control the inputs or the outputs?

Superannuation is a tax-concessional environment designed to encourage people to save for their retirement. The tax-concessional environment that superannuation offers implies that the federal government is forgoing tax revenue it would have otherwise collected. Estimates of how much tax revenue is forgone vary greatly; however, there is no doubt that it amounts to billions of dollars a year and it has a significant budgetary impact.

The key policy issue is how concessional does a tax-concessional environment need to be in order to entice individuals to save for their retirement? If the environment is too concessional, the federal government will lose significant tax revenue, which may compromise its ability to provide a full range of services. If the environment is not concessional enough, federal government tax revenues will be higher but people will be saving less for retirement, and the end result will be greater budgetary outlays in the future to meet the burden of increased social security payments.

How can people be encouraged to save enough to fund their retirement but not so much as to exploit the tax-concessional nature of superannuation? Essentially, either the amount of money flowing into superannuation must be controlled or the amount of money flowing out of superannuation must be controlled.

Prior to 2007, the limit for concessional contributions was a function of the individual's age. Concessional contributions occur where a tax deduction can be claimed for a contribution. We will discuss these in more detail later in this chapter. Prior to 2007 the government also imposed reasonable benefit limits (RBLs) which taxed money being withdrawn from superannuation that was in excess of the RBLs at a much higher rate than the tax on a usual withdrawal. These limits were meant to encourage individuals to carefully monitor how much they put into the tax-concessional superannuation environment in the first place.

As part of the Howard–Costello reforms to superannuation, RBLs were abolished; however, the limit on concessional contributions that could be made into superannuation was tightened. This shift to restricting money flowing into superannuation mitigated individuals taking advantage of the tax-concessional superannuation environment.

In 2017 the Turnbull government introduced a range of superannuation reforms. These reforms included a **transfer balance cap** of $1.6 million which could be held in a tax-free pension mode. The transfer balance cap has since risen, and superannuation amounts in excess of $1.9 million must now be held in accumulation mode, which means that a tax of 15% is applied to earnings. These reforms also reduced the non-concessional contribution cap. Non-concessional contributions are personal contributions made with after-tax money and there is no deduction for the individual.

Is this the right balance? Is the superannuation environment concessional enough to attract contributions but not so attractive that it seriously reduces government tax revenue? Should we control the money going into superannuation, or out of superannuation or both?

Is everybody treated equally?

Prior to 1988, contributions to, and earnings inside, superannuation funds were not taxed. In 1988, a 15% tax was introduced on all contributions and earnings.

An individual who earns $200 000 might decide to **salary sacrifice** $10 000 into superannuation. If this $10 000 was taken as income, the individual would be taxed at their marginal tax rate of 45% and they would lose $4500 of this amount in tax. If, instead, the $10 000 was sacrificed into superannuation, the individual's employer would be able to claim this as a tax deduction and the full $10 000 would be remitted to the superannuation fund. The fund would then be obliged to deduct 15% in contributions tax; that is, the individual would lose $1500 in tax. By salary sacrificing the amount, the individual has saved $3000 in tax. We will discuss the process of salary sacrifice later in the chapter.

An individual who earns $50 000 might also decide to salary sacrifice $10 000 into superannuation. If this $10 000 was taken as income, the individual would be taxed at their marginal tax rate of 32.5% and they would lose $3250 of this amount in tax. If, instead, the $10 000 was sacrificed into superannuation, the individual's employer would be able to claim this as a tax deduction and the full $10 000 would be remitted to the superannuation fund. The fund would then be obliged to deduct 15% in contributions tax; that is, the individual would lose $1500 in tax. So, the individual has saved $1750 in tax through salary sacrificing. Is it fair that a high-income earner saves $3000 in tax whereas the middle-income earner saves only $1750?

In 1996, the federal government introduced the superannuation surcharge. The surcharge added an extra 15% to the existing 15% contributions tax for high-income earners resulting in an effective tax rate of 30% on contributions. The surcharge was very unpopular — perhaps it was the political influence of those subject to the surcharge, or perhaps the superannuation environment was not sufficiently tax concessional anymore but either way the surcharge was removed in 2005. In 2013, however, the federal government effectively reinstated the surcharge by passing legislation which resulted in individuals who earned more than $300 000 paying contributions tax at the rate of 30%. As part of its 2017 superannuation reforms, the Turnbull government reduced the threshold at which the 30% contributions tax applied from $300 000 to $250 000.

FIGURE 8.3   Overview of the superannuation environment

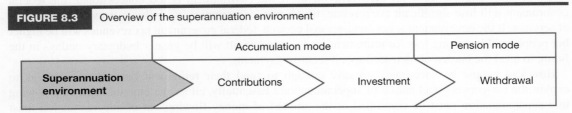

Australia's three pillars (or tiers) policy

Tier 1
A taxpayer funded social security pension (a safety net) which is means tested.

Tier 2
Compulsory employer contributions to superannuation for employees.

Tier 3
Tax incentives for voluntary contributions to superannuation.

The legislative context of superannuation
The legislative environment is dominated by federal legislation. While many Acts impinge on superannuation the cornerstone of this legislative framework is the *Superannuation Industry (Supervision) Act 1993*.

The legislative framework controls how funds are *contributed*, how they are *invested* and how they are *withdrawn* from superannuation.

The regulators
• Australian Prudential Regulation Authority
• Australian Securities and Investments Commission
• Australian Taxation Office
• Australian Financial Complaints Authority

Types of funds
Funds can be viewed from a number of different perspectives.

Superannuation funds are either accumulation funds (also known as defined contribution funds) or defined benefit funds. Most working Australians will have an accumulation fund(s).

Funds can also be viewed from the perspective of the provider of the funds. The main providers are:
• corporate funds
• industry funds
• public sector funds
• retail funds
• small funds.

Historical development of superannuation
The history of superannuation in Australia is full of recurrent themes. Understanding these themes helps in predicting where superannuation might go in the future.

Another way of injecting more equity into the superannuation tax environment is to provide low-income earners with a contributions tax rebate. In 2012, the Gillard–Swan federal government introduced a rebate for low-income earners which effectively negated the contribution tax for people earning less than $37 000. The Turnbull 2017 superannuation reforms have ensured that this rebate/offset continued beyond 1 July 2017.

Figure 8.3 provides a brief summary of the superannuation environment we have discussed in this chapter.

8.6 Superannuation contributions

LEARNING OBJECTIVE 8.6 Differentiate between concessional and non-concessional contributions to superannuation.

Before discussing concessional and non-concessional contributions it should be noted that there are several conditions placed on these contributions, such as:
- the age of the contributor
- their work status
- the respective contribution caps
- the total superannuation balance cap.

Table 8.1 summarises the age restrictions on contributions.

TABLE 8.1   **Age restrictions on accepting contributions**

Age of member at the time of contribution	Contribution type
Under 55	All contributions can be accepted, except downsizer contributions.
55–74 years old	All contributions can be accepted. Personal deductible contributions age 67–75 the individual must meet work test to allow deduction.
75 years old or over	Can only accept mandated contributions.

Source: ATO 2022.

The work test is that an individual must be in gainful employment (i.e. paid work) for at least 40 hours over 30 consecutive days in that financial year in which the contribution is made.

Overview of concessional and non-concessional contributions

A **concessional contribution** to superannuation is a contribution for which a tax deduction has been claimed, by either an employer or the individual themselves. When a superannuation fund receives a concessional contribution, it deducts 15% contribution tax.

For example, if Jenny's salary is $100 000 per year and her employer contributes $10 000 to her superannuation under its superannuation guarantee obligations, the employer is able to claim $110 000 as a tax deduction. If Jenny asks her employer to salary sacrifice $12 000 of her salary to superannuation, the employer will pay Jenny $88 000 and send $22 000 to her superannuation fund. Either way, the employer claims $110 000 as a tax deduction.

Prior to 1 July 2017, if an individual wished to make a personal contribution to superannuation and claim this contribution as a personal tax deduction, that individual would need to prove their self-employed status. The Turnbull government, as part of its 2017 reforms to superannuation, removed this requirement thereby allowing any individual, regardless of their employment status, to claim a personal tax deduction for any contributions made.

Concessional contributions are capped at $27 500 in 2023–24. This figure is indexed to average weekly ordinary times earnings (AWOTE) and increments are accumulated until they reach $2500.

Therefore, continuing on from the example above, Jenny can make a further concessional contribution of $3000 from funds held in her bank account for example and claim a tax deduction for that contribution. This would result in her concessional contributions reaching the cap of $27 500 (i.e. $11 000 super guarantee contributions, plus $12 000 salary sacrifice contributions and $4500 personal deductible contributions). The superannuation fund would deduct 15% contributions tax (i.e. $4125).

The 2017 reforms to superannuation also allowed individuals to make 'catch-up' concessional contributions from 1 July 2018. If an individual has a total superannuation balance of less than $500 000, they can carry forward any unused concessional cap space on a rolling 5-year basis. For example, if Vivian has $200 000 in superannuation in 2018–19 and makes $10 000 in concessional contributions in that year, she then has $15 000 in unused concessional cap that can be carried forward to 2019–20. That would give her a 'catch-up' cap of $40 000 in that financial year, given the actual 2019–20 concessional cap remained at $25 000.

An individual can continue to receive concessional contributions into their superannuation even if their total superannuation balance exceeds $1.9 million. Concessional contributions which exceed the annual cap will be refunded to the individual and taxed at the individual's marginal tax rate. These excess contributions are also subject to an interest penalty to reflect the delay faced by the ATO in collecting the tax payable.

Concessional contributions into accumulation accounts are reasonably easy for an individual to calculate to ensure that they stay below the concessional contribution cap. Concessional contributions into defined benefit schemes are more difficult to measure. To get around this problem, each superannuation fund offering a defined benefit plan will publish a notional taxed contribution (NTC) for each defined benefit member according to a prescribed formula. For example, a member who earns $100 000 might have an NTC of 17%, which means the concessional contribution is assumed to be $17 000. If the concessional contribution limit is $25 000 per financial year, the individual could salary sacrifice up to $8000 and stay below the limit. An individual may split concessional superannuation contributions with their spouse. A concessional contribution will be received by the individual's superannuation fund and the 15% contributions tax deducted. The balance may then be split with their spouse. The contributions will be counted under the contributor's concessional contribution cap and not the receiving spouse.

A **non-concessional contribution** to superannuation is a contribution for which a tax deduction has *not* been claimed. That is, individuals have taken their after-tax dollars and contributed this into the superannuation environment and not claimed a tax deduction for doing so. When a superannuation fund receives a non-concessional contribution, the 15% contributions tax is not deducted so the full contribution amount is added to the individual's superannuation balance.

Non-concessional contributions are limited to four times the concessional contribution limit. Therefore, the non-concessional contributions cap in 2023–24 is $110 000 p.a.. As the concessional cap increases over time due to indexation so too will the non-concessional cap increase. Individuals, under age 65, can 'bring forward' on a rolling 3-year basis their non-concessional cap thereby allowing them to make a non-concessional contribution of up to $330 000.

Individuals can only make non-concessional contributions provided their superannuation is below the total superannuation balance cap of $1.9 million on 30 June of the previous financial year to when the contribution will be made. If an individual's total superannuation balance was less than $1.7 million on 30 June then in the following financial year they could exercise the 'bring forward' rule and make a non-concessional contribution of $300 000. If the total superannuation balance was between $1.7 and $1.8 million, the bring forward contribution would be limited to $200 000. A total superannuation balance of $1.8 to $1.9 million would still allow a non-concessional contribution of $100 000 in the following financial year. Therefore, an individual's total superannuation balance may end up being more than $1.9 million at the end of the financial year in which the non-concessional contribution is made.

Types of concessional contributions

The superannuation guarantee scheme

The superannuation guarantee (SG) scheme is an arrangement whereby an employee is guaranteed that their employer will make a minimum contribution to the employee's superannuation fund. Up to 30 June 2021, the SG rate was 9.5% of the employee's ordinary quarterly earnings. The legislation requires annual increments of 0.50% from 1 July 2021 until it reaches 12% on 1 July 2025.

SG contributions are classified as concessional contributions and are to be made at least quarterly, but may be made monthly. The ATO administers the scheme and, if employers do not contribute the required minimum amounts, they are liable to pay an SG charge which comprises the shortfall plus an interest and administration charge.

The legislation that established and governs the scheme are the *Superannuation Guarantee (Administration) Act 1992* (SGAA) and the *Superannuation Guarantee Charge Act 1992* (SGCA). The SG scheme is a self-assessment scheme. Employers must ensure they have contributed at the required minimum levels or report the shortfall to the ATO and pay the SG charge.

Obviously, for an employer the definition of an employee is very important when the labour cost can increase by the SG rate. Under the SGAA, an employee is defined within its ordinary common-law meaning as a person who works for salary or wages, but is expanded to include, among others, directors of companies and board members of associations (who are not normally employees), members of parliament and entertainers under contract to entrepreneurs and film producers. The difficulty lies, as it always has with taxation law, with employee-like persons such as independent contractors. Contractors can work for one customer at a time or for many customers at a time.

Case law has concluded that there are many indicators to be considered in each case, but no one indicator is the deciding determinant. The factors that have been used and would tend to suggest a person is a contractor rather than an employee are:

- the client has limited control over the worker's actions — the worker decides what to do and how to do it
- the worker has their own business organisation
- the worker mostly has a number of clients
- the worker is paid on the basis of a result and usually provides a quote before commencing the work
- the worker bears the risk (i.e. time and cost) to fix errors in their work
- the worker has the freedom to employ others to complete the work
- the worker mostly provides their own tools.

The ATO has provided guidance on this issue with the commissioner's view given in *Superannuation Guarantee Ruling SGR 2005/1*. A difficulty arises with people who work under genuine contracts but must perform the work themselves, provide principally their own labour, work with the employer/client's tools, machinery or assets, and are paid by time rather than outcome. The commissioner regards these people as employees rather than contractors for the purposes of the SG scheme.

ILLUSTRATIVE EXAMPLE 8.1

Tim Jones is a local electrician. He does repairs and new work for householders. Is Tim an employee or a contractor for the purposes of the SG scheme? Clients tell him what needs to be done in general terms but do not normally stipulate where the wires should be run or how the job is to be carried out; he has a business structure; he works for many clients; when he gives fixed quotes, he bears the risk of cost increases and of rectifying his work; he may employ others; he provides his own tools. Therefore, Tim is an independent contractor and the people who engage him will not make a separate payment to cover the SG charge. It will be up to Tim whether or not he decides to contribute some of his personal income to superannuation.

ILLUSTRATIVE EXAMPLE 8.2

Brian Need is a computer programmer who specialises in complex shipping-industry design programs. He works for a small number of clients each year, sequentially rather than at the same time. He must use his own skills, works on large mainframe computers and is paid for hours worked fortnightly. The ATO considers him an employee for SG purposes and therefore people who employ Brian will also need to contribute the SG to his nominated superannuation fund.

The ATO website contains a useful *employee or contractor decision tool*.

Employers are required to calculate their SG contributions on their employees' **ordinary times earnings (OTE)**. OTE are defined in the SGAA and include:

- total earnings for ordinary hours of work
- over-award payments
- shift loadings
- commissions.

OTE do not include:
- general bonuses
- overtime pay
- car allowances paid as cents/km
- fringe benefits
- maternity and paternity leave payments
- annual leave loadings
- payments in lieu of notice and redundancy pay.

Whilst the SG rate is the minimum contribution rate the employer must pay, there is also a maximum income level per employee to which the SG contribution rate applies. In 2023–24 the maximum superannuation contribution base is $62 270 per quarter. This figure is subject to indexation. If, for example, an employee earns $70 000 in a particular quarter and the SG contributions payable by the employer would be limited to the maximum superannuation contribution base amount.

Some employees do not qualify for SG contributions and this may be due to:
- employees receiving less than $450 per month (based on actual cash receipts in a month)
- part-time (less than 30 hours per week) employees under 18 years of age
- people who do work of a domestic nature for not more than 30 hours per week. This work includes housework or cleaning, child care in the home, doing minor repairs and gardening.

The ATO website contains a useful *superannuation guarantee eligibility decision tool*.

Failing to pay superannuation guarantee

The SGAA specifies that employers will be liable to pay SG charges if the level of superannuation support paid on behalf of an employee does not at least equal the required level of employer contributions. The SG charge for any employer who incurs a liability is the sum of the following.
- *The SG shortfall in contributions for the employee.* This charge is not tax deductible, whereas the original contributions would have been deductible. This charge is collected by the ATO and passed on to the employee's superannuation fund.
- *The nominal interest component.* The interest charge is calculated at the rate of 10% p.a. The nominal interest component is a charge to compensate employees suffering shortfalls for the earnings their superannuation funds could have made if contributions had been received on time. This charge is collected by the ATO and passed on to the employee's superannuation fund.
- *An administration fee of $20 per affected employee.* The administration fee is retained by the ATO.

Once an SG charge debt is raised by the ATO, it is a debt due to the Commonwealth of Australia and the ATO may sue for recovery of the funds. Where employers become insolvent, unpaid superannuation contributions have the same priority as unpaid wages. Generally, employee entitlements rank behind secured creditors.

Shortfalls do occur following errors in calculations, where employees have highly variable OTE and with firms having cash flow problems. The ATO does randomly audit employers' compliance with their SG obligations and generally there is a high level of compliance. Where it does find non-compliance, the ATO publishes a list of at-risk industries on its website as a means of encouraging compliance. A perennial favourite is the café and restaurant business.

Salary sacrifice

An employee may decide to sacrifice some of their pre-tax salary as a contribution to superannuation. The contribution is a tax deduction for the employer, the contribution is a concessional contribution and the individual must ensure that they stay within the concessional contribution cap. A decision to salary sacrifice must be made before the income is earned. All concessional contributions are taxed at 15% when they enter the superannuation fund. The tax saving from salary sacrificing is a function of the employee's marginal tax rate (MTR) — the higher the MTR the higher the tax saving. This is illustrated in table 8.2.

A decision to salary sacrifice is a trade-off between current consumption and future consumption, since superannuation is not likely to be accessible until retirement. A younger person might be less willing to trade current consumption for future consumption — they want disposable income now to buy their first car and their first home. Indeed, buying their first home might be the first step to building wealth which will ultimately set them up for partially funding their retirement. An older person, however, who has accumulated assets and is possibly earning a higher income might find it more useful to salary sacrifice.

The older person may also see that they can access their superannuation within a reasonably short time frame as opposed to a younger person who might have to wait 30 years or more before they can access their superannuation.

TABLE 8.2   Tax saving from salary sacrificing $10 000 compared to various MTRs

MTR	Net income $	Net contribution $	Saving $
19.0%	8 100	8 500	400
32.5%	6 750	8 500	1 750
37.0%	6 300	8 500	2 200
45.0%	5 500	8 500	3 000

Prior to the Howard–Costello government reforms to superannuation in 2007, the concessional contribution limit was a function of age. Under that contribution regime individuals over the age of 50 could make the highest annual concessional contributions (compared to their younger counterparts) so that superannuation could be topped up very quickly later in a person's working life. The current flat concessional contribution cap means that this is no longer the case. If individuals are to accumulate enough superannuation to afford a comfortable retirement they need to start salary sacrificing more, and earlier, in their working lives. The issue with this is that younger people need to be convinced that forgoing current consumption for the sake of future consumption is worthwhile. Many younger people ignore the issue because it is too distant, too abstract and too complicated and simply don't have the financial capacity to divert additional money to superannuation.

Low income superannuation tax offset (rebate)

Individuals who have an adjusted taxable income of less than $37 000 p.a. are entitled to a tax offset of up to $500. If an individual through salary sacrifice, and/or their employer via their superannuation guarantee obligations, has made concessional contributions to superannuation, the first $500 of any contribution tax paid by the superannuation fund will be refunded by the federal government to the fund and added back to the individual's account. For every dollar of income in excess of $37 000 the $500 cap is reduced by 1.5 cents.

For example, Paul has an adjusted taxable income of $30 000 and has concessional contributions of $3000 in the current financial year. This $3000 would have 15% contribution tax applied by the fund resulting in $450 in tax payable. The federal government will refund this $450 in tax paid by the fund and this would be added back to Paul's account.

Sally has an adjusted taxable income of $40 000 and has concessional contributions of $4000 in the current financial year. This $4000 would have 15% contribution tax applied by the fund resulting in $600 in tax payable. Sally earns $3000 more than the income threshold so her maximum offset is reduced to $455 ($500 – (($40 000 – $37 000) × 1.5 cents)). The federal government will refund this $455 in tax paid by the fund and this would be added back to Sally's account.

PROFESSIONAL ADVICE

Salary sacrifice

Brianna is 26 and works 4 days a week in a hardware shop. Her employer contributes the standard superannuation guarantee amount into her nominated superannuation fund. Brianna does not salary sacrifice into superannuation but her employer is happy to organise this if she wants. Brianna has also been undertaking contract interior design work. Last year, Brianna earned $32 000 more than the threshold at which the 37% marginal tax rate commences. She was annoyed that she lost $11 840 in tax on this income. This year, she is determined not to let this happen and has decided to salary sacrifice into superannuation. The problem is that her income level fluctuates so much she is not sure how to organise this.

QUESTIONS

1. What advice can you give Brianna with respect to the concessional contribution cap?

2. Does Brianna need to qualify as a self-employed person in order to make a personal concessional contribution to superannuation?

▶

Non-concessional contributions

As we discussed earlier, a non-concessional contribution to superannuation is a contribution for which a tax deduction has *not* been claimed. That is, individuals have taken their after-tax dollars and contributed the money to superannuation. When a superannuation fund receives a non-concessional contribution, no contributions tax is deducted.

Non-concessional contributions are limited to $110 000 per year calculated on a rolling 3-year basis. This means an employee could contribute $330 000 today but it would be 3 years before they could make non-concessional contributions again, providing they meet the age and work status requirements.

Non-concessional contributions are a useful way for an individual to build their superannuation balance. Often non-concessional contributions are motivated by particular legislative provisions which in turn are generally tax driven. For example, non-concessional contributions might be made to derive the government co-contribution or the eligible spouse rebate or to take advantage of the proceeds from the sale of a small business. Non-concessional contributions are also a valuable tool for people with SMSFs who wish to make in-specie contributions, that is 'contributions' of existing assets rather than cash.

Government co-contributions

The government introduced the co-contribution scheme in 2003 to encourage low-income earners to build their superannuation balances by making a non-concessional contribution which would be matched by the government.

The amount of the government matching payment has varied over the years. Since 2012–13 *eligible* non-concessional contributions have been matched $0.50 for each $1 of contribution up to a maximum government co-contribution of $500.

This maximum government co-contribution is reduced by 3.333 cents for each $1 that the individual's income exceeds the lower income threshold. In 2023–24 this threshold is $43 445. For example, if an individual earned $46 000, their maximum non-concessional contribution *eligible* for matching would be reduced to $415 ($500 − (($46 000 − $43 445) × 3.333 cents)).

If a person earning less than the lower income threshold makes an *eligible* non-concessional contribution of:
- $1000 it will be matched with a government co-contribution of $500
- $1200 it will be matched with a government co-contribution of $500 ($500 is the maximum government co-contribution)
- $200 it will be matched with a government co-contribution of $100 ($0.50 for each dollar contributed).

Therefore, if a person who earns $46 000 makes an *eligible* non-concessional contribution of:
- $1000 it will be matched with a government co-contribution of $295 (the maximum government co-contribution for someone with this income level)
- $1200 it will be matched with a government co-contribution of $295 ($0.50 for each dollar contributed up to the maximum government co-contribution for someone with this income level)
- $200 it will be matched with a government co-contribution of $100 ($0.50 for each dollar contributed).

If a person's income in 2023–24 exceeds $58 445 they will not be eligible for any government co-contribution.

Spouse contribution tax offset

The government provides a tax offset for an individual who makes a non-concessional contribution into the superannuation account of a low-income earning spouse (considered as legally married or de-facto).

The offset is equal to 18%. The maximum eligible non-concessional contribution is $3000. Therefore the maximum offset is equal to $540 ($3000 × 0.18).

The offset is payable on the lesser of 18% of:
- $3000 reduced by every dollar the low-income spouse earns in excess of $37 000, or
- the value of the spouse contributions.

For example, Sue makes a non-concessional contribution of $3000 on behalf of her spouse Carl. Carl earns $37 800 p.a. Sue will receive a tax offset of $396 (($540 − ($37 800 − $37 000)) × 0.18). If Sue had made a non-concessional contribution of $2000 instead, then she would receive a tax offset of $360 ($2000 × 0.18) and not $396 (($540 − ($37 800 − $37 000)) × 0.18).

Proceeds from the sale of a small business

The federal government introduced a series of special capital gains tax (CGT) provisions for small business owners in recognition that many small business owners build up and reinvest in their businesses rather than in superannuation throughout their working lives. The provisions enable small business owners to remove or reduce their CGT liability which would otherwise arise from the sale of their small business while at the same time making a non-concessional contribution to superannuation that it is not counted under the non-concessional contributions cap, but rather a higher CGT concessional cap.

A small business is generally defined as a business which has an annual turnover of less than $2 million or the CGT assets of the business are less than $6 million. For more detail, refer to the ATO website and search 'Small business CGT concessions'.

Small business owners are able to access any of the following four CGT concessions when they dispose of an active asset and realise a capital gain from that disposal:
- a 15-year active asset exemption
- a small business retirement exemption
- a 50% active asset reduction
- a rollover exemption

An active asset can be the business itself such as goodwill, or the business premises or any other asset that was active in the course of carrying on the business for at least half of the time the asset was owned.

ILLUSTRATIVE EXAMPLE 8.3

Tania is 62 years old and is planning to retire. Fifteen years ago, she purchased a shop in the main street of her local town. For the first five years, she operated a café from the premises and then leased the premises and business for seven years. Three years ago she returned to operating the café. Given that Tania used the shop for her café business for 8 of the last 15 years it will satisfy the active asset definition.

There is a certain order to applying these four concessions as some are more effective than others in reducing the capital gains tax liability.

15-year active asset exemption

The most generous CGT exemption is the 15-year active asset exemption. This allows the entire capital gain arising from the sale of the business active assets owned for 15 years been to be exempt from CGT provided the individual is over 55 and retires or is permanently incapacitated. The small business owner can then choose to contribute some or all the sale proceeds into superannuation as a non-concessional contribution counted towards the CGT contribution cap.

In 2023–24 the CGT cap is $1.705 million and is subject to indexation. The cap is a lifetime limit which means that it can be used only once and any unused portion can be carried forward to offset future gains. The CGT cap can be used in conjunction with the other contribution caps. Any amount of sale proceeds over the CGT cap can be contributed to superannuation as a voluntary concessional or non-concessional cap and counted towards those respective contribution caps.

ILLUSTRATIVE EXAMPLE 8.4

Alan is 61 years old and is planning to retire. He has just sold his small business for $1.75 million which includes a capital gain of $1.2 million. The sale satisfies the conditions associated with the 15-year active asset exemption. Alan will receive this gain of $1.2 million tax-free and he can make a non-concessional

▶

---

contribution of $1 705 000 to superannuation under the CGT cap. The balance of the sale proceeds of $45 000 can be made as voluntary deductible concessional contribution up to the cap of $27 500 or as a non-concessional contribution.

50% active asset reduction

If the 15-year exemption doesn't apply to the active asset, then the 50% active asset reduction can apply, after already utilising a 50% discount where available, before accessing the retirement exemption. If the active asset is owned by a company or trust, they may in fact opt out of the 50% active asset reduction before utilising the retirement exemption as this allows a higher amount to be contributed. If the individual doesn't qualify for the retirement exemption, then after applying any discount and active asset reduction, they can make a regular concessional or non-concessional contribution subject to the relative contribution caps.

Small business retirement exemption

The small business retirement exemption allows the first $500 000 of a capital gain arising from the disposal of a business' active assets to be exempt from tax. This $500 000 is a lifetime limit and is not subject to indexation and it also reduces the CGT cap.

If the small business owner is over 55 years of age the individual can decide whether they want to keep this capital gain or contribute it to superannuation. If the small business owner is under 55 years of age the capital gain will remain CGT exempt only if it is contributed to superannuation.

ILLUSTRATIVE EXAMPLE 8.5

Steve is 50 years old and a sole trader. He has just sold his small business for $1.4 million and made a $800 000 capital gain. Steve has owned the business for 6 years and therefore does not satisfy the requirements of the 15-year active asset exemption. Given that Steve has owned the small business for more than 12 months he will be entitled to the regular 50% CGT discount which means his net gain is $400 000. Steve opts out of using the 50% active asset reduction. Steve will be able to claim the small business retirement exemption (capped at $500 000) which will clear his assessable gain of $400 000 completely. Steve must then contribute the $400 000 to superannuation as he is under age 55. If Steve was over age 55 he can then choose whether or not to contribute the $400 000 capital gain to superannuation after claiming the small business retirement exemption. Steve's remaining CGT cap is $1 165 000 (i.e. $1 565 000 less the $400 000 retirement exemption contribution).

Note that the 'rollover' CGT exemption is not relevant here as it is simply using the capital gain to acquire a replacement active asset.

Downsizer superannuation contributions

From 1 July 2018, individuals over the age of 65 can make non-concessional contributions of up to $300 000 from the proceeds of selling their principal residence owned for at least ten years. Whilst this is considered a non-concessional contribution it is not counted under the cap. The contribution has to be made within 90 days of settlement.

It is not unusual for only one spouse to be on the title of the home, however if the sale proceeds allow for it, the spouse not on the title can also make a downsizer superannuation contribution.

In-specie contributions

In specie means a contribution 'in kind' rather than in cash. An SMSF is able to accept **in-specie contributions** provided its trust deed allows it and the investment rules that apply to the fund are complied with. For example, a member of an SMSF might contribute $100 000 in shares to their fund. An in-specie contribution can be made on a concessional or non-concessional basis. However, it is important to note that, if the contribution is made in-specie as a concessional contribution, 15% contributions tax will need to be paid.

Choice of fund

The Howard–Costello government announced in 1997 that employees should be allowed to make a choice of super fund, rather than a fund of the employer's choosing. Fund choice was finally put in place from 1 July 2005.

This policy is important for a number of reasons. Firstly, being able to choose the fund was an incentive for each individual to take an interest in superannuation. Secondly, choice of fund fosters competition between funds and thus encourages fund managers to examine their processes to gain efficiencies and cut fees, and to invest as well as possible to maximise returns in order to retain existing members and attract new ones.

However, some superannuation funds are for members of a defined group only; for example, TelstraSuper is open only to existing employees and their family members, and former Telstra employees. A person who is not a member of the defined group cannot choose the fund; however, most industry funds and all retail funds are public-offer funds.

Employers must give employees a standard choice form within 28 days of commencing employment. The standard choice form nominates the **default fund** to which the employer will make contributions.

Ironically, while most Australians have a choice of superannuation fund and a choice of investment options within that fund, most people do not exercise that choice. Most Australians allow their employer to make perhaps the two most critical superannuation decisions on their behalf. Firstly the employer will have a default fund into which superannuation contributions will be made. Most people will simply accept this as their preferred fund notwithstanding the fact that they have a choice of funds. Secondly the fund will have a **default investment option**, typically a balanced investment option. Again, most people will simply accept this as their preferred investment option notwithstanding the fact that they have a choice of investment options.

Motivated in part by this superannuation apathy, the federal government introduced the MySuper reforms in order to provide a low cost default superannuation option. Superannuation funds began offering MySuper accounts from 1 July 2013. Since 1 January 2014 employees who have not exercised their choice of fund will have had their contributions placed into a MySuper account as the default option.

Prior to the introduction of the MySuper reforms, individual accounts with small balances, that is balances of less than $1000, were protected from being eroded by administration fees. This protection was criticised by the Cooper Inquiry of 2010 on a number of grounds including the fact that it provided little incentive for individuals to consolidate their disparate superannuation balances. Most of these small accounts will now end up in the default MySuper investment choice and therefore will be subject to a low-cost standard fee environment. However, it is important to note that they are no longer protected from erosion by fees.

A range of criteria are used to determine if a superannuation account is inactive and lost and these are outlined on the ATO website (www.ato.gov.au). Not surprisingly, small account balances are more frequently lost than large account balances. Small account balances are periodically swept up and transferred to the ATO. Currently balances of less than $6000 which are lost are transferred to the ATO.

Bankruptcy provisions

The High Court has affirmed that it is possible for all funds held in superannuation to be protected from creditors in the case of bankruptcy. However, the legislative response to the High Court's decision has been to allow creditors access to the superannuation funds of a bankrupt provided it can be proven that the transfer of assets to a superannuation fund was done for the purpose of denying creditors their entitlements. The legislation also provides some guidance on how proof might be established, for example:
- if it can be reasonably assumed that the individual was insolvent at the time assets were transferred to the superannuation fund
- if a transfer to a superannuation fund was out of character, for example, it would generally be seen as out of character for a person who in the past has made no contributions to superannuation to make a $300 000 contribution the day before they declare bankruptcy.

Contributions overview

Figure 8.4 summarises the types of contributions that can be made to superannuation.

FIGURE 8.4 Overview of superannuation contributions

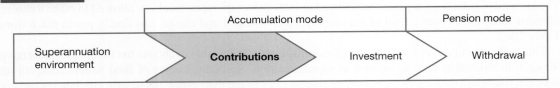

Concessional contributions

A contribution to superannuation for which a tax deduction has been claimed — for example, employer superannuation guarantee contributions (tier 2) or a salary sacrifice contribution (tier 3).

Will be taxed at 15% inside the superannuation fund. If the amount contributed had been taken as salary instead it would be taxed at the individual's marginal tax rate.

Amount is generally limited to $27 500. Amount is indexed by average weekly ordinary times earnings — amount will jump in increments of $2500.
Concessional contributions include:
• superannuation guarantee
• salary sacrifice
• personal contributions where the individual has claimed a tax deduction.

Non-concessional contributions

A contribution to superannuation for which a tax deduction has *not* been claimed, that is, a contribution of after-tax money.

Will be *not* be taxed inside the superannuation fund.

Amount is limited to $110 000. The amount is 4 times the concessional limit.

Non-concessional contributions include:
• personal contributions where the individual has NOT claimed a tax deduction
• downsizer contributions
• government co-contributions
• spouse tax offset (rebate)
• proceeds from the sale of a small business
• in-specie contributions.

PERSONAL FINANCE BULLETIN

Women's super gap hits record low as Australia inches towards equality

Women have closed the gap with men in the superannuation stakes to a record low, and are on track to reach parity within a decade, research shows.

The latest *Financy Women's Index*, which tracks women's economic progress, shows the gap between the average super balance for men and women has narrowed to 28 per cent.

While that means women are still notably worse off than males, it also marks a rapid improvement in women's retirement outcomes since 2015–16, when the gap was as high as 34 per cent.

Since 2004, the report said, the gap has actually halved across most age groups.

And if the current pace of change is maintained, women's average super balances should be on par with men's in just 11 years.

Speaking to *The New Daily*, Financial Services Council chief executive Sally Loane said the findings were a 'really positive surprise'.

The significant improvement in balances for women aged between 55 and 64 (which has fallen from 49 per cent in 2003–04 to 26 per cent this year) is particularly promising, Ms Loane said.

'Older women are still the group of Australians who are most vulnerable to becoming homeless, and they're the fastest-growing group of homeless Australians,' Ms Loane said.

'The fact that gap is closing is a very positive sign, and I'm very pleased to see this happening.'

More progress needed elsewhere

Financy founder Bianca Hartge-Hazelman said it is 'great to see this progress', but cautioned that challenges remain.

'It's kind of like a two-steps-forward-one-step back approach, and the reason for that is that all the things contributing to a woman's progress tend to happen at different paces,' she said.

The recent drop in the number of women represented on the boards of Australia's 200 largest publicly listed companies illustrates Ms Hartge-Hazelman's point.

The Australian Institute of Company Directors' (AICD) latest Gender Diversity Report shows women made up 29.5 per cent of board positions for companies in the ASX200 at the end of September.

That's down from 29.7 per cent in July. The AICD also noted the rate at which women are being appointed to board roles has slowed sharply, from 45 per cent in 2018, to a paltry 31.7 per cent in 2019.

Those figures, according to Ms Hartge-Hazelman, put 2019 'on track to be the worst year in the past decade for board appointments'.

But the situation isn't as dire as it might appear.

'When we look at the data over the longer term, the gains in women's board appointments have been significant, and that's contributing to us being able to achieve gender equality on boards in about six years time,' she said.

Super system exacerbates inequality

Sandra Buckley, chief executive of advocacy group Women in Super, however, told *The New Daily* that closing the super gap in only 11 years seems unlikely.

'Women in Super would seriously question the assumption that the rate of change in the gender retirement gap will move more rapidly than the other key drivers of inequality,' Ms Buckley said.

'Typically the compounding effect of long-term savings, like superannuation, sees underlying differences between male and female pay, paid-work participation rates and other factors make the retirement gap larger and slower to close.'

Ms Buckley noted that almost half of Australian women work part time, half the female workforce earns $40 000 per year or less, and the gender pay gap has seen 'no changes'.

'Given superannuation is based on a percentage of income earned, it would be difficult for the majority of women to contribute similar amounts to men over their full working lifetime,' she said.

Source: Plastow 2019.

8.7 Investment and superannuation

LEARNING OBJECTIVE 8.7 Discuss the main investment constraints that apply to superannuation.

Contributions to a superannuation fund need to be invested by the trustees of the fund on behalf of, and for the benefit of, the members. For members with accumulation style superannuation accounts, positive investment earnings will increase their account balances. For members of defined benefit schemes where the investment risk has been passed to the employer, the impact of short-term investment returns is of less consequence for the members themselves. Nonetheless, it is vital for the long-term viability of the fund that the trustees of defined benefit schemes also properly manage the investment of contributions.

Investment objectives and strategies

Trustees of superannuation funds must formulate an investment objective and support investment strategies pursuant to the SIS Act s. 52(2)(f). If a fund offers more than one investment choice, each must have its own objective and supporting strategies.

A published investment objective(s) helps members and potential members decide on which superannuation fund and which investment choice suits their needs. The objective also becomes a benchmark by which the actions of the trustees can be judged. For example, a fund might offer a balanced investment choice which aims to return 2% above the rate of inflation on a rolling 5-year basis.

Once an investment objective is established, the fund must formulate and implement strategies to support that objective. Specifically, these strategies must address the:
- *risk and return* — how will investments that are likely to produce the return specified in the objective while at the same time managing risk, be chosen?
- *diversification* — how will investments be spread across different asset classes to reduce volatility?
- *short-term liquidity* — how will the fund manage its day-to-day cash flow?
- *long-term liquidity* — how will the fund invest its assets such that the assets release cash over the longer term to meet the needs of members who leave the fund and/or retire?

Investment choices

Most large superannuation funds offer a range of investment choices to accumulation account members. Most funds use fairly standard and conventional terms to describe their investment choices — typically the most conservative investment choice will be labelled 'cash' and the most aggressive might be labelled 'high growth' and sitting somewhere in between will be a 'balanced' investment choice. Sometimes more exotic labels are used by funds, so it is important for a member to look beyond the label and review the asset allocation strategy adopted by the particular investment choice.

Members have different investment needs and different attitudes to risk. High-growth investment choices tend to be more volatile and better suited to members with longer investment time horizons and a willingness to accept a degree of risk. Members closer to retirement or already retired may prefer a more conservative investment choice.

Typically, funds allow members to switch their investment strategy. Some members do switch their investment choice frequently, which seems illogical given the long-term nature of superannuation as an investment. Conversely, some members never switch, which might mean they have accepted the long-term nature of superannuation and are happy with their investment choice, or it might mean that they have not given the matter any thought at all and have simply retained the original default investment strategy option.

Investment restrictions

As there are significant tax benefits associated with superannuation, trustees might be tempted to use the superannuation environment for purposes other than providing for retirement. This may be particularly so in the case of SMSFs. The government has placed numerous investment restrictions on superannuation in an attempt to ensure that the superannuation environment is used for its intended purpose. These restrictions, described next, include the sole purpose test, the in-house assets rule, borrowings, loans and financial assistance to members and the need for transactions to be conducted on an arm's length basis.

Individuals intending to set up their own SMSF need to consider these investment restrictions (and the responsibility of adhering to them) against the tax advantages on offer. SMSFs are discussed in more detail in the appendix at the end of this chapter.

Sole purpose test

Section 62 of the SIS Act requires that the trustee of a regulated fund must ensure that the fund is maintained *solely* for one or more of specific retirement-related issues such as the provision of benefits:

- upon retirement
- upon reaching age 65
- to dependants in the event of death.

However, where an investment provides an incidental advantage to a member (i.e. not one of the three specific retirement related issues), this will not automatically cause the fund to fail the sole purpose test. For example, a fund might own a ski chalet which is vacant for one weekend a year and it might let members stay there for that weekend at a reduced rate. This incidental advantage is unlikely to cause the fund to fail the sole purpose test. However, if the chalet is never rented out and provides no commercial return but members can use it free of charge any time they like, the regulator may well ask whether this advantage is more than incidental; that is, is the fund seeking to provide retirement benefits to members or is it seeking to provide them with cheap holidays partially funded by a concessionally taxed superannuation environment?

The regulator is concerned with the purpose of the investment not what the investment is; it is possible for a superannuation fund to invest in quite exotic investments and still meet the sole purpose test.

In-house assets rule

Trustees are generally not permitted to acquire assets from a related party of the fund. An exception is where the value of the asset acquired does not exceed 5% of the total fund's assets. A superannuation fund is meant to provide for retirement benefits, it is not meant as a vehicle to invest in the business and other assets of members and associates.

Another exemption is that certain assets are exempt from the rule and funds are allowed to acquire these particular assets from a related party regardless of the value. The most common assets that fall into this exemption are business real property and listed securities.

Borrowings

There is a general prohibition on superannuation funds borrowing money. There are some exceptions. Superannuation funds can borrow small amounts of money for transactional purposes for periods up to 90 days — for example, when having to make a payment to a member and not being able to sell down an asset in time.

Superannuation is a controlled and heavily regulated environment, making it a relatively safe investment environment. Whilst investment returns for accumulation account members are not guaranteed, superannuation funds are not allowed to borrow money leveraging against the fund's existing assets (creating a charge over existing assets) increasing the risk of the portfolio.

However, s. 67A of the SIS Act allows for superannuation funds to enter into limited recourse borrowing arrangements (LRBAs) which means that the superannuation fund can take opportunity of leveraged investments, without creating a charge over its existing assets. LRBAs are explained in more detail in the appendix at the end of this chapter.

Loans and financial assistance to members

Trustees are not allowed to lend money or provide financial assistance to members or relatives of members, even if its short term or what might be considered insignificant.

Transactions on an arm's length basis

All investments are to be made on an arm's length basis, that is on strictly commercial terms. The purchase and sale price of an asset should always reflect the true market value. Income from assets should always reflect the true market rate of return.

In the case of *APRA vs. Derstepanian* [2005] FCA 1121, the defendant was a trustee of the Tunstall Bond Superannuation Fund. The defendant was also the sole director of Tunstall Bond Pty Ltd. The defendant transferred jewellery-making equipment as an in-specie contribution to the superannuation fund to satisfy their superannuation guarantee obligations on behalf of their employees.

In the accounts of the superannuation fund, this equipment was valued at $285 000; however, the equipment was largely obsolete and had a real value of approximately $10 000. Had the transaction been conducted on an arm's length basis on commercial terms, it would have been readily apparent that the jewellery-making equipment was not worth $285 000.

The Federal Court ruled that the defendant had breached arm's length rules and ordered that the defendant pay the $225 000 owing to employees, a further $70 000 to the ATO and a $100 000 fine.

Investment performance

Given that superannuation contributions are preserved until a condition of release is satisfied, they should be seen as a long-term investment decision.

The Association of Superannuation Funds of Australia (ASFA) regularly report on the short- and long-term investment performance of superannuation funds in Australia. Investment returns for the previous 50 years to 30 June 2019 averaged 9.7% p.a., during the same period average weekly earnings increased by 3.9% p.a. and inflation increased by 4.4% p.a. (AFSA 2020).

Analysts should always be cautious in interpreting averages. Some funds will obviously perform better than average, some less than average — for the individual contributor the key is how their fund has performed. In the last 10 years, average returns have continued to exceed average weekly earnings and inflation but by a significantly lower margin than the figures noted above.

Figure 8.5 provides a brief summary of the superannuation investment environment.

8.8 Taxation of superannuation funds

LEARNING OBJECTIVE 8.8 Demonstrate how superannuation funds are taxed.

The taxation arrangements of superannuation funds are important because the tax paid effectively reduces the balances of members' accumulation accounts.

In Australia, the principal legislation governing the taxation of superannuation fund income and capital gains are the *Income Tax Assessment Act 1936* (ITAA36) and the *Income Tax Assessment Act 1997* (ITAA97). In 2007, ITAA97 was amended by the *Tax Laws Amendment (Simplified Superannuation) Act 2007*.

The basic framework for taxing the income of superannuation funds is very similar to that used for individuals. That is, the superannuation fund must determine its assessable income and then subtract allowable deductions to result in the taxable income of the fund.

FIGURE 8.5   Overview of superannuation investment environment

	Accumulation mode	Pension mode
Superannuation environment	Contributions **Investment**	Withdrawal

Investment objectives and strategies
Contributed funds and accumulated balances are invested. All superannuation funds must have a published investment objective and strategies to support that objective. The fundamental purpose of all investment is to build wealth.

Investment choice
Most Australians can choose which superannuation fund they contribute to.

Most superannuation funds offer a range of investment choices from very conservative to very aggressive. The individual member can select the investment choice which suits their risk profile.

Tax-concessional environment
Earnings are taxed at 15%. If these earnings had been made outside a superannuation environment they would be taxed at the individual's marginal tax rate.

Investment restrictions
The Federal government provides tax concessions for superannuation and wants to ensure that this money is used to fund retirement. Therefore it imposes investment restrictions on superannuation money.

Investment restrictions include:
• the need for investments to be for the sole purpose of providing retirement benefits
• limits on assets acquired from members via the in-house asset rule
• limits on borrowings
• prohibition on loans and financial assistance to members
• the need to conduct transactions on an arm's length basis.

Assessable income

Income includes both ordinary income and statutory income but excludes exempt income. Income from investments, such as dividend income, will generally meet the description of ordinary income and will need to be included by superannuation funds in their assessable income.

ITAA97 provides a full list of statutory income for superannuation funds. Concessional contributions are, in essence, a receipt of capital; however, the relevant legislation (in this case ITAA36) defines these contributions as income which must be included in the superannuation fund's assessable income.

Where the superannuation of an individual member has been previously taxed and rolled over into a new superannuation fund, the receipt of this rollover by the new superannuation fund does not represent a contribution and is not taxable income for the fund. However, where the superannuation of an individual member has *not* previously been taxed and is rolled over into a new superannuation fund, the receipt of this rollover by the new superannuation does represent taxable income for the fund.

Capital gains realised from the sale of investments held by the superannuation fund are also, in essence, capital; however, as with individuals, the superannuation fund must declare part of this gain as income. For assets bought after 21 September 1999, two-thirds of any gain is assessable income for a superannuation fund and one-third is exempt and does not have to be included in assessable income.

Other exempt income for superannuation funds include:
• contributions to superannuation where no tax deduction has been claimed (i.e. non-concessional contributions)
• income and realised capital gains attributable to investments which are dedicated to the purpose of paying current pensions.

Allowable deductions

Deductions are expenses necessarily incurred by a superannuation fund to earn assessable income. The legislative provisions about general deductions and specific deductions are set out in sections 8.1 and 8.5 of ITAA97 and a table covering each particular deduction is in s. 12.5 of the Act.

Some deductions are administrative in nature, for example, the costs of running an office and employing staff to answer member inquiries. Some deductions are more a function of how the fund operates, for example, contributions received by superannuation funds for the purpose of paying insurance premiums are generally deductible. The chapter that focuses on risk management and insurance will look further into the circumstances under which insurance premiums are deductible for a superannuation fund.

Taxable income

Taxable income is assessable income less allowable deductions. The taxable income of complying superannuation funds is taxed at 15%. A superannuation fund with a taxable income of $100 000 will have to pay $15 000 in tax; however, tax credits may mean that the actual tax paid will be less than $15 000. The two most important tax credits are as follows.

- *Dividend imputation credits.* Fully franked dividends, which provide 30% tax credits, are a valuable tool for trustees in managing their fund's tax liability. Imputation credits have the power to negate the tax payable on dividend income and reduce the tax otherwise payable on other sources of income.
- *Foreign tax credits.* Where an Australian superannuation fund holds investments overseas in a country with which Australia has a tax treaty, any tax paid in that country is offset against income from that country. Therefore, tax would be payable on this income only if the tax rate was less than 15%.

There are, however, occasions where additional tax will be payable by the superannuation fund, including the following.

- Where the individual member has not supplied a tax file number (TFN), the fund is obliged to tax any contributions received at the highest personal marginal tax rate. The TFN is a discrete identifier issued to taxed entities by the ATO to help reduce identity fraud. It is important to remember that an individual may have many superannuation funds and could claim concessional contributions for each of these funds. The matching of TFNs by the ATO is designed to prevent this abuse.
- Where an individual has made concessional contributions in excess of their concessional contribution limit and the excess has not been withdrawn.
- Where a fund is non-complying, all taxable income will be taxed at the highest personal marginal tax rate.

ILLUSTRATIVE EXAMPLE 8.6

During the financial year, the Three Crows Superannuation Fund receives the following amounts. Three Crows is a complying superannuation fund.

	$
Superannuation guarantee contributions	200 000
Salary sacrifice contributions (includes $10 000 which are contributions received to pay for life insurance)	100 000
Cash received from fully franked dividends	84 000
Unfranked dividends	20 000
Non-concessional member contributions	80 000
Proceeds from sale of property (cost $140 000 in 2003)	200 000
Income from investments used to fund pensions	50 000

What is the assessable income of the fund and how much tax will be payable by the fund?

Assessable income	$
Superannuation guarantee contributions (defined as assessable income under ITAA97)	200 000
Salary sacrifice contributions (defined as assessable income under ITAA97)	100 000
Fully franked dividends (the cash received needs to be grossed up)	120 000
Unfranked dividends	20 000
Non-concessional member contributions (no tax concession has been claimed and therefore not taxed inside the fund)	0
Capital gain from sale of property ($200 000 – $140 000) × 2/3 assessable (defined under the ITAA as assessable income)	40 000
Income from investments used to fund pensions (exempt income and not included)	0
Total assessable income	**(480 000)**
Allowable deductions	
Contributions received to pay for life insurance (defined under the ITAA as an allowable deduction)	(10 000)

Taxable income	470 000
Tax payable (taxed at 15%)	70 500
Less franking credits (grossed up amount less cash received = $120 000 – $84 000)	(36 000)
Net tax payable	**34 500**

8.9 Relationship breakdown and the splitting of superannuation

LEARNING OBJECTIVE 8.9 Understand how superannuation is divided in the case of a relationship breakdown.

Superannuation is often the most valuable non-housing asset owned by a couple. In many cases, one member of the couple may have substantially more in superannuation than their partner. We have seen earlier in this chapter that men have, on average, substantially more in superannuation than women. In any division of assets resulting from relationship breakdown, superannuation is a significant asset which needs to be considered.

The *Family Law Act 1975* and the *Superannuation Industry (Supervision) Act 1993* provide for the division of superannuation as a result of a relationship breakdown. The Act applies to spouses who are legally married and to spouses who are in de facto relationships whether they are opposite sex or same sex relationships.

Where spouses agree, they are able to enter into a superannuation agreement which, if ratified by the Family Court, outlines how their superannuation is to be divided. Where spouses are unable to agree, the Family Court will make a determination as to how the superannuation should be divided. The Family Court may order an interest split or a payment split. An interest split is where the account is split immediately and one account becomes two — each party then independently manages their own separate superannuation account. A payment split is where the split occurs at the time of payment which is generally at retirement. In both interest splits and payment splits, the components that make up the original superannuation balance are split proportionally.

ILLUSTRATIVE EXAMPLE 8.7

Thelma has $500 000 in a superannuation account which comprises a $100 000 tax-free component (20%) and a $400 000 taxable component (80%). The Family Court determines that Thelma's superannuation should be split 60% to Thelma and 40% to Louise. After the split, Thelma will have $300 000 in superannuation comprising a $60 000 tax-free component (20%) and $240 000 taxable component (80%). Louise will have $200 000 in superannuation comprising a $40 000 tax-free component (20%) and $160 000 taxable component (80%).

(The difference between tax-free and taxable components is discussed in the chapter on retirement planning.)

Rather than an interest or payment split, spouses may initiate, or the Family Court may impose, a flagging order. The flagging order is a form of injunction on the superannuation account and limits what actions can be taken until the flag is lifted. Being such a valuable asset, this can often cause problems for the Family Court in arriving at an equitable distribution of assets which meets the needs of both parties.

ILLUSTRATIVE EXAMPLE 8.8

Bonny and Clyde own a house that is worth $600 000 and Clyde has $400 000 in superannuation. Other than an everyday bank account with a very low balance, they have no other assets. Bonny cares for their two children. The Family Court determines that the assets should be split 60% to Bonny and 40% to Clyde. Bonny gets to keep the house to assist with the raising of the children and Clyde gets to keep his

---

superannuation. The problem for Bonny is that, although she has the house, she has very little cash flow and the problem for Clyde is that he cannot access his superannuation until he reaches his preservation age, nor can he use his superannuation as security for a loan — he too will have cash flow problems.

8.10 Fees and charges

LEARNING OBJECTIVE 8.10 Outline the various fees and charges which apply to superannuation.

The financial planning industry has been subject to considerable criticism over the complexity and lack of transparency with respect to how fees are charged and this has led in part to the Future of Financial Advice (FOFA) reforms discussed in the chapter on personal financial planning. It is hoped that these reforms will, over time, simplify and make more transparent the way fees are charged on all financial investments including superannuation.

We discussed earlier, under the heading of MySuper, how apathy often results in individuals letting others make key superannuation decisions on their behalf. Where an individual makes their own superannuation decisions (or their employer or the MySuper system makes them on their behalf), no adviser service fees are applicable. However, on some occasions individuals will seek professional financial advice with respect to their superannuation and other investments.

One of the key elements of the FOFA reforms was to eradicate conflicted remuneration. In the past, product issuers would charge a product fee and some, or all, of this fee would be rebated to the adviser. This arguably could influence the adviser to recommend a product that may not be in the best interests of the individual, hence the conflict. This product fee was in effect a contribution fee which meant that for every $100 contributed something less than $100 ended up in the superannuation fund. The FOFA reforms lead to more fees being charged upfront as adviser service fees that the client had to pay for directly to reduce conflict and improve transparency. The initial adviser service fee may be charged as a flat dollar fee or as a percentage of the amount invested. Similarly, any ongoing fees may be charged as a flat dollar fee or as a percentage of the amount invested.

The *Royal Commission into misconduct in the banking, superannuation and financial services industry* was conducted during 2018. The final report published 1 February 2019 reiterated that conflicted remuneration must be banned and no grandfathering provisions allowed.

Superannuation fees and charges

Once money enters the superannuation environment, it is subject to a range of fees and charges which can have a significant bearing on the final amount accumulated in superannuation over time.

Fees and charges must be disclosed in the product disclosure statement associated with the fund. These documents can be long and complex, often making it difficult for the individual to understand what fees actually apply.

Fees for superannuation can be broadly classified into direct and indirect fees. Direct fees are fees that are charged directly to the investor's/member's account when a given transaction occurs. Indirect fees are usually expressed as a percentage of the funds under management and are subtracted from investment returns to produce an investment return net of indirect costs.

Direct fees

Direct fees include establishment fees, contribution fees, switching fees and withdrawal fees. This list is not exhaustive and different funds will use different terminology to describe the particular fees that apply to their funds.

Establishment fees are fees payable when money is initially contributed to superannuation. Contribution fees are payable when money is periodically contributed to superannuation. Many superannuation funds do not charge an establishment or contribution fee, but when they do the fees are typically charged as a percentage of the amount contributed. Establishment and contribution fees can have a significant impact on the dollar amount accumulated depending on the percentage applied. If, for example, a superannuation fund charges a 2% establishment fee on the initial superannuation contribution and a 2% contribution fee on all additional contributions, the amount accumulated will be 2% less than for a comparable fund which does not charge these fees, all other things being equal. This 2% differential applied to a large superannuation balance as a person approaches retirement has a significant dollar effect.

A switching fee is usually charged when an individual wishes to change their selected investment option. For example, if an individual wishes to switch from a balanced option to a growth option this will incur a fee. Most funds will limit the frequency with which investors can change their investment option (typically this would be monthly). Most funds will also have an established cycle as to when switches take place and it is important for the individual to realise that, having made the request to switch, there may be some time lag before this switch takes place.

A withdrawal fee is generally payable when an individual seeks to withdraw a full or partial lump sum when they are in pension mode. This withdrawal fee will also often apply to rollovers to other funds and contribution splitting.

Indirect fees

Indirect fees include the annual management fee and all other fees which cannot be directly attributed to an individual member's account including legal, accounting, auditing and other operational and compliance costs.

The annual management fee is often separately identified by the fund. The dollar amount incurred is aggregated, then expressed as a percentage of the funds under management. This measure is generally known as the **management expense ratio (MER)**. All other indirect fees — legal, accounting and so on — are similarly aggregated and expressed as a percentage of funds under management. If, for example, the MER was 1% and the other indirect fees were equal to 1% of the funds under management, the **indirect cost ratio (ICR)**, which is an aggregation of the MER and the other indirect fees, would be 2%. It is important to remember that the MER is a subset of the ICR and that the ICR is the most valuable fee-based measure by which funds can be compared.

For accumulation-style superannuation funds, the ICR is subtracted from the investment returns that would otherwise be credited to members' accounts. If the investment returns were a positive 7% before the application of the ICR and the ICR was 2%, this would mean that accounts would be credited with a net 5% return. Similarly, if investment returns were a negative 4% before the application of the ICR and the ICR was 2%, this would mean that accounts would be credited with a net 6% negative return.

For defined benefit superannuation funds the indirect costs are effectively built into the formula which determines the defined benefit entitlement. Once a superannuation balance gets reasonably large, the indirect fees are a much more significant consideration than the direct fees.

ILLUSTRATIVE EXAMPLE 8.9

Jiang has done his research on where he wants his superannuation money to go and has narrowed the choice to two funds, A and B. He believes that both funds are very similar and that the only significant difference between them is that fund A has an ICR of 1% while fund B has an ICR of 2%.

If Jiang was to contribute $10 000 p.a. for the next 30 years and the investment return for each fund was 8% p.a. before the application of the ICR, what would be the future value of Jiang's superannuation in each fund?

In Excel Future Value (FV) = (rate, number of periods, amount)

Fund A FV = $944 607 (7%, 30, 10 000)

Fund B FV = $790 581 (6%, 30, 10 000)

The promoters of Fund B may well argue that not all funds are equal. They may argue that they employ expert fund managers who are likely to outperform other funds and more than compensate for their higher ICR. They could also argue that they offer a greater range of services. The ICR is a very useful starting point in comparing funds; however, it is not the only factor to be considered.

8.11 How much will I accumulate in superannuation?

LEARNING OBJECTIVE 8.11 Model how much a person might accumulate in superannuation.

There are a number of superannuation calculators available on the internet which will calculate how much you will accumulate in superannuation for a given set of assumptions. Sometimes these assumptions are quite explicit as the calculator prompts you for inputs; for example, the expected annual increase in your income or future additional contributions. Sometimes, however, the assumptions are implicit in the model and the model itself becomes a 'black box' where you feed data in one end and results come out the other end without you really understanding the basis of the calculations.

ILLUSTRATIVE EXAMPLE 8.10

Gina currently earns $60 000 per year and her employer contributes 12% of this amount to superannuation. She currently has $100 000 in superannuation. Gina would like to know how much she will accumulate in superannuation over the next 10 years. She makes the following assumptions.
• Her salary will grow by 5% p.a.
• Her investment choice inside superannuation will earn 7% return p.a. after fees but before tax.
• The inflation rate will be 3% p.a.
   To make the modelling simpler, we will model in calendar years and assume that contributions are made in December each year so that they do not attract investment earnings in the current year (figure 8.6).

FIGURE 8.6	Gina's superannuation projection

Assumptions and data	
Salary	$ 60 000
Rate of growth of salary	5.00%
Opening balance of superannuation	$100 000
Earnings after fees but before tax	7.00%
Earnings tax	15.00%
Earnings after fees and after tax	5.95%
Employer superannuation contribution before tax	10.00%
Contribution tax	15.00%
Employer superannuation contribution after tax	8.50%
Inflation	3.00%

Workings				
Salary ($)	Year	Opening Balance ($) (OB)	Earnings after fees and after tax $ (earn) = OB × 5.95%	Employer superannuation contribution after tax $ (cont.) = S × 10.20%	Closing balance ($) (CB) = OB + earn + cont.
63 000	1	100 000	5 950	6 426	112 376
66 150	2	112 376	6 686	6 747	125 810
69 458	3	125 810	7 486	7 085	140 380
72 930	4	140 380	8 353	7 439	156 172
76 577	5	156 172	9 292	7 811	173 275
80 406	6	173 275	10 310	8 201	191 786
84 426	7	191 786	11 411	8 611	211 809
88 647	8	211 809	12 603	9 042	233 453
93 080	9	233 453	13 890	9 494	256 838
97 734	10	256 838	15 282	9 969	282 088

If the assumptions hold true, Gina will have accumulated $282 088 in superannuation in 10 years. The problem for Gina is that she is not sure what $282 088 will buy in 10 years. She can see that her salary will increase significantly over this time but knows that part of this is due to inflation. The $282 088 superannuation balance is a nominal figure; that is, it includes an inflationary component. We can remove this inflationary component and convert it to a real figure.

Assume that currently $100 will buy groceries that last a week for 1 person. In 10 years time with inflation of 3% per annum, the $100 loses its current value and will be worth only $74 in today's prices — the shopping trolley would be only three-quarters full and only last five days.

$$\frac{100}{(1+3\%)^{10}} = \$74.41$$

$$\frac{282\,088}{(1+3\%)^{10}} = \$209\,859$$

As the formula shows, Gina's superannuation in 10 years will buy the equivalent of what $209 859 will buy today. Is this enough? Does she need to start salary sacrificing? Should she be more aggressive in her investment selection? In the chapter on retirement planning we discuss the difficult question of how much we need to accumulate in order to fund our retirement.

SUMMARY

Superannuation is a means of saving and investing to accumulate wealth and then using that wealth to fund retirement, usually in the form of an income stream. Superannuation has progressed from humble beginnings in 1992 and, with the introduction of the superannuation guarantee, has grown to having nearly $3.5 trillion worth of assets. During that time, there has been a perceptible shift in expectations from reliance on the state to provide for retirement to reliance on the individual to fund their own retirement. Individuals need to understand the different types of superannuation accounts available and the characteristics of the different providers of these accounts so that they can make informed choices about their superannuation.

The political and legislative context of superannuation is highly dynamic. Understanding how we have got to where we are today provides some insight into where we might go in the future. Individuals and their advisers need to be aware of history as well as have a keen eye for current and future developments.

There is one key aspect of Australia's superannuation system which has bipartisan support, the three pillars (or tiers) policy of superannuation: Tier 1 — a taxpayer funded social security pension (a safety net) which is means tested; Tier 2 — compulsory employer contributions to superannuation for employees; Tier 3 — tax incentives for voluntary contributions to superannuation. The federal government has effectively gained legislative control of superannuation in Australia. The cornerstone of this legislative framework is the *Superannuation Industry (Supervision) Act 1993* (SIS Act).

For a superannuation fund to be able to claim the tax concessions associated with being a superannuation fund, it must be a complying superannuation fund. Four bodies are primarily charged with the regulation and control of the superannuation industry: the Australian Prudential Regulation Authority (APRA), the Australian Securities and Investments Commission (ASIC), the Australian Taxation Office (ATO) and the Australian Financial Complaints Authority (AFCA).

The most common type of superannuation account held by an individual is an accumulation account. Less common, but still a significant part of the superannuation industry, are defined benefit schemes. Money needs to be contributed to superannuation. Concessional and non-concessional contributions are treated differently when they enter the superannuation environment and they are also treated differently when they leave the superannuation environment. Money needs to be invested by the trustees of superannuation funds. The rules for investment inside superannuation are quite different from those outside superannuation. Contributions and earnings are taxed and trustees always need to be mindful of the tax consequences of their actions.

Superannuation is often the most valuable asset owned besides the family home. It is also an asset often in dispute when a relationship breaks down. In an ideal world, both parties would have a similar amount in superannuation. However, as we have seen for tax and work-related reasons there is often a significant difference between the superannuation balances for each individual. The Family Court is often called upon to determine how superannuation should be split between spouses.

Over the longer term, fees and charges can have a significant impact on the amount ultimately accumulated in superannuation. Individual fund members should know the indirect fees they are being charged and make a conscious decision that the services they receive from their fund justify the fees being charged. The advent of MySuper would suggest that there is a low level of public interest in superannuation and as a result most fund members would have very little understanding of the fees and charges they are currently paying on their superannuation.

A number of superannuation calculators are available on the internet which will calculate how much is likely to be accumulated in superannuation given a set of assumptions about income and investment earnings. More important are the calculators that can calculate the gap between the current situation and the capital required for retirement.

KEY TERMS

accumulation account A type of superannuation fund where the investment risk is borne by the member and in which contributions and positive earnings increase the accumulated amount and negative earnings reduce the accumulated amount.

actuarial calculations To evaluate mathematically the likelihood of certain financial events and their associated costs; for example, what percentage of the total superannuation fund membership is likely to retire in the next 12 months and how much should be set aside to meet this likelihood.

codify Legal principles that have been developed by the courts (common law) and included in legislation.

complying superannuation fund A superannuation fund which is resident in Australia, has made an irrevocable decision to be regulated by the SIS Act and meets the conditions for compliance as outlined in the SIS Act.

concessional contribution A contribution to superannuation for which a tax deduction has been claimed.

condition of release Criteria that, if satisfied, enables an individual to withdraw their money from superannuation.

corporate fund A superannuation fund that is offered from employers to employees. Historically employers, and a small number today still, operate their own fund by appointing a board of trustees. Generally, corporate funds are operated as a subset via a retail or industry fund with membership restricted to that company's employees. Some older corporate funds have defined benefit schemes as well as accumulation accounts.

default fund An employer-nominated superannuation fund where the member does not exercise their choice of fund.

default investment option A trustee-nominated investment choice where the member does not exercise their investment choice.

defined benefit scheme A type of superannuation account where the balance is determined by a formula which often includes salary and years worked; generally the investment risk is borne by the employer sponsor of the fund.

fiduciary responsibilities To act in good faith and to put the interest of others (members) ahead of your own.

fully funded scheme A superannuation fund where contributions and earnings have been set aside to meet the commitments to members as they fall due.

grandfather(ing) provisions Conflictedremuneration which was paid to intermediaries (i.e. financial advisers) on products sold prior to the FOFA reforms.

indirect cost ratio (ICR) An aggregation of all management costs (MER) and other indirect costs which cannot be attributed to individual member accounts expressed as a percentage of funds under management.

industry fund Historically these funds were established for employees of a particular industry and generally as a result of negotiations of the union representing employees with employer groups in that industry. There are some industry funds that have defined benefits. However, industry funds are now offered to any member of the public, hence referred to as 'public offer funds', are mostly accumulation accounts. Industry funds are membership based so all profits earned are returned to the fund members' accounts.

in-specie contributions Contributions made in kind rather than in cash; for example, a self-employed person may contribute listed shares already owned in their personal name to their SMSF.

limited recourse borrowing arrangement (LRBA) Borrowing arrangements whereby the lender's recourse is limited to the acquired asset should the borrower be unable to make repayments.

management expense ratio (MER) A ratio of fees charged to the value of the assets under management.

non-concessional contribution A contribution to superannuation for which a tax deduction has not been claimed (formerly known as undeducted contributions).

ordinary times earnings (OTE) Prescribed in legislation as including some items, for example earnings for ordinary hours worked, and excluding other items, for example overtime pay.

preservation age The minimum age at which funds can be withdrawn from superannuation.

prudential To monitor risk-taking behaviour.

public-sector fund A superannuation fund that is offered to government employees and not offered to members of the public. These type of funds have both defined benefits and accumulation accounts. Profits earned are returned to the fund.

retail fund A superannuation fund that is offered by financial institutions or investment companies and open to any member of the public to join as member (i.e. a 'public offer fund'). Some of the profits made on the investment of members' money will be retained by the institution/company that offers the fund. Retail funds are regulated by APRA and do not offer defined benefits.

salary sacrifice Where an employee asks their employer to take some of their income and redirect this to pay for a benefit on behalf of the employee; the most commonly salary sacrificed benefit is superannuation.

self-employed person An individual who earns less than 10% of their income from employment related activities.

self-managed superannuation fund (SMSF) A superannuation fund that is limited to only four members who are known to each other (i.e. family and friends) and all members must also act as trustees of the fund. Trustees must ensure the SMSF complies with regulations to retain its complying status and are also responsible for investment and administration of the SMSF. The ATO regulates SMSFs, while all other types of superannuation which are regulated by APRA.

small APRA fund (SAF) A superannuation fund, similar to an SMSF, limited to four members who have control and flexibility in investment decisions. SAFs are regulated by APRA and must be administered by a licensed trustee.

superannuation A trust structure that offers tax concessions in saving and investing to accumulate wealth for the purpose of growing wealth to fund retirement.

superannuation guarantee An arrangement whereby employees are guaranteed that their employers will contribute to their superannuation funds a minimum percentage of their ordinary times earnings.

total superannuation balance The accumulation of all superannuation interests/balances that are both in accumulation and retirement modes, plus any outstanding balances of a limited recourse borrowing arrangement (LRBA) held by an associate or where there is a nil cashing restriction, less any structured settlement/compensation paid into the fund.

transfer balance cap The maximum amount of superannuation which can be transferred from accumulation mode to pension mode.

transition to retirement (TTR) income stream A scheme that allows workers to continue to work part-time (or full-time) and supplement their income by drawing down some of their superannuation.

trustee A person who administers a trust fund; a superannuation fund is a form of trust fund.

unfunded scheme A public-sector superannuation fund where contributions and earnings have not been set aside to meet the commitments to members as they fall due; the balance in a member's account is effectively only a promise to pay.

work bonus scheme A scheme that encourages people over age pension age to continue working by allowing them to earn a higher amount of income before their age pension payments are reduced.

PROFESSIONAL APPLICATION QUESTIONS

8.1 Given that we have the age pension in Australia, why do we need superannuation?

8.2 Feng, aged 38, has $250 000 to invest in order to help fund his retirement but is unsure how to do this. Assume each of the following investments are returning 5% p.a. — superannuation, share portfolio and rental property. How would you advise Feng?

8.3 What is the three pillars policy? What tax incentives drive the third pillar?

8.4 Superannuation in Australia is primarily regulated by the *Superannuation Industry (Supervision) Act 1993*. What are the key underlying principles upon which this Act is based?

8.5 Distinguish between the roles of APRA, ASIC and the ATO with respect to the regulation and control of the superannuation industry.

8.6 Why has there been a shift away from defined benefit schemes and towards accumulation schemes in Australia?

8.7 Why are actuarial calculations and estimations critical to the viability of defined benefit schemes?

8.8 Distinguish between funded and unfunded superannuation schemes. How will the commitments to unfunded schemes be met?

8.9 What public policy initiatives have been introduced to encourage Australians to stay at work longer?

8.10 What is the difference between a concessional and a non-concessional contribution? What are the different tax consequences when these contributions enter the superannuation fund?

8.11 Why is it important to distinguish between an employee and a contractor? How do we distinguish between them?

8.12 Each investment choice within a superannuation fund must have investment objectives that must be supported by investment strategies. What are the key investment strategies that must be addressed?

8.13 How have the FOFA reforms and subsequent outcomes from the Royal Commission shifted advice fees from the product to the adviser?

8.14 Distinguish between direct and indirect superannuation fees. In the longer term which fees are likely to have the most impact on the amount accumulated? Why might an individual choose a fund that has higher indirect fees?

PROFESSIONAL APPLICATION EXERCISES

★ BASIC | ★★ MODERATE | ★★★ CHALLENGING

8.15 Tax saving from concessional contributions ★

Claudia is self-employed and earns $200 000 p.a. If she makes a concessional contribution to superannuation of $8000, how much tax will she save?

8.16 Eligible spouse offset (rebate) ★

Carol's assessable income and reportable fringe benefits is $38 800. Her spouse, Sam, makes a non-concessional contribution of $3000 on her behalf. What tax rebate is Sam entitled to?

8.17 Impact of fees on amount accumulated ★

Jiang has received his Choice of Superannuation Funds form from his employer. He is undecided whether to contribute to the FlexE Superfund or the PeqSA Superfund. He believes that both funds are very similar and that the only significant difference between them is the FlexE Superfund has an ICR of 0.9% while the PeqSA Superfund has an ICR of 2.2%.

If Jiang was to contribute $5000 p.a. for the next 20 years and the investment return for each fund was 7% p.a. before the application of the ICR, what would be the future value of Jiang's superannuation in each fund?

8.18 Maximum concessional contributions — accumulation ★★

Justin is 29 and earns $110 000 p.a. As part of the applicable industrial award, his employer contributes an amount equal to 11% of his salary to his nominated superannuation fund. Justin would also like to salary sacrifice into superannuation. What is the maximum amount that Justin can sacrifice and still stay within the concessional contribution limit?

8.19 Maximum concessional contributions — defined benefit ★★

Janice is 31 and earns $100 000 p.a. She is a member of her employer's defined benefit scheme. She has just received a notice from her superannuation fund which indicates that her notional taxed contribution is 17%. Janice would also like to salary sacrifice into superannuation. What is the maximum amount that Janice can sacrifice and still stay within the concessional contribution limit?

8.20 Determining SG obligation ★★

Akmal believes that his employer has not contributed enough in SG payments. The table shows what Akmal has earned over the last financial year. If we assume a SG rate of 11%, how much should the employer contribute?

	$
Earnings for ordinary hours of work	40 000
Overtime pay	6 250
Over award payments	3 320
Loadings for night shift	4 800
Annual leave loading	500
Christmas bonus	1 000
Total	**55 870**

8.21 Government co-contribution — under the income threshold ★★

How much government co-contribution will each of the following people be entitled to?
(a) Barney earns $38 000 p.a. and makes a non-concessional contribution of $1000.
(b) Pam earns $38 000 p.a. and makes a non-concessional contribution of $700.
(c) Ralf earns $38 000 p.a. and makes a non-concessional contribution of $2000.

8.22 Government co-contribution — over the income threshold ★★

How much government co-contribution will each of the following people be entitled to?
(a) Ed earns $45 000 p.a. and makes a non-concessional contribution of $1000.
(b) Darren earns $45 000 p.a. and makes a non-concessional contribution of $250.

8.23 Government co-contribution — an efficient co-contribution amount ★★

Audrey earns $57 455 p.a. She wants to make the smallest non-concessional contribution possible and still get the maximum government co-contribution payment available. How much will she need to contribute?

8.24 Investment restrictions ★★

The trustees of Uripper Superannuation fund have made the following investment decisions. As auditor of the Uripper Fund, advise the trustees as to whether you believe the decisions comply with the investment restrictions outlined in the *Superannuation Industry (Supervision) Act 1993* and its associated regulations.

(a) The trustees of the fund have bought a beach house for the exclusive use of members.

(b) The trustees have acquired shares in Uripper Pty Ltd which amount to 40% of the total assets of the Uripper fund. Uripper Pty Ltd is owned by 2 of the members of the Uripper Superannuation Fund.

(c) In order to fund a payout to a recently retired member the fund has borrowed $100 000 for a period of 2 years.

(d) The fund has loaned Kita, who is a member of the fund, $200 000 to help fund a new business venture. The loan has been offered on commercial terms.

(e) Masami, who is a member of the fund, has sold a parcel of vacant land to the fund at a price which is considerably below its market value.

8.25 Determining the taxable income of a superannuation fund ★★★

During the financial year, the Stone Masons superannuation fund receives the following amounts. The Stone Masons fund is a complying superannuation fund.

	$
SG contributions	500 000
Salary sacrifice contributions (includes $20 000 which are contributions received to pay for life insurance)	285 000
Cash received from fully franked dividends	61 000
Unfranked dividends	20 000
Non-concessional member contributions	180 000
Income from investments overseas (includes $10 000 in tax withheld — the country has a reciprocal tax agreement with Australia)	100 000
Proceeds from sale of property (cost $120 000 in 2009)	310 000
Income from investments used to fund pensions	60 000

What is the assessable income of the fund and how much tax will be payable by the fund?

8.26 Determining the balance of a defined benefit account ★★★

Tran is a member of a defined benefit superannuation scheme. His superannuation entitlement is determined by the following formula.

$$\text{Final average salary} \times \text{Years of service} \times \text{Percentage factor}$$

Final average salary is determined by taking the average salary over the last 3 years of work. His annual salary over the last 3 years has been $80 000.

Years of service is equal to the number of equivalent full-time years he has worked for the firm. Tran has worked with the firm for over 25 years; however, some of that has been part-time work and there was also a period of 6 months where he took leave without pay. Tran has the equivalent of 18 years full-time service.

The factor which is relevant to Tran is determined by a number of variables. The key variable is the rate of salary sacrifice that Tran has made to the fund over the years. The choices for Tran were 0%, 5% and 7%. Tran has salary sacrificed 5% during his working career. As a result his factor is 15%.

(a) What is Tran's current superannuation balance?

(b) Tran has noticed that if his rate of salary sacrifice was 7% rather than the current 5% his factor would rise to 18% and this would give him a superannuation windfall. Advise Tran on the benefits of increasing his rate of salary sacrifice.

(c) Tran has recently been offered a promotion which would increase his salary by 40%. The new position is highly stressful, however, and Tran is not sure how long he would be able to cope with the stress. Advise Tran on the arguments for and against taking the promotion.

CASE STUDY

SALARY SACRIFICE TO ACHIEVE AN ACCUMULATION TARGET

Ferda is an engineer who likes precision in everything she does. Ferda is 55 years old and wants to retire in 10 years. She has been doing some reading about retirement incomes. If Ferda was 65 years old today and was to retire today she has calculated that she would require $587 574 to afford the type of income stream she desires in retirement. However, Ferda is 55 years old, not 65 — she has 10 years to accumulate this amount. Ferda also knows that inflation over the next 10 years will mean that she will need to accumulate more than $587 574.

Ferda has worked out that $789 650 received 10 years from today has the same value as $587 574 today assuming an inflation rate of 3% p.a.

As her financial adviser, you explain that the broad scope of the assumptions which underpin such modelling mean that such precision is very difficult to achieve. Nonetheless, any plan is better than no plan even if it is necessary to come back to the plan from time to time and adjust the assumptions.

Ferda wants you to build a model which accumulates a nominal $789 650 in superannuation over the next 10 years. She has supplied you with the following information and assumptions.

- Her opening superannuation balance is $367 823.
- Her income is $70 000 p.a. and will grow in nominal terms by 4% per year.
- Her investment choice inside her fund is expected to earn 6% nominal returns p.a. after fees but before taxes.
- Her employer contributes an amount equal to 12% of her income to superannuation.

To make the modelling simpler, we will model in calendar years and assume that contributions are made in December each year so that they do not attract investment earnings in the current year.

The missing variable is the percentage of salary sacrificed into superannuation. Ferda is happy to sacrifice as much as possible to achieve her goal provided she stays within her concessional contribution limit. Ferda uses spreadsheets a lot in her work and has found the GOALSEEK function very useful in trying to solve problems like this. Construct a model similar to figure 8.6 and answer the following questions.

QUESTIONS

1 What percentage of her salary must Ferda sacrifice into superannuation in order to accumulate $789 650 in nominal terms in 10 years?

2 Explain to Ferda how salary sacrificing represents a trade-off between current consumption and future consumption and the factors she should take into account in determining the appropriate level of salary sacrifice.

3 What other factors besides salary sacrificing might Ferda alter in order to achieve her accumulation goal?

4 If Ferda was 15 years from retirement rather than 10 years, would her goal of accumulating a real amount of $587 574 in superannuation alter if her desired retirement income stream remained the same? Would her goal of accumulating a nominal amount of $789 650 in superannuation alter?

APPENDIX

SELF-MANAGED SUPERANNUATION FUNDS

Introduction

At 30 June 2023, there were 600 000 SMSFs representing 1.1 million individual accounts with $876.4 billion invested. This is in contrast to 153 APRA regulated funds (with more than four members) that have almost $2.3 trillion invested (APRA 2023).

Self-managed superannuation funds (SMSFs) are supervised by the ATO. In SMSFs, the members are the trustees, or directors of the trustee company.

This brief introduction to SMSFs will outline how individuals establish an SMSF and the important decisions, including what type of trustee structure, that need to be made at this time.

Whilst this chapter has covered many of the rules and investment restrictions that apply across all the different types of superannuation funds, it is important to consider the differences here.

Reasons for a self-managed superannuation fund

Managing an SMSF can be a complex and time-consuming business; however, the rate of growth of SMSFs, particularly in the last decade, has been significant. There are three prominent reasons individuals may wish to establish their own SMSF:

1. *control* — particularly investment control
2. *flexibility* — including the flexibility to accept in-specie contributions; that is, contributions other than cash
3. *cost* — notwithstanding the fact that SMSFs can cost several thousand dollars to establish and to administer, there is a point where control, flexibility and the amount of funds to be invested make the cost feasible and on par with the large-scale superannuation funds.

People are often attracted to SMSFs by the notion that they can do it all themselves and in the process save a significant amount in fees that would otherwise be payable to advisers. However, very few people have the breadth of tax, accounting and legal knowledge necessary to establish an SMSF.

Setting up a self-managed superannuation fund

The key legal document to establish the SMSF is the trust deed. To prepare this document, decisions need to be made about what trustee structure will be used and who will be admitted as members. Once this is done, an investment and insurance plan needs to be developed. The assets of the fund must be clearly distinguishable from the personal assets of the members.

The rapid growth in the funds under management by SMSFs has resulted in a corresponding growth in the number of professionals who offer advice and assistance in the establishment of SMSFs, including accountants, financial advisers and legal practitioners.

Given the amount of funds under management and the structure of trustees being members who may not have much trustee experience, the SMSF market is vulnerable to exploitation. For example, a number of property developers run workshops where individuals are encouraged to establish/use their existing SMSF to borrow under a limited borrowing arrangement (LRBA) to fund the purchase of property within that SMSF. In many cases these individuals may not have sufficient funds to justify the creation of an SMSF and, if they then do create an SMSF, they may find that the resulting fund is highly illiquid and impracticable when it comes time to creating an income stream.

Establishing the trust deed

The key legal document in any SMSF is the trust deed.

The trust deed effectively sets out the rules by which the fund will be conducted. It is a complex legal document that requires careful drafting and usually requires specialised legal assistance.

The trust deed will:
- state the objective of the fund
- outline how trustees can be appointed and removed
- describe who is eligible to be a member of the fund
- explain how contributions can be made to the fund
- outline how and when benefits can be paid from the fund.

The trust deed works in conjunction with the relevant superannuation legislation, particularly the *Superannuation Industry (Supervision) (SIS) Act* to direct the actions of the trust. A trust deed can be narrower than the SIS Act; that is, a trust deed might prevent a trustee from acting in a manner that normally would be permitted under the SIS Act and SISR. However, a trust deed cannot be broader than the SIS Act; that is, the trust deed cannot authorise the trustee to act in a manner that goes beyond the scope of what is permitted under the SIS Act and SISR.

The trust deed must be signed and dated by all trustees and properly executed under the relevant legal jurisdiction.

Regardless of how the trust deed is structured, the SIS Act contains a number of covenants that **codify** the common law responsibilities of trustees and which are automatically included in all superannuation funds' trust deeds. These responsibilities include to:
- act honestly in all matters
- exercise the same care, skill and diligence as an ordinary prudent person
- act in the best interests of the fund members.

For an SMSF to be able to claim the tax concessions associated with being a superannuation fund it must be a complying superannuation fund. To be a complying superannuation fund, the fund must:
- be resident in Australia
- have made an irrevocable election to be regulated by the SIS Act
- meet the conditions for compliance as outlined in the SIS Act.

Trustee structure

If an SMSF has between two and four members, all members must be trustees and all trustees must be members. Rather than having individuals as trustees, the SMSF may decide to have a corporation act as the trustee. In this case, all members of the fund must be directors of the trustee company and all directors must be members.

If an SMSF has a single member, the individual cannot be the only trustee as the legal and equitable notion of trust has not been established. A single-member SMSF must have two individual trustees, one of whom is the member. An individual can, however, establish a separate company with the individual as the sole director of the company. This company can then act as the corporate trustee of the single-member fund. In this case, the notion of trust has been established because the corporate trustee has a separate legal identity from the member.

The choice between an individual and corporate trustee is a critical decision in setting up an SMSF. Seventy-eight per cent of SMSFs opt for the individual trustee structure and for most people this works out well. However, in the case of *Shail Superannuation Fund and the Commissioner of Tax (2011)* AATA 940, a husband and wife set up an SMSF as individual trustees. The husband withdrew over $3 million from the fund contrary to the rules of the fund and subsequently disappeared. The ATO declared the fund non-complying and, as a result, the fund incurred tax payable in excess of $1.5 million. The wife, who all agreed was the innocent party in this event, was left with a $1.5 million tax bill for which she was personally liable as an individual trustee. The wife would not have been personally liable if the fund had used a corporate trustee structure instead.

Trustees are not allowed to be paid for the services they provide to the fund as a trustee.

SMSF members are usually connected in some way; for example, family members or business partners. However, no member (and therefore trustee) of an SMSF is allowed to be an employee of another member of the fund unless they are a relative. Generally, self-employed professionals and small business owners have been the main users of SMSFs.

Resident status

In order to be complying, a fund must 'reside in Australia'. Residency requires that the fund:
- was established in Australia
- satisfies the active asset test
- is managed and controlled in Australia.

Trustees/members of SMSFs are generally able to travel overseas for periods of up to two years without jeopardising the residency status of their SMSF.

If a trustee travels overseas and their return date is uncertain or they remain away for more than two years, then determining the residency status of their SMSF becomes more complex.

The ATO will employ an activity test. If a person who is a resident (including a resident who is travelling overseas) contributes to their SMSF in the current financial year, they are an active member and their accounts will represent active assets. The SMSF can satisfy the activity test by having:
- no active members and therefore no active accounts, or
- more than 50% of the fund's assets held in active accounts.

With careful management, the trustees might comply with the active asset test, but they also need to be mindful that extended stays overseas may cause the ATO to question whether the central management and control of the fund remains in Australia. A stay overseas in excess of two years does not automatically mean that the ATO will deem the central management and control is no longer in Australia.

The ATO will look at the individual circumstances of the fund and how it is being administered. The ATO will be more concerned about where the higher-level strategic decisions are being made rather than where more routine operational tasks are performed. Therefore, having locally based accountants and administrators performing operational tasks is unlikely to satisfy the ATO management and control requirements. The trustees might consider establishing an enduring power of attorney which passes management and control to an Australian-based representative. The ATO will, however, want to be reassured that the attorney has real management and control and is not simply acting under instruction from the trustees.

Setting the investment objectives/strategies

As part of setting up an SMSF, trustees must develop and officially record a clear investment objective and strategies to support that objective.

Where a fund has one member, a single investment objective and supporting strategies need to be developed. The objective will be strongly influenced by the individual's circumstances. For example, if the individual is close to retirement the investment objective might be more conservative.

Where a fund has multiple members and all assets are managed within a single pool, the fund will need to develop a single investment objective and supporting strategies. This could be relatively straightforward if all members had similar characteristics; however, it becomes more complex when members have divergent characteristics; for example, if one member is retired and another member is 10 years from reaching retirement.

Supporting strategies need to address how the fund will manage risk and return, diversification, short-term liquidity requirements and longer-term liquidity requirements as members seek to withdraw their money from the fund.

In outlining how the fund will address risk and return, the fund may specify what types of assets it will and won't invest in. In addressing diversification it may then attribute weighting to various asset classes. In addressing liquidity it may develop specific rules; for example, the fund will keep at least $10 000 cash in an at-call account at all times.

A clearly articulated and regularly reviewed investment plan which includes objective(s), strategies and rules is likely to avoid or minimise disputes between members as to how assets are invested, and will also make it easier to justify investment decisions to auditors and regulators.

Establishing the insurance plan

Trustees are obliged to consider the type and level of insurance for each fund member. This consideration needs to be formally recorded either in the fund's investment strategy or in the minutes of the trustee meetings.

If an individual decides to roll over their superannuation from a large fund to an SMSF, they cannot take their life insurance coverage with them, in which case they will need to seek out new insurance cover. For an insurer to provide insurance coverage for four members or less means that each of those members needs to be individually risk assessed by the insurer and the premiums determined accordingly. In some cases, insurance may not be available and, in other cases, it may be available but at a much higher premium. This is an important factor to take into account before the rollover decision is made.

Issues concerning totally and permanently disabled (TPD) and trauma insurance are essentially the same for SMSFs and large funds, and these are discussed in the chapter on risk management and insurance.

Assets owned by the fund also need to be insured, particularly collectables and artwork. Similarly, property owned by the fund needs to be insured, including any property which is subject to a limited recourse borrowing arrangement.

Holding assets

It is important that the resources of the fund are kept separate and distinct from the personal assets of the individual members.

All investments should be held in the name of the fund, for example:
- if the fund has individual trustees — Fred and Wilma Rubble as trustees for the Bedrock Superannuation Fund
- if the fund has a corporate trustee — Bedrock Pty Ltd as trustee for the Bedrock Superannuation Fund.

Where ownership is shared between an SMSF and other parties, the assets should be held as tenants in common rather than as joint tenants.

With **joint tenants** each tenant effectively owns the whole property and the death of one tenant means that the property is then owned by the surviving tenant. Most couples own their home as joint tenants, that is, the death of one tenant (spouse) means that the surviving tenant (spouse) then owns the whole property. Because the ownership interest is not severable, the ownership of assets through joint tenancy is not appropriate for an SMSF.

With **tenants in common** each tenant owns a share of the property and, in this case, a superannuation fund could be one of the tenants in common. The trustee(s) will need to decide whether the ownership interest is one which could be reasonably severed without damaging the interests of the fund.

The fund should also have its own bank account. If an individual member pays for an expense of the fund, this could be deemed a contribution unless an immediate reimbursement is claimed. Conversely, if an individual member receives cash that belongs to the fund, this could be deemed a withdrawal. If the member is not entitled to make withdrawals from the fund, this could lead to serious consequences for the fund.

Auditors are required to report to the ATO whenever there is insufficient separation between the assets of the fund and the assets of the individual. Moreover, the creditor protection afforded by holding assets inside the fund might be put at risk where there is some uncertainty as to whether assets are assets of the fund or assets of the individual member.

CONTRIBUTIONS

Contributions to SMSFs are essentially bound by the same rules, regulations and tax incentives that apply to large superannuation funds. There are, however, some important differences we should review including the:

- ability to make in-specie contributions
- distinction between selling and contributing to an SMSF.

In specie

An SMSF is able to accept in-specie contributions provided its trust deed allows it and the investment rules that apply to the fund are complied with. **In specie** means a contribution in kind rather than in cash.

In-specie contributions are limited to:
- ASX listed securities
- widely held managed funds
- real business property
- cash-based investments such as bonds and debentures.

A member of an SMSF might, for example, contribute their personal holding of $20 000 in National Australia Bank Ltd (NAB) shares to their fund.

An in-specie contribution might be claimed by the individual as a tax deduction, that is as a concessional contribution, or it might be made on an after-tax basis, that is as a **non-concessional contribution**. In-specie contributions are subject to the same limits as cash contributions.

As explained earlier, assets might be owned as tenants in common with one of the tenants being the SMSF. This strategy is often employed when the SMSF has insufficient resources to buy the asset and/or contributing to the asset would breach the contribution limits. Alternatively, the individual member might consider setting up a company or unit trust structure to own the asset, thereby simplifying the progressive contribution, or sale of shares or units to the SMSF in the future.

An in-specie contribution is a disposal of an asset, therefore the member needs to be mindful of the CGT consequences.

Contribution versus sell

It is important to distinguish an in-specie contribution from a purchase by the SMSF. For example, if the member makes a non-concessional contribution of $20 000 in NAB shares, these shares are subject to the non-concessional contribution limit and the member receives nothing in return for their contribution other than having their account credited with the $20 000 contribution. Alternatively, the member might decide to sell the shares to their SMSF. In this case, the non-concessional contribution limit does not apply because it is not a contribution and the member will receive $20 000 in cash from the SMSF as the proceeds from the sale.

All SMSF investments are required to be made on an *arm's length basis*, that is on strictly commercial terms. The purchase and sale price of an asset should always reflect the true market value. Tax Ruling 2010/1 states that when a 'fund acquires an asset for less than market value the difference between market value and actual purchase price is deemed to be a superannuation contribution'.

Investment choices

SMSFs basically have the same range of investment choices as large funds; however, there are three very important investment opportunities available to SMSFs that are not available to large funds. SMSFs can:
- invest in collectables and personal use items
- leverage their investment portfolio through the use of **instalment warrants**
- invest in business real property without the constraint of the 5% in-house asset rule.

Collectables and personal use items

As noted earlier, one of the key attractions of establishing an SMSF is the investment freedom they provide, particularly when compared to large superannuation funds. This freedom extends to investing in collectable and personal use items. Section 62A of the SIS Act outlines the rules associated with investing in collectables. Regulation 13.18AA(1) lists the collectable assets, which include:
- artwork
- jewellery
- antiques
- coins, medallions or bank notes
- postage stamps or first-day covers
- rare folios, manuscripts or books
- memorabilia
- wine or spirits
- motor vehicles.

The use by SMSF members of collectable and personal use assets owned by the fund does raise questions of compliance with the sole purpose test. In response to the uncertainty associated with permissible use and clear cases of inappropriate use, the SIS Act was amended. Since 1 July 2016, if an SMSF holds investments in collectables and personal use assets, it must ensure that the assets are not:

- leased to any related party of the fund
- stored or displayed in the private residence of any related party of the fund
- used by any related party of the fund.

Trustees must keep a written record of the reasons for the decisions about where to store the assets and keep the record for 10 years.

Instalment warrants and leveraged investment

An instalment warrant is where an asset is purchased via a series of payments which effectively extinguish a loan that is used to finance the purchase. There has been significant growth in the purchase of residential and commercial property using instalment warrants by SMSFs in recent years.

If an SMSF buys an investment asset financed via an LRBA, the legal title to the asset must be held in a trust separate to the SMSF. This separate trust is usually called a **bare trust**. However, all the cash flows associated with the investment asset such as interest payments, rent, maintenance and so on pass through the accounts of the SMSF in the same way that cash flows associated with investment assets that are fully owned by the SMSF pass through the accounts of the SMSF.

In addition to creating a bare trust, trustees must ensure the:

- SMSF has the right to acquire legal ownership by making a series of payments (instalments)
- lender's **recourse** against the SMSF is limited to the underlying asset, that is the lender has no recourse to the other assets of the fund
- investment is in line with the fund's investment objectives and strategies.

The ATO's *Self-managed superannuation funds ruling (SMSFR) 2009/2* outlines what constitutes borrowing for an SMSF. An SMSF can purchase an instalment warrant issued over any asset that an SMSF can normally purchase; however, the asset must be a single acquirable asset. A portfolio of shares is not a single acquirable asset; however, the shares of an individual company would be. It is important to remember that the other investment restrictions discussed earlier still apply, including the prohibition against acquiring assets from related parties which exceed 5% of the total assets.

An SMSF can invest in all types of property, including residential, commercial, industrial, and listed and unlisted property.

There are a number of restrictions and disadvantages of holding a leveraged residential or commercial property inside an SMSF. These include the following.

- The increased complexity of the lending arrangements combined with the limited recourse nature of the loan means that lenders will limit the amount that they will lend. Typically residential property would be limited to 75% to 80% of the property value. For commercial property, it might be limited to 60% to 65% of the property value. Lenders are also likely to charge higher fees initially and insist on higher interest rates than would apply outside an SMSF environment.
- An SMSF can purchase an investment asset and maintain that asset (e.g. a physical investment property). The SMSF can also use their own funds (as opposed to borrowed funds) to improve the asset. However, the SMSF cannot improve an asset to the point where a replacement asset is created.
- An SMSF must be careful to not infringe the investment restrictions that apply to superannuation funds. A purchase of a property from a related party is likely to breach the in-house asset rule unless it is covered by the business real property exemption. Similarly renting the property to a related party is likely to be in breach of the investment restrictions.
- If a rental property is negatively geared, the tax shield associated with these annual losses is only equal to the tax rate applicable to superannuation funds, namely 15%. Therefore an annual pre-tax loss of $1000 on the property effectively becomes an $850 post-tax loss.
- Tax advantages rarely turn a bad investment into a good investment. A poorly selected property is likely to produce disappointing results both inside and outside an SMSF environment. Selecting the right property is really a first-order decision and determining the right tax vehicle is a second-order decision.

These restrictions need to be balanced against the potential advantages of holding a leveraged residential or commercial property inside an SMSF, which include the following.

- An individual may not hold sufficient cash resources outside the superannuation environment to enter into a leveraged property investment.

- The legal title to the property sits in a bare trust funded in part by a limited recourse loan. If the SMSF was to default on the loan, the other assets within the SMSF are protected from the lender as are the other non-superannuation assets of the individual members of the SMSF.
- If the rental property is positively geared, the taxable income is taxed at only 15%. Therefore an annual pre-tax gain of $1000 on the property effectively becomes an $850 post-tax gain.
- Other income derived by the fund can be used to reduce the principal on the loan. For example, concessional contributions that are taxed at 15% inside the superannuation fund can be used to reduce the principal on the loan. If the property was held outside an SMSF environment the investor would need to pay their marginal tax rate of up to 49% to release these funds to help extinguish the principal.
- If the investment asset is sold during the accumulation phase, the asset will be subject to capital gains tax. As discussed in the chapter on superannuation, the effective rate on capital gains for a superannuation fund is 10% (two-thirds of 15%) compared to capital gains made outside a superannuation fund where the rate could be as high as 24.5% (half of 49%).
- If the investment asset is sold during the pension phase, the asset will not be subject to capital gains tax. However, if the gains were made outside a superannuation fund, the rate could still be as high as 24.5%.

It is therefore not surprising that SMSFs have been eagerly acquiring residential and commercial property. The ability to extinguish the principal with dollars that have been taxed at 15%, and the opportunity to sell the investment during retirement and incur no capital gains have been the primary drivers of this boom.

Business real property

As we noted earlier trustees are permitted to acquire assets from a related party of the fund only where the acquisition of the asset will not result in the in-house assets of the fund exceeding 5% of all assets. SMSFs are, however, allowed to acquire business real property from related parties which exceeds 5% of all assets. This exemption to the in-house asset rule is primarily aimed at small business owners who have effectively built up wealth in their business in order to fund their retirement and now wish to move some of that wealth into a superannuation environment.

Business real property is defined in the ATO SMSF Ruling 2009/1. It is property that is used wholly and exclusively for business purposes. The property must be unencumbered by loans unless the property is acquired via the use of instalment warrants discussed earlier. The SMSF is allowed to own the property and then lease the property on commercial terms. Often the property is leased back to the member so that they can continue to run the small business.

Business real property also includes property that is used for primary production purposes. Where the property includes a residence on no more than 2 hectares, the property can still be considered business real property.

While for small business owners the real business property exemption provides considerable tax advantages, it does sometimes cause concern with respect to the investment objectives of diversification and liquidity. Real business property could constitute 100% of the SMSFs assets, in which case the fund is not diversified and is highly vulnerable to changes in the value of a single asset. If the fund has more than one member, and some members are approaching retirement then a single, large, non-divisible asset presents challenges in terms of releasing cash to pay retirement incomes.

For more detailed information and podcasts on topical issues please refer to the ATO website and search 'self-managed superannuation funds'.

REFERENCES

APRA 2023, *Annual Superannuation Bulletin June 2015 to June 2022 - superannuation entities*, January, www.apra.gov.au/sites/default/files/2022-01/Annual%20superannuation%20bulletin%20highlights%20-%20June%20 2021.pdf

Association of Superannuation Funds of Australia (ASFA) 2020, 'Superannuation statistics', February, www.superannuation.asn.au/ArticleDocuments/269/SuperStats-Feb2020.pdf.aspx?Embed=Y.

ATO 2022, 'Age restrictions on contributions', Australian Government, 22 March, www.ato.gov.au/individuals-and-families/super-for-individuals-and-families/self-managed-super-funds-smsf/in-detail/smsf-resources/smsf-technical/returning-contributions/contributions-a-fund-must-not-accept#ato-Agerestrictionsoncontributions

Australian Bureau of Statistics (ABS) 2019, '3302.0.55.001 — Life Tables, States, Territories and Australia, 2016–2018', www.abs.gov.au/ausstats/abs@.nsf/mf/3302.0.55.001.

Australian Institute of Health and Welfare (AIHW) 2023, 'Older Australians: Demographic profile', Australian Government, www.aihw.gov.au/reports/older-people/older-australians/contents/demographic-profile

Dixon, D 2017, 'Defined benefit members should take the income stream not the lump sum', *The Sydney Morning Herald*, 4 November, www.smh.com.au/money/super-and-retirement/defined-benefit-members-should-take-the-income-stream-not-the-lump-sum-20171102-gzdoxx.html.

Future Fund 2020, 'Australia's sovereign wealth fund – Facts at a glance as at 31 December 2019', www.futurefund.gov.au.

Merton R 2014, 'Superannuation: make income the outcome', *The Conversation,* July 25, https://theconversation.com/superannuation-make-income-the-outcome-29547.

Parliament of Australia 2019, *Budget review 2019–20*, Research Paper Series, 2018–19, April, Commonwealth of Australia, https://parlinfo.aph.gov.au/parlInfo/download/library/prspub/6903434/upload_binary/6903434.pdf.

Plastow, K 2019, 'Women's super gap hits record low as Australia inches towards equality', *The New Daily*, 1 November, https://thenewdaily.com.au/finance/superannuation/2019/10/31/super-gender-gap-financy-close.

The Treasury 2021, *2021 intergenerational report*, Australian Government, https://treasury.gov.au/publication/2021-intergenerational-report

ACKNOWLEDGEMENTS

Extract: © The New Daily
Extract: © The Conversation

CHAPTER 9

Retirement planning

LEARNING OBJECTIVES

After studying this chapter, you should be able to:

9.1 explain why it is important to plan for retirement

9.2 outline the three phases of retirement

9.3 calculate how much funds are required to fund retirement needs

9.4 differentiate between ordinary money and superannuation money

9.5 determine the various options a member has at retirement with accumulated superannuation funds

9.6 explain the implications of the transfer balance cap in determining retirement options

9.7 outline the tax consequences of withdrawing a lump sum from superannuation to fund retirement

9.8 differentiate between the different types of retirement income streams

9.9 contrast and compare account-based and non-account-based income streams

9.10 describe other income support available in retirement

9.11 discuss what constitutes an adequate retirement income.

Anne is a 64-year-old administrator at a local council. She is single and works full-time and earns around $85 000 p.a.

Anne would like to retire or, at the very least, cut back on her work commitments and start to ease into retirement; however, she is worried that she may not have saved enough to retire.

Anne divorced 8 years ago and was forced to return to the workforce after an absence of 20 years and is struggling to be able to boost her investments. She has a home worth $820 000, a holiday home which she estimates to be worth $650 000 and a share portfolio which is currently valued at $120 000, although its value has been highly volatile in recent times. Anne also has $25 000 sitting in a bank account earning no interest and $240 000 in an industry-based superannuation fund.

Some of the issues that Anne needs to consider include the following.
- If she was to retire immediately how would she replace the sense of belonging and achievement that often comes through working?
- Should she retain her highly volatile share portfolio as she approaches retirement?
- How will her income needs change throughout the various phases of retirement?
- Will her accumulated superannuation and other savings be sufficient to provide for her financial needs in retirement?
- Should she take a lump sum or retirement income stream when she retires?

These issues will be explored in this chapter.

Introduction

Despite the mandated employer superannuation guarantee contribution system being introduced in 1992 requiring all employers to contribute superannuation payments for their employees, there are still many Australians that have not had the opportunity to accumulate an adequate level of retirement funds during their working life to support their financial needs in retirement. To try and boost their superannuation and other forms of savings prior to retirement, some individuals may seek to take on other jobs, defer their retirement, or undertake a range of pre-retirement strategies such as salary sacrificing aimed at maximising their wealth to support their needs in retirement. Upon retirement, however, most people have little opportunity to grow their savings and what they have accumulated at that point needs to provide them with sufficient income to last their lifetime. Accumulating sufficient funds to provide a comfortable retirement is a key concern for those approaching the end of their working life. While this chapter focuses primarily on the financial aspects of retirement, we will also briefly consider some of the non-financial aspects of retirement.

Planning for retirement and seeking appropriate advice generally leads to better outcomes than simply hoping that the person's retirement savings will be sufficient. Too many Australians either undertake no planning or leave their retirement planning too late. Retirement planning cannot commence on the day a person retires; it cannot commence a year before they retire. Retirement planning is a long-term process. In this chapter, we will review each of the components of a long-term retirement plan.

Part of the retirement planning process is determining how much a person needs to accumulate in order to fund their desired lifestyle in retirement. This is often an iterative process where what is desirable is traded off against what is achievable.

Having accumulated a certain amount of retirement funds, decisions then need to be made about how these funds are invested and what form the withdrawal should take to fund the person's retirement needs. Should the individual take a lump sum or an income stream? If the individual takes an income stream, what type of income stream should they take? What are the tax implications of the different forms of withdrawal?

This chapter concludes by reviewing the question of what constitutes an adequate retirement income. Can an adequate level of income be generally prescribed or is the level different for each individual? If the level is different, what factors make it different?

9.1 What is retirement planning?

LEARNING OBJECTIVE 9.1 Explain why it is important to plan for retirement.

Planning involves making choices. Retirement planning requires an individual to make many choices — some of them are very difficult.

In accumulating wealth to fund retirement, an individual must consider the following.

- How much current consumption am I prepared to forgo in order to fund future consumption?
- How aggressive should my investment strategy be?
- Should I accumulate wealth inside or outside a superannuation environment?
- How long should I seek to accumulate wealth as opposed to using that wealth to enjoy my retirement?
- How much do I need to accumulate in order to fund my desired lifestyle in retirement?
- Will part of my retirement savings be required to pay off debt, such as the home mortgage?
- Will additional funds be required to fund aged care, such as moving into an aged care facility?

Having 'retired' there are still many choices to be made, including the following.

- What does retirement actually mean? Does it mean stopping work or working less? How will I know when I am ready to retire?
- How will I manage the change in lifestyle associated with being retired? Will I be happy in retirement? What if I change my mind? Can I return to the workforce?
- How do I access my retirement savings?
- How do I best manage the risk of longevity? That is, the risk of outliving my retirement funds. Am I able to access any government support?

Individuals' needs in retirement

An individual's basic needs do not change in retirement; however, the post-retirement lifestyle within which those needs are fulfilled does change, and it does so dramatically. Individuals need to plan for this change such that their needs are fulfilled. Maslow (1987) identified a hierarchy of individual needs. One of the key aspects of Maslow's hierarchy is that higher-level needs cannot be satisfied unless lower-level needs in the hierarchy have been satisfied first.

At the base level, we all have physiological needs that must be satisfied, for example, water, food, shelter and basic health. In Australia, we are fortunate that most people have these basic physiological needs satisfied. Health issues are of particular concern for retirees. People who envisage that they will become fit and healthy when they retire are likely to be disappointed. For this to occur, changes to lifestyle patterns need to happen well before retirement if they are to be enduring and effective. Increased life expectancies mean that most people will enjoy longer and more active retirements. However, as people age, it is reasonable to expect that health concerns and health costs will increase.

Moving up the Maslow hierarchy are safety needs, for example feeling safe at home and outside of the home. As people get older, security concerns become more prominent — many people decide to defend themselves via deadlocks, alarm systems, gated communities and retirement villages; however, we also want to live in a society where extreme defensive measures are not required.

All people have the need for belonging and love — to sustain personal and family relationships, and to be members of their communities. Many people form significant relationships at work and lose some contact with these friends when they retire. Developing new friendships can be difficult. Some retirees intend to join groups when they have more time in retirement; if at all possible, it would be better to join these groups while working and increase participation once retired. (It is no good waiting until you are retired to take up golf only to find that you don't like the game.) Many retired Australians participate in voluntary work both as an aide to the community and as a means of maintaining belonging to the community.

The death or loss of a partner is generally recognised as one of the most significant psychological events in a person's life. Sometimes the end of a long-term relationship coincides with retirement and unpreparedness for retirement compounds the effects of other difficulties in a relationship. Such events cannot really be planned for but their effect on the need for love and belonging can be mitigated somewhat by a good support network of family and friends.

Everyone has the need for self-esteem and to be respected by others. One of the first questions often asked by a new acquaintance is 'what do you do?' In many ways, work defines who we are. This can lead to difficulties in retirement — work provides people with the opportunity to complete a task well and to earn the respect of others for doing so, an opportunity that can be difficult to replicate in retirement.

All people have what Maslow calls self-actualisation needs, for example to be creative, to acquire knowledge and enjoy the aesthetic. Retirement often provides people with the time they need to pursue these needs. It is important, however, that retirement also provides people with the money they need to do so — to stand in front of the pyramids is a joyous experience, but it costs money.

9.2 The three phases of retirement

LEARNING OBJECTIVE 9.2 Outline the three phases of retirement.

The concept of retirement is relatively new. Up until the end of the nineteenth century, people expected to work until they died. If a person was unable to continue working for any reason, there was often an extended family to provide some level of support.

The average Australian retiring today might reasonably expect a retirement period of around 25 years. Over that period, the individual might go through a number of phases. The phases can be categorised into active, passive and support phases. There are no clear boundaries between these phases as they are affected by a number of factors; for example, the transition from active to passive may take a number of years, and the age at which these transitions take place will depend on the individual's circumstances.

The active phase of retirement

The traditional notion of the workforce made up of mainly men working for a single employer for many years, retiring, having a going away party, receiving a gold watch and never again working in paid employment was always a generalisation and is even less the case today. Nonetheless, in the past, it did reflect some aspects of the working life of many Australians. However, today, female participation in the workforce is much higher, and people change jobs more frequently, move between full-time and part-time work for the same or different employers more often, and provide consulting services or start small businesses from home. As a result of these and other changes, today many people find it hard to identify if and when they have retired. Maybe a new term needs to be invented that means 'working less' or 'transitioning into retirement'.

The active phase might also include having more time for pursuits that were previously constrained by full-time work such as hobbies, sport, travel and voluntary work. Surveys of retirees highlight the importance of these pursuits in helping the individual ease from full-time work to part-time work to no work.

The income generated from part-time or contract work can provide a useful supplement to other retirement income. Active retirement can involve expensive outlays such as for overseas travel, sporting activities and socializing, which may require a considerable income flow and place significant demands on retirement savings.

The passive phase of retirement

Generally, in the passive phase, the individual will no longer be working in paid employment, although many older Australians still participate in voluntary work. Hobby and sporting interests are likely to be somewhat less energetic than during the active phase and more expensive pursuits such as travel are likely to be reduced. In the passive phase, the individual is capable of caring for themselves in their own home although they may need some support such as Meals on Wheels or home nursing care. Many may decide to move into a retirement village. The income needs in the passive phase are generally less than in the active phase because the individual or couple are less active.

The support phase of retirement

In the support phase, the individual is no longer able to care for themselves in their own home, even with the support services. The individual may need to move into an aged-care facility or nursing home. Provision needs to be made in any retirement plan to cover the costs associated with moving into such alternate accommodation. Accordingly, the funds needed during the support phase tend to increase again, taking into account increased medical and pharmaceutical costs, and aged care support.

9.3 Funding retirement

LEARNING OBJECTIVE 9.3 Calculate how much funds are required to fund retirement needs.

The active, passive and support phases of retirement all need to be funded. Surveys of retirees show that their number one concern is whether they will have adequate wealth to fund their retirement income needs for the rest of their life.

Perhaps the best way to answer the question of how much wealth is adequate to fund retirement is to start with a simple example and then make it slightly more complex (and realistic). For example, Kate is 60 years old and is retiring today. She wants an income stream of $50 000 per year for the next 10 years. Kate needs to save $500 000 to afford this income stream. She can place the $500 000 under her bed and each year she can reach down under her bed and take out $50 000 to fund her retirement lifestyle.

This approach, however, has several problems. Firstly, $50 000 in year 10 will purchase a lot less than $50 000 in year 1 because of the effects of inflation. We might adjust for this by increasing the desired income stream by the rate of inflation each year. If we assume inflation of 3% p.a., Kate would need an income of $51 500 in year 1, $53 045 in year 2 and so on. To afford this income stream, Kate would need to put a total of $640 390 under her bed.

Most retirees do not, however, put their money under their bed. They consume some of their capital in the current year as income and invest the remaining capital. The investment returns on unused capital mean that Kate can start with a smaller accumulated amount and achieve the income stream she desires. If we assume that Kate invests her unused capital at 7% p.a. and she draws down her income at the end of the year she would need $407 907 to afford her desired income stream. This is illustrated in table 9.1.

TABLE 9.1   Kate's retirement funding

Year	Opening balance $	Earnings (invested at 7%) $	Income drawn down (adjusted for 3% inflation p.a.) $	Closing balance $
1	407 907	28 553	51 500	384 960
2	384 960	26 947	53 045	358 863
3	358 863	25 120	54 636	329 347
4	329 347	23 054	56 275	296 126
5	296 126	20 729	57 964	258 891
6	258 891	18 122	59 703	217 310
7	217 310	15 212	61 494	171 028
8	171 028	11 972	63 339	119 662
9	119 662	8 376	65 239	62 800
10	62 800	4 396	67 196	0

Kate is only 60 years old. She has estimated that she will require her retirement income stream for 10 years; however, there is every likelihood that she will outlive this income stream. The risk that the individual will outlive their retirement income/savings is generally referred to as **longevity risk**. Current life expectancy is 81.3 for males and 85.4 for females. Table 9.2 illustrates the **life expectancy** of men and women aged 55 to 70.

TABLE 9.2   Male and female life expectancies

Age (years)	Life expectancy (years)	
	Male	Female
55	28.35	31.49
56	27.47	30.57

(continued)

TABLE 9.2 *(continued)*

Age (years)	Life expectancy (years)	
	Male	Female
57	26.60	29.66
58	25.73	28.75
59	24.87	27.84
60	24.02	26.93
61	23.17	26.03
62	22.33	25.14
63	21.50	24.24
64	20.67	23.36
65	19.86	22.47
66	19.04	21.60
67	18.24	20.73
68	17.45	19.87
69	16.67	19.02
70	15.90	18.18

Source: Extracts from Australian Government Actuary 2023.

Thus, aged 60, Kate has an average life expectancy of another 26.93 years. If we extended table 9.1, Kate would need over $826 000 to fund her desired income stream for 26.93 years rather than 10 years. However, Kate might still outlive her income stream; life expectancies are just that, they are not certainties. In contrast, Kate might die before her life expectancy and might have wished that she had enjoyed more of her savings during her life.

An alternative to creating a spreadsheet like the one shown in table 9.1 to determine how much a client needs to accumulate to fund their retirement is to use the present value (PV) function, either in a financial calculator or a spreadsheet. The PV function requires three inputs. Once the inputs are determined, the amount a client needs to accumulate in retirement savings in order to afford their desired income stream in retirement can be estimated.

1. *The real rate of return.* This is a function of the nominal rate of return and the rate of inflation. Generally, the more aggressive the investment strategy, the higher the nominal rate of return. It is important to remember that, once a client is in **pension mode** rather than **accumulation mode**, they are unable to recover from investment losses that occur by working harder/longer. Therefore, their investment strategy is likely to be less aggressive compared with when they were working. However, it is important for the client to be aware of the ramifications of becoming too conservative in their investment strategy. Given that Kate might live for a further 26.93 years or longer, she will be concerned to ensure that her retirement funds last her lifetime. The risk of investing too conservatively may result in Kate's retirement funds running out early. Taking on too much risk may result in investment losses. This highlights the importance of careful planning and an appreciation of risk versus return.

   In Kate's example, 7% is the nominal rate of investment return including an inflationary component. If the inflation rate is 3%, then the real rate is approximately 4%. More precisely, to allow for a small compounding effect the real rate is 3.88%:

$$\frac{1 + \text{Nominal rate}}{1 + \text{Inflation rate}} - 1$$

2. *The number of periods.* How much longevity risk does Kate wish to bear? In this case, we have assumed 26.93 years.

3. *The payment required.* It is important for the client to determine whether this payment is relative to how much they earned prior to retirement or more of an absolute figure. For example, in June 2023, a single person was estimated to need $50 207 income p.a. for a comfortable lifestyle in retirement. As a result:

$$PV = (\text{rate, number of periods, desired income})$$
$$PV = (3.88\%, 26.93, \$50\,207) = \$829\,771$$

If Kate was some years away from retiring, she would need to build an accumulation strategy that would achieve the equivalent of $829 771 in real terms by the time she retired. This process is discussed in the chapter on superannuation. Often the process is an iterative one. The client may have unrealistic retirement income expectations, the adviser will calculate the amount that needs to be accumulated to fund this income, and it will become clear that the client will not be able to accumulate this amount during their working life. The client will often need to both boost the amount they accumulate and modify their retirement income expectations.

In undertaking this planning process, it might be useful to provide the client with a scenario analysis. The financial planner must decide which variables to change.

Changing one variable at a time provides the client with a one-dimensional view of the data which can be displayed as a list.

Changing two variables at a time provides the client with a two-dimensional view of the data which can be displayed in a table format. Figure 9.1 varies the nominal rate of return and the number of periods the income stream will last for Kate. The client can then see the impact of the individual variable as well as its interaction with the other variable.

FIGURE 9.1	Scenario analysis for Kate's retirement

Income of: $50 207

Assume inflation rate of: 3.00%

Nominal	3.00%	4.00%	5.00%	6.00%	7.00%	8.00%	9.00%	10.00%
Real	0.00%	0.97%	1.94%	2.91%	3.88%	4.85%	5.83%	6.80%
Periods								
15	$ 753 105	$ 697 741	$ 648 028	$ 603 288	$562 934	$526 456	$493 085	$463 114
25	$1 255 175	$1 109 827	$ 987 154	$ 883 094	$794 382	$718 377	$652 314	$595 786
35	$1 757 245	$1 483 993	$1 266 997	$1 093 124	$952 555	$837 896	$742 665	$664 503

Changing three variables at one time provides the client with a three-dimensional view of the data. Results of this analysis cannot be displayed in a single table; a series of tables would be needed. Moreover, understanding the interactions between the three changing variables becomes more complex.

Any number of variables can be varied at one time but it becomes increasingly difficult to display and interpret the results for both the client and the financial planner.

The data in figure 9.1 highlights that higher nominal returns means less has to be accumulated to afford the desired income stream. However, higher nominal returns means potentially higher risk and the client should identify what level of risk they are comfortable with. The table also highlights that, the longer the desired income stream is expected to last, the more that has to be accumulated.

Kate might believe that a 6% nominal return is as risky as she is comfortable with. Kate might also be worried about longevity risk and choose an income stream for 35 years. This means she would need to accumulate $1 093 124 in retirement savings in real terms by the time she retires. However, if Kate has only $650 000 accumulated in retirement savings, she would need to modify some combination of the total amount she accumulates, the nominal return she seeks, the desired term of her income stream, and the desired amount of her retirement income stream.

9.4 Ordinary money versus superannuation money

LEARNING OBJECTIVE 9.4 Differentiate between ordinary money and superannuation money.

In the chapter on superannuation, we recognised that individuals can accumulate wealth to fund their retirement both inside and outside of a superannuation environment. If money is accumulated outside of a superannuation environment it is known as **ordinary money**. If money is accumulated inside a superannuation environment, it is known as **superannuation money**. It is likely that most individuals will have some combination of ordinary money and superannuation money available to fund their retirement.

Ordinary money is after-tax money. It could be held in many forms, including cash, term deposits, bonds, shares, investment bonds and property. One of the advantages of using ordinary money to fund retirement, rather than superannuation funds, is that it does not need to satisfy a condition of release in order for retirement funds to be accessed. If, for example, an individual wishes to withdraw some of their cash to fund an extended overseas holiday, the decision is entirely up to the individual. That is, no other conditions need to be satisfied and no tax has to be paid to release the funds.

Superannuation money is held inside the tax-concessional superannuation environment. This money must be maintained (**preserved**) in a superannuation environment until a condition of release is reached which includes the following situations:
- the individual has reached age 65
- the individual is aged between 55 and 60 and has reached preservation age (see table 9.3) — also the normal employment arrangement must have ceased and the superannuation trustee must be convinced that the individual does not intend to work more than 10 hours per week in the future
- the individual is aged between 60 and 65 and has reached preservation age — also the normal employment arrangement must have ceased, but the individual may continue in another employment situation
- the individual is permanently incapacitated or suffering from a terminal medical condition
- the death of the individual
- the individual experiences severe financial hardship or funds are needed for compassionate grounds.

Note that, as a result of Federal Government support for the COVID-19 outbreak, members experiencing financial distress were able to withdraw up to $10 000 from their superannuation accounts in 2019–20 and another $10 000 in 2020–21. Withdrawals under this temporary measure were tax free.

Preservation ages are based on the member's date of birth and are shown in table 9.3.

TABLE 9.3   Preservation age based on date of birth

Date of birth	Preservation age
Before 1 July 1960	55
1 July 1960 – 30 June 1961	56
1 July 1961 – 30 June 1962	57
1 July 1962 – 30 June 1963	58
1 July 1963 – 30 June 1964	59
From 1 July 1964	60

Source: Australian Taxation Office 2023.

If, for example, a superannuation fund member wishes to use some of their superannuation money to fund an extended overseas holiday, they must ensure that they have satisfied a condition of release from their superannuation. In some circumstances, taxes may be payable on the release of the funds. The amount of tax payable will be a function of three factors:
1. the type of superannuation money held in the individual's account
2. the age of the individual
3. whether the money is withdrawn as a lump sum or as an income stream.

A member's superannuation benefit is divided into two main tax components: a tax-free component and a taxable component.

The taxable components may be subject to tax when withdrawn by the member, depending upon their age, whereas the tax-free component will always be tax-free when withdrawn. An explanation of the two components is provided below.

1. **Tax-free component** includes **non-concessional contributions** that individuals have contributed to superannuation voluntarily from after-tax income. These personal contributions are tax free when subsequently withdrawn in retirement.
2. The **taxable component** refers to the balance of the member's superannuation account and is made up of concessional contributions plus earnings.

In certain situations, the taxable component may comprise two elements — a taxed element and an untaxed element. The taxed element includes that part of the taxable component that has been subject to the 15% contributions tax by the super fund. This will typically make up the major portion of the taxable component. The untaxed element represents that part of the taxable component where the 15% contributions tax has not been levied by the superannuation fund. This will arise in situations where the superannuation fund is a public sector superannuation fund, a constitutionally protected fund or where the member's superannuation account includes a life insurance payout. Because the 15% contributions tax has not been levied by the super fund, the member may need to pay a higher rate of tax upon withdrawal of funds.

9.5 Options that a member has upon retirement with their accumulated superannuation funds

LEARNING OBJECTIVE 9.5 Determine the various options a member has at retirement with accumulated superannuation funds.

When an individual satisfies a condition of release, they have four available options as illustrated in figure 9.2.

FIGURE 9.2 Superannuation options after meeting a condition of release

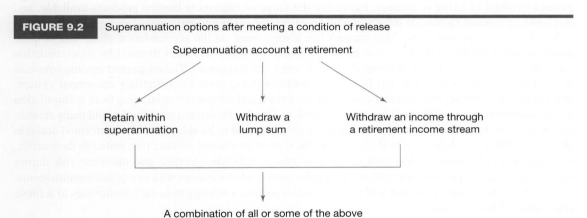

The four options are as follows.

1. Retain the funds in their superannuation account if the member doesn't need to withdraw funds at this stage. Funds can be retained within a superannuation account indefinitely and can always be withdrawn at a later date. A 15% tax will continue to apply on all earnings generated by the fund.
2. Withdraw their superannuation as a lump sum to spend as they see fit. A lump sum tax may be payable which will be covered later in this chapter.
3. Purchase or 'roll over' their superannuation funds into a retirement income stream, such as an account-based pension. The retirement income stream may be subject to tax which will be covered later in this chapter.
4. Withdraw part of their superannuation as a lump sum and roll over the remainder into an account-based pension.

There are several benefits associated with moving superannuation funds across into an income stream or pension fund in retirement. The main benefits are:

• it provides a regular income stream where members can decide to receive payment monthly, quarterly, six-monthly or annually, to substitute for their previous regular salary
• all investment earnings generated with the pension phase are tax free when compared with earnings generated within the superannuation phase which are taxed at a maximum rate of 15%

- all withdrawals after the age of 60 are completely tax free to the member from a taxed superannuation fund (taxed element) and at concessional tax rates for an untaxed element for amounts up to the untaxed plan cap which will be covered later.

Where funds are transferred to commence an account-based pension at retirement, there is a requirement to withdraw a minimum income each year which is determined by the member's age. This will be discussed in a later section. A member can also withdraw a lump sum and depending upon the age of the member, lump sum tax may be payable.

The preferred option for a retired member will depend upon the individual circumstances and the age of the member. It needs to be remembered that funds can be retained within a superannuation fund indefinitely and there is no need to roll funds into a pension account at retirement or withdraw a lump sum. A member may decide to retain funds in their superannuation account in retirement because they do not need an income stream at the present stage, or perhaps they have reached their transfer balance cap, as explained below.

The process of rolling over funds from a superannuation account to a pension account is a relatively straight forward process. Most superannuation funds also offer pension accounts that a member may wish to utilise in order to provide them with an income stream in retirement. If a member is happy to use the same superannuation organisation to hold their pension account, the rollover this can be achieved by completing an internal transfer form. Otherwise, funds can be rolled over / transferred if the member feels that another organisation may provide them with greater benefits, such as lower fees. Most members have choice as to which superannuation organisation they hold their pension fund with. The only requirement is that it is a regulated complying superannuation fund, which includes a self-managed superannuation fund (SMSF).

Retirement income covenant

The retirement income covenant (RIC) came into effect on 1 July 2022 and requires superannuation trustees to formulate a retirement income strategy for their members with the objective of increasing the general standard of living of retirees, increasing the range of retirement income products available, and empowering trustees to provide members with an easier transition into retirement.

The focus of superannuation fund trustees has always been on the accumulation phase and helping members build wealth in their account balances. Much less effort has been directed by superannuation funds in considering the needs of members transitioning into retirement. The retirement income covenant is intended to address this gap and is a long overdue enhancement to Australia's retirement system, particularly given the significant number of superannuation fund members transitioning from accumulation phase into retirement over the next few years. Decisions faced at retirement are complex and many retirees do not have the knowledge or level of financial literacy required to be able to make an informed decision about such things as: their options at retirement, the type of retirement product best suited to their needs, the taxation implications of decisions made, how best to maximise income and minimise risk during retirement, the impact of longevity risk and how retirement products interact with age-pension entitlements.

The retirement income covenant will require trustees to have a strategy to assist beneficiaries to achieve and balance three objectives:
- maximising their expected retirement income
- managing expected risks to the sustainability and stability of their expected retirement income
- having flexible access to expected funds during retirement.

Superannuation fund trustees have a requirement to have their retirement income strategy developed and recorded, with a summary publicly available on the fund's website.

9.6 Implications of the transfer balance cap

LEARNING OBJECTIVE 9.6 Explain the implications of the transfer balance cap in determining retirement options.

One of the issues for consideration in planning for retirement and looking to rollover superannuation into a retirement income stream is the transfer balance cap (TBC). Prior to 1 July 2017, there was no limit on the amount of superannuation funds an individual could transfer from the accumulation phase to the pension phase. Post 1 July 2017, the Turnbull government superannuation reforms limited the amount of superannuation that can be transferred and held in a pension account in order to restrict the tax concessions available to members holding relatively large retirement balances. The transfer balance cap restricts how much superannuation funds can be held in a retirement income stream to $1.9 million, effective from 1 July 2023. The cap is indexed in $100 000 increments according to the Consumer Price Index (CPI). A member can continue to make multiple transfers of funds into their pension account for as long as the total funds in pension phase remain below the cap. All pension account balances are included in determining whether the cap has been reached.

If an individual transfers $1.9 million from their superannuation account to a retirement pension account in the 2023–24 financial year, they will have used 100% of their transfer balance cap and therefore will not be eligible to transfer any further funds from accumulation phase to pension phase, even if the $1.9 million cap increases in the future due to indexation. Any excess pension balance above the transfer balance cap has to be either retained or transferred back into a superannuation account, where earnings are taxed at 15%, or the excess withdrawn as a lump sum and invested outside of superannuation. It is important to note, however, that changes in the market value of investments held within the pension account do not impact upon the member's transfer balance cap. For example, if a member's retirement pension account suffers poor investment returns such that the balance in their pension account falls below $1.9 million, this does not entitle the individual to transfer more superannuation money into their pension account. Conversely, if an individual enjoys good investment returns in their pension account such that their balance increases beyond $1.9 million, the amount in excess of $1.9 million does not have to be returned back into their superannuation account.

If, for example, Marina retires and transfers $950 000 from her superannuation account to a pension account in the 2023–24 financial year, she will have used 50% of her TBC of $1.9 million and has 50% of her transfer balance cap remaining. If, due to indexation, the TBC increases to $2.1 million in a future year (i.e. increases by $200 000) then Marina will only benefit from a proportion of the indexation which is 50% of her unused cap of the $200 000 (i.e. $100 000). This means her personal TBC will increase to $2 million. With 50% of her transfer balance cap remaining, she would be entitled to transfer up to $1 050 000 from accumulation to pension mode in that year.

The general rule applying to the $1.9 pension transfer balance cap is modified in the case of a person receiving a defined benefit pension. The reason for the different treatment is that defined benefit pensions are typically paid for the life of the member and include rules which make it non-commutable and, therefore, it is not possible to convert or withdraw part or all of the defined benefit income stream funds and transfer them back to accumulation phase. Defined benefit income streams that do not ordinarily have an account balance, have an account value determined for the purpose of the TBC based on a formula contained in the legislation. The calculation is as follows.

$$\text{Account value} = \text{Annual income} \times 16$$

The value of a defined benefit pension does not give rise to an excess transfer balance because the underlying capital cannot generally be removed to reduce the amount assessed against the cap. However, tax may be payable on the income stream payments.

For high income earners, where their accumulated superannuation balance is close to, or already exceeds the transfer balance cap, the member needs to plan their preferred strategy. That is, whether is it beneficial to still continue to maximise their contributions to superannuation, whether it might be beneficial to, instead, build up their spouse's superannuation funds in order to utilise two transfer balance caps, or whether it might be preferable to build wealth outside of the superannuation environment, such as commencing a share portfolio, investing into an investment bond or purchasing an investment property.

At the time the transfer balance cap was introduced, the Treasurer estimated that fewer than 1% of superannuation fund members would be impacted by this cap.

9.7 Withdrawing a lump sum in order to fund retirement

LEARNING OBJECTIVE 9.7 Outline the tax consequences of withdrawing a lump sum from superannuation to fund retirement.

As discussed earlier in this chapter, withdrawing a lump sum from ordinary money to fund retirement is a simple and straightforward process. Funds are withdrawn from after-tax money (capital) by disposing of the investment and CGT may be payable.

Withdrawing a lump sum from either a superannuation account, once a member satisfies a condition of release, or at any time from a retirement income stream, is also a relatively straight forward process and may have significant tax advantages. This will be discussed later in this chapter.

The calculation of tax on the withdrawal of a lump sum from superannuation monies, whether in accumulation phase or pension phase, is based on two components:

- tax-free component
- taxable component.

The tax-free component of a member's superannuation comprises the total of a member's contributions segment and the crystallised segment. The contributions segment generally includes all non-concessional contributions made after 30 June 2007. The crystallised segment is made up of a number of different tax-free components that applied under complex superannuation rules that existed prior to 1 July 2007. On 1 July 2007, the superannuation rules relating to the taxing of lump sums were simplified and any tax-free components that a member had at that time were consolidated and the balance able to be carried forward as a crystallised (tax-free) segment.

All superannuation money which is not tax free is taxable and includes concessional contributions and all earnings generated over the years. Table 9.4 and the following illustrative examples show the tax implications of withdrawing a lump sum from superannuation. The examples are based on the member satisfying a condition of release and therefore able to access their superannuation.

TABLE 9.4   Taxed superannuation money — withdrawing a lump sum

Type of superannuation money	Age	Tax consequences
Tax free component		Tax free
Taxable (taxed)	Over 60	Tax free
	Under 60	Tax free up to the low-rate cap[a].
		Above the low-rate cap[a], taxed at 15%[b]

[a] The low rate cap for 2023–24 is $235 000. The low rate cap is indexed in line with AWOTE, in increments of $5000 (rounded down). At the time of writing the low rate cap for 2024–25 isn't available.

[b] Tax payable also subject to 2% Medicare levy.

Source: Australian Taxation Office 2023.

ILLUSTRATIVE EXAMPLE 9.1

Sally is 59 years old and has $500 000 in superannuation. Her superannuation comprises a tax-free component of $100 000 and a taxable superannuation component of $400 000. Sally has satisfied a condition of release and would like to withdraw a $300 000 lump sum. Money must be withdrawn from a superannuation environment in proportion to the tax-free/taxable components that exist within the individual's superannuation fund. A member is not able to determine what component they wish to use as part of the withdrawal.

Sally's superannuation fund consists of a tax-free component of 20% ($100 000 / $500 000) and therefore has a taxable component of 80% ($400 000 / $500 000). Any lump sum that Sally withdraws must therefore be in the proportion of 20% tax free and 80% taxable. If Sally withdraws $300 000 as a lump sum, $60 000 (20%) will be tax free and $240 000 (80%) will be taxable. The amount of tax required to be paid by Sally on the lump sum withdrawal of $300 000 is shown below.

Component	Amount released	Tax payable	Note
Tax-free component	$ 60 000	0	Tax free
Taxable component	240 000	0	Up to low-rate cap of $235 000, tax free.
			Balance of $5 000 taxed at 15% plus Medicare
		$850	levy ($5 000 × 17%)
Total	$300 000	$850	

As Sally is under the age of 60, $850 in tax would be payable on the $300 000 lump sum withdrawal. If Sally waited until she was 60 years of age, the taxable component would also be totally exempt from tax and no tax would be payable. This reflects the Howard–Costello 2007 changes to superannuation where individuals over the age of 60 years with taxed superannuation money are able to withdraw their superannuation money entirely tax free.

If an individual has an untaxed element, the tax treatment associated with withdrawing a lump sum (shown in table 9.5) is not quite so generous. This reflects the fact that the member has not paid taxes on contributions and investment earnings on their superannuation fund during the accumulation phase.

TABLE 9.5 Untaxed element — withdrawing a lump sum

Type of superannuation money	Age	Tax consequences
Tax free	Not applicable	Tax free
Taxable (taxed)	Over 60	Up to the untaxed plan cap[a], taxed at 15%
		Above the untaxed plan cap[a], taxed at 45%
	Preservation age to 59	Up to the low-rate cap[b], taxed at 15%
		Above the low-rate cap[b] but below the untaxed plan cap[a], taxed at 30%
		Above the untaxed plan cap[a], taxed at 45%
	Under preservation age	Up to the untaxed plan cap[a], taxed at 30%
		Above the untaxed plan cap[a], taxed at 45%

Tax rates are also subject to 2% Medicare levy.

[a] The untaxed plan cap for 2023–24 is $1.705 million.

[b] The low-rate cap for 2023–24 is $235 000.

Source: Australian Taxation Office 2023.

ILLUSTRATIVE EXAMPLE 9.2

Ben is 59 years old and has $500 000 in superannuation. His superannuation comprises a tax-free component of $100 000 and an untaxed element of $400 000. Ben has satisfied a condition of release from superannuation and would like to withdraw a $300 000 lump sum. Ben will need to pay $41 550 in tax to release a $300 000 lump sum from superannuation as shown in table 9.6.

TABLE 9.6 Ben's tax payable on a lump sum withdrawn from an untaxed element at 59 years (preservation age to 59) is shown below.

Component	Amount released	Tax payable	Note
Tax-free component	$ 60 000	0	$100 000 / $500 000 = 20% tax free $300 000 × 20% = $60 000
Taxable component (untaxed element)	$240 000		Taxable component = $300 000 − $60 000 = $240 000
		$39 950	Up to low-rate cap of $235 000, taxed at 17% (15% plus Medicare) $235 000 × 17%
		1 600	Above the low-rate threshold but below the untaxed plan cap of $1.705 million, taxed at 32% (30% plus Medicare) $5000 × 32%
Total	$300 000	$41 550	

If Ben waited until he was 60 years, the tax consequences would be as shown in table 9.7.

TABLE 9.7 Ben's tax payable on lump sum withdrawn from an untaxed element at 60 years

Component	Amount released	Tax payable	Note
Tax-free component	$ 60 000	0	Tax free
Taxable component (untaxed element)	$240 000	$40 800	Up to the untaxed plan cap of $1.705 million, taxed at 17% 240 000 × 17%
Total	$300 000	$40 800	

It's important to note that there is no difference in the tax rates or amount of tax payable between a lump sum withdrawn from a member's pension account or from their superannuation account. What is important, is the member's age and whether the taxed component is a taxed element or a non-taxed element.

Superannuation death benefits payable as a lump sum

The tax consequences of leaving a superannuation lump sum to a beneficiary upon the death of the member depend on whether the beneficiary is a tax dependent or a non-tax dependent. A tax dependent in this case is defined in the *Income Tax Assessment Act 1997* (ITAA97) as a person who at the date of death of the deceased is a:

- spouse or former spouse of the deceased (includes de facto and same sex spouses)
- child of the deceased under the age of 18
- person who is financially dependent on the deceased
- person who has an interdependency relationship with the deceased.

Superannuation death benefits can only be paid to dependents defined under the SIS Act. The definition of a dependent under the SIS Act contains two main differences to the definition of a dependent contained within the Taxation Act. A SIS dependent does not include a former spouse and a child can be of any age. Whilst the SIS Act informs a trustee as to whom a death benefit can be paid to, the Taxation Act informs the trustee how that benefit is to be taxed. Superannuation funds paid to beneficiaries as a lump sum upon the death of the member are free of tax to those classified as tax dependents. When paid to beneficiaries who are non-tax dependents, the calculation of tax is more complex and is determined as:

- the tax-free component is not subject to tax
- the taxable component is taxed at 15% plus Medicare levy
- if the taxable component contains an untaxed element, this will be taxed at 30% plus the Medicare levy.

The trustees of a superannuation fund have discretion as to who a superannuation death benefit is payable to, unless the superannuation fund member makes a binding death nomination. In estate planning terms, it is usually preferable to make a binding death nomination in favour of a tax-dependent, if at all possible, to reduce the amount of tax that would otherwise be payable. If non-tax dependents need to be provided for, it may be preferable to provide for them by way of non-superannuation assets via the individual's will.

ILLUSTRATIVE EXAMPLE 9.3

Aileen, aged 62 years, dies and leaves $500 000 in superannuation, which includes a tax-free component of $100 000 and a taxed component of $400 000. Therefore, 20% of Aileen's superannuation is tax free ($100 000 / $500 000) and 80% is taxable. The binding death benefit nomination within her superannuation account leaves 50% of the superannuation balance to her husband Callum and 50% to her 24 year old son Rick who has left home and is financially independent.

$250 000 left to husband Callum

Callum, her husband, is a tax dependent and therefore the amount will be totally tax-free in his hands.

$250 000 left to son Rick

Rick, being over 18 years old and financially independent, is a non-tax dependent and therefore he may be liable to tax. Whilst the taxable proportion is subject to tax, the tax-free proportion is tax free to Rick. The proportions can be determined as:

- Tax-free component: $50 000 (20% × $250 000) is tax free
- Taxable component: $200 000 ($250 000 – $50 000) is taxable and will be taxed at a tax rate of 15% plus Medicare levy = $34 000.

Splitting the lump sum as a result of divorce or separation

The *Family Law Act 1975* allows the Family Court to split superannuation between separating couples. Where the superannuation money is held in an accumulation-style account, the splitting process is relatively straightforward — the components of the old superannuation account are split proportionally into two new accounts.

Ray and Janice recently divorced. As part of the Family Court's determination, Ray's superannuation of $400 000 is to be split 70% to Ray and 30% to Janice. Ray's superannuation includes a $100 000 tax-free component.

After the split, Ray will have $280 000 in superannuation, which includes a tax-free component of $70 000. Janice will have $120 000 in superannuation, which includes a tax-free component of $30 000. Both Ray and Janice are now free to manage their superannuation accounts as they wish.

Where the superannuation money is held in a defined benefit account, the process of splitting is more complex. Defined benefit accounts do not have an account balance. In these cases, the court might order a payment split; that is, the funds will remain in the defined benefit account until the current owner of the account retires, at which time part of the payment received will pass to the other party.

Re-contribution of a lump-sum withdrawal

We have previously seen that, when withdrawing a superannuation lump sum, there are considerable tax advantages associated with having as large a tax-free component as possible. Later in this chapter, we will also see that a larger tax-free component will also have tax advantages for members seeking to receive an income stream.

A common strategy to maximise the tax-free component of a member's superannuation balance is for the member to contribute additional non-concessional contributions. Non-concessional contributions form part of the tax-free component of a superannuation balance so, the more non-concessional contributions a member makes to their superannuation fund, the higher the tax-free component and the lower the taxable proportion. For example, where a member has a superannuation balance of $500 000 with a $50 000 tax-free amount, their current tax-free component is 10% and taxable proportion is 90%. If the member makes a non-concessional superannuation contribution of $200 000 to their superannuation fund, their tax-free component will now be $250 000 / $700 000 = 35.7% and their taxable proportion will fall from 90% to 64.3%.

Another very common strategy developed by financial planners for members that have satisfied a condition of release and are still able to contribute funds into their superannuation account is called the re-contribution strategy. The aim of the strategy is to convert part of a member's taxable component into a tax-free component within their superannuation account.

A re-contribution strategy involves making a lump sum withdrawal from superannuation and preferably paying either no tax, or a very small amount, and then recontributing the amount back into their superannuation account in the form of a non-concessional contribution.

Barney is 59 years old and has $600 000 in superannuation which includes a tax-free component of $120 000 and a taxable component of $480 000. Therefore, 20% of Barney's superannuation is tax free and 80% is taxable.

Barney has satisfied a condition of release from superannuation and decides to withdraw $300 000 as a lump sum and then immediately recontribute this amount back into his superannuation account as a non-concessional contribution.

Remember that the lump sum withdrawal from superannuation must be made in proportion to the components of his superannuation fund as detailed below:

- $60 000 (20% × $300 000) is tax free
- $240 000 ($300 000 – $60 000) is taxable — however, the first $235 000 (the low-rate cap for 2023–24) of the taxable component is tax free leaving $5000.

Therefore, Barney can release a lump sum of $300 000 from his superannuation and pay tax of: $5000 × 17% (15% plus Medicare) = $850.

Barney can then recontribute the $300 000 back into superannuation as a non-concessional contribution under the 3-year bring forward rule, as long he has not triggered the bring forward rule in the past 3 years. Barney will still have $600 000 in his superannuation account but the components will now be comprised of the following:

Employment termination payments (ETP)

Employees sometimes receive a lump sum payment from their employer associated with the termination of their employment. While this might occur at any stage during a person's working life, it is more likely to occur as a person approaches retirement.

Prior to 2007, it was possible for some employer payments to be paid directly into the superannuation account of the recipient and avoid tax. Since 2007, all employer payments are required to be paid directly to the recipient and may be subject to tax. The employee then has a choice as to how the after-tax funds are used — they may decide to spend this money, save it or contribute it to their superannuation account. Payments classified as Employer Termination Payments (ETPs) are prescribed in ITAA97 and are subject to concessional tax treatment. They include:

- payment in lieu of notice
- payment for unused sick leave
- golden handshakes (gift upon retirement)
- invalidity payments (for permanent disability)
- compensation for loss of job or wrongful dismissal
- genuine redundancy payments in excess of the tax-free amount.

ETPs do not include:

- lump sum payments for unused annual or long service leave
- the tax-free part of a genuine redundancy payment or an early retirement scheme payment
- superannuation benefits
- compensation for personal injury.

Payments which are not considered ETPs are included within the assessable income of the employee and generally taxed at marginal tax rates.

As with superannuation lump sum payments, ETPs are also divided into tax-free and taxable components. The taxable amount up to an ETP low-rate cap is treated in a tax-concessional manner. In 2023–24, the low-rate threshold was $235 000.

An ETP has a tax-free component if part of the payment relates to:

- employment that relates to the period before 1 July 1983
- invalidity of the member.

ETPs are also divided into life benefit termination payments (LBTP) where the employee receiving the ETP is still living, and death benefit termination payments (DBTP) where sadly the employee is not alive to receive the payment.

Life benefit termination payments (LBTP)

The tax-free component of a LBTP is exempt from tax. The taxable component is taxed as follows.

- If the recipient is above their preservation age, the amount up to the low-rate threshold is taxed at 17%. Amounts received in excess of the low-rate cap are taxed at 47% (tax rates include Medicare).
- If the recipient is below their preservation age, the amount up to the low-rate threshold is taxed at 32%. Amounts received in excess of the low-rate cap are taxed at 47% (tax rates include Medicare).

One of the payments that may be paid to an employee is as a result of redundancy. Any payments that meet the conditions of a genuine redundancy are tax free up to a limit based on years of service with the employer. The tax-free limit is calculated as follows.

$$\text{Base amount} + (\text{Service amount} \times \text{Completed years of service})$$

Indexation changes the tax-free limit on 1 July each year. For 2023–24, the tax-free limit is $11 985 (base amount), plus $5994 (service amount).

ILLUSTRATIVE EXAMPLE 9.6

Marge is aged 63 and has worked for her employer for 10.5 years. She has just received a redundancy payout of $100 000. The tax payable is calculated as follows:

$$\text{Tax-free amount} = \$11\,985 + (10 \times \$5994) = \$71\,925$$

Note that only completed years of service are taken into account. This will leave Marge with a taxable component of her ETP (the balance of the redundancy payment) of $28 075 ($100 000 – $71 925). As Marge is above her preservation age, the ETP will be taxed at a tax rate of 17% up to the low rate cap, $28 075 × 17% = $4772.75.

ILLUSTRATIVE EXAMPLE 9.7

Continuing from illustrative example 9.6, now assume that the reason for the $100 000 payment received by Marge was not due to redundancy but some other reason and classified as an employer termination payment.

Does Marge have a tax-free component? Given that Marge has worked for her employer for 10.5 years, all her work must have been after June 1983. Also, we can assume that the reason for the payment is not due to her invalidity. As a result, all her ETP represents a taxable component. At age 63, Marge is past her preservation age and will need to pay $17 000 ($100 000 × 17%) in tax on her ETP. Marge is then free to spend this money, save it or contribute it to superannuation as a concessional or non-concessional contribution.

Death benefit termination payments (DBTP)

The tax payable on a DBTP depends on who is the recipient of the DBTP. Tax dependents are treated more generously on the ETP than non-tax dependents. For tax dependents:

- the tax-free component of a DBTP is exempt from tax
- the taxable component up to the low-rate threshold ($235 000 for 2023–24) is also exempt from tax
- amounts in excess of the low-rate threshold are taxed at the highest marginal tax rate.
  For non-tax dependents:
- the tax-free component of a DBTP is exempt from tax
- the taxable component up to the low-rate threshold is taxed at 30% plus the Medicare levy
- amounts in excess of the low-rate threshold are taxed at the highest marginal tax rate.

9.8 Sources of income streams in retirement

LEARNING OBJECTIVE 9.8 Differentiate between the different types of retirement income streams.

Once a condition of release has been satisfied, many Australians see the ability to withdraw all or some of their money from superannuation as a lump sum as a right. Under the current rules, members are able to withdraw their entire superannuation balance at retirement as a lump sum. In contrast, most countries with retirement savings schemes do not allow individuals to withdraw all their money as a lump sum, although some do allow limited lump sum withdrawals.

Most Australians, however, do not withdraw all their superannuation as a lump sum. During their working lives, an individual earns a regular income, pays bills each month, and budgets their expenditure in this way. People see retirement in much the same way and therefore often need to use their superannuation account to create a regular income stream in retirement. However, due to lack of information or poor financial literacy, many Australians make poor decisions at retirement and may decide to withdraw a lump sum to fund holidays, buy an expensive new car, a caravan or an extravagant lifestyle only to find that their superannuation runs out very quickly and they have insufficient income to fund their lifestyle. Given the significant increase in house prices and the resultant increase in the amounts of home mortgages taken out, many Australians find that they still have an outstanding home mortgage at the time of retirement and seek to withdraw funds from superannuation to pay off any outstanding loans. Whilst this does pay off debt, it also has the impact of reducing a member's retirement funds with the risk that their accumulated superannuation funds will not adequately provide for their retirement needs.

The rules and regulations that apply to the retirement phase are much less stringent than in the accumulation phase where there are strict rules governing what can go into superannuation, when it can go in, the amounts that can be contributed and when the funds can be released. As a result, many Australians unfortunately make inappropriate decisions on how best to fund their retirement which may last for another 20–30 years.

Commencing an income stream means moving from accumulating phase into retirement phase to generate an income in retirement.

Source of income in retirement

Income generated in retirement can come from a variety of sources, including:
- retirement income stream originating from superannuation or external funds
- part-time work
- the government age pension
- running a business
- return or capital from investments.

9.9 Main forms of retirement income streams

LEARNING OBJECTIVE 9.9 Contrast and compare account-based and non-account-based income streams.

There are two types of income streams available in Australia today: account-based income streams and non-account-based income streams. An **account-based income stream** is funded from a member's superannuation account and provides the individual with significant control over their retirement account in terms of how the funds are invested and how income is withdrawn, much the same way as with superannuation. Account-based income streams are the most popular type of income stream for Australians who convert their accumulated superannuation into an income stream. Account-based income streams can only be acquired with superannuation monies and are offered by superannuation funds.

Non-account-based income streams are funded from either superannuation funds or ordinary money and are offered by either a superannuation fund or a life office. In return for a capital sum, they provide the person with an income stream over a period specified in a contract. Usually, an income stream from a superannuation fund is called a pension, and an income stream from a life office is called an annuity.

The characteristics of account-based and non-account-based income streams are shown in table 9.8.

TABLE 9.8   Comparing account-based and non-account-based income streams

Characteristic	Account-based income streams	Non-account-based income streams
Superannuation or ordinary money	Can be purchased only with superannuation money.	Can be purchased with superannuation money or ordinary money.
Investment assets	Held in the name of the individual.	Held by the income-stream provider.
Investment selection	Made by the individual.	Made by the income-stream provider.
Investment risk	Borne by the individual.	Borne by the income-stream provider.
Income level	Determined by the member. Prescribed minimum annual payment must be taken, which is a function of age. No maximum annual payments. (See discussion on minimum income levels for account-based income streams later in the chapter.)	Amount of income is specified in a contract with the provider at the time of commencing the income stream and is fixed thereafter. Amount can be contracted at commencement to increase subject to indexation.

Consequences of death	Balance remaining is made to SIS beneficiaries as per superannuation death benefit nomination or determined by trustee. (See discussion of tax of retirement income streams on death later in the chapter.)	Can be contracted that income reverts to a dependent on death (known as a reversionary beneficiary), usually at a lower rate (e.g. 60% of the original pension payment is paid to the surviving spouse).If a lifetime income stream with a guarantee period is acquired, the present value of the remaining payments within the guarantee period will be paid to the estate. If the lifetime income stream product has no guarantee period or the guarantee period has expired, the remaining capital is forfeited upon death.
Longevity risk	Borne by the individual.	If a fixed-term income stream, then borne by the individual after the fixed term has expired. If a lifetime income stream, then borne by the income-stream provider.
Taxation of fund earnings	Investment earnings are exempt from tax.	When purchased with superannuation money, investment earnings are exempt from tax. Otherwise, earnings are taxable.
Taxation on income paid to member		If funded from superannuation, taxation is the same as for account-based pension.
• If the member is over 60 years of age	Totally tax free if funded by taxed superannuation money.	If purchased with ordinary money, income is fully assessable less any deductible amount, representing the return of capital over the period of the annuity.
• If member is aged between preservation age and age 59	Tax-free component is tax free. Taxable component is assessable at marginal tax rates but member entitled to a 15% pension tax offset.	
• If member is under preservation age	Tax-free component is tax free. Taxable component is assessable at marginal tax rates.(See discussion on taxation of retirement income streams later in the chapter.)	
Commutation[a]	Can be commuted at any time.	Generally not possible to commute.
Ability to make additional contributions	Additional contributions cannot be made to an existing pension account. However, if a member is still able to pay funds into a superannuation account, a second pension account could be commenced. Otherwise, a member could commute an existing pension account, transfer funds back into a superannuation account and then commence a brand new pension account with the combined funds.	Income-stream provider will not accept additional contributions; however, a separate accumulation account could be started. Individual generally cannot commute; therefore, they are locked into their income stream.

[a] Commutation is the ability to make a lump sum withdrawal from the income stream

Determining income levels for account-based income streams

For an account-based pension, it is a requirement that a member must withdraw an annual income stream. A minimum annual payment amount must be paid each year once an account-based pension commences (table 9.9). It is calculated using a percentage factor based on the member's age. There is no restriction on the maximum amount of pension paid each year. Whilst an annual income is required to be withdrawn each year, the frequency of payment is determined by the member which may be monthly, quarterly, semi-annually or annually based on the needs of the member. At the commencement of each financial year, the superannuation fund trustee contacts the member to determine two items. Firstly, what level of income is required for the year, given minimum income level requirements and secondly, how frequently does the member seek an income stream? This is usually monthly, but can be paid quarterly, semi-annually or once a year.

TABLE 9.9 Minimum percentage factor for each age group

Age	Minimum percentage payment
Under 65	4%
65–74	5%
75–79	6%
80–84	7%
85–89	9%
90–94	11%
95 and over	14%

Source: Adapted from Australian Taxation Office 2023.

The table illustrates that a minimum percentage must be drawn down by the individual each year and that the percentage required to be withdrawn increases with the individual's age. This is designed to encourage individuals to progressively use their superannuation to fund their retirement rather than not spending their accumulated superannuation and, upon death, passing funds to the next generation. The federal government provides generous tax concessions when individuals are in pension phase (e.g. earnings inside the superannuation fund are tax exempt). Accordingly, the government does not want individuals to simply park their wealth in this tax-concessional environment to leave to beneficiaries.

Note that, as a result of federal government support for individuals affected by the COVID-19 pandemic, the government temporarily reduced minimum drawdown requirements for account-based pensions by 50% for the 2019–20 through to the 2022–23 income years. The aim of the decrease to minimum drawdown requirements was to assist members preserve their capital in a falling financial market while still having to draw down an income from superannuation.

Thus, if Michael is aged 72 and drawing an income from his account-based pension, he would be required to draw down at least 5% of his account balance in the form of a pension income. However, Michael can withdraw any income amount above the minimum required. During the years 2019–2023, Michael was only required to draw a minimum income of 2.5%.

Taxation of retirement income streams

If the individual uses taxed superannuation money to fund their retirement income stream, and they are over 60 years of age, the tax consequences are very simple: there is no tax payable by the member on the income, regardless of whether the pension is an account-based or non-account-based pension. The tax treatment is the same. The lack of tax payable on superannuation pensions for those aged 60 and over provides a powerful incentive to accumulate wealth within a superannuation fund. The tax consequences for members under the age of 60 are similar to the taxation of lump sum withdrawals covered in an earlier section. That is, the tax-free and taxable component needs to be determined using the proportion rules when the pension first commences. Once the proportion of the tax-free and taxable components are determined, they are locked in from that point onwards. For all future years, the proportions remain the same. Therefore it is important for a member to maximise their tax-free component before they actually commence their account-based pension.

A summary of the tax implications of superannuation pensions is provided in table 9.10. The tax-free component is always tax free.

TABLE 9.10 Tax payable on taxable component — taxed element

Age of recipient	Income stream
Age 60 years or more	Tax free
At or above preservation age and under 60 years	Taxed at member's marginal tax rates — member entitled to a 15% pension tax offset.
Under preservation age	Taxed at marginal tax rates with no tax offset

Source: Adapted from Australian Taxation Office 2023.

Toby, aged 58, retires on 1 July of the current year after satisfying a condition of release. His accumulated superannuation account totals $500 000 including a tax-free amount of $100 000. Toby transfers his superannuation account into an account-based pension. What is the minimum amount of income Toby is required to withdraw for the current year?

As Toby is aged under 65 years of age, he is required to withdraw a minimum income of 4%. That is $500 000 × 4% = $20 000.

This is the minimum amount he is required to withdraw but there is no maximum amount of income. Assume Toby decides to withdraw an income of $40 000 for the current year.

What amount of tax is payable on the $40 000 of income received by Toby?

The first step is to determine the proportion of the retirement income stream that is tax free on the date that the pension account commences.

With Toby, the tax-free proportion is $100 000 / $500 000 = 20%. From this point onwards, 20% of all pension income withdrawn each year will be tax free and 80% will be taxable.

Thus, if Toby withdraws an income of $40 000:
- $8000 will be tax free (20%)
- $32 000 ($40 000 – $8000) will be taxable.

The amount of $32 000 will be included in Toby's assessable income and will be taxed at his marginal tax rates. The same tax-free proportion will apply in the following year when Toby turns 59 years of age. Once Toby turns 60 years of age, all pension income will be completely tax free in his hands. While the tax-free and taxable proportions will not affect Toby's tax situation once he turns 60 years of age, the proportions are still important if Toby dies and leaves a superannuation death benefit to his non-tax dependents. Non-tax dependents are subject to a tax rate of 15% plus Medicare on the taxable amount they receive from a superannuation death benefit. Accordingly, it is still beneficial for Toby to undertake strategies after the age of 60 to reduce the taxable proportion.

Pension tax offset

Members who receive an income from an Australian retirement income stream may be eligible for a pension tax offset equal to 15% of the taxable component included in the assessable income of the member.

Assume that Toby receives a pension from his account-based pension of $40 000 as well as net rental income from an investment property amounting to $15 000. The tax payable is shown in table 9.11.

TABLE 9.11   Retirement income tax consequences for Toby aged 59

Scenario	Amount $
Taxable component of the account-based pension ($40 000 × 80%)	32 000
Rental income	15 000
Assessable income	47 000
Tax payable (2024–25)	4 888
Less: Pension rebate (15% of taxable component of the pension ($32 000 × 15%))	4 800
Less: LITO: $700 – [($44 000 – $37 500) × 0.015]	88
Note: Eligibility to a tax offset, other than a franking credit, is restricted to the amount of tax payable (i.e. tax offsets cannot provide a refund). Accordingly, the LITO is restricted to $88.	
Tax payable	0
Add: Medicare levy	940
Net tax payable	940

Taxation of retirement income streams on death

A retirement income stream can **revert** only to a tax dependent upon the death of a member. The tax-free component is exempt from tax. The amount of tax payable on the taxable component is a function of whether the:
- money used was taxed or untaxed
- deceased was under or over 60 years of age
- tax dependent beneficiary was under or over 60 years of age.

As previously discussed, if a lump sum death benefit is paid to a tax dependent, the benefit is completely tax free. If it is paid to a non-tax dependent, tax is applied to the taxable component of the death benefit at a rate of 15% (plus Medicare levy).

In respect of a retirement income product held by the deceased member, the situation is a little different and depends on the circumstances of the beneficiary. This is shown in tables 9.12 and 9.13.

TABLE 9.12 Taxation of taxable element of death benefit income stream received by a tax dependent

Age of deceased	Both deceased member and tax dependent are under age 60	Either deceased member or tax dependent are 60 or over
Tax rate	Marginal rate less 15% pension offset	Tax free

Source: Adapted from Australian Taxation Office 2023.

TABLE 9.13 Taxation of untaxed element of death benefit income stream received by a tax dependent

Age of deceased	Age of tax dependent < 60 years	Age of tax dependent > 60 years
< 60 years	Taxable at marginal rates	Taxable at marginal rates with 10% rebate
> 60 years	Taxable at marginal rates with 10% rebate	Taxable at marginal rates with 10% rebate

Source: Adapted from Australian Taxation Office 2023.

If the death benefit is paid to a reversionary beneficiary upon the death of the member as a pension, and either the deceased member or the tax dependent are aged 60 years and over at the date of death, the pension benefit will be paid entirely tax free.

It is important to note that superannuation death benefits in the form of an income stream cannot be paid to a non-tax dependent. The payment must be paid via a lump sum. Payments can be paid to minors. However, once a child turns 25, they cannot generally continue to receive the death benefit income stream and must cash it in as a lump sum.

Choosing between an account-based and non-account-based income stream

As can be seen from table 9.14, many factors need to be traded off against each other in deciding between an account-based or non-account-based income stream.

TABLE 9.14 What type of income stream is preferred by a member?

Characteristic	Prefer an account-based income stream	Prefer a non-account-based income stream
Managing investment risk	More aggressive risk profile	Less aggressive risk profile
Fluctuations in investment returns	More aggressive risk profile	Less aggressive risk profile
Longevity risk	Less concerned or has a large account-balance	More concerned about longevity
Wants the option to draw a lump sum if required (commutation)	Can be done	Not possible
Potential to re-enter the workforce and move the pension back to accumulation phase	Can be done if member is under 75	Difficult
Potential to leave unused retirement savings to beneficiaries upon their death	Can be done	Depends on income stream chosen (not possible for a lifetime income stream beyond guarantee period)

It is important to remember that, in order to best manage their individual circumstances in retirement, an individual has the option of commencing either an account-based or a non-account-based income stream (lifetime income stream) with superannuation monies.

The use of annuities to provide retirement income.

As noted above, individuals may decide to use their superannuation money to buy an annuity from a life office rather than select an account-based pension with their superannuation provider. Annuities include an insurance component in their offer. Annuities can also be acquired with ordinary monies but a member will not be entitled to the tax concessions applying to superannuation pensions. Income payments received from annuities derived from ordinary money will be fully assessable to the member. While the number of life offices offering annuities has declined in recent years, the range of features associated with the annuities on offer has increased considerably. This has been encouraged by the introduction of the retirement income covenant discussed earlier. It would be expected that better features and innovations in retirement income products will continue to develop over the next few years. Up until 2020, there was minimal development and innovation in lifetime annuities which has restricted their market uptake. The lack of control over investment choice, low returns and limited access to capital has meant that most retirees have gravitated towards account-based pensions where the member has control, is able to access capital at any time and can vary the level of income withdrawn each year. However, as a result of the retirement income covenant, innovation in lifetime annuities has started to take place with a number of providers launching lifetime income stream products that are investment-linked. Investment-linked lifetime annuities provide members with a choice of investment options and the ability to switch between those options. This provides a similar feature to that provided by account-based pensions. The ability of members to select their own investment option means that the level of income paid can change from year to year to reflect the return of the underlying investment options.

Annuities can be as short as one year or as long as a person might live, if they purchase a lifetime annuity. Other features that some annuity products include are:
- income that is:
  - fixed each period or indexed to some measure which is typically movements in the CPI
  - paid for the agreed term (fixed-term annuity) or paid for as long as a person lives (lifetime annuity)
  - paid to the owner of the annuity only (single life) or with reversion to a spouse on the death of the owner of the annuity (joint lives)
- capital that is:
  - completely or partially returned at the expiration of the fixed term of the annuity (residual capital value); or
  - entirely consumed during the fixed term of the annuity (residual capital value is zero)
  - returned to the estate if the owner of the annuity dies within a guarantee period or forfeited if there is no guarantee period or the guarantee period has expired (lifetime annuity).

By agreeing to pay a fixed or indexed income stream regardless of how financial markets are performing, life offices are insuring the individual against the volatility of investment markets. Similarly, by offering lifetime annuities, life offices are insuring the individual against the prospect of living beyond their life expectancy. This insurance component within annuities means that an individual should expect the rate of return on these income products to be less than the rate of return on similar income products which do not offer this insurance component.

Because of this insurance component, life offices generally do not disclose the rate of return implicit in the income streams they provide. Instead, they might disclose their offer in the following terms; for example, for every $100 000 invested, a 60-year-old male can buy a life expectancy income stream of $3014 p.a.

Using a financial calculator or the RATE function in Excel it is possible to work out the rate of return implicit in a fixed-term non-account-based income stream.

If a 60-year-old male commences a life expectancy income stream, it will have a fixed term of 24.02 years. If they invest $400 000 in the non-account-based income stream and receive an annual payment of $12 056 ($3014 × 4), the implicit rate of return is 2.44%.

$$\text{Rate} = (\text{number of periods, payment, present value})$$
$$= (24.02, -\$12\,056, \$400\,000) = 2.44\%$$

In times of turbulent financial markets, such as the global financial crisis or the COVID-19 pandemic, there is normally a significant increase in individuals buying annuities with their superannuation in order to receive a guaranteed income to fund their retirement income needs. Life offices have been successful in marketing the relative safety of annuities in uncertain economic times and how individuals can insure against a rapid reduction in income and capital levels precipitated by other market shocks. Individuals have been prepared to accept the very low implicit rates of return associated with these short-term annuities in return for the income and capital certainty they provide.

It is important to remember that buying an annuity from superannuation monies keeps funds within the tax-concessional superannuation environment. If an individual was to withdraw their money from superannuation and buy, for example, a fixed-term deposit with a bank, the interest on that capital would be taxable. Buying an annuity also gives the individual some time to determine how to best fund their long-term retirement income needs.

Life expectancy

The Australian Government Actuary periodically publishes life expectancy tables. Table 9.2 earlier in the chapter shows the life expectancies for males and females aged 55 to 70 years from the most recently published tables. Table 9.15 shows a selection of male life expectancies over the past century.

TABLE 9.15   **Selected male life expectancies**

Age (years)	Males 1891–1900	Males 1960–1962	Males 2019–2021
0 (birth)	51.1	67.9	81.3
1	57.9	69.5	81.6
15	62.0	70.1	81.7
25	63.9	70.8	82.0
45	69.0	72.4	82.9
65	76.3	77.5	85.3
85	88.8	89.1	91.6
95	97.2	97.3	98.1

Source: Australian Bureau of Statistics 2023.

We can see from the table that life expectancy at all age levels has increased significantly over the last 100 years. A male born in 1891 had a life expectancy of 51.1 years, whereas a male born in 2020 has a life expectancy of 81.3 years. More recent statistics gathered by the Australian Bureau of Statistics and actuaries working for major Australian superannuation funds suggest that current life expectancies exceed those shown in table 9.15. Increased longevity means a longer retirement period needs to be funded.

We can also see a survivor bias in the table. This is evident in each of the time periods but most pronounced in the 1891–1900 figures. For example, a baby born in 1891 was expected to live, on average, a little over 51 years. However, a baby that survived to the age of 15 had a life expectancy of another 47 years which means that they would live, on average, to 62 years. In other words, less developed health systems and higher rates of infant mortality meant that, if you were able to survive this period, your life expectancy would increase.

In modelling retirement income streams, it is important to allow for this survivor bias. For a male born between 1960–1962, a 65-year-old male is expected to live for another 12.5 years on average; that is, they are expected to live until 77.5 years of age. It is important to remember that, if your 65-year-old client comes back to see you 5 years later when they are 70, this does not mean that their life expectancy is 7 years (12.5 − 5).

It is also important to remember that life expectancies are averages. If we have 100 males at age 65 their average life expectancy is 19.86 years (as detailed in table 9.2). We would expect approximately 50 of these males to still be alive at a little over 84 years, we would expect 20 to be alive at age 90 and 10 to be alive at age 93. Should individuals be encouraged to spend their money while they can, just in case they die before their life expectancy, or should they be encouraged to be more frugal just in case they are one of the 10% who live to 93?

The headline gave me hope: 'Innovative income product now available for retiring Australians'

It was July 2017. The description of this new product was promising as it was 'designed to help Australians more easily and confidently manage their superannuation in the lead up to and during retirement.'

But then, like so many times before . . . '[A]n account-based pension that offers a flexible and simple way for people to convert their superannuation into a steady income stream.'

How is that innovative? What is new about an account-based pension? It might have been an adequate product for some in the past and maybe in the future, but more innovation is required to help individuals and society deal with the retirement crisis that is emerging driven by continued increases in life expectancy. For many Australians living to 90 years of age and beyond is becoming commonplace. Funding longer lives is a challenge for individuals, and society.

A good working definition of innovation is 'fresh ideas that create value'. This is required as more and more people transition from full-time work into the next phase of their lives — a phase that is becoming longer and more complicated to navigate as each year passes.

Let's take a look at fresh ideas in retirement incomes. Some are too new to know if they will create value, others have come and gone having failed to deliver on their promise. It is important to learn from these failures when developing new solutions.

There have been many innovations in wealth management that have also impacted retirement incomes such as ETFs and robo advisors, but let's drill down into those offerings specific to retirement and retirement incomes.

Many of us are aware of the retirement income challenges facing society as our population ages — putting a strain on both public and private retirement income finances. Retirement adequacy is a concern for many, and new solutions are required to reflect the changing dynamics.

Innovation in retirement products

For many years, the pension and annuity standards in the Superannuation Industry (Supervision) Regulations were seen as a barrier to innovation in retirement income products. The new standards, introduced in July 2017, removed these regulatory barriers but there has not been a flood of new products into the market.

As with the example described at the start of this article, most of the innovations in retirement income products in Australia have been variations of account-based pensions and offer no longevity risk protection whatsoever. This includes applications of the so-called bucket strategy commonly employed by financial planners that have won awards for innovation. This involves dividing assets into different short, medium, and long-term buckets.

Variable annuities have been widely used in North America and Asia for many years. Only a small number of providers have released these products into the Australian market. They have only found a small niche and are not considered as mainstream solutions as they were launched before the regulatory changes mentioned above and had to be adapted to deal with the old rules — which led to complexity.

There have been a number of failed attempts at addressing the longevity risk problem by pooling. These also pre-dated the regulatory changes, and this may have contributed to their failure. There are one or two still on the market but with very small uptake. More recent innovations include a life insurer entering into a group annuity arrangement with superannuation funds.

It is into this landscape that Optimum Pensions has launched the Real Lifetime Pension, an investment-linked annuity that is available as an immediate or deferred annuity and may provide superannuation funds with an efficient way of helping their members manage longevity risk.

Innovation in retirement services

It is widely recognised that helping people navigate the risks and challenges of transitioning from full-time work needs more than just retirement income products. A number of innovations are addressing some of the broader issues facing retirees including behaviour and lifestyle.

▶

There are a number of Australian startups with saving for retirement at the core of their proposition including new superannuation products and digital wealth managers (aka robo advisors).

Two of the latter category that are more focused on the retirement challenges are: OnTrack, a digital retirement planning system that allows the user to build individual retirement plans incorporating financial and non-financial goals and takes into account personal health and lifestyle information; and Retirement Essentials, that offers a digital solution that helps Australians navigate the complexity of the Age Pension.

A successful retirement is much more than financial, and it is great to see innovations addressing the whole person and even whole couple including Changing Gears and Full Time Lives. Both these companies have developed tools and frameworks designed to assist people to make a successful transition from full-time work.

Looking overseas

In the USA, Blueprint Income has built a digital platform to facilitate the purchase of annuities to create a personal pension. The objective is to encourage clients to think about retirement in terms of income, rather than assets.

Emerging technologies are being employed across financial services including helping improve retirement outcomes. A number of digital wealth management platforms are deploying artificial intelligence (AI) in both the planning phase and in the spending phase. Dream Forward has compiled a Confusion Index based on queries its AI technology fielded from its users covering topics such as understanding the different withdrawal options available in the USA given the individual circumstances of the user.

Virtual reality (VR) is another emerging technology that is being piloted by financial advisors. Fidelity Investments has teamed up with Amazon to develop a digital financial adviser, which people can interact with through a VR headset. Another application of VR is to help people 'play out' how certain financial decisions will impact them in the future.

There are a number of organisations applying blockchain to the administration of pension schemes and one, TontineTrust, has gone further to combine this new technology with an old product idea and is developing blockchain-secured tontines as an alternative to traditional pensions and annuities. Will this be a viable, practical solution? It's too early to tell but innovation needs experimenting, failing and learning from these failures.

Everyone is watching the big tech firms and their moves into financial services. Whilst an iPension might still be a fair way off, at the end of 2018 there was an announcement that BlackRock and Microsoft are coming together to 'Reimagine Retirement'. There are no details yet but expect some interesting innovations to arise from this partnership.

New challenges need new solutions

We are facing new challenges as populations continue to age, life expectancy continues to grow, and the nature of work continues to evolve. The financial services industry must step up to this challenge and design products and services to better meet the needs of all Australians. This will require a range of retirement income products along with a combination of digital and human advice to assist people to make better choices.

Source: Huppert 2019.

PROFESSIONAL ADVICE

Income streams

Your client is Belinda, aged 63. Belinda's husband looked after all of the couple's finances and Belinda is now struggling to know how best to manage the finances since her husband died earlier this year. Belinda has 3 children aged 23, 17 and 15. Her husband has left a superannuation balance amounting to $600 000 consisting of a $150 000 tax-free component. Belinda is a relatively low risk investor and thinks that the security of a regular income stream sounds very appealing.

QUESTIONS

1. What advice would you provide Belinda in respect to longevity risk? Given her circumstances, how is she likely to be affected by longevity risk? Given life tables, for how many years on average is Belinda likely to require an income stream?

2. What are the implications if part of the husband's death benefit superannuation is distributed to their children?

3. Belinda is concerned that she does not have the skills or interest to manage the investment decisions associated with the $600 000 superannuation death benefit. Does this effectively rule out an account-based pension as an option?

4. Based on Belinda's circumstances, would you advise that she commence an account-based income stream or a non-account-based income stream?

9.10 Other income support available in retirement

LEARNING OBJECTIVE 9.10 Describe other income support available in retirement.

The assessment of superannuation accounts for age-pension purposes

Most retiring Australians will need to supplement their self-funded retirement income with a full or part pension provided by Centrelink. Centrelink delivers a range of government social security payments and services on behalf of Services Australia, which is the Australian Government agency responsible for delivering income support payments and other services to Australians.

In the 2023–24 Federal budget, social security and welfare spending amounted to around $250.3 billion. The biggest component of social security spending is the age pension and other income support for seniors. More than $100 billion will go to aged welfare payments in the next financial year. The bulk of that money will go towards income support for seniors and aged care services. The increase is largely the result of demographic factors rather than policy decisions. Under preservation rules, Australians are able to access their superannuation at age 55 if born before 1 July 1960, and at age 60 if born after 1 July 1964 and they declare to being permanently retired from the workforce. However, they are not currently eligible to access the government age pension until they have reached age-pension age. Age-pension age is dependent upon date of birth as per table 9.16.

TABLE 9.16   Pension age

Period within which a person was born	Pension age	Date pension age changes
From 1 July 1952 to 31 December 1953	65 years and 6 months	1 July 2017
From 1 January 1954 to 30 June 1955	66 years	1 July 2019
From 1 July 1955 to 31 December 1956	66 years and 6 months	1 July 2021
From 1 January 1957 onwards	67 years	1 July 2023

Source: Department of Social Services 2023.

There has been some discussion in the financial media about lifting the preservation age for superannuation so that it is in line with the age pension entitlement age. This would be a difficult political move for any party to make and the likelihood is that the disparity will remain for some time. As such, individuals will continue to access and use some (or all) of their superannuation before being entitled to the age pension.

Australian Prudential Regulation Authority (APRA) statistics reveal that, in the year ending June 2023, benefit payments from superannuation totalled $102.1 billion, comprising lump sum benefit payments of $58.8 billion (57.6% of total benefit payments) whilst pension payments amounted to $43.3 billion (42.4% of total benefit payments) (APRA 2023). The proportion of lump sum withdrawals has increased over the past few years relative to pension payments, which may be explained by a number of reasons including the fact that many Australians are retiring with an outstanding mortgage on their home and are using their superannuation to pay off debt.

The withdrawal and use of lump sums prior to reaching the age pension entitlement age reduces the assessable assets of the individual and increases their entitlement to the government age pension. This process has been called 'double-dipping' and clearly places additional strain on the federal government in funding its retirement income responsibilities.

Centrelink entitlements are typically means tested and for the age pension, both an assets and an income test is used to determine an individual's age-pension entitlements. The following discussion concentrates on the treatment for age-pension purposes of superannuation held in accumulation-style accounts, which are the most commonly held form of superannuation. The Centrelink treatment of defined benefit style accounts is slightly different and outside the scope of this chapter.

Treatment of superannuation where a member is under age-pension age

Where a member is under age-pension age, amounts held in superannuation are excluded from both the assets and income tests. Accordingly, a useful strategy with a couple is to try and maximise the superannuation balance of the member under age-pension age and to minimise the superannuation balance of the member of age-pension age because their superannuation balance is assessed for age-pension purposes. It is important to note that, where a member has converted their superannuation into an account-based pension, the pension is assessed for aged pension purposes no matter the age of the member.

Treatment of superannuation where a member is of age-pension age

Assets test

When the individual is above the age pension entitlement age, amounts held in superannuation or a retirement income stream are classified as an assessable asset and assessed according to the value of the account balance existing at that time.

Income test

For both amounts held in superannuation and an account-based pension, Centrelink applies deeming rules to determine how much income is assessed. Deeming is a set of rules used to determine the amount of income generated from financial investments, including superannuation. It assumes a certain rate of return no matter the return actually earned.

Deeming rates from 1 July 2023 are as follows.

- For a single pensioner, the first $60 400 of worth of the financial investments has a deeming rate of 0.25% applied. Anything over $60 400 is deemed at a rate of 2.25%.
- For a couple where at least one member is entitled to the age pension, the first $100 200 of the worth of the combined financial investments has a deeming rate of 0.25% applied. Anything over $100 200 is deemed to earn 2.25%.

ILLUSTRATIVE EXAMPLE 9.9

Cameron, aged 68 and single, has $400 000 held in an account-based pension account which comprises a taxed component of $300 000 and a tax-free component of $100 000. The account-based pension commenced on 1 July 2022. During the year, Cameron withdrew an income of $24 000. How will the retirement income stream be assessed for age-pension purposes?

Under the asset test, the account balance of $400 000 will be assessable.

Under the income test, income will be assessed under deeming rates as follows.

The first $60 400 of the account balance is assessed at a rate of 0.25%	$ 151
The balance of the pension ($400 000 – $60 400 = $339 600) is assessed at a rate of 2.25%	$7 641
Total income assessed	$7 792

Thus, while Cameron withdrew an income of $24 000 from the income stream, he is only assessed for age-pension purposes on an amount of $7792.

However, for the following income streams, Centrelink uses a different means to assess income for age-pension purposes.
- a non-account-based pension
- an account-based pension that commenced before 1 January 2015. Assessment rules are described below and are similar to the assessment of lifetime pensions. However, if the member changes their existing account-based income stream after this date to another account-based income stream product, the income stream changes to being assessed under the deeming rules described above.

New rules only apply to an investment in a lifetime income stream (non-account-based pension) made on or after 1 July 2019.

Asset test

The new rules will generally assess:
- 60% of the purchase price of the lifetime income stream until age 84, subject to a minimum of 5 years
- 30% of the purchase price thereafter.

This concessional treatment of the lifetime pension can make these pensions attractive relative to other pension products where 100% of the asset is assessable and therefore an investment in a lifetime income stream could improve a person's age pension eligibility.

Income test

The new rules will assess 60% of payments from lifetime income streams under the income test. For example, where a lifetime income pays an annual income of $5000, only $3000 will be assessed under the income test.

This might again make lifetime pension a viable option for maximising age-pension entitlements.

For non-account-based pension prior to 1 July 2019, Centrelink uses the following formula to determine assessable income.

$$\text{Gross payment received} - \text{Deductible amount}$$

The deductible amount is calculated as the purchase price divided by the term of the income stream (e.g. if lifetime pension, use life expectancy) with the amount representing the return of capital each year over the period of the income stream. The income received less the deductible amount equals the assessable income.

Under the asset test, a formula is used to reduce the value of the initial investment by an annual sum that represents the using up of part of the capital value each year over the lifetime of the product.

Figure 9.3 provides an overview of how funds are withdrawn from a superannuation environment and the interaction with the age pension.

Reverse mortgages

For older people with a large amount of equity in their family home but with little disposable income, reverse mortgages can provide a useful means by which home equity can be turned into *income*. We have used the word income in italics because it is not income as such, it is actually a progressive consumption of capital. Indeed, some providers prefer to use the term 'home equity conversion loans'.

Under a **reverse mortgage**, the home owner borrows a sum of money secured against the family home. Rather than paying regular amounts of interest (and principal), the interest accrues over time with the total interest accrued and principal paid back as a lump sum from the proceeds of the sale of the family home once it is eventually sold or the home owner dies.

The terms and conditions which apply to reverse mortgages can be very complex and difficult to understand. There can also be an incentive for commission-based sellers of these products to encourage clients to borrow more than is prudent for their circumstances.

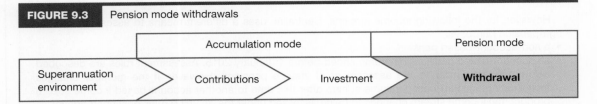

FIGURE 9.3   Pension mode withdrawals

Ordinary money
While we have concentrated on superannuation it is important to remember that many people build wealth outside a superannuation environment and then use this ordinary money to fund their retirement. This money does not have to be withdrawn as such.

Superannuation money
Superannuation money is money that is held inside a superannuation environment and needs to be withdrawn (released) to fund retirement. Superannuation money can be held in one of three forms: taxed, untaxed and tax-free.

Taxable component
For most Australians their concessional contributions and earnings are taxed at 15% — this results in taxed superannuation money.

For some Australians their concessional contributions and earnings are *not* taxed — this is known as an untaxed element.

The taxed and untaxed elements form what is known as the **taxable component.**

Tax-free contributions
Where an individual has made an after-tax contribution to superannuation.

Non-concessional superannuation money is combined with superannuation which is attributable to superannuation that was accrued prior to June 1983 to form what is known as the **tax-free component.**

Tax payable on withdrawal of money from superannuation
The amount of tax payable is a function of four factors:
1. Whether the taxable component contains a taxed or untaxed element
2. The size of the tax-free component relative to the taxable component
3. The age of the individual — persons over the age of 60 are treated more generously than persons under the age of 60
4. Whether the individual wishes to take a lump sum, an income stream or some combination of both.

Lump sum or income stream from superannuation
A range of factors need to be taken into account in deciding whether to take a lump sum, an income stream or some combination of both. These factors are outlined in the chapter.

If an income stream is selected then should the individual take an account-based income stream, a non-account-based income stream or some combination of both?

Interaction with Centrelink
All Australians who meet the qualifying requirements are entitled to the aged pension *(Tier 1).* One of the qualifying requirements is that the retiree meets the asset and income tests. Withdrawing money from a superannuation environment and/or using ordinary money to fund retirement will have an impact on Centrelink entitlements.

Gran is a 70-year-old widow. She lives in the family home which is worth $500 000. She relies on the single age pension for income. She would like to release some of the equity in her home to provide some additional income. She decides to borrow $200 000 against the equity in her house using a reverse mortgage. Assume the rate of interest on the reverse mortgage is 8%. Assume that her home increases in value by 4% p.a. Figure 9.4 outlines Gran's equity in her home.

FIGURE 9.4   Gran's reverse mortgage

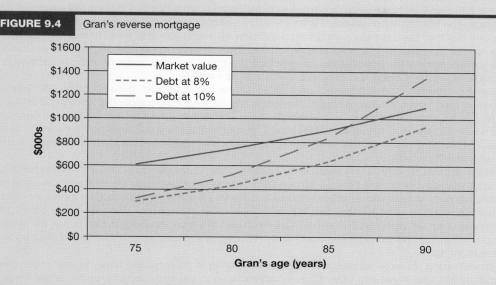

The blue line represents the market value of Gran's home over time. The green line represents the accumulated debt. Because the interest cost of 8% is greater than the rate of appreciation of the value of the home of 4% the 2 lines begin to converge over time. That is, the amount of equity Gran has in her house diminishes. At the age of 75 and 80, Gran still has a considerable amount of equity in her home; however, by the time she turns 90 her equity is seriously diminished. If she needs to sell the family home in order to fund moving into other accommodation, she may not have enough left to do so after repaying the loan.

The orange line represents an interest rate on the loan if it was 10%. If Gran's loan is a variable-rate loan and if interest rates suddenly jump to 10% soon after she enters the loan agreement, then the solid and dashed lines will converge more quickly and equity will be lost more rapidly.

On 18 September 2012, the federal government legislated to ensure that all reverse mortgages issued from that date had a **no negative equity guarantee (NNEG)**.

Individuals also need to be aware that the cash/income provided by a reverse mortgage may affect their age-pension entitlement. The family home is exempt from the age-pension asset test; however, the cash released via the reverse mortgage is not exempt and will be assessed unless all spent. The cash released that is held will also be subject to deeming and will therefore have age pension income test consequences.

The ASIC website Moneysmart (moneysmart.gov.au) also has a warning with respect to home reversion schemes. In a home reversion scheme, you sell a fixed percentage of the future value of your home. For example, you might own a house that is currently worth $600 000 and you sell 50% of its future value. You might expect the lender to provide $300 000 for this right; however, they will offer significantly less than this.

Reverse mortgages

People often have strong views on reverse mortgages without much understanding of what they entail. One view is expressed below.

People spend much of their working lives trying to pay off their mortgage so that they can fulfil the Australian dream and own their home. The day that they make that last mortgage payment and legal title passes from the bank to the homeowner is often a very special day in people's lives. Reverse mortgages are an insidious thing — they undo all that hard work, they turn that psychology upside down — you end your days living in a house owned by the bank. I saw an article in the paper the other day that said 'Reverse mortgages aren't for everybody', well I would go further — I would say that 'Reverse mortgages aren't for anybody'.

There is no doubt that in Australia many people have a strong desire to own their own home. Most people feel that they own their home when they move in, notwithstanding the fact that they are still paying off their mortgage. The final mortgage payment is an important symbolic event; however, most people will feel at that point that they have already owned their own home for a long period of time. To suggest that taking out a reverse mortgage would make people feel that their home is now not theirs might be overstating the argument somewhat. Nonetheless, re-establishing a mortgage after years of trying to extinguish a mortgage represents a significant psychological hurdle for many people.

Interest on reverse mortgages is not paid on an annual basis. Instead, it compounds. The younger the person taking out a reverse mortgage, the longer the compounding period. For instance, a female at age 65 has a further life expectancy of [over] 22 years. This is a long time for interest to compound and the amount of debt ultimately accumulated could be substantial, leaving little or no equity in the family home. The older the client, the less the effect of compounding interest and the lower the amount of debt ultimately accumulated.

The age pension provides a very basic level of income support. If a person lives in a $1 million home but has no other means of income besides the age pension they would generally be referred to as asset rich and income poor. In this case, a reverse mortgage may release some valuable income for the individual, and because they are asset rich they may still retain substantial equity in their home even after allowing for the amount of accumulated debt. However, if a person lives in a more modestly valued home, the amount of equity left in their home might be substantially reduced by the amount of accumulated debt under a reverse mortgage.

With increasing life expectancies and fewer people living in an extended family environment, many Australians will now move into alternative accommodation in old age. The sale of the family home is often used to help fund this alternative accommodation and it is important that the sale proceeds, net of any reverse mortgage payout obligation, are sufficient to fund this accommodation. Many people also see the family home as an asset that should be passed on to dependents unencumbered by reverse-mortgage obligations.

If you have a 95-year-old client who is living in a $5 million house who is not too worried about any inheritance they might leave and whose only source of income is the age pension, the argument in favour of the client taking out a reverse mortgage is fairly strong. This is as long as they can overcome the psychology of owing the bank money again.

In summary, to say that 'reverse mortgages aren't for anybody' is perhaps an overstatement. However, reverse mortgages are not for everybody. Financial planners need to balance several variables in determining whether or not a reverse mortgage is suitable for a client.

QUESTIONS

1. Given the rate of interest payable, are reverse mortgage arrangements viable?

2. Would it be preferable for most Australians to rather seek a bank loan rather than take out a reverse mortgage if they require additional funds?

3. Given that house prices are growing exponentially, are concerns of an increasing debt position justified for the children of the couple?

Home Equity Access Scheme

Services Australia offers a pensions loan scheme which has some similarity to a reverse mortgage. If an individual satisfies the requirements to be eligible for the age pension, they may be able to take out a pension loan.

Where either of the couple are of age-pension age, this loan offers Australians the ability to take out a loan which provides a fortnightly income stream to supplement their retirement income, a lump sum payment or a combination of the two. Retirees are able to access a maximum loan amount which is based on the age of the retiree and how much equity they own in their home. This amount can be up to 1.5 times the maximum payment rate of the eligible age pension each fortnight.

To work out the maximum loan amount, Services Australia reduces the security value down to the nearest $10 000, divides it by 10 000 and multiplies that by the age component amount. The loan needs to be secured against real estate and does not have to be repaid unless the property is sold or the individual passes away. The amount borrowed and the associated interest continues to accumulate in much the same way as the balance of a reverse mortgage accumulates. Services Australia currently charges an annual interest rate of 3.95% p.a. (2023) that compounds fortnightly on the outstanding loan balance.

9.11 What is an adequate retirement income?

LEARNING OBJECTIVE 9.11 Discuss what constitutes an adequate retirement income.

Most people who rely on the age pension as their only source of income in retirement will tell you that the age pension is not adequate.

We referred earlier to an example which suggested that a comfortable retirement for a single person in June 2023 required $50 207 p.a. Is this adequate?

Should an adequate income stream be determined as a fixed amount or as a relative number? If it is a relative number, what is it relative to; income levels, expenditure levels?

Some commentators suggest that retirement income should relate to a person's pre-retirement income. That is, someone who earns $200 000 p.a. prior to retirement will have higher expectations in retirement relative to someone who earns $70 000 p.a. Various percentages have been suggested over time. For instance, former prime minister Paul Keating suggested '65 at 65'; that is, individuals should aim for a retirement income of 65% of pre-retirement income at age 65. A retirement income of less than 100% of pre-retirement income reflects the fact that generally less tax is paid in retirement and other financial commitments are lower because the member is no longer working and as active compared to when they were younger.

Should retirement income be a function of your commitments? If the mortgage still has to be paid and if dependent children are still at home, there are considerable commitments that still need to be met.

The federal government recognises that the superannuation guarantee system will not, in its current form, produce an adequate income in retirement for many Australians, and as a result, has legislated to increase the superannuation guarantee contribution (SGC) rate each year until it reaches 12% in 2025.

The adequacy of retirement income streams is one of the questions considered within the Retirement Income Review conducted by the government. This review was recommended by the Productivity Commission in its report *Superannuation: assessing efficiency and competitiveness* (*Productivity Commission 2018*): 'The review will consider the incentives for people to self-fund their retirement, the fiscal sustainability of the system, the role of the three pillars of the retirement income system, and the level of support provided to different cohorts across time (Australian Treasury 2019)'.

As we mentioned earlier in the chapter, there is still a very heavy reliance on the age pension in Australia and this reliance looks set to continue for many years yet notwithstanding increases in the superannuation guarantee scheme and the tax incentives encouraging us to save for our retirement.

ILLUSTRATIVE EXAMPLE 9.11

Jodie is 60 years old and has just retired. Her gross income in the last year prior to retirement was $140 000. She would like to receive 65% of this figure as a retirement income, that is $91 000 for her life expectancy. She would also like the real value of this $91 000 income stream maintained over time. She estimates that she will be able to invest her unused superannuation at a real rate of 2%, that is, a rate over and above the rate of inflation. Her life expectancy at age 60 is 86.93 (a further 26.93 years as per table 9.2). How much superannuation does she need to fund her retirement income desires?

$$PV = (2\%, 26.93, \$91\,000) = \$1\,880\,630$$

While the concept of adequacy can be discussed at great length, the reality is that the majority of retirees in the near and medium term are unlikely to produce the level of retirement income they desire.

ILLUSTRATIVE EXAMPLE 9.12

At the beginning of this chapter, we introduced the case of Anne. Anne was working full-time and relatively long hours. For Anne, retiring immediately would represent a dramatic change in lifestyle. Work for many people provides a sense of belonging that might be hard to replicate in retirement — it is not clear how much retirement planning Anne has done. Many people these days seek to ease themselves into retirement rather than retire immediately, but this is not always possible.

▶

Anne is 64 years old and earns around $85 000 p.a. If Anne wanted to generate a real income of 65% of her pre-retirement income of $55 250 (and we assume real investment returns of 2%) she would need to have accumulated around $1.023 million in wealth [PV = (2%, 23.36, $55 250)]. Her life expectancy at age 64 is a further 23.36 years. At the moment, her accumulated wealth is $835 000 ($450 000 + $120 000 + $25 000 + $240 000). This would produce an income stream of $45 093 per year if all was transferred into her superannuation fund [PMT = (2%, 23.36, $835 000)] which is approximately 53% of her pre-retirement income. With $835 000 in assets, Anne is likely to exceed the upper threshold of the age pension asset test and therefore not be entitled to any age pension. The level of Anne's assets could, however, decrease below the upper threshold between now and when she reaches age pension entitlement age as she consumes assets to fund her retirement income. Nonetheless, any entitlement to the age pension is likely to be small. It is unlikely that Anne will see this as an adequate retirement income.

Anne might need to work beyond the age of 64 and this has a twofold benefit. Firstly, the existing accumulated wealth is not eroded and hopefully is increased through additional contributions and positive investment returns. Secondly, the period of retirement to be funded is shorter. An extra five years of work can have a significant impact on the level of retirement income that is achievable, however Anne might also have to modify her retirement income expectations.

Financial considerations need to be blended with non-financial considerations. The thought of working for more years in the same job might be completely unacceptable to Anne — health, lifestyle and social issues all need to be factored into the planning.

SUMMARY

Planning does not guarantee a good outcome; however, most people concede that planning generally produces better outcomes than not planning. Retirement is a significant life event and it needs to be appropriately planned. Retirement planning has many dimensions.

We all have needs in our life — Maslow describes them as a hierarchy of needs. These needs must be satisfied in our working lives and in our retired lives. Retirement provides a different context within which these needs must be satisfied — retirement planning must address issues such as how we will maintain our sense of belonging and self-esteem in retirement.

There are active, passive and support phases of retirement. Most retirement income modelling assumes a uniform income flow over the retirement period; however, maybe more income should be directed to the active phase and less to the passive phase, while at the same time ensuring there is a sufficient safety net for the support phase.

Retirement income can be funded by ordinary money or superannuation money or some combination of both. Inside the superannuation environment, money can exist in one of three forms: taxable (taxed element), taxable (untaxed element) and tax free. Understanding the characteristics of each helps the client and the financial planner determine the tax consequences of withdrawing money from their superannuation accounts.

Money can be withdrawn from a superannuation environment as a lump sum or an income stream, or both. A person over the age of 60 with taxed superannuation money can withdraw a lump sum or an income stream from superannuation completely tax free. Where a person is under the age of 60, or has some taxed component within their superannuation fund, some tax may be payable on withdrawal.

Most Australians withdraw their superannuation in the form of an income stream. The individual must then decide whether to commence an account-based income stream, a non-account-based income stream or some combination of the two. Account-based income streams are distinctly different from non-account-based income streams and it is important to match the needs of the individual to the characteristics of the income stream.

Retirement income can also be funded by a variety of other means including releasing cash from property through the use of reverse mortgages and downsizing the family home.

Federal government budget papers highlight that most Australians will not be able to achieve an adequate self-funded retirement income for many years in which case self-funding will still need to be supplemented by the age pension. However, the modest income support provided by the age pension is unlikely to satisfy the average Australian's needs for an adequate retirement income, so working Australians need to reassess their wealth accumulation and retirement income strategies in an iterative process until an achievable outcome is obtained.

This chapter has largely concentrated on the financial dimensions of retirement; however, it is wrong to assume that a person with a large amount of accumulated wealth leading into retirement will automatically have a happy retirement — just as it is wrong to assume that a person with little accumulated wealth leading into retirement will have an unhappy retirement. Retirement planning has many dimensions, and these dimensions stretch far beyond financial considerations alone. Nonetheless, surveys of retirees and those approaching retirement consistently highlight their number one concern as having insufficient financial resources for retirement.

Retirement planning should be one aspect of a comprehensive financial plan which is commenced long before retirement.

KEY TERMS

account-based income stream A flexible income stream product that generates a regular income, acquired from a superannuation account when a member retires.

accumulation phase The phase where an individual is still contributing to superannuation.

assessable income Income that is assessed for tax and measured under taxation law.

condition of release Regulations that specify the conditions that must be satisfied before a member is able to withdraw their money from their superannuation account.

deductible amount That amount of an income stream representing a return of capital.

life expectancy How long a person is expected to live based on their gender and current age as determined by the Australian Government Actuary's life expectancy tables.

lifetime income stream An income stream that pays an income for the life of the person.

longevity risk The risk that the individual will outlive their retirement income/savings.

no negative equity guarantee (NNEG) A guarantee that the accrued interest and principal obligations under a reverse mortgage will not exceed the value of the real estate pledged as security.

non-account-based income stream A retirement income stream product that generates a regular income under the terms of a contract where there is no account balance attributable to the member. The income is usually guaranteed for life or for a fixed term.

non-concessional money An after-tax contribution paid to superannuation for which a tax deduction has not been claimed.

ordinary money Money held outside a superannuation environment.

pension phase The phase where an individual has retired and has begun drawing down their superannuation in order to fund their retirement.

preserved Money that must be maintained in a superannuation environment until a condition of release has been satisfied.

re-contribution The process by which some funds are withdrawn from superannuation and then re-contributed back into superannuation in order to boost the tax-free component of the superannuation balance.

reverse mortgage An arrangement to mortgage a home in order to receive payments from the fund provider in return for a percentage ownership in the home or an accumulated debt to be paid when the home is sold or the home owner dies.

reversion An income stream that reverts or passes to the dependant of the deceased.

superannuation money Money held inside a superannuation environment.

taxable component That part of a superannuation balance that excludes the tax-free component.

taxable component — taxed element That part of a superannuation account where a 15% contributions tax has been levied on concessional contributions and earnings.

taxable component — untaxed element Money held inside a superannuation environment which has not been subject to the 15% contributions and earnings tax.

tax-free component That part of superannuation which is exempt from tax comprising non-concessional contributions.

PROFESSIONAL APPLICATION QUESTIONS

9.1 What is the difference between superannuation money and ordinary money?

9.2 What are the main conditions that must be satisfied before funds can be released from superannuation?

9.3 Differentiate between taxed, untaxed and tax-free superannuation money.

9.4 For the purposes of superannuation, who is considered a SISA-dependent as compared to a tax-dependent?

9.5 What is a binding death benefit nomination? Why is it important for a member to have this document in place?

9.6 Outline the difference in how superannuation is assessed for age pension purposes between a person of age-pension age compared to a person below age-pension age.

9.7 The life expectancy tables demonstrate a survivor bias. What is survivor bias? How does this impact on the modelling for a client?

9.8 Describe the difference in tax treatment between a member aged under the age of 60 who withdraws a lump sum from their superannuation account compared to a member aged 60 or over?

9.9 Outline the main differences between account-based and non-account-based income streams.

9.10 What are the ramifications of a retired member who has a total of $2.2 million held in the superannuation environment — a superannuation account contains $500 000 and their account-based pension contains an amount of $1.7 million? The member is seeking to roll over their remaining superannuation into a second account-based pension.

9.11 The federal government insists that individuals holding an account-based pension must draw down a minimum pension income each year. Why?

9.12 Why do annuities have relatively low implicit rates of return?

9.13 Longevity risk is an issue that all retirees face. What is longevity risk and what are the ways in which a member might best manage this risk in retirement?

9.14 What is the transfer balance cap? Why was it introduced? What impact does it have on an individual's contribution strategies?

9.15 What are some of the reasons why it might be preferable for a couple's superannuation funds to be spread between the partners rather than all superannuation funds held in the name of just one of the partners?

9.16 The withdrawal and use of lump sums from superannuation prior to reaching age pension entitlement age is often referred to as double dipping. What does this mean and should people be allowed to double dip?

PROFESSIONAL APPLICATION EXERCISES

★ BASIC | ★★ MODERATE | ★★★ CHALLENGING

9.17 Present value function ★

Using the present value function in Excel or a financial calculator, how much would an individual need to accumulate in superannuation in order to fund a real retirement income of $60 000 p.a. for 20 years if the real rate of return was 4%?

9.18 Impact of divorce: lump sum split ★

Brendan and Annie recently divorced. As part of the Family Court determination it has been decided that Brendan's superannuation of $400 000 should be split 60% to Brendan and 40% to Annie. Brendan's superannuation includes a $300 000 taxed component and a $100 000 tax-free component. What will be the component parts of Brendan's and Annie's superannuation after the split?

9.19 Lump sum taxes: taxable component ★★

Kim is 59 years old and has $500 000 in superannuation. Her superannuation comprises a tax-free component of $150 000 and a taxable component of $350 000. Kim has satisfied a condition of release from superannuation and would like to withdraw a $345 000 lump sum. How much lump sum tax would be payable?

9.20 Lump sum taxes: untaxed element ★★

Joe is 59 years old and has $700 000 in superannuation. His superannuation comprises a tax-free component of $100 000 and a taxable component (untaxed element) of $600 000. Joe has satisfied a condition of release from superannuation and would like to withdraw a $250 000 lump sum. How much lump sum tax would be payable?

9.21 Income stream: taxable component ★★

Jane is aged 58 and commenced an account-based pension on 1 July of the current financial year with an amount of $400 000. The balance comprises a $100 000 tax-free component and a taxable component of $300 000.

(a) What is the minimum and maximum income that Jane is able to withdraw from her pension account?

(b) Calculate Jane's net tax payable if she withdraws an income of $45 000 for the year. (Ignore any entitlement to low-income tax offsets.)

(c) Is Jane able to withdraw a lump sum from her account-based pension during the year?

9.22 Income stream: taxing of ordinary monies and superannuation monies ★★

Murray is 59 years old and has $450 000. What will be the difference in his net tax payable between the following two situations (Ignore the LITO).

• The funds are held in a share portfolio generating a return of 5% of fully franked dividends.

• The funds are held in a retirement income stream consisting of an $80 000 tax-free component and Murray withdraws a pension income of $22 500 for the year.

9.23 Income stream: superannuation money ★★

Petra is 59 years old and has $700 000 in superannuation money. This includes a tax-free component of $200 000 and a taxed superannuation component of $500 000. During the year, Petra withdraws an income stream during the year of $35 000. Petra also earns net rental income of $12 000 and interest income of $4000.

(a) What will Petra's assessable income be for tax purposes for the year?

(b) Calculate Petra's net tax payable for the year?

9.24 Superannuation contributions prior to retirement ★★★

Paul is aged 59, has retired, has satisfied a condition of release and is looking to commence an account-based pension. Paul's superannuation account totals $600 000 including a tax-free component of $80 000. Paul's other investments consist of a $120 000 share portfolio (cost base of $60 000) and a term deposit of $100 000. Paul is looking to withdraw an income of $50 000 from his retirement income stream.

(a) Calculate Paul's net tax payable for the year if he acquired an account-based pension on the basis of the above information and withdraws an income of $50 000 for the year. Ignore income from the share portfolio and term deposit.

(b) Would Paul still have been able to contribute funds held outside of his superannuation account (in the share portfolio and term deposit) into his superannuation account as a non-concessional contribution before commencing the account-based pension? Would there have been any tax ramifications?

(c) Assume that Paul sells his share portfolio, cashes in his term deposit and makes a non-concessional contribution into his superannuation account with a net amount of $200 000 prior to commencing an account-based pension. Calculate Paul's amended net tax payable for the year on the basis that Paul still withdraws an income of $50 000 for the year. Ignore income from any investments still held outside of his pension account and any CGT on sale of shares.

9.25 Recontribution strategy ★★★

Chuck is 59 years old and has $800 000 in superannuation which includes a tax-free component of $200 000 and a taxed superannuation component of $600 000. Chuck has satisfied a condition of release from superannuation and decides to withdraw $300 000 as a lump sum and then immediately recontribute this $300 000 back into his superannuation account as a non-concessional contribution.

(a) Will Chuck be subject to any lump sum withdrawal tax?

(b) What will be Chuck's tax-free component after the re-contribution takes place?

(c) Why might Chuck be seeking to increase his tax-free component when he is nearly 60 years of age?

(d) Can you suggest a more tax-efficient amount for Chuck to withdraw and recontribute?

CASE STUDY

RETIREMENT INCOME STREAMS

Peter is 58 years old, has just been made redundant from his job and received a redundancy payment of $90 000. He was with his employer for the past 12.5 years.

Peter is married to Maggie. They have two grown-up daughters who live away from home and are financially independent. Both daughters are engaged to be married with weddings likely in the next 18 months.

For the past 12.5 years, Peter has worked as an insurance assessor. In his last year of work, he earned $120 000. He currently has $500 000 in superannuation which includes a tax-free component of $50 000. Peter also owns a $250 000 share portfolio (cost price of $140 000) generating fully franked dividends of $10 000 from a publicly listed company. It is 1 July, Peter is looking to now retire and is thinking about his retirement options. He satisfies a condition of release.

QUESTIONS

1 Would you advise Peter to invest all of his superannuation funds into a lifetime pension? Discuss.

2 Calculate any tax payable on the redundancy payment received by Peter.

3 If Peter was to withdraw a $320 000 lump sum from his superannuation fund, how much tax would be payable?

4 Assume that, instead of withdrawing a lump sum, Peter will acquire an account-based pension. Prior to commencing the pension, Peter is looking to sell his share portfolio, pay any tax and contribute the balance into his superannuation account as a non-concessional contribution.

(a) What will be the minimum and maximum income that Peter is able to withdraw from the account-based pension during the year?

(b) Calculate the amount of net tax payable if Peter withdraws an income of $60 000 from his account-based pension during the year (ignore any income from the redundancy payment and LITO).

(c) If the account-based pension generates a return of 7% during the year, calculate the amount of tax payable within the fund.

REFERENCES

Australian Government Actuary (AGA) 2023, 'Australian Life Tables 2015-17', Australian Government, https://aga.gov.au/publications/life-tables/australian-life-tables-2015-17

Australian Prudential Regulation Authority (APRA) 2023, 'Statistics: quarterly superannuation performance statistics highlights: June 2023 (released 22 August 2023)', Australian Government, www.apra.gov.au/news-and-publications/apra-releases-superannuation-statistics-for-june-2023

Australian Taxation Office (ATO) 2024, 'Super withdrawal options, Australian Government, 8 October, www.ato.gov.au/Individuals/Super/Withdrawing-and-using-your-super/Super-withdrawal-options/#Conditionsofreleaseofsuper

Australian Treasury 2019, 'Retirement income review', Australian Government, https://treasury.gov.au/review/retirement-income-review

Australian Treasury 2020, 'Retirement income covenant', Australian Government, https://treasury.gov.au/publication/p2020-100554

Department of Social Services 2023, 'Age pension', Australian Government, https://www.dss.gov.au/seniors/benefits-payments/age-pension

Huppert, S 2019, 'Innovations in Retirement Income Solutions', *Super Review*, www.superreview.com.au/features-analysis/expert-analysis/innovations-retirement-income-solutions

Maslow, AH 1987, *Motivation and personality*, 3rd edn, Harper & Row, New York.

Productivity Commission 2018, 'Stage 3: assessing efficiency and competitiveness', Australian Government, www.pc.gov.au/inquiries/completed/superannuation/assessment#report

ACKNOWLEDGEMENTS

Extract: © Super Review

Table 9.2: © Australian Government Actuary

Tables 9.3, 9.4 and 9.5: © Australian Taxation Office

Tables 9.15 and 9.16: © Australian Bureau of Statistics

CHAPTER 10

Social security

LEARNING OBJECTIVES

After studying this chapter, you should be able to:

10.1 explain briefly the history of, and rationale for, social security in Australia

10.2 outline the role of Services Australia in the delivery of social security services

10.3 provide an overview of the range of benefits available under social security

10.4 outline pension and allowance benefit entitlements and eligibility rules

10.5 outline the assistance provided to retirees

10.6 explain the means testing regime for eligibility for the age pension

10.7 outline the assistance provided to families raising children

10.8 outline the assistance provided to people with disability

10.9 explain the support provided for those undertaking study or an Australian apprenticeship

10.10 outline the taxation of pensions and allowances

10.11 describe the accommodation alternatives in retirement.

Con and Maria are aged 66 and 62 respectively. Many of his friends have retired from the workforce and Con is now considering either changing to part time work (and earning $20 000 p.a.) or retiring altogether. Maria enjoys working two days a week and earns $18 000 p.a. She does not plan to retire in the near future. The couple own their home, but are looking to downsize. They plan to sell their home, purchase a smaller and cheaper house and gift $50 000 to their son who is experiencing financial difficulties.

The couple's assets consist of the following.

Asset	Amount $	Notes
Home	860 000	No mortgage against home.
Contents	45 000	
Cars	40 000	
Caravan	15 000	
Bank account	17 000	Earns interest of 1.0% p.a.
Managed funds	85 000	Investment return of 3.8% p.a.
Australian shares	50 000	Fully franked at 2.8% p.a.
Superannuation — Maria	180 000	Investment return of 6% p.a.
Superannuation — Con	350 000	Investment return of 6% p.a.

There are some issues for the couple to consider.
- Is the couple entitled to the age pension or any other social security entitlements?
- Are any strategies available to Con to help maximise his age pension entitlement?
- What are the tax and social ramifications of the couple downsizing their home and gifting $50 000 to their son?

Illustrative examples used throughout this chapter relate to the information contained within this case study.

Introduction

The social security system in Australia is the means by which the government provides a level of care and assistance to people in society who need help. Over time, the range of benefits provided by Australian society has been extended dramatically, although in recent years rationalisation has taken place to reduce the number of specific benefits available and to better target those in need.

In 2021–22, the Australian government spent around $220 billion or 37% of total budgeted revenue on social security and welfare. Assistance is provided to the aged, veterans and their dependants, people with disability, families with children, the unemployed and the sick, youth, and Indigenous people. In this chapter we will examine in some depth the three areas of social security which between them account for around 80% of the annual funding: assistance to the aged (34%), families with children (17%) and people with disability (28%) (Treasury 2022).

10.1 History of social security in Australia

LEARNING OBJECTIVE 10.1 Explain briefly the history of, and rationale for, social security in Australia.

Since the early 1900s, Australian governments have passed legislation to support a basic standard of living for virtually all citizens through a range of social security policies. Before 1900, voluntary charitable organisations accepted responsibility for care of the destitute. However, the effects of the 1890s depression, the emergence of the political power of the trade union movement through the Labor Party, the recognition that welfare policies could play a part in consolidating the gains of the industrialisation era, and the desire to avoid workhouses for the poor (which constituted the welfare policy of Britain) all combined to produce policies that accepted state responsibility for alleviation of financial distress that was beyond the control of the individual. In the early 1900s, Australia was a world leader in social reform.

The first legislation centred on the provision of assistance to alleviate financial hardship of the unemployed elderly. It is of interest to note, however, that the first steps were somewhat tentative, as the qualifying age of 65 years for the **age pension** for men (established from 1 July 1909) was in fact older than the average life expectancy of men at the time. Additionally, the legislators of the time could not escape the social morality of the period — help was made available only to those who were considered deserving. For instance, people could be disqualified from receiving the age pension if they were not of good character or if they had deserted their spouses without just cause.

The social security safety net was expanded in the 1940s. In 1942, the widow's pension was introduced and, from 1 July 1945, the government introduced a suite of unemployment, sickness and special benefits. These benefits were aimed at supporting an active working population. The 1980s saw another period of expansion of benefits with carers' and sole parents' pensions either introduced or reformed and several other allowances introduced. The home and community care program was also introduced during this period.

However, despite the extension of the types of benefits, there has been rationalisation during the past 10 years to reduce the number of specific benefits in favour of more generally applicable benefits. Additionally, conditions of eligibility have been tightened to try to ensure only the needy have access to community support.

Rationale underlying the provision of social security

The reasons that a community allocates taxation revenue to the payment of social security benefits vary from the lofty and philosophical to the mundane and practical. The philosophical reasons include:

- *altruism* — support for others who are worse off than oneself is considered to be one facet of a civilised society
- *humanitarianism* — enjoyment of basic necessities of living is a fundamental human right and all societies should strive to provide these for all members
- *utilitarianism* — individuals' marginal utility (happiness) derived from the expenditure of money decreases as expenditure increases, so redistribution from the better-off to the worse-off will increase the total stock of happiness in a society.

Practical arguments include:

- *economic* — help given to the needy at relevant times (e.g. the unemployed or temporarily disabled) may facilitate their recovery to become productive members of society and thus the continuation of their contribution to society
- *reduction in crime* — needy people given community support do not need to resort to crime to survive, thus protecting the assets of the better-off.

There are, of course, people who are against the provision of social security and they refute most of the arguments described above. Their views usually centre around the notion that financial help reduces work incentives for both the helped and the helpers and that it is economically inefficient to continually levy the high-fliers with increased taxation to help the poor.

10.2 Centrelink and Services Australia

LEARNING OBJECTIVE 10.2   Outline the role of Services Australia in the delivery of social security services.

In 1997, the federal government restructured the way social security services were delivered to Australians and established the Commonwealth Services Delivery Agency, more commonly known as **Centrelink**. Centrelink is the access point for social service beneficiaries. Social security and compensation payments are also provided to defence-service veterans and their dependants by the Department of Veterans' Affairs (DVA) either directly by DVA or through Centrelink.

Centrelink is managed through a federal government department (a department which has been the subject of continual change), Services Australia (formerly known as the Department of Human Services (DHS)). Services Australia is responsible for the development of service delivery policy and provides access to social, health and other payments and services. The *Human Services Legislation Amendment Act 2011* integrated the services of Medicare Australia, Centrelink and CRS Australia on 1 July 2011 into the former DHS. The creation of Centrelink as an agency can be seen as part of a broader shift to the use of market-like mechanisms in the running of public programs. The work is increasingly carried out under an agreement or contract even though those agents are themselves public service organisations.

The other main government department involved in the development and provision of social policy outcomes is the Department of Social Services (DSS). It is responsible for integrated service delivery to the Australian public of a wide range of Commonwealth programs designed to improve the lifetime wellbeing of people and families in Australia. Table 10.1 gives details of the estimated costs of social security and welfare payments.

TABLE 10.1   Social security estimates 2022–23 to 2026–27

Expense	2022–23 $m	2023–24 $m	2024–25 $m	2025–26 $m	2026–27 $m
Social welfare — assistance to the aged	54 867	59 182	61 672	64 577	67 308
Assistance to veterans and dependants	4 420	4 425	4 323	4 209	4 100
Assistance to people with disabilities	29 961	32 582	34 038	35 531	36 415
Assistance to families with children	27 993	31 387	33 392	34 832	36 201
Assistance to the unemployed	13 867	13 830	15 483	15 999	15 915
Student assistance	2 708	3 105	3 329	3 495	3 643
Other welfare programs	1 937	961	953	973	958
Financial and fiscal affairs	723	641	693	747	521
Vocational and industry training	85	249	359	305	257
Other	8 924	7 892	11 521	15 257	22 135
Total personal benefits expense	**145 485**	**154 254**	**165 763**	**175 925**	**187 453**

Source: Data derived from Treasury 2023.

The main growth area in estimated and projected payments is the income support for seniors (age pension) and people with disability, particularly with the introduction of the National Disability Insurance Scheme which was launched in July 2013. The expected increase in expenses is associated with home care, home support, and the residential and flexible aged care programs, reflecting demographic factors.

10.3 The range of social security benefits

LEARNING OBJECTIVE 10.3 Provide an overview of the range of benefits available under social security.

Services Australia has reported that it pays more than 140 different types of benefits. Table 10.2 lists a number of the main social security benefits available and explains the purpose of each benefit. To obtain a current list of benefits and their eligibility conditions, refer to the Services Australia website (servicesaustralia.gov.au).

TABLE 10.2   The main benefits available from Services Australia

Type of benefit	Purpose of benefit
For aged people	
Age pension	Ensures that elderly people receive a minimum level of income to meet their retirement income needs.
For people raising children	
Family tax benefit (A)	Assists families with the cost of raising children and is paid per child. Eligibility requirements relate to the age of the children and satisfying an income test.

Family tax benefit (B)	Provides extra assistance to single-parent families and families with one main income. Eligibility requirements relate to the age of the children and satisfying an income test.
Parenting payment	Income support for parents or guardians to help with the cost of raising children.
Child care subsidy	Assists with the cost of approved and registered child care. Eligibility criteria based on the child attending approved or registered child care, and the parent or carer being liable to pay child care fees and satisfying an income and hours of activity test.
For people who are ill, injured or disabled	
Disability support pension	Provides minimum level of payments to people who are unable to work because of a physical, intellectual or psychiatric impairment.
For people who are unemployed looking for work	
JobSeeker payment	Payments to a person who is registered as unemployed and is aged between 22 and age pension age. Person must satisfy the rules for either of these conditions: (i) be unemployed and looking for work, or (ii) be sick or injured and incapable of performing the usual work or study.
Youth allowance	Provides income support for full-time students and apprentices aged 16–24. Job seekers aged under 21 must be looking for work, or combining this with part-time study, or undertaking any other approved activity. Paid also to 15-year-olds who have left school and are living independently.
For people caring for others	
Carer payment	Income support to a person who provides constant care for an adult and that adult's dependent child; a person who has physical, intellectual or psychiatric disability; a profoundly disabled child; or two or more disabled children who need care for an extended period.
Carer allowance	Payments to a person who provides daily care and attention to a person with disability who is a family member aged 16 or over or a dependent child under 16.
For students	
Youth allowance	Provides income support for full-time students and apprentices aged 16–24. Job seekers aged under 21 must be looking for work, or combining this with part-time study, or undertaking any other approved activity. Paid also to 15-year-olds who have left school and are living independently.
Austudy payment	Payment to a person who is over 25 and satisfies the activity test by undertaking qualifying study or a full-time apprenticeship.
ABSTUDY	Payments to students who are Aboriginal Australians or Torres Strait Islanders and are studying an approved course of study at an approved education institution or undertaking a full-time apprenticeship.
Concession cards	
Pensioner concession card	Concession card that provides fringe benefits to persons in receipt of certain pension and allowance support. The card provides concessions on pharmaceutical prescriptions, a telephone allowance and access to a number of state, territory and local government concessions.

(continued)

TABLE 10.2 *(continued)*

Type of benefit	Purpose of benefit
Health care card[a]	Concession card that is issued to persons who do not qualify for a pensioner concession card but who are receiving a number of other government income support payments or for those people on low incomes. The card provides concessions on pharmaceutical prescriptions and access to a number of state, territory and local government concessions.
Commonwealth seniors health card[a]	Concession card that is targeted at self-funded retirees of age-pension age who do not qualify for an age pension due to assets or income levels. To qualify, the person must have an adjusted level of income of less than $95 400 for singles and $152 640 for couples (effective from 1 January 2020). The card provides concessions on pharmaceutical prescriptions and access to the seniors supplement.

[a] Entitlements to the health care card for low-income earners and to the Commonwealth seniors health card are based on an adjusted taxable income which comprises taxable income plus: the value of any adjusted fringe benefits, target foreign income, total net investment losses and reportable superannuation contributions.

10.4 Pension and allowance benefit entitlements and eligibility rules

LEARNING OBJECTIVE 10.4 Outline pension and allowance benefit entitlements and eligibility rules.

It is important to note that benefit entitlements and eligibility rules change on a regular basis and the rates provided in the text below may not be the most current available. While the latest rates and eligibility rules are obviously important, these can be readily looked up through the Services Australia website (servicesaustralia.gov.au).

What is more important is an understanding of the entitlements available for individuals in need of income support and the principles governing their application.

Pension and allowance benefit entitlements

The rate of payment for the majority of **government pensions** is shown in table 10.3.

TABLE 10.3 Maximum pension entitlements (effective from 20 March 2024)

Status	Maximum payment per fortnight
Single	$1116.30 including the maximum pension and energy supplements
Couple (each)	$841.40 including the maximum pension and energy supplements

Source: Services Australia 2024.

The **pension supplement** is an extra payment received by those in receipt of a pension or other form of eligible income support. The **energy supplement** is a tax-exempt payment that provides assistance for pensioners, families who receive family assistance, income support payment customers and Commonwealth Seniors Health Card holders.

Table 10.4 illustrates the maximum allowance entitlement for a number of **government allowances** including the JobSeeker payment.

TABLE 10.4 Maximum allowance entitlements (effective from 20 March 2024)

Status	Maximum benefit per fortnight
Single, no children	$762.70
Single, with children	$816.90

| Single, aged 55 and over, after 9 months on allowance | $816.90 |
| Couple (each) | $698.30 |

Source: Services Australia 2024.

Pension and allowance benefit eligibility rules

Means testing

Social security pensions are subject to a **means test** to ensure they are paid only to people most in need. The means test is based on a person's assets and their income. A person's pension entitlements are based on the test that produces the lowest payment. Means testing will be considered in further detail later in the chapter.

Residence requirements

To qualify for a social security pension, a person must be a permanent resident by being:
- an Australian resident for at least 10 years with more than 5 years of continuous residence, with the exception of refugees
- in Australia at the time of applying.

An Australian resident residing outside of Australia, but residing in a country with which Australia has entered into an international social security agreement, may still be eligible for payment.

10.5 Assistance provided to retirees

LEARNING OBJECTIVE 10.5 Outline the assistance provided to retirees.

To ensure that retirees have an adequate level of income in retirement, the government provides retirees in need with access to income support and a range of concessions. The main form of income support for retirees in need is known as the age pension. The age pension is administered through Centrelink and is paid on the basis of a retiree satisfying certain eligibility criteria.

The age pension is paid fortnightly and is reviewed twice yearly, in March and September, to keep in line with the consumer price index (CPI) and changes in the male total average weekly earnings (MTAWE). Commencing from March 2010, the age pension is indexed against the MTAWE at a rate of 27.7% for singles and 41.76% for couples combined.

Age test eligibility for the age pension

As well as satisfying residency requirements and a means test qualification, retirees accessing the age pension are also required to satisfy an **age test**. The age test is currently 67 years of age for both males and females.

One of the recommendations of the 2009 Henry review looking into Australia's future tax system was that the age pension age should be lifted further. The following is an extract from that report.

> The age at which pensions become available should be responsive to the increase in life expectancy and longevity. For a century, the Age Pension age has been 65 years for men. To support system sustainability, and fairness, and to ensure that social policies adapt to changes in the life circumstances of people, the Age Pension age should rise modestly and gradually to age 67 years. This would provide a strong social signal about work and retirement expectations and their link to increasing life expectancies. The increase in the Age Pension age should be part of a suite of polices [sic] to increase the social and workforce participation of older Australians (Commonwealth of Australia 2009, pp. 16–17).

This recommendation was adopted by the government and as a result, the age pension age has been increased progressively to age 67 commencing in 2017, as detailed in table 10.5.

TABLE 10.5 Increase in pension age eligibility for the age pension

Effective from	Age pension age
1 July 2019	66 years
1 July 2021	66.5 years
1 July 2023	67 years

Source: Services Australia 2023.

The age service pension is the equivalent of the age pension but is paid to eligible ex-defence service claimants. The age requirements are the same as for the age pension.

10.6 Means testing

LEARNING OBJECTIVE 10.6 Explain the means testing regime for eligibility for the age pension.

In order to determine how much benefit is paid to an applicant, a means testing system is generally used. The means testing regime considers both an asset test and an income test subject to some important exceptions. Each test comprises a threshold level and an upper limit with a shade-out zone between these levels. For applicants with incomes or assets levels which are less than the thresholds, the benefit payments are made at the maximum or full rates. Where incomes or assets are greater than the thresholds, the benefits are reduced, and where the upper limits are exceeded no benefits are payable.

The principal rules for the application of the assets and incomes tests are as follows.

- Both tests are applied to pension applications. Asset and/or income levels that exceed a lower threshold reduce the level of pension payment. The test on assets or income that produces the lower benefit is ultimately applied.
- Both tests are applied to allowance applications. However, under the assets test, the lower threshold is a cut-out point which causes the payment to be decreased to zero. No allowance is payable where the person's holding of assets exceeds this lower threshold.
- Some other types of payments are not means tested or are not subject to the assets test (e.g. family tax benefit).

Assets test

The values applied under the assets tests differ according to the applicant's home ownership status and whether they have a partner. Table 10.6 provides the threshold and upper limits effective from 20 March 2024.

TABLE 10.6 Assets test thresholds and upper limits effective from 20 March 2024

Value		Homeowner	Non-homeowner
Threshold for full benefit	single	$ 301 750	$ 543 750
	couple	$ 451 500	$ 693 500
Upper limit for part benefit	single	$ 674 000	$ 916 000
	couple	$ 1 012 500	$ 1 254 500

Source: Services Australia 2024.

From the data in the table, it can be seen that a single pensioner who owns their own home may have up to $301 750 in assessable assets and receive the full age pension. Where a person's assessable assets exceed the lower threshold, the maximum pension entitlement is reduced by a reduction factor. The reduction factor is calculated as a reduction in the maximum pension entitlement of $3.00 for singles ($1.50 for each member of a couple) for every $1000 of assets up to the upper limit. Once assessable assets exceed the upper limit or threshold, no pension is payable.

You may notice that the difference between the allowable values for homeowners and non-homeowners for each component in the test is $242 000. This is the notional value of a house and is unlikely to represent the values of homes in Australia's capital cities. The notional value of a house has increased only slightly over the years.

Assessable assets

The most important questions in relation to an assets test is 'what assets are counted?' followed by 'how are they valued?' The answer to the first question is 'almost all assets are counted', but there are some limited exemptions from assessment. The main exemption from the asset test is a person's principal home. Other exempt assets include:

- prepaid funeral expenses and funeral bonds (up to $15 000 per person)
- superannuation assets if under age-pension age (exemption ceases after reaching age-pension age)
- life interests in assets created by others excluding the applicant's partner
- gifts of up to $10 000 per person or couple in a 12-month period provided no more than $30 000 has been gifted in the last 5 years (see gifting rules)
- accommodation bonds paid on entry to residential aged care
- the proceeds of the sale of a principal home for up to 12 months, as long as the proceeds are used to buy another home.

The assets taken into account and assessed include both financial and physical assets. Financial assets are investments such as term deposits, shares, units in managed funds or insurance policies with surrender values. Physical assets include cars, home contents and businesses. Other than the above exemptions, most other assets and investments are assessed.

Superannuation accounts are exempt under both the assets and income tests for social security purposes until a person reaches age-pension age. Withdrawals of superannuation by persons under age-pension age are also not assessable under either test. The exemption of superannuation from both the assets and income tests may provide opportunities for couples to structure their affairs in order to minimise their asset assessment. Thus, where one member of a couple is under age-pension age, for example where the husband is aged 65 and the wife is aged 59, funds may be transferred from the husband into the wife's superannuation account and be exempt under both the assets and income tests. However, the amount of the transfer/contribution is subject to normal super contribution limits.

Once a person reaches age-pension age, the account balance under both a superannuation and account-based pension account is treated as an assessable asset.

Principal home

The most significant assets test exemption is the principal home. The principal home may be a house, unit, flat, houseboat, caravan or shack — there is no limit placed on the value. It could be a **life interest** gained under a will in a home owned by someone else. It might also be a $6 million mansion, but it is unlikely such an owner would be applying for the age pension. Included within the principal home category are permanent fixtures such as garages, swimming pools and garden features, carpets and fixed internal fittings such as dishwashers and stoves. Also included with the house is up to 2 hectares of land on a single title. Some people with a larger area of residential land on more than 1 title currently have an exemption on this greater area. This is known as the 'private land use test'.

From 1 January 2007, rural applicants have benefited from a concession in that land areas greater than 2 hectares may be exempted, provided the:

- land is on one title
- applicant has had a long-term (20-year) continuous attachment to the land and house
- applicant must be making effective use of the land within their physical capacity to do so.

General asset valuation methodology

The general rule for asset valuations including real estate and businesses is net market value. Net market value is fair market value less any debts owing on the asset. Thus, an investment house is valued at market value at the time of the estimate less any debt owing. Services Australia generally asks clients to make these valuations, but can call in registered valuers if required to make estimates.

Special rules apply to home equity conversion loans. Home equity conversion loans, commonly known as **reverse mortgages**, are a loan product whereby a homeowner can convert some home equity to immediate cash by taking out a loan on which both interest and principal repayments are deferred until death or the owner voluntarily leaves the house. If a single lump sum is withdrawn under the loan contract, the first $40 000 is exempt from the assets test for 90 days. Any amount after $40 000 not spent becomes an assessable asset. Any excess loan over $40 000 is assessable as an asset from the time of receipt.

If the loan is taken out in the form of regular payments, the payments are not assessable under the assets or income test as long as they are spent immediately on the cost of living.

ILLUSTRATIVE EXAMPLE 10.1

Referring to the case study presented at the start of this chapter with Con and Maria, the couple's assessable assets consist of the following.

Asset	Value	Status
Family home	$860 000	Exempt
Contents	45 000	Assessable
Cars	40 000	Assessable
Caravan	15 000	Assessable
Bank account	17 000	Assessable
Managed funds	85 000	Assessable
Shares	50 000	Assessable
Superannuation — Maria	180 000	Exempt (under 67 years of age)
Superannuation — Con	350 000	Assessable
Total assessable assets	**$602 000**	

Income test

Like the assets test, the income test also imposes limits on the amount of income that can be earned for eligibility to either full or part benefits. The income test differs between pensions and allowances. Table 10.7 shows the income limits for the full and part pension for singles and couples.

TABLE 10.7   **Income limits for the full and part pensions effective from 20 March 2024**

Status	Full pension per fortnight	Part pension per fortnight
Single, no dependent children	$204.00	$2 397.40
Couple, no dependent children	$360.00	$3 666.80

Source: Services Australia 2024.

The pensions payable under the income test are reduced by 50 cents per fortnight for every dollar of income in excess of the full-pension limit for single pensioners (25 cents each for every dollar of income in excess of the full-pension limit for each member of a couple). Thus, for a married couple with a combined assessable income of $1800 per fortnight, the reduction in their maximum age pension benefit would be ($1800 − $360) × 0.25 = $360 per fortnight each.

Assessable income

For social security purposes, assessable income encompasses income derived from most sources. It includes income derived from both inside and outside Australia and, if you have a partner, their income and assets are taken into account when working out payment rates. The types of income generally assessable for social security purposes include:
- gross income from wages and salaries, including reportable fringe benefits and amounts that are salary sacrificed into superannuation
- income from carrying on a business
- net rental income
- family income trust distributions
- total losses from rental property
- longer-term annuities. Short-term annuities with a term of 5 years or less and account-based pensions are subject to deeming rules (discussed in the next section)
- **deemed income** earned from financial assets (discussed in the next section).

Deeming of income from financial assets

To discourage the practice of pensioners holding large sums in low-earning accounts, such as cheque accounts, in order to minimise assessable income and thus maximise pension payments, the government introduced deeming provisions in 1996. Deeming provisions apply predetermined rates of return on all financial investments held by a pensioner to determine assessable income regardless of the actual return generated. In other words, the values of all financial assets are added together and it is assumed that they earn certain set rates of return. People are free to invest their money wherever they like, but they have an incentive to invest in assets which earn at least the deeming rates. Any return earned above the deeming rates is non-assessable.

Table 10.8 shows the deeming rates and thresholds effective from 20 March 2024. The thresholds are changed periodically, as are the deeming rates (in line with market interest rates).

TABLE 10.8 Deeming rates for benefit recipients effective from 20 March 2024

Status	Initial rate %	Threshold $	Upper rate threshold %
Single	0.25	60 400	2.25
Couple	0.25	100 200	2.25

Source: Services Australia 2024.

Financial investments generally include most forms of investments held by a pensioner such as bank accounts, shares, managed funds, account-based pensions and short-term income streams. However, the following are excluded:
- life insurance policies
- rental properties, holiday homes and other real estate
- long-term annuities of greater than 5 years.

As discussed previously, superannuation fund balances for those under age-pension age are exempt under both the assets and income tests. Once a pensioner reaches age-pension age, superannuation and account-based pensions are both treated as financial investments and subject to deeming rules.

ILLUSTRATIVE EXAMPLE 10.2

Referring to the case study presented at the start of this chapter with Con and Maria, the couple's financial assets and income would consist of the following.

Financial investments	
Bank account	$ 17 000
Managed funds	85 000
Shares	50 000
Superannuation — Con	350 000
Total	**$502 000**

As Maria is below age-pension age, her superannuation account balance is exempt under both the assets and income tests.

Deemed income	
First $100 200 assessed at 0.25%	$ 250.50
Balance of financial investments ($401 800) assessed at 2.25%	9 040.50
Total deemed income	**$9 291**
Income assessed for taxation purposes	
Bank account — $17 000 @ 1.0%	$ 170
Managed funds — $85 000 @ 3.8%	3 230
Shares — $50 000 @ 2.8%	1 400
Plus imputation credit — 30/70	600
Total	**$5 400**

Assume that Con retires. Maria's salary of $18 000 would need to be added to the above figures for both social security and taxation purposes.

▶

As can be seen, while the couple's income for tax purposes, excluding Maria's salary, would be assessed at $5400, Services Australia would assess the couple's income at $9291 — this is $3891 more than the taxable assessable amount. The main reason is that Con's superannuation account is treated as a financial investment and subject to deeming rates.

Is this difference likely to encourage Con and Maria to sell their investments in favour of higher yielding investments? Probably not — it depends on the capital gain they would make, the associated capital gains tax and the outlook for the shares held. Is the couple able to do anything with Con's superannuation account to reduce the income that is assessed by Services Australia? Some strategies will be examined later in this chapter.

When only one member of the couple is entitled to the age pension

Situations may arise when only one partner is entitled to an age pension. This may occur when only one of the partners satisfies age requirements. In such cases, all of the couple's combined assets and income are used to determine eligibility under the assets and income test regardless of which partner owns the assets or receives the income. Pension payments and reduction factors are based on individual partner rates.

ILLUSTRATIVE EXAMPLE 10.3

Based on the case study involving Con and Maria provided at the commencement of this chapter and assuming that Con retires, his age pension entitlement would be calculated as provided below. As only Con satisfied the age eligibility requirement, his pension entitlement will be based on the individual partner rate as will all reduction factors.

Assets test

The couple's assessable assets total $602 000 (see illustrative example 10.1).

Pension payable under assets test

Con's pension entitlement is calculated as the maximum pension entitlement less a reduction factor.

$$\text{Pension entitlement} = \$755.70 - [(\$602\,000 - \$451\,500) / \$1000 \times \$1.50]$$
$$= \$755.70 - \$225.75$$
$$= \$529.95 \text{ per fortnight}$$

Income test

Based on the calculations determined earlier (see illustrative example 10.2), the couple's financial investments total $502 000 and generate deemed income of $9291. Total assessable income is determined as follows.

Wages	$18 000
Deemed income	$ 9 291
Total income	$27 291

Their fortnightly income is $27 291 ÷ 26 weeks = $1049.65 per fortnight.

Pension payable under income test

Con's pension entitlement is calculated as the maximum pension entitlement less a reduction factor.

$$\text{Pension entitlement} = \$755.70 - [(\$1049.65 - \$360) \times 0.25]$$
$$= \$755.70 - \$172.41$$
$$= \$583.29 \text{ per fortnight}$$

Pension payable

The test that provides the lower pension applies. In this case, the age pension payment under the assets test ($529.95/fortnight) will apply.

Work bonus

The work bonus was introduced by the government in its 2009–10 budget as an incentive for pensioners of age-pension age to remain in the workforce.

All pensioners over age-pension age, other than recipients of the parenting payment, are eligible for the work bonus. Under the bonus, the first $300 of employment income per fortnight is not assessed and is not counted under the pension income test. The work bonus applies to income from employment, including:
- wages paid in Australia and outside Australia
- annual and long-service leave paid where the employee remains with the same employer
- director's fees.

Pensioners over age-pension age are able to accrue any unused part of the $300 fortnightly work bonus exemption amount in a work bonus income bank, up to a maximum of $7800. The income bank amount offsets future employment income from the pension income test.

Exempt income

The income test exempts some cash flows which are not really income but are payments of capital (such as **home equity conversion (HEC) loans** or **reverse mortgages**), as well as income flows paid by government and the non-cash estimated value of any free board and lodging. Cash inflows exempt under the income test include:
- lump sums received as home equity conversion loans
- general insurance receipts from claims for damage to property
- capital gains realised on the sale of assets
- rent subsidies and most other government transfer payments, such as child support payments and carer allowances
- emergency relief payments
- medical benefits.

In relation to home equity conversion loans, the lump sum received as a loan is exempt as income. However, if the amount is deposited into a bank account and interest is earned, the income will be assessed under deeming rules.

Gifted assets

Gifted assets are assets that have been disposed of for less than market value or given away. Pension applicants may be tempted to give away some of their cash or other assets to family members and then claim higher pension entitlements due to a lower holding of assessable assets and/or income earned. The **gifting rules** allow an applicant to give away, without affecting the pension entitlement, a maximum of:
- $10 000 annually, and
- $30 000 over a 5-financial-year rolling period.

Any amounts given away above these limits are assessed as assets and income in the hands of the applicant and continue to be so assessed for 5 years. Any gifts made in the 5-year period prior to the initial application for a pension will also be assessed.

Retirement income stream products

Upon retirement, a retiree will normally look to use their superannuation to acquire a financial product that pays them a regular income stream to cover their living costs. In return for providing a lump sum, income-stream products covering pensions and annuities provide a regular income flow to the recipient. While many income-stream products are typically acquired with a person's superannuation account balance, some income-stream products can also be acquired with non-superannuation monies, such as with personal savings or through the sale of an investment property.

The issue that needs to be determined is how retirement income-stream products are assessed for social security purposes. The assessment of retirement income-stream products for the purposes of the assets and income tests falls under one of the following three categories.
1. **Asset-test-exempt income streams** — non-commutable income streams that have a nil residual value.
2. *Asset-tested income streams (long-term)* — long-term (more than 5-year) income streams which are assessed on the account balance (such as account-based pensions).
3. *Asset-tested income streams (short-term)* — short-term (less than 5-year) income streams which are assessed on the account balance (such as short-term annuities).

Rules of assessment under the assets test

For asset-test purposes, most income-stream products under categories 2 and 3 above are generally assessed on the actual account balance at any point in time. However, asset-test-exempt income streams (category 1), such as lifetime or life expectancy pensions and annuities and term-allocated pensions, are exempt under the assets test as follows.

- 100% exempt if purchased before 20 September 2004.
- 50% exempt if purchased on or after 20 September 2004 and up to 19 September 2007.

All income-stream products acquired after 20 September 2007 are fully assessable.

For pensions and annuities for which there is no account balance, such as with a lifetime pension or annuity, the value of the asset is calculated under a method called the original purchase price depletion method. This method calculates the value of the asset based on the original purchase price reduced periodically for income payments made by the product provider. The following formula is used where income payments are made to the recipient more than once a year and there is no capital sum returned at the end of the term, that is there is no **residual capital value (RCV)**.

$$PP - \left(\frac{PP}{RN \times 2} \times \text{Completed half years} \right)$$

where: PP = purchase price of the income stream

RN = the relevant number of the income stream.

Completed half years = the number of half years that have passed since the commencement of the contract.

Where the income stream does not have a specified term, for example a lifetime pension, the relevant number used is the member's life expectancy at the time of taking out the income stream. For a 10-year fixed annuity, the relevant number is the term of the contract.

Rules of assessment under the income test

Income-stream products provide regular income payments to the member. In return for providing a capital sum at the commencement of the income stream, the product provider pays the member an ongoing income stream.

All new account-based pensions commencing after 1 January 2015 are treated as a financial asset and therefore income is assessed using the deeming rules discussed previously.

For asset-test-exempt income streams and asset-tested long-term income streams, excluding account-based pensions commencing after 1 January 2015, assessable income is calculated by reducing the gross annual payments by a deduction amount that reflects a return of the purchase price. The deduction amount reduces the gross income received each year on the basis that part of the income payment received each year from the pension or annuity provider represents a return of the original purchase price (capital) to the member.

The deduction for the capital component, known as the deductible amount, is calculated by apportioning the whole of the initial capital invested or the purchase price over the term of the contract or the life expectancy of the beneficiary. It should be noted that the deductible amount is determined at the date of original acquisition of the pension and remains fixed thereafter. Thus, assessable income is determined as follows.

$$\text{Gross annual income} - \frac{\text{Purchase price}}{\text{Life expectancy or term of pension or annuity}}$$

Current life expectancy tables can be found on the Australian government website 'Guides to Social Policy Law' (guides.dss.gov.au/guide-social-security-law/4/9/5/49).

Short-term income products (category 3) taken out for less than 5 years, are generally assessed under deeming rules.

ILLUSTRATIVE EXAMPLE 10.4

Continuing on from the case study based on Con and Maria, assume that Con decides to roll over his superannuation account balance of $350 000 into an account-based pension. Assume that Con's life expectancy at the time of acquiring the income stream is 19.06 years.

In 2 years, with Con aged 68, how will the income stream be assessed for Services Australia purposes given that the balance of the account-based pension has risen to $360 000 and Con takes an income

---

withdrawal of $25 000 for that year? The value of the asset for age pension purposes is calculated as the current balance of the account-based pension, that is $360 000.

Con's assessable income under the income test for age pension purposes is calculated below.

If the account-based pension commenced after 1 January 2015, the income will be subject to deeming rules as follows.

First $100 200 assessed at 0.25%	$ 250.50
Balance of financial investment to $360 000 ($259 800) is assessed at 2.25%	5 845.50
Total deemed income	**$6 096.00**

If the account-based pension commenced prior to 1 January 2015, the income will be determined by reducing from the gross income received, the deductible amount based on the return of capital to the member as follows.

$25 000 – ($350 000 / 19.06) = $6637

Note that the deductible (tax-free) amount is based on the value of the account-based pension and the life expectancy at the time that the account-based pension was first acquired. In other words, the deductible amount remains the same each year.

Means testing of allowances

Allowance recipients use the same assets test thresholds as shown in table 10.6. However, unlike pension payments, no allowance is paid where the level of assets exceeds the lower threshold. The income test for the payment of allowances is slightly more complicated. Table 10.9 shows the threshold and upper-limit rates for a number of allowances including the JobSeeker payment. Fortnightly income in excess of $150 and up to $250 reduces the payable benefit by 50 cents per dollar, and income above $250 reduces the benefit by 60 cents in the dollar.

TABLE 10.9   Income test limits for allowances from 20 March 2024

	Limits ($ per fortnight)	
Status	**Full allowance**	**Part allowance**
Single, no dependent children	150	1 454.50
Single, dependent children	150	1 545.00
Partnered (each)	150	1 344.67
Single, principal carer with dependent children	150	2 233.00

Source: Services Australia 2024.

10.7 Assistance provided to families raising children

LEARNING OBJECTIVE 10.7   Outline the assistance provided to families raising children.

Services Australia provides assistance to families through a range of benefits. The chief benefits are **family tax benefit** part A, family tax benefit part B, parental leave payment, dad and partner pay, child care rebate and parenting payment.

For the purposes of satisfying an income test for eligibility to a number of family benefits, including family tax benefits, child care benefit and parental leave payment, an income test based on **adjusted taxable income (ATI)** is used.

An individual's ATI is made up of:
- taxable income
- the value of any adjusted fringe benefits (total reportable fringe benefit amounts multiplied by 0.535)
- reportable employer superannuation contributions
- target foreign income
- total net investment losses
- tax-free pension or benefit.

Family tax benefit part A

The family tax benefit part A provides assistance to low- and medium-income families for the cost of raising children. Residency and income testing eligibility rules apply, but some allowance is made when a family may be required to live temporarily overseas. Claimants must be living in Australia on a permanent basis and be Australian citizens, holders of permanent visas, New Zealand citizens or holders of one of some specific temporary visa. The benefit is payable to families with dependent children under 16 years of age, dependent children aged 16 or 17 years completing a year 12 or equivalent qualification, or for children aged 16–19 years (up to the end of the calendar year they turn 19) and undertaking full-time education or training in an approved course leading to a year 12 or equivalent qualification.

Payment is made for each dependent child. The payment is not assets tested. The maximum rates of benefits are shown in table 10.10.

TABLE 10.10	Maximum rate of family tax benefit part A payable from 20 September 2023	
For each dependent child	**Payment per fortnight**	**Payment p.a. (includes supplement of $879.65)**
Under 13 years	$213.36	$6 442.25
13–19 years	$277.48	$8 113.95
In an approved care organisation aged 0–19 years	$ 68.46	$1 784.85

Source: Services Australia 2023.

The supplement is paid after the end of the financial year once a tax return has been lodged.

Maximum family benefits are payable where family adjusted taxable income is less than $62 634 p.a. (effective from 20 September 2023). Part payments are available as family income rises. In most cases Services Australia determines an FTB part A payment using two income tests.
1. The payment will reduce by 20 cents for each dollar above $62 634 until the payment reaches the base rate of FTB part A.
2. The payment will stay at that rate until the family income exceeds $111 398 p.a. when the family tax benefit payment reduces by 30 cents in the dollar above $111 398 until the payment is nil.

The base rate of FTB part A for each child is currently $68.46 per fortnight.

Family tax benefit part B

The government has extended assistance to single-income families with children and to families with one main income earner where one parent chooses to stay at home to look after the children through the family tax benefit part B. To be eligible for a part B benefit, a family must have a dependent child under the age of 16 or have a qualifying dependent full-time student up to the age of 18 (who does not receive a youth allowance or a similar benefit).

The maximum amount of family tax benefit part B payable depends upon the age of the youngest child as shown in table 10.11.

TABLE 10.11	Maximum rate of family tax benefit part B payable from 20 September 2023	
Age of youngest child	**Payment per fortnight**	**Payment p.a. (includes supplement of $430.70 per family)**
Under 5 years	$181.44	$5 161.10
5–15 years (or 16–18 years if a full-time student)	$126.56	$3 730.30

Source: Services Australia 2023.

The supplement is paid after the end of the financial year once a tax return has been lodged.

Income test for sole-parent families

Sole parents will receive the maximum part B benefit if they have an income of $112 578 or less.

Income test for two-parent families

The maximum part B benefit will be payable where the higher income earner in a couple has an income of $112 578 or less. A part B payment will not be payable where the primary earner receives an income in excess of $112 578. Where the primary earner's income is less than $112 578, the income of the lower income earner determines how much part B benefit the family will receive. The lower income earner can earn up to $6497 p.a. before the maximum part B benefit is reduced. The maximum benefit is reduced by 20 cents for each dollar of income earned over $6497 p.a.

A couple will still receive some part B payment if the income of the lower income earner is less than:
- $32 303 a year, if the youngest child is under 5 years of age, or
- $25 149 a year, if the youngest child is 5 to 18 years of age.

Members of a couple are ineligible to receive the FTB part B where the youngest child is 13 years of age. FTB part B is payable to single parents, grandparents or great-grandparent carers where the youngest child is 13 years of age. However, members of a couple must have their youngest child aged 12 or younger to be eligible.

Parental leave pay scheme

The parental leave pay scheme offers financial support allowing parents to take time off work to care for their children following birth or adoption. The eligibility and benefits are summarised in table 10.12.

TABLE 10.12 **Eligibility for and benefits of parental leave pay scheme from 20 September 2023**

	Parental leave pay
Care requirement	• be caring for a newborn or newly adopted child • the parent of a newborn child • the adoptive parent of a child • another person caring for a child under exceptional circumstances.
Work test	Must worked for at least: • 10 of the 13 months before the birth or adoption, and • 330 hours in that 10-month period. Must also be on leave or not working whilst in receipt of paid parental leave.
Income test	Have an individual adjusted taxable income of $168 865 or less.
Pay rate	$882.75 per week before tax, based on the weekly rate of the national minimum wage.
Pay period	Payable up to 20 weeks.

While government parental leave pay is currently paid on top of any leave provided by an employer, the government has proposed legislation whereby it would only top-up parental leave pay to cover any shortfall in employer leave payments.

Child care subsidy

A child care subsidy is paid to parents who use approved child care. Eligibility for the child care subsidy is based on:
- using approved child care
- being responsible for paying the child care fees for the child aged under 14
- the child being immunised (or on an immunisation catch-up schedule) or is exempt from the immunisation requirements
- meeting the residency requirements.

The amount of fortnightly child care subsidy paid to parents for each child depends on the:
- family income
- hourly rate cap
- hours of activity.

Family income

Families with a combined income of up to $80 000 could have up to 90% of their child care costs subsidised. This percentage decreases as the family income increases, as shown in table 10.13 below.

TABLE 10.13   Family income and child care subsidy percentage from 20 September 2023

Combined family income	Standard child care subsidy rate
Up to $80 000	90%
More than $80 000 to below $530 000	Decreasing from 90% by 1% for every $5000 over $80 000
$530 000 or more	0%

Source: Services Australia 2023.

The child care subsidy percentage is applied to either the hourly fee charged by the child care provider or their hourly fee, whichever produces a lower subsidy.

Hourly rate cap

Table 10.14 shows how the hourly rate cap differs, depending on the type of approved child care used.

TABLE 10.14   Hourly rate cap and types of child care provider from 20 September 2023

Type of child care	Hourly rate cap
Centre based day care — long day care and occasional care	$13.73
Family day care	$12.72
Outside school hours care — before, after and vacation care	$13.73
In home care	$37.34, per family

Source: Services Australia 2023.

Hours of activity

Recognised activities and subsidised care

The number of hours of subsidised child care payable to families fortnightly for each child varies with the number of hours of recognised activities undertaken by the parents (see table 10.15).

TABLE 10.15   Recognised activities and hours of subsidised care from 20 September 2023

Hours of recognised activities each fortnight	Hours of subsidised care each fortnight
Less than 8 hours	0 hours if you earn above $80 000 24 hours if you earn $80 000 or below
More than 8 to 16 hours	36 hours
More than 16 to 48 hours	72 hours
More than 48 hours	100 hours

Source: Services Australia 2023.

Recognised activities can include:
- paid work including being self employed
- paid or unpaid leave, including paid or unpaid parental or maternity leave
- unpaid work in a family business
- unpaid work experience or unpaid internship
- actively setting up a business
- doing an approved course of education or study
- doing training to improve work skills or employment prospects
- actively looking for work
- volunteering
- other activities on a case by case basis.

10.8 Assistance provided to those with disability or impairment

LEARNING OBJECTIVE 10.8 Outline the assistance provided to people with disability.

A number of support services are available to people with disability and to carers of people with severe disability. These services include the disability support pension, sickness allowance and carer payment.

Disability support pension

The **disability support pension** provides a level of income for people who have physical, intellectual or psychiatric impairment assessed under impairment tables at 20 points or more. To qualify for a disability support pension, a person must:
- be over 16 but less than age-pension age,
- be unable to work for 15 hours or more per week for the next 2 years as a result of the impairment,
- meet the requirements for Australian residency and the income and assets tests for pensions,
- be unable to undertake a training activity due to the impairment which would equip the person for work within the next 2 years, or
- be permanently blind.

In situations where a person has been working and has suffered an injury as a result of the working environment, a range of other factors are taken into account before any disability support pension may be payable.

The rate for the disability support pension is the same as the age pension (detailed earlier in this chapter), except where the claimant is aged less than 21 years and has no children. The benefit is means tested under the assets and income tests as a pension payment.

Carer payment

The carer payment is payable to eligible carers who provide daily care for either an adult or child who is being nursed at home. The carer payment is paid at the same rate as the age pension.

The person being cared for must:
- be assessed as having physical, intellectual or psychiatric disability under the Adult Disability Assessment Tool, or
- be assessed as having severe disability or a severe medical condition under the Disability Care Load Assessment (Child) Determination, and
- meet the care receiver income and assets tests, or
- be receiving an income support payment from Services Australia or a service pension, or
- not be receiving an income support payment only due to not meeting residency requirements.

The carer must be providing constant care for a:
- person who has physical, intellectual or psychiatric disability, or
- disabled adult who has a dependent child in their care.

10.9 Support for those undertaking study or an Australian apprenticeship

LEARNING OBJECTIVE 10.9 Explain the support provided for those undertaking study or an Australian apprenticeship.

The government pays a number of allowances to support those undertaking study or an apprenticeship.

Austudy

Austudy provides income support to students aged 25 years or over undertaking qualifying study or a full-time Australian apprenticeship. Courses approved for Austudy payment include secondary education, undergraduate courses, graduate courses (excluding most Masters degrees and all doctorates), TAFE courses and associate diplomas. Full-time students under the age of 25 may be eligible for the youth allowance.

The basic rate of payment at 1 January 2024 is:
- $602.80 per fortnight for a single or partnered person with no children
- $760.40 per fortnight for a single person with children
- $652.60 per fortnight for a partnered person with children.

Assets and income means tests

The assets means test is the same as for pensions and a number of other allowances.

Under the income test, gross income is assessed. The full benefit under Austudy will be paid where the student's or apprentice's income is less than $480 per fortnight. Income between $480 and $575 reduces payment by 50 cents in the dollar and income above $575 reduces payment by 60 cents in the dollar.

Austudy students are also allowed to accumulate up to $12 000 of any unused portion of their $480 fortnightly income-free area which can be used to offset against income earned in excess of $480. Australian apprentices can accumulate up to $1000 of any unused portion of their income-free area. This is known as the income bank.

Youth allowance

The youth allowance is payable to full-time students and Australian apprentices aged between 16 and 24 or students who are temporarily incapacitated for full-time study aged 22–24. Job seekers under 22 years, either looking for work or combining part-time study with job search, or undertaking other approved activity or are temporarily incapacitated for work or study, may also be eligible. Those aged 25 and over may also qualify if they were receiving the youth allowance immediately before turning 25.

If the recipient is not independent, a parental income test and a family assets test will apply. Otherwise the recipient will be subject to personal income and assets tests. If not independent, the rate reduces if the parents' combined adjusted taxable income exceeds the income threshold of $62 634 (to 30 June 2023). The reduction factor is 20 cents in the dollar over the threshold. If the recipient is independent (considered independent if aged 22 years of age or over), the personal income test applies. For students and Australian apprentices who earn money from paid work, an income bank helps to build up income credits. Australian apprentices and students can earn up to $480 a fortnight before their income support payment is reduced.

Rates of payment (from 20 March 2024) are shown in table 10.16.

TABLE 10.16   Rates of payment (from 20 March 2024)

Single no children	
— aged under 18 and at home	$395.30/fortnight
— aged under 18 and away from home	$639.00/fortnight
Single with children	$806.00/fortnight
Partnered with children	$691.80/fortnight

Source: Services Australia 2024.

10.10 Taxation of pensions and allowances

LEARNING OBJECTIVE 10.10 Outline the taxation of pensions and allowances.

The taxation of social security benefits introduces more complexity to the social security field. Some pensions and allowances are taxable and some are not. In addition, some social security benefits attract a tax offset to reduce a person's overall tax liability. A tax offset directly reduces the tax payable by taxpayers on their taxable income, whereas a tax deduction reduces taxable income and therefore the tax payable.

Some of the more common taxable pensions and allowances are:

- age pension
- age service pension
- Austudy
- carer payment with some exceptions
- disability support pension — for person of age-pension age
- JobSeeker payment
- parenting payment
- youth allowance.

Some of the more common non-taxable pensions and allowances are:

- carer allowance
- carer payment — if both carer and the cared-for are under age-pension age
- child care benefit
- disability support pension — if under age-pension age
- disaster relief
- double orphan pension
- family tax benefit (A) and (B).

The benefits that are taxable are, in the main, those that are paid in substitute of employment income. For example, **JobSeeker payment**, age pensions and disability support pensions are paid to people as a result of their inability to find work or because they are regarded as too old to work. In contrast, benefits that are not taxable are those designed to top-up other income and give individuals and families specific financial assistance for special purposes such as maternity, pharmaceuticals, rent and living in a remote area.

Seniors and pensioners tax offset (SAPTO)

SAPTO is payable to persons of age-pension age who are self-funded retirees. The tax offset provides a tax concession for those retirees on a low income who satisfy eligibility for an Australian government pension but who do not qualify because of the application of the means test. Each member of a couple is tested separately for SAPTO eligibility.

The rebate amount and thresholds for 2022–23 are detailed in table 10.17.

TABLE 10.17 The SAPTO tax offset and thresholds for 2022–23

Family status	Maximum tax offset	Shade-out threshold	Cut-out threshold
Single	$2 230	$32 279	$50 119
Couple (each)	$1 602	$28 974	$41 790
Couple (separated due to illness)	$2 040	$31 279	$47 599

The shade-out threshold is the level of income at which individuals will be entitled to the maximum tax offset. The tax offset reduces by 12.5 cents for each dollar of rebate income in excess of the shade-out threshold.

The income test for SAPTO is based on income known as 'rebate income', which includes:

- taxable income
- adjusted fringe benefits (that is, the total reportable fringe benefits amount multiplied by 0.535)
- reportable employer superannuation contributions and deductible personal superannuation contributions
- deductible personal superannuation contributions
- total net investment loss.

10.11 Accommodation in retirement

LEARNING OBJECTIVE 10.11 Describe the accommodation alternatives in retirement.

One of the considerations that people need to make as they grow older is the need for some form of alternative accommodation. This is an important issue when planning a retirement strategy not only because of the emotional stress of moving, but also because of the costs and charges levied with the alternative accommodation and the effect that moving will have on social security entitlements.

The various accommodation options available to a person in retirement include:
- remaining in their principal residence
- special residence options
  - retirement villages
  - granny flats
- home care
- residential aged care.

The Australian government spends more than $11 billion annually on residential aged care facilities. Aged care homes (a preferred term for a nursing home or an aged care facility) are quite separate from the facilities provided in retirement villages and granny flats, which constitute a different segment entirely of the housing market.

Special residence

Retirement villages

Retirement villages generally accommodate people, both singles and couples, aged over 55. Some complexes include both retirement villages and aged care homes. According to research conducted by the Property Council of Australia in 2021, there are about 263 000 Australians living in retirement villages, or 6% of the over-65 population. This rate is projected to increase to 7.5% by 2041 meaning that there will be approximately 495 000 people wanting to live in a retirement village in 2041. Retirement villages are funded by residents' payments, loans or donations (also known as entry contributions) and by ongoing fees and charges. When buying into a retirement village, depending on the type of tenure being sought, a resident will either pay an entry payment (sometimes known as an entry fee or entry price) or a purchasing price. Leaseholds and licences (tenures) are generally set up so the entry payment is usually the current market value of the property. Under strata, community and company titles, residents generally pay a purchase price for the legal title to the property.

The amount of entry contribution required will vary according to the retirement village and the kind of accommodation chosen. Some villages base their entry contribution on the actual purchase price or market value of a unit in the facility. Residents of a retirement home also need to pay ongoing fees and charges for services and facilities. Fees for those residents living in a self-care or serviced unit are set by the retirement village. There is no government legislation that sets these fees. A departure or exit fee is normally also payable on leaving the retirement village and is usually determined by a formula that takes into account entry costs, sale proceeds and years of occupancy. This fee will vary between retirement villages.

Granny flats

Under the Guide to Social Security Law (para. 4.6.4.50) a granny flat is defined as: .

> A life interest or right to accommodation for life where:
> - the person 'pays' for a life interest or right to accommodation for life, AND
> - the life interest or right to accommodation for life is in a private residence that is to be the person's principal home.

A granny flat interest does not include where a person is the owner or part-owner of the property. In this case, the person has the right to live in the property because of their ownership. The assessed value of a granny flat interest is normally the same as the amount paid for the interest and could include the value of the transfer of the title of their home, the costs paid for the construction and fit-out of premises, or where a property has been purchased in another person's name in return for a life interest or the right to accommodation for life.

Granny flats — a lifestyle alternative for the elderly

Introduction

Whilst most people express the desire to remain in their own home for as long as they can, for many, moving to some sort of alternative accommodation in later years becomes necessary. This could be the consequence of physical or mental frailty or just the desire for social company that, for example, a retirement village offers elderly people.

Retirement living can include alternative retirement village settings or aged care for the frail and infirm. An alternative is mum or dad (or both) living with one of the children, frequently known as a 'granny flat' option. Granny flat living is becoming a favoured alternative — particularly in light of social security gifting concessions where Centrelink requirements are met.

What is a granny flat?

The Social Security Act defines a 'granny flat interest' in a person's home if:
- the residence is the person's principal home as a private residence and
- the person acquired for valuable consideration or has retained:
  - a right to accommodation for life in the residence, or
  - a life interest in the residence.

Where a genuine granny flat interest has been acquired for Centrelink purposes, the elderly person's son or daughter/carer cannot revoke that interest simply because the child/carer may want to sell the property. Indeed, if the child wants to sell the property they can only do so if the child/carer:
- ensures the parent's right to live there is a condition of the sale (obviously unacceptable to a third party buyer)
- transfers the granny flat interest to another property (the more likely scenario) or
- provides money/assets to the parent in return for the loss of mum or dad's interest.

Payment by the parent in consideration for the right to reside in a property for house improvements etc. is considered an exempt asset for Centrelink gifting purposes and so the asset deprivation or gifting rules will not apply; provided Centrelink requirements are met.

So, if the parent has:
- transferred title in their own property to a child/carer in exchange for a lifetime right to live there, or
- paid for building improvements in a property owned by a child/carer to suit their own needs, or
- purchased a property in a child's name in exchange for a lifetime right

then Centrelink will not assess any of these contributions under the gifting rules. If however the consideration for the occupation right is something different or in addition, then Centrelink will assess it against a reasonable value test. In that instance, if Centrelink deems an amount to be paid over and above a reasonable sum (based on its own assessment), then that surplus will be deemed to have been gifted to the child/carer. That has implications for the parent's pension.

This all means that where a parent and a child are looking at a granny flat interest, great care must be taken in the arrangement to ensure there are no Centrelink/pension impacts.

But in addition to the impact on the parent there can be implications also for the child/carer. This is because there can be CGT implications of the child/carer if they receive a payment from a parent which exceeds the market value of the right created. The CGT considerations are quite involved. Suffice to say that there can be revenue implications, both for the parent and for the child if careful planning is not carried out.

How should the arrangement be structured?

One of the key aspects of a granny flat interest is to assess how best to structure the arrangement. Should assets be gifted or lent and should security be taken? For example, is it best that the parent gift the amount of the intended home improvements to the child/carer (with consequential impact on the value of the elderly person's estate) or should those monies be loaned? If monies are loaned, are there financial implications for the parent and should the loan be repaid to the estate on death?

To meet Centrelink granny flat interest requirements, the parent cannot obtain a legal interest in the property in which he or she lives and so that would generally inform the decision that Mum or Dad ought to lend monies to a child if home improvements are required. Then there is the issue of the implications for the parent's pension income because of the deeming rate applying to interest payable on the loan — even if the loan agreement provides that interest is not payable.

So, once again, careful planning has to be considered because the amount of the loan made will influence the deemed income/interest return on monies lent and so has a potential implication on the parent's pension income.

▶

The importance of a granny flat agreement

Irrespective of the manner in which a granny flat interest is structured and the dollars involved, both parties to the arrangement should consider a formal agreement to document the arrangement. This is particularly important where there are other siblings involved — if only to ensure that everyone is on the same page to mitigate the risk of argument and disharmony on Mum's or Dad's death.

What should be covered in a granny flat agreement?

Granny flat agreements need to address:

- who the parties to the agreement are
- a detailed recital to explain the family circumstances and dynamics which ought to demonstrate the process come to and the involvement of other family members
- the nature and purpose of the contribution to be made by the older person being cared for
- how the interest of the older person's contribution is to be secured and perhaps if not, why not
- the care and services which are to be provided to the older person
- the legal status of the older person's occupation of the property (e.g. life tenant)
- how outgoings are to be apportioned
- how absences and respite care for the carer are to be dealt with
- appropriate indemnities and insurance provisions
- voluntary and involuntary termination of the agreement (e.g. deal with termination as a consequence of relationship breakdown as well as death/incapacity)
- dispute resolution
- ensure that the agreement is binding upon the estate of a deceased party
- how incapacity might be addressed (consider appropriate enduring power of attorney provisions).

As always, the devil will be in the detail. Some of the challenges of old age which need to be thought through to focus on what the elderly person is to receive under the arrangement will include such things as:

- how the proposed agreement will affect other family members; will they feel dispossessed
- precisely what household tasks will the older person have done for them
- how will food and utility costs be shared
- is there to be an expectation that the older person will provide childcare services for grandchildren
- will there be access to a car, telephone or internet
- is the older person in a position to enjoy a separate social life and how will that change
- will there be separate access to the older person's living accommodation arrangements
- will the older person be able to have a pet.

There have been a lot of cases in recent years where argument has arisen as a consequence of shared living arrangements between elderly parent and child. One of the issues from the cases is that, ideally, the parties to a granny flat agreement should be separately represented by lawyers to avoid arguments of duress or unconscionable conduct.

Conclusion

Granny flats offer a sensible and, from the government's perspective, a simpler and cheaper lifestyle alternative for a lot of elderly people. They are not for everybody but if a family is considering this option for an elderly parent or parents, then it is important that careful consideration is given to Mum's or Dad's financial position; particularly for pensioners. Further, there could be quite unwittingly financial implications for the child/carer as well and these need to be thought through.

Careful advice is required and we strongly recommend the arrangement be documented by an appropriate agreement for which both parties are separately represented.

Source: Paxton-Hall Lawyers 2019.

Social security implications of entering special residences

One of the issues in moving into special residences, such as a retirement village or granny flat, is how any age pension entitlement will be affected. For Services Australia purposes, the amount of the entry contribution to a retirement village or granny flat determines whether the age pension recipient is assessed as a homeowner or non-homeowner. Where the entry contribution paid to enter a special residence is greater than the difference between the pension single/couple asset test threshold for a homeowner and that of a non-homeowner ($242 000 effective from 20 September 2023), the person will be assessed as a homeowner under the assets test. The amount of the entry contribution in this case will not be assessed as an asset. If the entry contribution is less than $242 000, the person will be considered a non-homeowner under the assets test. In this case, the entry contribution will be considered an assessable asset but not subject to deeming rates.

If a person is living in a special residence and retains their former principal home, the home will be assessable under the assets test and any rental income will be assessable under the income test. Where a person's former principal home is sold, the proceeds from sale will be treated as an assessable financial investment and subject to deeming rates. If some or all of the proceeds are to be used to pay for the entry contribution to the special residence, the amount will be treated as an exempt asset for up to 12 months until payment is made. However, the whole proceed will still be subject to deeming rates.

The other issue of particular concern for granny flats is whether the amount paid for the accommodation is reasonable and whether the gifting rules have been breached. In these cases, a reasonableness test is applied.

Aged care accommodation

There are two types of aged care accommodation — nursing homes and supported residential services (SRS). Nursing homes are government funded and must give a certain level of service in order to be accredited. SRSs are generally private businesses that provide accommodation and care for residents on a fee basis. They are not Commonwealth funded and therefore not governed by the *Aged Care Act 1997*. SRSs are able to set their own fees and charges.

Residents considering moving into an aged care home will first need an assessment with a member of an aged care assessment team (ACAT). ACATs assess people in terms of their ability to cope with their clinical needs, personal hygiene, daily living, communication, and social and emotional support structures. Clients are currently assessed on a scale containing eight grades.

Residents of residential aged care are required to pay a range of accommodation costs consisting of:
- accommodation payments
- a basic daily fee
- a means-tested care fee
- fees for extra optional services.

Accommodation costs

Since 1 July 2014, residents entering an aged care home for the first time will need to have their income and assets assessed by Services Australia if they want to receive government assistance with their care and accommodation costs. This assessment will be used to determine the costs residents could be asked to pay and the amount of government assistance received. All residents can be asked to pay fees and charges as a contribution towards their accommodation, care and living expenses.

The accommodation costs for residential aged care are detailed in table 10.18.

The costs for aged care homes changed on 1 July 2014. If the resident entered a home before 1 July 2014, they will continue to pay the costs under the old fee arrangement.

Social security implications of entering residential aged care

Where a resident retains their principal home, they will be assessed as a homeowner. The former principal home is exempt from the pension assets test for two years for all people entering residential care. While the home is occupied by a partner, spouse or dependent child, it is classed as an exempt asset. Additionally, this exemption will remain in force for two years after the second member of a couple leaves the home.

From 1 January 2016, all new residential care recipients have any rental income generated from their former principal home included in their aged care means test. For residents entering aged care prior to 1 January 2016, rental income from the former principal home was not assessed.

A lump sum refundable accommodation deposit paid to an aged care provider is exempt from the age pension assets and income test.

TABLE 10.18   Residential aged care costs (effective from 20 September 2023)

Accommodation payments	A basic daily fee	Means-tested care fee	Fees for extra optional services
• Residents will normally be required to pay a charge for their accommodation costs. This charge may be in the form of a lump sum, known as a refundable accommodation deposit (RAD), a daily periodical-type payment called a daily accommodation payment (DAP) or a combination of these two. • The daily accommodation payment (DAP) is based on the amount of the refundable accommodation deposit (RAD) and subject to a government set interest rate, which is currently 8.15% (from 1 October 2023). • The combination method allows residents to pay a partial refundable deposit, ensuring that they are left with the minimum permissible asset level (currently $58 500), and then pay the balance of the agreed price by daily payments. Residents can elect to have the daily payments deducted from the refundable deposit.	• A basic daily fee is used to contribute towards the resident's day-to-day living costs. • For new residents, the maximum basic daily fee is 85% of the single person rate of the basic age pension.	• This is an additional contribution towards the cost of care that some residents may be required to pay. • Services Australia will work out if the resident is required to pay this fee based on an assessment of their income and assets. • Annual and lifetime caps apply to the means-tested care fee.	• Additional fees may apply if the resident chooses a higher standard of accommodation or additional services.

PROFESSIONAL ADVICE

Negotiating aged care accommodation deposits

Donna is single, has become too frail to continue living in her home and is looking to move into a residential facility near her family. Donna's family have looked at a number of facilities around the area and have chosen one that has been newly renovated and has a good reputation.

After discussions with the manager of the facility, the family are advised that the refundable accommodation deposit required to be paid is set at a minimum of $500 000 and may be higher based on the size of the room required and the resident's level of assessable assets.

Donna's family has undertaken a number of strategies over the past few years, with the result that Donna has been left with her home and contents worth $420 000 and $60 000 contained in some bank accounts and term deposits. The ACAT team have provided Donna with an asset assessment form which Donna completes and sends into Services Australia. Services Australia will verify the information in the form to calculate her level of assessable assets and the maximum refundable accommodation deposit she is eligible to pay. The maximum deposit is calculated as the assessable assets less $58 500. Donna's assessable assets amount to $480 000 and she receives a letter from Services Australia stating the maximum bond she can pay is $421 500.

A week later, Donna's family receives a phone call to say that a place has become available and an appointment is made to discuss the opportunity for her to move in. However, the facility is firm that the minimum refundable accommodation deposit is $500 000. To admit Donna, they would need to accept a lower deposit.

QUESTIONS

1. Does the facility have to offer Donna a place based on a refundable accommodation deposit of only $421 500?

2. If the facility demands a refundable accommodation deposit of $500 000, is it too late for Donna's family to gift funds to Donna to bring her assessable assets up to $500 000?

3. How will the refundable accommodation deposit be assessed under the asset and income test for age pension purposes?

SUMMARY

The provision of social security measures has expanded dramatically during the last century in Australia although the eligibility requirements are gradually being tightened. Protagonists argue that helping our fellow community members financially is one mark of a civilised society and there are also humanitarian, utilitarian and economic arguments for such expenditures. The range of possible social security benefits is wide and has grown to include benefits designed to assist a diverse community in almost any form of need. About one-third of Australia's population receives some form of income assistance, to a greater or lesser extent.

The government's purse, however, is not bottomless, even in these times of relative prosperity. Thus, there is a comprehensive system of means testing for most benefits. Means testing involves both assets and income testing to ensure that benefits are only paid to those in need.

Age pension benefits have been part of Australian culture for over 100 years and currently form the basis of retirement income for 70–80% of the retired population. The work bonus scheme and the Commonwealth Seniors Health Card supplements the age pension as mechanisms to assist the aged.

Families raising children enjoy a comprehensive set of financial benefits to help compensate them financially for the extra costs they bear in raising children who, to some extent, provide population benefits to the whole of our society. These family based benefits include general benefits such as the family tax benefits, and specific benefits such as the child care benefit and the maternity immunisation allowance.

People with disabilities who are unable to work to support themselves are able to apply for the disability support pension if they are likely to be disabled for at least the next two years, while those with temporary sickness or disability may apply for the JobSeeker payment. There are also other allowances to assist disabled people.

The taxation of government pensions and allowances is a complex area. Some pensions and allowances are taxed at normal rates and others are not. Generally, the benefits that are taxed are those which are substitutes for employment income, while those untaxed include supplements to employment income.

With regard to the issue of housing for the aged who can no longer live in their own home, a number of different alternatives exist including special residence and residential aged care, depending upon the ability of the person to care for themselves. The government provides funding for residential aged care as well as government funding for home and community care to keep people at home as long as possible.

KEY TERMS

adjusted taxable income (ATI) Adjustments made to taxable income to determine eligibility for a number of family assistance and Services Australia payments, and tax offsets and rebates.

age pension A pension paid to eligible members of the community based on their age and subject to an income and assets test.

age test A test that requires persons to reach a certain age before being eligible for the age pension.

approved child care Child care that has been approved by the Australian government for child care benefit purposes because it meets certain standards and requirements.

asset-test-exempt income stream An income-stream product where part or all of the account balance is exempt under the assets test.

Austudy An Australian education assistance scheme that provides financial support to those aged 25 years and under and studying or undertaking an Australian apprenticeship full-time.

Centrelink The federal government agency which administers the payments of government pensions and allowances.

deemed income A notional rate of earnings used by Services Australia to calculate the investment returns from assets of eligible age pensioners.

disability support pension A pension paid to people who have a physical, intellectual or psychiatric impairment.

energy supplement Additional support to those in receipt of a pension to provide assistance for pensioners, families who receive family assistance, income support payment customers and Commonwealth Seniors Health Card holders.

family tax benefit Income support paid to eligible families to assist them with the cost of raising children.

gifting rules The rules that restrict the amount of assets able to be given away by pensioners before their age pension entitlements are affected.

government allowance Income support payments for persons in need of short-term assistance.

government pension Income support payments for persons in need of medium- to long-term assistance.

home equity conversion (HEC) loan (reverse mortgage) A loan or an amount by which a homeowner may draw funds based on the equity or ownership value of the home.

JobSeeker payment An allowance paid to unemployed persons while they are looking for work or to persons who are sick and unable to perform their usual work or study.

life interest An interest in property for the remaining life of the owner or occupant.

means test A test that reduces a person's entitlement to a pension or allowance based on exceeding certain asset and income thresholds.

pension supplement Additional support paid to those in receipt of a pension and replacing a number of individual allowances and supplements.

residual capital value (RCV) The capital amount payable on termination of a pension or annuity.

reverse mortgage An arrangement to mortgage a home in order to receive payments from the fund provider in return for a percentage ownership in the home or an accumulated debt to be paid when the home is sold.

youth allowance Financial support for young people who are studying, undertaking training or an Australian apprenticeship, looking for work or sick.

PROFESSIONAL APPLICATION QUESTIONS

10.1 Should every person reaching the age of 67 be entitled to receive a certain amount of age pension based on the fact that they have paid taxes all their working life? Discuss.

10.2 Is the Work Bonus scheme sufficient to encourage ongoing worker participation?

10.3 Why are there still so many Australians receiving the age pension when most employees have been receiving a superannuation guarantee contribution since 1992?

10.4 Is exempting the family home from the social security assets test fair? Discuss.

10.5 John is an age pensioner and he wishes to gift $12 000 to his daughter in the next month. How would this affect his age pension benefit?

10.6 Catherine, aged 36, sustains an injury and is unable to work for at least 2 months. What social security benefits could she apply for?

10.7 For the purposes of maximising an age pension entitlement, is it better for a pensioner to retain their retirement funds in superannuation or roll over their funds into a retirement income stream? Discuss.

10.8 Despina sells her family home and pays her son an amount of $410 000 to acquire an interest in a granny flat behind her son's house. The granny flat has a market value of $300 000. What issues might Services Australia have with the amount paid by Despina for the granny flat?

10.9 What is included within the definition of 'adjusted taxable income' and why do you believe the government introduced this concept as a means of determining eligibility to family assistance?

10.10 Is it fair that an older person might be forced to sell their family home in order to fund a refundable accommodation deposit? Explain.

PROFESSIONAL APPLICATION EXERCISES

★ BASIC | ★★ MODERATE | ★★★ CHALLENGING

10.11 Asset test assessment ★

Caroline is single and aged 68 years. She lives in her own home and has $426 000 in various assessable assets. How much would the assets test reduce her age pension per fortnight?

10.12 Income test assessment ★

Frank is a single age pensioner. He has just sold his house and entered an aged care facility. After paying his mortgage loan and the refundable accommodation deposit (RAD), he is left with total assets of $210 000 in cash. Regardless of where he holds these funds, what is his annual deemed income?

10.13 Austudy entitlement ★

Mark, aged 26, is single and lives at home with his parents. He is working full time as an apprentice and he earns $600 per fortnight. Mark also has $400 in his savings account and no other assets or income. Would Mark be entitled to Austudy and if so, how much?

10.14 Gifting rules ★

Lan and Vinh are age pensioners and have assets of $480 000. They wish to gift their son, Hoang, an amount of $35 000 to help him acquire a new home. How should they do this without affecting their age pension entitlement?

10.15 Aged care accommodation ★

Sanjay is an age pensioner who owns a unit worth about $520 000. He is assessed by an aged care assessment team (ACAT) and enters an aged care facility. He also has $42 000 in cash. What is the most likely assessed amount of the refundable accommodation deposit (RAD) that Sanjay will be asked to pay? Why?

10.16 Parental leave pay scheme entitlement ★★

Clarence is a full time business analyst with an adjusted annual taxable income (ATI) of $165 000. His wife Matilda is a speech therapist. She works at a primary school three days a week where she earns an annual ATI of $45 000. Following the birth of the couple's first child, Matilda takes 9 months maternity leave and Clarence takes two weeks paternity leave. What entitlements would Clarence and Matilda receive under the parental leave pay scheme?

10.17 Age pension entitlement ★★

Oscar and Lucinda are age pensioners and have the following assets.

Home	$870 000
Contents	$ 45 000
Car	$ 12 000
Investment property — net rental income of $14 000	$530 000
Shares — dividend yield of 2.5%	$ 65 000
Bank account — interest rate of 0.5%	$ 15 000
Superannuation — return of 4%	$155 000
Term deposit — interest rate of 1%	$ 35 000

Calculate their entitlement for the age pension.

10.18 Age pension entitlement ★★

Mr and Mrs Leong are a pensioner couple. They own their own home and have no dependants. Their home is valued at $920 000 and needs repair, and they have the following assets.

Superannuation — Mr Leong	$235 000
Bank account, interest rate 1% p.a.	125 000
Balanced managed fund, income return 4.5% p.a.	170 000
Shares, actual dividends $4800	75 000
Funeral bonds	9 000
Total	**$614 000**

Mr Leong has just retired. Mrs Leong still works on a casual basis with her son and earns a salary of $18 000 p.a. (assume the Work Bonus income bank already holds the maximum balance). During the year, the couple gave their daughter $24 000 to help with buying a new car.

Calculate the couple's entitlement to the age pension. Suggest ways the couple might be able to improve their pension entitlement.

10.19 Aged care accommodation ★★

Lilian is an age pensioner who enters a retirement village and pays an entry contribution of $320 000.

(a) Will Lilian be treated as a homeowner or non-homeowner for age pension purposes?

(b) How is this entry contribution treated under the assets and income test?

(c) What are the implications for social security purposes if Lilian retains her former family home and rents it out?

10.20 Family tax benefit ★★★

Scott and Larissa are a young married couple. Larissa, aged 41, earns a salary of $51 000 plus the 11% employer superannuation contribution. Scott is aged 44 and earns a salary of $85 000 after salary sacrificing $4000 into his superannuation account. He also has $6500 of reportable fringe benefits. The couple has 3 children aged 5, 8 and 15. Calculate the couple's family income for the purposes of determining eligibility for the family tax benefit part A and determine whether the couple would be eligible for any benefit under the family tax benefit part A.

10.21 Assessment of retirement income streams ★★★

Corina is aged 60 and still working, while Caleb is aged 67 and is a self-funded retiree. They own their home and the couple's combined income consists of Corina's employment income of $34 000, income from an account-based pension acquired by Caleb in 2014, as well as dividends and bank interest. Caleb acquired the account-based pension at age 64 for $480 000 and it is currently worth $400 000. Caleb withdraws an income from his pension account of $30 000 p.a. The couple's share portfolio is valued at $630 000 and generates a dividend yield of 3% p.a. The couple also has a term deposit of $175 000 which earns an interest rate of 1.5% p.a. and a savings account holding $50 000 earning 1% p.a.

(a) Calculate how the account-based pension would be assessed under the asset and income tests.

(b) How would Services Australia's treatment of the income from the retirement income stream differ from its treatment for income tax purposes?

(c) Will the couple be entitled to any age pension? Calculate.

(d) Explain any strategies the couple might consider using to reduce their assessable assets and income for social security purposes.

(e) If the couple were not able to receive any age pension entitlement, are there any other social security benefits or tax concessions they may be entitled to?

CASE STUDY 1

FAMILY TAX BENEFIT AND CHILD CARE SUBSIDY ENTITLEMENTS

Gupinder and Miranda have twin girls aged 4. Gupinder works full time with an annual income of $110 000. Miranda works part time and earns an annual income of $30 000. Each week, the twins are sent to an approved family day care centre for 18 hours while Miranda is at work. The child care fee is $20 per hour per child.

QUESTIONS

1 Calculate the amount of family tax benefit (FTB) part A that Gupinder and Miranda may be entitled to receive.

2 Calculate the amount of FTB part B that Gupinder and Miranda may be entitled to receive.

3 Discuss if the couple would be entitled to receive any child care subsidy.

4 Gupinder receives a pay rise and now earns an ATI of $155 000 p.a. Explain, with supporting calculations, how this new salary impacts on the couple's FTB and child care subsidy entitlements.

5 With Gupinder earning a higher salary, Miranda now wonders if she could stop working and apply for carer payment. She believes she would be caring for her children, so this could qualify her for the carer payment. Discuss if this is correct.

CASE STUDY 2

AGE PENSION AND ASSESSMENT OF GRANNY FLATS

Verna is single and age 72 and has been receiving the age pension for the past few years. Recently, Verna's health has steadily declined and her daughter Josie is concerned about her mother living by herself.

Josie and her husband have suggested that Verna moves in with Josie's family into a granny flat which they would build for her.

Verna has the following assets and income.

Asset	Current market value $	Income return
Home	610 000	Nil
Contents	35 000	Nil
Bank account	15 000	1% p.a.
Term deposit	50 000	2% p.a.
Account-based pension	180 000	4% p.a. (withdraws an income of $25 000 p.a.)
Share portfolio	85 000	3% p.a. (fully franked)
Prepaid funeral expense	10 000	Nil

It has been agreed that in return for the transfer of her home to Josie, Verna will receive ownership of the granny flat and a cash amount of $100 000. The account-based pension was acquired when Verna was aged 66 for $270 000.

QUESTIONS

1 Calculate the cash income *and* taxable income of Verna prior to the granny flat arrangement.
2 Calculate Verna's age pension entitlement prior to the granny flat arrangement proceeding.
3 Based on the granny flat arrangement proceeding as detailed above, calculate the impact on Verna's age pension entitlement.
4 Verna is wondering whether she is able to add the $85 000 received from her daughter into her existing account-based pension or into a new superannuation account. Discuss. What other investment options does Verna have if she wants to minimise the impact of the funds on her income assessed for age pension purposes?

CASE STUDY 3

FINANCIAL IMPLICATIONS OF ENTERING AN AGED CARE HOME

Mr Churchill, aged 72, is a widower and due to his poor health has decided to move into residential aged care. Mr Churchill has been offered a place at the Green Valley Aged Care Home for $380 000, which is located 10 minutes away from where his daughter lives. Mr Churchill owns his home worth $480 000 and has other assets of around $160 000.

After considerable negotiations, the aged care home provider agrees to charge Mr Churchill a refundable accommodation deposit (RAD) of $380 000. Mr Churchill is worried that if he pays a lump sum for the full RAD, he will be left with very few funds to cover the facility daily care fees, emergency payments and other cost of living expenses. He would also need to sell his home which he does not want to do. Mr Churchill has been told by the aged care home that he can pay the RAD by way of a lump sum, in periodic payments or a combination of both. The owner explains that Mr Churchill is able to make the periodic payments either monthly or fortnightly.

Mr Churchill agrees to pay a lump sum of $190 000 towards the cost of the RAD and pay the remaining $190 000 balance by way of regular payments. To pay for the periodic payments, Mr Churchill has decided to rent out his home which he believes should be able to earn a net amount of around $250 per week.

Unfortunately, after 4 years, Mr Churchill dies. Mr Churchill's entire estate is to be left to his daughter.

QUESTIONS

1 What is the maximum RAD that Mr Churchill could have been asked to pay by the care provider?
2 In terms of maximising his age pension benefit, would Mr Churchill have been better paying the total amount of the RAD as a lump sum or by way of a mixture of a lump sum and periodic payments?
3 If Mr Churchill wanted to minimise his monthly outgoings, calculate the minimum monthly periodic payment that he would have to have paid on the $190 000 owing on the RAD.
4 How will the following items be assessed for social security purposes: the RAD; Mr Churchill's former home that is being rented out; and the rental income generated?
5 Upon Mr Churchill's death, will the RAD be refunded to the estate plus interest earned on the RAD over the period of Mr Churchill's residence in the aged care home?

REFERENCES

Australian Government 2016, Guide to social security law.

Commonwealth of Australia 2009, *Australia's future tax system, the retirement income system: report on strategic issues*, May, https://treasury.gov.au/review/the-australias-future-tax-system-review/retirement-report.

Paxton-Hall Lawyers 2019, 'Granny flats — a lifestyle alternative for the elderly', 26 September, www.paxton-hall.com.au/2019/09/granny-flats-a-lifestyle-alternative-for-the-elderly.

Property Council of Australia 2023, 'Retirement living statistics', www.propertycouncil.com.au/advocacy/our-divisions/retirement-living-council.

Services Australia 2023, 'A guide to Australian Government payments', www.servicesaustralia.gov.au/sites/default/files/2023-09/co029-2309.pdf.

Treasury 2022, *Final budget outcome 2021–22*, Commonwealth Government, Canberra, https://archive.budget.gov.au/2021-22/fbo/download/fbo_2021-22.pdf.

Treasury 2023, 'Budget paper no. 1: budget strategy and outlook', Commonwealth Government, Canberra, https://budget.gov.au/content/bp1/download/bp1_2023-24_230727.pdf.

USEFUL WEBSITES

Department of Health, health.gov.au.
Department of Social Services, dss.gov.au.
Services Australia, servicesaustralia.gov.au.

ACKNOWLEDGEMENTS

Extract: © The Treasury
Table 10.1: © Commonwealth of Australia
Tables 10.3–10.15: © Services Australia

CHAPTER 11

Estate planning

LEARNING OBJECTIVES

After studying this chapter, you should be able to:

11.1 understand the importance of estate planning and the role of the financial planner in helping clients achieve their estate planning objectives

11.2 understand the role of a valid will within estate planning

11.3 explain the consequences of dying without a valid will

11.4 analyse the impact of taxation on distributions from deceased estates

11.5 understand the role and benefits of testamentary trusts in the minimisation of taxation and protection of assets

11.6 understand the rules applicable to superannuation death benefits

11.7 discuss the purpose of a power of attorney.

Jen, aged 58, died last month leaving investments totaling $1.5 million. Jen separated from her husband last year. Jen has a will in place that was drawn up 5 years ago leaving 50% to her husband, 40% to her daughter Felicity and 10% to her son Michael. Michael married 2 years ago and Jen and the daughter-in-law don't get along. Jen is hesitant to leave Michael much in her will on the basis of Michael and his wife separating in the near future and the daughter-in-law having access to her estate. However, Michael only has the one income in his family and is struggling a little. They have a one-year-old child. Felicity is married with two young children and is on the highest marginal tax rate.

At the date of Jen's death, her investments consist of the following:

House and contents (cost price $400 000 in 1994) Jointly owned 50/50 with ex-husband	$ 900 000
Car	20 000
Fixed interest	100 000
Investment property (cost price of $200 000 in 2010) Owned 50/50 under joint tenancy agreement with her sister	820 000
Managed funds (cost price of $70 000 in 2012)	100 000
Life insurance policy (owned in Jen's name)	300 000
Superannuation fund (non-binding death benefit nomination leaving 100% to ex-husband) incorporating an $80 000 tax-free component	280 000
Total	**$2 520 000**

Some of the issues that need to be considered include the following.
- What effect does separation and divorce have on a will? Will Jen's ex-husband be entitled to a share of Jen's estate?
- Under what circumstances might Michael be able to successfully challenge his mother's will and receive a larger share of her estate?
- Which of Jen's assets are covered by her will?
- What is the ramification of Jen having a non-binding death benefit nomination in place within her superannuation fund?
- If upon inheriting the home and contents and the share portfolio, the daughter Felicity subsequently sold them 9 months later, would there be any capital gains tax implications? If so, how much tax would be payable?

Illustrative examples used throughout this chapter will relate back to the information contained within this case study.

Introduction

Traditionally, the **will** has been the major focus of **estate planning**. Although it is important to ensure clients have valid and up-to-date wills, client needs in estate planning must be viewed more broadly as a means of protecting and maximising net assets available for distribution to chosen beneficiaries and ensuring those beneficiaries receive the assets in a tax-effective manner. Increasingly, a significant portion of a person's wealth is held in superannuation, insurance and business structures that are not directly owned by the person. These assets may not form part of a will but are still an important consideration in estate planning. The area of estate planning is dynamic and affected by legislative changes in the areas of wills, taxation and superannuation, and by societal changes in attitudes to inheritance and increasing amounts of wealth to pass on.

Another increasingly important area, given Australia's ageing population, relates to the provision of a Powers of Attorney. This is a legal document that an individual can use to appoint a person to make decisions relating to their property, financial affairs or future medical treatment should they lose mental capacity or decision-making capacity. Another related issue that has been reported widely in the media is to how best to deal with vulnerable clients. How does a planner or other adviser determine if a client has diminished capacity or loss of decision-making capacity and how does society deal with problems associated with abuse of the elderly.

11.1 Obligations of the financial planner

LEARNING OBJECTIVE 11.1 Understand the importance of estate planning and the role of the financial planner in helping clients achieve their estate planning objectives.

Estate planning is part of the overall financial planning process and a financial planner has an important role to play in ensuring that the estate planning objectives and needs of a client are met. As with any other financial product or service, financial planners have an obligation to ensure that their advice is appropriate to the client's circumstances and complies with the statutory best interest provisions that exist under section 961 of the *Corporations Act 2001* (Cwlth). Much of the work in estate planning needs to be undertaken in conjunction with other professionals, typically lawyers but also accountants. However, financial planners are in a unique position of possessing detailed understanding and comprehension of the client's overall goals and needs. Some of the needs and concerns of the client might consist of the following.

- I'm getting too old to properly manage my finances.
- Do I need a will and what are the ramifications of not having one?
- How do I leave money to a particular beneficiary?
- How can I ensure that children from a previous marriage are protected upon my death?
- What happens to my superannuation account balance upon my death?
- How can I best protect the interests of a disabled child upon my death?
- How can I minimise the tax payable by beneficiaries in receipt of an inheritance?
- What rights does my ex-partner have to my estate and how best do I protect myself?

It is useful to think of estate planning in terms of the before- and after-death stages, and financial planners can provide important guidance to their clients in both areas. The following are major considerations for financial planners in estate planning.

1. *Identify objectives and wishes.* Identifying a client's objectives and wishes is the first step in the estate planning process. Who does the client want to benefit from their estate and how much is to be left to each **beneficiary**? Are there any specific objectives, such as maintaining lifestyle of dependants in the event of early death, supporting a spouse in retirement, or passing on control of any family businesses? Are there any special circumstances that need consideration, such as disabled beneficiaries or beneficiaries who are financially at risk? Is a beneficiary likely to be exposed to bankruptcy or divorce, and potentially lose an inheritance to the trustee in bankruptcy or to an ex-partner? Another example of a beneficiary at risk is a drug-dependent beneficiary who may easily be taken advantage of and use the inheritance to pay for drugs.

2. *Identify assets available to the estate for distribution and non-estate assets.* What is the value of the deceased's estate and how are the assets to be distributed among beneficiaries? For those assets not forming part of the will, how will ownership be passed to the intended beneficiary? Who will benefit from any insurance policies and/or superannuation assets?

3. *Identify any tax implications on the estate plan.* Tax planning is an important element of estate planning, both to maximise the amount of assets available for distribution and to minimise the amount of tax to be paid by the estate and individual beneficiaries.

4. *Ensure a valid and up-to-date will is executed.* A current legal will helps to ensure that the client's assets go where intended. Consideration needs to be given to any potential claims on the estate by disgruntled potential beneficiaries. Selection of an appropriate executor is also important as this is the person who will carry out the instructions contained in the will.

5. *Establish an enduring power of attorney.* An **enduring power of attorney** is especially important if a client becomes ill and loses decision-making capacity. Different forms of enduring powers of attorney may need to be considered for different situations that might arise, such as managing the financial affairs of a person, or making medical and accommodation decisions on behalf of the person. To illustrate, when a person is assessed as needing to enter an aged care facility, the enduring power of attorney has the power to arrange such accommodation needs by locating and arranging the placement of the person into the facility. Powers of attorney are discussed in more detail later in this chapter.

While legislation in most states prohibits persons other than legal practitioners from providing legal advice, financial advisers are ideally placed to assume a facilitator role and coordinate the various professionals involved in the estate planning process to ensure proper execution of the plan.

11.2 The role of a will within estate planning

LEARNING OBJECTIVE 11.2 Understand the role of a valid will within estate planning.

A will specifies how property is to be dealt with upon the willmaker's death. It provides directions about who the willmaker wants to distribute their assets to, how much each beneficiary is to receive and nominates the person responsible for finalising the affairs of the deceased in accordance with the directions of the will. Although there are many reasons why having a valid will is important, it is not required by law.

Drawing up a valid will

A will is a legal document that must be made in accordance with the relevant legislation applicable to where the will is made. In Australia, making a will falls under state jurisdiction and each state has its own legislation dealing with wills. Although there are many similarities between the states, there are some differences. This chapter deals with making a will in general terms and does not examine the differences in state legislation.

The person making the will is known as the willmaker or testator. Wills must be in writing and signed by the willmaker in the presence of witnesses. Generally, there needs to be at least two witnesses who are independent of the willmaker and must not be beneficiaries. The number of witnesses required and who is allowed to witness wills differs between states. Although it is not a requirement, it is preferable that the willmaker and witnesses use the same pen when signing. Otherwise, the validity of the will may be open to challenge on the basis that the witnesses and willmaker were not present at the same time. It is important that the willmaker sets out all his or her wishes in the body of the will. Any details written in another place and not referred to in the main body of the will, or any instructions appearing after the signatures, may not form part of the will. Some people make a separate list of belongings and nominate the person they want to leave them to. Although this list may be useful, unless it is referred to in the will it may not be legally enforceable if a dispute over any of the nominated items arose among the beneficiaries.

States have different rules in relation to survivorship. In Victoria and New South Wales for example, a beneficiary must survive for 30 days before he or she can inherit. If this person dies within 30 days of the deceased person, they are treated as if they had died before the deceased and accordingly they (or their estate) would generally not be entitled to the gift under the will. However, an executor can make a distribution of funds to the spouse, partner or child of a deceased within this 30-day period. The distribution needs to be made by the executor in good faith, and must be for the purpose of providing maintenance, support or education to the beneficiary. The amount distributed will also be deducted from the relevant person's entitlement under the will.

A willmaker does not have to engage a solicitor to prepare the will. There are many do-it-yourself will kits available that can be used to construct an effective will; however, a will is a very important document and must be validly constructed and executed. In all but the simplest cases, it is well worth getting advice from a solicitor to ensure that no mistakes are made. Remember, if there is no valid will, the willmaker's assets may not go to the people intended to have them.

When a person wants to make a minor adjustment to a will they can prepare a **codicil** (a 'little will'). The codicil will contain the minor amendments but needs to be witnessed in the same manner as a normal will. If major changes are to be made then it is advisable to prepare a new will.

While most people consider drawing up a will to be an important matter to ensure that their family is adequately looked after upon their death, there are many examples of unusual wills in existence. For example, the famous escape artist and daredevil Harry Houdini, who died in 1926, left his wife, Bess, a secret code that contained 10 words that he said he would use to contact her from the afterlife. He also stated in his will that he wanted a séance to be held each year on the anniversary of his death (Halloween). Bess abided by this request and held a séance every Halloween for 10 years; Houdini never appeared (Investopedia 2011).

Another example is of a Californian rancher named Thomas Shewbridge who left his shareholder rights of his estate to his two dogs. These dogs inherited 29 000 stock shares in an electric company and were active members of stockholders' and board of directors' meetings (Investopedia 2011).

Who can make a will?

Anyone over the age of 18 years can make a will, providing they have **testamentary capacity**. Testamentary capacity can be difficult to define, but a useful guide is that the willmaker should:

- understand the nature of making a will
- understand the extent and character of the property left in the will

- understand the claims of potential beneficiaries such as family
- have no mental disorders which may influence the decision.

A will made by someone who does not have testamentary capacity is invalid and can be challenged. Any potential beneficiaries who think they should have been left more in a will may challenge the will on the grounds that the willmaker did not have testamentary capacity at the time of making the will.

The existence or otherwise of testamentary capacity is a growing area for concern today because people are living much longer and there is increasing incidence of dementia. Solicitors and financial planners taking instructions from elderly clients or clients who have suffered from mental illness are well advised to attempt to establish testamentary capacity. Unfortunately this is often a difficult assessment as each individual is different and there are no easy procedures or processes that can be applied objectively across the board. In such cases, it is a good idea to have the will signed in front of a solicitor, who can then give evidence if the will is challenged. Additionally, a statement from the client's doctor or health professional providing their professional judgement on the client's testamentary capacity at the time of making the will should be attached to it. In some states, the court can allow a minor to make a will and can authorise a will to be made for a person who does not have testamentary capacity.

The need to update a will

To ensure that a will continues to accurately represent the wishes of a willmaker, it is essential that the will be reviewed and updated on a regular basis. There may be a range of situations that necessitate the need to update a will, including the birth of children, the death of dependants, disputes with beneficiaries, windfalls, starting a business, and divorce and marriage.

Generally a will is cancelled upon the marriage or remarriage of a person. The only exception to this is if the will is made in contemplation of the marriage. While a divorce in most states of Australia does not automatically cancel a will, it will cancel any distribution to the ex-spouse as well as cancelling their appointment as an executor, trustee or guardian of children.

Appointing an executor

The person appointed in the will to look after and distribute the assets in accordance with the willmaker's wishes after death is called the **executor**. Some of the tasks usually undertaken by the executor are:
- organising the funeral
- managing the legal and financial affairs of the estate
- obtaining grant of probate
- locating, protecting (such as changing the locks) and insuring estate assets
- paying outstanding debts from the estate
- distributing the remaining assets in accordance with the will
- defending the will if there is a challenge.

Grant of probate

Obtaining the grant of probate confirms the last will and testament and provides the executor with authority to proceed to collect the assets and distribute them to the beneficiaries. Probate simply means 'proof of the will'. On death, the assets of a person are frozen and cannot be dealt with by anyone other than the personal representative upon production of a document stating grant of probate. The grant of probate is awarded by the Supreme Court, which undertakes an assessment of the validity of the will, confirms the appointment of the executor(s), and confirms the major assets and liabilities owned by the estate. When estates are of relatively low value (such as $20 000), grant of probate may not be required.

Letters of administration apply when, for example, an executor has died and no replacement has been named in the will. Letters of administration are also granted by a court when a person dies without a will. Letters of administration give court authority to a person to carry out the functions of administering the estate.

The role of the executor is a very important one and the person chosen should be carefully considered. Some of the questions that should be considered in the selection of the person include the following.
- Is the person likely to outlive you?
- Is the person competent to undertake the tasks required?
- Does the person have the time to carry out the tasks required of an executor?
- Will the person be impartial if a dispute arises between the beneficiaries?
- Is the person trustworthy?

It is usually best to check that the person chosen both understands the duties and is happy to accept the role. The executor should also be told where the will and other important documents are kept. It is a good idea to appoint an alternative executor in case the first one is unable to do the job when the time comes.

What can you leave in your will?

It may seem unnecessary to say that any assets that a willmaker owns or is entitled to at the time of their death can be left in the will. However, many willmakers may be surprised to learn that some of their major assets cannot be left in their will. For estate planning purposes, it is necessary to classify a person's assets into two categories.

1. **Estate assets**. These are assets owned solely and independently by the willmaker. These assets form part of the willmaker's estate and their distribution to beneficiaries is determined in accordance with their will.

2. **Non-estate assets**. These are assets that are either owned jointly or are owned and controlled through another entity or tax structure, such as a family company or trust, or a superannuation fund. The distribution of non-estate assets is not determined by the will of the deceased and other forms of estate planning apply to these assets.

As noted, only estate assets are governed by the terms of a will. Examples of non-estate assets include:
- bank accounts in joint names
- jointly owned property
- superannuation accounts
- some life insurance policies where there is a nominated beneficiary
- assets held in a family company or trust.

Jointly owned property can be divided into two categories: **joint tenancy** and **tenancy-in-common**.

In the case of *joint tenancy*, both parties own the entire asset. Upon the death of one of the owners, ownership automatically passes to the surviving owner and does not form part of the deceased's estate. For example, in the case of a husband and wife who have money in a joint bank account, if the husband died, the whole account balance would be transferred to the surviving wife. The same is true for a jointly owned family home. These assets bypass the will and can be paid to the other owner directly and quickly. Also, because these assets do not go through a will, their distribution cannot be challenged. This will be discussed in a later section.

For assets owned as *tenants-in-common*, each party owns a separate, defined portion of the asset, typically with respect to property. In this case, the willmaker is able to leave his or her share of the property to a chosen beneficiary in their will and hence these are estate assets. For example, two brothers may each hold a 50% interest of an investment property valued at $800 000 under a tenants-in-common arrangement. If one of the brothers was to die, their 50% interest in the property ($400 000) would form part of their individual estate and the terms of their will would determine the distribution to their beneficiaries.

Assets owned within a family company structure, or held in a family trust structure, are not estate assets. The assets held within these structures are owned by the respective entities, not the individual. However, the actual shares held by the shareholder of a company structure are an estate asset and can be transferred to a beneficiary under a will. Similarly, units held in a unit trust are estate assets and, accordingly, the ownership of the units can be transferred to a beneficiary through the will of the deceased. While shareholdings and ownership of units in a trust can be transferred to a beneficiary in a will, the entity and its assets remain in existence. The distribution of superannuation will be discussed in a later section.

Rights of beneficiaries

In general, beneficiaries have the right to have the estate administered efficiently and the right to their allocation in accordance with the instructions in the will. While the estate is in the hands of the executor, the beneficiaries have no claim to the assets or income of the estate, even if they have been left a specific bequest or legacy. Beneficiaries are not entitled to borrow against assets of the estate until it is settled and proper title has passed to them.

However, if the executor makes a distribution to a beneficiary but then realises that an estate debt is still outstanding, the executor cannot demand the beneficiary return the distribution. The executor would have to pay the debt personally. Accordingly, the executor needs to be very careful before making a final distribution.

Beneficiaries can bring the executor to court to apply for a grant of probate if the executor fails to lodge the application with the Probate Office within the statutory time frame. Beneficiaries have the ability to challenge a will if they feel they have been inadequately provided for or they believe the will is invalid.

Contesting a will

As a general principle, people can leave their estate to whomever they wish. There is no obligation by law, for example, for willmakers to treat their children equally or fairly. However, a disgruntled beneficiary, or potential beneficiary, has some scope to challenge a will. There are two main situations where an estate could be contested by a person who feels they deserve a share of the estate. The will can be contested on the basis that:

1. the will is invalid
2. inadequate provision has been made for a beneficiary.

It should be noted that, when a will is challenged, the executor(s) is entitled to pay for the estate's legal costs from the estate's funds. If costs become extensive and the challenge to the will is drawn out, there will be less available to distribute to beneficiaries.

Challenging the validity of a will

The validity of a will can be challenged on any of the following grounds:

- lack of testamentary capacity
- **undue influence**
- incorrect execution.

If beneficiaries or potential beneficiaries believe that the willmaker did not have testamentary capacity at the time the will was executed, they can challenge it. If potential beneficiaries believe the willmaker was unduly influenced by another person when giving instructions for a will, they can also mount a challenge to the will.

If there is an omission or error in drafting and/or executing a will, it may be voided. For example, if the willmaker signed the will and then later took it to work to have a colleague witness their signature, the will would be void as it was not witnessed appropriately at the time of signature. However, in some states, the court has discretion to rectify a will that does not fully comply with legal requirements if the court is satisfied that the document was intended by the willmaker to be their last will.

If the court finds that the will is invalid on any of these grounds and it does not use its discretion to validate it, the estate will be distributed in accordance with any earlier valid will. If there is no earlier valid will, it will be distributed in accordance with the applicable laws of **intestacy**. (The laws of intestacy are examined later in this chapter.) This may mean, of course, that disgruntled beneficiaries may not necessarily be any better off, even if their challenge is successful.

The time limits for contesting a will vary from state to state. For example, in Victoria and Western Australia claims against an estate must generally be commenced within 6 months of the date of the grant of probate, while in New South Wales and the ACT claims against an estate must generally be commenced within 12 months of the date of death.

Inadequate provisions for certain beneficiaries

The second ground for contesting a will stems from the notion that the family members of a deceased person should be looked after and supported out of the proceeds of the estate wherever possible. The laws in each state differ in terms of the classes of people who have the right to make claims for a share, or an increased share, of the estate. Such proceedings are called testator's family maintenance (TFM) proceedings.

In general, the classes of potential claimants are restricted to various family members, including former spouses. However, which family members are eligible to make claims differs between states. For example, same-sex spouses are eligible claimants in some states but not all. New South Wales and Victoria extend eligible claimants beyond family members. In New South Wales, a person who has been a member of the deceased's household and partly or wholly dependent on the deceased can make a claim. In Victoria, the claimants need to be closely related to the person who died such as a spouse or domestic partner or former partner; a parent, child or stepchild; or someone treated as a child by the willmaker. A registered carer or grandchildren may also be eligible if they can show that they were dependent on the willmaker.

To help prevent TFM proceedings, it is important that financial planners alert willmakers to the possibility of a challenge to their will. One suggestion for anyone thinking of omitting a family member is to make a small provision in the will for that person. This may reduce the chance of a successful challenge to the will. In addition, the reasons for the omission should be documented and kept with the will to be used if a challenge is mounted. A letter prepared by the willmaker and left with the will which explains why a family member has been left a smaller entitlement under the will may be an effective means to reduce a likely challenge to a will. Although adoption of these strategies will not guarantee the failure of any challenge, a judge will at least understand the willmaker's reasoning for excluding the particular person from the will or for leaving that person only a small amount, and can make a decision in the light of that knowledge.

As noted in the case study at the start of this chapter, Jen's son Michael has been largely left out of his mother's will, due to issues with Michael's wife. Michael's family is struggling financially. Michael may decide to challenge his mother's will on the basis that he has not been sufficiently looked after and supported from his mother's estate. The success of any challenge may depend upon the extent to which a judge is able to understand Jen's reasoning for largely excluding Michael from the will.

Given the increasingly complex family structures that exist in today's society, a common concern often raised is, how can a person safeguard the interests of their children in the event of their spouse remarrying after they die?

In determining whether or not provision should be made for a dependant or applicant, the court will consider a range of factors including the relationship between the deceased person and the dependant; the nature and length of the relationship between the parties; the extent to which the deceased had obligations or responsibilities towards the dependant or any other persons; the size and nature of the estate; and the needs of the beneficiary or other parties.

The foundation case governing this issue was established in 2004 in the case of *McKenzie vs. Topp* ('McKenzie'). In this case, the Victorian Supreme Court was required to consider the rights and entitlements of an adult son who was making a claim against the estate of his deceased stepmother. The applicant's father had previously passed away, leaving everything to the applicant's stepmother. The applicant contested his stepmother's will on the basis of not being adequately provided for. The court took into consideration not only the time and effort that the applicant put into caring for his elderly stepmother, but also the fact that the stepmother had a moral obligation to provide for the adult son in these circumstances. The judge noted that while it was appropriate for the father to provide for his wife above other dependants, it was appropriate that children from a previous marriage should still rank for their fair share.

11.3 Dying intestate

LEARNING OBJECTIVE 11.3 Explain the consequences of dying without a valid will.

If a person dies without a valid will, they are said to have died intestate. In such cases, the estate will be distributed in accordance with the individual state's intestacy laws. The fundamental principle is that the estate will pass to the deceased's next of kin. The state laws prescribe the precise order of persons who will share in the estate. For example, under Victorian intestacy rules:

- the entire estate goes to the surviving partner if there are no children. Partner means the person's spouse, a domestic partner or registered caring partner at the time of death
- if there are both a surviving partner and children, the entire estate goes to the surviving partner
- if there is a surviving partner and children born of a different relationship, then the partner will receive all the personal chattels, the first $451 909 and 50% of the balance with the remaining 50% distributed amongst the children
- if there are children but no partner, the children share the estate equally
- if there are no children and no partner, any surviving parents receive the estate
- if there are no children, no partner and no surviving parents, any surviving siblings receive the estate
- if there are no other remaining family members, the estate is distributed equally between the aunts and uncles, and then to the aunt's/uncle's children
- if there is no family or next of kin, the property of that person is passed to the Crown.

Burke & Associates Lawyers (2022) have written a guide explaining intestacy rules in Victoria.

In Queensland, for example, if there is a partner and one child, the partner receives $150 000, the personal chattels and half of the balance. The child receives the other half of the balance. If there is more than one child, the partner receives $150 000, the personal chattels and a third of the balance. The remaining two thirds will be divided equally between the children. If there is no partner and no children, the distribution is similar to that within Victoria.

Naturally, intestacy laws are unlikely to match precisely the wishes of the deceased, and dying intestate may mean that the deceased's assets are distributed to people who he or she may not have wanted.

Dying intestate can have even worse ramifications in the case where both parties to a marriage die at the same time. It is a generally accepted rule of law that if it is not possible to determine the actual time of death, the older person is presumed to have died first. In this event, the estate of the older spouse will pass firstly to the younger one. The estate of the younger spouse will then include both of the couple's assets. It is possible that these will then be distributed to the younger partner's next of kin and nothing will pass to the family of the older spouse. This scenario depends on the relevant state laws.

The New South Wales Trustee and Guardian (n.d.) provide a number of real-life examples on its website of how things can go wrong when a valid will is not in place.

- A reclusive woman decided to write her own will. The only relative with whom she had contact was a niece. However, after writing her own will, she asked the niece's husband to sign the will as her witness. On her death she left an estate worth $400 000, but unfortunately the niece was not able to inherit the estate due to the fact her husband had signed the will as a witness. The will fell into intestacy due to the fact that a spouse of a beneficiary should not be a witness. The estate was distributed to the next of kin and the niece received nothing.
- An 18-year-old man had been living with his girlfriend for only 6 months when he died without a will. The court decided that his girlfriend was his legal de facto spouse, and she received his entire substantial estate. The man's parents received nothing.
- Jim had looked after his uncle Wayne for many years and had been assured that he was included in the will. When Wayne died, Jim searched the house for a will but to no avail. He checked all the local solicitors, banks and anyone else who might have dealings with his uncle. There was no evidence of a will anywhere or anything to suggest Wayne ever made a will. Under the laws of intestacy, Jim shared his uncle's estate with several other nieces and nephews who barely knew their uncle and never attended to any of his needs.
- A 21-year-old girl with no will was killed in a motor vehicle accident during the course of her employment. There was $200 000 accident cover. The estate passed to her mother and father equally on intestacy but the father had deserted the family weeks before she was born. He had had no contact since but was entitled to $100 000.
- A family consisting of 3 stepchildren fought for 3 years over the division of antique furniture that was valued at $6000. Legal costs incurred by the children amounted to $55 000.

11.4 Estate planning and taxes

LEARNING OBJECTIVE 11.4 Analyse the impact of taxation on distributions from deceased estates.

The basics of taxation have already been covered in the chapter on taxation planning. This section examines some of those concepts and discusses their relevance to, and implications for, estate planning. The area of taxation in estate planning is highly technical and complex. This section covers the main areas that financial planners should be aware of, but it is not meant to be a definitive statement on taxation law. In cases where complex taxation issues arise, financial planners are advised to refer their clients to a tax specialist.

Most willmakers will be concerned with minimising the impact that income tax and capital gains tax is likely to have on estate assets that are left to beneficiaries. The main areas of tax consideration in relation to estate planning are:
- capital gains tax
- the '3-year rule'
- **testamentary trusts**.

It is important to note that there is no inheritance tax in Australia and no tax is payable by beneficiaries upon receipt of estate assets. However, tax consequences may arise when the beneficiary disposes of an inherited asset.

Capital gains tax

Capital gains tax (CGT) (refer to the chapter on taxation planning) is an important consideration in estate planning. For CGT purposes, the death of the owner of an asset does not constitute a CGT event; that is, it is not considered to be a disposal of the asset for CGT purposes. However, it does constitute an acquisition by the beneficiary inheriting the asset. Hence, there is no CGT paid at the time of death, but CGT may be levied at some later date when the asset is sold by the beneficiary. Table 11.1 provides a summary of the CGT position on the inheritance of certain assets.

TABLE 11.1   CGT position on the inheritance of certain assets

Asset type inherited	CGT consequences
Family home	CGT-free if sold within 2 years of date of death or the home continues to be used as the principal residence of the beneficiary.
Investment assets (e.g. shares and property)	**Purchased by deceased before 20 September 1985** The cost base to the beneficiary is the market value at date of death of the deceased and CGT will be payable at the time of sale by the beneficiary on any gain since date of death. The 50% CGT discount will apply only where the disposal takes place more than 12 months after the deceased acquired the asset. **Purchased by deceased after 19 September 1985** The beneficiary takes on the original cost base of the deceased at the date of death. CGT is payable at the time of disposal by the beneficiary on any gain made from date of acquisition by the deceased to the date of sale, either by the estate or the beneficiary. The asset must be held for a total of 12 months (by the deceased and/or the beneficiary) to attract the 50% discount.
Personal assets (e.g. cars, jewellery, furniture)	CGT-free (unless they are collectables, e.g. antiques, art work, expensive jewellery).

In estate planning, as in other applications of CGT, the date an asset is acquired determines how the asset will be treated for CGT purposes. Assets can be categorised into two time periods:
1. assets acquired before 20 September 1985
2. assets acquired after 19 September 1985.

Assets acquired before 20 September 1985

Assets acquired by the deceased before 20 September 1985 will incur CGT only when sold by the beneficiary or executor. The CGT payable will be on gains made from the date of death of the deceased to the date of disposal by the beneficiary. The cost base takes on the market value of the asset at the date of death of the deceased. For the CGT discount to apply, the disposal must take place at least 12 months after the death of the deceased.

Assets acquired after 19 September 1985

Similarly, assets acquired by the deceased after 19 September 1985 will also incur CGT only when sold by the beneficiary or executor. As detailed above, the beneficiary takes on the original cost base of the deceased at the date of death.

The method used for calculating CGT is determined upon the date of death of the deceased. Where the deceased died between 19 September 1985 and 20 September 1999, the CGT rules allow owners to choose to calculate their capital gain by either the frozen indexation method or the discount method, whichever gives the better result. Where the deceased died after 20 September 1999, the CGT discount method must be used to determine the capital gain. However, for the CGT discount to apply, the disposal of the asset must occur at least 12 months after the deceased originally acquired the asset.

CGT exemptions

The principal residence of the deceased is normally exempt from CGT upon disposal by the beneficiary providing one or more of the following conditions are met.
- The property is used by the beneficiary as their principal residence for the entire period of ownership prior to sale.
- The residence is disposed of by the beneficiary within 2 years of the date of death of the deceased.
- While the residence is under the control of the executor, it is the principal residence of the deceased's spouse.

A partial CGT exemption will apply if the property was used as the principal residence of the deceased for only part of their period of ownership, but not at the date of death, or if the property was used for only part of the period of ownership by the beneficiary as their principal residence prior to sale. The partial exemption is based on the total period of time for which the property was used as a principal residence relative to the total period of ownership.

The 3-year rule

The *Income Tax Assessment Act 1936* allows executors up to 3 years to finalise an estate. During this period, the estate itself is taxed as if it were an individual. The estate is entitled to a tax-free threshold and will be taxed at normal adult marginal tax rates for amounts in excess of the threshold. Depending on the tax position of the beneficiaries, this may provide some scope to minimise the tax paid on distributions from the estate. For example, if there are two beneficiaries entitled to all of the estate assets, both of whom are on the highest marginal rate, the executor can choose to retain the assets within the estate and delay distribution until towards the end of the 3-year period. The effect of this is that the estate will have paid tax only on income above the tax-free threshold for those 3 years and, depending on the size of the estate, at lower marginal tax rates. If the estate had been distributed promptly, the beneficiaries would have paid tax on the full amount of income at the highest marginal tax rate.

ILLUSTRATIVE EXAMPLE 11.2

Refer to the case study presented at the start of this chapter.

Part of Jen's estate consists of the managed funds that were acquired in 2012. The managed funds were acquired for $70 000 and, at the date of Jen's death, their value had increased to $100 000. Assume that her daughter, Felicity, inherits the managed funds and subsequently sells them for $120 000 nine months after Jen's death.

What will be the CGT ramifications of the sale of the managed funds by Felicity?

The disposal of the managed funds by Felicity will be subject to CGT. For the purposes of determining the CGT payable, Felicity will be subject to CGT based on the difference between the disposal value and the cost base. As the managed funds were acquired by Jen after 19 September 1985, Felicity's relevant cost base will be the same as that of Jen's, that is, $70 000.

Thus, the capital gain upon disposal would be $50 000 ($120 000 – $70 000).

As the managed funds had been held for a period greater than 12 months since the date of acquisition by Jen, Felicity will be entitled to the 50% CGT discount upon disposal. Accordingly, the assessable capital gain forming part of Felicity's taxable income for the year will be $25 000 ($50 000 less 50%).

Stamp duty

Under state legislation, stamp duty is typically payable on the transfer of assets between entities or individuals based on the value of the asset. Assets subject to stamp duty include real estate and shares. However, stamp duty is usually not levied on assets where they are distributed to beneficiaries under the terms of a will. Full stamp duty is payable where dutiable property is transferred while the deceased is still alive or where an asset is distributed to a beneficiary not in accordance with a will.

11.5 Estate planning and trusts

LEARNING OBJECTIVE 11.5 Understand the role and benefits of testamentary trusts in the minimisation of taxation and protection of assets.

Two of the more important objectives in effective estate planning lie in:
1. establishing a tax-effective structure by which estate assets and income are able to be distributed to intended beneficiaries
2. providing the willmaker with control over how their estate assets will be distributed and managed after their death.

One of the commonly used tools to achieve these objectives is the establishment of a testamentary trust established through a will.

A trust is a unique legal entity recognised by law, which involves separation of the legal and beneficial ownership of an asset. There are two main types of trusts in the context of estate planning: a *living trust*, also known as an **inter vivos trust** (established during a person's lifetime) and a *testamentary trust* (established by will after the death of the person), sometimes referred to as a will trust. A testamentary trust is established by a will and comes into effect only upon the death of the willmaker. Assets of the estate are passed into the testamentary trust rather than being paid directly to the beneficiary. This might provide for a number of benefits including inherited assets being distributed to beneficiaries in a more tax-effective manner, as well as retaining a degree of control where assets are to be distributed to at-risk beneficiaries.

Essential elements of a trust

A trust has the following essential elements.

- *A settlor* — the person who settles a sum of money or property to establish the trust. Usually a trust created during a person's lifetime is established by a settlor, who starts by placing a small amount of money in trust. The settlor is usually a lawyer, accountant or friend who settles the trust with a small sum (usually $10). A settlor should never be a beneficiary of the trust. Note that for a testamentary trust, the willmaker (as future settlor) is able to instruct their legal representative in the appointment of the trustee for the trust. The willmaker can also nominate the trustee under his/her will.
- *An appointer* — a person nominated by the settlor to appoint a trustee for the trust. The appointer has ultimate control of the trust (i.e. they can appoint and discharge the trustee).
- *A trustee* — the person or party who holds trust property on behalf of beneficiaries and who has the personal obligation attached to that property. The trustee is appointed and manages the trust in accordance with the conditions set out in the trust deed. The trustee can be one or more persons or a corporation.
- *A beneficiary* — the person or persons nominated to receive the beneficial interest in the trust property; they are entitled to receive distributions of income and/or assets from the trust.
- *Trust property* — the property held in the trust, it is legally vested in the trustee.
- *A personal obligation* — the trustee has a personal obligation and a fiduciary duty to deal with trust property for the benefit of the beneficiaries. A fiduciary duty means that the standard of care that a trustee should exhibit in carrying out their responsibility for the beneficiaries is at a higher standard than simply showing a normal duty of care. It is highlighted by concepts of good faith and loyalty.

How a trust is controlled

For a living trust, once the settlor has created the trust, the person who wants the trust established nominates an appointer who can appoint and dismiss the trustee of the trust at any time. If the trust is created by the will (i.e. a testamentary trust) then the trustee may be named either in the will or by the executor of the will.

A trustee has control over the trust assets and authority to distribute the income and capital of the trust in accordance with the trust deed. The person with ultimate control over the trust and its assets is the person who controls the trustee; that is, the appointer of the living trust. For a testamentary trust, the executor or legal representative takes the role of appointer and can remove the trustee if necessary.

Types of trusts

Trusts can be described in a number of different ways, for example, in accordance with the entitlements of the beneficiaries, such as a fixed or discretionary trust. A fixed trust (or unit trust) gives beneficiaries a fixed entitlement in respect of the income and capital of the trust in proportion to the number of units they hold. Whenever a distribution is made from the trust, the beneficiary must receive this proportion of the available income.

A discretionary trust gives beneficiaries an entitlement to distributions from the trust but does not give them a right to distributions. The trustee has complete discretion on how any income is to be distributed among the beneficiaries. This enables the trustee to distribute income in a tax-effective manner through, for example, distributing income between family members.

A testamentary trust is normally established as a discretionary trust in order to provide the trustee with this discretion.

Trusts can also be named in accordance with their purpose, for example, family trusts, charitable trusts and child support trusts.

Use of trusts in estate planning

There are four significant reasons why a business, or the assets or investments of an individual may be preferred to be held in a trust rather than in the individual's personal name:

1. tax minimisation
2. asset protection
3. succession
4. provision for minor and/or disabled dependants.

These reasons apply to both inter vivos (living) trusts and testamentary (or will) trusts. The discussion here focuses on the use of trusts in estate planning, which includes both preserving assets available to the estate before death and protecting assets after death.

Tax minimisation

Trusts can provide significant tax-minimisation benefits. Trusts do not generally pay income tax where the trustee distributes all the trust's net income to beneficiaries. Income distributed from a trust retains its original character on distribution to the beneficiaries. This would include such items as franked dividends and any associated franking credits, and assessable capital gains and any CGT discount that might apply. The establishment of a discretionary trust provides a significant degree of flexibility in the way that income is distributed and split between the potential beneficiaries of the trust. In a discretionary trust, the trustee has complete discretion over how trust income is distributed each year. The receipt of trust income by beneficiaries is taxed at their marginal tax rate. One of the major benefits of a trust is the ability to divert income to beneficiaries, such as family members, on a lower marginal tax rate. This can be achieved through the use of either an inter vivos trust, while still alive, or a testamentary trust that is established upon death. Upon the death of the person, the establishment of a testamentary trust allows income to be distributed across a range of beneficiaries, which might include a spouse and children, rather than being left solely to the spouse who is taxed on all of the income under their individual name.

Taxation of minors

Rather than distributing income to adult beneficiaries, significant tax benefits may arise where income is able to be distributed to children. As discussed in the chapter on taxation planning, penalty tax rates apply to the 'unearned income' of minors. Unearned income up to $416 p.a. is tax free. Any amount above this is taxed at penalty rates.

One of the main considerations in distributing income to a minor is that unearned income is taxed at these penalty rates. However, an exemption from this penalty tax rate is given to any income derived from an estate that is held and distributed through a testamentary trust established under a will. Income distributed from a testamentary trust to minor beneficiaries is taxed at normal adult tax rates, thereby providing an opportunity to gain significant tax advantages in a family situation where there are minors. Accordingly, each minor is able to receive $18 200 of trust income tax free. One of the important issues to note when distributing income to minors is that the minor has a legal entitlement to any amount distributed to them. It is important to note that income distributed to minors from an inter vivos (living) trust is treated as unearned income in the hands of a minor and subject to penalty rates of tax.

ILLUSTRATIVE EXAMPLE 11.3

Refer to the case study presented at the start of this chapter.

Upon the death of Jen, a testamentary trust was established for the benefit of Felicity. During the current year, the trust derives the following classes of income:

- fully franked dividend income: $7000 p.a.
- rental income: $11 000 p.a.
- interest income of $2000 p.a..

The total income is $20 000. The trustee is able to distribute the income to beneficiaries in the most tax-effective way possible. Rather than assets being distributed directly to Felicity who would then need to pay tax on the total income at her marginal tax rate, assets can be directed into a testamentary trust with the result that any investment income earned within the testamentary trust can be distributed equally among Felicity's family. This would include Felicity and her husband, and their two minor children who would be taxed on the income at normal adult resident marginal tax rates. As each child's share would be less than $18 200 (assuming no other income), if the total income was distributed between the two children, the family would not be subject to any tax at all.

If all the income had been received by Felicity in her personal name, the investment income of $20 000 would be added to any other income that she earned for the year from her salary and other income, and the total income be taxed at her marginal tax rate of 45% plus the Medicare levy.

The tax effectiveness of distributing income to Felicity's two children through a testamentary trust can be illustrated by the following:

▶

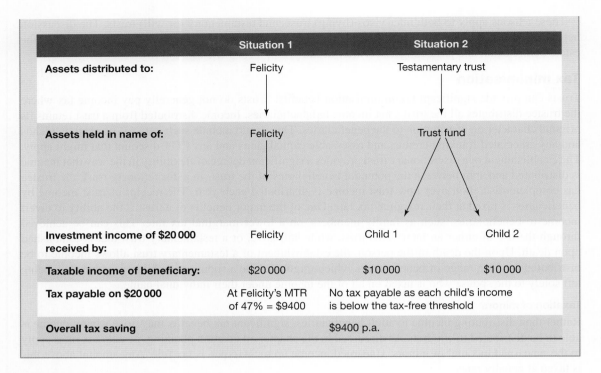

	Situation 1	Situation 2	
Assets distributed to:	Felicity	Testamentary trust	
Assets held in name of:	Felicity	Trust fund	
Investment income of $20 000 received by:	Felicity	Child 1	Child 2
Taxable income of beneficiary:	$20 000	$10 000	$10 000
Tax payable on $20 000	At Felicity's MTR of 47% = $9400	No tax payable as each child's income is below the tax-free threshold	
Overall tax saving		$9400 p.a.	

Asset protection

The separation of legal and beneficial ownership protects trust assets from claims made on the beneficiaries by third parties. For example, many professionals prefer not to own assets in their own name because of the possibility of a negligence claim arising from their work. Any such claim could result in assets held in their own name being liquidated to pay any damages awarded. A negligence claim can greatly reduce the assets available to an estate.

A discretionary trust can be used to protect assets from creditors. When a person places assets into a trust, legal ownership of the assets vests in the trustee. Trust assets are generally not available for the benefit of creditors in the event of a bankrupt trustee or appointor, except if the trust has been specifically or deliberately set up as a means of hiding assets from creditors.

From an estate planning perspective, a testamentary trust can also be used to protect assets from beneficiaries who have problems such as drug or gambling addictions or who are spendthrifts. Often these people are in need of parental support, and parents may wish to continue to provide such financial support after they die. Leaving an inheritance to people with these problems may result in the money disappearing quickly to support their lifestyle or habit. Leaving the assets in trust under the control of a trustee provides the means of being able to provide the beneficiary with ongoing financial support without giving them access to a large amount of money.

Succession

The separation of legal and beneficial ownership of trust assets can also assist in preserving an estate for intended beneficiaries and future generations. Potential claims against beneficiaries could arise as a result of bankruptcy, litigation or family breakdown. The ownership of assets within a trust structure helps to protect assets from claimants, ensuring the assets are available to future generations.

One application of this is protecting assets from inadequate provision claims. With the broadening of the class of potential Testator Family Maintenance (TFM) claimants in some states, a growth in such claims can be expected. One way to prevent TFM claims and ensure assets go to the intended beneficiaries is to place the assets into a trust during the willmaker's lifetime (an inter vivos trust). Assets held within a trust cannot be contested. Under the trust deed, the trustee would be obliged to hold assets for the intended beneficiaries after the death of the settlor. However, as opposed to an inter vivos trust, a testamentary trust is established under a will, and therefore assets forming part of the deceased's estate are able to be contested under a TFM claim prior to them being transferred into the testamentary trust.

Discretionary trusts, both inter vivos and testamentary, can also offer protection from any potential divorce settlement. Division of assets as a result of divorce can substantially reduce the assets available to an estate. The use of a testamentary trust can protect assets inherited by one spouse from claims by the other in a divorce settlement. The benefit of trusts to thwart divorce settlements, however, is somewhat minimised as the Family Court has broad powers in determining divorce settlements. Although Family Court judges are not always able to access trust assets for distribution, they do take into account funds held within the trust and rights to distributions when making their judgements. This can result in the spouse who is entitled to trust assets and distributions being awarded a smaller proportion of other family assets.

Provision for minor and/or disabled dependants

Discretionary trusts are also useful vehicles to provide for minor and/or disabled dependants who are unable to manage their affairs. Under a testamentary trust, the assets are preserved and distributions from the trust can be applied for the benefit of the dependant(s). The taxation benefits associated with testamentary trusts for minors were discussed earlier in this chapter.

In formulating an estate plan, the client, in conjunction with the financial planner and other professionals, needs to establish whether it is preferable to keep assets out of an estate and paid directly to a beneficiary or rather left within an estate so as to allow for assets to be potentially transferred into a testamentary trust.

Issues to consider include:
- the likelihood of the estate being challenged
- the costs versus benefits of establishing a testamentary trust
- how quickly probate may occur
- the need to control estate assets for at-risk beneficiaries
- potential tax savings.

11.6 Superannuation death benefits

LEARNING OBJECTIVE 11.6 Understand the rules applicable to superannuation death benefits.

For many people, superannuation will be one of the largest assets they have to pass on to their beneficiaries. In addition to the increasing popularity of superannuation as a retirement savings vehicle, many people also hold their life and other personal risk insurance covers within their superannuation funds. Accordingly, the way in which superannuation balances are distributed upon the death of a member will be of increasing importance. However, for many people, their superannuation may not form part of their estate and, therefore, will not be distributed through their will.

Binding death benefit nominations

As previously stated, superannuation is not normally treated as an estate asset. If the member has established a death benefit nomination, super funds may be paid directly to that dependant and not form part of the deceased's estate and therefore not subject to being contested. If the member does not have a death benefit nomination, the trustee of the superannuation fund will determine which of the deceased's dependants will receive a share of the super death benefit.

Members can make a non-binding nomination where the member nominates their preferred beneficiaries and the superannuation fund trustee takes the member's nomination into account in the distribution, but is not compelled to. **Binding death benefit nominations** enable superannuation fund members to direct the trustee of the super fund on how they want their super funds distributed upon their death. Strict provisions apply to the effective execution of these nominations — they must be signed and witnessed by two witnesses, they are normally only valid for three years, and must be confirmed or renewed at that time. However, many funds have established provision for the establishment of non-lapsing death benefit nominations that continue indefinitely until amended.

When a member joins a super fund, they will be given the opportunity to complete a binding or non-binding death benefit nomination form and can amend the nomination form at any time.

Who can you leave your superannuation to?

Upon the death of a member, superannuation funds must be paid to dependants, as defined by the SIS Act, or to the estate of the deceased. Both the SIS Act and the *Income Tax Assessment Act 1997* (Tax Act) have similar definitions of 'dependants', but there are some important differences worth noting. Both definitions of dependants include: spouse (including de facto spouses); children, both adopted and ex-nuptial; and a person in an interdependent relationship with the deceased just before death. Somebody financially dependant on the deceased is also likely to be classified as a SIS dependant. It is worth noting that a member is unable to nominate a person within their death benefit nomination that is not classified as a dependant under the SIS Act.

However, under the Tax Act, section 302-195 provides for the following definition of a tax dependant:

(a) the deceased person's spouse or former spouse; or

(b) the deceased person's child, aged less than 18, or

(c) any other person with whom the deceased person had an interdependency relationship under section 302-200 just before he or she died; or

(d) any other person who was a dependant of the deceased person just before he or she died.

The major difference between the two definitions is that a tax-dependant includes:
- not only a current spouse or de facto spouse but also a former spouse or former de facto spouse
- a child of the deceased is included but only if they are under 18 years of age.

Under the Tax Act, a child over the age of 18 would be classified as a non-tax dependant, unless they could show financial dependence on the deceased.

An interdependent relationship between two people is one in which:
- they have a close personal relationship
- they live together
- one or each of them provides the other with financial support
- one or each of them provides the other with domestic support and personal care.

People in such a relationship can receive the death benefit of a deceased fund member.

Whilst in the majority of cases, it is preferable to distribute death benefit funds directly to the beneficiary, there may be circumstances where it is preferable to have the superannuation death benefit paid directly into the estate of the deceased and made subject to the deceased's will. This might arise where a will provides for the establishment of a testamentary trust and tax benefits would be derived from having superannuation death benefits transferred to a testamentary trust rather than being paid directly to a beneficiary. To allow for superannuation death benefits to be paid into the deceased's estate, superannuation funds may allow a member to nominate that their superannuation death benefit be paid to their **legal personal representative**.

Taxation of superannuation death benefits

Taxation of superannuation death benefits depends on whether the money is distributed to a dependant as defined under the Tax Act or not. Different tax rates will apply to the various superannuation components and to different categories of beneficiaries.

As detailed above, the definition of a dependant under the income tax legislation is somewhat more restrictive than that adopted under the SIS Act. A superannuation death benefit can generally be paid to a SIS dependant in the form of a lump sum and/or a super pension (such as an account-based pension). Note that an existing superannuation pension can't be paid to a non-dependant on death and must be paid as a lump sum.

However, a restriction does apply on the ability to pay an income stream product to a child. Where a child is over 18 and under 25 years of age, a pension can only be paid where the child was financially dependent on the deceased at the date of death. All income streams paid to a child cease when the child turns 25 and then must be paid out as a lump sum to the child.

On the death of a member, a superannuation benefit is completely tax free if paid to a tax dependant. On the other hand, tax may be payable if a super distribution is received by a non-tax dependant. When paid to a non-tax dependant, such as an adult child, the taxable component of a superannuation death benefit is assessed as a death benefit lump sum and taxed at 15% plus the Medicare levy. Note that the tax-free component will always be tax free. Table 11.2 indicates the tax levied on death benefits paid either as a lump sum or as a pension.

For a superannuation fund member aged 60 and above, the tax components of their superannuation account are not particularly relevant as all lump sum withdrawals and income payments are tax free to the member. However, the tax components become relevant upon the death of the member where death benefits are paid to non-tax dependants. As previously detailed, the taxable component of a lump sum death benefit paid to a non-tax dependant will be subject to a 15% tax rate plus Medicare levy. Accordingly, estate planning and superannuation strategies remain a critical issue throughout the life of a person to ensure that wealth is passed on to beneficiaries in the most tax-effective manner possible. Thus, a member aged 60 and over may still be interested to ensure that the tax-free proportion of their superannuation account balance is maximised so as to minimise tax payable on super death benefits distributed to non-tax dependants upon their death. An interesting issue that provides some scope for strategic planning, is that while a 15% tax rate plus Medicare levy is payable on super death benefits paid to non-tax dependants, no tax is payable by the member aged 60 and over who withdraws superannuation funds prior to their death and then provides a 'gift' to the same non-tax dependant. A member might consider gifting some of their super monies to their beneficiaries prior to death, especially where there are non-tax dependants, in order to avoid the dependants paying the 15% tax plus Medicare levy.

TABLE 11.2 — **Summary of tax treatment for superannuation death benefits (taxable component — taxed element)**

Lump sums	Dependant	Tax treatment
Death benefit	Tax dependant	Nil
	Non-tax dependant	15%[a]
Income stream (tax dependants only)		
Death pension	Either the deceased or the dependant is aged 60 or above	Nil
	Both the deceased and dependant are under age 60	Marginal tax rates[a] with a 15% tax offset

[a] Plus Medicare levy.

Source: Information derived from ATO 2024.

ILLUSTRATIVE EXAMPLE 11.4

Refer to the case study presented at the start of this chapter.

When Jen died, her superannuation benefit amounted to $280 000 with a tax-free amount of $80 000 (a tax-free proportion of 28.5%). As Jen did not have a binding death benefit nomination in place, the trustee of Jen's superannuation fund will determine how her funds are to be distributed. Assume that the trustees decide to split the superannuation balance 50% to Jen's husband and 50% to her son Michael.

The lump sum superannuation death benefit would be taxed in the hands of the beneficiaries as follows.

- Death benefit received by Jen's husband of $140 000 — as he is a tax dependant (former spouse), all of the lump sum death benefit would be tax free in his hands.
- Death benefit received by Michael of $140 000 — as he is a non-tax dependant due to his age, the taxable component of the death benefit received would be subject to a tax rate of 15% plus Medicare levy.

That is:

Tax-free component = $140 000 × 28.5% (tax-free proportion) = $39 900
Taxable component = $140 000 − $39 900 = $100 100

Michael would be subject to a tax rate of 17% (including Medicare levy) on the taxable component — $17 017.

PROFESSIONAL ADVICE

Binding death benefit nominations for self-managed superannuation funds (SMSF)

To ensure that the benefits are distributed in accordance with the member's wishes, a valid binding death benefit nomination should be put in place.

The Australian Taxation Office's determination SMSFD 2008/3 states that a member of an SMSF can make a valid binding death benefit nomination if it is permitted by the fund's trust deed. The ruling also states that the binding nomination does not have to satisfy certain requirements of the SIS Act, including the need for it to be:

- witnessed by 2 individuals
- updated every 3 years.

This means that SMSFs can offer binding nominations that do not have to be updated on a regular basis to remain valid, that is, non-lapsing binding nominations. A non-lapsing binding nomination remains valid until the member changes it or revokes it.

▶

If the member dies and there is no valid binding nomination directing how the benefit is to be distributed, the trustees must refer to the trust deed. Generally, the trust deed includes one of the following options.

- The trustees identify all potential dependants and decide to whom the benefit should be paid. The trustees can also decide to pay the benefit to the deceased member's estate.
- Automatic payment is made to the deceased member's estate.

The trustees of a SMSF are likely to be closely related and emotional issues may impact upon how decisions are made if superannuation death benefits are paid without a valid binding nomination.

Example

Jason has 2 children, Grace and Jack. Grace works with Jason in the family business, is a member of Jason's SMSF and is also his LPR (legal personal representative). Jack is neither a member of the fund nor an LPR.

Jason passes away and, before his death, did not think it worth completing a binding death benefit nomination. Jason wanted his share of the SMSF to be distributed equally between his two children upon his death.

Source: Adapted from Miles 2009.

QUESTIONS

1. Why is there a need to consider binding death benefit nominations for members within an SMSF when all members are also required to be trustees of the fund?
2. What persons are able to be nominated as beneficiaries within a binding death benefit nomination?
3. Discuss the ramifications of Jason's death in terms of control over the funds of the SMSF and the potential distribution of Jason's superannuation death benefits.
4. If a dispute was to arise in the distribution of Jason's death benefits, what means of redress would SMSF beneficiaries have?

11.7 Power of attorney

LEARNING OBJECTIVE 11.7 Discuss the purpose of a power of attorney.

A power of attorney is a legal document that authorises another person to act on your behalf. The person delegating the power is known as the donor, and the person receiving the power is known as the attorney. The attorney has the same power as the donor and can sign legal documents on behalf of the donor and make decisions, which are binding on the donor. Therefore, a power of attorney gives the attorney extensive powers to act on behalf of the donor, such as to buy and sell property, invest and enter into contracts on behalf of the donor. The only legal act an attorney is unable to do on behalf of the donor is make the donor's will.

The granting of powers of attorney comes under state legislation, and the legislation differs between states. However, a validly made power of attorney made in one state or territory is generally recognised in other states of Australia.

Types of powers of attorney

In general, there are two types of powers of attorney: (1) general power of attorney, and (2) enduring power of attorney. Although each authorises the attorney to act on behalf of the donor, there are differences in the extent and duration of the powers.

General power of attorney

A general power of attorney authorises the attorney to stand in your place and make any financial and legal decisions for you. It will remain in force until it is specifically cancelled by the donor. The power of attorney will also lapse if the donor dies or becomes mentally incompetent.

Enduring power of attorney

An enduring power of attorney grants the same extensive powers to an attorney as a general power of attorney. One significant difference between an enduring power of attorney and other powers of attorney is that an enduring power of attorney remains in force even if the donor is unable to make decisions due to mental incompetence or they become unable to make decisions for themselves.

A number of states also provide for medical powers of attorney or a medical treatment decision maker that empower the attorney or decision maker to make decisions about what medical treatment the donor should receive if they are unable to make a decision themselves. For example, in Queensland, a person can set up an Advanced Health Directive in order to assign someone the ability to make decisions about their special health issues. Victoria also provides for an advanced care directive appointment that is designed to provide the donor with the opportunity to document their values and preferences about their future medical treatment.

Powers of guardianship empower the guardian to make lifestyle and accommodation decisions on behalf of the donor. (See the appendix at the end of this chapter for information on the legislation and where to access sample forms.) It is important to realise that enduring powers of attorney aren't limited to just elderly people. One never knows when misfortune may strike with a consequence of not being able to make decisions for oneself.

Medical advanced care planning and directives

Different states and territories in Australia have different laws and terminology in relation to advance care planning and the appointment of a medical treatment decision maker. If illness or serious injury prevents a person from making decisions about their future health care, advance care planning aims to ensure that the person's values, preferred outcomes, and preferences for treatment and care are understood and acted upon. Illness or serious injury can happen to people of all ages, especially as they move towards the end of their life. The substitute decision maker can make decisions on the donor's behalf and is required to act in accordance with any lawful directions contained in the form. They can also consent to, or refuse treatment, on the donor's behalf.

Different states provide for different substitute decision makers to be appointed. For example in Victoria, the substitute decision maker is the first of the following who is available, willing and able to make decisions.

1. Medical treatment decision maker(s) appointed by you.
2. Guardian appointed by the Victorian Civil and Administrative Tribunal (VCAT) to make decisions on your medical treatment.
3. Person with a close and continuing relationship with you (medical treatment decision maker), chosen in the following order:
   • spouse or domestic partner
   • primary carer
   • adult child (eldest to youngest)
   • parent (eldest to youngest)
   • adult sibling (eldest to youngest).

In Queensland, the substitute decision maker will be one of the following:

1. Attorney or attorney for an Advance Health Directive appointed by you.
2. Guardian appointed by the Queensland Civil and Administrative Tribunal to make decisions on your medical treatment.
3. The first of the following (statutory health attorney):
   • spouse or domestic partner
   • carer
   • close relative or close friend.

A person is also able to complete an Advance Care or Health Directive. In the document, a person is able to:

• write an instructional directive with legally binding instructions about future medical treatment you consent to or refuse. If your directive relates to refusing or withdrawing life-saving treatment, certain criteria will need to be met for it to apply
• write a values directive that documents your values and preferences for your attorney to consider when making decisions for you
• appoint your attorney or guardian for personal/health matters.

See www.advancecareplanning.org.au/understand-advance-care-planning/advance-care-planning-exp lained#:~:text=Advance%20care%20planning%20is%20the,%2C%20and%20substitute%20decision%2 Dmaking for more information.

Executing a power of attorney

The laws relating to powers of attorney are complex, differ between states and do not always transcend state boundaries. For example, a power of attorney issued in one state may, in some situations, not give the attorney power to act on behalf of the donor in transactions conducted in other states. As we have seen, the granting of a power of attorney gives the attorney broad powers to act on behalf of and legally bind the donor. For these reasons, it is recommended that professional legal advice be sought before granting a power of attorney.

Cancelling a power of attorney

A power of attorney becomes valid as soon as the legal document is signed and witnessed and continues to be valid until it is revoked. In most cases, a power of attorney can be cancelled verbally simply by telling the attorney that his or her authority to act has been cancelled. The problem with simply telling the attorney is that there is no evidence of the cancellation and those who have been dealing with the attorney may not be aware that authority has been withdrawn. It is wise to cancel the power of attorney in writing and to inform those people who have been dealing with the attorney of the cancellation. All copies of the power of attorney, including the copy held by the attorney, should be destroyed.

If the donor wishes to alter the power of attorney, this can be done either by simply amending the original one or by cancelling it and making a new one. The second option is preferable, as amending the original power of attorney could result in it becoming messy and confusing.

A power of attorney is valid only while the donor is alive and automatically ceases when the donor dies. Therefore, granting a power of attorney is not a substitute for making a will.

Choosing a power of attorney

Granting a power of attorney gives extensive power to the attorney to make decisions that are legally binding on the donor. Although powers of attorney can be very useful, they should be used carefully and the attorney must be chosen carefully. The chosen attorney should be someone the donor can trust completely, who is likely to outlive the donor and who is competent and has the time to undertake the tasks required. The person chosen must understand the nature and effect of the power of attorney, and understand the need to be trustworthy. The attorney cannot delegate the powers to anyone else.

Issues to consider in appointing a power of attorney or medical decision maker

It is normally beneficial for partners to hold an enduring power of attorney or be a medical decision maker for each other. This would enable each spouse to take control of and make financial and legal decisions about the assets held by the other partner, or their medical decisions in the event of loss of mental competence of either of them. Additional problems can arise where the family has made use of business structures for asset protection and tax minimisation purposes. These structures can cause difficulty and hardship when the person owning or controlling the structure becomes mentally incompetent and cannot deal with legal and financial affairs. The person's family may find that they do not have access to the income and assets intended for their benefit. An enduring power of attorney prevents the added hardship of being denied access to vital financial resources in such tragic times.

Appointment of each spouse as the sole attorney or medical decision maker for the other partner may not always provide the outcome sought. Consider the ramifications of both the husband and wife becoming mentally or physically incompetent at the same time, for example, if both partners were involved in a serious accident leaving them both in a coma for a period of time, or they both became elderly and incompetent. In the case of either of these events, family members would be in a much better position to provide for the couple if another, or substitute, attorney or medical decision maker had been appointed. The role of an attorney or medical decision maker is similar to that of an executor of a will. The same questions should be considered in making such an appointment. These include the following.

- Does the person understand the role required?
- Do they have the time to carry out the tasks required?
- Does the person live close by? Are they located conveniently for day-to-day requirements?
- Will the person act in the best interests of the donor?

In many cases, the attorney may be a son or daughter (or both) so that the duties can be shared.

SUMMARY

Estate planning is an important part of the wider financial planning discipline. A thorough estate plan looks beyond the need for a valid will to potential threats to the assets of the estate both before and after the death of the willmaker. There can be potential challenges to the will from disgruntled beneficiaries (and potential beneficiaries). Taxation has an impact on estate distributions and estate assets may be passed to outside claimants in the event of bankruptcy or divorce. An effective estate plan deals with both estate and non-estate assets, including superannuation fund distribution. Assets can be protected from vulnerable beneficiaries while still allowing them access to the benefits of those assets.

The establishment of a testamentary trust within a will can provide a number of potential benefits in minimising the imposition of tax on beneficiaries and in the protection of the assets of an estate. One of the important decisions to be made within estate planning is the extent to which assets should form part of a deceased's estate. Some of the issues to be considered include the size of the estate, the ability to transfer estate assets into a testamentary trust and the potential for estate assets to be contested.

As superannuation is increasingly likely to form a significant part of the assets of deceased estates, proper planning can ensure that death benefits are distributed to the beneficiaries of choice in the most tax-effective manner.

An important consideration in the estate planning of a person is the appointment of a power of attorney and medical decision maker, or writing a directive. This is a critically important document for all persons, but especially as a person starts to age and finds it increasingly difficult to properly manage their affairs or wants to provide direction on their medical care.

Through careful estate planning, a financial planner can help clients identify their estate-planning goals and objectives, and put in place a plan to build and preserve assets for their estates, and ensure those assets will be distributed to the intended beneficiaries.

KEY TERMS

beneficiary A person nominated to receive a payout from an insurance policy, a superannuation fund or the assets of an estate.

binding death benefit nomination A declaration by a superannuation fund member that upon their death the balance of their superannuation must be paid to those beneficiaries nominated by the member; the trustees are bound to follow this direction.

codicil A legal document that amends an existing will without revoking the will in its entirety.

enduring power of attorney A power of attorney (POA) is a legal document given by a person (donor) that authorises another person (attorney) to act on their behalf; an enduring POA continues to be valid even after the donor becomes mentally incompetent.

estate assets Assets owned in the personal name of the willmaker, which are capable of being disposed of by a will.

estate planning The planning and management of a person's estate following their death.

executor The personal representative or manager of a deceased person's estate.

inter vivos trust A trust established during the lifetime of a person.

intestacy The situation that arises when a person dies without having a valid will and, as a result, their assets are distributed in accordance with a government formula.

joint tenancy A form of ownership of an asset where two or more persons each hold the rights over the entire asset and in which the surviving tenant receives total ownership of the asset.

legal personal representative The person responsible for managing the estate of a deceased who is appointed through either being named as the executor in a will or, if there is no will, by being appointed administrator of the estate by the Supreme Court.

medical decision maker The appointment of a substitute decision maker who is able to make decisions on their behalf relating to their health care, advance care planning, beliefs and preferences for treatment

non-estate assets Assets that are not owned in the personal name of the willmaker and their distribution is not governed by a will.

power of attorney A legal document in which one person nominates and gives legal authority to another person to make decisions on their behalf in respect of their legal and financial affairs.

tenancy-in-common A form of ownership of an asset where two or more people each have a distinct share in the ownership of an asset and in which the share of the deceased's interest forms part of their estate.

testamentary capacity The mental capacity required of a willmaker to be able to make a valid will.

testamentary trust A trust established under the terms of a will that comes into effect upon the death of the willmaker.

undue influence A situation that arises where one person is able to take advantage of a position of power over another person.

will A legal document that directs how a willmaker's assets are to be distributed or disposed of upon their death.

PROFESSIONAL APPLICATION QUESTIONS

11.1 What are the key estate planning matters that financial planners should identify when advising clients?

11.2 What are some of the circumstances that might require a person to update their will?

11.3 Describe the difference in treatment of assets upon the death of a person between those that are jointly owned compared with those held in a tenancy-in-common arrangement.

11.4 Discuss the purpose of a medical/advanced care directive? What factors should be taken into account in appointing a substitute decision maker to make medical decisions on behalf of a person?

11.5 After hearing the contents of his mother's will, Jacqui is upset to learn that her brother, Mick is to inherit the family farm valued at $3 million whereas she will receive a cash sum of $350 000 and a share portfolio valued at $550 000. Mick works on the farm whereas Jacqui moved away four years ago and is working and living in the city. Is Jacqui able to contest the will, and, if so, on what basis? Give reasons why Mick might argue that the distribution is fair.

11.6 Jasmine receives a distribution from her father's estate, which includes a property. Jasmine sells the property four years later and wants to know if there are any CGT implications. Discuss.

11.7 What is the purpose of a binding death benefit nomination? What are the consequences and risks of having a non-binding death benefit nomination?

11.8 Discuss the circumstances by which it would be preferable for a person's superannuation death benefits to be paid to their estate, rather than directly to a dependant, and explain how this could be achieved.

11.9 Janelle, a widow, is updating her will and has heard from one of her friends that she should establish a family trust for her three adult children. Explain to Janelle the type of trust that would be provided for in a will and discuss the possible benefits of Janelle's estate being transferred to the trust upon her death.

11.10 Jim, aged 72, dies leaving an estate worth $2 million. Jim is survived by his spouse Beth and their four children and two grandchildren. Jim went to a solicitor three years ago to prepare his will. Jim was very keen to leave $100 000 to each of his grandchildren to cover their private education costs and to leave $100 000 to the Cancer Council Australia where he worked as a volunteer. However, upon his death, his will in unable to be located. Explain how Jim's estate is likely to be distributed and whether Jim's estate planning objectives are likely to be satisfied.

11.11 Lisa is looking to amend her will and has an estate worth approximately $2 million. She wants to leave $1 million to her eldest daughter Gail and $500 000 each to her other two children, Sheena and Adrian. Under what circumstances would Sheena and Adrian be able to challenge the will and how could Lisa ensure that her wishes are adhered to as far as possible?

11.12 Travis is aged 47, single and is updating his will. He wants to know how the difference in the definition of 'dependant' between the Tax Act and the SIS Act would affect funds paid from his superannuation fund to the following beneficiaries upon his death:
  • his mother
  • his sister, aged 44, and living with her husband
  • his child, Beatrice, aged 14, and living with his former wife but supported by Travis through child maintenance payments.

11.13 Explain the purpose of a power of attorney including the difference between a general and enduring power of attorney.

11.14 What factors should be taken into account when considering the appointment of an executor of a will?

PROFESSIONAL APPLICATION EXERCISES

★ BASIC | ★★ MODERATE | ★★★ CHALLENGING

11.15 Wills ★

Why is it important to differentiate estate assets from non-estate assets when drafting a will? Other than a will, are there any additional estate planning issues that may be required by a person in dealing with the distribution of their assets to intended beneficiaries?

11.16 Power of attorney ★

Frank and Litisha are aged in their seventies and concerned about who will look after their son, aged 38, who has a drug addiction. There are no other family members with the financial means to look after him and they are concerned that, if they leave funds to him in their will, he will spend the funds on drugs. What are the couple's options?

11.17 Estate planning ★★

Barbara seeks financial planning advice from your office in respect of her estate. Barbara is single, aged in her 60s and has an estate worth $800 000. She is looking to leave her estate to her two children — Ian, aged 40, who runs a very successful business and earns a taxable income of around $250 000 p.a., and Susan, aged 36 and single, who is disabled and is financial dependent upon Barbara. Ian has a spouse Louise who works on a casual basis and earns around $10 000 and three children aged 16, 14 and 9.

Advise Barbara on the issues she needs to consider in her estate planning requirements and give guidance on how she can best provide for Susan and Ian upon her death.

11.18 Death benefits ★★

Joe is aged 58 and has a terminal illness. Joe has a superannuation account worth $500 000 of which 18% represents a tax-free proportion. His binding death benefit nomination states that his superannuation death benefit is to be distributed equally between his two adult children.

Joe seeks advice from a financial planner who advises him that a significant amount of tax will be payable by his beneficiaries from the superannuation death benefit they receive.

(a) Calculate the tax payable by Joe's beneficiaries upon receipt of the superannuation death benefit.

(b) What strategies could be implemented by Joe prior to his death to reduce the amount of tax payable by his children upon receipt of the superannuation death benefit?

11.19 Death benefits ★★

Paul has just died leaving a superannuation balance totaling $1.8 million, which contains a $300 000 tax-free component. Assume the following.

Paul leaves behind a spouse and three children. The eldest child, Louise, aged 26, is married and financially independent; Travis is aged 22, still lives at home and is studying a Masters course in physiotherapy; and Jessica is aged 17, lives at home and goes to school.

Paul wants to leave $200 000 to his sister, who is disabled and lives with Paul and the family and is dependent upon Paul's family, and the balance equally between his wife and three children.

Advise what the tax implications would be on each member of the family if they received a share of Paul's $1.8 million superannuation balance.

11.20 Intestacy ★★

Janine and Rick are living in a de facto relationship. Janine is 37, a widow and has two children — Meg, aged 8, and Jack, aged 6. Rick, aged 35, has three children who live with his former wife. They were divorced 4 years ago. Janine and Rick have been living together for 3 years. Neither Janine nor Rick has a will. Janine owns the house (valued at $650 000) that they are living in, and has $20 000 in the bank and $100 000 in her superannuation fund. Rick has $5 000 in a bank account and $80 000 in his superannuation fund. Janine and Rick have a car accident and Janine is killed instantly. Rick is seriously injured and lies in a coma for 5 weeks before he dies. Describe what will happen to the estate under intestacy laws in your state.

11.21 Estate distribution and CGT ★★

Angela has the following assets at date of death:

Asset	Cost and date of purchase	Market value at date of death
Home	Acquired in May 1994 for $420 000	$ 750 000
Holiday house (50% share held under a tenancy-in-common arrangement with sister)	Acquired in July 1985 for $180 000	$ 520 000
Bank account		$ 40 000
Shares	Acquired in 2003 for $80 000	$ 100 000
Investment property	Acquired in 2005 for $400 000	$ 580 000
Superannuation account Binding death benefit nomination to her daughter Shana (comprises 20% tax free component)		$ 200 000
Life insurance, owned in the name of Shana		$ 500 000

In her will, Angela leaves everything to her daughter Shana. For the next 12 months, Shana retains all of the inherited assets and uses her mother's home as her primary residence. After 12 months, Shana decides to sell the following assets that she inherited:

Asset	Market value at date of disposal
Home	$ 820 000
Shares	$ 120 000
Investment property	$ 620 000

You are required to provide details on the following issues.

(a) At the date of Angela's death, explain whether Shana would have been liable to any tax upon the distribution of the inherited assets.

(b) If a testamentary trust had been established within Angela's will, which of her assets would have been able to be transferred into the trust structure?

(c) Calculate the amount of CGT likely to be payable by Shana upon the disposal of the inherited assets.

11.22 Estate planning ★★★

Nick and Foula were recently married, each for the second time after knowing each other for about 4 years. Nick lost his wife 5 years ago and Foula divorced 7 years ago. Both Nick and Foula have children from their first marriages, and each has a will in place that was drawn up during their first marriage. As part of the process of starting a new life, they sold their respective homes and bought a new one under a tenants-in-common arrangement.

As part of their estate planning needs, the couple has the following questions for you.

(a) Given their recent marriage, how would their respective estates be distributed under current circumstances?

(b) How could Nick and Foula ensure that, upon the death of either of them, the other could continue to live in the house for the remainder of their life?

(c) How are the interests of Nick and Foula's children able to be best safeguarded upon the death of either parent?

(d) Upon his death, how would Nick's account-based pension be treated for tax purposes if he wanted the income from the pension to continue to be paid tax-free to his adult daughter?

11.23 Testamentary trusts ★★★

Tim is an accountant and has a $1 million life insurance policy in place owned by his wife Melanie. Tim also has $800 000 held in his superannuation account with a non-binding death benefit nomination in place leaving 50% of the funds to his two adult children and 50% to his brother Callum who has a gambling issue. The couple's home is jointly owned by Tim and Melanie, as is the couple's share portfolio. Tim also owns a holiday home owned as tenants in common with Callum. They inherited the holiday home from their parents. Tim has a will in place that provides for the establishment of a testamentary trust upon his death and Tim is seeking to maximise the amount of his estate that is able to be held in the testamentary trust. Discuss the following issues.

(a) How is each of Tim's assets likely to be distributed upon his death?

(b) What modifications would be required to help Tim achieve his objective of maximising the amount of his estate transferred into the testamentary trust?

(c) What potential problems could be faced by the brother upon the distribution from Tim's superannuation fund and can you suggest any solution?

CASE STUDY 1

Milenko and Amy have made an appointment with you to discuss their financial planning needs. They provide the following information.

Milenko is aged 58 and Amy is aged 56. Milenko works as an accountant and earns $120 000 p.a. including the SG contribution. Amy works 2 days a week and earns $30 000. The couple has one child from their marriage, Catherine, aged 14. The couple has been married previously and both have children from their first marriage. Milenko has two children from his first marriage, Peter and Jack. Both are aged in their early thirties. Jack is severely disabled and needs full-time care. Milenko pays support towards Jack's ongoing medical and care costs. Peter is married with two children but is experiencing some marriage problems. Amy has one child from her previous marriage, Sharon, aged 26. Sharon was very upset when her mother remarried and Amy and Sharon have little contact.

The couple has the following assets and liabilities (current market value):

	$
Home and contents	920 000
Cars	35 000
Bank account	20 000
Holiday home	480 000
Shares	120 000
Superannuation accounts	
Milenko	410 000
Amy	180 000
Life and TPD policy	
Milenko	500 000
Amy	250 000
Liabilities	
Home mortgage	320 000

Milenko and Amy advise that their objectives are as follows.

- Milenko hopes to be able to retire in 4 years.
- The couple would like the home mortgage paid off as soon as possible.
- The couple would like to continue to send Catherine to a private school for the next 4 years.
- In the event of their death, the couple would like to ensure the following distribution of their estate.
  - Milenko — Amy and Catherine to receive 25% each of his estate, his son Jack to receive 35% and his other son Peter to receive the remaining 15%. Milenko is particularly concerned to ensure that Jack is looked after in the event of his death.
  - Amy — her daughter Sharon to receive a fixed amount of $200 000. The balance of her estate to be split equally between Milenko and Catherine.

  Other issues raised are as follows.
- In the event of Milenko's death, Amy would sell the holiday home and the shares. In the event of Amy's death, Milenko would sell the holiday home. The holiday home is jointly owned by the couple and its cost was $240 000 in 2010. The shares were acquired by Milenko in 2006 for $100 000.
- Both Milenko and Amy would like each other to make all of their financial, legal and medical decisions in the event that either of them was unable to do so.
- Milenko checks his superannuation statement, which reveals he has a non-binding death benefit nomination in place.

QUESTIONS

1 To be able to properly analyse the couple's estate planning needs, what additional information would be needed and why?

2 Explain to Milenko what a death benefit nomination is and its purpose. What advice would you give to Milenko about the type of death benefit nomination that he should establish and who he can and should nominate as his dependants?

3 In the event of Milenko's death, what recommendations can you provide as to how any financial distribution to his son Jack should be structured to ensure that Jack's best interests are looked after?

4 In the event of Milenko's death, how would the CGT legislation affect the amount of funds inherited by Amy? If Amy was to sell the holiday home and shares at their current market value, how much CGT would she be liable to pay?

CASE STUDY 2

ESTATE PLANNING

Peter and Amity are in their mid-fifties and have three children from their marriage: Mark, aged 23; Drew, aged 17; and Imogen, aged 15. Peter has been married before and has one child from that marriage — Alice, aged 26. Alice has no contact with her father and blames him for the financial hardships that her mother has experienced since their divorce.

Peter is employed as an architect while Amity is a fashion consultant. The couple's assets, at current market value, consist of the following:

	$
Home and contents (home acquired for $450 000 in 2000)	1 050 000
Bank account	30 000
Shares (acquired for $20 000 in 1986)	130 000
Holiday home (acquired for $380 000 in 2010)	680 000
Managed funds (acquired for $80 000 in 2007)	40 000
Life insurance policy	800 000
Self-managed superannuation fund — total (Peter and Amity — 50/50)	550 000
Superannuation account — Amity	60 000

The couple raises the following issues.

- All of the couple's assets are jointly owned between Peter and Amity.
- The couple gave Alice $180 000 to establish a business 3 years ago on the basis that she has no further claim on Peter's estate. However, the couple is convinced that Alice will nevertheless contest Peter's will upon his death.
- Peter's life insurance policy is owned by Amity.
- Amity's individual superannuation fund contains a $150 000 life and TPD policy and Amity has decided to retain this account in order to preserve the insurance policy. Amity completed a binding death benefit nomination 4 years ago nominating 100% to be paid to Peter in the event of her death. Both Peter and Amity have completed binding death benefit nominations within their SMSF.
- The couple each has a will in place leaving everything to each other. They have each nominated their son Drew as executor of their respective estates. Peter and Amity have appointed each other as their respective general power of attorney.
- Amity's mother, aged 90, owns an apartment in Queensland. However, the mother is in an aged care facility and in bad health and is no longer living in the apartment. The mother is looking to leave the property to Amity. The property cost $130 000 in 1989 and has a current market value of $510 000.
- The couple's son, Drew, has been married for the past 3 years but he and his spouse have experienced marriage problems for some time. Peter and Amity would like to gift Drew $180 000 to use as a deposit on a house but, given the marriage problems, do not want the money to be lost in a divorce.
- The couple would like the family assets distributed in a tax-effective manner upon their death.

QUESTION

Peter and Amity are looking to review their wills and seek some advice from you on how best to structure their estate-planning needs. You are required to analyse the couple's situation and detail relevant issues and recommend advice that the couple should consider.

CASE STUDY 3

Bill and Cassy are aged 66 and 64 years respectively and have both just retired from running a newsagency together for many years. They intend to become 'grey nomads' for the next 12 months and tow a caravan around Australia. However, before they set off on their journey, they decide that they had better get their personal estate plans put into action. They make an appointment to see Jim, the financial planner whom they have consulted with over the past few years, to review their finances and to make plans in the event that they die while on their trip.

Jim prepares notes based on the information provided by Bill and Cassy. They advise him of the following.

- Their home is valued at $920 000 and has no debt. It was purchased in 1980 for $140 000.
- They own an investment property currently valued at $720 000 but they still owe $150 000 on the property. The property cost them $320 000 in 2006.
- They have a share portfolio currently valued at $240 000. The portfolio was purchased in two lots: $40 000 was acquired in 1982 with the proceeds of a distribution from Cassy's aunt (now worth $90 000); and $100 000 was purchased in 1990 (now worth $150 000).
- The couple plan to fund their retirement income from account-based pensions paid from the couple's superannuation fund - the ABC Master Superannuation Fund. Bill's balance is $500 000 (30% tax free) and Cassy's balance is $250 000 (100% taxable).
- All assets except for the balances held in the superannuation fund are held in joint names.

Jim does some calculations based on the couple's account-based pensions, their share dividends and the rent they receive from their investment property and, after allowing for various expenses, calculates an approximate income that they can expect to receive while they are away which seems to meet their expected expenditure needs whilst on their 'round Australia trip'.

Jim is reminded that Bill and Cassy have three adult children, all of whom are married and are living independently. With thoughts about estate planning, Jim specifically asks about whether the marriages of the children are happy or not. Bill and Cassy both express some concern about two of the marriages and admit that they would not be surprised if divorce were the outcome. Jim uses the opportunity to ask about whether they would like to put in place some plans for their estates.

Bill and Cassy tell Jim that they want to ensure that their children are treated equally on their death and that their funds are passed on for the benefit of their children and grandchildren. Jim explains the implications of property settlement when a couple decides to divorce and that the assets are likely to be split equally between the two parties. Bill and Cassy foresee that, if they do not properly plan, some portion of their accumulated assets are likely to be taken away from the family by one or more marriage break-ups.

Through their discussions with Jim, Bill and Cassy propose that, upon their death, all of their assets (including their home) are sold and converted to cash and the proceeds distributed to their beneficiaries accordingly. They also assume that the balances held in the superannuation fund would be paid by the trustees to their estate prior to distribution to beneficiaries. Bill and Cassy plan to make their best friends the executors of their will.

Jim suggests that he write some notes based on their conversation and then brief an estate-planning lawyer. Bill and Cassy agree that Jim can assist them with this matter and even take up his offer to attend the meeting with the lawyer when they meet to discuss the estate plan.

QUESTIONS

1 If the three children agreed not to sell the shares but to split the shareholding of those shares equally between them:
   (a) describe the CGT impact on such a proposal at the time of the inheritance
   (b) are the three children able to request that the shares not be sold as proposed by Bill and Cassy? Explain how this may be done.
2 Identify the taxation impact on the sale of each of the assets forming part of the couple's estate.
3 Determine the likely amount to be distributed to each of the children after taxes have been paid.
4 Consider how a testamentary trust might be used by Bill and Cassy to help protect the family assets if a divorce occurred with any of their children.
5 Describe how the establishment of three separate testamentary trusts, one for each child, may provide a better outcome than the creation of only one testamentary trust covering all of their children.

APPENDIX

POWERS OF ATTORNEY

In Australia, the law regarding powers of attorney is made by the individual states and territories. All of this legislation may be found on the internet at austlii.edu.au.

The relevant state Acts are as follows:

State	Legislation
Australian Capital Territory	*Powers of Attorney Act 2006*
New South Wales	*Powers of Attorney Act 2003*
Northern Territory	*Powers of Attorney Act 1980*
Queensland	*Powers of Attorney Act 1998*
South Australia	*Powers of Attorney and Agency Act 1984*
Tasmania	*Powers of Attorney Act 2000*
Victoria	*Powers of Attorney Act 2014*
Western Australia	*Powers of Attorney and Guardianship Act 2018*

Sample forms may be found on the internet, usually on state justice departments' websites. In Queensland, for example, a sample form may be found at the Department of Justice and Attorney-General website (justice.qld.gov.au). However, as this 'short form' comprises 20 pages of forms and instructions, it is not reproduced here. Look on the internet for your state justice department's site to see if a sample form is available.

REFERENCES

Australian Government, *Income Tax Assessment Act 1997* (Cwlth), www.legislation.gov.au/Series/C2004A05138.

Australian Taxation Office (ATO) 2024, 'Super lump sum tax table', Australian Government, 14 April, www.ato.gov.au/rates/key-superannuation-rates-and-thresholds/?anchor=Superlumpsumtaxtable#.

Burke & Associates Lawyers 2022, 'NO WILL, NO SAY. A guide to Victoria's intestacy provisions', www.burkelawyers.com.au/wp-content/uploads/2020/08/No-will-no-say.-A-guide-to-Victorias-intestacy-provisions.pdf.

Investopedia 2011, '10 strange will and testaments', *Forbes*, 12 April, www.forbes.com/sites/investopedia/2011/04/12/10-strange-will-and-testaments/#7c94cb226b10.

Miles, A 2009, 'Tax strategies for SMSFs in estate planning', *Money Management*, 21 July, https://www.moneymanagement.com.au/news/financial-planning/tax-strategies-smsfs-estate-planning.

New South Wales Trustee & Guardian (TAG) n.d., 'Case studies', www.tag.nsw.gov.au.

USEFUL WEBSITES

Basic information on estate planning, https://moneysmart.gov.au/wills-and-powers-of-attorney.

A range of articles on estate planning, www.turnbullhill.com.au/articles/category/estate-planning.

ACKNOWLEDGEMENTS

Table 11.2: © Commonwealth of Australia

Extracts: © Commonwealth of Australia

CHAPTER 12

Development of a statement of advice

LEARNING OBJECTIVES

After studying this chapter, you should be able to:

12.1 describe the regulatory requirements relating to financial product advice

12.2 understand the disclosure documents required in respect of the provision of a financial product

12.3 outline the legal obligations behind the provision of financial advice

12.4 explain when a statement of advice is required and its purpose

12.5 explain the circumstances under which a statement of advice is not required

12.6 outline the main types of statement of advice documents used in the marketplace

12.7 appreciate the importance of effective communication in a statement of advice

12.8 understand the importance of the planner–client relationship

12.9 explain the 6-step financial planning process used to prepare a statement of advice

12.10 understand the various ethical and legal compliance issues involved in developing a financial plan

12.11 construct a statement of advice to meet the needs of a client and to satisfy regulatory requirements.

Cory and Amy are seeking financial advice. You are employed as a para-planner with Good Advice Financial Planners and are just about to enter the first meeting with the clients and the practice's financial planner. Cory and Amy have supplied the practice with some preliminary financial information prior to the meeting. A summary of the information is provided below.

Cory is aged 33 and Amy is aged 29. Cory works as a self-employed builder while Amy is a physiotherapist. Cory earns an annual net income from his business of around $80 000 before tax and Amy earns a salary of $72 000 p.a. including the employer SG contribution. The couple is currently renting and after paying all their living costs, have a disposable income of $35 000 p.a. The couple's investments currently consist of:

- a savings account of $20 000 earning 2% p.a.
- a share portfolio of $25 000 paying a fully franked dividend of 2% p.a.
- superannuation accounts: Cory has a balance of $40 000 invested in the CBUS industry super fund (conservative investment option), while Amy's superannuation is invested with the ABC retail super fund with an account balance of $35 000 (balanced investment option).

The couple's superannuation accounts are invested as follows:

- Cory: cash 15%; Australian fixed interest 40%; property 10%; Australian shares 25%; international shares 10%
- Amy: cash 7%; Australian fixed interest 28%; property 10%; Australian shares 35%; international shares 20%.

The couple is hoping to buy a home in the next 6 months and have seen a property worth around $650 000 which they like. The couple is seeking some advice on how best to save for a deposit, what deposit amount they need to accumulate for the purchase and how much they can afford to borrow from the bank. The couple is also looking to go on an overseas trip in four years and will need to save an amount of $20 000. They want to know how they should save for this cost.

The couple has specifically requested that they do not want advice in respect of any other aspect of their financial circumstances. They have asked for information on how the financial planning practice charges for their advice.

Some of the issues to consider in this case include:

- the matters that should be discussed with the couple at the first meeting and the documentation required to be provided to the couple at the various stages of the financial planning process
- how a financial planner deals with the situation where a client wants to limit the scope of the advice sought
- the disclosure requirements in respect of the provision of financial advice
- the different charging options available to a financial planning practice and what disclosure requirements (if any) are needed with the provision of financial advice.

The illustrative examples used throughout this chapter will relate back to the information contained within this case study.

Introduction

Personal financial planning provides a framework for people to effectively manage their finances to satisfy their goals and objectives. This is manifested in the design, implementation and review of a personal financial plan that incorporates an integrated set of actions and transactions that best achieves and maintains the financial goals and wellbeing of the individual.

The financial planning process should provide the basis for a systematic and organised approach to preparing a financial plan for a client. The planning process should detail the client's goals and objectives, put forward appropriate strategies and recommendations, describe the manner in which the recommendations will achieve the client's agreed goals and establish a framework from which the planner intends to put the plan into action. However, to be effective, it is vital that there is clear communication with the client throughout all stages of the process.

Personal financial planning encompasses many different disciplines, including investments, business structures, personal risk insurance, taxation, superannuation, retirement and estate planning. A comprehensive analysis of all these disciplines will need to be considered in a typical financial plan, in the context of the client's circumstances and requirements.

As a result of the implementation of Part 7.7 of the *Corporations Act 2001* (the Act), a financial plan is now formally referred to as **statement of advice (SOA)**. Section 946A provides that financial advisers must give a client an SOA when required and sections 947B and 947C detail the main disclosure requirements of an SOA. The regulations prescribe a range of issues that need to be addressed within an SOA to ensure that the advice is in the best interests of the client and that the advice allows the client to be able to make an informed decision.

An SOA is the means by which a financial planner's advice and recommendations are communicated to a client in a clear, concise and effective manner. However, an SOA has a much greater role to play than simply setting out recommended advice, strategies and financial products to a client. An effective SOA should provide the planner with the opportunity to communicate with the client, to educate and inform them and, importantly, to encourage client engagement with and ownership of their SOA.

The government's Quality of Advice review's final report contained 22 recommendations and was submitted to government on 16 December 2022. In response, the government created the Delivering Better Financial Outcomes package to be implemented in three phases:

1. removing red tape that just adds to the cost of producing advice with no consumer benefit
2. expanding access to retirement income advice
3. finding new mediums for advice by expanding the provision of personal advice by other institutions. Phase one includes:
- the abolition of safe harbour steps for meeting the 'best interest' duty
- replacing the SOA with a financial advice record
- simplifying fee consent and renewals, including standardising wholesale and sophisticated investors
- added flexibility to FSG requirements
- further bans in conflicted remuneration.

At the time of writing, none of these changes have been implemented. Importantly, the concepts and values of the disclosure regime will not be diminished with the reforms coming through. Therefore, this chapter provides details of what is in place currently.

12.1 Regulation of financial advice

LEARNING OBJECTIVE 12.1 Describe the regulatory requirements relating to financial product advice.

Part 7.7 and Div. 2 of Pt 7.7A of the Act requires those who provide financial product advice to retail clients to comply with certain conduct and disclosure obligations. These obligations are designed to ensure that retail clients receive advice that is in their best interest and that the information is disclosed in a manner that allows the client to fully understand the ramifications of acting upon the advice.

The disclosure obligations vary depending on whether the financial product advice is personal advice or general advice (RG 175.1). Subject to some limited exclusions, a person who provides financial product advice to retail clients must hold an Australian financial services (AFS) licence and comply with the disclosure and conduct obligations in Pt 7.7 of the Act.

All financial product advice falls under one of two types: general advice or personal advice. An investor receives personal advice where the adviser has (or could reasonably be expected to have) considered one or more of the investor's objectives, financial situation or needs. General advice does not take into account the particular circumstances of the client and the client must be warned that the advice is general in nature (s. 949A).

Every client is deemed to be a retail client unless they satisfy one of the requirements to be classified as a wholesale client under sections 708, 761G and 761GA of the Act. Generally, a wholesale client is someone who satisfies either the definition of a sophisticated, experienced or professional investor.

A sophisticated investor is someone who has the financial means and this is certified by a qualified accountant that gross personal annual income over the previous two years has been greater than $250 000 or net assets greater than $2.5 million.

A professional investor holds their own Australian Financial Services licence or controls gross assets greater than $10 million.

An experienced investor is categorised if the licensee is reasonably satisfied that the client has enough previous experience in investing into securities (shares, bonds) that the client can determine for themselves the merits and risks of accepting the offer.

12.2 Disclosure documents required in respect of the provision of financial products

LEARNING OBJECTIVE 12.2 Understand the disclosure documents required in respect of the provision of a financial product.

Part 7.7 of the Act and ASIC's Regulatory Guides set out the various disclosure documents that are required to be provided by a planner prior to the purchase of a financial product or provision of a financial service by a retail client. The three main documents are:

- *financial services guide* — who the financial planner is and what financial services are able to be provided
- *statement of advice* — a statement setting out the advice and recommendations provided by the planner
- *product disclosure statement* — details on the financial product that is being acquired by the client.

These obligations are designed to ensure that retail clients receive appropriate information about financial products and advice, so they are able to make informed decisions.

Financial services guide (FSG)

Prior to the provision of financial advice, a client must be provided with a financial services guide (FSG). The FSG provisions (ss. 941–943 of the Act) are designed to ensure that retail clients are given sufficient information to enable them to decide whether or not to obtain financial services from the financial planner. The FSG is required to provide information to a client concerning:

- who is providing the service
- what financial services are being offered
- who the service provider is acting for
- details of how the planner is remunerated
- details of any potential conflicts of interest.

The financial planner must provide the client with a copy of their FSG at the earliest possible opportunity prior to any advice being given.

Statement of advice (SOA)

A retail client provided with personal advice from a financial planner must be issued with an SOA in such a way that they are able to make an informed decision about whether to act on the advice given and whether to acquire a financial product. The SOA must be provided to the client when, or as soon as practicable after, that advice is provided. An SOA must include various information including:

- the name of the party providing the advice
- a statement setting out the advice
- the reasoning or basis that led to that advice
- the remuneration and other benefits received by the provider of the advice
- all conflicts of interest that may affect the advice.

There are two main types of advice statements — a comprehensive advice statement and a scaled advice statement which is more limited in scope. There is also a record of advice which is a simplified version of a statement of advice but is generally only used for existing clients that already have a statement of advice and the adviser needs to provide further related advice.

Finally, there is execution only statement or nil-advice where a client is not seeking advice but simply requests you to carry out a transaction, such as buying some shares.

Product disclosure statement (PDS)

A PDS is prepared by the financial product issuer and must contain sufficient information to enable a retail client to be able to make an informed decision about whether to purchase a financial product (Pt 7.9 of the Act). Briefly, a PDS includes information such as:

- fees payable in respect of a financial product
- risks of the financial product
- benefits of the financial product
- significant characteristics of the financial product.

A PDS is generally required to be provided to a retail client at or before the time a recommendation is made to buy a financial product. Shorter PDSs are permitted to be issued by product providers for most superannuation funds, simple managed funds and margin lending facilities. The shorter PDS is restricted to eight pages (four pages for margin lending) and its purpose is designed to make it easier for retail clients to find and understand key financial information.

ILLUSTRATIVE EXAMPLE 12.1

What can Cory and Amy expect from the first meeting with the financial planner and what documentation should they be provided with?

A financial planner is required to provide a client with a financial services guide (FSG) at the earliest possible opportunity, before any advice is provided or recommendations made.

The first meeting provides an opportunity for both the financial planner and client to establish whether there is confidence and a rapport between them. The meeting provides the planner with an opportunity to detail who they are, what services they can provide, and how the adviser is remunerated for the services and advice they provide. It also provides the client with an opportunity to decide if the planner is likely to be able to help the client achieve their goals and objectives.

The FSG can be used during this first meeting to ensure all the planner provides all the necessary disclosures and that the client understands.

12.3 The legal obligations relating to the provision of financial advice

LEARNING OBJECTIVE 12.3 Outline the legal obligations behind the provision of financial advice.

The financial planner's obligations relating to disclosure and conduct obligations of advice documents are detailed within Pt 7.7 of the Act. Part 7.7A deals with the 'best interest' duty.

ASIC's RG 175 *Licensing: Financial product advisers — conduct and disclosure* provides guidance on the best interest duty and the key obligations are shown in figure 12.1.

FIGURE 12.1   Key obligations contained in RG 175

Relevant section of the Corporations Act	Obligation imposed	How the obligation would be satisfied
s. 961B	Acting in the best interests of the client	• Identify the objectives, financial situation and needs of the client. • Identify the subject matter of the advice sought by the client. • Make reasonable enquiries to obtain complete and accurate information. • Assess whether the advice provider has the expertise required to provide the advice sought. • Conduct a reasonable investigation into the financial products and assess the information gathered in the investigation. • Base all judgements on the client's relevant circumstances. • Take any other step that would be in the best interests of the client.
s. 961G	Providing appropriate advice	Advice must only be given if it is reasonable to conclude that it is appropriate for the client.
s. 961H	Warning the client if advice is based on incomplete or inaccurate information	The client must be warned if it is reasonably apparent that the advice is based on incomplete or inaccurate information about the client's objectives and needs.
s. 961J	Prioritising the interests of the client	Advice providers are required to prioritise the interests of the client over their own interests.

Source: ASIC 2017a.

Best interest duty and safe harbour provisions

The best interest duty means that a planner has a duty to:

1. act in the client's best interests
2. provide advice that is appropriate
3. provide an advice warning
4. prioritise the client's interests in the event of a conflict.

1. A duty to act in the client's best interests

The term 'best interests' is not defined in the Act or RG 175, although ASIC interprets it to mean advice provided that would leave the client in a 'better position' (RG 175.235). The overarching standard used to assess whether a client would be left in a better position is what an experienced and reasonable advice provider (financial planner) would believe to be the outcome if the client followed the advice. It is important to note that ASIC does not require the advice to be 'perfect' to establish that the client is in a better position.

Section 961B(2) provides a safe harbour for advice providers. If an advice provider can show that they have taken the steps in section 961B(2), they are considered to have complied with the best interests duty.

The financial planner must be able to demonstrate compliance with these requirements and accordingly the planner's records must be able to support and provide evidence of the work undertaken in analysing both the client and the financial products recommended.

The safe harbour provisions require an advice provider to take a number of factors into account as outlined in figure 12.2.

FIGURE 12.2   Safe harbour provisions

(a) Identify the objectives, financial situation and needs of the client that were identified through instructions.

(b) Identify:
   i. the subject matter of the advice sought by the client (whether explicitly or implicitly); and
   ii. the objectives, financial situation and needs of the client that would reasonably be considered relevant to the advice sought on that subject matter (the client's relevant circumstances).

(c) If it is reasonably apparent that information relating to the client's relevant circumstances is incomplete or inaccurate, make reasonable enquiries to obtain complete and accurate information.

(d) Assess whether you have the expertise to provide the advice sought and if not, decline to give the advice.

(e) If it would be reasonable to consider recommending a financial product,
   i. conduct a reasonable investigation into the financial products that might achieve the objectives and meet the needs of the client that would reasonably be considered relevant to advice on the subject matter; and
   ii. assess the information gathered in the investigation.

(f) Base all judgements on the client's relevant circumstances.

(g) Take any other step that, at the time the advice is provided, would reasonably be regarded as being in the best interests of the client, given the client's relevant circumstances.

Source: ASIC 2017a.

The provisions of the safe harbour rules are expanded upon below.

The client's circumstances disclosed through instructions

This requires an advice provider to determine what the client's objectives, financial situation and needs are (i.e. the client's circumstances), based on the information that has been disclosed. The adviser should use the client needs analysis to identify, set and prioritise, specific and measurable goals and objectives with the client based on their circumstances and information. The planner is also required to ascertain relevant client circumstances for any financial product advice.

Advice providers may need to exercise their judgement in determining what the client's objectives, financial situation and needs are from the instructions given by the client. Many clients do not know or fully understand what their objectives, financial situation or needs are. Clients may also provide instructions that are unclear or seem inconsistent with their circumstances.

It is important that the planner clearly documents their client's circumstances in the SOA in order to demonstrate that the adviser has understood the client's financial situation and that the information is accurate.

The subject matter of the advice sought by the client

This requires the advice provider to identify the subject matter of the advice sought by the client.

Determining the subject matter of the advice should not be limited to what the client advises the planner of what they want and need. The subject matter of advice sought by a client may be explicit from the client's request for advice or implicit from the client's financial situation. For example, the client may seek advice on an inheritance they have received, but also have considerable debt. Even though the client may seek investment advice, it would be implicit that the client should also be provided with advice about managing and repaying their debt.

RG 175.291 sets out a range of factors that may assist the adviser to identify the particular subject matter of the advice sought such as:

- what the client's instructions are
- why the client is seeking financial advice
- the outcomes the client wants to achieve if they follow the advice (i.e. their goal in seeking advice)
- how much the client is willing to pay for the advice, if this amount is reasonable. Clients will not always understand how much it costs to provide advice on the subject matter they are seeking.

As part of the process of identifying the subject matter, the adviser should assist the client to develop objectives that are specific and measurable and consider whether the client may have other needs besides what they have stated. If two or more of the client's objectives conflict, discuss these with the client and assist them with prioritising the more urgent of these or assist them with reaching a compromise.

Scoping of the advice

It is essential that the client and adviser agree upon exactly what areas the advice is intended to address. This requires the adviser to not only state what the advice does address but also what the advice does not cover. An advice provider can determine the **scope of the advice** only after identifying the subject matter of the advice sought by the client (RG 175.282).

Either an adviser or the client may suggest limiting or scoping the subject matter of advice sought by the client. In some situations, the client might prefer to receive more targeted advice on a matter that is particularly concerning them rather than comprehensive advice. This might arise where the client seeks to limit the cost of the advice being sought. As long as the adviser acts ethically and in the client's best interest in this process, the adviser will not be in breach of their duty. In other circumstances, the adviser initiates scoping the advice because they do not have the skill or expertise to provide advice in a particular strategy, or the client seeks advice on a particular financial product that is not on the advisers' approved product list (APL).

When scoping advice for whatever reason, it is important that the client understands the nature of the advice that is going to be and not going to be provided. This must also be documented very clearly in the client's SOA. The adviser is required to use their ethical obligations and professional judgement to determine if the scope of the advice the client is seeking is in their best interest.

Identifying the client's relevant circumstances

Once the scope of advice is starting to take shape it is expected that an ethical and competent financial adviser is required to make reasonable enquiries to obtain complete and accurate information about their client's *relevant* circumstances. A client initially offers information regarding their circumstances, such as their objectives, financial situation and needs. However, it is the adviser who is required to extend this and seek further information from the client that as a professional they believe may be relevant to the scope of advice.

If it is reasonably apparent that information about a client's relevant circumstances is incomplete or inaccurate, an adviser must make reasonable enquiries to obtain complete and accurate information.

Where advice relates to financial products with an investment component, the adviser should examine the client's relevant circumstances to determine the needs and requirements of the client, including the need for income versus capital growth, the importance of fees, the risk profile of the client, their time horizon, the investment portfolio and the debt position of the client. (RG 175.309)

Assessing the expertise of the advice provider

After assessing the financial needs and requirements of the client, the adviser may conclude that they do not have the necessary authorisation, qualification and expertise to advise on specific subject matter. In this case, the adviser must refrain from providing any advice on that subject matter and it must be scoped out of the adviser's advice.

The adviser may refer the client to an adviser who does have the authorisation, qualification and expertise to provide the advice (RG 175.319).

Recommending financial products

Whenever advice is provided in respect of a financial product, it is important that the adviser conduct a reasonable investigation into the recommended financial products that would be considered relevant to the subject matter of the advice. While advisers may rely on financial products recommended by their licensee, or on research conducted by research providers, it is important to note that the financial adviser remains responsible to the client for the advice that they give. One way an adviser can conduct a reasonable investigation into financial products is by benchmarking the product against the market for similar products to establish its competitiveness on factors such as:

- performance history over an appropriate period
- features
- fees
- risk.

If the adviser is recommending that the client change products, also referred to as 'switching advice', it will be important to provide clients with sufficient information to enable them to adequately assess the recommended product against their current product. Section 947D of the Act requires the adviser to disclose costs and any benefits lost as a result of the switch from their existing product to the recommended product.

RG 175.340 provides a scenario to illustrate the requirement to examine not just the recommended product(s) but also the client's existing product(s).

PROFESSIONAL ADVICE

Scenario

An advice provider is considering recommending that their client redirect their superannuation contributions to a self-managed superannuation fund (SMSF) that the advice provider will help the client set up.

Commentary

In conducting a reasonable investigation for the purposes of section 961B(2)(e)(i), the advice provider would need to investigate both the existing superannuation fund and the SMSF.

Source: ASIC 2017a, example 16.

Many licensees restrict the range of products that their financial advisers are able to provide advice on through an APL. APLs are used to assist advisers to meet their legal obligations when providing financial product advice.

Often a financial adviser will be able to conduct a reasonable investigation into the financial products they intend to recommend to their clients as the products are listed on their licensee's APL. It is important to note that, if the adviser is looking to recommend a financial product that is not on their APL, they must ensure that they have the appropriate authorisations and approvals from their licensee. If the adviser finds that they are unable to provide advice on a financial product that is not listed on their APL, they are required to scope out any advice in respect of the financial product.

In other cases, an adviser may also be required to conduct reasonable investigations into financial products not on the APL because either the client's existing product could already be well suited for the client needs but isn't on the APL, or the client has requested the adviser to consider a specific product not on the APL.

An adviser must use their ethics and judgement to decide what is the right course of action in conducting reasonable investigations particularly when there is a need to divert from the APL (RG 175.349).

2. Ensuring your advice is appropriate for your client

Advice must only be provided if it would be reasonable to conclude that the advice is appropriate to the client. ASIC's key measure of appropriate advice is whether it would be reasonable to conclude, at the time the advice is provided, that:

(a) it is fit for its purpose — that is the advice is likely to satisfy the client's relevant needs and objectives

(b) the client is likely to be in a better position if they follow the advice.

The definition of what is a better position is not restricted to a financial gain after implementing the advice. There are a few examples in RG175.251 of what ASIC considers to be advice that put the client in a better position. It could be reducing the level of risk in their portfolio or implementing insurance that covers their personal risk. It could even be to give the client reassurance that they do not need to change anything in their current investments and strategies they have implemented themselves.

To meet their ethical and professional requirements, an adviser must make recommendations based on the premise that it is in the client's best interest. This means that an adviser's recommendations will not be based on a recommended financial products' projected returns.

3. Advice warning

It is important that the financial adviser uses their professional judgement when determining whether the client has provided all relevant information needed to enable the adviser to provide advice that is in the best interests of the client. If the adviser is of the opinion that the client has provided inaccurate or incomplete information, they are required to warn the client that the advice may not be appropriate to meet the needs and objectives of the client.

It is important to note that RG175.389 stipulates that this warning does not relieve the adviser from the obligation to make reasonable inquires if they do suspect the client is withholding or unable to provide relevant information.

An adviser may need to work more closely with the client to investigate and gather the information required. It would be unethical and unprofessional to superficially ask questions that the client is unlikely to have answers for, and then not offer assistance to the client to attain that information. The inaccurate or incomplete information warning cannot be used to relieve the adviser of this duty (RG 175.389).

4. Prioritise your client's interests

An adviser must prioritise the interests of the client if they know, or reasonably ought to know when they give the advice, that there is a conflict between the interests of the client and their own interests or the interests of their licensee or other associated parties.

The requirement to prioritise the client's interest relates to identifying and managing any conflicts the adviser and related parties may have in relation to the advice that is provided to the client.

Giving priority to a client's interests is where the adviser refrains from recommending a product on the basis that it provides revenue for the adviser or a related party but a benefit for the client cannot be proven. An adviser must be ethical and, if the client's circumstances only require a new strategy that does not involve a financial product then the adviser must avoid manipulating the clients circumstances to support a financial product recommendation and keep recommendation to strategies only.

An adviser must also refrain from over complicating recommendations if the purpose is to ensure that the client needs to pay the adviser for ongoing assistance in managing the complexities. Of course, an adviser must be compensated or remunerated for their time, knowledge, skill and expertise, but this payment should not depend on a financial product recommendation or an over-complicated strategy.

An adviser must use their ethical and professional judgement in determining if they can honestly put the client's interest first. If they cannot put the client's interest first, for whatever reason (e.g. they do not have a suitable product to recommend the client), the adviser must decline to provide the advice.

RG 176.402 provides an example of a remuneration conflict.

PROFESSIONAL ADVICE

Scenario

An advice provider is providing a client with a review of their life insurance policy, which currently sets a death benefit of $300 000. The advice provider advises the client that they require additional cover of $100 000. The advice provider recommends that the client obtain a new policy for $400 000 and then ▶

cancel the existing policy, rather than apply for additional cover within the existing policy. The terms of the life insurance policies and the annual premiums are the same. The advice entitles the advice provider to a commission of 120% of the annual premium of the whole insured amount (i.e. $400 000), rather than just the increased amount (i.e. $100 000). The client follows the advice. As a result, they need to have medical checks, which they would not have needed if their level of cover was increased. The client was nearing the 4-year anniversary of their existing policy. If they had continued to hold their existing policy and increased their level of coverage, they would have been entitled to a 5% increase in the level of cover at no extra cost.

Commentary

In this situation, we consider that section 961J has been breached. The advice provider has given priority to maximising the non-client source of remuneration over the interests of the client.

Source: ASIC 2017a, example 21.

PROFESSIONAL ADVICE

A client approaching retirement meets with an advice provider (financial planner) to seek advice on what to do with their superannuation when they retire. They have been told that SMSFs are an easy way to maximise the value of their superannuation. The client has a healthy superannuation balance because they have been contributing to their superannuation for the past 35 years. They have no experience with investing.

The client's existing employer-sponsored superannuation fund has no pension option. The client understands that they need to start making some decisions about their superannuation but, because they have no previous investment experience, they are nervous about this process. They want a simple, cost-effective solution that they can easily understand and does not require too much of their time. They are looking forward to retirement and do not want the burden of watching the market every day, as they have seen some of their colleagues do.

The advice provider recommends an SMSF and reassures the client that they do not need to be too involved because the advice provider will look after it for them.

Source: ASIC 2017a, example 22.

....

QUESTIONS

1. What factors might account for why the financial planner might have recommended the establishment of an SMSF for the client?
2. There has been a significant growth rate in the establishment of SMSFs over the past decade. What are some of the reasons that might explain this growth?
3. Is the advice likely to be in the best interests of the client?

12.4 When is an SOA required and what is its purpose?

LEARNING OBJECTIVE 12.4 Explain when a statement of advice is required and its purpose.

Part 7.7 of the Act sets out the financial service disclosure requirements in respect of the provision of financial services or advice. Included within these provisions is a requirement that, when providing advice to a client, a financial planner must provide the client with an SOA at the same time as, or as soon as practicable after, the advice is provided (s. 946A) (see also RG 175.163).

The purpose of an SOA is to communicate advice and recommendations concerning the financial affairs of a client. To be effective, an SOA must disclose sufficient information to enable a person to make an informed decision about whether the advice is appropriate to their situation and whether they should act upon the advice.

There has been ongoing concern within the financial planning profession about the appropriate length of an SOA and the amount of detail that needs to be provided within the document given the detailed regulatory disclosure requirements. There is no set rule that governs the appropriate length of an SOA. The level of detail provided is important in determining whether the financial plan is likely to be of value in helping the client to make informed decisions concerning their financial situation. In determining the suitability of an SOA, what is important is the extent to which the plan is tailored to the needs of the client while taking into account the client's level of financial literacy and the complexity of the advice provided.

12.5 When is an SOA not required?

LEARNING OBJECTIVE 12.5 Explain the circumstances under which a statement of advice is not required.

Although an SOA is generally required whenever personal advice is provided to a client, the Act provides for a limited number of situations where an SOA does not need to be provided (see RG 175.166 (ASIC 2017a)). They are:
- when the client is not a retail client
- where the advice relates to a general insurance product, a cash management trust, basic deposit products, non-cash payment products related to a basic deposit product or traveller's cheques
- when providing further advice to a client
- when providing personal advice to clients having a small amount of funds to invest (less than $15 000)
- where the advice does not involve the purchase of a financial product and where the entity providing the advice does not receive any remuneration.

The obligations relating to the provision of further advice

In situations where a client is provided with further advice, RG 175.170 and section 946B of the Act sets out the circumstances where an SOA may not need to be provided. The circumstances prescribed include:
- the client had previously been given an SOA by the adviser setting out the client's personal circumstances in relation to the advice
- the client's personal circumstances in relation to the further advice have not significantly changed
- the basis of the advice is not significantly different from the advice in the previous SOA.
  In these circumstances, the planner may provide the client with a **record of advice (ROA)** instead of an SOA. The ROA must be given to the client when the advice is provided or as soon as practicable after the advice is given. The ROA must include as a minimum:
- a brief description of the recommendations made and the basis on which the recommendations are made
- information on the extent of any benefits lost, any charges made and any other significant consequence for the client, if the advice includes a recommendation that the client replace one financial product with another
- information about the remuneration the adviser will receive and details concerning any conflicts of interest.
  In situations where an adviser provides further advice to a client, there is no prescriptive format for the ROA. Although the ROA may simply be a record in the client's file in the form of a summary and bullet points, a written advice statement may be more practical and reliable in demonstrating that the adviser has discharged their responsibilities.

ILLUSTRATIVE EXAMPLE 12.2

As Cory and Amy are looking to save costs in respect of the financial planning advice they are seeking, and wish to limit the advice to a two-page letter, would the financial planner be able to provide the clients with an ROA instead of an SOA?

An ROA can be provided only in circumstances where the advice is provided to an existing client and where the client had previously been given an SOA setting out their personal circumstances. As Cory and Amy are new clients, an SOA would need to be prepared in accordance with all the regulatory requirements regardless of the wishes of the client. The client should be aware that the disclosure requirements are designed to protect their interests and the planner is not permitted to disregard their legal obligations.

12.6 Types of SOAs

LEARNING OBJECTIVE 12.6 Outline the main types of statement of advice documents used in the marketplace.

Financial planning advice can generally be classified into three main types.

- *Issue specific or scaled advice.* This addresses particular aspects of a client's personal finances, for example, the most effective way to make personal super contributions.
- *Comprehensive or holistic financial advice.* This is about developing a comprehensive financial plan to help meet a client's overall financial needs and goals. It would generally cover issues including investing, taxation, personal risk insurance, superannuation and retirement planning, estate planning and social security.
- *Ongoing advice.* This is advice provided to a client on an ongoing basis to ensure that financial strategies remain in line with the client's objectives, or new strategies are developed to meet changing circumstances or to take advantage as new opportunities arise.

Through RG 244 *Giving information, general advice and scaled advice* and the updates to RG 175, ASIC has allowed for scaled advice to be given, provided certain requirements are met to encourage access to affordable advice. Scaled advice is personal advice that is limited in scope, either by being in response to a limited range of issues or by addressing specific areas of the investor's needs. While the best interest duty requirements of the adviser are the same as for comprehensive advice, the adviser should make their intention to scale clear to their client and act accordingly.

Scaled advice is often sought and requested by clients seeking financial advice on a particular issue or specific circumstance, for example, an investigation into negative gearing strategies, the investment of an inheritance or the effectiveness of a salary packaging arrangement (see appendix 12D). ASIC has stated that all advice is scaled in some way and has suggested that the appropriate way to look at personal advice is to see it as positioned on a spectrum, with one side being fully comprehensive in nature and the other scaled to a very specific area.

It is important to note that the same rules, including the best interest duty and related obligations, apply to all personal advice on a particular topic, regardless of the scope of the advice.

In certain circumstances, the financial planner may be asked to execute a particular transaction, but not to provide any advice. An example is where the planner is asked to transfer a client's superannuation balance from one fund to another. It is prudent in such circumstances for the planner to ask the client to sign a **no-advice statement** — this is in the form of a disclaimer document where the client confirms that they have not sought financial advice. This is important in order to protect the planner against future claims that state the client acted upon the advice of the planner (see appendix 12A).

A comprehensive SOA considers all aspects of the client's personal circumstances and situation. It is also known as holistic advice. The planner needs to complete a thorough fact finder, analyse all aspects of the client's circumstances and produce a comprehensive set of integrated solutions that helps to achieve all of the client's goals, needs and objectives.

PERSONAL FINANCE BULLETIN

Testing the boundaries: industry funds and advice

Superannuation funds ought to be the box seat when it comes to delivering affordable financial advice to the masses. Yet most funds still only provide financial advice to a small fraction of their members, possibly because not all funds equally value the benefits of advice, or perhaps because they're simply not adequately resourced to deliver it at scale.

Some of our recent research suggests there may be other dimensions to the advice challenge facing super funds, namely, meeting the advice-scope expectations of members themselves, and the apparent indifference of those members to whether or not the individual they get advice from is employed by their super fund.

CoreData's Q1 2020 Trust Research shows that almost six in 10 (57.2%) people expect a fund's financial adviser to be allowed to give them advice on more than just superannuation, whether they actually needed that broader advice or not.

And more than half (53.3%) of them would be more likely to seek advice from another adviser if their super fund's adviser were permitted only to give advice on superannuation, not on broader financial planning issues.

Almost six in 10 (58.1%) people expect a fund's adviser to be allowed to recommend an alternative superannuation fund to them, if the adviser considers the alternative fund to be better suited to the member.

For various reasons, the specific issues — advice extending beyond super, and recommending alternative super funds — isn't a feature of all super funds' advice offerings.

Funds themselves have created a variety of advice solutions, including developing in-house teams, setting up referral arrangements with carefully selected panels of advisers, and proactively working to engage with the general financial planning industry.

Whether an adviser is employed by a superannuation fund or not seems to make little difference to the member: about a quarter (24.6%) say they would trust an adviser somewhat or significantly more if the adviser were employed by the fund, and a similar proportion (25.6%) say they'd trust the adviser somewhat or significantly less.

For around four in 10 members (40.6%) the employment status of the adviser makes no difference; and around one in 10 (9.2%) members say they don't know if they'd trust the adviser more or less.

This raises an issue for industry funds who may have traditionally been reluctant to expose members to the broader financial advice industry for fear of potentially losing members to competitor funds (often retail funds) recommended by those advisers. CoreData's findings suggest that fund members are not likely to trust a fund's in-house advisers more than external advisers.

Trust in advice in general remains a barrier to its greater take-up by the Australian community generally — our research shows trust in advice stands at 38%*, down from 42.4% in Q4 2019, but broadly consistent with how it's tracked ever since the royal commission.

And a referral by a fund to an adviser likewise makes little difference to the member's level of trust in the adviser: most (47.4%) say they'd neither trust the adviser more or less if they were referred to the adviser by their fund; around one in five (21.5%) say they'd trust the adviser more as a result of a referral; and a similar proportion (20.1%) say they'd trust the adviser less. One in 10 (10.9%) say they don't know how their trust in the adviser would be affected.

This paints a bit of a picture about the sort of advice — and the sort of adviser — superannuation fund members might expect to encounter when or if they seek advice from their fund. It appears from these initial results that fund members don't care too much who gives them the advice — whether it's an employed adviser or it's an adviser they're referred to — nearly as much as they care about the scope of advice they can get from whichever adviser they see.

And it illustrates the challenges for super funds to develop a workable advice proposition. Current intrafund advice rules restrict the scope of advice that funds can provide to members, apparently contrary to the scope of advice members say they want.

Spending time, money and effort creating a full-service in-house advice capability might not have any meaningful impact on member advice take-up, because the level of trust in the in-house adviser is likely to be no greater than the level of trust in an external adviser to whom the member may be referred.

There remains little question, however, that financial advice is a potentially enormously valuable service for super fund members. Research by CoreData has shown on numerous occasions that receiving good financial advice leads to measurable financial and non-financial benefits for the recipient.

For many Australians superannuation is the most significant financial asset they will ever own, not counting their family home. Their superannuation fund remains well placed to be the provider of advice to help them make the most not only of their superannuation but also non-superannuation financial assets.

A number of submissions to the government's Retirement Income Review have backed the idea of allowing advice to be paid for from MySuper accounts. But even before the question of how to pay for advice in superannuation is settled, it would seem to be a fine idea to make sure the advice offer available to members is relevant and attractive to them in the first place.

* Simon Hoyle is head of market insights for CoreData Group. Hoyle was previously editor of Professional Planner magazine.

Source: Hoyle 2020.

12.7 The importance of effective communication in an SOA

LEARNING OBJECTIVE 12.7 Appreciate the importance of effective communication in a statement of advice.

An SOA should provide details on recommended strategies and products, and projected outcomes to demonstrate how these are intended to achieve the client's stated objectives. Most importantly, the details must cover the benefits and the risks so clients can make an informed decision.

To ensure that the client fully understands the advice, it is important that the SOA is written in plain English and prepared with the client's level of financial literacy in mind. In this way, the adviser helps to ensure that the client 'owns' the plan and commits to its implementation.

Where a client's level of financial literacy and understanding is low, information needs to be presented in such a way as could reasonably be understood from a layperson's point of view. For clients who have more experience or a higher level of financial literacy, the level of detail and form of explanation may be expanded upon. The adviser needs to carefully balance the need for illustrating the technical aspects of the strategy against the need for the client to understand what is being recommended. The adviser needs to be ethical in deciding what is pertinent information for the client and provide that information in a manner that is at the client's level of financial literacy.

RG 168 *Disclosure: Product Disclosure Statements (and other disclosure obligations)* contains ASIC's **Good Disclosure Principles** to help product issuers and financial planners comply with the disclosure requirements and also promote good disclosure outcomes for consumers (ASIC 2011). According to the Good Disclosure Principles (RG 168.4), disclosure should:

(a) be timely
(b) be relevant and complete
(c) promote product understanding
(d) promote product comparison
(e) highlight important information
(f) have regard to consumers' needs.

12.8 The importance of the planner–client relationship

LEARNING OBJECTIVE 12.8 Understand the importance of the planner–client relationship.

Having excellent technical knowledge and a comprehensive knowledge of financial products will not be sufficient in fostering an effective working relationship between the client and the financial planner. Many clients face difficulty opening up and confiding personal information to a planner, who they may suspect is looking out for their own interests. It is important that, in gathering client information, a financial planner complies with the *Privacy Act 1988* and explains to the client the personal information that is going to be requested from them and the reason why the financial planner is requesting it.

Communication is a critical aspect in both establishing and maintaining effective client relationships. A planner needs to exhibit excellent communication skills in order to develop a thorough understanding and appreciation of the client's personal, financial and emotional situation. In addition, an effective planner also needs to exhibit competence in communicating strategies and concepts in terms that are understood by the client and in a way that encourages the client to appreciate the importance of acting upon the advice.

Jaffe & Grubman (2011, p. 1) argue that 'the most effective and successful advisers in the industry are ones who can truly listen, build trust, interview effectively, make the client feel understood, and manage the delicate issues money can evoke'.

A significant body of research has looked into some of the more important factors that determine an effective client–professional relationship. The financial planning discipline is no different to other professions, with the key attributes being the ability to communicate well and the ability to develop trust. A report by Wharton University entitled *Bridging the Trust Divide: The Financial Advisor–Client Relationship* found that three types of trust are important (Wharton University of Pennsylvania 2007).

- *Trust in technical competence and knowhow* — investors are primarily looking for someone whose level of competence and experience inspires trust.
- *Trust in ethical conduct and character* — does the client associate with the personal character and ethics of the planner and do these attributes instill trust that the planner will look after the client's best interests?
- *Trust in empathic skills and maturity* — does the client have trust in the adviser to handle personal issues and sensitive information with empathy and tact?

Obligations at the initial client meeting

Prior to engaging the services of a financial planner, an introductory meeting between the financial planner and the client is normally arranged and serves a number of purposes such as to:

- establish the relationship between the planner and the client
- provide the planner with an opportunity to learn about the client, the client's circumstances and needs, and to determine what the client is hoping to accomplish from the relationship

- provide the client with an opportunity to learn about the planner, the services they offer and whether the planner is likely to be able to satisfy the client's requirements.

The initial meeting or interview provides the means by which a financial planner and client are able to ascertain the extent to which they have the confidence and trust to work constructively together. If, for any reason, either party does not feel comfortable with the relationship they should not continue.

The meeting allows the client to learn about the planner and their practice, the services the planner offers and how the client will be charged for the services provided. The client is likely to ask questions that will allow them to judge the ability of the planner to appropriately manage their finances and to act in their best interests. The initial meeting also provides an opportunity for the planner to learn about the client, their goals and concerns, their plans for the future and their personality. At the first meeting, the planner would normally provide the client with a copy of their FSG, run through the main provisions of the document and give the client an opportunity to ask questions and seek clarification on any issues.

Once the client and planner have agreed to commence the financial planning process and work towards the preparation of an SOA, a planner may decide to issue an engagement letter setting out the parameters of the engagement.

One of the important disclosure obligations imposed on the planner is to provide the client with a financial services guide (FSG). A financial planner is required to provide a client with an FSG at the earliest possible opportunity, before any advice is provided or recommendations made. To provide evidence that the client has been provided with an FSG, many planners will ask the client to sign a written acknowledgement or statement that they have received a copy of the planner's FSG.

Another obligation imposed on the planner relates to the *Anti-Money Laundering and Counter-Terrorism Financing Act 2006* (AML/CTF Act), which imposes ongoing transaction and compliance reporting obligations on the planner as part of the process of preventing and detecting money laundering and terrorism financing activities. These obligations relate to customer identification and identity verification, record keeping, and ongoing client due diligence and reporting.

A planner should not provide a client with financial advice until they are able to personally identify and verify the identity of the client. This will require the planner to verify and keep on the client's file documentation relating to the client's identification, such as a driver's licence or passport. As the planner works with the client and gathers information from the client it may be that the planner detects some suspicious activity or situation.

AUSTRAC regulates the AML/CTF Act and has produced a one-page reference guide for financial planners showing some of the indicators (or 'red flags') in a client's circumstances that the planner must look into. If necessary, a suspicious matter report (SMR) must be lodged with AUSTRAC. Some of the important indicators are shown in figure 12.3.

12.9 The 6 steps of the financial planning process

LEARNING OBJECTIVE 12.9 Explain the 6-step financial planning process used to prepare a statement of advice.

In preparing an SOA for a client, a financial planner will normally follow a structured process to help understand the needs and requirements of the client and facilitate the design and implementation of appropriate strategies. While the process should be carried out in a logical sequence and will be similar for most clients, the depth and flexibility of the process will vary depending on the complexity and needs of the client.

The Financial Advice Association Australia (FAAA) generally recommends a 6-step financial planning process; however, other formats and processes may be equally relevant and appropriate in compiling a client-specific SOA. The 6-step process is discussed in detail next and is summarised in figure 12.4.

Step 1. Gather client information

Client information is normally gathered in a data-collection questionnaire (also referred to as a fact finder) and forms the basis for the preparation of the SOA (see appendix 12B). Completing a data-collection questionnaire is provides evidence that a financial planner has made reasonable enquiries into the personal circumstances of the client (RG 175.302–305) and satisfied the 'best interests' duty imposed under section 961B of the Act.

FIGURE 12.3 Financial crime red flags — a guide for financial planners

	Crime type:	Red flag:
1. Client/planner relationship established	• Money laundering/tax evasion • Money laundering/tax evasion • Money laundering • Tax evasion	• Customer enquires whether planner accepts large cash deposits • Customer requests advice on overly complex company/trust structures that go beyond their financial needs • Customer is reluctant to provide identification or behaves nervously • Customer requests advice on how to evade tax
2. Client information is collected, analysed and evaluated	• Fraud • Money laundering/tax evasion • Money laundering • Money laundering • Welfare fraud • Tax evasion • Tax evasion • Terrorism financing	• Customer documents not expected formats, appear altered or inconsistent (e.g. date of birth) • Customer has unexplained wealth inconsistent with economic situation • Customer requests unusual/uneconomic investments • Customer uses company/trust structures with unclear beneficial owners • Customer reveals they are misleading Centrelink for welfare benefits • Customer has suspicious property ownership arrangements • Customer has money in, or corporate entities based in, tax havens • Customer's name appears on the Department of Foreign Affairs & Trade's list of sanctioned persons ("Consolidated List")
3. Financial planner provides advice	• Fraud • Money laundering • Money laundering/Fraud	• Customer asks how to make an insurance claim before an insurable event takes place • Customer receives advice but chooses to implement the advice without the planner • Customer asks to establish a self-managed super fund (SMSF) without being able to show source of funds/ ownership for the initial transfer
4. Financial planner arranges products	• Fraud • Money laundering	• The members or trustees of an SMSF change several times over a short period of time • Funds from several sources are consolidated into customer's account
5. Financial planner reviews or makes variations to portfolio	• Cyber-enabled fraud • Cyber-enabled fraud • Cyber-enabled fraud • Money laundering/tax evasion • Money laundering	• Product issuer receives email instructions from a financial planner however it appears financial planner's email has been compromised • Customer changes bank details by email or online soon after changing contact details • Email request from customer expresses urgency • Customer makes structured or large cash deposits into their bank account to facilitate investments • Customer requests radical change to financial strategy
6. Withdrawal/ closure	• Money laundering • Cyber-enabled fraud • Terrorism financing • Fraud	• Customer quickly withdraws funds soon after making initial investment • Planner receives withdrawal request from customer by email, but customer usually makes contact via telephone • Customer requests funds transfer to a conflict zone, or country neighbouring a conflict zone • Planner receives request for funds to be sent to a third party overseas

Source: AUSTRAC 2019.

It is important for the client to be made aware that the planner is unable to provide appropriate advice unless the client provides accurate and complete information concerning their personal and financial circumstances. Some clients may not wish to disclose certain information about their circumstances. If withheld information is pertinent to the subject matter of the advice being sought, under section 961H the adviser must warn the client that the advice is based on inaccurate and incomplete information. In this case, the client is responsible for considering the appropriateness of advice.

Throughout the data-gathering stage, the financial planner needs to look beyond the quantitative information provided by the client and ensure that qualitative issues are also considered. This is where relationship building skills of the planner come into play. Some of the qualitative issues that the planner may be interested in exploring may include the client's financial and non-financial objectives, concerns, health, degree of financial literacy, and any preconceptions or investment behaviour biases the client may have.

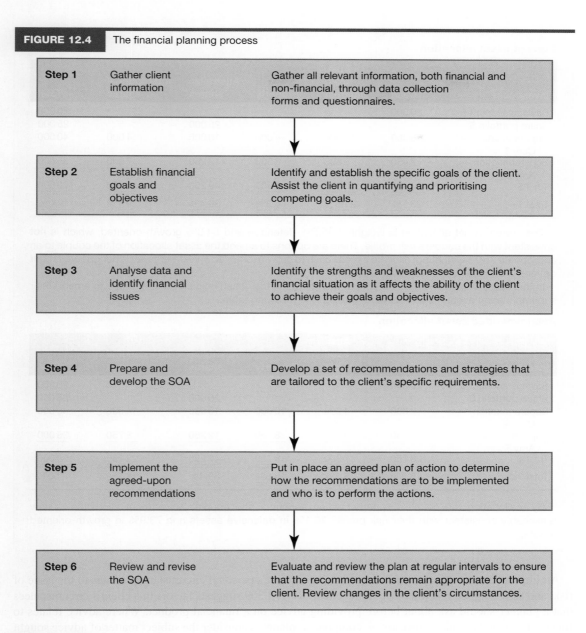

FIGURE 12.4 The financial planning process

Step 1	Gather client information	Gather all relevant information, both financial and non-financial, through data collection forms and questionnaires.
Step 2	Establish financial goals and objectives	Identify and establish the specific goals of the client. Assist the client in quantifying and prioritising competing goals.
Step 3	Analyse data and identify financial issues	Identify the strengths and weaknesses of the client's financial situation as it affects the ability of the client to achieve their goals and objectives.
Step 4	Prepare and develop the SOA	Develop a set of recommendations and strategies that are tailored to the client's specific requirements.
Step 5	Implement the agreed-upon recommendations	Put in place an agreed plan of action to determine how the recommendations are to be implemented and who is to perform the actions.
Step 6	Review and revise the SOA	Evaluate and review the plan at regular intervals to ensure that the recommendations remain appropriate for the client. Review changes in the client's circumstances.

Risk profiling

At this stage, the planner normally assesses the client's risk profile as well. Risk profiling is also an integral part of the safe harbour step to identify relevant client's circumstances (s. 961B(2)). Once the client's risk profile is identified, this can be used to guide the proposed asset allocation. The asset allocation is usually investment assets including superannuation but excludes personal and lifestyle assets.

ILLUSTRATIVE EXAMPLE 12.3

You have assessed the risk profile of Cory and Amy and have determined them as moderately aggressive, with a recommended investment allocation weighted 75% to growth-oriented investments (shares and property) and 25% to defensive investments (cash and fixed interest).

From the information provided, prepare both a current and recommended asset allocation.

▶

Current asset allocation

Investment	Cash	Aust. fixed interest	Property	Australian shares	International shares	Total
Savings account $	20 000					20 000
Share portfolio $				25 000		25 000
Superannuation — Cory $	6 000	16 000	4 000	10 000	4 000	40 000
Superannuation — Amy $	2 450	9 800	3 500	12 250	7 000	35 000
Total $	28 450	25 800	7 500	49 250	11 000	120 000
Total %	23.7%	21.5%	6.3%	39.4%	9.1%	100%

The current asset allocation is weighted 45.2% defensive and 54.8% growth-oriented, which is not consistent with the couple's risk profile. There are options to amend the asset allocation of the couple to an appropriate 25/75 weighting; allocate excess cash to growth-oriented investments and change investment options within their superannuation accounts.

In this case, we assume that the couple wish to retain their cash holding but are happy to amend their superannuation accounts as illustrated through the following table.

Recommended asset allocation

Investment	Cash	Aust. fixed interest	Property	Australian shares	International shares	Total
Savings account $	20 000					20 000
Share portfolio $				25 000		25 000
Superannuation — Cory $	2 000	4 000	10 000	10 000	14 000	40 000
Superannuation — Amy $	1 750	3 500	8 750	12 250	8 750	35 000
Total $	23 750	7 500	18 750	47 250	22 750	120 000
Total %	19.8%	6.3%	15.6%	39.4%	18.9%	100%

By reallocating the couple's superannuation accounts, the couple's investment allocation is now reasonably consistent with their risk profile; 26.1% in defensive assets and 73.9% in growth-oriented assets.

An important consideration when investigating a client's personal circumstances relates to the issue of risk, and assessing the risk tolerance of the client. RG175.309 suggests factors in a client's circumstances that a planner should ask about before providing advice on a financial product. Where advice relates to financial product(s) with an investment component, planners consider the subject matter of advice sought by the client and the relevant circumstances which may include the client's:

(a) need for regular income (e.g. retirement income);
(b) need for capital growth;
(c) desire to minimise fees and costs;
(d) tolerance for the risk of capital loss, especially where this is a significant possibility if the advice is followed;
(e) tolerance for the risk that the advice (if followed) will not produce the expected benefits. For example, in the context of retirement advice, this may include considering longevity risk, market risk and inflation risk;
(f) existing investment portfolio;
(g) existing debts;
(h) investment horizon;
(i) need to be able to readily 'cash in' the investment;
(j) capacity to service any loan used to acquire a financial product, including the client's ability to respond to any margin call or make good any losses sustained while investing in leveraged products; and
(k) tax position, social security entitlements, family commitments, employment security and expected retirement age.

Note: This is not an exhaustive list.

Reconciling a client's risk profile is not always an easy and straightforward process, especially where each individual in a couple have differing tolerances to risk. In the end, it is up to the clients to decide what risk they are prepared to accept and feel comfortable with. In illustrative example 12.3, it is possible that Cory increases the level of growth-oriented assets within his superannuation account and Amy does not change her superannuation asset allocation at all. The planner can play an important role in educating the client about the significance of a risk profile and the interrelationship between this and potential investment returns to achieve financial objectives. For example, a client should be made aware that a conservative risk profile is unlikely to help them retire at age 65 and fund their desired retirement lifestyle. Likewise, if a client is taking unnecessary risks in their portfolio, the planner may recommend to reduce that risk without it impacting their goal of reaching their financial objectives.

While an assessment of the client's risk profile is an integral part of the financial planning process, there is no generally accepted view within the industry on how it should be assessed or applied in formulating appropriate advice for a client. Many advisers use some form of risk profiling questionnaire and an example is provided in appendix 12C. Under this approach, a series of questions is drawn up for the client to answer. The answers the client provides are used to indicate the level of risk that a client can tolerate and, leading on from this, what would be an appropriate asset allocation. An alternative approach is a psychological assessment, which attempts to uncover a client's psychological response to risk and decision making. Whatever methodology is used to determine the risk profile of a client, the planner will need to ensure that the tool used is valid, thorough and justifiable. In addition to this formal assessment, a planner must also pay attention to what the client is saying in general conversation to get a holistic view of the client's risk profile. It is all well and good that a client answers risk profiling questions but there are other factors in a client's circumstances that impact the appropriate asset allocation for them.

Despite each person possessing different goals and differing abilities to cope with risk, it is generally accepted that investors can usually be grouped into a number of core risk profiles. Table 12.1 provides an illustration of how an asset allocation can be determined based on the various risk classifications.

TABLE 12.1   **Examples of asset allocations for different risk and return profiles**

	Capital stable	Conservative	Balanced	Growth	High growth
Cash	25%	15%	10%	5%	5%
Fixed interest	50%	45%	30%	25%	15%
Property	5%	10%	10%	10%	10%
Australian shares	15%	20%	30%	35%	40%
International shares	5%	10%	20%	25%	30%
Overall asset allocation (growth/defensive)	25/75	40/60	60/40	70/30	80/20
Investment term	2 years	3 years	5 years	7 years	7+ years

Step 2. Establish financial goals and objectives

During this stage, the planner's role is to help the client define and prioritise their personal and financial objectives. Each client will have different goals, objectives and time frames and it is up to the financial planner to determine the extent to which the client's objectives are achievable, realistic or optimistic.

ILLUSTRATIVE EXAMPLE 12.4

Cory and Amy are looking to acquire a family home in 6 months for a cost of around $650 000. Is this objective and expectation realistic? How might a planner deal with this?

Part of the financial planner's role is to educate the client on expectations and order of priorities. The financial commitments required in owning a property would need to be discussed with the client as well as their ability to fund an appropriate deposit on the purchase and repay mortgage repayments. Issues that the planner should cover with the client might include the following.

▶

As clients have different objectives, each financial plan needs to be tailored to fit the individual circumstances of the client. The planner's role is to help clients develop and clarify their objectives in terms of whether they are short-term (e.g. taking a holiday, paying off credit cards), medium-term (e.g. saving a deposit for a car or a home) or long-term (e.g. estate or retirement planning).

Client objectives need to be clear, specific and measurable. An effective objective statement should contain a well-defined target that is expressed in a time frame that is achievable and details how the objective is to be funded. For example, the client is seeking to accumulate $60 000 in savings towards putting a deposit on a house in 5 years.

The financial planner then needs to identify any problems or conflicts that might arise between the client's objectives and the possible strategies and recommendations.

Step 3. Analyse data and identify financial issues

Having obtained all the necessary information relevant to the preparation of a comprehensive personal SOA, the financial planner then undertakes a detailed analysis of the client's quantitative and qualitative data and clarifies all areas of doubt regarding the client's perceptions and intentions.

This analysis will help the financial planner to determine what strategies may be appropriate to overcome problems or weaknesses in the client's financial position. Every area of financial planning has to be considered in the context of the client's circumstances for appropriate strategies to be developed. For example, in the area of tax planning, strategies such as negative gearing, salary sacrifice, income splitting, business and investment ownership structures, franking credits and capital gains and losses all need to be examined when relevant to the client's situation. Unless all of the client's circumstances are fully analysed, appropriate recommendations and strategies cannot be determined and put in place. This is consistent with the best interest duty required of financial planners under section 961B(2) of the Act.

A comprehensive analysis of a client's situation would normally involve:
- ascertaining cash inflows and outflows to determine saving capacity
- assessing income tax obligations
- assessing the appropriateness of the asset allocation
- determining the extent to which the current wealth creation of a client is likely to generate sufficient funds for retirement
- assessing social security entitlements
- determining whether personal insurance cover is adequate and appropriate
- comparing proposed strategies and investment products with the client's risk tolerance and objectives.

To assist in the analysis and interpretation of the client's position, the planner may prepare a set of personal financial statements from the data gathered. This normally consists of a balance sheet, income statement and cash flow statement. Financial planners may use a range of analytical techniques to monitor and review the data — for example, the use of financial ratios as discussed in the chapter on financial planning skills. The analysis will indicate such things as:
- what investments the client owns
- whether the investments are held in the most beneficial name or structure for tax purposes
- the amount and nature of the liabilities
- whether there is a cash deficit (to be rectified) or a cash surplus (investment opportunities)
- the tax position.

The planner may also undertake financial modelling to determine whether or not the client's goals are likely to be achieved based on existing conditions. For example, is the client likely to achieve their desired income upon retirement? Once the client's personal data is analysed, it can be related to the client's goals and objectives to determine possible problem areas. For example, a client may desire to invest some funds to achieve a high rate of return with low risk and low tax. Such an objective may prove impossible and require a trade-off between competing wishes. The planner would need to explain the nature of risk and returns to the client and see if a more realistic and achievable objective can be established. Other examples of problems may include inadequate holdings of liquidity to fund a holiday; spending in excess of income levels; inadequate funds to support retirement at age 60; and inadequate levels of insurance to pay out all debts and provide for dependants in the event of the premature death of the main income earner.

Step 4. Prepare and develop the SOA

Once the client's personal situation has been comprehensively analysed, the planner can develop appropriate financial planning recommendations and strategies. One of the key skills and obligations of a planner is to be able to communicate their recommendations effectively and in a manner that will enable a client to make an informed decision. This is facilitated through the preparation and presentation of a comprehensive and detailed SOA.

Within the SOA, careful planning is needed to ensure that the plan is well structured, clear and concise. The strategies need to be sufficiently articulated so that a client is able to determine what is being proposed, the rationale for the proposal, the amounts involved, any tax implications, and the risks and benefits. The client should not have to go searching through different sections of the financial plan to determine what the recommendations are, or be left guessing exactly what is being proposed.

A financial planner's recommendations are often based on a number of assumptions. It is important that all of these assumptions are clearly stated and attached to the plan. Only those issues that relate to future events that cannot be verified (e.g. economic indicators and expected returns) should be assumed. However, the assumptions need to be both reasonable and justifiable at the time they are made.

Some of the assumptions that would normally be included in an SOA include:
- tax rates (i.e. use current year's tax rates)
- inflation (e.g. assume an annual CPI increase of 3.0%)
- interest rates
- income and capital investment returns
- life expectancy of the client.

Step 5. Implement the agreed-upon recommendations

The SOA has to be formally agreed upon, signed and consented to before it can be implemented. The SOA should describe in a clear manner the implementation process and the agreed-upon recommendations. This may take the form of a chronological list of actions to be undertaken. It is most important that the client fully understands the contents of the plan so that they become a shared owner of the ideas and are satisfied that implementation of the recommendations are in their best interests.

Implementation procedures will normally include the following documents for the client to sign:
- an 'action to proceed' section within the SOA
- an 'authority to proceed' document
- application forms to transact the financial products recommended.

The action to proceed section should indicate clear responsibilities and a time line for implementation (see the following for an example).

Who	When	What
Client	Immediately	Organise with employer salary sacrifice of $1500 per month into their superannuation fund.

The purpose of an authority to proceed document is for the client to be able to confirm acceptance of the strategies detailed within the plan and to confirm all product recommendations that have been proposed including the name of the product, in whose name the product is to be acquired and the amounts involved. The authority also provides the opportunity for the client to confirm that they have received an SOA and an FSG. The authority to proceed document should be signed by the client.

Once the client's consent is obtained, the financial planner should take full control of time lines, check and network with all parties involved, and monitor the implementation stage. The planner and client should agree on *who* is going to implement *what* and *when*. The financial planner should be vigilant in every aspect of the implementation and processing stages and closely monitor the various steps of the action plan in an agreed-upon process. As part of this process, the planner may need to refer the client to other professionals, such as solicitors for estate planning matters, stockbrokers for the purchase of equities, and accountants for setting up business structures and tax advice.

Tax (financial) advice

One important thing to note is that a planner who wants to provide tax (financial) advice is required to be registered to do so by the Tax Practioners Board (TPB). This is in addition to holding an AFS licence, or being an authorised representative of one.

Tax (financial) advice as defined in section 90-15 of the *Tax Agent Services Act 2009* (TASA). Fundamentally, it is an estimation of a tax liability or interpretation of tax laws relevant to a client's circumstances (or recommended strategy and product) in the provision of personal financial advice. TPB (2014) provides the following definition.

> A tax (financial) advice service consists of five key elements:
>
> 1. a tax agent service (excluding representations to the Commissioner of Taxation)
> 2. provided by an AFS licensee or representative (including individuals and corporates) of an AFS licensee
> 3. provided in the course of advice usually given by an AFS licensee or representative
> 4. relates to ascertaining or advising about liabilities, obligations or entitlements that arise, or could arise, under a taxation law
> 5. reasonably expected to be relied upon by the client for tax purposes.

Step 6. Review and revise the SOA

Periodically, the client's financial position should be reviewed to ensure the recommendations and strategies developed under the SOA remain appropriate. This normally occurs on an annual basis, although it could also be undertaken at a frequency that has been agreed upon with the client. The financial planner should describe the process of review, the frequency proposed and the fee for providing this service.

A review is much more than just a current valuation of the portfolio. It also evaluates whether the existing plan continues to meet the client's needs or requires adjustment. A review should therefore include consideration of the appropriateness of the portfolio in the context of any changes to the client's personal or family situation, new liabilities or changes to their goals and objectives.

It is important that the client understands the level of service they are paying for on an ongoing basis. To some, the term 'monitoring' implies a 24-hour vigil, with prompt corrective action implemented in accordance with the client's prior consent. Some financial planning practices may well have the infrastructure and facilities to accommodate this. The review process undertaken by most financial planners, however, is normally done on a periodic basis, as required.

As discussed previously, Part 7.7 of the Act requires that a written advice document be provided to a client each time financial product advice is given. One of the issues arising from this obligation is whether a comprehensive SOA is required to be prepared each time a review of a client is undertaken and, as a result, whether the planner is required to duplicate information already contained in an earlier SOA. Where the recommendations and strategies continue to meet the needs of the client and no significant changes have occurred in the client's financial circumstances or in the recommended financial products, the review may take the form of an ROA as previously discussed. Otherwise, a new SOA will need to be issued.

12.10 Ethical and legal compliance issues

LEARNING OBJECTIVE 12.10 Understand the various ethical and legal compliance issues involved in developing a financial plan.

Financial planners must be familiar with all regulatory requirements as well as their professional obligations if they are members of a professional association. Members of the FAAA are required to comply with the FAAA Professional Code. Essentially, the code is based on the planner having a fiduciary obligation to look after the best interests of the client without bias or conflict and in a manner that establishes a relationship of trust, confidence and discretion.

Overarching is the legal requirement under section 921E of the Act for planners to comply with the Code of Ethics developed by the standards body. The standards body is the Financial Adviser Standards and Ethics Authority (FASEA) and they have developed the Financial Planners and Advisers Code of Ethics 2019. There are some particular differences with this code (that is enforced by the Act) that make it more specific than those standards prescribed under the professional association's codes.

Client records

It is important that all information contained within a client's file is stored safely and kept confidentially. This includes records such as SOAs, ROAs, letters, authorities to proceed, client invoices and receipts. A 7-year period is specified by the Corporations Act and *Anti-Money Laundering and Counter-Terrorism Financing Act 2006*, as well as being required by the professional associations in respect of the retention of client records (see FPA Rule 7.26). A prudent planner will, however, keep those records for longer periods than specified. Regular backups of electronic and other physical data should be made and stored at remote premises.

Financial planners must also strictly adhere to the guidelines of the *Privacy Act 1988*. (The website of the Office of the Privacy Commissioner, oaic.gov.au, has further information on the Act.) The aim of the privacy provisions is to ensure that organisations that collect information about people retain the information responsibly. The provisions set out how organisations should collect, use, keep, secure and disclose personal information. Individuals are also given a right to know what information an organisation is holding about them and a right to correct that information if it is wrong.

Access to client records

The courts and ASIC have the right to access client records as part of any investigation. The dealer or licensee will also have access to the client files of their financial planners and will check/audit client records on a periodic basis to ensure that the planner is adhering to all regulatory and compliance issues. The licensee is responsible for the actions of their authorised representatives and for any breaches that put the licensee at risk.

Ownership of client records

Clients have the right, at all times, to be able to identify the licensee who bears the ultimate liability for the advice provided. As such, the ownership of the client's records lies with the licensee and not the planner. In the event that a financial planner moves to another licensee, the client's records remain the property of the original licensee unless the client decides to move with their planner. However, for years the financial planning industry has worked on the unwritten rule that the planner 'owns' the client, and, in the event that a planner leaves a licence holder, the client moves with the planner. From time to time, this arrangement has been challenged and planners who leave their licensees are discovering that it is not so easy to gain access to clients, even those who were brought into the licensee's business by the planner from a previous business arrangement.

Regardless of one's stance on such a contentious issue, it is vital to remember that clients are the people who decide whether they stay with the licensee or follow the adviser. The client's decision will be determined by their assessment of who has offered them the best value and the best advice.

Disclosure of remuneration

The issue of the disclosure of fees and remuneration received by financial planners has become an important and contentious issue within the financial planning profession. Consumers are demanding an increasing level of integrity, honesty and transparency from their planners.

Financial planners have an ethical and legal obligation to disclose all fees, commissions and any material interests that may result from their recommendations. RG 182 requires that various costs, fees, charges, expenses, benefits and interests related to the planner's remuneration, costs related to the purchase of a financial product or other costs incurred by the client as a result of the planner's recommendations be stated in dollar amounts in an SOA and Product Disclosure Statement (ASIC 2017b). This requirement is also set out in sections 947B, 947C, 947D, 1013D and 1017D of the Act and RG 175, which also requires that various costs, fees, charges, expenses, benefits and interests must be stated as dollar amounts in an SOA.

There is a range of remuneration models within the financial planning industry and includes the following.

- *Commissions* — this remuneration model is based upon the product provider, such as an insurance provider, paying a fee directly to the planner (a **commission**) out of the product costs charged to the client (i.e. the insurance premium). While the client does not pay a fee to the planner directly, they do pay for the service indirectly through the insurance premium. The contentious issue with this remuneration model is that there is the potential for it to lack transparency and that it influences the planner to recommend a product that may not be appropriate for the client. It is likely that commissions will be banned, without 'grand-fathering' in the near future.
- *Fee-for-service* — under a **fee-for-service** model, amounts are charged by the planner based on an agreement with the client. The client may pay the fee directly or, more commonly, the product provider might execute or pay the fee on behalf of the client out of the client's funds. The fee is negotiated with the client and may be based on an agreed level of service, the complexity of the advice or the size of the investment (i.e. percentage based on funds under management). For example, a planner might negotiate an initial fee for the provision of the SOA of $2500 plus an ongoing fee of 1% p.a. based on the amount of the client's funds that are managed by the planner.
- *Hourly rate* — under this model, the client is charged an hourly rate based on the amount of time spent by the planner. For example, a planner may charge a fee of $150 per hour for advice provided to a client with respect of the establishment and operation of a self-managed superannuation fund.

The FAAA (previously the FPA) decided to move away from a commission-based remuneration model effective from 2012 and members were required to adopt a fee-based model (FPA 2009). The Future of Financial Advice reforms amended the Act so that, from 1 July 2013, it was illegal to charge commissions on investment products as it was deemed to be 'conflicted remuneration'. ASIC RG246 *conflicted and other banned remuneration* provides more details. However, for the time being, the Act allows commission payments to continue for risk and insurance products.

12.11 Important components of an SOA

LEARNING OBJECTIVE 12.11 Construct a statement of advice to meet the needs of a client and to satisfy regulatory requirements.

A client must be provided with an SOA when, or as soon as practicable after, advice is provided and before any action is taken associated with that advice. Each SOA needs to be tailored to the specific needs of the client. Every client has different needs, objectives and therefore strategies, and accordingly each SOA must be specifically tailored to the individual client and take into account their level of financial literacy and general understanding.

It is important to note that while there is no set format or template for an SOA, section 947B(2) of the Act does set out a range of issues that are common to every SOA. The test applied by ASIC is based on what a person would reasonably require for the purpose of deciding whether or not to act on the advice.

To illustrate how an SOA might be constructed, the following section provides reference to two different scaled (limited) SOAs. The first example has been provided by ASIC in RG 90 *Example Statement of Advice: Scaled advice for a new client*. The example SOA has been kept deliberately short and concise with the focus being on the key sections that help clients make informed decisions about the advice given. The ASIC example SOA provides a guide to industry best practice. However, this is only one example of an acceptable format; many other and different formats are acceptable and being used throughout the industry. What is important is that the disclosures are in accordance with prescribed regulations, the strategies are appropriate for the client's needs and objectives, and the information is communicated in a clear and concise manner.

The second example (scaled) SOA provides an alternative format for consideration. The client's background personal and financial information has been made available, as has the client's objectives, and the information forms the basis of the recommendations contained within the SOA. The example SOA is provided in appendix 12D.

The main components of an SOA are outlined next.

The main components of an SOA

RG 175.151 sets out the information that is required to be disclosed within an SOA. The title 'statement of advice' must be disclosed on the cover or at the front of the SOA. Other issues requiring disclosure include:

- the name and contact details of the holder of the Australian Financial Services Licence (AFSL)
- the name and contact details of the financial planner and the organisation they work for
- a statement setting out the advice and the basis for the advice
- information about remuneration or other benefits that the adviser may receive arising from the advice
- information about any conflicts of interest that may prejudice the advice
- a warning that the advice provided by the financial planner may not be suitable or totally appropriate for the client's circumstances if information supplied by the client is incorrect or where the client is seeking limited or scaled advice only.

Covering letter

A covering letter should always accompany any client correspondence. The covering letter that accompanies an SOA may contain some or all of the following:

- references to the meeting(s) with the client, the attached SOA, and the FSG provided at the first meeting with the client
- a request that the client review the SOA, make further enquiries if needed, check the accuracy of their personal details and bring any inaccuracies to the attention of the financial planner
- a summary of the main recommendations
- an offer to help with implementing the SOA
- recommendations as to a time frame for the SOA and its validity, that is, a sunset clause (which is a date limit for the recommendations to remain valid)
- a suggestion of a date and time for a follow-up appointment.
  In all correspondence with a client, it is important that the following details are provided:
- licensee's identification, including name, licence held, address and contact information
- planner's identification, including name, authority held, address and contact information.

Contents page

Given the comprehensiveness of the SOA presented to a client, the pages should be numbered and an easy-to-follow contents or index page should be included to facilitate referencing. The client can then see at a glance the various components of the SOA.

Cover page

The cover page introduces the nature of the report, whether an SOA or ROA, and sets out basic information the client needs to know before they read the contents, including the name of the providing entity and their contact details, what the advice statement is about and why the client should read it.

Executive summary

An executive summary is normally included at the front of most SOAs and should include in a simple, clear and concise way:

- the main strategies recommended
- the risks and benefits associated with each of the strategies
- how the strategies meet the needs of the client
- the fees and charges
- how to proceed.

These elements should be viewed from a *macro* point of view, with details provided within the body of the SOA. The executive summary should normally be around one page long and is designed to be a quick summary of issues for the client.

Scope of the advice

To ensure that both parties are clear as to the nature and coverage of the advice sought, the SOA should detail the extent to which the plan is limited or restricted in any fashion. This is known as the scope of the advice. Limitations may arise in terms of the information provided by the client, areas of the client's circumstances that are to be excluded from the review, or restrictions placed by the licence holder on the planner's ability to recommend certain financial products. Where the advice is based on incomplete or inaccurate information provided by the client, the planner is required to warn the client that they should consider the appropriateness of the advice having regard to their personal circumstances (s. 961H of the Act).

For example, the scoping section of an SOA may appear as follows.

What my advice covers

When we discussed your relevant circumstances, you instructed me to limit the scope of my advice for the following reasons — you are concerned with the cost of the advice and are prepared to limit the scope of the advice provided in order to reduce the cost of the advice sought.

Accordingly, the advice provided in this SOA does not include the following areas:

- personal risk and insurance
- estate planning needs
- your share portfolio.

As you requested, we have limited our recommendations, so please consider the appropriateness of our advice in the context of your personal as well as financial goals, objectives and aspirations.

Important information about the client

The financial planner must ensure that the client's present position, financial circumstances, attitude and risk are clearly identified and form an integral part of the SOA. A current balance sheet and cash flow statement is normally provided here. The current asset allocation of the client should also be detailed and analysed in terms of the client's risk profile to establish a target or direction for the asset allocation going forward. This information should be organised and displayed in an easy-to-follow manner.

As the SOA's strategies and recommendations are based on the information gathered from the client, it is imperative that the information is accurate. Clients should be encouraged to review their personal details in the SOA carefully and refer any errors or omissions immediately to the planner.

What the client wants to achieve

Under this section, the client's goals and objectives are listed. The objectives should be prioritised, quantified where possible and categorised into time periods.

The advice to the client

The SOA needs to detail specific strategies to meet the clients' specific needs and objectives. The SOA needs to be sufficiently detailed and specific for the client to be able to clearly determine what is recommended, the basis for the recommendation, how much, with who and when. However, the planner needs to be mindful of not overloading the SOA with so much detail that the nature of the advice itself is lost.

The recommendations should enable the client to understand fully what has been proposed and to engage with the advice provided. Therefore, it is important to disclose in appropriate language:
- what the advice is
- the basis of the advice
- why the advice is appropriate
- the benefits of the advice
- the risks and disadvantages associated with the advice
- how the advice enables the client to achieve their goals and objectives.

To facilitate understanding and comprehension, advice may best be illustrated through the use of graphs, tables, diagrams and charts. The wording and detail of the information provided will be determined largely by the financial literacy of the client. RG 90.46 noted the following in its example statement of advice.

We have used the following strategies to make the SOA easier to read and understand:

(a) where possible, technical words and phrases have been replaced with more commonly understood terms;

(b) where legal or technical terms have been used, their meaning and implications are explained in simple, plain language;

(c) acronyms and abbreviations have only been used where necessary and are defined at the first point of usage;

(d) short, simple sentences have been used, with no complex sentence structures;

(e) where possible, tables and bullet points have been used to break up the text and present information in a clear, accessible way, and to make it easier for clients to find and compare information; and

(f) different types of information have been identified and separated into two 'voices', using a different style to represent each voice:

  (i) the first 'voice' (in normal text) is the voice of the adviser and sets out key information, facts and recommendations; and

  (ii) the second 'voice' (in italics with an arrow bullet) provides further explanation or expands on the implications of what the first voice has said.

It is important that the advice provided to a client covers all aspects of the client's circumstances. Any issue that is omitted leaves the financial planner open to possible litigation. Any restriction or limitation to the advice provided or sought should be detailed in the scope of the advice section.

ILLUSTRATIVE EXAMPLE 12.5

As part of your comprehensive analysis of Cory and Amy's circumstances, you identify that the couple are significantly underinsured for life, trauma and income protection. You discuss this issue with the couple at a meeting and the ramifications that a premature death or disability would have on their family's lifestyle. The couple agree they probably need more insurance, but state that they cannot afford the cost of the premiums at this stage and they have other priorities.

Should the planner still refer to the client's insurance shortfall and provide recommendations within the SOA regardless of the client's statement that insurance is a low priority, or can the planner safely ignore the insurance needs of the client within the plan?

Despite Cory and Amy stating that they cannot afford the cost of insurance premiums, the planner should still provide what they believe is appropriate for the client and in their best interest. Imagine if the planner made no reference to their insurance needs and 2 months later Cory was killed in a car crash. Amy may challenge the planner to explain why they had not tried to educate them on importance of taking out appropriate insurance. Without documented evidence to show that the advice was actually provided, the planner would also be potentially exposing themselves to possible litigation on the basis of not providing advice appropriate to the client's needs. The client can choose to ignore the advice or scope out personal risk insurance. In the end, it is up to the client to determine whether they take up the insurance or not. However, the planner does have a responsibility to raise the issue with the client and provide advice that is in the client's best interests.

Other disclosure requirements

The cost of the advice and how the planner is paid

Under this section, all costs, fees, commissions and potential conflicts of interest associated with the SOA need to be detailed to the client.

With respect to the purchase or replacement of a financial product, all product costs need to be disclosed. These may include brokerage costs and stamp duty in respect of the purchase of shares, indirect cost ratio (ICR), entry and exit costs and buy/sell spreads for managed funds, and stamp duty and legal expenses for the purchase of property. For specific details on the costs of the financial products recommended, the client should be provided with a copy of the product disclosure statement (PDS) of the financial product or, if appropriate, provide the client with a link to the product's website.

Any potential tax implications associated with the purchase or disposal of a financial product, such as CGT payable, should also be referred to in the SOA.

The legal requirement to disclose the remuneration of the planner (such as costs, fees, expenses, benefits, interests and commissions) in the SOA, is contained in both the Act and RG 175. An example is provided in appendix 12D. Remuneration may be charged by the planner for preparing an SOA, implementing the recommendations contained within an SOA and for the provision of ongoing advice and review. The regulations prescribe that, no matter what form the remuneration takes, the planner is required to disclose all fees, costs, benefits, charges and interests as a dollar amount within the SOA.

An example of the disclosure of fees is provided in illustrative example 12.6.

The following disclosure is illustrative of the type of disclosure that might be provided on the planner's remuneration within the SOA.

ABC Financial Planners will charge you a fee of 1% plus GST on the establishment of your investment plan. ABC Financial Planners will rebate all upfront and ongoing insurance commissions back to you, the investor. ABC Financial Planners will also charge an ongoing fee of 0.5% p.a. plus GST based on the amount of funds under management.

	Amount	Advice fee		Ongoing fee	
	($)	(%)	($)	(%)	($)
MNO Master Trust	120 000	1.1	1 320	0.55	660
DEF Retail Fund	80 000	1.1	880	0.55	440
LMN Insurance (premium)	5 000	66%	3 300	22%	1 100
LMN Insurance (rebate)			−3 300		−1 100
Total	200 000		2 200		1 100

These fees and commissions are inclusive of the goods and services tax (GST).

Note: As the holder of the AFSL, XYZ Dealer Group receives all fees, retains 10% and pays the balance to us as the financial planner. This equates to the licence holder receiving $220 p.a. of the initial fee and $110 p.a. of the ongoing fees.

Specific disclaimers

Disclaimers are often used within an SOA in an attempt to restrict the liability of the planner for situations outside the planner's direct control. There are certain statutory obligations that cannot be disclaimed, such as the fiduciary obligation imposed on financial planners under common law to act in the best interests of their clients and to exercise a duty of care. However, in the preparation of an SOA, and in dealings with the client, specific disclaimers can be used to assist in clarifying the role and responsibility of the planner and client.

The following are examples of such disclaimers.
- No responsibility is given to any person other than the client(s) addressed in the SOA.
- No guarantees are provided on future performances.
- Taxation issues should be referred to the client's tax accountant, even if the planner is a registered tax (financial) adviser.
- The recommendation is valid for 60 days after date of issue.
- The plan is prepared from information provided by the client, to suit their particular needs and objectives. If the information is not accurate, the onus is on the client to bring it to the planner's attention.

How to proceed

The client needs to fully understand the agreed-upon recommendations and the implementation process going forward, including responsibilities, time lines and amounts. Where referrals to other professionals are required in order to implement the plan, these should be detailed in the plan and it is the financial planner's responsibility to facilitate and coordinate the process. The client should be asked to check the accuracy of the information contained within the SOA and to notify the planner if the information is incorrect or has changed so that the strategies can be reviewed and amended if necessary.

The SOA has to be formally agreed upon, signed and consented to before it is implemented. The client should be asked to sign and return an 'authority to proceed' document in order to signify acceptance of the recommendations contained within the SOA.

SUMMARY

The practice of financial planning encompasses many disciplines — investments, retirement planning, superannuation, insurance, taxation planning, portfolio management, social security, debt management and financial analysis, to name a few. The objective of the financial planning process is to analyse these aspects in the context of the client's circumstances and provide recommendations and strategies in the form of a compliant and comprehensive SOA that meets the needs and requirements of the client. All personal advice must comply with the best interest duty detailed in the Act.

The Act sets a requirement that, when providing advice to a retail client, a financial planner must provide the client with an SOA. While this may be in the form of a comprehensive SOA, increasingly clients are seeking scaled advice in relation to a limited range of issues. The nature of the arrangement with the client and the type of advice sought will determine which of these SOAs will be appropriate.

The Act also provides for an alternative advice document in a limited number of situations, known as a record of advice (ROA).

While it is important that the planner be technically competent and able to provide detailed strategies, the advice and recommendations will be of little use if the client does not fully understand the strategies and the rationale for them. Effective communication and trust are vital if the client is to accept and act upon the advice provided by the planner. Without an open, trusting and honest relationship between the planner and client, it is unlikely that the goals and objectives of the client will be satisfied. The first meeting between the planner and client is not only important for establishing this relationship, but the regulations also impose a number of requirements on the planner, including the need to provide the client with an FSG and obligations relating to the prevention and detection of money laundering and terrorism activities.

The 6-step financial planning process provides a framework for the development of an SOA and highlights the compliance issues imposed on the financial planning profession.

A considerable number of regulations have been imposed on the financial planning industry to ensure that clients are given appropriate and reasonable advice at a fair price. Financial planners have a professional and fiduciary obligation to look after the interests of a client without bias or conflict, be compliant with all regulations and act in a manner that is transparent and ethical.

Finally, the various components of an SOA were outlined including reference to two example scaled SOAs.

This chapter aims to apply the knowledge and skills acquired from earlier chapters to the preparation, presentation, implementation and review of an SOA. This case study approach is used to help foster and develop those skills considered essential for the professional financial planner — critical thinking, analysis and interpretation, and problem solving.

KEY TERMS

commission A fee paid to a planner by a product issuer for recommending that particular issuer's products to a client.

fee-for-service A remuneration model where the client is billed directly by the financial planner for the service they provide based on an agreement with the client.

Good Disclosure Principles Principles promoted by ASIC to help promote good disclosure outcomes for clients.

no-advice statement A document signed by a client stating that no advice was given by a planner in respect of a transaction.

record of advice (ROA) An alternative advice document to the SOA able to be used when providing further advice to existing clients.

scaled advice Advice about a specific area of an investor's needs or about a limited range of issues.

scope of the advice The nature of the advice sought by the client, including any client or planner limitations.

statement of advice (SOA) A written personal financial plan prepared for a client by a financial adviser.

PROFESSIONAL APPLICATION QUESTIONS

12.1 When must an FSG be provided to a client? List five items in an FSG that convey information about the planner to a client.

12.2 How might a planner develop comprehensive insight and knowledge about the client in order to satisfy the best interests duty imposed under the Act and ultimately provide appropriate advice?

12.3 What is 'scaled advice' and what are the advantages and risks for a client?

12.4 What are some reasons why a financial adviser may scope their advice?

12.5 Does a disclaimer in an SOA assist the client in any way? If so, how? In what way might a disclaimer be used to assist the financial planner?

12.6 In practice, it is common for a financial planner to disclose their recommendations and provide an SOA by using a practice template. What advantages and disadvantages can you foresee with this practice?

12.7 There is often a disagreement between the licensee and the financial planner about who 'owns' the client. Why does this happen? Who do you think owns the client? Discuss your answer from the view of the licence holder, the financial planner and the client.

12.8 An SOA should be developed to accommodate a client's aims and goals. On the basis that these goals are likely to change over a client's lifetime, by what means can a financial planner ensure the goals continue to be achieved?

12.9 What should a planner do if they believe they don't have the expertise to be able to appropriately advise the client on a certain topic for the client?

12.10 Explain some of the methods that a planner may adopt to present their recommendations in a way that engages the client.

12.11 Explain the purpose of an executive summary in an SOA.

12.12 When discussing a particular strategy or investment within an SOA, how does the planner determine how much general information and description should be included?

12.13 What are the conditions that allow an ROA to be prepared instead of an SOA?

PROFESSIONAL APPLICATION EXERCISES

★ BASIC | ★★ MODERATE | ★★★ CHALLENGING

12.14 Compliance and regulatory obligations ★

Jeremy seeks some financial advice from you on behalf of his brother Todd who is migrating to Australia in 3 months. Jeremy provides information about Todd's personal circumstances. Jeremy claims that Todd is similar in personality to him so would have the same risk profile. Todd wishes to invest $10 000 in a particular managed share fund and Jeremy asks, on Todd's behalf, whether you will accept cash and organise the investment. What are some of the issues or obligations that you should consider in providing financial advice to Jeremy's brother?

12.15 Analysing issues and developing strategies ★

Jamal seeks some assistance from you in respect to buying a property. At this stage, he is unsure whether he will live in it straight away or use it as an investment property initially and then move into it in a few years. Jamal has $30 000 sitting in a cash management account and $20 000 held in a managed fund; he will borrow the rest. Jamal advises that he is looking to buy a property worth around $450 000 and is keen to get into the market as soon as possible as he believes property will continue to boom given historically low interest rates. Jamal is single and earns a salary of $70 000 p.a. plus SG contributions.

(a) What are some of the issues you would raise with Jamal about the purchase of a property and the related borrowing?

(b) If Jamal decided to wait a few years before purchasing a property, what investment options would you recommend to help him save for a deposit?

12.16 Type of disclosure advice statement ★★

Walter is an existing, long-standing client aged 59. In 2016, you established a self-managed super fund for Walter with recommendations documented in an SOA dated 23 February 2016. The fund now has $720 000 of assets. In 2011, Walter stated that he intended to retire at age 65 and that he would not expect to access the funds before then. The plan provided an asset allocation strategy for the fund. Walter was made aware at the time that there may be a need to change some of the managed funds from time to time.

Since then, you have provided Walter with a review of the managed funds every 12 months. These reviews have included changes to the investment portfolio by way of portfolio re-weighting and changing fund managers from time to time. The risk profile and asset allocation strategy has not changed.

For each of the following situations occurring this financial year, explain whether you could provide the client with an ROA or whether an SOA would be required.

(a) In July, the fund has available cash of $40 000 to invest. You recommend that Walter allocates the cash among his existing investment products based on maintaining his agreed asset allocation.

(b) In August, your research provider issues a sell on the State Australian share fund. During your next review you recommend that Walter sells his holding in the share fund, worth $50 000, and invest the proceeds into the Capital Australian share fund which hasn't been used before.

(c) In September, during discussions with Walter, he expresses a desire to reduce the tax he pays and undertake some sort of gearing strategy (he hasn't previously geared before). You recommend a limited recourse borrowing arrangement through the ANZ.

(d) In November, upon turning 60 years of age, you recommend to Walter that he implements a transition to retirement strategy. This involves him rearranging his affairs to salary sacrifice to the super fund and to commence drawing a pension from the fund.

12.17 Satisfying the needs of a client ★★

Mary has sought advice from you on her financial position. Mary is aged 38 and married; the couple's combined earnings are around $160 000 p.a. The couple's home is worth $800 000 and they have a $500 000 outstanding mortgage owing. The couple also has $20 000 owing on one of their cars. The couple are in good health but you note that there is a history of heart-related issues within Mary's family. You complete an SOA providing advice on the couple's superannuation funds, managed fund portfolio and their personal insurance cover. You recommend that the couple each take out a $1 million life and total and permanent disability cover, an income protection insurance policy for up to 75% of their salary and a trauma policy for an amount of $200 000 each.

At a meeting that you have with the client prior to the presentation of the SOA, the couple appear happy to accept your recommendations on the superannuation and managed funds but raises concerns about the level of insurance cover that you have recommended and the cost of the premiums. They advise that they would want only half the amount of insurance that you have recommended.

(a) What sort of issues would you likely have taken into account in determining an amount of $1 million for the couple's life and TPD coverage?

(b) How should you with the situation where the client wants only half the amount of personal cover that has been recommended? Should your advice provided in the SOA reflect the client's preferences?

(c) Discuss the importance of requiring a client to sign an 'authority to proceed' document prior to the implementation of the recommendations.

12.18 Regulatory obligations and developing strategies ★★

My name is Emilia, I am 52 years old and a widow. I am employed to run exercise programs for senior citizens. My gross salary is $75 000 p.a. plus an SG contribution. Together with investment income of $1500, I am left with a disposable income of $6000 p.a. I have one child who lives independently. I am currently renting near where I work and have decided to sell my family home which I have rented out for the past 7 years. I want to buy an apartment closer to work as I expect to stay in the area in which I am now living. My assets consist of the following: family home, $600 000 (no mortgage); bank deposits, $10 000; managed share portfolio, $30 000; and superannuation, $120 000 invested in a balanced fund.

I purchased the family property 21 years ago for $180 000 but have been advised that, because I have been away from the family home for over 6 years, I cannot claim a full exemption from capital gains tax. I am told that it is exempted from capital gains tax for the time that it was my principal place of residence, but I must pay capital gains tax on that proportion of the gain accrued during the remainder of the time when it was rented to another party. After selling the family home, buying another property and paying all costs and taxes, I expect to have surplus funds of approximately $100 000. I require some advice on how best to invest the funds.

(a) What issues should be covered with Emilia in the initial meeting?

(b) In order to reduce costs, is the planner able to provide Emilia with an ROA detailing strategies and recommendations?

(c) Determine Emilia's likely capital gains tax liability if she sells the property and uses the CGT discount method to determine the CGT liability.

(d) What are the advantages and disadvantages of contributing the proceeds from the sale of the property into her superannuation fund? Are there any restrictions on the amount of the proceeds that can be contributed into Emilia's superannuation account this year?

(e) If, as a result of the extra funds, Emilia salary sacrifices an amount of $40 000 into her superannuation fund this year, what would be the tax consequences for both her employer and herself?

12.19 Analysing issues and developing strategies ★★

Ian approaches you for advice concerning his superannuation fund account. He is aged 38, earns a gross income of $80 000 p.a. and has $95 000 invested in superannuation. His super fund is invested in a conservative investment option and has achieved an average return of 5.5% p.a. over the past 3 years. Ian is attracted by a number of television advertisements that promote returns for an industry superannuation fund that, because of lower fees, has achieved an average return of 7.5% p.a. over the past 3 years.

(a) Ian wonders why his fund may have underachieved compared with the one advertised on the television. Explain.

(b) What factors would you need to discuss with Ian if he was considering transferring his superannuation account to the industry fund?

(c) What factors might you consider to determine Ian's risk tolerance?

(d) If Ian wanted more control over his superannuation fund with greater investment choice and the ability to acquire direct shares, what type of superannuation structure might be recommended?

12.20 Analysing issues and developing strategies ★★

My name is Jamil and I am aged 28. My fiancée, Taliah, is aged 30. Taliah and I still live with our parents and expect to remain there until our marriage in 9 months. Two years ago, I used $100 000 that I had saved and borrowed $350 000 from a bank and bought an investment property for $450 000. Apart from $10 000 in a savings account, I have no other investments. My fiancée has $20 000 invested in fixed-term deposits. We are unsure what our living arrangements will be once we marry. We could sell the investment property and use the proceeds to buy a home, or use our savings as a deposit and borrow further funds to acquire a home to live in, or we could live in the investment property for a couple of years before selling it and buying a bigger home. Alternatively, we could rent a property for the next 5 years and continue to invest our savings.

(a) What are some of the qualitative issues that you may discuss with Jamil and Taliah in helping them with their decision?

(b) What capital gains tax issues need to be considered if they were to sell the investment property?

(c) If the couple chose to use their savings to buy their own home and retain the investment property, what factors would you need to consider before recommending that the couple further increase their debt levels?

(d) Why might the couple decide to rent and, if they do decide to rent, do you consider renting to be a viable long-term solution to a client's housing needs?

12.21 Analysing issues and developing strategies ★★

Kim works as a retail assistant in a large department store. She earns $52 000 p.a. after salary sacrificing $5000 into her superannuation fund. Kim is also entitled to an SG contribution on her total remuneration package of $57 000. Kim also earns $3000 of interest income. Kim's husband recently retired, aged 59, and has a taxable income of $9500 for the year. Kim is looking to retire next year when she will be aged 56. Kim is interested in contributing further funds into her superannuation account in order to maximise taxation benefits and entitlements and has considered investing $2000 of savings into her superannuation fund so that she can claim the government co-contribution. However, one of her colleagues has told her that she would be better off salary sacrificing the amount into her superannuation account while another friend has told her about contributing the funds into her spouse's superannuation account in order to claim the superannuation contributions spouse tax offset. Kim comes to you for your advice.

(a) Is Kim entitled to make a superannuation contribution and claim a tax benefit or concession under the three alternatives? Explain.

(b) Which of the three alternatives would you recommend for Kim in terms of maximising her tax benefits and concessions? Provide calculations to justify your answer.

(c) Once Kim retires, she will need to receive an income stream from her superannuation fund account. What type of income-stream product is Kim able to choose from and what would you recommend?

(d) Assume that upon her retirement, Kim's superannuation balance amounts to $350 000 including a tax-free component of $60 000. If Kim rolls the super money into an account-based pension and withdraws an income of $40 000, how much tax would be payable on her taxable income? You can assume Kim continues to receive interest income of $3000.

12.22 Compliance and regulatory issues ★★★

Teresa recently visited a financial planner to help sort out her financial affairs. After 2 short interviews, one being over the telephone, the planner sent her a six-page SOA. Teresa received no other documentation from the financial planner nor did she complete any forms. She says she is uncomfortable with some of the recommendations and does not understand a number of the strategies. When she asked about the fees, the planner replied that the SOA was absolutely free and there was no charge to her. Teresa is aged 38, divorced and has 2 primary school-aged children. She earns $52 000 p.a. and has around $200 per month available to invest. She owns a house and is paying off a mortgage of $80 000. She has $20 000 invested in a savings account which her parents have given her for emergency expenses and to help with the education of her children. Teresa's financial planner has recommended that she takes out something called a margin lending facility totalling $100 000 and together with her $20 000 savings account, acquire units in an international share fund for an amount of $120 000. Teresa says she does not understand what a margin loan is and she is not sure whether investing in an international share fund is suitable for her.

(a) How appropriate do you think a margin lending strategy is for Teresa? Discuss.

(b) Describe the various methods of remuneration available to financial planners.

(c) Suppose the PDS of the international share fund indicates that the fund's ICR is 2.1% p.a. Prepare a table to indicate what fees the financial planner should have included in the financial plan given to Teresa.

(d) It is obvious that the financial planner has breached several ethical, professional and legal obligations. Discuss the various areas of non-compliance by the financial planner.

(e) Discuss some of the ways in which financial planners can seek to limit their exposure to possible litigation and breaches of their ethical, professional and legal obligations.

12.23 Analysing issues and developing strategies ★★★

Paul and Anne are both 59 years of age. They are considering whether to commence a TTR pension. They operate a family business and pay themselves a salary of $90 000 p.a. each plus the SG contribution. They are considering a proposal to salary sacrifice $16 000 each into their respective superannuation accounts, receive a cash salary of $74 000 and both commence withdrawing a TTR pension of $12 500. They each have $450 000 in superannuation funds which they will roll over into a TTR pension. Assume that their superannuation and pension funds earn a 6% return net of tax.

(a) Calculate the amount of personal income tax that Paul and Anne are currently paying. Prepare a table to illustrate their income and taxation liability.

(b) Prepare another table to illustrate the taxation effect of the proposal to salary sacrifice $16 000 each into superannuation and commence a TTR pension with an income of $12 500 each. You can assume that the taxable proportion of their superannuation is 100%.

(c) How will the salary sacrifice/TTR strategy impact upon the couple's accumulated wealth when they retire at age 65? Determine the future value of the couple's combined superannuation accounts and TTR pension accounts to age 65.

(d) Given the salary sacrifice/TTR strategy, explain the taxation impact on their income when they both turn 60 years of age.

(e) Describe any other benefits that may be derived with the couple undertaking the TTR strategy.

CASE STUDY 1

THE DEVELOPMENT OF STRATEGIES

Phil, a new client, has approached your financial planning practice seeking some advice. The practice's financial planner had a telephone conversation with Phil last week. The planner asks you to undertake a few tasks as part of the process of providing advice and recommendations for Phil and his wife.

After speaking with Phil, the financial planner provides you with the following information concerning the couple's financial situation.

1. Personal situation

Phil is aged 37 and his wife Jill is aged 36. Phil is a self-employed architect while Jill works 2–3 days a week as a solicitor.

They have 2 children, Tessa aged 11 and Matthew aged 10. The couple would like the children to attend a private school from age 14, which is expected to cost around $15 000 p.a.

2. Assets and liabilities consist of the following

Assets

Home (joint ownership) $900 000, contents (joint ownership) worth $80 000, 2 cars (one car in each name) worth approximately $60 000, savings account with Westpac Bank for $6000 (in Phil's name), shares (in Phil's name) with a current market value of $70 000 (cost price of $90 000 acquired in May 2014), superannuation balances — Phil $120 000, Jill $70 000.

Phil acquired the shares 3 years ago on the advice of a friend. However, the shares have never done well and Phil has no interest or time in following the share market.

The couple do not take an active interest in their investments.

Liabilities

Eighteen-year home mortgage of $590 000 with a variable interest rate of 5.5% p.a., monthly repayments of $4372.

Five-year car loan of $15 000 with a variable interest rate of 6.6% p.a., monthly repayments of $300.

Credit card average monthly balance of $6000 (used to pay for living expenses).

The couple are finding that a lot of their monthly income is going towards paying off their large amount of debt. They are worried that they have taken on too much debt and would like to reduce outstanding debt as fast as possible.

3. Cash income and expenses consist of the following

The couple feel they pay an excessive amount of tax and are looking at ways of minimising tax payable as far as possible.

Income:	$ p.a.
– salary	40 000
– net profit from business	130 000
— bank interest	120
— fully franked dividends (cash receipt)	2 250
— unfranked dividends (cash receipt)	400
Payments:	
Living expenses (excluding loans and interest charges)	40 000
Mortgage and loan repayments	56 064
Private health insurance	3 200
Professional membership fees	
— Phil	700
— Jill	800
Travel expenses for work purposes:	
— Jill	400
Tax preparation (split 50/50)	2 000
Donations (split 50/50)	1 500
Holidays and entertainment	10 000

4. The couple's superannuation accounts consist of the following

Phil:	

(i) Australian Industry Super Fund
  — invested in the balanced option
  — includes death and TPD cover for $100 000
	$20 000

(ii) Self-managed superannuation fund — invested 50% in shares and 50% in cash	$100 000
Jill:	
(i) Invested with Australian Industry Super Fund — invested in the balanced option	$60 000
(ii) Self-managed superannuation fund — invested 50% in shares and 50% in cash	$10 000

Other than detailed above, the couple have no other personal insurance cover.

The couple's SMSF was established 4 years ago by their accountant. However, they have no real understanding of how the SMSF works or what the benefits are in contributing.

Jill's current employer pays her SG contribution into the Australian Industry Super Fund. Phil contributes to his SMSF on an irregular basis when he remembers to contribute or his accountant happens to mention it before the end of the year. However, Phil has not taken an active interest in his superannuation affairs and has not contributed for the past 2 years.

The asset break-up of the Australian Industry Super Fund balanced fund account is approximately as follows.

Cash	5%
Australian fixed interest	15%
International fixed interest	5%
Australian shares	35%
International shares	23%
Property	10%
Alternative investments	7%

The couple now feel that they need to take a more active interest in their wealth creation and retirement planning but are not sure how best to go about it. Their objective is to retire when Phil turns 58 so they can travel around Australia. Accordingly, they have sought the advice of your financial planning practice.

The financial planner had a brief telephone conversation with Phil a couple of months ago and the client emailed the above details. The financial planner has asked you to prepare some appropriate strategies for Phil that will assist in meeting his goals and needs.

You are required to provide a discussion and explanation of the broad strategies that you would recommend for the couple taking into account their objectives and assumed risk profile, and explain how your recommended strategies meet Phil's objectives. For each broad strategy, you should also detail the main benefits and risks to the client.

CASE STUDY 2

ESTABLISHING A FRAMEWORK FOR CONSTRUCTING A LIMITED STATEMENT OF ADVICE

The aim of this case study is to help the reader apply the financial planning principles and practices that have been covered in this text by analysing a typical client situation and providing appropriate recommendations and strategies.

Given that there is, in most cases, more than one appropriate solution to achieving a client's objectives in a dynamic and ever-changing financial environment, and that financial planners take different approaches when forming recommendations, the authors do not provide solutions to the questions arising from the case study. Rather, the reader is provided with a framework and a methodology within which a limited advice SOA can be constructed.

The case study on Fui Ling and Tin Nguyen is dealt with by applying the 6 steps of the financial planning process. Students are encouraged to refer to ASIC's RG 90 *Example Statement of Advice: Scaled advice for a new client* or to the Example Statement of Advice provided in appendix 12D and use the examples as the basis to prepare a suitable SOA for Fui Ling and Tin.

Fui Ling Nguyen is a prospective client who phones your financial planning practice. She says she is approaching you as a financial planner to seek financial guidance and to ask you to prepare a financial plan for a particular matter. She would like to make an appointment to see you and has sent you the following letter detailing the couple's background.

> Dear financial planner
>
> I am 30 years old and my husband Tin is 32. We both have well-paying secure jobs. We have no children and are not planning to have any for at least 3–4 years. We both have very busy work and social lives that leave little time to organise our finances. There is a mortgage on our house, but we are gradually reducing the amount owing as we have been paying extra amounts to get it paid off sooner. We own two cars and have a loan on one of them. There is very little else I can tell you except that we have not been able to invest much at all despite our reasonably high income levels. However, we now want to start building up a managed fund portfolio of Australian shares by borrowing funds. We are not sure whether we should use some of the equity in our home now that we own more than half of the house; whether we should use margin lending; or whether we should start an instalment gearing plan. We tend to favour the idea of an instalment gearing plan to get us started. What do you think? and can you advise us on the gearing options?

The financial planning process

First, you send Tin and Fui Ling your FSG, identifying the fact that you are acting as an authorised representative of an AFSL holder, and providing information on the advisory services you offer, your experience, specialisations, remuneration details and complaints-handling mechanism. You also send a confidential client questionnaire and ask them to read the two documents, to complete as much as possible of the client questionnaire and bring it along with supporting documentation to their first appointment.

In developing an appropriate SOA for the couple, you should refer to the best interest duty and safe harbour provisions as well as the 6-step financial planning process discussed earlier in this chapter. Your plan must comply with all legal, professional and ethical standards that have been outlined in this chapter.

STEP 1. Gather the clients' data

At the first appointment, you should do the following.

- Introduce yourself and your organisation and ask if Fui Ling and Tin have any questions arising from the FSG.
- Briefly introduce the couple to the financial planning process and explain how you normally go about preparing your recommendations, the follow-up meetings, the implementation process, reviews, remuneration and so on.
- Discuss the terms of your engagement, scope of advice and legal ramifications of accepting the engagement and providing advice.
- Develop a rapport with the clients to gain an understanding of their circumstances and to assist them to relax and feel comfortable about openly discussing financial matters.
- Extract a more detailed account of the couple's circumstances to complete the client questionnaire — even though you have been requested to consider only one aspect of their financial circumstances.
- Maintain a professional image and presentation at all times.

From the results of the client questionnaire, you can summarise the clients' situation as follows.

Personal information

- Tin Nguyen   Date of birth: 10 May 1985
- Fui Ling Nguyen   Date of birth: 9 August 1987
- Contact information: Address, telephone and facsimile numbers were recorded.
- Children/dependants: None
- Employment details:
  - Tin Nguyen, Chemical engineer. Gross income: $95 000
  - Fui Ling Nguyen, Osteopath. Gross income: $65 000
- Other information:
  - Both enjoy good health and are non-smokers.
  - Neither Tin nor Fui Ling has a will in place.

– They are fully insured for their home contents, cars and medical costs. However, they have not thought about taking out any personal insurance coverage as they both have term life insurance and income continuance insurance within their superannuation funds.

Income and expenses

Cash flow reveals the following.

	Tin	Fui Ling	Combined
Income[a]	>$70 000	>$48 000	>$118 000
Less: Expenses			83 000
Net surplus			$ >35 000

[a] After tax and superannuation contributions

Note: A detailed and itemised expenditure list was not provided. The couple has been allocating extra amounts from their surplus to reduce their mortgage.

Assets at market value

Home and contents	$600 000	
Cars	$55 000	
Bank savings account	$6 500	earning 2% p.a.

Superannuation

Tin	$106 000	Balanced fund earning 5.5% p.a.
Fui Ling	$55 000	Balanced fund earning 5% p.a.

Liabilities

Immediate financial goals

- Pay off credit card debt within 12 months.
- Commence an investment plan using borrowed funds.
- Go on an overseas holiday in 3 years — estimated cost $15 000.
- Perhaps start a family in 3–4 years.
- Pay off car loan within 3 years.

Home mortgage	$280 000
Credit cards	$15 000
Car loan	$20 000

Personal investment preferences

- They do not require any further income from the proposed investment plan. They are mainly seeking capital growth over a long-term time frame. They intend to reinvest any dividend payments received.
- They prefer to have a reasonable amount of liquidity on hand to cover emergencies — say, a minimum of $5000.
- They are seeking a real rate of return of at least 6% from the investments.
- They are prepared to accept a reasonably high level of risk in order to obtain a reasonable rate of return.
- Tin and Fui Ling have no problems with any of the classes of investments suggested in the questionnaire. They feel comfortable about borrowing money to invest.
- They realise that the share market is subject to volatility and are prepared to invest for the long-term.
- The client questionnaire was duly signed and dated by both Tin and Fui Ling and by the financial planner.

STEP 2. Identify the clients' goals

The couple's short- and medium-term goals and objectives should be detailed as specifically as possible and, where appropriate, expressed in dollar terms. These goals should be confirmed in the executive summary to the client.

Short-term goals	Medium-term goals
• Pay off credit card debt within 12 months. • Commence an investment plan in Australian shares.	• Go on an overseas holiday in 3 years — estimated cost $15 000. • Maybe start a family in 3–4 years. • Pay off car loan within 3 years.

The long-term plans of Fui Ling and Tin do not need to be considered at this stage as the couple have specifically asked about their short-term proposal of investing in shares using borrowed funds. Comments about the longer-term may be confined to the projected amounts and issues concerned with the investment plan as proposed.

STEP 3. Analyse the clients' financial position and identify financial problems

Having gone through the personal investment (risk profile) questionnaire (appendix 12C) with Tin and Fui Ling, you identify their risk profile to be that of a moderately aggressive type. This means that they accept volatility in both income and capital returns, they look for capital appreciation more than an income stream, and they have a long-term investment time frame.

At this point, all information about the client should be restated to ensure that strategies are based on accurate information. The analysis of the clients' financial position will cover some of the following areas.
- A balance sheet is compiled and the current net worth of the clients is established.
- A cash flow statement is drawn up based on the clients' details. An itemised expenses list has not been provided but it has been revealed that:
  - the car loan will be paid off in 3 years
  - the credit cards will be paid off over the next 2 years
  - the home mortgage requirement is $2500 per month but they have been paying up to $4000 per month in some months.
- Relevant personal financial ratios should be calculated.

The objective of the analysis should be to highlight potential problem areas in the clients' situation and to identify possible recommendations and strategies.

STEP 4. Prepare written recommendations

It is important at this stage to detail the assumptions used in the SOA. All assumptions used must be reasonable and justifiable in the circumstances. Following are some of the assumptions that should be referred to in this case:
- the latest tax rates
- inflation is assumed to be 3.0% p.a.
- details of projected investment earnings for the various asset classes together with the type of returns the clients can expect to earn
- the couple will remain in secure employment for the foreseeable future.

The financial planner needs to ensure that facts concerning the clients are not assumed. The specific focus of the SOA needs to be examined in depth. The benefits of establishing an appropriate investment plan should be explained to the clients, including the principles of investing. You need to consider each of the proposed borrowing types and discuss the advantages and disadvantages of each. Items to consider include franking credits, capital gains, interest rate on borrowings and capacity to repay the interest.

Fui Ling and Tin favoured an instalment gearing plan and so (assuming you agree with them and it is in their best interests) you should explain how such a plan works and provide some projections of the plan. You should also indicate the flexibility of the plan and any other specific features to help them understand how the plan works. Critical issues to address are the benefits, risks and costs of the recommended plan (and financial product selected) and the suitability of the plan and products for your clients' circumstances. You will also need to detail the managed funds that will be acquired with the borrowings, including such information as fees, past performance, fund profile, amounts to be invested, fund ratings and the rationale for the recommendation. The recommendations need to be considered in light of the client's risk profile and target asset allocation.

You may comment upon their current strategy of reducing non-tax-deductible personal debt as a worthwhile pursuit. You may also question their level of expenses and whether they can be reduced, with any surplus used to go towards the investment plan or to reduce the mortgage.

You will also be required to scope your advice to detail the areas of your plan that you have not addressed, the reasons for the exclusion and the risks, and ramifications the client faces in having areas of their financial situation excluded from the advice statement. Such areas include: risk management and insurance, retirement planning and estate planning.

You will need to ensure that all costs and fees associated with the recommendations are detailed in the plan including your remuneration. This will need to be expressed in dollar terms and include any fees and remuneration for preparing the plan and implementing the plan, as well as any fees received from the instalment gearing provider.

STEP 5. Implement the agreed-upon plan

The SOA should set out how the financial planner will put the recommendations into place and will include a breakdown of responsibilities. The plan will include an authority to proceed, together with an appropriate step-by-step action plan.

STEP 6. Review, revise and maintain the SOA

The plan must indicate benchmarks for the clients' current financial position and expected position at the time of the review. The planned reviews and the frequency should be indicated in the original plan, together with the types of services offered and the associated costs.

APPENDIX 12A

NO ADVICE STATEMENT

The following adaptation is an example of a no advice statement, provided by Integrity Financial Planners Pty Ltd.

Integrity Financial Planners
AFSL #110099

The Directors
XYZ Financial Planners Pty Ltd
319 East Doncaster Road
Melbourne 3109

Dear..............................

I/we confirm that I/we do not seek your advice in relation to the amount specified below, and that I/we do not require you to make any investigation or recommendation in relation to any other of my/our assets nor do I/we require a full analysis of my/our financial situation.

I/we request that you purchase/sell on my/our behalf the following.

Amount	$ market price
Details	1000 units of Telstra Direct Shares at market price + brokerage
Name(s)	Mr John Citizen and Mrs Ann Citizen
	2 McKeons Drive
	Mulgrave 3170

Signature(s) ....
....

Date ..../............/............   ..../............/............

Declaration by authorised representative

No advice is given, on the basis of your specific instruction that you do not wish me to make a full analysis of your financial situation but wish me to execute on your behalf the purchase/sell of 1000 **Telstra Direct Shares** as per your instructions.

Authorised representative: Josette Chikhani CFP

Signature:.. **Date**............/............/............

Note: All parties must sign this disclaimer, with a copy being retained by each.

APPENDIX 12B

CONFIDENTIAL CLIENT QUESTIONNAIRE

The following adaptation is an example of a confidential client questionnaire, provided by Integrity Financial Planners Pty Ltd.

Name: Mr & Mrs Mark Stephan
Date............/............/............
Adviser: David M. Smart
Referred by Mr Joe Stephan

CONFIDENTIAL CLIENT QUESTIONNAIRE
Important notice to client

In order for an adviser to make an investment or insurance recommendation, the adviser must have reasonable grounds for making that recommendation. This means that the adviser must conduct an appropriate investigation as to the investment objectives, financial situation and particular needs of the person concerned. The information requested in this form is necessary to enable a recommendation to be made on a reasonable basis and will be used for that purpose only.

You should allow 1–2 hours to complete this questionnaire. We cannot stress how important that time will be in properly planning your future standard of living. If you have any queries or do not understand a question, then ask your adviser for an explanation.

Please note that you have a 14-day cooling-off period from the time your managed investment transaction confirmation is received by you, or 5 days after your units are issued, to notify the funds in writing that the investment does not suit your needs.

Integrity Financial Planners Pty Ltd
ABN 24 069 537 855
Holder of an Australian Financial Services Licence

What is your main reason for seeking advice?

Personal information

Name .... **Date of birth** ....

Partner's name .... **Date of birth** ....

Contact information

Telephone H .... **W** ....

Mobile.. **Fax** ....

Street address...

.... **Postcode**..

Postal address...

.... **Postcode**..

Children/Dependants Name(s)	Date of birth	Dependant? Y/N
1	....	....
2	....	....
3	....	....
4	....	....

Employment details

Client's occupation..

Business name.. Start date............/................/...............

Business address..

Tax file number (optional)..

Retirement age.. Date ..../................/...............

Partner's occupation..

Business name.. Start date ..../................/...............

Business address..

Tax file number (optional)..

Retirement age.. Date................../................/...............

Health

Client   Are you in good health? Y/N

               (If no, please give details on last page)

               Are you a smoker? Y/N

Partner   Are you in good health? Y/N

               (If no, please give details on last page)

               Are you a smoker? Y/N

Legal details

Client's will　　　　Last updated.................../..................../.................. Held by..........................

Testamentary trust?　　　Y/N　　　Power of attorney?　　　Y/N

Solicitor's name...

Solicitor's address...

....Postcode..

Income and expenses/cash flow

Estimated income per annum, net after tax:

Client $...　　Partner $...

Your projected or regular expenses per annum

(please attach list) $...

Net surplus/(shortfall) per annum $...

Do you expect any significant change in income or expenses in the next year? Y/N

Description...

....

....

....

ASSETS

Should insufficient space be provided, please supply details on a separate attachment.

General assets	Description	Original cost of investment	Owned by (client, partner or jointly)	Original date invested dd/mm/yyyy	Current income per annum	Current value
Home						$
Business					$	$
Motor vehicles					Insured value	$
Home contents						$
Investments					$	$
Property					$	$
Shares					$	$
					$	$
					$	$
Unit trusts					$	$
					$	$
Insurance bonds						$
						$
Other bonds: investment value of insurance policies						$
						$
						$
						$
						$
Bank accounts, term deposits, debentures etc.					$	$

			$	$
			$	$
Private pensions/ annuities			$	$
			$	$
			$	$
Superannuation account			$	$
			$	$
Other investments or assets (e.g. boat)			$	$
			$	$
			$	$
Other assets and investments as per attachment			$	$
Total general assets and investments			$	$

LIABILITIES

Short term: (personal loans, credit cards, leases etc.)

Description	Rate of interest (% p.a.)	Owned by (client, partner or jointly)	Repayments per month	Amount owing
			$	$
			$	$
			$	$

Long term: (mortgages, investment loans etc.)

Description	Rate of interest (% p.a.)	Owned by (client, partner or jointly)	Repayments per month	Amount owing
			$	$
			$	$
			$	$

Explanatory notes ....
....
....
....

What financial goals and needs do you have?

For example, children's education, home renovations, overseas travel, new home, new car, luxury items, savings targets, retirement, gifts.

Short-term (less than 3 years)

$...

$...

$...

Medium-term (3–5 years)

$...

$...

$...

Long-term (more than 5 years)

$...

$...

$...

Estimated costs

$...

$...

$...

$...

$...

$...

$...

$...

$...

Your personal investment preferences

We need to understand how you feel about investments.

1. Do you need any income from your investments to help you meet your day-to-day living expenses?	Yes: Attach details	No
2. Do you have a loan payment or other financial commitment that requires a fixed amount from your investments in the future?	Yes: Attach details	No
3. What is the main objective for your investments?		
4. What is the time frame for your investment program?		
5. What level of funds do you prefer in investments that can be accessed at short notice (less than 7 days)?		

You should spend time with your adviser in completing this section.

6. What do you believe would be a realistic real return on these different asset classes? Your adviser will explain the risks associated with each type of investment.	Cash Fixed interest Property Shares

7. How comfortable are you with the following investments?
(1 = uncomfortable, 4 = very comfortable)

	1	2	3	4
Shares: Australian regional/international				
Direct property				
Indirect property				
Cash				
Fixed interest: term deposits				
bonds debentures				
Speculative investments				

8. What do you feel about borrowing to fund your investment portfolio?	Uncomfortable	☐
	Neutral	☐
	Comfortable	☐
	Very comfortable	☐

9. What type of investor do you see yourself as?   Client   Partner
   Conservative: capital secure, stable income stream
   Moderately conservative: capital security but with aspects of growth
   Balanced:
   moderate growth over a spread of investments
   Moderately aggressive:
   higher growth potential from a spread of growth assets
   Aggressive:
   high level of capital growth and volatility

Existing insurance program details

We need to know about your existing personal insurance program.

1. Existing life/trauma insurance details

Policy details (co., commencement date & policy no.)	Owner's name	Type	Premium	Sum insured (death, TPD, trauma)	Reason for cover

2. Existing disability income insurance details

Policy details (co., commencement date & policy no.)	Owner	Premium (per month or per annum)	Benefit payable (per month)	Benefit period (accident/ illness)	Waiting period	Benefit ceasing age

I have requested to be insured for the amounts specified:		
Death cover	Sum insured	$...
Total and permanent disability cover	Sum insured	$...
Trauma cover	Sum insured	$...
Income protection	Monthly benefit	$...

Special planning considerations

What is your desired annual retirement income (in today's dollars)? $...

Do you, your partner or children expect to receive an inheritance in the near future? Y/N

If yes, please provide details ....

....

....

....

Other information for consideration (e.g. expected changes to your income or debt level, proposed sale of assets, tax liability)

....

....

....

....

....

Superannuation and tax considerations

So that we may clarify your superannuation and tax, please complete the following.

Superannuation (please attach copies of statements)

Fund manager	Personal/employer/SGC	Start date	Contributions per annum	Current value
			$	$
			$	$
			$	$
			$	$

If you are about to leave your job, please list the payments you expect to receive. Please attach copies of statements.

	Client	Partner
Superannuation: account balance	$	$
start date	$	$
preserved amount	$	$
Redundancy payments: ex-gratia	$	$
other	$	$
Long-service leave (net after tax)	$	$
Annual leave (net after tax)	$	$
Other payments	$	$
Expected payment date		

Client statement/acknowledgement

	Yes (initial please)	No (initial please)
The information provided in this form is complete and accurate to the best of my knowledge		
OR I have chosen to only disclose a limited amount of information shown in this form		
OR I have chosen and requested that no formal analysis is to be conducted for my circumstances.		

Detailed insurance analysis form

You may wish to complete the following insurance needs calculator for your own purposes.

Death, permanent disability and trauma insurance calculator			
Balance outstanding on:	**Client**	**Partner**	**Example**
Home mortgage	$	$	$50 000
Other investment loans	$	$	20 000
Credit cards	$	$	1 000
Business loans	$	$	Nil
Foreseen one-off capital requirements	$	$	10 000
			81 000

Future income needs			
Annual income requirement	$	$	($25 000 × 15) = $375 000
How long can the family go without regular income? (e.g. 14, 30, 90 days)	$	$	Nil
Subtotal (a) total commitments	$	$	$456 000

Each partner does contribute to household income even if one partner is not earning an income. As a rule of thumb, it will be necessary to convert your surviving partner's income needs into a lump sum. In this example, we have multiplied the family income needs by 15 (i.e. $25 000 × 15 = $375 000). (This number takes account of your age and would be higher if you were younger.)

Less	Client	Partner	Example
Net value of existing assets (excluding family home) Current level of cover	$	$	$ 50 000
Subtotal (b)	$	$	250 000
			$300 000
Subtract (a) from (b) **Surplus/(Shortfall)**	$	$	$ (156 000)

General information

1. We need to know of any circumstances that may, or may have in the past, affected an application for insurance on your life. Things to consider may include your own health, your parents' health, any participation in hazardous sports, previous illnesses or accidents, or if you have ever been declined insurance cover. Please provide details.

....

....

....

....

2. As a life broker representative, by law we are required to operate in your best interests, which means that we shall choose insurance products designed to meet your needs. There are a range of features contained in risk products which, by way of our experience and training, would allow us to tailor an insurance program to *best fit* your needs as determined by the information you have provided to us within this form.

If you are happy to accept our recommendations with this in mind, please tick the yes box. If not, we shall be happy to provide a detailed table and an explanation of product features.

Yes ☐   No ☐

3. Additional information or explanatory notes

....

....

....

....

I understand and acknowledge that by not completing a fact finder analysis/questionnaire, advice may not be appropriate to my needs and objectives.

....

Client signature   **Partner signature**

Date........../.........../...........   Date........../.........../...........

..../............/............

Adviser signature   Date

ADDITIONAL INFORMATION

....
....
....
....
....
....
....

Future financial plan reviews: quarterly 6-monthly annually

APPENDIX 12C

RISK TOLERANCE CLASSIFICATIONS

There are a number of risk tolerance classifications used by financial planners. The chapter on personal financial planning has an example of a risk profile questionnaire that uses classification based on the income versus growth needs of a client. The example below provides a classification of risk based on a client's likely attitude towards risk.

However, it is important to note that the definition of the degree of risk tolerance is more important than the classifications used. Risk classifications can differ markedly depending on the design and terminology used within the questionnaire. It is recommended that advisers look beyond the terminology and understand the underlying meaning assigned to the classifications. This appreciation is very important because of its impact on the determination and design of an appropriate asset allocation model for the client.

Questions to ask yourself to determine your risk profile

1. Do you like to make all your investment decisions yourself?
2. Do you expect to leave your investments where they are for the next 5–10 years?
3. When considering long-term investing, do you aim to maximise returns accepting the possibility of short-term declines in the value of your investment?
4. Is your major investment objective to grow your investment portfolio quickly?
5. Do you want your investments to significantly outpace inflation?
6. Have you ever put money into shares or other volatile investments?
7. If the value of one of your investments fell by 15% 6 months after you bought it, would you consider buying more?
8. Do you decide on your investments quickly before the opportunity is gone?
9. Does the opportunity of increasing the value of your investments outweigh concern about market fluctuations?
10. Would you be willing to consider an investment which returned 50% in a good year and −25% in a bad year?

Count how many times you answered yes to these questions and choose the risk profile which fits your answers.

You have answered yes to 1 or 2 questions
Conservative investor
You are a conservative investor and you typically select investments with little or no risks associated with capital loss, such as fixed-term deposits. You are willing to accept other risks to avoid capital loss, such as a rate of return that does not keep pace with inflation.

You have answered yes to 3 or 4 questions
Moderately conservative investor
You are a moderately conservative investor and you are willing to accept a slightly higher risk of capital loss than a conservative investor but you still focus on avoiding potential capital losses and volatility. Typically, you are most comfortable with investments that normally have less severe and less frequent changes in their value.

You have answered yes to 5 or 6 questions
Moderate investor
You are a moderate investor and you are willing to tolerate more possibilities of suffering capital losses. Typically, you are 'middle of the road' with regard to both potential risks and rewards. You do not mind some fluctuations but will stay away from investments that have more dramatic or frequent changes. You are not as

---

concerned as a more aggressive investor with investment timing but are more willing than a conservative investor to accept risks associated with inflation and reinvestment. Your portfolio will often have some investments that fluctuate in value, balanced with investments subject to less frequent fluctuation.

You have answered yes to 7, 8 or 9 questions
Moderately aggressive investor
You are a moderately aggressive investor and you are willing to tolerate a greater chance of capital loss and will be more comfortable with market fluctuations than a more conservative investor. You will usually have some investments that are subject to greater fluctuation than those of a more conservative investor. Your portfolio will be made up of a combination of direct investments in shares and property.

You have answered yes to all questions
Aggressive investor
You are an aggressive investor and you are willing and usually eager to accept a greater chance of capital loss in return for potentially higher returns. You sometimes focus on short-term market timing as opposed to long-term investing. You are comfortable accepting a high level of risk in the hope of greater opportunity for returns. Typically, you are less concerned with the rate of inflation and ability to reinvest earnings at the same rate. Your investment portfolio will typically include Australian shares, investment property, a direct investment in a private company and exposure to overseas markets.

APPENDIX 12D

EXAMPLE STATEMENT OF ADVICE

The following case study provides an example of an SOA prepared to industry standards. Client information is provided on Jack and Jill Smith who are seeking assistance in relation to their income needs in retirement as well as their social security entitlements.

We gratefully acknowledge the assistance and support provided by Integrity Financial Planners — a dealership and financial planning practice based in Melbourne.

Client information

Jack and Jill Smith seek some assistance from the financial planning practice that you are employed with. The couple is an existing client of the practice and you have previously provided advice in respect of Jill's retirement and the commencement of an account-based pension, as well as the couple's eligibility for the age pension. Jack is now looking to retire as well and is seeking advice on what should be done with his existing superannuation account to provide an income upon his retirement, as well as to recalculate the couple's Centrelink entitlements as a consequence of Jack's retirement.

The Smiths provide you with the following information in respect of their financial situation.

Ages:	Jack is aged 67 and Jill is aged 65.		
Children:	The couple has 3 children and they are all financially independent.		
Cash inflows:	Jack was previously a technician but is currently on long-service leave leading to retirement. He normally receives a weekly wage of $1827 per week. Jill currently receives income from an account-based pension of around $909 per month.		
Cash payments:	The couple's living costs amount to approximately $62 000 p.a.		
Assets:	**Item**	**Owner**	**Market value**
	Home	Joint	$590 000
	Home contents	Joint	$25 000
	Motor vehicles:		
	Family sedan	Jack	$15 000
	Small sedan	Jill	$10 000
	Bank account	Joint	$10 000
	Term deposit	Joint	$35 000
	Netwealth superannuation	Jack	$267 836
	Netwealth account-based pension	Jill	$218 234

Liabilities:	None
Insurance:	The couple is fully covered for private health insurance.
	The couple has no other personal insurance coverage.

Primary objectives:
- Jack to retire in next couple of months
- To maximise social security entitlements
- To determine how to structure Jack's superannuation account to provide an income upon his retirement
- To target a combined retirement income of at least $52 000 p.a. tax free in today's dollars.
- To have an investment portfolio that is easy to manage and provides flexibility.

Other information:
- After completing a risk profile for the couple, you have assessed their risk tolerance as balanced with a target asset allocation of 50% allocated to growth investments and 50% allocated to defensive investments.
- The couple both have up-to-date wills as well as enduring power of attorney documents.
- Jack's superannuation is invested in a growth option while Jill's account-based pension is invested in a conservative investment option.
- Both Jack and Jill are happy with their super and account-based pension funds held with Netwealth and are not looking to move to another provider at this stage.
- Jack and Jill both have non-binding death benefit nominations in place within their account-based pension/superannuation accounts.
- The couple is seeking limited advice in relation to Jack's superannuation account and age pension entitlements only.
- The couple do not wish you to consider any other aspect of their financial situation other than issues that relate to the goal of making the most effective use of Jack's superannuation upon his retirement.

ACE Financial Services

25 June 2023
Mr J & Mrs J Smith
23 Bona Vista Road
BAYSWATER Vic. 3153

Dear Jack & Jill,

Statement of Advice

Thank you for allowing us to present the enclosed recommendations. We are pleased to enclose your personal financial plan which outlines our strategies and recommendations.

This Statement of Advice has been prepared based on your objectives and your current financial situation. Please take the time to carefully read and understand it, to ensure that it is consistent with your views and reflects the information we discussed.

Our recommendations are based on information you have previously provided. If this information does not in any way accurately reflect any part of your current situation, please let us know so that we can check whether any part of the plan needs to be modified.

At our earlier meeting, we provided you with a copy of our most recent financial services guide. If you have any questions about this guide, please do not hesitate to contact us.

Our aim is to maintain an ongoing relationship with you as a client by providing an exceptional level of service now and in the future. Please take time to read through the enclosed plan in detail and contact us if you wish to discuss any matters further. We look forward to receiving your instructions to proceed.

Please note that you should not act on any advice in this plan after 45 days from the above date without first checking with us that the advice remains appropriate.

Yours sincerely,

Gayle Jones
Jones Private Clients Pty Ltd
Authorised Representatives of ACE Financial Services

Australian Financial Services Licence #225051

65 Main Street, Melbourne 3000

STATEMENT OF ADVICE

Prepared for:

Mr J & Mrs J Smith

23 Bona Vista Road

BAYSWATER Vic. 3153

Prepared by:

Gayle Jones

Jones Private Clients Pty Ltd

Authorised Representatives of

Ace Financial Services

Australian Financial Services #225051

25 June 2023

Our contact details

You can contact us on: **(03) 9999 1111**

Our email address: Gaylej@jonesfp.com.au

Postal address: 65 Main Street, Melbourne 3000

CONTENTS

EXECUTIVE SUMMARY

RECOMMENDATIONS

- Convert Jack's superannuation account held with Netwealth Investments to an account-based pension drawing an income of $17 000 p.a.
- Increase the withdrawal of pension income from Jill's account-based pension from $12 000 p.a. to $17 000 p.a.

- Invest the account-based pensions of both Jack and Jill into a balanced investment option in-line with their risk profile.
- Both Jack and Jill to complete application for a binding death benefit nomination within their respective account-based pensions to nominate beneficiaries.
- Jack and Jill to submit application for an age pension entitlement from Centrelink.

WHY MY ADVICE IS APPROPRIATE

- You will receive sufficient income to support you through your retirement.
- You will maximise your eligibility for a Centrelink age pension and thereby gain access to the pensioner concession card.
- Your superannuation portfolio will be easy to manage, simple to administer and will enable you to retain investment flexibility.
- Funds held in account-based pensions are fully liquid and can be accessed at any time after the age of 65.
- The portfolio asset allocation is in-line with your risk profile, which will assist you to meet your financial goals.
- Completing a binding death benefit nomination will ensure that your respective account-based pensions are paid to your nominated beneficiaries upon death.

WHAT ARE THE RISKS ASSOCIATED WITH MY ADVICE?

- Your pension account balances are likely to fall over time. We have recommended you both withdraw $17 000 a year from your pension accounts in order to meet your income needs. However, given rates of return currently available in the marketplace, your capital will reduce over time.
- Projected superannuation returns will depend on movement of markets. Over the long run, in our projections we have assumed your investments will generate a return of at least 6%. While we do not believe this is unreasonable, this is by no means guaranteed.
- An account-based pension does not provide a guaranteed income in retirement and you may outlive your retirement savings.
- Income receipts may not be sufficient for your needs, requiring you to eat into your capital over time.
- Legislation changes. The government may decide to change the superannuation rules again in the future — for instance, increase the tax rates on pension accounts.

FEES AND COMMISSIONS

Based on your current combined superannuation/account-based pension account balance of $486 070, our ongoing fee will be $4277 as detailed within our FSG.

The fund manager or responsible entity operating the recommended investments will charge other ongoing fees and/or deduct expenses for managing the investment. These fees and expenses are generally applied prior to the manager declaring a unit price or rate of return.

WHAT TO DO NEXT

As you are reading this plan, please write down any questions that you may have about the information provided. We will attempt to satisfactorily answer your questions and you can indicate any changes that you wish to make to the recommendations outlined earlier. You should read any other information given to you and let us know if you have any queries.

If you are happy to proceed with these recommendations, please sign the authority to proceed and return it to our offices.

SECTION 1 INTRODUCTION

1.1 SCOPE OF ADVICE

What is the scope of our advice?

Jack and Jill, you have sought our advice in relation to the following specific issues:
- review the investment of Jack's superannuation assets now that he is retired and there are no longer any further contributions going into your superannuation fund
- determine whether you are eligible to apply for an age pension from Centrelink.

We understand that you have provided us with complete information in relation to the above specific issues.

At your request, we have not provided advice on:
- estate planning
- insurances
- non-superannuation assets.

As we have not reviewed your entire situation, you must decide whether it is appropriate to proceed with this advice in light of your total situation.

It is recommended that you consult with other professionals as part of the recommendations given. You should consult with your accountant to consider the extent of any capital gains tax payable upon the transfer of investment funds as well as a lawyer for estate planning issues.

1.2 LIMITED INFORMATION WARNING

It is perfectly reasonable to seek advice regarding specific issues as you have done. You should be aware that by limiting advice in this way you risk neglecting issues of significance and that you could incur financial loss in relation to issues not covered by this advice. Where we become aware of such issues we will bring them to your attention; however, we are limited in our capacity to do so by the information you have provided. If you wish to undertake a broader analysis of your financial affairs you should let us know before proceeding with this advice.

If you believe we have misinterpreted or overlooked some relevant information, it is your responsibility to bring this to our attention before proceeding with this proposal. You should be aware that if you have not disclosed information that is relevant to this advice you risk making a financial decision that may not be appropriate to your needs and circumstances.

Jones Financial Planners is licensed to provide advice on a range of financial products as set down in the financial services guide we previously provided. We are not licensed to provide advice on derivatives (futures and options), nor on general insurance products such as car or household insurances.

We do not provide advice regarding every financial product that is available. We can only recommend products that are on our approved product list which generally only includes products that have been assessed by our chosen external professional researchers.

SECTION 2 WHERE ARE YOU NOW?

Before we provide you with recommendations, it is appropriate that we reflect on your current situation. Please check the following information carefully to ensure that no detail has been omitted or is inconsistent with your understanding. If the advice provided in this report has been based on incorrect information, it may be inappropriate for you.

2.1 PERSONAL DETAILS

	Jack	Jill
Date of birth	14 Feb 1953	26 Sep 1954
Age last birthday	67	65
Marital status	Married	Married
Health	Good	Good
Smoker	Non-smoker	Non-smoker
Employment status	Employed – currently on long service leave	Retired
Occupation	Technician	Supervisor

Children and dependants

You have 3 children — Catherine, 40, Robert, 39, and Jamie, 35 — who are not financially dependent on you.

2.2 ASSETS AND LIABILITIES

Your asset holding at 25 June 2023 is as follows.

Lifestyle assets

Description	Owner	Market value
Real estate — principal residence	Joint	$590 000
Contents/personal property (market value)	Joint	25 000
Motor vehicle — Family sedan 4dr auto	Jack	15 000
Motor vehicle — Small sedan 4dr auto	Jill	10 000
Total		$640 000

Financial assets

Description	Owner	Market value
Bank account	Joint	$ 10 000
Term deposit	Joint	35 000
Netwealth superannuation (growth option)	Jack	267 836
Netwealth account-based pension (conservative option)	Jill	218 234
Total		$531 070

You have no outstanding debt.

2.3 CASH FLOW

Based on the information that you provided during our meeting, we estimate your present monthly income situation is as follows.

	Jack	Jill	Total
Income			
Interest ($840 p.a.)	$ 35	$ 35	$ 70
Wages and salary ($88 000 p.a.)	7 340		7 340
Netwealth account-based pension ($12 000 p.a.)		1 000	1 000
Total monthly income	$7 375	$1 035	$8 410

2.4 YOUR OBJECTIVES AND GOALS

Jack and Jill, you have stated that your primary objective is to restructure your investments to provide an ongoing income now that you have both retired.

Beyond this goal, your other short- and long-term objectives are as follows.

- You would like to know more about your potential eligibility for any Centrelink benefits both now and in the future.
- To structure superannuation accounts to ensure a sustainable income in retirement that will last for as long as possible.
- You wish to structure your investments in the most tax-effective means available and obtain effective diversification.
- You wish to maintain control of your financial affairs but require professional help planning and putting plans into action.
- Minimise taxation.
- To receive an income in retirement of around $52 000 p.a.

2.5 RISK PROFILE

For the purpose of developing a suitable investment strategy, we discussed your understanding of, and tolerance to, risk and investment return volatility, as well as the types of investments you already hold and are familiar with.

There are two main areas in which your money can grow — shares and property. The other asset classes, cash and fixed interest provide you with income and minimal capital growth.

The important issues to consider when deciding on an appropriate level of risk for your circumstances are as follows.

- You are at a stage in your life where you are relying on your superannuation investments to support your cost of living.

Given the above, we recommend you have a holding across all asset sectors within your portfolio with a balance of income producing and growth investments. Following our discussions, we have agreed that a balanced allocation is appropriate for your needs given your desire to preserve capital while also achieving a reasonable rate of return. We recommend an asset allocation of 50% in defensive asset classes such as cash and fixed interest and 50% in the growth-oriented asset classes such as shares and property. This will enable your portfolio to focus on providing you with sufficient income to fund your retirement, while generating a moderate amount of capital growth without taking excessive risk to counter the effects of inflation.

Numerous research studies show that diversification across all asset classes will reduce risk and improve long-term returns. Risk is increased when a portfolio is too heavily exposed to any one sector.

Investment theory states that returns over the long-term will be greatest for shares, property, fixed interest [bonds] and cash in that order. While past returns and risk are no indication of future performance these facts should be kept in mind. There are other ways of reducing risk within your investment portfolio and this is to include different investment styles within each asset sector [mainly the growth sectors].

Another risk reduction tool is to blend together investments that do not follow the same pattern that is, some investments can be expected to underperform or in fact fall in value in the short-term while still providing good long-term returns. It is important to diversify investments so that when one is suffering from short-term underperformance other investments, subject to different economic influences, are outperforming to compensate.

2.6 ASSET ALLOCATION

Asset allocation and security selection are the two fundamental decisions in the implementation or realisation of investment objectives.

Asset allocation involves making the decision of how much to invest within each asset class or investment sector.

Investment selection involves making the decision of how to invest within each asset class.

Considering the above information regarding risk and returns, and that your investment needs are to provide income with some capital growth over the longer term, we recommend the following asset allocation for your portfolio.

	Target	Range
Cash	10%	0–20%
Australian fixed interest	35%	20–60%
Alternative income	10%	0–20%
Australian property	10%	5–20%
Australian shares	25%	5–35%
International shares	10%	5–20%

The above allocation provides you with a spread over all asset sectors with 50% of your funds invested in growth-oriented investments. You need to note that a portfolio that has 50% of its funds invested in growth investments statistically is likely to have 1 year of negative returns in a 12-year period.

Your exposure to asset classes may differ from the long-term benchmark portfolio because of adjustments based on the latest research of medium-term risks and to account for individual considerations.

As investment markets move, profits should be taken periodically to rebalance the portfolio back to the desired asset allocation to ensure you are not over-exposed to any one asset sector and to increase exposure to sectors, which may be under-valued. In this way, the risk of exposure to over-valued market sectors is reduced and long-term returns are improved.

We will review your risk profile and your asset allocation on an ongoing basis to ensure that it remains suitable for your goals and objectives. If you do not feel that this description is an accurate reflection of your risk profile you should let us know. Please feel free to raise any queries you may have.

SECTION 3 RECOMMENDATIONS AND ANALYSIS

3.1 RECOMMENDATIONS

(i) Convert Jack's superannuation account held with Netwealth Investments to an account-based pension drawing an income of $17 000 p.a.

Earlier this year, we provided advice to convert Jill's superannuation account to an account-based pension held with Netwealth Investments. Now that Jack is looking to retire and is seeking ongoing income, we recommend that Jack also now transfers his superannuation account to an account-based pension held with Netwealth Investments. You have advised that you wish to retain your funds with Netwealth Investments and after undertaking research, we believe the fund continues to be appropriate for your needs and is likely to assist in helping you achieve your retirement goals.

The information following has been previously provided when Jill acquired her account-based pension; however, we have repeated it here so that you understand the process and can discuss any queries you have with us prior to proceeding. We have previously detailed the features, risks and benefits of investing your super monies into Netwealth Investments.

What is an account-based pension?

An account-based pension is a retirement income stream that is drawn from an investment in a superannuation fund. An account-based pension has no guaranteed term or return. Exactly how long the pension payments will last is dependent on the performance of the underlying investments and the amount withdrawn from your pension account (either as pension payments or lump sums).

Advantages of account-based pensions

Account-based pensions are a secure, tax effective and flexible way of drawing down income in retirement. They provide flexibility, both in terms of investment choice and the amount of income drawn. Investment in an account-based pension provides you with many important advantages.

Flexibility

You are able to vary the income you receive, and you will have the option of monthly, quarterly, biannual or annual payments. Currently, account-based pension investors can also withdraw (commute) lump sums from their account at any time.

Tax concessions

- The commencement of an account-based pension counts as a rollover, so lump sum tax does not apply on the commencement of the pension.
- The returns generated within your account-based pension account are entirely free of tax within the pension fund.
- As you are already over the age of 60, any pension payments or lump sum withdrawals from your account-based pension will be completely free of personal tax.
- If any assets are sold down within your pension account, they are exempt from capital gains tax.

No mortality risk

Importantly, there is no mortality risk with an account-based pension. If you die before the capital (plus any investment earnings) is exhausted, the balance can be paid to your nominated beneficiary detailed in your binding death benefit nomination.

Assessment for social security purposes

Your account-based pension will be treated as a financial investment and subject to deeming rates which from 1 May 2023 are 0.25% on the first $100 200 of financial investments for a couple and 2.25% on the value of financial investments that exceed $100 200.

Pension payments

Pension payments from an account-based pension must be made at least annually and are required to be above a set minimum amount which varies depending on your age at 1 July each year. These amounts are recalculated at the start of each financial year.

The minimum amount that must be withdrawn each year is as follows.

Age	Minimum percentage of pension
Under 65	4.00%
65–74	5.00%
75–79	6.00%
80–84	7.00%
85–89	9.00%
90–94	11.00%
95 and over	14.00%

The minimum payment amount is imposed to ensure that there is no unreasonable build-up of assets in the tax-free environment.

Jack, as you are 67 years of age, the minimum pension that you are currently required to draw is 5.00% of your account balance. It is important to note that this is a minimum amount; no maximum limit is set. You do need to be aware, however, that your account balance is not guaranteed to last you for the rest of your life.

To generate the amount of income required in retirement, we recommend that Jack withdraws an annual income of $17 000 p.a. or $1417 per month. Because you are commencing the pension part-way through the year, the pension withdrawal for the first year will be pro-rated.

(ii) Increase the withdrawal of pension income from Jill's account-based pension from $12 000 p.a. to $17 000 p.a.

Jill currently withdraws an income of $12 000 p.a. from her account-based pension. As Jill is aged over the age of 60, all pension payments are completely tax-free.

In order to generate the amount of income required in retirement, we recommend that Jill increases her pension withdrawal from an amount of $12 000 p.a. to $17 000 p.a. This will mean that your retirement funds will be depleted a little quicker but will provide the level of income you require in retirement.

(iii) Invest the account-based pensions of both Jack and Jill into a balanced investment option in-line with your risk profile

To ensure that funds held in your account-based pensions are invested in such a way so as to be consistent with your risk profile and generate sufficient returns so as to ensure that your retirement funds last as long as possible, we recommend that:

- Jill moves funds held in her Netwealth account-based pension from a conservative investment option to a balanced investment option. The asset allocation we are recommending is 50% into defensive asset classes and 50% into the growth asset classes
- Jack invests into a balanced investment option when transferring his retirement funds from the Netwealth super account to the Netwealth account-based pension.

Netwealth's balanced investment option holds approximately 50% of the funds in defensive asset classes and 50% in growth asset classes, and would be appropriate for your needs in retirement.

(iv) Both Jack and Jill to complete applications for a binding death benefit nomination within your respective account-based pensions to nominate beneficiaries

Both of you currently have non-binding death benefit nominations in place within your respective superannuation/account-based pension accounts. What this means is that the trustee of the superannuation fund, Netwealth Investments, has the final say as to how your super funds will be distributed among your dependants upon your death, although they are likely to take note of your preference in your nomination. Preferences noted in your nomination form are not binding on the super fund trustees. The risk of having a non-binding death benefit nomination in place is that the trustee of the super fund pays the death benefits to a beneficiary not of your choosing.

We are therefore recommending that both of you complete a binding death benefit nomination which will allow you to nominate which of your dependants will receive the super funds upon your death. It is binding on the trustee and therefore cannot be challenged except under extreme circumstances. As Netwealth offers non-lapsing binding nominations, your nominations will not expire or change unless you make a new nomination.

This type of nomination can be made only to a dependant; this is either your partner, child, someone who is financially dependent upon you at the time of your death or someone under an interdependency relationship. An interdependent relationship exists if:
• two people have a close personal relationship; and
• they live together; and
• one or each of them provides the other with financial support; and
• one or each of them provides the other with domestic support or personal care.

(v) Jack and Jill to submit application for an aged pension entitlement from Centrelink

There are a number of eligibility requirements to claiming an age pension for the both of you, including:
• residency
• age
• asset and income means test.

You will both satisfy the residency and age requirements. Note that combined assets and income of the family are included under the assets and income means tests.

From 1 July 2023, the asset test threshold for a couple cuts out once total assets exceed $1 003 000. Assessable assets exclude the family home. The income test threshold currently cuts out at an income of around $3666.80 per fortnight or $95 336.80 p.a. On this basis, both of you will be entitled to a part pension payment and with this, an entitlement to the pensioner concession card which will provide access to Australian Government health concessions and provide help with the cost of living by reducing the cost of certain goods and services.

How much age pension will you receive?

After Jack's salary ceases, we believe Centrelink will calculate your entitlement as follows.

Assets test

Description	Owner	Market value	Included for assets test?
Real estate — principal residence	Joint	$590 000	No
Contents/personal property (Centrelink value)	Joint	$25 000	Yes
Motor vehicle — Family sedan 4dr auto	Jack	$15 000	Yes
Motor vehicle — Small sedan 4dr auto	Jill	$10 000	Yes
Bank account	Joint	$10 000	Yes
Term deposit	Joint	$35 000	Yes
Netwealth account-based pension	Jack	$267 836	Yes
Netwealth account-based pension	Jill	$218 234	Yes

Total assessable assets amount to $581 070. A couple can currently hold a total value of $451 500 in assets before the fortnightly pension amount is reduced by $3 per fortnight for every $1000 above the threshold.

Therefore, under the assets test, we believe you will be entitled to approximately *$632.35 each per fortnight* from Centrelink. Note that this may vary depending upon the current balance of your bank account.

Income test

Centrelink includes all financial assets in their calculations when estimating your entitlement under the income test. This includes superannuation and account-based pension accounts as well as most other forms of investments including your bank and term deposit accounts, which are deemed to earn a certain level of income, whether they actually earn this income or not. Accordingly, income actually earned is ignored and you are deemed to earn a specified rate of return. This is called deeming rates and the current rates from 1 May 2023 are 0.25% on the first $100 200 of financial investments for a couple and 2.25% on the value of financial investments that exceed $100 200.

Your current holding of financial investments totals $531 070 – note that motor vehicles and home contents are not counted. A couple can currently earn an income of $360 per fortnight before the fortnightly pension amount is reduced by 50 cents in the dollar earned in excess of the full pension income level.

Therefore, under the income test, we believe you will be entitled to approximately *$810.70 each per fortnight* from Centrelink.

Centrelink age pension entitlement

As Centrelink will pay the lower amount under both the income and assets tests, we believe each of you will receive a pension payment of $632.35 per fortnight or $1264.70 combined ($32 882.20 p.a. combined).

3.2 OTHER STRATEGIES CONSIDERED

- We considered leaving Jack's superannuation in the accumulation phase. This alternative was not recommended as converting to pension phase is the most tax-effective outcome and would also allow you to maximise your Centrelink entitlement.
- We considered taking a larger amount of income from Jack's and/or Jill's pension accounts. By withdrawing a relatively low amount, you will ensure your pension funds last as long as possible. If you decide that you don't have enough income to live on, you can increase your level of income at any time or take a lump sum withdrawal from either of your pension accounts.
- We considered withdrawing all or some of the funds from your superannuation/account-based pensions and investing outside of the super environment, into shares or managed funds. However, retaining funds inside the super environment is the most tax-effective means for accumulating wealth. Not only are earnings generated within an account-based pension completely free of tax, but all pension or lump sum withdrawals after the age of 60 are completely tax free.
- We considered transferring your super/account-based pension funds out of Netwealth Investments and into another super fund. However, given the features and low cost of the Netwealth Investments Wrap Super Fund, we believe that the fund is appropriate for your circumstance and in your best interest.

3.3 OUTCOMES OF THE RECOMMENDED STRATEGY

By implementing the recommendations made in this document:
1. you will have sufficient income to support you through your retirement
2. you will maximise your eligible Centrelink pension
3. your superannuation portfolios will be easy to manage, simple to administer and will enable you to retain investment flexibility. The portfolio asset allocation is in-line with your risk profile; this will assist you to meet your financial goals
4. you will both have a tax-effective account-based pension to provide an income during your retirement
5. completing a binding death benefit nomination within your account-based pensions will ensure funds are paid to your preferred dependants upon your death.

After the recommendations have been implemented, a revised estimate of your annual income should be as follows.

	Jack	Jill	Total
Income			
Interest	$ 420	$ 420	$ 840
Centrelink – age pension	16 441	16 441	32 882
Netwealth account-based pension	17 000	17 000	34 000
Total annual income	$33 861	$33 861	$67 722

3.4 WHAT ARE THE RISKS ASSOCIATED WITH MY ADVICE?

Naturally there are risks associated with any financial planning strategy. Here are some of the more specific ones that relate to our advice for you.
- Your pension account is likely to diminish over the years of your retirement. We have recommended you both withdraw a level of income close to the minimum permitted. However, depending upon the

level of income generated within your funds each year, the balance will fall over time. Jill, you will be withdrawing $17 000 p.a. from your pension account, which represents approximately 6.8% of your current balance. This means that your account would need to generate at least a return of this to prevent dipping into the capital. Jack, we have recommended you withdraw an amount of $17 000 or 6.3% of your account balance, which is a little over the minimum permitted of 5.0% of your balance. This means your account would need to generate at least a return of 6.3% p.a. to prevent dipping into your capital.

- Projected superannuation returns will depend on movement of markets. Over the long run, in our projections we have assumed your investments will generate a return of at least 6%. While we do not believe this is unreasonable, this is by no means guaranteed.
- Investment returns are volatile and financial markets do go up and down over time. With your balanced investment option, there is the risk of volatility of returns and/or loss of capital.
- Legislation changes. The government may decide to change the superannuation rules in the future — for instance, increase the tax rates on pension accounts.

SECTION 4 INVESTMENTS

4.1 APPROVED PRODUCTS THAT I CAN RECOMMEND

It is worth noting that I am only able to recommend investment products available on an approved product list (APL) prescribed by my dealer (Ace Financial Services) who holds an Australian Financial Services Licence. This list of approved products restricts the range of products that I am able to recommend to you. I have not considered any products that are not on this list.

The approved list is compiled based on research by our external research consultant, Zenith Investment Partners. By drawing upon external research, I ensure a wide coverage of available products and that assessment has been made by experienced professionals specialising in this area. The external researchers also monitor ongoing developments and changes to products to ensure they remain suitable.

I have selected appropriate approved products that have been assessed as:

- meeting your investment objectives
- blending together well to provide an appropriate diversified portfolio
- matching your attitude towards investing
- appropriately managing your exposure to financial risk.

4.2 DETAILS OF INVESTMENTS RECOMMENDED IN THIS REPORT

I recommend that your account-based pension accounts be held with Netwealth Investments and invested in the balanced investment option which invests according to the following proportions.

Cash account	15%
Fixed interest	35%
Property	15%
Australian shares	25%
International shares	10%

Product	Amount	Performance	Cost (MER) p.a. $	Cost (MER) p.a. %	Zenith rating
Netwealth Investment balanced investment option					
Jack	$267 836	6.8% p.a. 3 years average	2 946	1.1	Recommended
Jill	$218 234		2 401	1.1	Recommended

4.3 RESEARCH AND PRODUCT DISCLOSURE STATEMENTS

I have attached the latest research on the above funds at the back of this SOA.

The research material is independently appraised by a credible research house (Zenith Investment Partners) and provides an overview of the key features and costs of the fund as well as a website address for more information about the fund.

The PDS for the Netwealth account-based pension is available from the Netwealth Fund website at netwealth.com.au

If you are unable to access the PDS in this manner or have difficulty doing so, please contact me and I will arrange for you to receive a copy of the PDS.

All financial products involve an element of risk. The risks associated with each of the recommended products are explained in the respective product disclosure statements. You should read these documents and in particular, the sector which describes the risks of the products and ask me if you have any concerns.

SECTION 5 IMPLEMENTING THE PLAN

5.1 WHAT TO DO NEXT

As you are reading this plan, please write down any questions that you may have about the information provided.

We will attempt to satisfactorily answer your questions and you can indicate any changes that you wish to make to the recommendations outlined earlier.

You should read any other information given to you and let us know if you have any queries.

Each of you will need to sign the attached authority to proceed where indicated and return it to us.

5.2 IMPLEMENTATION

Action required?	By who?	When?
Sign the enclosed authority to proceed (ATP)	Jack and Jill	Now
Convert Jack's Netwealth super wrap to an account-based pension p.a.	Jack and Jones Private Clients (JPC)	After ATP has been received
Apply for an aged pension from Centrelink	Jack and Jill and JPC	After ATP has been received
Increase Jill's pension withdrawal to $17 000 p.a.	JPC	After ATP has been received
Complete application for binding death benefit nomination in pension accounts	JPC	After pension has commenced

5.3 DISCLOSURE OF FEES AND COMMISSIONS

Financial planning document

As you are an existing client, you will not be charged for the preparation of this report.

Implementation

No fees are payable on the implementation of our recommendations.

Ongoing fees and commissions

As previously advised and noted in our financial services guide, Jones Private Clients will charge a fee for ongoing advice and review of your portfolio. This fee will be 0.8% p.a. plus GST of your account balances within your respective account-based pensions.

Based on your current combined account balances in your Netwealth account-based pensions of $486 070, this fee would be $4277 per year. Of this amount, the licence holder, Ace Financial Services, will be paid an amount of $642.

For your investments in Netwealth, this fee will be deducted from your account each month and paid to Jones Private Clients (JPC).

The amounts shown in the table prior will vary over time according to the mix of investments and changes to the account balances. The amount shown is only an estimate for the first year.

GST

The above fees and commissions are inclusive of the goods and services tax (GST).

Adviser's interest

You have been provided advice by Gayle Jones in her capacity as an Authorised Representative and Director of Jones Private Clients Pty Ltd.

Jones Private Clients pays Ace Financial Services a fee for the provision of services such as licensing, research, training etc.

Gayle Jones is owner of Jones Private Clients and will benefit from income and profits earned by Jones Private Clients.

Other costs

The table prior shows charges deducted from your account and ongoing commissions paid to JPC.

The fund manager or responsible entity operating the recommended investments will charge other ongoing fees and/or deduct expenses for managing the investment. These fees and expenses are generally applied prior to the manager declaring a unit price or rate of return. They are not deducted from your account but will impact on the returns from your investment.

The indirect cost ratio (ICR) is an estimate of the total of these fees and expenses expressed as a percentage of the funds held. The ICR is used rather than showing a list of all fees and expenses to enable meaningful comparisons between products.

These fees are not paid to your adviser or Ace Financial Services.

In addition, investment products often have a spread between the buying and selling price of the investment. This represents a cost for trading investments which will occur only when units in the investment are bought or sold. This cost usually does not exceed 2% and is generally less than 0.5% of an investment's unit price.

We have not attempted to itemise these costs for each investment. You should refer to the product disclosure statements accompanying this statement of advice to determine the actual costs for particular products recommended. If you have any questions regarding this information please ask us.

SECTION 6 DISCLAIMER AND AUTHORITY TO PROCEED

DISCLAIMERS

The law requires that recommendations made to clients are consistent with their financial needs and objectives and have a reasonable basis. This statement of advice is based on information that you have provided. If you believe we have misinterpreted or overlooked some relevant information, it is your responsibility to bring this to our attention before proceeding with this proposal.

The scope of this advice is limited to areas defined in the statement of advice. No responsibility is accepted in relation to any other aspect of your financial circumstances. You are warned that there may be issues beyond the scope of this advice which may impact on outcomes. We have made reasonable efforts to identify such issues, where it is in our power to do so. If there is any information that has not been provided to us, or about which you have not sought our advice, you risk making a financial decision that may not be appropriate to your needs and circumstances and financial loss may occur.

In preparing this plan, we have relied on information supplied to us by you and by others, which, where reasonable, we have assumed to be correct. While reasonable efforts have been made to substantiate such information, no responsibility can be accepted if the information is incorrect or inaccurate.

This advice is prepared solely for the use of the client to whom it is addressed and we do not accept any liability whatsoever to third parties.

Advice in this report is based on current information and should only be considered current for 45 days from the date of this report. After that time you should not act on any of the recommendations without further reference to us.

In the event that any advice or other services rendered by the company constitute a supply of services to a consumer under the *Trade Practices Act 1974* (as amended), then the Company's liability for any breach of any conditions or warranties implied under the Act shall not be excluded but will be limited to the cost of having the advice or services supplied again.

While every effort has been made to include relevant tax and social security considerations, you are advised to discuss your annual tax liability and the tax and social security implications of this advice with your tax adviser as the estimates contained herein are intended as a guide only.

Estimates of income and capital growth are based on assessments of current and likely future economic conditions, as well as investment past and likely future performances. Such figures are purely estimates and may vary with changing circumstances. They are not guaranteed to occur.

Each paragraph of this disclaimer shall be deemed to be separate and severable from each other. If any paragraph is found to be illegal, prohibited or unenforceable, then this shall not invalidate any other paragraphs.

AUTHORITY TO PROCEED

I hereby authorise Gayle Jones Authorised Representative of Jones Financial Planners Pty Ltd, to arrange for the implementation of the recommendations specified in the statement of advice dated 25 June 2023, and as per the attached summary.

I have read the statement of advice, agree that the client information on which it is based is complete and accurate and accept the advice provided.

I acknowledge that every care has been taken to ensure the accuracy of information included in this document and that neither Jones Financial Planners nor its representative will accept responsibility for any errors or omissions made by me regarding the information we have provided.

I understand that no guarantee is given that investments will meet the expectations stated in this report and that adverse market conditions may result in a reduction in the capital value of my investments.

At my instruction, advice has been limited to the funds, circumstances and issues specified in the statement of advice. I do not require advice regarding any other aspect of our financial affairs. I understand that, by limiting the advice in this manner, I risk making an investment or purchase that may not be appropriate to my overall needs and objectives.

I understand that I will be charged a fee for ongoing services which will not currently exceed 0.88% p.a. (inc. GST) of the value of my portfolio.

I have also been provided with a Financial Services Guide (FSG).

I authorise Jones Financial Planners Pty Ltd to retain my tax file number while acting on my behalf and to quote my tax file number to the Australian Taxation Office and to investment companies when making investments on my behalf.*

I wish to advise that my tax file number is ____ ____ ____ **(Jack)**

*(*Please note, you do not have to provide your tax file number nor authorise its use. Please delete these paragraphs if you do not wish us to retain your TFN.)*

Signed:_____   Date: _____/_____/_____
     Jack Smith

Signed:_____   Date: _____/_____/_____
     Jill Smith

Confidential Personal Financial Plan for Jack Smith and Jill Smith   25 June 2023

Prepared by Gayle Jones

REFERENCES

ASIC 2011, *Disclosure: product disclosure statements (and other disclosure obligations)*, Regulatory Guide 168, October, asic.gov.au.

ASIC 2017a, *Licensing: financial product advisers — conduct and disclosure*, Regulatory Guide 175, November, asic.gov.au.

ASIC 2017b, *Dollar disclosure*, Regulatory Guide 182, December, asic.gov.au.

ASIC 2017c, *Example statement of advice: scaled advice for a new client*, Regulatory Guide 90, December, asic.gov.au.

AUSTRAC 2019, 'Financial crime red flags: a guide for financial planners', Australian Government, 17 July, www.austrac.gov.au/business/how-comply-guidance-and-resources/guidance-resources/financial-crime-red-flags-guide-financial-planners.

Hoyle, S 2020, 'Testing the boundaries: industry funds and advice', *Professional Planner*, 27 March, www.professionalplanner.com.au/2020/03/testing-the-boundaries-industry-funds-and-advice.

Jaffe, DT & Grubman, J 2011, 'Core techniques for effective client interviewing and communication', *Journal of Financial Planning*, October.

Tax Practitioners Board (TPB) 2014, 'Tax (financial) advice services', Australian Government, 30 June, www.tpb.gov.au/tax-financial-advice-services.

Wharton University of Pennsylvania 2007, 'Bridging the trust divide: the financial advisor–client relationship', https://knowledge.wharton.upenn.edu/special-report/bridging-the-trust-divide-the-financial-advisor-client-relationship-2.

ACKNOWLEDGEMENTS

Figures 12.1 and 12.2: © ASIC
Extracts: © ASIC
Extract: © Professional Planner
Extract: © Tax Practitioners Board

INDEX